PRENTICE HALL
THE AMERICAN NATION
Beginnings Through 1877

James West Davidson
Author

PEARSON
Prentice
Hall

Upper Saddle River, New Jersey
Boston, Massachusetts

Dr. Michael B. Stoff
Senior Consultant

Dr. Herman J. Viola
Senior Consultant

Collections of the Fort Ticonderoga Museum

Acknowledgments appear on page 664, which constitutes an extension of this copyright page.

ISBN 0-13-181764-7
9 10 V057 10

Author

James West Davidson who earned his Ph.D. at Yale University, is coauthor of *After the Fact: The Art of Historical Detection* and *Nation of Nations: A Narrative History of the American Republic.* Dr. Davidson has taught at both the college and high school levels. He has also consulted on curriculum design for American history courses. Dr. Davidson is an avid canoeist and hiker. His published works on these subjects include *Great Heart,* the true story of a 1903 canoe trip in the Canadian wilderness.

Senior Consultant

Dr. Michael B. Stoff received his Ph.D. in history from Yale University. He currently teaches at the University of Texas at Austin, where he also directs the graduate program in history. He is the author of *Oil, War, and American Security: The Search for a National Policy on Foreign Oil, 1941-1947,* coauthor of *Nation of Nations: A Narrative History of the American Republic,* and co-editor of *The Manhattan Project: A Documentary Introduction to the Atomic Age.* Dr. Stoff has won numerous grants, fellowships, and teaching awards.

Dr. Herman J. Viola, curator emeritus with the Smithsonian Institution, is a distinguished historian and author. Dr. Viola received his Ph.D. in American history from Indiana University. He founded the scholarly journal *Prologue* at the National Archives. Dr. Viola also served as director of the National Anthropological Archives at the Smithsonian Institution. A nationally recognized authority on American Indians, the history of the American West, and the Civil War, Dr. Viola is the author of many historical works for both adults and young readers.

AmericanHeritage® **American Heritage** magazine was founded in 1954, and it quickly rose to the position it occupies today: the country's preeminent magazine of history and culture. Dedicated to presenting the past in entertaining narratives underpinned by scrupulous scholarship, *American Heritage* today goes to more than 300,000 subscribers and counts the country's very best writers and historians among its contributors.

Program Reviewers

Academic Consultants

David Beaulieu, Ph.D.
Professor, School of Education
University of Wisconsin–Milwaukee
Milwaukee, Wisconsin

William R. Childs, Ph.D.
Associate Professor of History
Ohio State University
Columbus, Ohio

Theodore DeLaney, Ph.D.
Associate Professor of History
Washington & Lee University
Lexington, Virginia

Emma Lapsansky, Ph.D.
Professor of History and
  Curator of Special Collections
Haverford College
Haverford, Pennsylvania

William A. McClenaghan
Professor of Political Science
Oregon State University
Corvallis, Oregon

Timothy R. Mahoney, Ph.D.
Professor of History
University of Nebraska–Lincoln
Lincoln, Nebraska

Ralph Mann, Ph.D.
Associate Professor of History
University of Colorado
Boulder, Colorado

Teacher Reviewers

Joanne Alexander
Reading Supervisor
Manassas City Public Schools
Manassas, Virginia

Chris Beech
Social Studies Teacher
Lamar Junior High School
Rosenberg, Texas

Bob Borjes
Social Studies Teacher
Hal Peterson Middle School
Kerrville, Texas

Phyllis Bridges
Social Studies Teacher
Chaffin Middle School
Ft. Smith, Arkansas

Clement Brown
Social Studies Teacher
Madison Junior High School
Naperville, Illinois

Susan Buha
Social Studies Teacher
Hobart Middle School
Hobart, Indiana

Marilyn Bunner
Social Studies Teacher
Decatur Middle School
Indianapolis, Indiana

Steve Bullick
Supervisor of Social Studies
Mt. Lebanon School District
Mt. Lebanon, Pennsylvania

Ronald Concklin
Social Studies Teacher
Will Rogers Middle School
Fair Oaks, California

Sandra Lee Eades, Ph.D.
Social Studies Content Leader
Ridgely Middle School
Lutherville, Maryland

Nancy Foss
Social Studies Teacher
Glenn Hills Middle School
Augusta, Georgia

Mike Harter
Social Studies Teacher
Austin Middle School
Amarillo, Texas

Contents

Building the Massachusetts Bay colony

vi

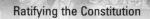
Ratifying the Constitution

Drum from the American Revolution

The Jefferson Memorial, Washington, D.C.

On the Oregon Trail

The 54th Massachusetts Regiment in battle, 1863

Special Features

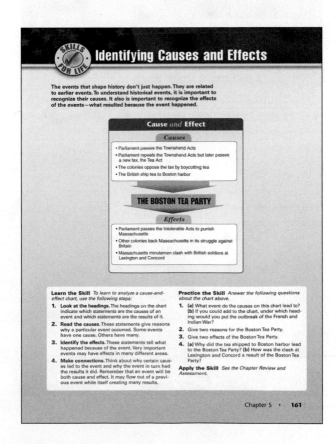

Special Features

Connecting With...

See how history has fascinating links with other subjects.

Connecting With... Economics

Women and the California Gold Rush

Women as well as men had the vision and willpower to make a profit in the mining towns of the California gold rush. One enterprising woman was Luzena Stanley Wilson, who in 1849 arrived at the gold mines near Sacramento with her husband and two sons. At first, the Wilsons built and ran a hotel in Sacramento, but lost it in a flood. Then, the family moved to Nevada City, where Luzena started a new business.

Miners' tools

Working a claim

"I determined to set up [another] hotel. So I bought two boards from a precious pile belonging to a man who was building the second wooden house in town. With my own hands I chopped stakes, drove them into the ground, and set up my table. I bought provisions at a neighboring store, and when my husband came back at night he found, mid the weird light of the pine torches, twenty miners eating at my table. Each man as he rose put a dollar in my hand and said I might count him as a permanent customer. I called my hotel 'El Dorado.'

"From the first day it was well patronized, and I shortly after took my husband into partnership."

Activity

Luzena Wilson wanted to run her own business. What were the advantages of running her own business? Divide a piece of paper into two columns, "Advantages" and "Disadvantages." List four items in each column.

Special Features

AmericanHeritage MAGAZINE   HISTORY **HAPPENED HERE**

Charleston, South Carolina

Fort Sumter

The Civil War began in 1861 when Confederate forces bombarded and captured Fort Sumter in Charleston Harbor, South Carolina. Later in the war, Union gunships reduced Sumter to rubble. The fort was rebuilt, and it remained part of the seacoast defenses until 1947. Today, Fort Sumter is a national monument. Tour boats to the fort leave regularly from downtown Charleston.

Go Online PHSchool.com

Virtual Field Trip For an interactive look at Fort Sumter, visit PHSchool.com, **Web Code mfd-1603.**

Special Features

History Through Literature

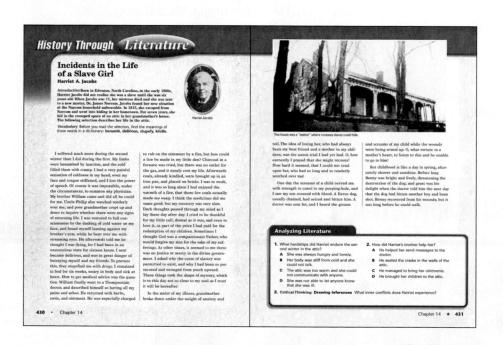

TEST PREPARATION

Special Features

An American Profile

Meet fascinating history makers.

Geography and History

The Negro Fort

The Negro Fort was built along the Apalachicola River, in the Spanish territory of Florida, about 60 miles from Georgia. At its height, some 1,000 African Americans farmed along the river. They worried Georgia planters, who feared they would encourage slaves to revolt.

The fort sat on a hill surrounded on three sides by forests and swamps. The weak side lay along the river. In early skirmishes against the Americans, the defenders beat their land forces. Then, the Americans launched an all-out attack by land and river. Gunboats bombarding the fort hit the room

Geography and History

Investigate the connection between history and geography.

Connecting to Today

Explore links between historical events and your world today.

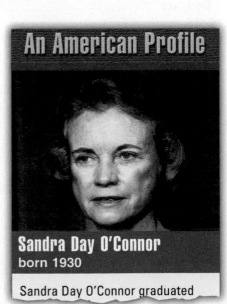

An American Profile

Sandra Day O'Connor
born 1930

Sandra Day O'Connor graduated

Special Features/Primary Sources

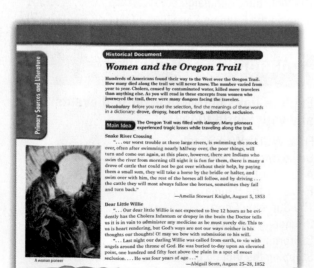

Primary Sources and Literature

Historical Document

Women and the Oregon Trail

Hundreds of Americans found their way to the West over the Oregon Trail. How many died along the trail we will never know. The number varied from year to year. Cholera, caused by contaminated water, killed more travelers than anything else. As you will read in these excerpts from women who journeyed the trail, there were many dangers facing the traveler.

Vocabulary Before you read the selection, find the meanings of these words in a dictionary: drove, dropsy, heart rendering, submission, seclusion.

Main Idea The Oregon Trail was filled with danger. Many pioneers experienced tragic losses while traveling along the trail.

Snake River Crossing

"... our worst trouble at these large rivers, is swimming the stock over, often after swimming nearly halfway over, the poor things, will turn and come out again, at this place, however, there are Indians who swim the river from morning till night it is fun for them, there is many a drove of cattle that could not be got over without their help, by paying them a small sum, they will take a horse by the bridle or halter, and swim over with him, the rest of the horses all follow, and by driving ... the cattle they will most always follow the horses, sometimes they fail and turn back."

—Amelia Stewart Knight, August 5, 1853

Dear Little Willie

"... Our dear little Willie is not expected to live 12 hours as he evidently has the Cholera Infantum or dropsy in the brain the Doctor tells us it is in vain to administer any medicine as he must surely die. This is us is heart rendering, but God's ways are not our ways neither is his thoughts our thoughts! O! may we bow with submission to his will.

"... Last night our darling Willie was called from earth, to vie with angels around the throne of God. He was buried to-day upon an elevated point, one hundred and fifty feet above the plain in a spot of sweet seclusion. ... He was four years of age ..."

—Abigail Scott, August 25–28, 1852

A woman pioneer

Primary Sources

In-text Primary Sources

> **❝**Everything we have, all our great institutions, hospitals, universities, libraries, this city, our laws, our music, art, poetry, our freedoms, everything is because somebody went before us and did the hard work. . . . Indifference to history isn't just ignorant, it's rude. It's a form of ingratitude.**❞**
>
> —David McCullough, *Why History?*

> **❝**This destruction of the tea is so bold, so daring, so firm . . . it must have such important and lasting results that I can't help considering it a turning point in history.**❞**
>
> —Diary of John Adams, December 17, 1773

> **❝**We hold these truths to be self-evident, that all men are created equal; that they are endowed by their Creator with certain unalienable rights; that among these are life, liberty, and the pursuit of happiness.**❞**
>
> —Declaration of Independence

Primary Sources

> ❝I doubt . . . whether any other Convention . . . may be able to make a better Constitution. . . . I cannot help expressing a wish, that every member of the Convention who may still have objections to it, would with me, on this occasion, doubt a little of his own infallibility, and . . . put his name to this instruction.❞
>
> —Benjamin Franklin, *Records of the Federal Convention of 1787*

> ❝We were worked in all weathers. It was never too hot or too cold; it could never rain, blow, hail, or snow too hard for us to work in the field. Work, work, work. . . . The longest days were too short for him and the shortest nights too long for him.❞
>
> —Frederick Douglass, *Narrative of the Life of Frederick Douglass, An American Slave*

> **❝**I have as much muscle as any man, and can do as much work as any man. I have plowed and reaped and husked and chopped and mowed, and can any man do more than that?**❞**
>
> —Sojourner Truth, speech at Akron women's rights convention, 1851

> **❝**This momentous question, like a fire bell in the night, awakened and filled me with terror. I considered it at once as the knell of the Union. . . . We have the wolf by the ears, and we can neither hold him, nor safely let him go.**❞**
>
> —Thomas Jefferson, Letter to John Holmes, April 22, 1820

> **❝**Veterans deserve to know that we as a people honor their service. Please honor their sacrifice. Pay tribute each day to their irreplaceable gift to our nation. And take a moment to thank tomorrow's veterans. It's never too early to let them know how deeply we recognize their passionate commitment to keep America safe.**❞**
>
> —2000 Veterans Day Speech, Army Public Affairs Division

Maps

Chapter Maps

(continued)

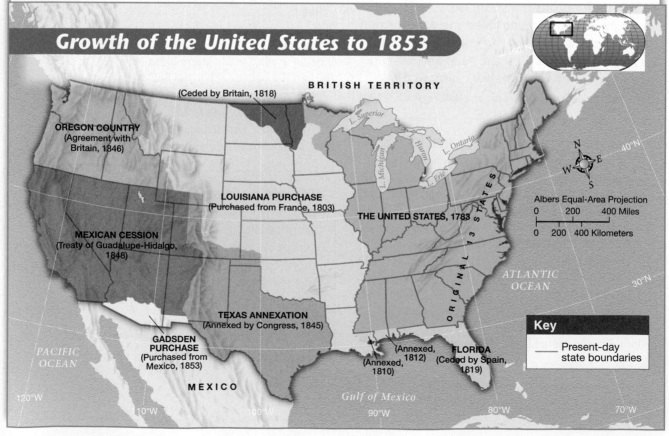

Growth of the United States to 1853

BRITISH TERRITORY

(Ceded by Britain, 1818)

OREGON COUNTRY
(Agreement with
Britain, 1846)

LOUISIANA PURCHASE
(Purchased from France, 1803)

THE UNITED STATES, 1783

MEXICAN CESSION
(Treaty of Guadalupe-Hidalgo,
1848)

TEXAS ANNEXATION
(Annexed by Congress, 1845)

GADSDEN
PURCHASE
(Purchased from
Mexico, 1853)

(Annexed,
1810)

(Annexed,
1812)

FLORIDA
(Ceded by Spain,
1819)

MEXICO

PACIFIC
OCEAN

ATLANTIC
OCEAN

Gulf of Mexico

L. Superior
L. Michigan
Huron
L. Ontario
Erie

ORIGINAL 13 STATES

Albers Equal-Area Projection
0   200   400 Miles
0   200   400 Kilometers

Key
Present-day
state boundaries

120°W   110°W   100°W   90°W   80°W   70°W
60°N   40°N   30°N

Maps/Political Cartoons

THE HORSE AMERICA, throwing his Master.

The Horse "America" Throwing His Master

Charts and Graphs

Charts and Graphs

(continued)

The Tariff of 1816

How a Protective Tariff Works

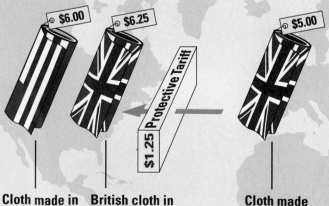

Cloth made in United States

Cost = $6.00

British cloth in United States

Cost = $5.00
    + $1.25 Tariff

Final Cost = $6.25

Cloth made in Britain

Cost = $5.00

Effects of a Protective Tariff, 1810–1840

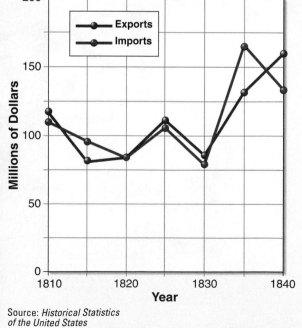

Source: *Historical Statistics of the United States*

Charts and Graphs

France Enters the War

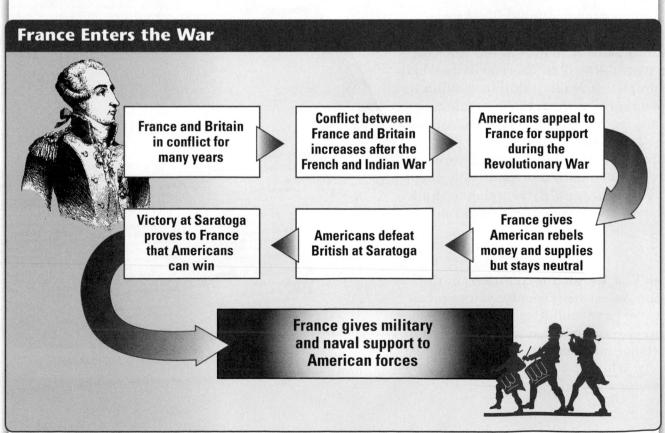

France and Britain in conflict for many years → Conflict between France and Britain increases after the French and Indian War → Americans appeal to France for support during the Revolutionary War → France gives American rebels money and supplies but stays neutral → Americans defeat British at Saratoga → Victory at Saratoga proves to France that Americans can win → France gives military and naval support to American forces

Use This Book for Success

You can use *The American Nation* as a tool to master American history. Spend a few minutes becoming familiar with the way the textbook is set up, and see how you can unlock the secrets of American history.

Read for Content Mastery

Before You Read You will begin each section of the text by reading the Section Objectives. These statements give you a purpose for reading and guide you to the critical content you need to master. Another helpful aid is the ⚙ **Target Reading Skills** exercise and graphic organizer at the beginning of each section. It encourages you to use reading skills to organize the content of the section. You will learn more about Target Reading Skills on pages xxxii–xxxiii.

As You Read *The American Nation* provides many opportunities for you to strengthen your reading skills. As you read the text, you will see ⚙ **Target Reading Skills** activities in the side column next to the text. These activities help you practice a reading skill in relation to the content you are actually reading. If you are reading about Native Americans of the Great Plains, it might ask you to construct questions you might have asked the Plains Native Americans about the roles of women. By stopping to think as you read, you will gain a better understanding of the text.

After You Read The questions in the Section Assessment require you to recall what you have read. Use these questions to assess your comprehension. Then, gain additional information by completing the activity. When you do activities, you continue to learn.

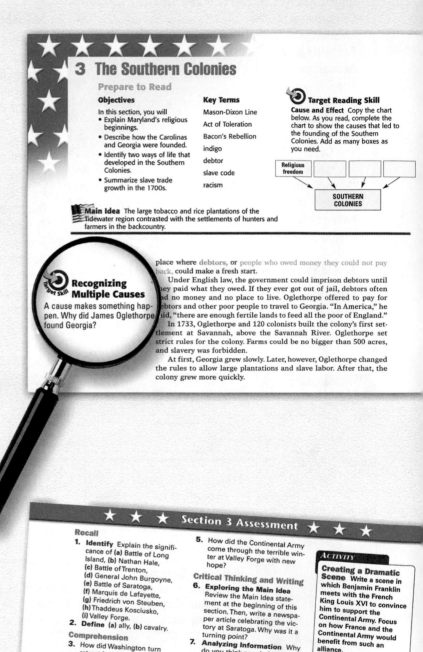

3 The Southern Colonies

Prepare to Read

Objectives

In this section, you will
- Explain Maryland's religious beginnings.
- Describe how the Carolinas and Georgia were founded.
- Identify two ways of life that developed in the Southern Colonies.
- Summarize slave trade growth in the 1700s.

Key Terms

Mason-Dixon Line
Act of Toleration
Bacon's Rebellion
indigo
debtor
slave code
racism

⚙ **Target Reading Skill**

Cause and Effect Copy the chart below. As you read, complete the chart to show the causes that led to the founding of the Southern Colonies. Add as many boxes as you need.

Religious freedom → → → SOUTHERN COLONIES

Main Idea The large tobacco and rice plantations of the Tidewater region contrasted with the settlements of hunters and farmers in the backcountry.

⚙ **Recognizing Multiple Causes**

A cause makes something happen. Why did James Oglethorpe found Georgia?

place where debtors, or people who owed money they could not pay back, could make a fresh start.

Under English law, the government could imprison debtors until they paid what they owed. If they ever got out of jail, debtors often had no money and no place to live. Oglethorpe offered to pay for debtors and other poor people to travel to Georgia. "In America," he said, "there are enough fertile lands to feed all the poor of England."

In 1733, Oglethorpe and 120 colonists built the colony's first settlement at Savannah, above the Savannah River. Oglethorpe set strict rules for the colony. Farms could be no bigger than 500 acres, and slavery was forbidden.

At first, Georgia grew slowly. Later, however, Oglethorpe changed the rules to allow large plantations and slave labor. After that, the colony grew more quickly.

★ ★ ★ **Section 3 Assessment** ★ ★ ★

Recall

1. **Identify** Explain the significance of (a) Battle of Long Island, (b) Nathan Hale, (c) Battle of Trenton, (d) General John Burgoyne, (e) Battle of Saratoga, (f) Marquis de Lafayette, (g) Friedrich von Steuben, (h) Thaddeus Kosciusko, (i) Valley Forge.
2. **Define** (a) ally, (b) cavalry.

Comprehension

3. How did Washington turn retreat into victory in New Jersey?
4. Explain the results of the Battle of Saratoga.

5. How did the Continental Army come through the terrible winter at Valley Forge with new hope?

Critical Thinking and Writing

6. **Exploring the Main Idea** Review the Main Idea statement at the beginning of this section. Then, write a newspaper article celebrating the victory at Saratoga. Why was it a turning point?
7. **Analyzing Information** Why do you think people from other lands, such as Lafayette and Pulaski, were willing to risk their lives to help the American cause?

ACTIVITY

Creating a Dramatic Scene Write a scene in which Benjamin Franklin meets with the French King Louis XVI to convince him to support the Continental Army. Focus on how France and the Continental Army would benefit from such an alliance.

Chapter 6 *Section 3* ★ **185**

Develop Your Skills

Each chapter has a Skills for Life feature. Use these features to learn and practice social studies skills. These skills will help you be successful in understanding American history. Complete the Skills Assessment at the end of every chapter to apply the skills that you have learned.

Use the Internet to Explore

With the click of a mouse, the Internet connects you to a wealth of American history resources. Use the Go Online activities to research and learn more about key concepts in American history. The Virtual Field Trips in the American Heritage® History Happened Here feature let you explore historic sites online.

For chapter summaries, Internet activities, and more, use **Web Code mgk-1000**.

Prepare for Tests

The American Nation helps you prepare for tests. Start by answering the questions at the end of every section and chapter. Go to **PHSchool.com** at the end of each chapter to take the practice Chapter Self-Test. Then, use the Test Preparation pages at the end of the unit to test your knowledge further.

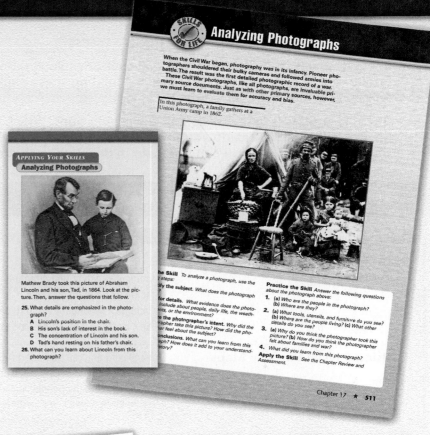

For chapter summaries, Internet activities, and more, use Web Code mgk-1000

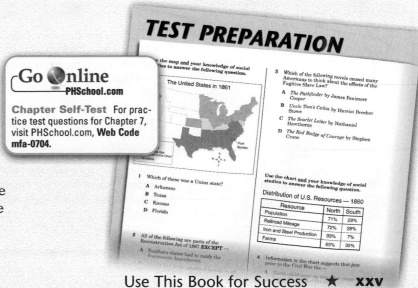

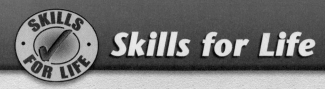
What are the keys to social studies success?

In every social studies course you will ever take, you will need to know how to use the following 20 core skills. Building these skills year by year will make you a stronger student.

Read through this list of skills and their definitions. Which ones do you know well? Which ones do you need to strengthen? Beside each definition, the page where you can find help in developing that skill is listed.

Skill	Definition	Example
GEOGRAPHIC LITERACY		
1. Using the Cartographer's Tools	The ability to use the • compass rose to find directions and relative location. • scale to estimate distance. • latitude and longitude grid to determine exact location. • key, or legend, to understand map symbols and colors.	p. 10
2. Using Special Purpose Maps	The ability to analyze and interpret maps of • natural features, such as elevation and climate. • features made by people, such as land use, roads, countries, population density, and battles.	p. 390
VISUAL ANALYZING		
3. Analyzing Graphic Data	The ability to read and interpret numeric information represented in • bar graphs. • line graphs. • circle graphs.	p. 258
4. Analyzing Images	The ability to identify and interpret symbols, tone, and message in • paintings and drawings. • photos. • posters and political cartoons.	p. 511
CRITICAL THINKING AND READING		
5. Identifying Main Ideas/ Summarizing	Identifying the main idea is the ability to distinguish the general idea of a passage from its supporting details. Summarizing is the ability to combine main ideas into an overview.	p. 61
6. Sequencing	The ability to organize items in order according to time, size, or priority.	p. 73
7. Identifying Cause and Effect/ Making Predictions	Identifying cause and effect is the ability to understand how an action or event leads to a result. Making predictions is the ability to use cause-and-effect understanding to determine the likely outcome of subsequent events or actions.	p. 161

Skill	Definition	Example
8. Drawing Inferences and Conclusions	Drawing inferences is the ability to determine the necessary consequences of an assumption: if this is true, that must be true. Drawing conclusions is the ability to analyze several inferences to make a reasoned judgment.	p. 295
9. Making Valid Generalizations	The ability to apply conclusions from specific circumstances to larger circumstances while maintaining accuracy.	p. 427
10. Distinguishing Fact and Opinion	The ability to separate those statements that can be proven to be true from those that reflect a personal viewpoint.	p. 369
11. Comparing and Contrasting	The ability to identify how different ideas, objects, historical figures, or situations are alike and/or different.	p. 347
12. Analyzing Primary Sources	The ability to evaluate a firsthand account for accuracy, tone, viewpoint, and frame of reference.	p. 219
13. Recognizing Bias and Propaganda	The ability to identify a stated or unstated viewpoint or slant that is designed to promote one set of beliefs over another.	p. 477
14. Identifying Frame of Reference and Point of View	The ability to identify an opinion expressed in writing or visual art and to understand the influences that shaped the writer's or artist's position.	p. 172
15. Decision making	The ability to state a question clearly, identify and evaluate possible choices, and select the option that seems to produce the best outcome.	p. 443
16. Problem solving	The ability to state a problem clearly, identify possible solutions, determine the likely outcome of each, select an option, and then evaluate its effectiveness.	p. 520
COMMUNICATIONS		
17. Using Reliable Information	The ability to locate and apply information for a variety of purposes that has been evaluated for its accuracy, age, authority, and bias.	p. 428
18. Transferring Information From One Medium to Another	The ability to translate numerical or visual information into text and to translate written information into graphs, tables, or diagrams.	p. 567
19. Synthesizing Information	The ability to analyze and combine information from several sources to draw conclusions and/or to create a new presentation of information.	p. 315
20. Supporting a Position	The ability to present evidence or reasoning that defends a given opinion or statement.	p. 72

Reading Informational Texts

Reading and understanding the material in a textbook is not the same as reading a novel or magazine article. The purpose of reading a textbook is to acquire information. There are many reading strategies that can help you get the most out of reading informational texts. In this section, we will focus on reading strategies that will help increase your comprehension of the information in your textbook. We will also look at ways to develop vocabulary as you read. Finally, we will examine a few skills that will help you read textbooks and other nonfiction materials with a more critical eye. On pages xxxii–xxxiii, you will read about some  **Target Reading Skills** that you will have a chance to practice as you read this textbook.

Reading Your Textbook

The reading strategies described below will help you before, during, and after you read. They will help you understand and remember what you have read.

Previewing: Prepare to Read

Before you begin reading a chapter or a section, take a few minutes to preview the text to get an idea of what you will be reading. Previewing will give you an overview of the chapter or section, help you consider what you already know, and give you some idea of what you are expected to learn.

- ❑ Read the chapter or section title.
- ❑ Read the objectives, key terms, and main ideas that begin each section.
- ❑ Check the Target Reading Skill and graphic organizer at the start of each section.
- ❑ Scan the headings and subheadings.
- ❑ Look at photos, maps, and charts.
- ❑ Check highlighted words and definitions.
- ❑ Read the questions at the end of the section or chapter.
- ❑ Read the section summaries that appear in the Chapter Review and Assessments.

Reading: Be an Active Reader

Become an active reader by learning to think about the meanings of new terms, main ideas, and the details that support the main ideas. Use the strategies listed here as you read. They will help you interact with your text.

- ☐ Take notes as you read.
- ☐ Turn headings into questions and look for the answers.
- ☐ Recall related information that you have previously learned.
- ☐ Use context clues and word structure to determine word meanings.
- ☐ Distinguish between facts and opinions.
- ☐ Identify the main ideas of sections, subsections, and paragraphs.
- ☐ Stop every so often and ask yourself, "Do I understand what I have read?"
- ☐ Reread to clarify words or ideas that you might not have understood the first time you read.

After Reading

Take time to be sure you understand and can remember what you have read. Use the strategies listed here to help you review and recall main ideas and details.

- ☐ Review the headings and subheadings.
- ☐ Summarize the main ideas and recall supporting details.
- ☐ Check the notes you took.
- ☐ Understanding informational texts often requires reading more than once. If you need to, read parts or all of the section again.
- ☐ If you still have questions about the content, get help from a classmate or your teacher.

Reading and Writing Handbook

Increase Vocabulary

Good readers try to increase their vocabulary. Using strategies that help you learn new words as you read will help you become a better reader.

Context

When you come across an unfamiliar word, you can sometimes determine its meaning from the context. The context is the surrounding words and sentences. Look for clues in the surrounding words, sentences, and paragraphs to help you understand the meaning of the unfamiliar word.

Word Analysis

Word analysis refers to strategies you can use to determine the meanings of unfamiliar words by breaking them into parts. Many words have a root and a prefix or a suffix. A root is the base of a word. It may be a word that has a meaning by itself. A prefix is placed at the beginning of a root and changes the meaning of the root. Think about the word *justice.* If you add *in-* as a prefix to *justice,* the word becomes *injustice. Justice* means "to be fair, right, or correct," while *injustice* is "the quality of being unfair."

A suffix is placed at the end of a root and changes the word's part of speech. If you add *-ment* to the root *amend,* it becomes *amendment. Amend* is a verb. *Amendment* is a noun.

Analyze Informational Text

Here are several reading strategies to help you think about and analyze informational text. They include analyzing the author's purpose, distinguishing between facts and opinions, identifying evidence, and evaluating credibility.

Analyze the Author's Purpose

Different types of materials are written with different purposes in mind. For example, a textbook is written to teach students information about a subject. The purpose of a technical manual is to teach someone how to use something, such as a computer. A newspaper editorial might be written to persuade the reader to a particular point of view. A writer's purpose influences how the material is presented.

Distinguish Between Facts and Opinions

It is important to distinguish between fact and opinion. A fact can be proved or disproved. An opinion reveals someone's personal viewpoint or evaluation.

For example, the editorial pages in a newspaper offer opinions on current events. You need to read newspaper editorials with an eye for bias and faulty logic. The newspaper editorial shown here shows factual statements in blue and opinion statements in red. The underlined words are examples of highly charged words and exaggerations. They reveal the writer's bias.

More than 5,000 people voted last week in favor of building a new shopping center, but the opposition won out. The margin of victory is irrelevant. Those <u>radical</u> voters who opposed the center are obviously <u>self-serving elitists</u> who do not care about anyone but themselves.

This month's unemployment figures for our area are 10 percent, which represents an increase of about 5 percent over the figures for last year. These figures mean that unemployment is worsening. But the people who voted against the mall probably do not care about creating new jobs.

Identify Evidence

Before you accept a writer's conclusions, you need to make sure that the writer has based the conclusion on enough evidence and on an accurate portrayal of the evidence. A writer may present a whole series of facts to support a claim, but the facts may not tell the whole story.

For example, what evidence does the writer in the newspaper editorial above provide to support his claim that shopping centers create more jobs? Isn't it possible that the shopping center might put local stores out of business, thus increasing unemployment rather than decreasing it?

Evaluate Credibility

Whenever you read informational texts, you need to assess the credibility of the writer. This is especially true of Web sites you may visit on the Internet. Here are some questions to ask yourself when evaluating the credibility of a Web site.

☐ Did a respected organization, a discussion group, or an individual create the Web site?

☐ Does the Web site creator include his or her name and credentials, as well as the sources he or she used to write the content?

☐ Is the information on the site objective or biased?

☐ Can you verify the information using two other sources?

☐ Is there a date on the Web site?

How to Read Social Studies

⤵ Target Reading Skills

The Target Reading Skills introduced on this page will help you understand the words and ideas in your textbook. Each chapter contains several of these strategies, and each strategy is paired with a graphic organizer. The graphic organizers help you visualize and organize the content you are reading. In the margins of your textbook, you will find Target Reading Skill sidenotes that will help you use the reading skill and the graphic organizer while you read the text. Good readers develop a bank of reading strategies. Then, they draw on the particular strategies that will help them understand what they are reading.

⤵ Reading Process

Reading actively will help you remember what you have read. The paragraphs below describe several ways to read actively. In addition, preparing an outline or using a chart, table, or concept web can help focus your reading.

❶ Set a Purpose

When you set a purpose for reading, you give yourself a focus. Before you read a section, study the objectives and look at headings and visuals to see what the section is about.

❷ Predict

Making predictions helps you remember what you read. After studying the objectives, headings, and visuals, predict what the text might discuss.

❸ Ask Questions

Before you read a section, write down one or two questions that will help you understand or remember something important in the section. Read to answer your questions.

❹ Use Prior Knowledge

Your prior knowledge is what you already know about a topic before you read. Building on what you already know helps you learn new information.

⤵ Clarifying Meaning

Clarifying meaning helps you understand what you have read. Reread difficult passages. Paraphrase, or restate in your own words, what those passages mean. Summarize, or state in the correct order, the main points you have read. Outlining and filling in charts, tables, or concept webs can help to clarify meaning.

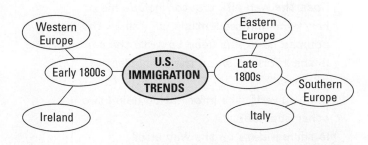

Main Idea

It is impossible to remember every detail that you read. Good readers therefore identify the main idea in every paragraph or section. The main idea is the most important point in a passage. Main ideas are supported by details that add more information. Use outlines and concept webs to help you identify main ideas and supporting details.

I. Differences Between the North and the South
  A. Views on slavery
    1. Northern abolitionists
    2. Southern slave owners
  B. Economies
    1. Northern manufacturing
    2. Southern agriculture

Comparison and Contrast

Comparing and contrasting can help you sort and analyze information. When you compare, you examine the similarities between things. When you contrast, you look at the differences. A Venn diagram is a good tool for comparing and contrasting people, places, events, or ideas.

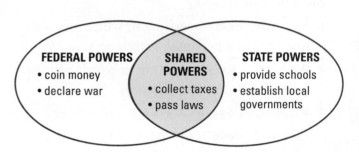

FEDERAL POWERS
• coin money
• declare war

SHARED POWERS
• collect taxes
• pass laws

STATE POWERS
• provide schools
• establish local governments

Sequence

A sequence is the order in which a series of events occurs. Noting the sequence of important events can help you understand and remember the events. You can track the order of events by making a flowchart. Write the first event, which sets the other events in motion, in the first box. Then, write each additional event in a box. Use arrows to show how one event leads to the next.

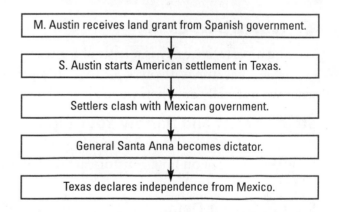

M. Austin receives land grant from Spanish government.

↓

S. Austin starts American settlement in Texas.

↓

Settlers clash with Mexican government.

↓

General Santa Anna becomes dictator.

↓

Texas declares independence from Mexico.

Cause and Effect

Determining causes and effects helps you understand relationships among situations or events. A cause makes something happen. An effect is what happens. Remember that there can be more than one cause for an event and more than one effect. Fill in a cause-and-effect chart to help you understand how causes lead to events and how effects are the results of events.

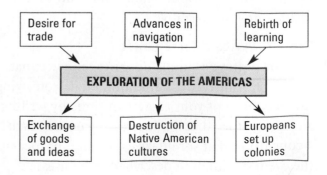

Desire for trade | Advances in navigation | Rebirth of learning

EXPLORATION OF THE AMERICAS

Exchange of goods and ideas | Destruction of Native American cultures | Europeans set up colonies

Writing for Social Studies

When you face a writing assignment, do you think, "How will I ever get through this?" Research shows that writing about what you have read actually helps you remember new content. And, of course, good writing skills are important for doing well on tests. Here are some tips to guide you through your social studies writing assignments, whether they are short-answer questions on a test, essays, or research papers.

Types of Writing

There are many different types of writing. Here are six types that are most often assigned:

1. **Narrative Essay**—writing in which you tell a story about a personal experience

2. **Persuasive Essay**—writing in which you support an opinion or a position

3. **Expository Essay**—writing in which you explain a process, compare and contrast, explain causes and effects, or explore solutions

4. **Research Paper**—writing in which you conduct research and write about a specific topic

5. **Writing Extended Responses on a Test**—writing essays for a test

6. **Writing Short Answers on a Test**—writing briefly to respond to short-answer questions

① Narrative Essay

Writing a narrative essay is a natural form of expression because it involves putting onto paper what we normally do when we tell a good story.

Step 1: Select and Narrow Your Topic

A narrative is a story. In social studies, a narrative essay might focus on how a historical event affected you or your family.

Step 2: Gather Details

Brainstorm for a list of details you want to include in your narrative.

Step 3: Write a First Draft

Start by writing a simple opening sentence that will catch your reader's attention while conveying the main idea of your essay. Continue by writing a colorful story that has interesting details. Write a conclusion that summarizes the significance of the event or situation described in your essay.

Step 4: Revise and Edit

Check to make sure you have not begun too many sentences with the word *I*. Replace general words with more specific, colorful ones.

Main idea →
Details →

My trip to Independence Hall in Philadelphia reminded me of two important U.S. documents. Here in 1776, delegates adopted the Declaration of Independence. Eleven years later, it was here that the Constitution of the United States was debated, drafted, and signed. That document is the world's oldest federal constitution in existence. As I stood in the hall, I could almost hear the arguments of delegates. I could understand why Benjamin Franklin was so pleased with the result of the debates. The trip to Independence Hall reminded me that ideas expressed on pieces of paper can be as powerful as any weapons of war.

Significance of narrative →

❷ Persuasive Essay

A persuasive essay is writing in which you support an opinion or a position.

Step 1: Select and Narrow Your Topic

Choose a topic that provokes an argument and has at least two sides. Your task will be to persuade most of your readers to understand your point of view.

Step 2: Gather Evidence

Create a table that states your position at the top and lists the pros and cons for your position beneath it.

Step 3: Write a First Draft

Write a strong thesis statement that clearly states your position. Continue by presenting the strongest arguments in favor of your position. Take time to acknowledge and refute opposing arguments, too.

Step 4: Revise and Edit

Check to make sure you have made a logical argument and that you have not oversimplified the argument. Add the following transition words to make your reasoning more obvious:

To show a contrast—*however, although, despite*

To point out a reason—*since, because, if*

To signal a conclusion—*therefore, consequently, so, then*

❸ Expository Essay

An expository essay is writing in which you explain a process, compare and contrast, explain causes and effects, or explore solutions to a problem.

Step 1: Select and Narrow Your Topic

Expository writing is writing that explains something in detail. It might explain the similarities and differences between two or more subjects (compare and contrast). It might explain how one event causes another (cause and effect), or it might explain a problem and describe a solution.

Step 2: Gather Evidence

Create a graphic organizer that identifies details to include in your essay. You might create a Venn diagram for a comparison-and-contrast essay, a diagram showing multiple causes and effects for a cause-and-effect essay, or a web for defining all the aspects of a problem and possible solutions.

Step 3: Write a First Draft

Write a strong topic sentence. Then, organize the body of your essay around the similarities and differences, causes and effects, or problem and solutions. Be sure to include convincing details, facts, and examples.

Step 4: Revise and Edit

Revise to include transition words between sentences and paragraphs.

To show similarities—*all, similarly, both, in the same way, closely related, equally*

To show differences—*on the other hand, in contrast, however, instead, yet*

Reading and Writing Handbook

④ Research Paper

A research paper is writing in which you conduct research and write about a specific topic. Research papers are very different from other types of writing. People who enjoy creative writing may find this form of writing more challenging. Others who do not enjoy creative writing may excel at writing research papers.

Step 1: Select and Narrow Your Topic

Choose something you are interested in, but make sure that the topic is not too broad. For example, instead of writing a paper on Panama, write about the construction of the Panama Canal. Ask yourself, What do I want to know about the topic?

Step 2: Acquire Information

Use several sources of information about the topic from the library, the Internet, or an interview with someone knowledgeable. Before you use a source, make sure that it is reliable and up to date. Take notes using an index card for each detail or subtopic, and note the source of the information. Use quotation marks when you copy the exact words from a source. Create a source index card for each resource, listing the author, title, publisher, and place and date of publication.

Step 3: Make an Outline

Decide on the organization of your report by creating an outline. Sort your index cards into the order of your outline.

Step 4: Write a First Draft

Write an introduction, body, and conclusion. Leave plenty of space between lines so you can go back and add details that you may have left out. Make sure that you have at least one new paragraph on each doubled-spaced page. If you don't, your paragraphs are probably too long and your reader may get lost or lose interest.

Outline
I. Introduction
II. Why the Canal Was Built
III. How the Canal Was Built

Reference
McCullough, David. *The Path Between the Seas: The Creation of the Panama Canal, 1870-1914.* N.Y., Simon and Schuster, 1977.

Good detail for body:
"In 1904, the U.S. government began the largest civil engineering project in its history. An enthusiastic President Theodore Roosevelt set the work in motion by urging the engineers to "Make the dirt fly!"

Introduction

Building the Panama Canal
Ever since Christopher Columbus first explored the Isthmus of Panama, people had been looking for a water route through it. They wanted to be able to travel from the Atlantic to the Pacific without having to sail around the southern tip of South America. However, it was not until 1914 that the dream became a reality.

Conclusion

It took eight years and more than 70,000 workers to make the Panama Canal. It remains one of the greatest engineering feats of modern times.

⑤ Writing Extended Responses on a Test

Step 1: Choose a Writing Prompt and Budget Time

In some testing situations, you may be given a choice of writing prompts, or topics. Before choosing one, consider how much you know about a topic and how much a topic interests you. To budget time, allow about

- 1/4 of your time to prepare to write,
- 1/2 of your time writing a first draft,
- 1/4 of your time revising and editing.

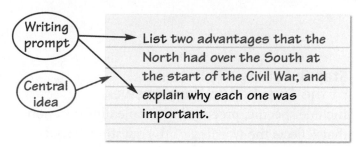

Writing prompt / Central idea

List two advantages that the North had over the South at the start of the Civil War, and explain why each one was important.

Step 2: Carefully Analyze the Question or Writing Prompt

Pay special attention to key words that indicate exactly what you are supposed to do:

Explain—Give a clear, complete account of how something works or why something happened.

Compare and Contrast—Provide details about how two or more things are alike and how they are different.

Describe—Provide vivid details to paint a word picture of a person, place, or thing.

Argue and Convince—Take a position on an issue and present strong reasons to support your side of the issue.

Summarize—Provide the highlights or most important elements of a subject.

Classify—Group things into categories and define the categories using facts and examples.

Persuade—Provide convincing reasons to accept your position.

Step 3: Gather Details

Take a few minutes to divide your topic into subtopics. Jot down as many facts and details as you can for each subtopic. Create a graphic organizer to organize the details.

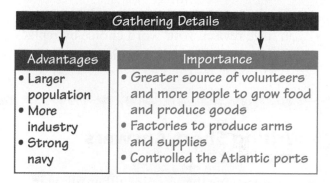

Gathering Details

Advantages	Importance
• Larger population • More industry • Strong navy	• Greater source of volunteers and more people to grow food and produce goods • Factories to produce arms and supplies • Controlled the Atlantic ports

Step 4: Write a First Draft

Write a single sentence that sums up your main point. Use this sentence as the centerpiece of an introductory paragraph. Then, consider the best plan for organizing your essay.

- For a summary or an explanation, organize your details in chronological order, as on a time line.
- For a comparison-and-contrast essay, present similarities first and then differences.
- For a persuasive essay, organize your points by order of importance.

Use the organization you've selected to write your first draft.

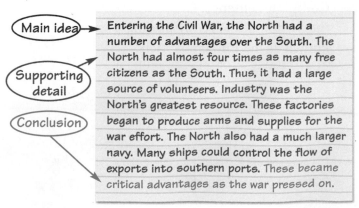

Main idea / Supporting detail / Conclusion

Entering the Civil War, the North had a number of advantages over the South. The North had almost four times as many free citizens as the South. Thus, it had a large source of volunteers. Industry was the North's greatest resource. These factories began to produce arms and supplies for the war effort. The North also had a much larger navy. Many ships could control the flow of exports into southern ports. These became critical advantages as the war pressed on.

Reading and Writing Handbook

Step 5: Revise

Read your response to make sure that

- the introduction includes a strong main idea sentence and presents subtopics.
- each paragraph focuses on a single topic.
- you have included transition words between sentences and paragraphs, such as *first, for example, because,* and *for this reason.*
- you have revised your word choice by replacing general words with specific ones.

Step 6: Edit and Proof

Read your response to make sure each sentence

- contains a subject and a verb.
- begins with a capital letter.
- ends with a period, question mark, or exclamation point.

Correct any spelling or punctuation errors.

⑥ Writing Short Answers on a Test

These are questions that require either filling in blanks, paragraph answers, or bullet-point answers.

Step 1: Use Key Words From the Question

Read the question carefully, noting key words.

Step 2: Write in Complete Sentences

When answering a short-answer question, always be clear and concise. Practice writing a structured response. Begin by introducing the key topic words you have jotted down.

Question: What was Great Britain's response to the Boston Tea Party?

Fragment: The Intolerable Acts

Complete sentence: Great Britain responded to the Boston Tea Party by passing a series of laws known as the Intolerable Acts.

Step 3: Follow the Pattern of the Question in Your Answer

Include specific, precise, and detailed information that reflects the wording of the question. Avoid vague answers.

Question: Who was Thomas Jefferson, and why is he remembered today?

Vague response: Jefferson was a Virginian who did many important things in the early days of American history.

Precise response: Jefferson wrote the Declaration of Independence and was the third President of the United States.

Step 4: Write a Draft

Write an introductory sentence. Then, provide an illustration or example that supports the introductory sentence. Be sure to answer only what the question asks.

Evaluating Your Writing: Rubrics

Most essays are scored on the following elements:

Purpose—distinct main idea, theme, or unified point

Organization—clear beginning, middle, and end; obvious relationship between one point and the next and between sentences and paragraphs using transitions

Elaboration—important details and specific, thorough, and correct word choices to explain the topic

Language—strong command of punctuation, capitalization, sentence structure, and spelling

Use the rubric below to help you evaluate your writing.

	Excellent	Good	Acceptable	Unacceptable
Purpose	Achieves purpose—to inform, persuade, or provide historical interpretation—very well	Informs, persuades, or provides historical interpretation reasonably well	Reader cannot easily tell if the purpose is to inform, persuade, or provide historical interpretation	Lacks purpose
Organization	Develops ideas in a very clear and logical way	Presents ideas in a reasonably well-organized way	Reader has difficulty following the organization	Lacks organization
Elaboration	Explains all ideas with facts and details	Explains most ideas with facts and details	Includes some supporting facts and details	Lacks supporting details
Use of Language	Uses excellent vocabulary and sentence structure with no errors in spelling, grammar, or punctuation	Uses good vocabulary and sentence structure with few errors in spelling, grammar, or punctuation	Includes some errors in spelling, grammar, or punctuation	Includes many errors in spelling, grammar, or punctuation

Unit 1

Roots of American History

An Untouched Landscape
Grand Canyon by William Robinson Leigh captures the natural beauty of the American continent.

> **"**For this is what America is all about. It is the uncrossed desert and the unclimbed ridge. It is the star that is not reached and the harvest sleeping in the unplowed ground.**"**
>
> —Lyndon B. Johnson, President of the United States (1965)

Geography, History, and the Social Sciences

PREHISTORY–PRESENT

1 **Thinking Geographically**
2 **Lands and Climates of the United States**
3 **The Tools of History**
4 **Economics and Other Social Sciences**

Early encounter between Europeans and Native Americans

Settlers clearing the land

AMERICAN EVENTS

1500s
The first global age begins with the meeting between Europeans and Native Americans.

1600s
England sets up colonies in North America.

1700s
Thirteen English colonies separate from Great Britain and form the United States of America.

Prehistory 1500 · · · · · · 1600 · · · · · 1700

▲ **1500s**
Europeans explore the Americas.

▲ **1600s**
European nations struggle for control of North America.

Physical Features of the United States

The United States is divided into different physical regions.

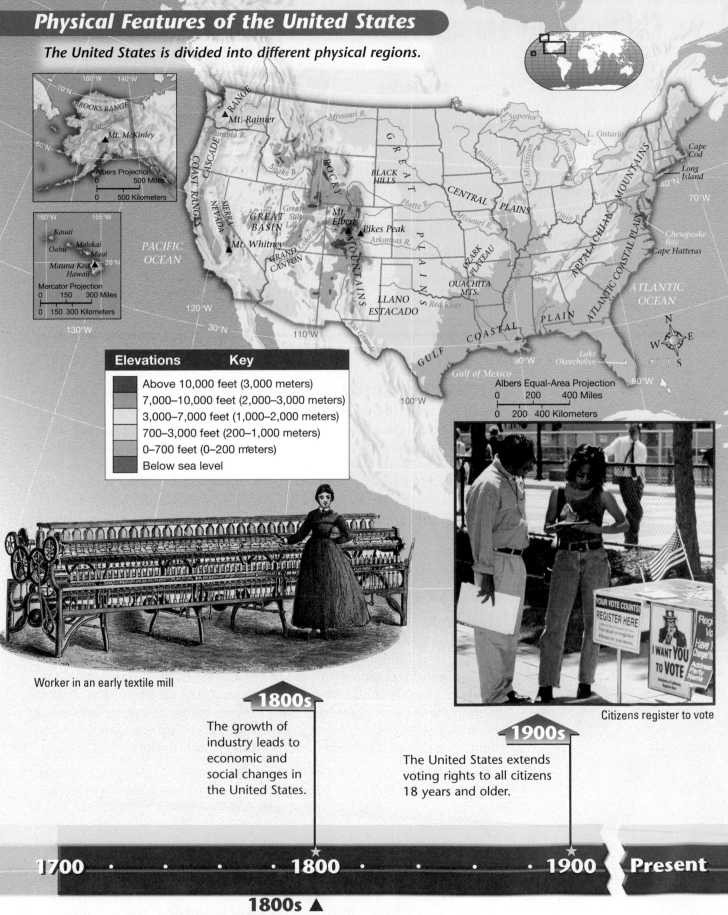

Elevations Key

- Above 10,000 feet (3,000 meters)
- 7,000–10,000 feet (2,000–3,000 meters)
- 3,000–7,000 feet (1,000–2,000 meters)
- 700–3,000 feet (200–1,000 meters)
- 0–700 feet (0–200 meters)
- Below sea level

Worker in an early textile mill

Citizens register to vote

1800s

The growth of industry leads to economic and social changes in the United States.

1900s

The United States extends voting rights to all citizens 18 years and older.

1700 · · · · · · 1800 · · · · · 1900 Present

1800s ▲
Millions of immigrants move to the United States.

1 Thinking Geographically

Prepare to Read

Objectives

In this section, you will

- Explain how the five themes of geography help define the connections between geography and history.
- Identify how geography influenced population trends in U.S. history.
- Describe how maps are made and used.

Key Terms

geography

latitude

longitude

natural resources

irrigation

cartographer

map projection

thematic map

Target Reading Skill

Reading Process Copy the chart below. As you read, fill in the chart with information about the five themes of geography. Add boxes for the remaining themes.

LOCATION	PLACE
• Exact Location: longitude and latitude	• •

Main Idea Geography helps us to understand the way people have lived in different places throughout history.

A map by Samuel de Champlain

Setting the Scene In a tiny Native American fishing village, a small group gathered around a man who began to draw in the sand. They watched closely as Samuel de Champlain, a French explorer, drew a sweeping line on the ground. The line represented the coastline where they stood. The local chief drew additional lines. A young man added piles of rocks to represent the village and nearby settlements. When they were done, they had an informal map of the local area.

Champlain and the Native Americans he met on Cape Ann in Massachusetts in the 1600s did not speak the same language. Yet, they both understood the basic language of geography.

Five Themes of Geography

Geography is the study of people, their environments, and their resources. Geographers ask how the natural environment affects the way we live and how we, in turn, affect the environment.

Geography is closely linked to history. Both historians and geographers want to understand how the natural environment affects people and events. To help show these connections, geographers have developed five themes: location, place, interaction between people and their environment, movement, and regions.

Location Often, the most basic question we ask about an event is, "Where did it happen?" The answer to this question involves the geographic theme of location. There are two types of location: exact and relative.

To describe the exact location of a place, geographers use a grid of numbered lines on a map or globe. Lines of **latitude** measure distance north and south from the Equator. The Equator is an imaginary line that lies at 0° (degrees) latitude. It divides the Earth into two halves, called hemispheres. Lines of **longitude** measure distance

The Five Themes of Geography

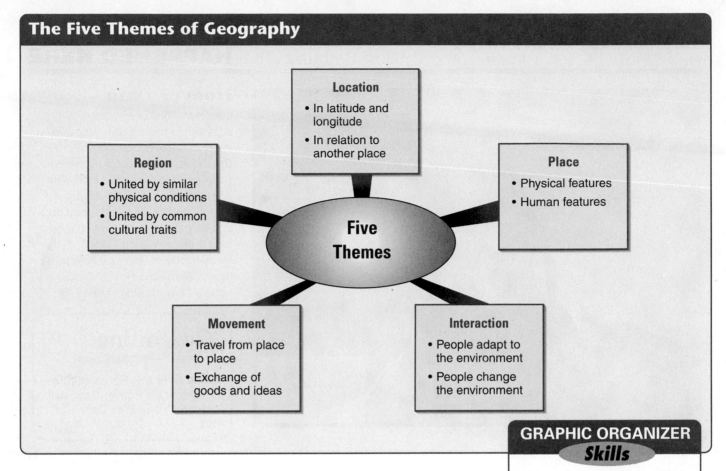

Location
- In latitude and longitude
- In relation to another place

Region
- United by similar physical conditions
- United by common cultural traits

Place
- Physical features
- Human features

Five Themes

Movement
- Travel from place to place
- Exchange of goods and ideas

Interaction
- People adapt to the environment
- People change the environment

east and west from the Prime Meridian, which runs through Greenwich (GREHN ihch), England. For example, the city of San Antonio, Texas, is located at 29 degrees (°) north latitude and 99 degrees (°) west longitude. This location is written as 29°N/99°W. In the same way, New York City is located at 41°N/74°W.

Sometimes, you will find it more useful to know relative location, or the location of a place in relation to some other place. For example, San Antonio is about 125 miles from the Mexican border. New York City is located where the Hudson River empties into the Atlantic Ocean. Relative location can help explain why people settled in certain areas or why battles took place at certain places.

Place Geographers use the theme of place to describe an area's physical and human features. Physical features include climate, soil, vegetation, animal life, and bodies of water. One of the most important aspects of a place is its **natural resources,** materials that humans can take from the environment to survive and satisfy their needs. For example, a mountain range may contain reserves of coal or iron, while a nearby river or ocean may supply fish.

People help shape the character of a place through their ideas and actions. The human features of a place include the kinds of houses people build, their means of transportation, their ways of earning a living, their languages, and their religions.

Interaction Interaction between people and their environment is a third theme of geography. Throughout history, people have adapted

Hoover Dam

Considered one of the greatest engineering projects ever, the building of the Hoover Dam demonstrates the successful interaction between people and their environment. The presence of the dam makes it possible for people to live in an area that is largely desert. Surrounding farmland is irrigated, and there is a ready supply of water and electric power. Today, the Hoover Dam is a national historic landmark.

Go Online
PHSchool.com

Virtual Field Trip For an interactive look at the Hoover Dam, visit PHSchool.com, **Web Code mfd-0101.**

---

to and changed their natural surroundings. Ancient American hunters learned to plant seeds and grow food crops. This adaptation meant they no longer had to move from place to place in search of food. Later, Native Americans in the Southwest developed methods of **irrigation,** or bringing water to dry lands. By digging ditches that channeled water from the Salt and Gila rivers, they turned arid, unproductive desert into farmland.

Today, advanced technology allows people to change their environment in even more dramatic ways. People have wiped out pests that destroyed crops and found ways to take oil from the ocean floor.

Movement A fourth geographic theme involves the movement of people, goods, and ideas. Movement occurs because people and resources are scattered unevenly around the globe. To get what they need or want, people travel from place to place. As they meet other people, they exchange ideas and technology as well as goods.

History provides many examples of movement. Early hunters populated the Americas as they followed herds of large animals. Much later, people from all over the world moved to the United States in search of opportunity or liberty. They brought customs and beliefs that have helped shape American life.

Regions A region has certain unifying characteristics. It may be defined by its physical characteristics, such as its climates or landforms. For example, the Great Plains is a region with fairly level land, hot summers, cold winters, and little rainfall. In the 1930s, when parts of the plains were hit by drought, the region was called the "Dust Bowl." The Pacific Coast region is known for rugged mountains, dense forests, and scenic ocean shores.

A region's characteristics may also be human and cultural. San Francisco's Chinatown is a region where Chinese Americans have preserved their language and culture. Bourbon Street in the city of New Orleans is associated with jazz.

Case Study: Population Trends and the Five Themes

As you study events and trends in history, you will often need to think geographically. For practice, let us see how population trends throughout the history of the United States relate to the five themes of geography.

When the United States won its independence in 1783, it was made up of 13 states located on the Atlantic coast (*region, exact location*). The majority of the population lived along the coast or near rivers (*relative location*), where water transportation was easy (*movement*). The Appalachian Mountains and other geographic features limited westward movement (*region, movement*). In 1790, the nation's center of population was located in Maryland.

The Nation Expands The United States added vast new territories in the early 1800s, eventually stretching to the Pacific Ocean (*movement, exact location*). As the nation expanded, its rapidly growing population shifted westward (*movement*). Settlers dug canals, built roads and railroads, and cut down forests to clear farmland and build log cabins (*interaction, place*).

A New Trend The westward trend continued in the late 1800s. As white settlers displaced Native Americans, the human and cultural characteristics of the West changed (*place*). By 1900, the center of population had shifted to Indiana.

In the mid-1900s, a new population trend began to emerge. Many people began to move from the Northeast to the Sunbelt, a region stretching from Florida across Texas to California (*region, movement*). Many people were attracted by the area's mild climate (*place*). In 1960, only 2 of the 10 largest American cities were located in the South or West (*region*). By 2000, six of them were: Houston, Dallas, San Antonio, Los Angeles, San Diego, and Phoenix. Furthermore, the center of the nation's population had shifted again, both southward and westward, to Missouri.

Maps and Globes

The most common tools used to understand geography are maps and globes. A map is a drawing of the surface of the Earth or part of the Earth. A globe is a sphere with a map of the Earth printed on it.

Maps and globes have different uses. Because a globe is about the same shape as the Earth, it can accurately show sizes and shapes of landforms. However, compared to a map, a globe is awkward to use. In addition, a map can show more detail than a globe and allows

Mercator Projection

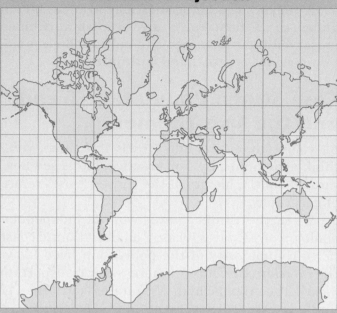

Robinson Projection

GEOGRAPHY
Skills

Map projections make it possible for mapmakers to show a round world on a flat map.

1. **Location** On the map, locate **(a)** North America, **(b)** Africa, **(c)** Asia.

2. **Place** What differences appear in the two projections of North America?

3. **Critical Thinking Comparing** On the Mercator map, which areas are most distorted?

you to see all of the Earth's surface at one time. Still, a flat map has the disadvantage that it distorts some parts of the Earth.

Map Projections Mapmakers, or **cartographers,** have developed dozens of ways of drawing the Earth on a flat surface. These methods are known as **map projections.** Each map projection has benefits and drawbacks. Some show the sizes of landmasses correctly but distort their shape. Others give continents their true shape but distort their sizes.

For hundreds of years, the most widely used map projection was the Mercator projection. It was developed in 1569 by the Flemish cartographer Gerardus Mercator. The Mercator projection was valuable because it gave sailors an accurate picture of ocean distances and the shapes of landmasses. Mercator boasted:

> 66 If you wish to sail from one port to another, here is a chart, and a straight line on it, and if you follow this line carefully you will certainly arrive at your destination. 99
> —Gerardus Mercator, "To the Readers of This Chart, Greeting!"

However, the Mercator projection distorts size, especially for places that are far from the Equator. For example, on a Mercator map, Greenland appears as big as all of South America, even though South America is more than eight times larger!

Today, many geographers use the Robinson projection. It shows the correct sizes and shapes of landmasses for most parts of the world. The Robinson projection also gives a fairly accurate view of the relationship between landmasses and bodies of water. There are many other types of map projections as well. On each map in this book, you will see a label identifying the type of projection used.

Types of Maps As you study American history, you will use various types of maps. Each one has a special purpose. Physical maps show mountain ranges, bodies of water, and other physical features. Political maps show features that are determined by people. These include the boundaries of countries and states, as well as the location of capitals and other cities. You will see examples of these types of maps in the Geographic Atlas in the Reference Section of this book.

You will also use a wide variety of **thematic maps,** or maps that deal with specific topics, that can help you understand the connections between geography and history. Population maps show the number of people who live in a particular area. Economic maps show how people make a living. Battle maps show the locations of major battles and the routes of advancing and retreating armies. Other thematic maps may provide information on natural resources, rainfall, vegetation, elections, or the religious or ethnic makeup of a place.

Making Accurate Maps The oldest surviving map in the world today was created by an ancient cartographer somewhere around 2300 B.C. Ever since, geographers have worked to make maps more accurate.

Today, cartographers create maps with the help of computers and satellites. This new technology provides incredibly complete information about the most remote corners of the Earth. As a result, today's mapmakers create maps that are more accurate than anyone had previously thought possible.

★ ★ ★ Section 1 Assessment ★ ★ ★

Recall
1. **Define** (a) geography, (b) latitude, (c) longitude, (d) natural resources, (e) irrigation, (f) cartographer, (g) map projection, (h) thematic map.

Comprehension
2. Briefly describe the five themes of geography.
3. List three population trends in the history of the United States. Give the theme, or themes, of geography illustrated by each.
4. Why does a globe show the Earth more accurately than a flat map?

Critical Thinking and Writing
5. **Exploring the Main Idea** Review the Main Idea statement at the beginning of this section. Name two ways that geography affects life in the community or state where you live. Write your findings in a paragraph.
6. **Synthesizing Information** Study the picture of the Hoover Dam on page 6. How does the dam illustrate the geographic theme of interaction?

ACTIVITY

Go Online
PHSchool.com

Connecting to Today
Use the Internet to research the satellite mapping program started in 1972. Choose a site with satellite images of the Earth. Select a picture. Print it out. In a paragraph, describe the picture. Explain how it would be useful to a cartographer. For help in completing the activity, visit PHSchool.com, **Web Code mfd-0102.**

Early maps were crude but useful pictures drawn on animal skins, clay tablets, and cloth. Today, maps are even more important tools in providing information about places on Earth. Learning how to read and interpret a map is also helpful in understanding how geography affects history.

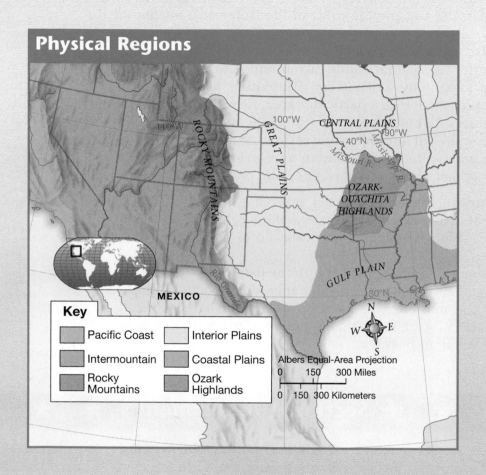

Physical Regions

Key
- Pacific Coast
- Intermountain
- Rocky Mountains
- Interior Plains
- Coastal Plains
- Ozark Highlands

Albers Equal-Area Projection

0   150   300 Miles

0   150 300 Kilometers

Learn the Skill *To review basic map-reading skills, use the following steps:*

1. **Read the title.** The title summarizes the basic information included on a map.

2. **Refer to the map key.** The key identifies what the different symbols on the map mean.

3. **Find the scales of distance.** Maps are miniature pictures of places on Earth, so they are drawn to scale. To determine actual distance, you need to know how many inches represent miles or kilometers.

4. **Use the compass rose.** The arrows on this symbol indicate directions on a map.

5. **Check for a locator map.** A locator map helps you see where on Earth a place is located.

Practice the Skill *Answer the following questions about the map above:*

1. What is the purpose of this map?

2. (a) What does the color tan represent on this map? (b) Through which physical regions does the Missouri River flow?

3. How many miles does one-half inch represent?

4. (a) What country is south of the United States? (b) In what direction are the Great Plains from the Mississippi River?

5. (a) What parts of the United States are not shown on the large map? (b) How do you know?

Apply the Skill *See the Chapter Review and Assessment.*

2 Lands and Climates of the United States

Prepare to Read

Objectives

In this section you will
- Identify the main physical regions of the United States.
- Explain how rivers and lakes affect American life.
- Describe how climates vary across the United States.

Key Terms

isthmus

elevation

erosion

tributary

weather

climate

precipitation

altitude

Target Reading Skill

Cause and Effect Copy the cause-and-effect chart. As you read, fill in additional factors that explain the causes and effects of climate.

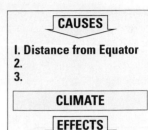

CAUSES
I. Distance from Equator
2.
3.

CLIMATE

EFFECTS
I. Hot and wet
2.
3.

Main Idea The United States is a nation of diverse landforms and climates.

Setting the Scene The view took her breath away. Katharine Lee Bates, a teacher from the East, had journeyed westward to Colorado in 1893. Standing atop the towering Pikes Peak, looking across the "sea-like expanse" below, Bates was moved to write a tribute to her land. Her poem was later set to music:

> ❝ O beautiful for spacious skies,
> For amber waves of grain,
> For purple mountain majesties
> Above the fruited plain!
> America America!
> God shed His grace on thee
> And crown thy good with brotherhood
> From sea to shining sea! ❞
>
> —Katharine Lee Bates, "America the Beautiful"

Pikes Peak

Besides plains and mountains, the United States is also a land of arid deserts and frozen tundras, quiet forests and crashing seas. This wide variety of climates and landforms has had a powerful impact on American life and history.

Physical Regions of the United States

North America is the world's third largest continent. It is surrounded on three sides by oceans: the Atlantic Ocean to the east, the Pacific Ocean to the west, and the icy Arctic Ocean to the north. To the south, an **isthmus** (IHS muhs), or narrow strip of land, links North America to South America.

The United States is one of the largest countries in the world. Its physical regions offer great contrasts. In some regions, the land is fertile. Other regions have natural resources such as coal and oil.

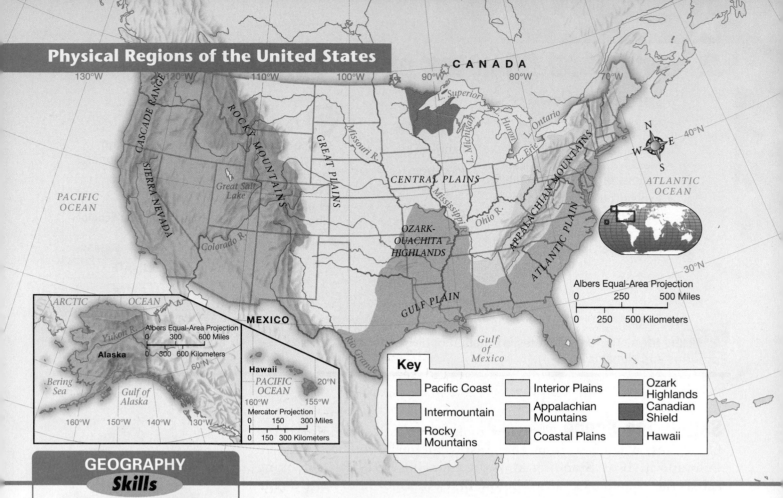

Key

Pacific Coast	Interior Plains	Ozark Highlands
Intermountain	Appalachian Mountains	Canadian Shield
Rocky Mountains	Coastal Plains	Hawaii

GEOGRAPHY *Skills*

Geographers divide the United States into different physical regions.

1. **Location** On the map, locate **(a)** Sierra Nevada, **(b)** Great Lakes, **(c)** Atlantic Plain, **(d)** Mississippi River, **(e)** Rocky Mountains

2. **Region** Through what three physical regions does the Mississippi River flow?

3. **Critical Thinking Comparing** Compare the Pacific Coast and the Rocky Mountain regions. Why do you think more people live on the Pacific Coast than in the Rocky Mountains?

Geographers divide the United States into different physical regions marked by contrasting landforms and physical features.*

Pacific Coast The westernmost region of North America is the Pacific Coast. It includes high mountain ranges that stretch from Alaska to Mexico. In the United States, some of these western ranges are near the Pacific Ocean. The Cascades and the Sierra Nevada stand a bit farther inland. Important cities of the Pacific Coast region include Seattle, Portland, San Francisco, San Diego, and Los Angeles.

A notable feature of the Pacific Coast region is the San Andreas Fault. This 600-mile fracture in the Earth's crust runs through California from northwest to southeast. Movement of the Earth's crust along this fault can cause earthquakes. For example, powerful quakes shook San Francisco in 1906 and Los Angeles in 1994, causing significant damage and loss of life.

Intermountain Region East of the Pacific Coast mountain ranges lies the Intermountain Region. This region is marked by mountain peaks, high plateaus, deep canyons, and dry, sandy deserts. The Grand Canyon, more than a mile deep, cuts through the Intermountain Region. Another prominent physical feature is the Great Salt Lake of Utah, the nation's largest saltwater lake.

---

*To review definitions of major landforms and other geographic terms, refer to the Glossary of Geographic Terms at the end of this section.

The rugged terrain limits where people can live in the Intermountain Region. Among the few major cities located there are Phoenix and Salt Lake City.

Rocky Mountains The Rocky Mountains stretch from Alaska through Canada into the western United States. They include the Bitterroot Range in Idaho and Montana, the Big Horn Mountains in Wyoming, and the Sangre de Cristo Mountains in Colorado and New Mexico. In Mexico, the Rockies become the Sierra Madre (MAH dray), or "mother range."

The Rockies include some of the highest peaks in North America—some with an **elevation,** or height above sea level, of more than 14,000 feet. Throughout history, visitors like Katharine Lee Bates have marveled at the beauty and grandeur of the Rocky Mountains. Today, Denver is a major city of the Rocky Mountain Region.

Interior Plains Between the Rockies in the West and the Appalachian Mountains in the East is a large lowland area called the Interior Plains. The dry western part of the region is called the Great Plains. The eastern part is called the Central Plains.

Scientists believe that a great inland sea once covered the Interior Plains. Today, some parts are rich in resources such as coal and petroleum. Other parts offer fertile soil for farming and grasslands for raising cattle. Major cities of the Interior Plains include Dallas, St. Louis, Chicago, Cincinnati, Detroit, and Indianapolis.

Ozark Highlands The Ozark Highlands extend across southern Missouri and northern Arkansas and into eastern Kansas. Thick with forests, the region includes mountains that rise more than 2,000 feet. The highest are the Boston Mountains in Arkansas. Important industries in the region include forestry, agriculture, and mining.

Appalachian Mountains The Appalachian Mountains run along the eastern part of North America. They stretch from Canada in the North to Georgia and Mississippi in the South. The Appalachians have different names in different places. For example, the Green Mountains, Alleghenies, and Great Smoky Mountains are all part of the Appalachians.

The Appalachians are lower and less rugged than the Rockies. The highest peak is Mt. Mitchell in North Carolina, with an elevation of 6,684 feet. Today, hearty hikers enjoy the challenge of walking the Appalachian Trail from Georgia to Maine.

Canadian Shield The Canadian Shield is a lowland area that lies mostly in eastern Canada. The southern part extends into Michigan, Wisconsin, and Minnesota. This region was once an area of high mountains. Centuries of **erosion,** or gradual wearing away, reduced the area to low hills and plains. The Canadian Shield is rich in minerals.

Coastal Plains The easternmost region of North America is called the Coastal Plains, a fairly flat, lowland area. This was the first region settled by Europeans who crossed the Atlantic Ocean. It is made up of two subregions, the Atlantic Plain and the Gulf Plain.

The Atlantic Plain lies between the Atlantic Ocean and the foothills of the Appalachians. The Atlantic Plain is narrow in the North, where major cities such as Boston, New York, and Philadelphia are located. It broadens in the South to include all of Florida.

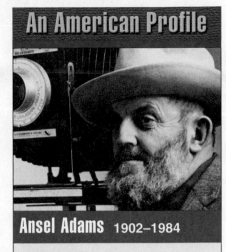

An American Profile

Ansel Adams 1902–1984

Ansel Adams was a landscape photographer known for his dramatic images of the American West.

Adams's photographs (one of which appears on page 14) have inspired millions of people to seek out the wilderness and preserve it.

In 1980, President Jimmy Carter awarded Adams the Medal of Freedom, which is presented to citizens for outstanding achievement in culture, world peace, or public service. "It is through [Adams's] foresight and fortitude," noted Carter, "that so much of America has been saved for future Americans."

How did Adams's art have a political effect?

The Gulf Plain lies along the Gulf of Mexico. This region is economically important because of its large deposits of petroleum. New Orleans and Houston are major cities of the Gulf Plain.

Hawaiian Islands The Hawaiian Islands lie far out in the Pacific, about 2,400 miles west of California. Much of Hawaii has a wet tropical climate and dense tropical rain forest vegetation. The region includes eight large islands and many smaller ones.

The islands are actually the visible tops of volcanoes that erupted through the floor of the Pacific many centuries ago. Mauna Loa (man uh LOH uh), on the island of Hawaii, is an active volcano that rises 13,680 feet above sea level.

American Rivers and Lakes

Great rivers crisscross North America, linking many of the different physical regions. Many of these rivers begin in the mountains. They collect runoff water from rains and melting snows and carry it to the oceans.

The Mississippi-Missouri River System The Mississippi and Missouri rivers make up the longest and most important river system in the United States. The system carries water thousands of miles through the Interior Plains to the Gulf of Mexico.

In addition to the two main branches, the Mississippi-Missouri river system includes many tributaries. A **tributary** is a stream or smaller river that flows into a larger one. Among the most important tributaries are the Ohio, Tennessee, Arkansas, and Platte rivers. These and other rivers provide water for the rich farmlands of the Interior Plains. The Mississippi River also serves as a means of transportation. Today, as in the past, barges carry freight up and down the river.

Other Rivers The United States includes dozens of other rivers, both large and small. The Colorado River begins in the Rocky Mountains and flows for about 1,450 miles through Colorado, Utah, Arizona, and Nevada. It forms the border between California and Arizona as it winds toward the Gulf of California.

Smaller rivers have also been important in American history. The Hudson River, for example, forms part of the border between New York and New Jersey. Only 306 miles long, it provided a vital link between New York City and the rich farmlands of upstate New York. In the 1960s, efforts to clean up pollution of the Hudson River helped launch the modern environmental movement.

Rivers form political boundaries between the United States and its neighbors. To the south, the Rio Grande forms part of the border between Texas and Mexico. To the north, the St. Lawrence River separates the Northeast from Canada.

The Great Lakes The Great Lakes also form part of the border between the United States and Canada. These five lakes—Superior, Michigan, Huron, Erie, and Ontario—form the largest body of fresh water in the world. Today, artificial waterways connect the Great Lakes to the St. Lawrence and Mississippi rivers. As a result, goods can be shipped from the Central Plains eastward to the Atlantic Ocean and southward to the Gulf of Mexico.

Climate and Weather

The condition of the Earth's atmosphere at a given time and place is its **weather.** The weather in one region can influence the weather in another area. It also affects the jobs we do, the leisure activities we enjoy, and the kinds of homes we build. In history, weather has determined the outcome of battles and even destroyed civilizations.

The average weather of a place over a period of 20 to 30 years is known as **climate.** Two main features that help define an area's climate are temperature and **precipitation** (pree sihp uh TAY shuhn), or water that falls in the form of rain, sleet, hail, or snow. A region may be hot and dry, cold and rainy, or any other combination.

Several factors influence climate. Perhaps the most important is distance from the Equator. Lands near the Equator are usually hot and wet all year. Closer to the North and South poles, temperatures are colder. **Altitude,** or height of the land above sea level, also affects climate. In general, highlands are cooler than lowlands. Other factors that affect climate include ocean currents, wind currents, and location of landforms such as inland mountains, large desert areas, lakes, or forests.

Identify Causes and Effects

Determining causes and effects helps you understand relationships among situations or events. A cause makes something happen. An effect is what happens. What is the effect of altitude on climate? Write the answer in your cause-and-effect chart.

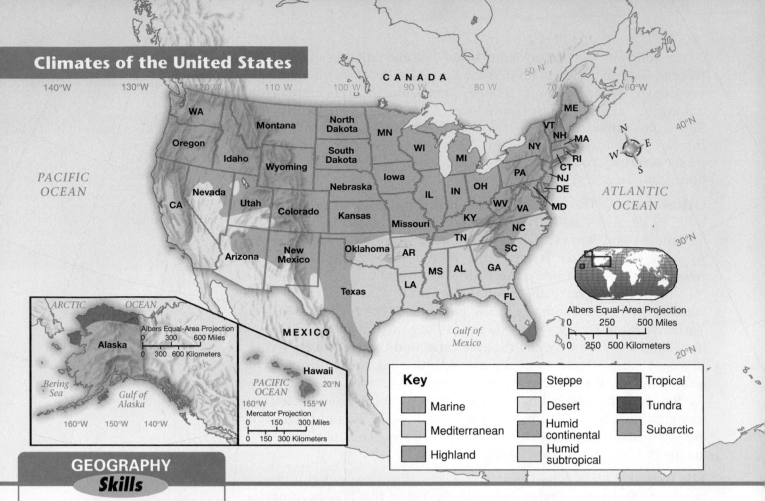

Climates of the United States

Key

- Marine
- Mediterranean
- Highland
- Steppe
- Desert
- Humid continental
- Humid subtropical
- Tropical
- Tundra
- Subarctic

GEOGRAPHY Skills

The United States is a land of many climates.

1. **Location** On the map, locate **(a)** an area with a Mediterranean climate **(b)** an area with a desert climate.

2. **Place** What states have three or more different climates?

3. **Critical Thinking Applying Information (a)** Identify a state or a part of a state where water is probably scarce. **(b)** Why is water in such short supply there?

Climates of the United States

The United States has 10 major climates. Today, as in the past, these climates strongly influence the nation's population patterns and economic activities.

Marine The strip of land from southern Alaska to northern California is sometimes called the Pacific Northwest. This region has a mild, moist marine climate, with warm summers and cool winters. The Pacific Northwest has many forests, making it a center of the lumber industry.

Mediterranean Much of California has a Mediterranean climate. Winters are mild and wet. Summers are hot and dry. Because of dry conditions, farmers and fruit growers must often irrigate the land. This region produces almost all of the nation's almonds, walnuts, olives, apricots, dates, and figs.

Highland In the Cascades, Sierra Nevada, and Rocky Mountains, a highland climate brings cooler temperatures. Conditions in a high-land climate vary according to altitude. For example, Mount Rainier in the state of Washington, at over 14,000 feet above sea level, is snowcapped all year. The highland climate attracts vacationers eager to ski in the winter and escape the heat during the summer.

Desert and Steppe Much of the southwestern United States has a desert climate, with hot days and cold nights. This dry region stretches as far east as the Rockies. The deserts of New Mexico, Nevada,

Arizona, and southeastern California get almost no rainfall. In many places, people irrigate the land so that they can grow crops.

East of the Rockies, the Great Plains have a steppe climate with limited rainfall, hot summers, and cold winters. In the 1800s, settlers brought cattle and built a prosperous beef industry in the region.

Humid Continental The Central Plains and the northeastern United States have a humid continental climate. This climate has more precipitation than the steppe. The seasons are marked by mild summers and cold winters. Tall prairie grasses once covered the Central Plains. Today, American farmers raise much of the world's food in this region.

At one time, the humid continental climate supported forests that covered much of the Northeast. While much of this forestland was cleared to build settlements and grow crops, the region still has a thriving lumber industry.

Tropical and Humid Subtropical Located near the Equator, Southern Florida and Hawaii have tropical climates. The hot, humid conditions make these regions good for growing such crops as pineapples and citrus fruits.

The southeastern United States has a humid subtropical climate. Warm temperatures and regular rainfall make this region ideal for growing crops such as cotton, soybeans, and peanuts.

Tundra and Subarctic Northern and western coastal regions of Alaska have a tundra climate. It is cold all year round. The rest of Alaska, as well as northern Canada, has a subarctic climate with long, cold winters and short summers.

Relatively few people live in these harsh climates. Farming is limited to a small fertile valley in southern Alaska. However, the dense forests that cover almost one third of Alaska are ideal for logging and production of paper pulp.

★ ★ ★ Section 2 Assessment ★ ★ ★

Recall
1. **Define (a)** isthmus, **(b)** elevation, **(c)** erosion, **(d)** tributary, **(e)** weather, **(f)** climate, **(g)** precipitation, **(h)** altitude.

Comprehension
2. Name the physical regions of the United States and describe one feature of each region.
3. How do rivers and lakes benefit the economy of the United States?
4. Describe the climate of the region in which you live.

Critical Thinking and Writing
5. **Exploring the Main Idea** List the physical regions and climates of the United States. Then, choose the three regions and climates where you would most like to live. Explain your choices.
6. **Linking Past and Present** **(a)** How do you think the role of rivers and lakes has changed over the course of the nation's history? **(b)** What are the most important roles of rivers and lakes today?

ACTIVITY
Mental Mapping Study the physical map of the United States on page 12. On a piece of paper, draw your own sketch map of the United States. Label the major physical features, including mountains, rivers, and other bodies of water. Use colors to outline and shade each physical region.

Glossary of Geographic Terms

The list below includes important geographic terms and their definitions.
Sometimes, the definition of a term includes an example in parentheses.
An asterisk (*) indicates that the term is illustrated on page 19.

altitude height above sea level

*archipelago chain of islands (Hawaiian Islands)

basin low-lying land area that is surrounded by land of higher elevation; land that is drained by a river system (Great Basin)

*bay part of a body of water that is partly enclosed by land (San Francisco Bay)

canal waterway made by people that is used to drain or irrigate land or to connect two bodies of water (Erie Canal)

*canyon deep, narrow valley with high, steep sides (Grand Canyon)

*cape narrow point of land that extends into a body of water (Cape Cod)

climate pattern of weather in a particular place over a period of 20 to 30 years

*coast land that borders the sea (Pacific Coast)

coastal plain lowland area lying along the ocean (Gulf Plain)

continent any of seven large landmasses on the Earth's surface (Africa, Antarctica, Asia, Australia, Europe, North America, South America)

continental divide mountain ridge that separates river systems flowing toward opposite sides of a continent

*delta land formed by soil that is deposited at the mouth of a river (Mississippi Delta)

desert area that has little or no moisture or vegetation (Painted Desert)

directional arrow arrow on a map that always points north

downstream in the direction of a river's flow; toward a river's mouth

elevation the height above sea level

fall line place where rivers drop from a plateau or foothills to a coastal plain, usually marked by many waterfalls

foothills low hills at the base of a mountain range

*gulf arm of an ocean or sea that is partly enclosed by land, usually larger than a bay (Gulf of Mexico)

hemisphere half of the Earth (Western Hemisphere)

*hill area of raised land that is lower and more rounded than a mountain (San Juan Hill)

*island land area that is surrounded by water (Puerto Rico)

*isthmus narrow strip of land joining two large areas or joining a peninsula to a mainland (Isthmus of Panama)

*lake body of water surrounded entirely by land (Lake Superior)

latitude the distance in degrees north and south from the Equator

longitude the distance in degrees east or west from the Prime Meridian

marsh lowland with moist soils and tall grasses

*mountain high, steep, rugged land that rises sharply above the surrounding land (Mount McKinley)

mountain range chain of connected mountains (Allegheny Mountains)

mouth of a river place where a river or stream empties into a larger body of water

ocean any of the five largest bodies of salt water on the Earth's surface (Arctic Ocean, Atlantic Ocean, Indian Ocean, Pacific Ocean, and Antarctic Ocean)

*peninsula piece of land that is surrounded by water on three sides (Delmarva Peninsula)

piedmont rolling land along the base of a mountain range

*plain broad area of fairly level land that is generally close to sea level

*plateau large area of high, flat, or gently rolling land

prairie large area of natural grassland with few or no trees or hills

*river large stream of water that empties into an ocean or a lake or another river (Pecos River)

*sea large body of salt water that is smaller than an ocean (Caribbean Sea)

sea level average level of the ocean's surface from which the height of land or depth of the ocean is measured

*source of a river place where a river begins

steppe flat, treeless land with limited moisture

strait narrow channel that connects two larger bodies of water (Straits of Florida)

*tributary stream or small river that flows into a larger river or stream

upstream in the direction that is against a river's flow; toward a river's source

valley land that lies between hills or mountains (Shenandoah Valley)

*volcano cone-shaped mountain formed by an outpouring of lava—hot, liquid rock—from a crack in the Earth's surface (Mount St. Helens or Mauna Loa)

weather condition of Earth's atmosphere at any given time and place

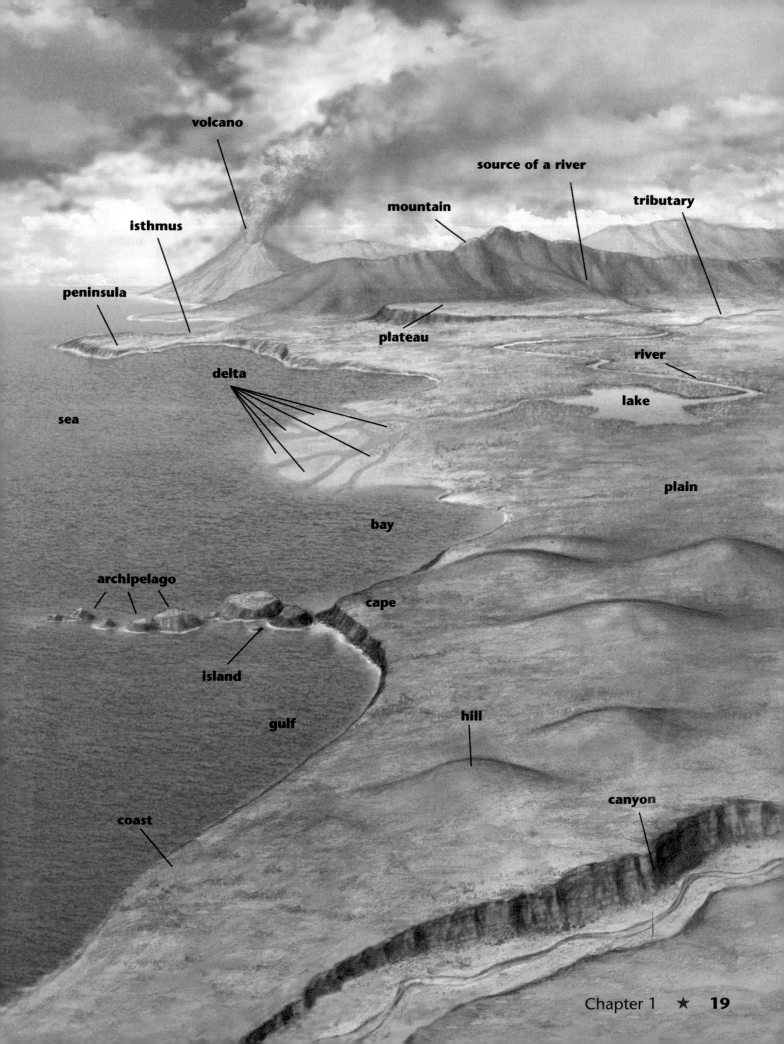

volcano

source of a river

isthmus

mountain

tributary

peninsula

plateau

river

delta

lake

sea

plain

bay

archipelago

cape

island

gulf

hill

canyon

coast

3 The Tools of History

Prepare to Read

Objectives

In this section, you will
- Explain how historians evaluate and interpret historical evidence.
- Summarize how archaeologists add to our knowledge of history.
- Explain what we can learn about history by understanding chronology and eras.

Key Terms

primary source

secondary source

authenticity

bias

artifact

archaeology

culture

chronology

Target Reading Skill

Reading Process As you read, prepare an outline of this section. Use roman numerals to indicate major headings, capital letters for subheadings, and numbers for the supporting details. The sample at right will help you get started.

> I. Using Historical Evidence
>   A. Primary and secondary sources
>   1. Official documents
>   2. Eyewitness accounts
>   B. Evaluating evidence
>   1.
>   2.
>   3.
>   C. Interpreting evidence
>   1.
>   2.
> II. Archaeologists Uncover the Past

Main Idea Historians have developed many tools to study and interpret history.

David McCullough

Setting the Scene "It has been coming on for a long time," warned David McCullough, "like a creeping disease." McCullough was not talking about a flu epidemic or an outbreak of measles. Instead, he was alarmed that young Americans did not know enough about their nation's past.

> 66 Everything we have, all our great institutions, hospitals, universities, libraries, this city, our laws, our music, art, poetry, our freedoms, everything is because somebody went before us and did the hard work. . . . Indifference to history isn't just ignorant, it's rude. It's a form of ingratitude. 99
>
> —David McCullough, *Why History?*

Historians like David McCullough have devoted their lives to making sure we do not forget our shared past and values. They have developed a wide variety of methods to accomplish this goal.

Using Historical Evidence

Studying the lives of people in different times and places is the work of the historian. The most basic tool for this work is historical evidence. Historians collect the evidence, then use it to interpret events.

Primary and Secondary Sources Historians look first for primary sources. A **primary source** is firsthand information about people or events. Primary sources include official documents such as laws or court decisions, public speeches, eyewitness accounts such as diaries and letters, and autobiographies. Primary sources may also include visual evidence such as a news photograph or a videotape. A special type of primary source is oral—or spoken—history, which may be based on interviews with people of today recalling the past.

Historians also make use of secondary sources. A **secondary source** is an account provided after the fact by people who did not directly witness or participate in the event. Secondary sources are usually based on primary sources. This textbook is an example of a secondary source. Encyclopedias, biographies, or books and articles written by historians are also secondary sources.

Evaluating Evidence When dealing with a primary source, the first job of a historian may be to determine whether it is authentic. **Authenticity** refers to whether or not the source is actually what it seems to be. For example, in 1928, a magazine published a series of newly discovered letters that were said to have been written by a young Abraham Lincoln. After careful detective work, historian Paul Angle concluded that the letters were clever forgeries. Angle described some of the questions historians ask when deciding if a source is authentic:

> 66 Is the paper of the proper age, and is the ink that of the period in which the documents are supposed to have been written? . . . Does [the handwriting] resemble that of letters and papers of undoubted genuineness? . . . Do specific incidents mentioned in the challenged documents check with [provable] historical fact? 99
>
> —Paul M. Angle, "The Minor Collection: A Criticism"

After showing that a source is authentic, historians must determine whether it is reliable. Reliability refers to whether or not the source gives an accurate account of the events being described. Was the person describing the event really an eyewitness or just passing on stories told by other people? How accurate was the witness's memory? Do the records of a meeting between two officials report their exact words? What was left out, and why? Such questions help a historian determine reliability.

In evaluating reliability, historians must always be on the lookout for bias. **Bias** is a leaning toward or against a certain person, group, or idea. Cultural background, personal experiences, economic status, and political beliefs may all contribute to bias. An account of a battle given by a soldier on one side may differ widely from an account of the same battle given by a soldier on the other side. A description of a political candidate may be affected by whether the writer is for or against that candidate. In this book, you will find lessons on how to look for signs of bias in order to determine the reliability of sources.

Interpreting Evidence In addition to evaluating sources, historians interpret what the sources mean. Often, the historian's goal is to determine the causes of a certain development or event, such as a war or an economic collapse. By explaining why things happened in the past, the historian can help us understand what is going on today and what may happen tomorrow.

Still, different historians may interpret the same evidence in different ways. Although historians try to be objective, they may be influenced by their own biases. Interpretations of events also change over time, influenced by current events, new ideas, and new sources.

Set a Purpose
When you set a purpose for reading, you give yourself a focus. Your purpose for reading "Evaluating Evidence" might be to find out how historians evaluate evidence. Add this information to your outline.

Primary Source

Preserving Historical Evidence

Historian Robin Winks tells how even the simplest documents can provide important evidence of the past:
"Precisely because the historian must turn to all possible witnesses, he is the most bookish of men. For him, no printed statement is without its interest. For him, the destruction of old cookbooks, gazetteers, road maps, Sears Roebuck catalogues, children's books, railway timetables, or drafts of printed manuscripts, is the loss of potential evidence. Does one wish to know how the mail-order business was operated or how a Nebraska farmer might have dressed in 1930? Look to those catalogues."

—Robin Winks,
The Historian as Detective

Analyzing Primary Sources
What can the historian learn from the items that Winks mentions?

"Good effort, Sam, but it was a water jug!"

Archaeologists Uncover the Past

Most of the evidence that historians use to study American history is in written form. However, when examining the distant past, historians must often rely on **artifacts** (AHRT uh faktz), or objects made by humans. Artifacts include items such as stone tools, weapons, baskets, and carvings.

The Science of Archaeology Artifacts are the building blocks of archaeology (ahr kee AHL uh jee). **Archaeology** is the study of evidence left by early people in order to find out about their way of life.

As ancient cultures disappear, their remains are buried by centuries of sand, dirt, and water. Later people then build new settlements in the same spot, burying the artifacts even deeper. In places like the desert Southwest, archaeologists dig into the earth. They carefully preserve, photograph, and label the artifacts they find. Each new find can provide valuable information about the past.

In laboratories, experts analyze the finds. By testing the level of carbon in a piece of pottery or bone, they can date it to within a few hundred years. They might study kernels of ancient corn through a microscope to find out about the climate in which it grew. They might compare clay pots from different areas to find out about the people who made them.

Studying Ancient Cultures From artifacts and other evidence, archaeologists form theories about the cultures of ancient peoples. A **culture** is the way of life that a people has developed. It includes their homes, clothing, economy, arts, and government. It also includes the customs, ideas, beliefs, and skills that they pass on from generation to generation.

By studying artifacts, archaeologists can determine approximately when the objects were made. They can also form theories about the people who made them. Modern technology, such as computers, helps the archaeologist study artifacts. A finely carved arrowhead suggests that a people knew how to make weapons and hunt. Woven plant fibers suggest that they were skilled basket makers.

In the Americas, archaeologists often focus on the cultures that existed before the arrival of Europeans. Their work has given us valuable insight into the lives of the first Americans, as you will see. Still, some Native Americans have objected to the disturbance of ancient burial grounds or other sites. In recent years, archaeologists have grown more aware of the need to respect Native American landmarks and traditions.

Chronology and Historical Eras

Perhaps you feel that the study of history is a collection of dates, names, and facts. Actually, it is much more than that. It is a story that has many parts.

Learn From the Past When you study history, you learn how the past is linked to the present. As you begin to study the past, you will find that it is like unraveling a fascinating mystery. There is always

Viewing History

Finding Artifacts Members of an archaeological team in Boston searched for and found artifacts from colonial Boston. The teapot and glass bottle were found at the site. **Analyzing Information** *What might these items tell archaeologists about the people who used them?*

23

Eras in American History

First Americans, or Pre-Columbian	**Before 1492**	Diverse cultures developed in North America and South America.
Era of Exploration	**1492–1600s**	Europeans explored and settled in the Americas. This began the meeting of peoples from three worlds—Europe, the Americas, and Africa.
Colonial Era	**1607–1775**	The thirteen English colonies were settled in North America. The era ended with the start of the American Revolution.
Revolutionary Era	**1763 – 1781**	Following a war for independence from Great Britain, the United States became a nation. Some historians mark the end of this era as 1789, when the Constitution went into effect.
Early Republic	**1789 – 1828**	The new United States government, with George Washington as its first President, took shape. The country began to expand, and its economy began to develop.
Jacksonian Era or the Age of Jackson	**1828 – 1840**	Andrew Jackson's inauguration symbolized a new era in which the interests of the people were addressed. Democratic rights were extended to more Americans.
Era of Expansion	**1840s – 1853**	The United States expanded from the Atlantic to the Pacific Ocean, adding many new territories.
Civil War Era	**1850s – 1877**	Disputes about the growth of slavery, as well as other conflicts, led to the Civil War between the North and South. Slavery was outlawed by the Thirteenth Amendment and the Civil War Era ended with Reconstruction, when the North and South reunited as one nation.
Progressive Era	**1898 – 1917**	Reformers sought to improve society. They were successful in passing laws for regulating business, limiting child labor, and protecting natural resources.
The Great Depression	**1929 – 1941**	After the boom of the 1920s, a severe economic crisis affected all Americans. Millions lost jobs as factories closed down.
Post–World War II	**1945 – Present**	As we get closer to the present day, it becomes more difficult to divide American history neatly. The years after World War II, however, are variously known as the Cold War Era, the Civil Rights Era, the Vietnam Era, the Atomic Age, and the Space Age.

CHART Skills

American history can be divided into several eras, or major periods of time.

1. **Comprehension** During which era did the United States begin to establish a new government?

2. **Critical Thinking Applying Information** Why is it useful to organize history into eras?

more to know. Often by studying how people solved problems in the past, we can apply these insights to solving today's problems.

History is the story of the men and women we honor as heroes. These exceptional men and women dared to believe they could change the world—and they did. Some were great leaders such as George Washington. Still others, such as Harriet Tubman; Abraham Lincoln; Dr. Martin Luther King, Jr.; and Charles Lindbergh, changed people's view of the world.

Learn About People History is also the story of ordinary people who do the everyday things that shape the character of our country. It is also the story of how people lived, where they traveled, and how they felt about their lives. Ordinary people work hard, raise families, and fight wars. In addition, ordinary people also settled the frontier, built cities, and participated in protest marches.

Furthermore, there is much that historians can learn from what we consider everyday items. Children's toys and games may give clues about a culture. The clothes people wear, the music they listen to, and even the kind of work people do can give clues to historians.

On the practical side, studying history provides you with useful skills. As you begin to analyze events, you will learn how to research topics, recognize different points of view, make connections, and understand causes and effects.

Absolute Chronology The study of history starts with chronology (kruh NAHL uh gee), the sequence of events over time. Just as geography answers the question *where*, chronology answers the question *when*.

There are two types of chronology: absolute and relative. Absolute chronology refers to the exact time an event took place. Depending on the information available, absolute chronology may be expressed in terms of centuries, years, days, or even hours. For example, according to eyewitnesses, President Abraham Lincoln died of an assassin's bullet on April 15, 1865, at 7:22 A.M.

Relative Chronology The time when an event took place in relation to other events is called relative chronology. For example, in 1773, Britain imposed a tea tax on its American colonies. Later that year, protesters in Boston raided British ships and dumped chests of tea into the harbor. Within three months, the British passed new laws to punish Boston. The phrases "later that year" and "within three months" show the relative chronology of the three events.

Relative chronology helps us understand connections between different events. Still, the fact that one event came before another one does not necessarily mean that the first event caused the second. For example, suppose your neighbor washes his car and an hour later there is a thunderstorm. Did washing the car cause it to rain? In January 1837, Martin Van Buren became President. Two months later the nation faced a terrible economic crisis. Did Van Buren's becoming President cause the crisis? Only careful study can help you decide if and how the two events are linked.

★ ★ ★ **Section 3 Assessment** ★ ★ ★

Recall

1. **Define** (a) primary source, (b) secondary source, (c) authenticity, (d) bias, (e) artifact, (f) archaeology, (g) culture, (h) chronology.

Comprehension

2. What steps must a historian take to evaluate historical evidence?
3. How do archaeologists learn about the past?
4. Why do historians divide history into eras?

Critical Thinking and Writing

5. **Exploring the Main Idea** Review the Main Idea statement at the beginning of this section. List five sources that a historian might use to write a history of your life. Then, evaluate them for authenticity, reliability, and bias.
6. **Solving Problems** How can archaeologists continue to study ancient remains without infringing on the rights of Native Americans?

ACTIVITY

Go Online
PHSchool.com

Exploring Primary Sources
Choose an era from the chart on page 24. Then, use the Internet to find a primary source from that era. Write a short summary of the source. Then, analyze it for authenticity, reliability, and bias. For help in completing the activity, visit PHSchool.com, **Web Code mfd-0103.**

4 Economics and Other Social Sciences

Prepare to Read

Objectives

In this section, you will
- Identify the basic questions that economists ask about society.
- List the benefits of free enterprise.
- Explain how the social sciences can support the study of history.

Key Terms

economics
consumer
cash economy
free enterprise system
social sciences
political science
civics
anthropology
sociology
psychology

Target Reading Skill

Main Idea Copy the concept web below. As you read, fill in the blank ovals with information about the study of economics. Add as many ovals as you need.

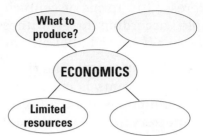

Main Idea The study of history is closely linked to economics and other social sciences.

Stacks of coins

Setting the Scene

If you were growing up in an Iroquois village 300 years ago, you would have depended on the local forests and rivers for all your needs. Americans living on the frontier in the 1800s also relied on what they could raise or hunt themselves. A lucky family might expand its supply of goods by growing a few pounds of cotton. They would then trade the cloth they wove from the cotton for a pig or a calf.

Today, Americans take for granted their ability to consume an almost limitless supply of goods from all over the world. With a short trip to the local shopping mall, we buy shoes from Italy or shirts from Hong Kong. Shopping on the Internet can bring leather backpacks and wool sweaters from Australia or stone carvings from Kenya.

People in every society have wants and needs. At the same time, every society—no matter how rich—has limited resources. In this section, we will examine the ways that different societies manage their limited resources to meet their wants and needs.

Three Economic Questions

The study of how people manage their limited resources to satisfy their wants and needs is called **economics.** Every society must answer three basic economic questions: (1) What goods and services should we produce? (2) How should we produce them? (3) For whom should we produce them? The answers to these questions define every society's economic system.

What Goods and Services Should We Produce? A society's first economic task is to fulfill people's basic needs—food, shelter, and clothing. After that, the society must make choices about how to use the rest of its limited resources. Should it focus on producing

---

consumer goods, such as cars and washing machines? Should it use its resources for education? Should it concentrate on heavy industry such as construction or trucking?

Decisions about what to produce vary according to the time and culture. Developing nations are less concerned about producing private automobiles. They are more concerned with building industries that will provide jobs and improve their quality of life. In the United States, on the other hand, we see cars as a necessity of life. Special situations also affect decision making. During World War II, for example, the United States government limited the manufacture of items such as cars and washing machines in favor of tanks and fighter planes.

How Should We Produce Goods and Services? Even when people agree on what to produce, they must choose how to produce it and how much of it to produce. Technology plays a major role in these decisions. For example, in the past, each family grew enough fruits, grains, and vegetables to meet its needs. Or small, family-run farms grew crops for the local community. With the invention of new farm machinery, agriculture changed. Today in the United States, most of the food we eat is grown on giant mechanized farms run by large corporations.

Advances in technology also changed manufacturing. At one time, most manufactured items were produced by hand in homes or small workshops. Then, the Industrial Revolution introduced new methods and machines that allowed large factories to mass-produce great quantities of manufactured goods. Today, computers and robot technology have once more revolutionized manufacturing.

For Whom Should We Produce Goods and Services? We are all **consumers,** or users of goods and services. However, just as resources are limited, supplies of goods and services are limited. What goods and services should be available to what consumers? How do consumers pay for what they want and need?

In past societies, consumers and producers were often the same people. They consumed the goods they produced themselves. Today, we live in a **cash economy,** that is, an economy where we exchange

Viewing History

Producing Goods and Services
Technology affects how goods and services are produced. On the farm (above) and in the textile factory (inset), machines do much of the work that was once done entirely by hand. **Drawing Conclusions** *What do you think are some of the economic benefits and drawbacks of technology?*

Identify Supporting Details

What details in this subsection discuss economic systems? Add this information to your concept web.

Glossary of Economic Terms

barter	the direct exchange of one set of goods or services for another
budget	a plan for spending and saving
capital	any human-made resource that is used to create other goods or services
command economy	an economy in which one organization decides what goods are produced and how much stores will charge for these goods
credit	any form of deferred payment
entrepreneur	ambitious leader who combines land, labor, and capital to create and market new goods or services
export	a good that is sent to another country for sale
free enterprise	an economic system characterized by private or corporate ownership of capital goods; investments that are determined by private decision rather than by state control
free market	an economic system in which individuals rather than the government make most of the decisions about economic activities
import	a good that is brought in from another country for sale
labor	the effort that people devote to a task for which they are paid
private property	something owned by an individual; especially land or buildings
profit	the amount of money a company has once it has sold its products
scarcity	limited quantities of resources to meet unlimited wants
supply and demand	a feature of the capitalist economy; when supplies of goods or services are plentiful, prices drop; when supplies are scarce, prices rise
surplus	situation in which quantity supplied is greater than quantity demanded; also known as excess supply

CHART Skills

This glossary gives the meaning of some basic economic terms.

1. **Comprehension** Which term refers to an economic system where ownership of goods can be private or corporate?

2. **Critical Thinking Making Decisions** Why might an entrepreneur be better off in a free-market economy than in a command economy?

money for goods and services. Your income and wealth determine the goods and services you can consume. How to supply basic needs to people who cannot afford to buy them is a difficult issue for governments, charities, religious communities, and individuals.

The American Free Enterprise System

The economy of the United States is based on an economic principle known as free enterprise. In a free enterprise system, the government plays a limited role in the economy. Businesses are owned by private citizens. Owners decide what products to make, how much to produce, where to sell products, and what prices to charge. Furthermore, competition is encouraged. Competition gives businesses an incentive, or reason, for working harder. Companies compete for consumers by making the best product at the lowest price.

The free enterprise system began early in the United States. After the War for Independence, Americans were free to engage in any economic activity without government interference. The Framers of the Constitution believed that the prosperity of the nation depended on a free-market economy. Provisions for private property and competition, for example, are included in the Constitution.

Until the late 1800s, the United States government did relatively little to control the economy. Since then, government has gradually taken on a more active role. Many Americans argue that government regulations are needed to end abuses or ensure against economic collapse. Others claim that government interference keeps the free enterprise system from working efficiently.

Despite such disagreements, Americans have long recognized free enterprise as one of the nation's greatest strengths.

The "know-how" of individual American traders, inventors, and investors helped create vast personal fortunes, as well as prosperity for the nation. Today, many nations around the world look to the American free enterprise system as a model.

The free enterprise system also allows consumers freedom to make economic choices. Through their buying decisions, consumers can tell businesses what to make, how much, and at what price. In this respect, the economic system is much like a democracy. People are allowed to express their preferences.

Other Social Sciences

Economics, history, and geography are considered social sciences because they relate to human society and social behavior. Other social sciences include political science, civics, anthropology, sociology, and psychology.

Political Science and Civics The study of government is called political science. Political scientists look at the ideas behind different forms of government, how these governments are organized, and how they work. Like economics, political science raises many basic questions. Who should have the most power in a government? How are decisions made? How do governments change?

Before 1776, Americans lived as subjects of a foreign king, to whom they owed loyalty and obedience. After throwing off that form of government, they built what Abraham Lincoln called a "government of the people, by the people, for the people." As citizens, Americans owe loyalty to the nation and have a say in their government. The basic principles and organization of American government are contained in the Constitution of the United States. You will learn more about the Constitution in later chapters.

Civics An important branch of political science is civics, the study of the rights and responsibilities of citizens. In 1776, the Declaration of Independence stated the idea that every person had basic rights that could not be taken away:

66 We hold these truths to be self-evident, that all men are created equal; that they are endowed by their Creator with certain inalienable rights; that among these are life, liberty, and the pursuit of happiness. 99

—Declaration of Independence

Throughout the nation's history, Americans have worked to expand and protect the rights of individuals. The addition of the Bill of Rights to the Constitution ensures individual rights to all

Americans. These rights include freedom of speech, which means the newspapers, books, and magazines you read can print the news. Your right to worship as you please and to freely assemble are also guaranteed. Americans have also recognized their responsibility to serve the nation in many ways, including obeying its laws, voting, and serving in the military.

Anthropology, Sociology, and Psychology The study of how people and cultures develop is called **anthropology** (an thruh PAHL uh gee). Anthropologists look at the ways people thought and behaved at different times and places. For example, an anthropologist might examine how the first Americans spread across North and South America and the different ways of life they developed. One branch of anthropology is archaeology, as discussed in Section 3.

Sociology is the study of how people behave in groups. Looking at a particular society, a sociologist might ask: Is this society divided into different social classes? How are families organized? How do the roles of men and women differ? What values and beliefs do people share? Even a single nation, such as the United States, contains many different social groups. For example, a sociologist may be interested in how life in a small farming community in upstate New York differs from life in a big-city neighborhood in New York, Los Angeles, or Houston. A sociologist might even study how different student groups in a middle school relate to one another.

Psychology is the study of how people think and behave. Psychology is linked to history because history is the study of human beings. For example, a person writing a biography of a well-known figure might look to psychology to understand why that person acted in a certain way. Psychology can also help us evaluate primary sources by helping us understand people's views and biases.

★ ★ ★ **Section 4 Assessment** ★ ★ ★

Recall

1. **Define** (a) economics, (b) consumer, (c) cash economy, (d) free enterprise, (e) social sciences, (f) political science, (g) civics, (h) anthropology, (i) sociology, (j) psychology.

Comprehension

2. What three basic economic questions must every society answer?
3. Explain why the free enterprise system was developed in the new nation.
4. Choose two of the social sciences discussed in this section. Describe how they support the study of history.

Critical Thinking and Writing

5. **Exploring the Main Idea** Review the Main Idea statement at the beginning of this section. Then, write three questions that you might ask about the development of the economy of the United States from independence to today.
6. **Identifying Alternatives** Why would a developing nation answer the three basic economic questions differently than a country like the United States?

ACTIVITY

Creating a Comic Strip Create a comic strip for Free Enterprise Publishers showing the steps an ambitious young American would take to start and run a new business. Be sure to include a panel showing how our hero would respond to competition from other businesses.

American Entrepreneurs

American history is filled with stories of successful entrepreneurs. Their success makes it easy to see why the United States is often called the "land of opportunity."

Walt Disney

Walt Disney owed his success to a mouse. In 1928, he introduced Mickey Mouse in the animated cartoon "Steamboat Willie." Mickey's worldwide popularity helped Disney build a business empire that came to include a movie studio and huge theme parks in Florida and California.

Madame C. J. Walker

Madame C. J. Walker's money-making idea was to market hair-care products for African Americans. Starting in 1905, she created her own formulas and sold them door-to-door. Five years later, she was running a factory that provided employment for some 3,000 people. By the time of her death in 1919, Walker was one of the first American women to have become a millionaire through her own efforts.

Junior Achievement

Since 1919, Junior Achievement has worked "to educate and inspire young people to value free enterprise, business, and economics." Junior Achievement volunteers run programs in schools across the country, including a competition in which students have an opportunity to experience running an actual business.

ACTIVITY

With a partner, write a plan for a new business. Describe the goods or services you plan to market, explain who your customers would be, and list what you would need to get started.

Review and Assessment

CHAPTER SUMMARY

Section 1
Geography is the study of people, their environments, and their resources. Geographers have developed five themes to help explain the connection between geography and history. Maps and globes are pictures of the Earth's surface.

Section 2
The United States is divided into nine physical regions and seven climate regions. Several great river systems and lakes have played important roles in American history.

Section 3
Historical evidence is the basic tool of historians. Archaeologists dig into the earth to find artifacts left behind by ancient cultures. The study of history starts with chronology, the sequence of events over time.

Section 4
Economics is the study of how people manage their resources to satisfy their wants and needs. The U.S. economy is based on the free enterprise system. The social sciences provide important clues about people who lived in the past.

Building Vocabulary

Review the chapter vocabulary words listed below. Then, use the words and their definitions to create a matching quiz. Exchange quizzes with another student. Check each other's answers when you are finished.

1. geography	6. primary source
2. cartographer	7. artifact
3. climate	8. chronology
4. precipitation	9. cash economy
5. altitude	10. free enterprise

Reviewing Key Facts

11. What are the different uses for maps and globes? (Section 1)
12. Describe three physical regions of the United States. (Section 2)

For additional review and enrichment activities, see the interactive version of *The American Nation,* available on the Web and on CD-ROM.

Chapter Self-Test For practice test questions for Chapter 1, visit PHSchool.com, **Web Code mfa-0104.**

13. Name three kinds of evidence that archaeologists study. (Section 3)
14. How does the American free enterprise system work? (Section 4)

Critical Thinking and Writing

15. **Connecting to Geography: Movement** How does the movement of people, goods, and ideas shape a society?
16. **Evaluating Information** Which would be more reliable: a map of North America from the 1500s or a map of North America from the 1900s? Explain your answer.
17. **Synthesizing Information** Look at the picture of Pikes Peak on page 11. **(a)** Describe the physical region in which Pikes Peak is located. **(b)** Describe the climate of that region.
18. **Applying Information** Imagine that you are an archaeologist living 1,000 years from now. What conclusions about our society might you draw from the following artifacts: **(a)** coins and dollar bills, **(b)** automobile, **(c)** fast food containers, **(d)** TV set, **(e)** cell phone?
19. **Making Decisions** Review the discussion on page 28 about the proper role of government in the economy. Do you agree with the Americans who argue for a smaller or a larger government role? Explain your answer.

In 1845, Lansford W. Hastings wrote a guide for people traveling to the West. In it, he made the following statements about the West:

66 The time is not distant, when those wild forests, trackless plains, untrodden valleys . . . will present one grand scene of continuous improvements . . . when those vast forests shall have disappeared before the hardy pioneer; those extensive plains shall abound with innumerable herds of domestic animals; those fertile valleys shall groan under the weight of their abundant products. 99

—Lansford W. Hastings, from *The Emigrants' Guide to Oregon and California*

20. How do you think Hastings felt about the changes he predicted?
   A. He feared them.
   B. He was unconcerned.
   C. He approved of them.
   D. He wanted to prevent them from happening.
21. Hastings probably would have been surprised by the
   A. increasing population of the West.
   B. emergence of the environmental movement.
   C. development of the lumber industry.
   D. rise of the beef industry.

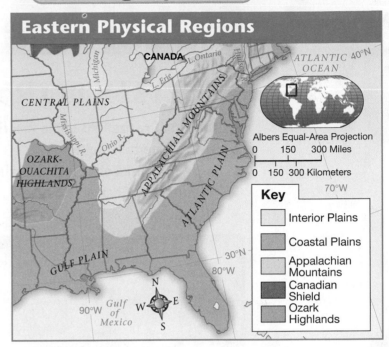

Eastern Physical Regions

22. What region is northwest of the Appalachian mountains?
   A. Ozark Highlands
   B. Atlantic Plain
   C. Gulf Plain
   D. Central Plains
23. Which is the smallest region? Describe its location.

ACTIVITIES

Connecting With . . .
Geography

Using the Five Themes Use the five themes of geography to describe the neighborhood, community, or state in which you live. Develop your description by writing one or two sentences for each of the five themes. Consider the following questions:
1. Where is the place located?
2. How do people interact with the environment?
3. How do people and ideas move between places?

Go Online
PHSchool.com

Connecting to Today

Creating a Chart Some scientists are worried that human activities such as driving cars and operating factories are causing a dangerous rise in the Earth's temperatures. Other scientists do not agree with this global-warming theory. They point out that the Earth has gone through warm and cold cycles in the past. Use the Internet to find out about the global-warming debate. Create a chart showing the arguments on both sides and the evidence used to support them. For help in starting this activity, visit PHSchool.com, **Web Code mfd-0105.**

Before the First Global Age

PREHISTORY—1600

1 The First Civilizations of the Americas
2 Native American Cultures
3 Trade Networks of Africa and Asia
4 Tradition and Change in Europe

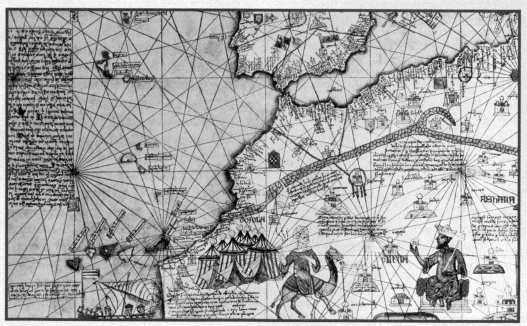

A Spanish map from the 1300s showing Mansa Musa seated on his throne

30,000 to 10,000 years ago

The first people arrive in the Americas.

Early 1300s

The African kingdom of Mali is at its most powerful. Its king, Mansa Musa, makes a famous pilgrimage to Mecca, Islam's holiest city.

Late 1300s

The Renaissance begins in southern Europe.

Prehistory · · · · 1300 · · · · · · 1400

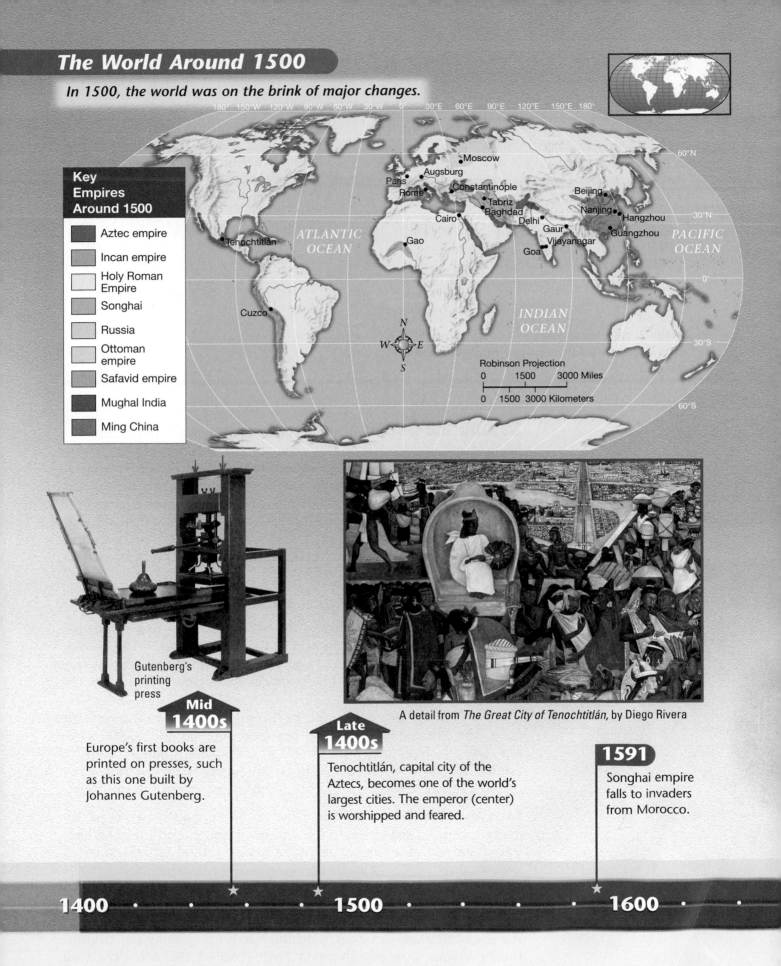

The World Around 1500

In 1500, the world was on the brink of major changes.

Key Empires Around 1500

- Aztec empire
- Incan empire
- Holy Roman Empire
- Songhai
- Russia
- Ottoman empire
- Safavid empire
- Mughal India
- Ming China

Moscow
Augsburg
Paris
Rome
Constantinople
Beijing
Tabriz
Baghdad
Nanjing
Hangzhou
Cairo
Delhi
Guangzhou
Gaur
Gao
Vijayanagar
Goa
Tenochtitlán
Cuzco

ATLANTIC OCEAN
PACIFIC OCEAN
INDIAN OCEAN

Robinson Projection
0 1500 3000 Miles
0 1500 3000 Kilometers

Gutenberg's printing press

A detail from *The Great City of Tenochtitlán*, by Diego Rivera

Mid 1400s

Europe's first books are printed on presses, such as this one built by Johannes Gutenberg.

Late 1400s

Tenochtitlán, capital city of the Aztecs, becomes one of the world's largest cities. The emperor (center) is worshipped and feared.

1591

Songhai empire falls to invaders from Morocco.

1400 • • • • 1500 • • • • 1600 • •

1 The First Civilizations of the Americas

Prepare to Read

Objectives

In this section, you will
- Explain how people first reached the Americas.
- Describe the Olmec, Mayan, Aztec, and Incan civilizations.
- Summarize the development of early cultures in North America.

Key Terms

glacier

surplus

causeway

quipu

terrace

culture

adobe

pueblo

Mound Builders

Target Reading Skill

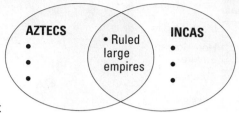

Comparison and Contrast Copy this incomplete Venn diagram. As you read, write key facts about the Aztecs and the Incas in the appropriate sections. Write common achievements in the overlapping section.

AZTECS
-
-
-

- Ruled large empires

INCAS
-
-
-

Main Idea In several parts of the Americas, the development of farming enabled some groups of people to build complex civilizations.

Ancient Indian spear points

Setting the Scene The hunters crept slowly forward. Ahead, a herd of bison grazed near a swamp. At a signal, the hunters leaped up, shouting loudly. The startled herd stampeded into the swamp. As the bison struggled in the deep mud, the hunters hurled their spears.

Scenes much like this took place on North America's Great Plains more than 10,000 years ago. Hunters tracking herds of bison were among the first people to reach the Americas. Over time, their descendants spread out across two continents.

Reaching the Americas

Like other early people around the world, the first Americans left no written records to tell us where they came from or when they arrived. However, scientists have found evidence to suggest that the first people reached the Americas sometime during the last ice age.

According to geologists, the Earth has gone through several ice ages. The last ice age occurred between 100,000 and 10,000 years ago. During that time, thick sheets of ice, called glaciers, covered almost one third of the Earth. In North America, glaciers stretched across Canada and reached as far south as present-day Kentucky.

Crossing the Land Bridge Glaciers locked up water from the oceans, causing sea levels to fall and uncovering land that had been under water. In the far north, a land bridge joined Siberia in northeastern Asia to Alaska in North America.

Most scientists think that bands of hunters reached North America across this land bridge. These hunters tracked herds of grazing animals. Other scientists disagree. They think that the first Americans crossed the icy arctic waters by boat, reaching North America by sea. Another theory claims that people could have reached the Americas from

South ... ... ied the ... ... ving in ... ... ands of ... ... merica, ... ca. The ... ... Native ... ... lateaus, ... odlands ... ... y differ- ... ... groups ... ... ms and

Adapting to New Conditions About 12,000 years ago, the last ice age ended. As temperatures rose, the glaciers melted. The land bridge between Siberia and Alaska disappeared under the Bering Strait.

About the same time, some types of large animals died out. This forced hunting bands to adapt to new conditions. Smaller animals, wild berries, nuts, grains, and fish became a larger part of their diets.

About 5,000 years ago, people in Central America learned to grow crops such as corn, beans, and squash. Farming brought great changes to those who practiced it. Farmers no longer had to keep moving to find food. Instead, they stayed in one place and began to build permanent villages. As farming methods improved, people produced more food, which in turn allowed the population to grow.

Olmec Civilization

Farming was a key advance. In time, some farming communities in Central America grew enough surplus, or extra, food to support large populations, and the first cities emerged.

Cities marked the rise of the first civilization in the Americas. A civilization is a society that has certain basic features. Among these are cities, a well-organized government, different social classes, a complex religion, and some method of record keeping.

The earliest known civilization in the Americas was that of the Olmecs in Central America. The Olmecs lived in the lowlands along the Gulf of Mexico, about 3,500 years ago. Scientists have found huge stone heads carved by the Olmecs. Some were ten feet tall and weighed several tons. Smaller figures showed creatures that were part human and part animal.

Olmec farmers supplied nearby cities with food. There, powerful leaders built stone temples. The Olmecs left few written records, but

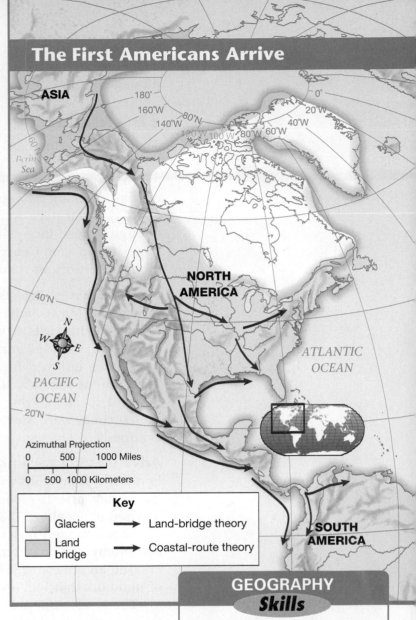

The First Americans Arrive

Key

▢ Glaciers   → Land-bridge theory

▢ Land bridge   → Coastal-route theory

Azimuthal Projection
0   500   1000 Miles
0   500   1000 Kilometers

GEOGRAPHY
Skills

The first Americans reached North America from Asia. Over thousands of years, these hunters populated two huge continents.

1. **Location** On the map, locate: **(a)** Asia, **(b)** Bering Sea, **(c)** North America, **(d)** South America.

2. **Movement** According to the land-bridge theory, in which direction did early hunters travel once they reached North America?

3. **Critical Thinking Drawing Conclusions** Why do you think many of the first Americans continued to travel south after reaching North America?

they did make many advances. They studied the stars and developed a calendar so they could predict the change of seasons and mark the passage of time.

The Mayas

The Olmecs influenced many later peoples, including the Mayas. The early Mayas lived in the rain forests of what are today Guatemala and Mexico. About 3,000 years ago, they began clearing the rain forest and draining swamps to create farmland.

Mayan farmers were able to produce great harvests of corn, enough to feed large cities. As Mayan population grew, cities began to spring up from Central America to southern Mexico. Trade flowed along a network of roads that linked inland cities and the coast.

Social Classes Priests held great power in Mayan society. Only priests, the Mayas believed, could perform the ceremonies needed to bring good harvests or victory in battle. Priests conducted these ceremonies in temples built on top of huge stone pyramids.

Nobles enjoyed high status, too. They served as warriors and government officials. Near the bottom of Mayan society were laborers and farmers, who grew corn, squash, and many other crops. Below them were slaves, most of whom were prisoners of war or criminals.

Advances in Learning Mayan priests had to know exactly when to honor the many gods who were thought to control the natural world. Every day, priests anxiously studied the sun, moon, and stars. They learned much about the movement of these bodies.

Based on their observations, priests made impressive advances in astronomy and mathematics. They learned to predict eclipses and created an accurate, 365-day calendar. They also developed a system of numbers that included the concept of zero.

Then, around A.D. 900, the Mayas abandoned their cities. Historians are not sure why. Perhaps they did so because of warfare, a drought—or both. The rain forests swallowed up the great Mayan temples and palaces. Although Mayan cities decayed, the Mayan people survived. Today, more than 2 million people in Guatemala and southern Mexico speak Mayan languages.

The Aztecs

Long after the Mayan cities were abandoned, a new civilization rose far to the north. Its builders were the Aztecs. The early Aztecs were nomads, people who moved from place to place in search of food. In the 1300s, the Aztecs settled around Lake Texcoco (tay SKOH koh) in central Mexico. From there, they built a powerful empire.

Tenochtitlán On an island in the middle of the lake, the Aztecs built their capital, Tenochtitlán (tay noch tee TLAHN). They constructed a system of **causeways,** or raised roads made of packed earth. The causeways linked the capital to the mainland.

The Aztecs learned to farm the shallow swamps of Lake Texcoco. In some places, they dug canals, using the mud they removed to fill

Compare and Contrast

As you read about the Aztecs and the Incas, check to see if you understand how their accomplishments were similar and how they were different. How were Tenochtitlán and Cuzco similar? How were they different?

in parts of the lake. In other places, they attached reed mats to the lake bottom with long stakes. Then, they piled mud onto the mats to create farmland. Aztec farmers harvested several crops a year on these *chinampas,* or floating gardens.

With riches from trade and conquest, Tenochtitlán prospered. Its markets offered a wide variety of goods. "There are daily more than 60,000 people bartering and selling," wrote a Spanish visitor in the 1500s.

Religion Like the Mayas, Aztec priests studied the heavens and developed complex calendars. Such calendars gave them the ability to tell their people when to plant or harvest. Priests also performed rituals designed to please the many Aztec gods.

The Aztecs paid special attention to the sun god. They believed that each day the sun battled its way across the heavens. They compared the sun's battle to their own, calling themselves "warriors of the sun." They believed that the sun required human sacrifices in order to rise each day. The Aztecs therefore sacrificed thousands of captives each year to please this powerful god.

A Powerful Empire By 1500, the Aztecs ruled a huge empire. It stretched from the Gulf of Mexico to the Pacific Ocean and included millions of people. The Aztecs took great pride in their empire and their capital. "Who could conquer Tenochtitlán?" boasted an Aztec poet. "Who could shake the foundation of heaven?"

The Aztec world was far from peaceful, however. Heavy taxes and the sacrifice of huge numbers of prisoners of war sparked many revolts. Across the empire, people conquered by the Aztecs were eager for revenge. As you will read in Chapter 3, enemies of the Aztecs would help outsiders from distant lands destroy the Aztec empire.

The Incas

Far to the south of the Aztecs, the Incas built one of the largest empires in the Americas. By 1500, their empire stretched for almost 2,500 miles along the west coast of South America.

The center of the Incan empire was the magnificent capital at Cuzco (KOO skoh), located high in the Andes. Cuzco was a holy city to the Incas. All nobles in the empire tried to visit it at least once in their lifetimes. The city had massive palaces and temples made of stone and decorated with gold ornaments. At the center was the

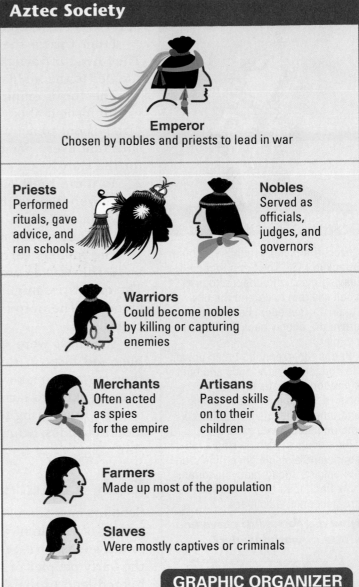

Aztec Society

Emperor
Chosen by nobles and priests to lead in war

Priests
Performed rituals, gave advice, and ran schools

Nobles
Served as officials, judges, and governors

Warriors
Could become nobles by killing or capturing enemies

Merchants
Often acted as spies for the empire

Artisans
Passed skills on to their children

Farmers
Made up most of the population

Slaves
Were mostly captives or criminals

GRAPHIC ORGANIZER
Skills

Like many other ancient civilizations, Aztec society was strictly divided into social classes.

1. **Comprehension**
   (a) Who occupied the highest position in Aztec society? **(b)** Which classes of people were equal to one another?

2. **Critical Thinking**
   Analyzing Information
   How does this graphic organizer suggest the importance of warfare in Aztec society? Give two examples.

palace of the emperor, who was known as the Sapa Inca. The emperor was regarded as a god who was descended from the sun god.

From Cuzco, the emperor ruled more than 10 million people. They lived in varied environments, from coastal deserts to lowland jungles to the highlands of the Andes.

The Incan empire was very well organized. The emperor kept well informed about affairs in all parts of his empire. He sent high officials out to act as governors of his domain. The governors made sure that every person worked at least part of the time on projects for the state.

To unite their empire, the Incas maintained a system of roads that covered more than 10,000 miles. Builders carved roads in rock cliffs and stretched rope bridges across deep gorges. Teams of runners quickly spread royal orders across the empire using these roads.

The runners carried with them a device known as a **quipu** (KEE poo). This was a cord or string with knots that stood for quantities. The quantities might be bags of grain, numbers of soldiers, or other amounts. The quipu was also used by government officials to keep records.

The Incas were skilled engineers. They built massive stone temples and forts. With only human labor, ropes, and wooden rollers, they moved stones weighing up to 200 tons. They used all their engineering skills to farm the dry, rugged mountain lands. They became experts at creating **terraces,** or wide steps of land, out of the steep mountainsides. Sturdy stone walls kept rain from washing away the soil.

Early Cultures of North America

Scholars have found evidence of Mayan and Aztec ideas among some groups of people farther north. Traders and migrating people carried foods, goods, arts, and beliefs from Central America and Mexico to the early peoples of North America. This flow of products and ideas helped lead to the development of many distinct cultures in North America. A **culture** is the entire way of life of a people. It includes their homes, clothing, economy, arts, and government.

People of the Southwest At least 3,000 years ago, knowledge of farming spread northward. Gradually, farming societies emerged in what is today the American Southwest. They included the Hohokams (hoh HOH kahmz) and Anasazis (ah nuh SAH zeez).

The Hohokams lived in present-day southern Arizona. About 2,000 years ago, they dug networks of irrigation ditches so they could farm the desert land. The ditches carried water from the Salt and Gila rivers to fields, where farmers produced corn, squash, and beans.

The Anasazis lived in the Four Corners region, where Colorado, Utah, New Mexico, and Arizona meet. Like the Hohokams, the Anasazis irrigated the desert in order to farm. They also created a network of roads to link dozens of towns. Traders traveled these roads, carrying cotton, sandals, and blankets woven from turkey feathers.

Anasazi Houses The Anasazis built large houses with walls of stone and **adobe,** or sun-dried brick. When the Spanish later saw these houses in the early 1500s, they called them **pueblos** (PWEHB lohz), the Spanish word for "village." (They also called the descendants of the Anasazis the Pueblos.)

About 1,000 years ago, some Anasazi villages faced attacks from warlike neighbors. To escape that threat, they built new homes along steep cliffs. Toeholds cut into the rock let people climb the cliff walls. Farmers planted their crops on land above the cliffs.

Mound Builders To the east, other farming cultures flourished in North America. Among them were the Mound Builders, various cultures that built large earth mounds beginning about 3,000 years ago. Thousands of these mounds dot the landscape from the Appalachian Mountains to the Mississippi Valley and from Wisconsin to Florida.

The first mounds were used for burials. Later mounds were used for religious ceremonies. They were similar in function to the pyramid temples of the Mayas.

The best-known groups of Mound Builders were the Hopewells and the Mississippians. Between A.D. 700 and 1500, the Mississippians built a large city at Cahokia (kah HOH kee ah) in present-day Illinois. As many as 30,000 people may have lived there at one time.

Viewing History

Cliff Dwellings
The cliff dwellings of Mesa Verde are examples of the homes of Native Americans in the canyons and cliffs of southwest Colorado. **Drawing Inferences** *Do you think the inhabitants of these dwellings were a peaceful or a warlike people? Explain.*

★ ★ ★ Section 1 Assessment ★ ★ ★

Recall

1. **Identify** Explain the significance of **(a)** Olmecs, **(b)** Mayas, **(c)** Aztecs, **(d)** Incas, **(e)** quipu, **(f)** Mound Builders.
2. **Define** **(a)** glacier, **(b)** surplus, **(c)** causeway, **(d)** terrace, **(e)** culture, **(f)** adobe, **(g)** pueblo.

Comprehension

3. In the opinion of most scientists, how did the first people reach the Americas?
4. Describe one achievement of each of the following early civilizations in the Americas: **(a)** Mayan, **(b)** Aztec, **(c)** Incan.

5. How did early people adapt to the desert Southwest?

Critical Thinking and Writing

6. **Exploring the Main Idea** Review the Main Idea statement at the beginning of this section. Then, write a paragraph explaining how farming was necessary for the first American civilizations to emerge.
7. **Applying Information** Review the subsection entitled "Early Cultures of North America." Then, make a list showing how the information in this subsection supports the idea that geography affects history.

2 Native American Cultures

Prepare to Read

Objectives

In this section, you will
- Describe how people lived in different culture areas of North America.
- Explain how climate and resources affected Native American cultures.
- List the beliefs shared by different Native American groups.
- Summarize life among the Iroquois.

Key Terms

culture area

tribe

diffusion

pit house

potlatch

kachina

clan

League of the Iroquois

sachem

 **Target Reading Skill**

Main Idea Copy the table below. As you read the section, fill in the ways that each Native American culture adapted to the climate and resources in its area.

CULTURE	CLIMATE/ RESOURCES	HOW ADAPTED
• Arctic • Great Basin • Northwest • Southeast • Eastern Woodlands	• Harsh, limited	• Hunted small animals

Main Idea Native American cultures in North America varied greatly due in part to differences in climate and resources.

Cheyenne shield made of buffalo hide

Setting the Scene When Christopher Columbus reached the Americas in 1492, he thought he had landed in the East Indies—islands off the coast of Asia. So, he called the people he met "Indios," or "Indians." Other Europeans picked up the term. Even after Europeans realized Columbus's error, they continued to call the people of the Americas Indians.

The term Indian is misleading for another, more important, reason. Native Americans do not belong to a single group. In 1492, as now, Native Americans included many different people with many distinct cultures. In North America alone, there were hundreds of Native American languages spoken. Native American cultures, too, varied greatly, much like the cultures of the people of Europe. In the years that followed Columbus's arrival, Europeans would have difficulty understanding this complexity.

Culture Areas of North America

The map on page 44 shows the major culture areas of North America, north of Mexico, around A.D. 1450. A **culture area** is a region in which people share a similar way of life.

Each culture area was home to many different tribes. A **tribe** is a community of people who share common customs, language, and rituals. Members of a tribe saw themselves as a distinct people who shared a common origin. Tribal leaders often made decisions for the group.

Hunting, Gathering, and Fishing Native Americans developed a variety of ways to meet their basic needs for food, clothing, and shelter. In some culture areas, tribes hunted animals and gathered the nuts and fruits that grew in the wild. Other tribes depended on the sea for food. They made boats out of animal skins or carved canoes out of trees. From their boats and canoes, they speared fish or hunted marine animals such as seals, walrus, and whales.

Farming Other tribes lived mostly by farming, planting corn, beans, and squash. Native American tribes farmed in many parts of North America, from California in the West to the Eastern Woodlands. Over time, farmers improved their crops. For example, more than 5,000 years ago, wild corn was tiny, about the size of a human finger. Indian farmers developed dozens of varieties of corn including ones with larger ears.

Trade Indian tribes traded with one another for goods not found within their own region. Trade networks linked people across large distances. Goods sometimes traveled more than 1,000 miles from where they were made.

In the Northwest, traders met near the Dalles on the Columbia River. Local Indians caught and dried salmon, which they exchanged for goods and produce from other places.

More than goods traveled from Indian group to group. New ideas and skills also spread. This process of spreading ideas from one culture to another is known as **diffusion.** Through diffusion, farming skills spread from one Native American group to another.

Climate, Resources, and Culture

Climate and natural resources helped shape Native American cultures in different regions. Climate and natural resources influenced the crops people grew and the animals they hunted. Climate also affected people's needs for clothing and shelter. Resources provided the materials for their clothing and shelter.

Climate and resources affected tribal organization. Where climates were harsh and resources limited, people struggled to find enough food and shelter. In such regions, people were often nomadic. They lived in small hunting bands. Each band included a number of families. In regions with more favorable climates and plentiful resources, people tended to live in larger groups and stay in one place for longer periods.

Cultures of the Far North and Plateau Regions Frozen seas and icy, treeless plains made up the world of the Inuits, who lived in the Arctic region. The Inuits used all the limited resources of their environment. In the short summer season, they collected driftwood along the ocean shore, using it for tools and shelters. For most of the year, the Inuits lived in **pit houses,** houses dug into the ground and covered with wood and skins. Lamps filled with seal oil kept their homes warm even in the bitter cold. Women made warm clothing out of furs and waterproof boots out of sealskins.

Geography and History

Living With Arctic Cold

The Inuit had to rely on the resources of the icy Arctic environment to survive. They built igloos and insulated them with seal skins and sod. They also used caribou and seal fur to make warm clothing. Because caribou hair is hollow, it traps air and offers good insulation against the cold. So, in the fall and winter, the Inuit wore caribou parkas.

Inuit parkas had two layers. The soft inner layer had the fur facing in. A heavier outer layer had fur on the outside. This design was comfortable and protected the wearer from the cold.

In the spring and summer, the coastal Inuit fished or hunted from boats. Because seal fur repels water, the Inuit wore sealskin during the spring and summer.

 How might Inuit culture have been different in a warmer climate?

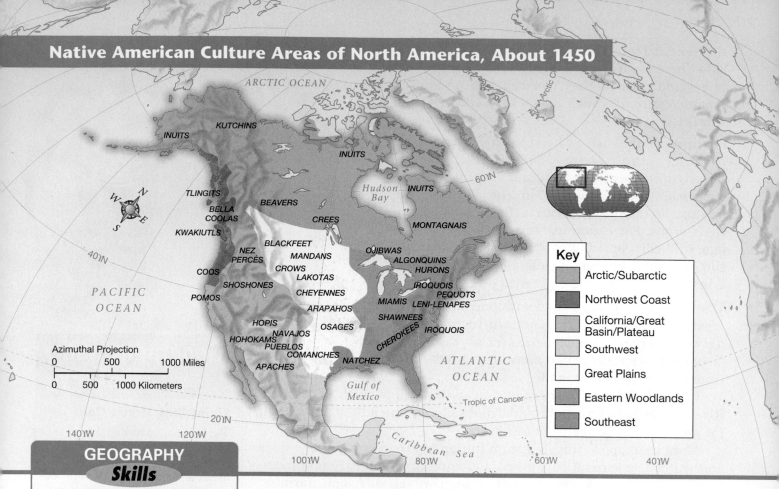

Native American Culture Areas of North America, About 1450

ARCTIC OCEAN

KUTCHINS
INUITS

INUITS

Hudson Bay

INUITS

MONTAGNAIS

TLINGITS
BEAVERS
BELLA COOLAS
CREES
KWAKIUTLS
BLACKFEET
NEZ PERCÉS
MANDANS
CROWS
LAKOTAS
SHOSHONES
CHEYENNES
POMOS
ARAPAHOS
HOPIS
NAVAJOS
OSAGES
HOHOKAMS
PUEBLOS
COMANCHES
APACHES
NATCHEZ
COOS

OJIBWAS
ALGONQUINS
HURONS
IROQUOIS
MIAMIS
PEQUOTS
LENI-LENAPES
SHAWNEES
IROQUOIS
CHEROKEES

PACIFIC OCEAN

ATLANTIC OCEAN

Gulf of Mexico

Tropic of Cancer

Caribbean Sea

Azimuthal Projection

0 — 500 — 1000 Miles
0 — 500 — 1000 Kilometers

60°N
40°N
20°N
140°W   120°W   100°W   80°W   60°W   40°W

Key
- Arctic/Subarctic
- Northwest Coast
- California/Great Basin/Plateau
- Southwest
- Great Plains
- Eastern Woodlands
- Southeast

GEOGRAPHY Skills

Native Americans spread out to populate North America. In the process, they developed many different cultures. Within these culture areas, tribes shared similar ways of life.

1. **Location** On the map, locate **(a)** Northwest Coast culture area, **(b)** Eastern Woodlands culture area, **(c)** Great Plains culture area.

2. **Place (a)** Name two tribes in the Southwest culture area. **(b)** With which culture area are the Cherokees associated?

3. **Critical Thinking Analyzing Information** In which culture areas could Native Americans probably not depend on the sea for food? Explain.

The Plateau region has a cold and dry environment. Surprisingly, however, numbers of hardy plants and animals thrive in the region.

Among the people of the Plateau region were the Utes (YOOTZ) and Shoshones (shoh SHOH neez). They collected pine nuts and dug for roots in the dry soil. They also hunted mountain sheep and rabbits. The Native Americans of the region had few possessions beyond digging sticks, baskets, and tools and weapons needed for hunting.

Cultures of the Northwest Elsewhere in North America the climate was kinder, which helped more complex cultures emerge. The people of the Northwest Coast enjoyed milder temperatures and abundant food supplies. They gathered rich harvests of fish from the sea. From nearby forests, they cut down tall cedar trees and split the trunks into planks for houses and canoes.

With plenty of food, the people of the Pacific Northwest stayed in one place. They built permanent villages and prospered from trade with nearby groups.

Within a village, a family gained status according to how much it owned. Families sometimes competed with one another. To improve its standing, a family might hold a potlatch, or ceremonial dinner, to show off its wealth. The potlatch could last for many days. The family invited many guests and gave everyone gifts. The more goods a family gave away, the more respect it earned. However, people who received gifts at a potlatch were then expected to hold their own potlatches and give gifts.

Native American Culture Groups of North America

ARCTIC/SUBARCTIC

Beavers, Crees, Inuits, Kutchins, Montagnais
Lived as nomadic hunters and food gatherers in cold climate; honored ocean, weather, and animal spirits

CALIFORNIA/GREAT BASIN/PLATEAU

Nez Percés, Pomos, Shoshones
Lived as hunters and gatherers in small family groups; ate mainly fish, berries, acorns

SOUTHWEST

Apaches, Hohokams, Hopis, Navajos, Pueblos
Lived in villages in homes made of adobe; built irrigation systems to grow corn and other crops; honored earth, sky, and water spirits

SOUTHEAST

Cherokees, Natchez
Grew corn, squash, beans, and other crops; held yearly Green Corn Ceremony to mark end of year and celebrate harvest

GREAT PLAINS

Arapahos, Blackfeet, Cheyennes, Comanches, Crows, Lakotas, Mandans, Osages
Lived in tepees; animals hunted by men; crops grown by women; relied on buffalo to meet basic needs of food, shelter, and clothing

EASTERN WOODLANDS

Algonquins, Ojibwas, Hurons, Iroquois, Leni-Lenapes, Miamis, Pequots, Shawnees
Lived in farming villages, but also hunted for food; long houses shared by several families; women shared social and political power

NORTHWEST COAST

Bella Coolas, Coos, Kwakiutls, Tlingits
Lived in villages; benefited from rich natural resources in forests, rivers, and ocean; held potlatches, or ceremonial dinners, where host families gave gifts to guests to show wealth and gain status

---

Cultures of the Southeast Many tribes inhabited the southeastern region of North America. Among them were the Natchez (NACH ihz). They benefited from the region's warm, moist climate. They hunted, fished, and farmed along the fertile coast of the Gulf of Mexico.

The Natchez calendar divided the year into 13 months. Each month was named after a food or an animal that the Natchez harvested or hunted. Their months included Strawberry, Little Corn, Mulberry, Deer, Turkey, and Bear.

The ruler of the Natchez was known as the Great Sun and was worshipped as a god. The Great Sun's feet never touched the ground. Either he was carried on a litter or he walked on mats. Below the Great Sun were members of his family, called Little Suns. Next came Nobles, then Honored People, and finally Stinkards, or commoners, who made up the majority of the people.

Marriage laws ensured that membership in each class kept changing. By law, Nobles had to marry Stinkards. Even the Great Sun chose a Stinkard as a wife. In this way, no one family could hold the position of Great Sun forever. In time, even descendants of a Great Sun became Stinkards.

Shared Beliefs

The many Native American groups had a wide variety of beliefs. Yet, they shared some basic ideas.

Identify Supporting Details

Which details in this paragraph give examples of how Native American cultures of the Southeast adapted to the climate and environment of their region? Use these details to fill in your table.

Knife River Indian Villages National Historic Site

For thousands of years, Native American groups were drawn to the Knife River in North Dakota by the herds of buffalo that came to the river to drink. Once the area was dotted with the Indians' earth-lodges. Time and weather have destroyed the earthlodges. However, visitors can still see depressions where lodges were located.

Knife River, North Dakota

Go Online
PHSchool.com

Virtual Field Trip For an interactive look at the Knife River Indian Villages, visit PHSchool.com, **Web Code mfd-0202.**

Respect for Nature Central to Native American beliefs was a deep respect for the earth. People felt a close bond to plants, animals, and the forces of nature.

Whether hunting, fishing, farming, or gathering wild plants, Native Americans had a great respect for the natural world. Their prayers and ceremonies were designed to maintain a balance between people and the forces of nature. They believed that they must adapt their ways to the natural world in order to survive and prosper.

Native Americans believed that the world was full of powerful, unseen forces and spirits. They honored those spirits, which were thought to act and feel like humans.

In the Pacific Northwest, many tribes relied on fishing. One such group was the Kwakiutls (kwah kee OOT lz). Each year when they caught their first fish of the season, they chanted this prayer:

> 66 We have come to meet alive, Swimmer,
> do not feel wrong about what I have done to you,
> friend Swimmer,
> for that is the reason why you came,
> that I may spear you,
> that I may eat you,
> Supernatural One, you, Long-Life-Giver, you Swimmer.
> Now protect us, me and my wife. 99

—Kwakiutl Prayer of Thanks

Special Ceremonies In farming areas, tribes held special ceremonies to ensure good rainfall. At midsummer, Pueblo villages in the

Cooking down the sap over heated rocks

Thickened syrup turns into taffy when poured on fresh snow

Collecting the sap from maple trees in early spring

Southwest rang with cries of: "The *kachinas* are coming!" **Kachinas** were spirits, who were represented by masked Native American dancers. The Pueblos believed that the kachinas had the power to bring good harvests.

At Pueblo festivals, the kachinas danced. Religious leaders prayed to the spirits and gave them gifts. Only if the spirits were treated well would they return each year with rain for the Pueblos' crops.

In the Southeast, many tribes held a Green Corn Ceremony when the corn ripened in the fall. The ceremony lasted for several days. It marked the end of the old year and the beginning of a new one. On the last day, a sacred fire was lighted. Dancers circled the flames, and the people enjoyed a great feast. Women then used coals from the sacred fire to make new fires in their own houses.

The Iroquois Confederacy

Among the many Native American groups in the Eastern Woodlands were the Iroquois (IHR uh kwoi) people. They lived mostly in present-day New York State.

The Iroquois called themselves "The People of the Long House." They took great pride in their sturdy dwellings, called long houses. A typical long house was about 150 feet long and 20 feet wide. Twelve or more families lived in a long house.

Women had a special place in Iroquoian society. They owned all the household property and were in charge of planting and harvesting. When a man married, he moved in with his wife's family.

Women also had political power. They chose clan leaders. A **clan** was a group of two or more related families. If a clan leader did not do his job well, the women could remove him from his position.

The Iroquois included five nations that spoke similar languages: the Mohawk, Seneca, Onondaga (ahn uhn DAW guh), Oneida (oh NI duh), and Cayuga (kay YOO guh). Each nation had its own ruling council. Until the late 1500s, the five nations were frequently at war.

Then, around 1570, the five Iroquois nations formed an alliance to end the fighting. According to legend, a religious leader named Dekanawida (deh kan ah WEE dah) inspired Hiawatha (hi ah WAH thah) to organize the alliance. It became known as the **League of the Iroquois.**

A council of 50 specially chosen tribal leaders, called **sachems,** met once a year. The council made decisions for the League. Here, too, women had a political role because they chose the sachems and watched over their actions.

Looking Ahead

Scholars do not know exactly how many people lived north of Mexico in 1500. Their figures range from about 1 million to 10 million. Many experts put the figure at about 2.5 million.

Across North America, hundreds of tribes followed their own ways of life. Trade and warfare brought some tribes into contact with one another. Yet, those contacts were limited. By the late 1400s, however, events were taking place on far-off continents that would forever change all of the Native American cultures.

★ ★ ★ **Section 2 Assessment** ★ ★ ★

Recall
1. **Identify** Explain the significance of **(a)** Natchez, **(b)** League of the Iroquois.
2. **Define** **(a)** culture area, **(b)** tribe, **(c)** pit house, **(d)** potlatch, **(e)** kachina, **(f)** clan, **(g)** sachem.

Comprehension
3. List three ways Native Americans in different culture areas met their needs for food, clothing, and shelter.
4. Give three examples of how climate and resources affected Native American cultures.
5. Describe one belief that Native Americans shared.

6. How did women play an important role in Iroquois culture?

Critical Thinking and Writing
7. **Exploring the Main Idea** Review the Main Idea statement at the beginning of this section. Choose the culture area that you think offered the most favorable conditions for people. Then, make a list of at least three reasons for your choice.
8. **Formulating Questions** Study the map and chart on pages 44–45. Then, pose a question that links the two graphics. Exchange questions with a classmate and answer his or her question.

ACTIVITY

Design a Magazine Cover Design a cover for a special issue of a magazine on the variety of Native American cultures. Include a cover illustration as well as the titles of three or four articles that will appear in the magazine.

Native American Dwellings

Native Americans developed a wide variety of dwellings to suit their different environments. Shown here are a pueblo from the Southwest, a tepee from the Great Plains, and a long house from the Eastern Woodlands.

Pueblo

The walls are made of sandstone blocks plastered with adobe.

Kivas are rooms used for religious ceremonies.

Winter cooking room

Roofs are used as a center for work and socializing.

Storage room

Sleeping room

Drainspouts and splash blocks keep moisture away from roofs and walls.

Tepee

Lodge poles

Smoke flaps

Buffalo sinew

Buffalo hide

Inner lining

Wooden stakes

This entrance almost always faced the rising sun in the east.

Long House

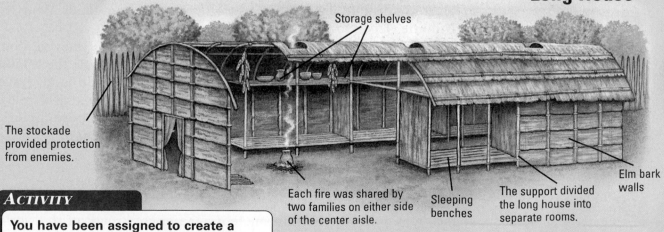

Storage shelves

The stockade provided protection from enemies.

Each fire was shared by two families on either side of the center aisle.

Sleeping benches

The support divided the long house into separate rooms.

Elm bark walls

ACTIVITY

You have been assigned to create a poster promoting an exhibit on different styles of Native American dwellings. Use the information in this chapter to create an original poster that will make people want to attend the exhibit.

3 Trade Networks of Africa and Asia

Prepare to Read

Objectives

In this section, you will
- Explain why trade flourished in the Muslim world.
- Identify the trading states that rose in Africa, and describe life in many African trading cultures.
- Describe how China's overseas trade expanded in the early 1400s.

Key Terms

first global age
Islam
Quran
Silk Road
caravan
city-state
savanna
extended family
kinship

Target Reading Skill

Main Idea As you read, prepare an outline of this section. Use roman numerals to indicate the major headings of the section, capital letters for the subheadings, and numbers for the supporting details. The outline has been started for you.

> I. The Muslim World
>   A. Rise and spread of Islam
>   1.
>   2.
>   B. Trade routes
>   1.
>   2.
>   C. Silk Road
> II. African Trading States and Cultures
>   A. City-states of East Africa
>   1.
>   2.
>   B. Trading kingdoms of West Africa

Main Idea Busy trade networks linked the peoples of Africa and Asia long before Europeans reached the Americas.

Ancient caravans across the desert

Setting the Scene

Ibn Battuta was just 21 years old in 1325 when he set off to see the world. During the next 30 years, he would cover more than 73,000 miles. Ibn Battuta visited lands from Spain and North Africa to the Middle East, India, and China. When he finally returned home for good, he wrote proudly of his travels:

> 66 I have indeed—praise be to God—attained my desire in this world, which was to travel through the earth, and I have attained in this respect what no other person has attained to my knowledge. 99
>
> —Ibn Battuta, *Rhila (Book of Travels),* 1355

Ibn Battuta was a scholar from North Africa who wanted to learn all he could about the many lands and the different peoples of the Muslim world. In the 1300s, that world reached from lands along the Atlantic Ocean to the borders of China.

Travelers like Ibn Battuta, as well as trade goods, moved along the land and sea routes that linked the peoples of Africa, the Middle East, and Asia. The amount of long-distance trade and travel increased dramatically in the 1400s. For the first time, far-off parts of the world began to be linked. For this reason, this period marks the beginning of what historians call the **first global age.**

The Muslim World

Arab merchants played a large role in this growing trade. Arabia's location in the Middle East made it a major crossroads of the world. It stood at the center of trade routes that linked the Mediterranean world in the west with Asia in the east and Africa in the south.

Rise and Spread of Islam The growth of trade was also linked to the growth of a new religion. In the early 600s, a new religion, Islam,

Trade Routes of Asia and Africa

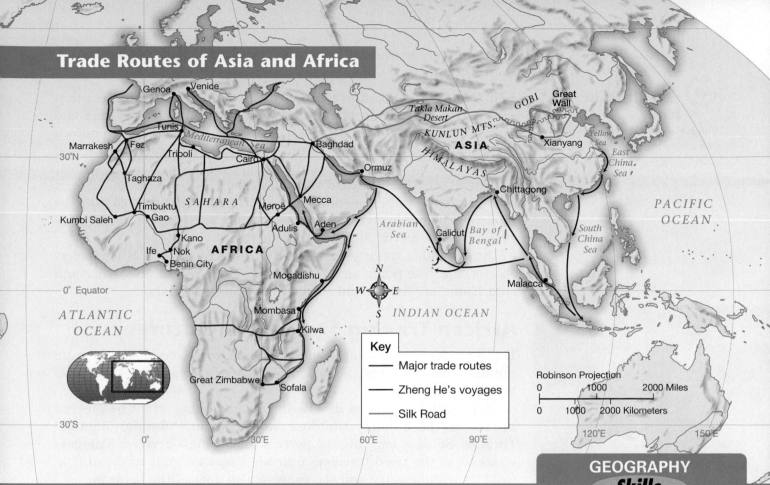

Key
— Major trade routes
— Zheng He's voyages
— Silk Road

Robinson Projection
0   1000   2000 Miles
0 1000 2000 Kilometers

emerged in Arabia. Its founder was the prophet Muhammad. The central teaching of Islam was belief in one God. (The Arabic word for God is *Allah*.) Followers of Islam, called Muslims, believed that the **Quran** (ku RAHN), the sacred book of Islam, contained the exact word of God as revealed to Muhammad.

Muhammad won many followers among the Arabs. After his death in 632, Islam spread rapidly. Devout followers carried Islam across North Africa and into Spain. Islam spread eastward, too, from Persia to India and beyond.

Islam expanded through trade and conquest. Many people in conquered lands chose to convert to the successful new religion. Elsewhere, Muslim merchants carried the new faith to people living along the trade routes of Asia and Africa.

Islam united Muslims from many lands. Muslims had a basic duty to make a pilgrimage, or journey, to the holy city of Mecca at least once in their lives. Every year, people from across the Muslim world traveled to Mecca. Muslims from North Africa, Persia, Afghanistan, India, Spain, and West Africa crowded Mecca's dusty streets. They prayed in Arabic, the language of Islam.

Trade Routes Muslim merchants traded across a vast area. They sailed to ports around the Indian Ocean. Their ships used large, triangular sails that allowed captains to use the wind even if it changed direction.

Muslim sailors had expert knowledge of wind and weather conditions of the Indian Ocean. As a result, merchants in ports around

GEOGRAPHY
Skills

Before the 1500s, Asian and African cultures had established important trade routes. This enabled the movement of goods and ideas between civilizations that had had few outside contacts.

1. **Location** On the map locate (a) the Silk Road, (b) Xianyang, (c) Baghdad.

2. **Place** Through what Asian desert did the trade route from Xianyang to Baghdad pass?

3. **Critical Thinking Drawing Conclusions** Why might large cities have developed on the eastern and western ends of the Silk Road but not in the middle?

Identify Main Ideas

Which sentence states the main idea under the red head "Silk Road"?

the region knew when the trading ships had to sail and when they would return.

Silk Road Some Muslim traders traveled the overland routes that crossed the grasslands, mountains, and deserts of Central Asia and linked China and the Middle East. These routes had become known as the **Silk Road** because prized Chinese silks had been carried westward along them for more than 2,000 years.

Travel on the Silk Road was dangerous. Desert storms, hunger, and bandits were a constant threat. Traders formed **caravans,** or groups of people who traveled together for safety. Despite the dangers, trade along the Silk Road prospered.

By the 1400s, trade goods flowed across a huge area. Muslim merchants sold fine porcelains from China, cloth from India, ivory and gold from East Africa, and spices from Southeast Asia.

African Trading States and Cultures

Trade routes played a large role in Africa, too. Long-distance trade routes crossed the vast Sahara, the desert linking West Africa and North Africa.

A peaceful afternoon in a West African village might be pierced by sounds of a horn. Children would shout, "Batafo! Batafo!" Traders! Soon, a long line of porters and camels arrived. Villagers watched as the tired travelers unloaded sacks of salt or dried fish. Gold, fabrics, jewelry, and slaves were also part of the caravan.

City-States of East Africa Trade had long flowed up and down the coast of East Africa. Small villages that had good natural harbors grew into busy trading centers.

Gold from Zimbabwe (zihm BAH bweh), a powerful inland state, was carried to coastal cities such as Kilwa and Sofala. From there, ships carried the gold, and prized goods such as hardwoods and ivory, across the Indian Ocean to India and China.

Wealth from trade helped local East African rulers build strong city-states. A **city-state** is a large town that has its own government and controls the surrounding countryside.

Many rulers of these city-states became Muslims. In time, Muslim culture influenced East African traditions. The blend of cultures led to the rise of a new language, Swahili, which blended Arabic words and local African languages.

Trading Kingdoms of West Africa A region of grasslands, called the **savanna,** covers much of West Africa. Several rich trading kingdoms emerged there. Among the best known were Mali and Songhai (SAWNG hi). The city of Timbuktu was the major trading center for both kingdoms.

The kingdom of Mali rose in about A.D. 1200 and flourished for about 200 years. Like the rulers of East Africa's city-states, many rulers in West African kingdoms adopted the religion of Islam.

Mali's most famous ruler, Mansa Musa, was a Muslim. In 1324, the emperor made a pilgrimage to Mecca. On the way, he and his caravan stopped in Cairo, Egypt. His wealth in gold amazed the Egyptians. In time, stories of Mansa Musa's immense wealth reached Europe. A

Primary Source

Timbuktu

Hasan al-Wazan, also known as Leo Africanus, described Timbuktu in 1526:

"The inhabitants are very rich.... The royal court is magnificent and very well organized.... There are in Timbuktu numerous judges, teachers, and priests, all properly appointed by the king. He greatly honors learning. Many hand-written books ... are also sold. There is more profit from this commerce than from all other merchandise."

—Hasan al-Wazan,
from *The Description of Africa,* 1526

Analyzing Primary Sources
What were some signs of prosperity in Timbuktu?

Spanish map from that time shows Mansa Musa on his throne, holding a golden object. The mapmaker wrote these words nearby:

> **66** So abundant is the gold in his country that this lord is the richest and most noble king in all the land. **99**
> —Catalan Atlas, 1375

In the 1400s, Songhai emerged as the most powerful kingdom in West Africa. Muslim emperors extended Songhai's power and made Timbuktu into a thriving city.

Village and Family Life Ways of life varied greatly across the huge continent of Africa. While powerful trading states flourished in some regions, most people lived outside these kingdoms. Many lived in small villages. They made a living by herding, fishing, or farming.

Family relationships were important in African cultures. Although family patterns varied across Africa, many people lived within an extended family. In an **extended family,** several generations live in one household. An extended family usually included grandparents, parents, children, and sometimes aunts, uncles, and cousins. The grandparents, or elders, received special respect for their wisdom and knowledge.

Ties of **kinship,** or sharing a common ancestor, linked families. People related by kinship owed loyalty to one another. Kinship ties encouraged a strong sense of community and cooperation.

Religious beliefs varied widely across Africa. Yet, African beliefs reflected some common threads. Links among family members lasted even after a person died. In their rituals and ceremonies, Africans honored the spirits of their ancestors as well as the forces of nature. Powerful spirits, they believed, could harm or could help the living.

Chinese Voyages of Trade and Exploration

Africa had many different cultures and kingdoms. By contrast, in China, power was centered on the emperor. Chinese rulers were often suspicious of outsiders. China was the most isolated civilization of the ancient world. Long distances and physical barriers separated it from Egypt, the Middle East, and India. This isolation contributed to the Chinese belief that China was the center of the Earth and the sole source of civilization. The ancient Chinese looked down on outsiders, who did not speak Chinese or follow Chinese ways.

Viewing History

Historic Journeys Between 1405 and 1433, the Chinese admiral Zheng He (bottom left) led a fleet of large ships like this one on journeys of exploration to Southeast Asia, India, and Arabia. By the time of Zheng He's death, Chinese influence had spread across a wide region. **Drawing Inferences** *What do you think it would take to maintain Chinese influence in these areas of Southeast Asia, India, and Arabia after Zheng He's death?*

Area visited by Zheng He

The Great Treasure Fleet The young emperor who came to power in 1402 was eager for trade. He ordered a huge fleet to be built and named Zheng He (DZUNG HEH) to command it. Zheng He's fleet numbered more than 300 ships. It carried tons of trade goods. The largest ships were more than 400 feet long.

Between 1405 and 1433, Zheng He made seven long voyages. His fleet traded at ports in Southeast Asia, India, Arabia, and East Africa. At every port, Chinese traders carried on a brisk business. They expanded Chinese trade and influence across a wide region.

The Voyages End The great fleet returned home with exotic goods and animals, such as giraffes, that the Chinese had never seen. However, China's overseas voyages soon ended. A new emperor decided that China had nothing to learn from the outside world. He outlawed foreign trade.

What Might Have Been Historians sometimes discuss what might have happened if events had taken a slightly different course. One question historians ponder is what if Zheng He had led his fleet around the southern tip of Africa or across the Pacific?

Chinese ships could certainly have made such long voyages. They were much larger than the ships commanded by Christopher Columbus in 1492. When Columbus sailed westward across the Atlantic Ocean, he had three tiny ships. They carried only 90 sailors, compared to the approximately 28,000 on Zheng He's ships.

If Zheng He had crossed the Pacific Ocean and reached the Americas, American history might have turned out very different. Instead, China stopped its voyages and closed its doors to trade. Within a few years, however, several small European nations began to hunt for new trade routes to Asia. Their eagerness for trade led to daring voyages across the Atlantic Ocean.

★ ★ ★ Section 3 Assessment ★ ★ ★

Recall

1. **Identify** Explain the significance of **(a)** Ibn Battuta, **(b)** first global age, **(c)** Islam, **(d)** Quran, **(e)** Silk Road, **(f)** Timbuktu, **(g)** Zheng He.
2. **Define (a)** caravan, **(b)** city-state, **(c)** savanna, **(d)** extended family, **(e)** kinship.

Comprehension

3. How did trade and religion link people in the Muslim world?
4. What were some common values that linked the people of many different African cultures?
5. How did China's emperor encourage overseas trade in the early 1400s?

Critical Thinking and Writing

6. **Exploring the Main Idea** Review the Main Idea statement at the beginning of this section. Then, write a paragraph describing networks linking Africa and Asia in 1400. Explain how these networks helped the movement of goods, people, and ideas.
7. **Solving Problems** Suppose a European ruler wanted to profit from trade with Asia. The routes through the Mediterranean and across Asia were already controlled by others, however. How might the ruler try to get a foothold in the Asian trade?

4 Tradition and Change in Europe

Prepare to Read

Objectives

In this section, you will
- Define Jewish and Christian traditions that influenced European civilization.
- Describe how ancient Greek and Roman traditions affected later Europeans.
- List the ways in which the events of the Middle Ages changed Europe.
- Identify the importance of the Renaissance.

Key Terms

salvation
missionary
direct democracy
republic
feudalism
manor
Crusades
astrolabe
Renaissance

Target Reading Skill

Clarifying Meaning Copy the concept web below. Add as many ovals as you need. As you read, fill in each blank oval with important facts about the traditions that shaped European civilization. Two ovals have been completed to help you get started.

Ancient Greek democracy

EUROPEAN TRADITIONS

Jewish tradition of obeying God's law

Main Idea European civilization emerged from a long period of isolation during the 1400s.

Setting the Scene

The sturdy ship dipped in and out of the rolling waves of the Atlantic Ocean. Above, stars dotted the night sky.

At the first hint of dawn, a cabin boy checked the hourglass, which was used to keep track of time. It took 30 minutes for sand to run from the top half of the glass into the bottom. So every half-hour, the boy had to turn the glass. Afterward, he prayed aloud:

66 Blessed be the light of day and the Holy Cross, we say; and the Lord of Truth and the Holy Trinity. Blessed be the immortal soul and the Lord who keeps it whole. 99

—Eugenio de Salazar, 1573

The boy's prayer was a tradition on European sailing ships. In the 1400s, bold Europeans set out to explore the world. They brought with them their traditions that, over time, would affect people in many lands.

Sailing the high seas

Jewish and Christian Traditions

European civilization emerged slowly during the long period from about A.D. 500 to 1400. As in other societies, religious beliefs played an important role in European life. They provided moral guidance and helped people understand their place in the world. European beliefs were shaped by two religions of the ancient Middle East, Judaism and Christianity.

Judaism and the Importance of Laws Judaism refers to the religious beliefs of the Israelites, who lived more than 3,000 years ago. (Later, the Israelites became known as Jews.) Jews believe in one God and feel a sacred duty to obey God's rules.

The history and laws of the ancient Jews were recorded in the Torah. The Jews credited Moses with bringing God's laws to them. Those laws included the Ten Commandments, a set of religious and moral rules.

The Jews believed that every Jew must obey the Ten Commandments and other religious laws. No one was above God's laws, even the most powerful ruler. That view differed from most religions of that time, which regarded rulers as gods. More than 2,000 years ago, many Jews left their homeland. This scattering of people sent Jews to different parts of the world. Wherever they settled, Jews maintained their identity as a people by obeying their religion's laws and traditions.

Christianity and the Teachings of Jesus About 2,000 years ago, a Jew named Jesus lived in a province of the Roman empire. Jesus believed in the Ten Commandments and other Jewish traditions. He preached about God's goodness and mercy. Some followers began to call him the Messiah, a savior chosen by God.

The Gospels, which recount the life of Jesus, tell how crowds flocked to hear Jesus teach and perform miracles. Local officials, however, saw Jesus as a political threat. They had him arrested, tried, and crucified—a Roman form of execution.

The life and teachings of Jesus inspired a new religion, Christianity. The new faith included many Jewish traditions, such as belief in one God and the Ten Commandments, along with the teachings of Jesus. Like Jewish teachers, Jesus emphasized love, mercy, and forgiveness.

Jesus taught that anyone, rich or poor, could achieve salvation, or everlasting life. That belief, which meant that everyone was equal in the eyes of God, appealed to many people. As Christianity spread across the Roman empire, officials sometimes persecuted Christians. However, the persecutions did not slow the growth of the religion. Eventually, around A.D. 391, Christianity became the official religion of the empire.

By then, Christians had organized a strong church with its own government and officials. The church sent out missionaries, people who spread Christian teachings across Europe. Slowly, missionaries brought many non-Christian peoples of Europe into the new faith.

Greek and Roman Traditions

Two ancient civilizations shaped European traditions over the centuries. They were the civilizations that grew up in ancient Greece and Rome.

Greek Ideas About Government Around 500 B.C., Greece entered a golden age. Greek artists created fine marble statues and designed elegant temples. Poets and playwrights created works that are still read today.

Greek thinkers, such as Socrates and Aristotle, valued human reason. Using reason, they said, individuals could understand the natural world. Other Greek thinkers made important contributions

---

Primary Source

The Greatness of Athenian Democracy

Pericles, a longtime leader of Athens, made a speech that has survived since ancient times. In it, he described Athenian greatness, especially its democracy:

"Our constitution is called a democracy because power is in the hands not of a minority but of the whole people. When it is a question of settling private disputes, everyone is equal before the law. . . .

Here a citizen is interested not just in his own affairs but in the affairs of state as well. Even citizens who are busy with their own affairs are very well-informed on politics. Unlike other states, we do not say that a man who takes no interest in politics is a man who minds his own business. We say that he has no business here at all."

—Pericles, Funeral Oration, 431 B.C.

Analyzing Primary Sources
What is Pericles' view of citizens who do not participate in government?

---

to science and mathematics. They developed the study of geometry and pioneered the idea that all matter is made up of small moving atoms. Greek doctors tried to diagnose and treat diseases using scientific methods. Greek thinkers debated many issues, including the best kind of government. Greek ideas about government would have a great impact on later European thinking.

Unlike in the large empires of the ancient world, the Greeks lived in small city-states. At first, a monarch ruled each city-state. Slowly, some city-states developed other kinds of government. In some, a king ruled. In others, a few wealthy people controlled the government. Ancient Athens, for example, first created direct democracy. **Direct democracy** is a form of government in which ordinary citizens have the power to govern.

Athenians were proud of their government. They believed that people could think and act for themselves. All citizens could attend the assembly and make laws for the city. Athenian democracy was very limited, however. Only free men whose parents had been born in Athens were citizens. Most people in Athens were not citizens. This included all women and slaves and men who came to Athens from other city-states.

Roman Government and Law As the Greeks entered their golden age, a few small villages in Italy were growing into the city of Rome. From a small city-state, Rome would one day become a huge empire. In the process, it absorbed ideas from many other peoples, including the Greeks. It also created its own traditions, especially in the fields of law and government.

In 509 B.C., the Romans overthrew their king and set up a republic. A **republic** is a system of government in which citizens choose representatives to govern them. In the Roman Republic, a senate and assembly made the laws.

As Rome expanded, the republic faced a series of crises that caused military leaders to seize power. Among them was Julius Caesar, who named himself dictator for life. After Caesar's murder, his nephew, Octavian, declared himself emperor in 27 B.C. He received the title Caesar Augustus.

The Roman empire lasted for almost 500 years. Rome spread its language, Latin, and ideas about law across a wide area. In Roman tradition, everyone was equal before the law. Accused people were considered innocent until proven guilty. Rome also set up rules about the use of evidence in court. Roman legal traditions would later influence Europe.

Decline of Rome The Roman empire declined slowly. Invaders attacked and overran many regions. Trade and travel slowed. In place of the Roman empire, Europe was splintered into many small, warring kingdoms.

During this time, the achievements of Greece and Rome were largely forgotten. A few Christian monasteries preserved ancient manuscripts. Others survived in the Islamic world. Much later, as you will read, Europeans would rediscover these ancient texts. Then, Greek and Roman traditions would, in turn, come to play a key role in American history.

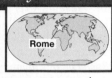

Paraphrase
When you paraphrase, you restate in your own words what you have already read. Paraphrase the information about how Roman government and law influenced European traditions. Include this information on your concept web.

Viewing History

Roman Senators
In the Roman Republic, forms of government were established to take power away from the few and give it to the many. The bas-relief below shows two Roman senators. **Summarizing** *Based on the information on Roman government, write two sentences explaining how the Romans established traditions of government that would influence later societies.*

The Middle Ages

The period from about A.D. 500 to about 1400 is known as the Middle Ages. During the early Middle Ages, invasion and war were common. Without Roman armies, people had to find other means of defending themselves.

Feudalism A new kind of government evolved during the Middle Ages. Kings and queens divided their lands among warrior nobles. In return, nobles promised to fight for the ruler when asked. This system of rule by lords who ruled their lands but owed loyalty and military service to a monarch is called **feudalism** (FYOOD 'l ihz uhm).

At the top of feudal society stood the king and the most powerful lords. Next came the lesser nobles. Most people in feudal society were peasants who farmed the lord's lands and could not leave the land without the lord's permission.

Daily Life Feudal life revolved around the **manor,** which included the lord's castle and the lands around it. Manor lands might include several villages.

Each manor was self-sufficient. That is, people made almost everything they needed. Life for peasants was hard. They struggled to produce enough food just to survive.

The most powerful force was the Roman Catholic Church. It ruled more than religious life. The Church owned large amounts of land and was the source of education. The clergy were often the only people who could read and write. Because of their efforts, much of the learning from the ancient world was preserved.

By about A.D. 900, life began to change. Peasants used new methods of farming to produce more food. Warfare declined and trade began to grow. Slowly, people began to look beyond their isolated villages.

The Crusades The pace of change increased between 1100 and 1300 in part because of the Crusades. The Crusades were a series of wars fought by Christians to control the Holy Land. The Holy Land included Jerusalem and the other places where Jesus had lived and taught. Muslims had controlled this region for centuries.

During the Crusades, tens of thousands of Christians journeyed to the Middle East. Fighting between Christians and Muslims continued for almost 200 years. Christians won some victories. But in the end, they failed to win control of the Holy Land.

Growth of Trade The Crusades had important effects on Europe, however. Crusaders traveled beyond their villages

Viewing History

Peasants and Lords

In the Middle Ages, it was the peasants' duty to farm the lord's lands. The lord in his magnificent castle had the duty of protecting the peasants. **Making Predictions** *Based on this painting from France in the early 1400s, and the information on the Middle Ages, what problems do you think could arise between peasant and lord?*

and came into contact with other civilizations. In the Middle East, they tasted new foods, such as rice, oranges, dates, and new spices. They saw beautiful silks and woven rugs.

Europe had traded with the Middle East for many years before the Crusades. However, returning Crusaders demanded more of the Asian foods, spices, silks, and rugs. Italian merchants realized that people would pay high prices for such goods. They outfitted ships and increased trade with the Muslim world.

New Tools for Navigation Trade brought new knowledge. From the Muslim world, Europeans acquired sailing skills and the magnetic compass. Muslims had earlier adopted the magnetic compass from the Chinese. The special needle of the compass always pointed north, which helped ships stay on course.

Another useful instrument was the **astrolabe** (AS troh layb), which helped sailors determine their latitude while at sea. These new instruments let Europeans sail far out to sea, beyond sight of land. By 1500, Portugal had taken the lead in this new overseas travel.

The Renaissance Expands Horizons

Increased trade and travel made Europeans eager to learn more about the wider world. Scholars looked in monastery libraries for manuscripts of ancient Greek and Roman works. Some traveled to the Muslim world, where many ancient works had been preserved.

As scholars studied ancient learning, they began to make their own discoveries. They produced new books on art, medicine, astronomy, and chemistry. This great burst of learning was called the **Renaissance** (REHN uh sahns), a French word meaning rebirth. It lasted from the late 1300s until the 1600s.

A new invention, the printing press, helped to spread Renaissance learning. A German printer named Johannes Gutenberg (GOOT uhn berg) is credited with this invention in the 1430s. Before then, books were scarce and costly because each was copied by hand. With the printing press, large numbers of books could be produced quickly and at a low cost. Soon more people began to read, and learning spread more quickly.

The Search for New Trade Routes During the Renaissance, trade brought new prosperity. European rulers began to increase their power. In England and France, kings and queens tried to bring powerful feudal lords under their control. In Spain and Portugal,

Portuguese Routes of Exploration

Key
- - → Bartholomeu Dias, 1487–1488
⟶ Vasco Da Gama, 1497–1499

Robinson Projection

0   1000   2000 Miles

0   1000   2000 Kilometers

GEOGRAPHY *Skills*

New technologies and new skills allowed Portuguese sailors to make historic voyages along the coast of Africa and across the Indian Ocean to India.

1. **Location** On the map locate (a) Portugal, (b) Cape of Good Hope, (c) Indian Ocean.

2. **Movement** Describe the route taken by Da Gama.

3. **Critical Thinking Drawing Inferences** Why do you think the Cape of Good Hope was an important landmark to sailors?

Christian monarchs drove out Muslim rulers, who had governed there for centuries.

Rulers in England, France, Spain, and Portugal were eager to increase their wealth. They saw the great profits that could be made through trade. However, Muslim and Italian merchants controlled the trade routes across the Mediterranean Sea. So, Western Europe's leaders began hunting for other routes to Asia.

European rulers also looked to Africa as a source of riches. Tales of Mansa Musa's wealth had created a stir in Europe, but no one knew the source of African gold.

Portuguese Voyages Portugal was an early leader in the search for a new trade route to Asia and for the source of African gold. In the early 1400s, Prince Henry, known as Henry the Navigator, encouraged sea captains to sail south along the coast of West Africa. Realizing that Portugal needed better navigators to accomplish the task, he set up an informal school to teach sailors techniques of navigation and the art of shipbuilding.

Under Henry's guidance, the Portuguese designed a new type of ship, the caravel (KAR uh vehl). With triangular sails and a steering rudder, caravels could be sailed into the wind. Portuguese caravels stopped at many places along the coast of West Africa. They traded cloth, silver, textiles, and grain for gold, ivory, and slaves.

Slowly, Portuguese explorers ventured farther south, hoping to find a sea route around Africa to the rich spice trade of Asia. In 1488, Bartolomeu Dias reached the southern tip of Africa.

Nine years later, in 1497, Vasco da Gama rounded the Cape of Good Hope at the southern tip of Africa. He then sailed up the coast of East Africa and across the Indian Ocean to India. The Portuguese pushed on to the East Indies, the islands of Southeast Asia and the source of valuable spices.

Viewing History

An African View of the Portuguese

West Africa

The ivory carving above was done by an African artisan in the 1500s. **Drawing Inferences** *How do you think Africans perceived the Portuguese?*

★ ★ ★ Section 4 Assessment ★ ★ ★

Recall
1. **Identify** Explain the significance of **(a)** Crusades, **(b)** Renaissance, **(c)** Johannes Gutenberg, **(d)** Prince Henry.
2. **Define** **(a)** salvation, **(b)** missionary, **(c)** direct democracy, **(d)** republic, **(e)** feudalism, **(f)** manor, **(g)** astrolabe.

Comprehension
3. Describe one tradition from Judaism and Christianity that influenced later Europeans.
4. What were three ideas that Europeans learned from ancient Greece and Rome?

5. How did the Crusades help bring changes to Europe?
6. Why did Renaissance rulers in Western Europe want to find new routes to Asia?

Critical Thinking and Writing
7. **Exploring the Main Idea** Review the Main Idea statement at the beginning of this section. Then, identify reasons for the European exploration of North America.
8. **Drawing Conclusions** Write an editorial explaining whether you think the Crusades were a success or a failure.

ACTIVITY
Writing a Diary You are a sailor on Vasco da Gama's voyage of 1497. With a partner, write two different diary entries that express your hopes and fears about the voyage.

History books are bursting with information. Although you can't remember every fact, you can learn to identify the main ideas and note the details that explain and support them. The passage below describes the growth of trade between Europe and other regions of the world. After you have read the passage, use "Learn the Skill" below to help you identify the main idea.

Toward the end of the Middle Ages, European nations developed an interest in trading with Asia. Several factors contributed to this interest. Perhaps the most important of these was the huge profit that European nations could gain through such trade. Rulers of countries including Spain, France, England, and Portugal quickly saw that increased prosperity from trade could be turned into increased power for them.

Trade with Asia promised several other benefits as well. The shimmering silks and colorful rugs of Asia pleased and intrigued Europeans. So, too, did foreign foods such as oranges, rice, and dates. Exotic spices such as ginger and pepper not only improved food but also helped to preserve it. Still other reasons that Europeans sought trade were a new awareness of the rest of the world and a curiosity to learn more about it.

Learn the Skill *To identify main ideas and supporting details, use the following steps:*

1. **Find the main idea.** The main idea is what the passage is about. Often, the main idea is stated in the first sentence of a paragraph. However, it can occur in other parts of a paragraph as well.

2. **Restate the main idea.** To be sure you understand what a paragraph is about, restate the main idea in your own words.

3. **Look for details.** These include facts, reasons, explanations, examples, and descriptions that tell more about the main idea.

4. **Make connections.** Note how the details support and expand the main idea.

Practice the Skill *Answer the following questions about the paragraphs above:*

1. What is the main idea sentence in each of the two paragraphs?

2. Restate the main idea in each paragraph in your own words.

3. Identify a detail that supports the main idea in the first paragraph.

4. (a) How do the details in the first paragraph help explain the main idea of that paragraph? (b) How do the details in the second paragraph expand the main idea of that paragraph?

Apply the Skill *See the Chapter Review and Assessment.*

Section 1

Asian wanderers who came to the Americas on a land bridge had to adjust to new conditions. A number of civilizations thrived in Central and South America. Other cultures blossomed in North America.

Section 2

The climates and resources of North America enabled many different groups to survive there. Native American cultures shared some beliefs. The Iroquois Confederacy linked several Native American nations.

Section 3

As Islam spread, Muslim merchants began to trade across Asia and Africa. The Chinese voyager Zheng He reached as far west as India, Arabia, and East Africa.

Section 4

The modern era has been influenced by many ideas from Jewish and Christian traditions, from Greek and Roman traditions, and from the Renaissance. The Crusades occurred during the Middle Ages.

For additional review and enrichment activities, see the interactive version of *The American Nation,* available on the Web and on CD-ROM.

Chapter Self-Test For practice test questions for Chapter 2, visit PHSchool.com, **Web Code mfa-0204.**

Building Vocabulary

Write sentences, using the chapter vocabulary words listed below, leaving blanks where the vocabulary words would go. Exchange your sentences with another student and fill in the blanks in each other's sentences.

1. **glacier**
2. **surplus**
3. **culture area**
4. **pit house**
5. **sachem**
6. **city-state**
7. **extended family**
8. **direct democracy**
9. **republic**
10. **feudalism**

Reviewing Key Facts

11. What civilizations emerged in present-day Mexico? (Section 1)

12. Name two Native American cultures that developed in North America and explain how each adapted to its environment. (Section 2)
13. How did trade affect East Africa and West Africa before the 1500s? (Section 3)
14. How did the Renaissance open new horizons for Europeans? (Section 4)

Critical Thinking and Writing

15. **Comparing** Make a list comparing the methods used by the Aztecs to farm swampy Lake Texcoco to those used by the Anasazi to farm the desert Southwest.
16. **Contrasting (a)** Make a list of differences between the cultures of the Great Basin and those of the Southeast. **(b)** Write a paragraph explaining how those differences were related to the climate and resources of each region.
17. **Connecting to Geography: Movement** The movement of people, goods, and ideas is another key link between geography and history. **(a)** Describe the trade networks that had grown up across Africa and Asia by the 1400s. **(b)** Give one example of how trade led to the exchange of ideas.
18. **Synthesizing Information** Write a paragraph describing how the Renaissance led Europeans to explore unfamiliar lands.

Analyzing Primary Sources

Not all primary sources consist of words. A painting can also be a primary source. For example, the painting below contains some valuable information about how the Aztecs lived. Study it, and then answer the questions below.

19. The seated person is the emperor. What is the other person doing?
    A. He is putting on a puppet show.
    B. He is bringing the emperor gifts.
    C. He is cleaning up the throne room.
    D. He is exterminating the throne room.
20. What do you think is the attitude of the person at right?
    A. He is defiant.
    B. He is aggressive.
    C. He is submissive.
    D. He is confused.

Finding Main Ideas and Supporting Details

Read the passage below, which comes from a high school American history textbook. Then, answer the questions that follow.

> 66 No matter how Native Americans adapted to their environment, they generally looked to the family to fulfill many of their social needs. Their families provided them with many of the services we expect today, from governments, churches, and private organizations. Such services included medical care, child care, settlement of disputes, and education. 99

—Andrew Cayton,
America: Pathways to the Present, 1998

21. Which statement best reflects the main idea of the selection?
    A. Families provide medical care.
    B. Families support people.
    C. Indian families were not important.
    D. Families provided for many social needs of Native Americans.
22. What details does the author use to support the main point of the selection?

ACTIVITIES

Connecting With . . .
Science and Technology

Identifying Causes and Effects By the 1400s, Europeans were beginning to use new instruments and knowledge about navigation. Several new technologies are discussed in the chapter. Write a news bulletin for two new technologies, describing how each one helped Europeans undertake voyages of exploration.

Go Online
PHSchool.com

Evaluating Internet Sites
Reviewing Sites About the First American Civilizations Use the Internet to find at least two sites with visual materials about the Mayas, Aztecs, or Incas. Write a review of these sites. In it, describe the kind of information they gave, the quality and quantity of visuals, and their usefulness in learning about the civilization. Include the addresses of the sites. For help in starting this activity, visit PHSchool.com, **Web Code mfd-0206.**

The Mother of Nations

Joseph Bruchac

Introduction Joseph Bruchac is a scholar of Native American culture and an author, poet, novelist, and storyteller. He has written more than 50 books and has won a Lifetime Achievement Award of the Native Writers' Circle of the Americas. Bruchac grew up and still lives in the foothills of the Adirondack Mountains in New York State. His story "The Mother of Nations" deals with the founding of the Iroquois Confederation.

Vocabulary Before you read the selection, find the meanings of these words in a dictionary: **longhouse, descendent, stockaded, exhort.**

Joseph Bruchac

Long ago there was a woman whose longhouse stood to the west at Oniagara. Her people, whom she led, were those known as the Cultivators, the Hadiyent-togeo-no and they were cousins to the Ongwe-oweh.

It was said that this woman was the direct descendent of the first woman born on the Earth. Her name was Jigonsahseh, the Lynx. Her longhouse stood by the warriors' path which ran from east to west. Though she was unable to stop the continual war which tore apart the nations in those days, still her words were respected. She always fed those who passed by her door and she was called by many "The Great Mother."

When The Peacemaker, who brought the great message from the Master of Life, set out into the world he went first to the land of the Cultivators. He crossed Sganya-dai-yo, the Great Beautiful Lake, in his canoe made of white stone. He saw that there were no cornfields planted because of the continual warfare. The towns were stockaded and filled with people who were hungry and quarrelling.

The Peacemaker went to the house of Jigonsahseh. She welcomed him and placed food before him. When he had finished eating she spoke. "You have come to bring a message," she said. "My mind is open to it. I wish to hear."

Then The Peacemaker spoke. He told her he was acting as the messenger of the Maker of Life. He said that his message was to bring justice, peace, and good laws for the people. The wars between the Ongwe-oweh, the True Human Beings, would cease.

"This message is good," said Jigonsahseh. "What form shall it take among the People?"

Then The Peacemaker explained. "It will take the form of the Longhouse. There will be many fires within the Longhouse, many families. But all will live together under the guidance of a wise Clan Mother. The five nations of the Ongwe-oweh will become of one mind and be known as the People of the Longhouse. Together they will seek the way of Peace which would be open to all the nations.

"My hands are open to this message. I reach out and grasp it," said Jigonsahseh.

Then it was decided that, since a woman was the first to accept this new way, from that day on the women would possess the titles and give them to the men who would speak for their nations in the Longhouse. These women would name from their clans the men who would serve the people. The Clan Mothers would give them the horns of office and if they did not do their jobs well the women could take back their titles.

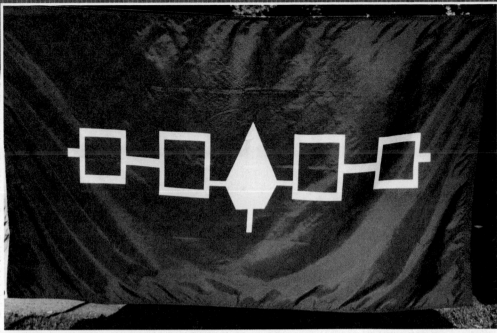

Iroquois flag showing the five-nation symbol

From that day on, the longhouse of Jigonsahseh would be known as the Peace House. All would now call her the Yegowaneh, "The Mother of Nations." In the land of her people there would be no war. The Cultivators would now be known as the Attiwendaronk, "The Neutral Nation."

So it came to be that in the land of the Yegowaneh, the Mother of Nations, there was no war. Her name was passed down from mother to eldest daughter. When it was necessary for the People of the Longhouse to deal with other nations who had not joined the League of Peace or when there were disputes between nations, the War Captains would always pass first through her land and deliver Peace Belts to the Yegowaneh.

She would give them food, as had been the custom of all those who carried the name of Jigonsahseh and were descended from the first woman born on Earth. Then the Mother of Nations would exhort them to seek peace and accept war only as a last resort. So it is said among the People of the Longhouse that the path of war runs through the House of Peace.

Analyzing Literature

1. Why was The Peacemaker troubled when he visited the land of the Cultivators?

    A   They were not worshipping him in the proper ways.

    B   They were not planting crops because they were fighting among themselves.

    C   They had gone off to war in far-off lands, leaving their families behind.

    D   They spent too much time hunting and trapping and not enough raising crops.

2. How did the longhouse symbolize the Iroquois?

    A   Many families lived under one roof in the longhouse, just as the tribes lived together in unity in the world.

    B   The longhouse was made of strong wood, just as the people were strong.

    C   Women built the longhouse, just as women held titles of power.

    D   People shared the longhouse, just as they shared land with the woodland animals.

3. **Critical Thinking and Writing Comparing** List three ways the information in this story supports the information about the Iroquois in Section 2 of Chapter 2.

Exploration and Colonization

1492–1675

1 **An Era of Exploration**
2 **Spain Builds an Empire**
3 **Colonizing North America**
4 **Building the Jamestown Colony**
5 **Seeking Religious Freedom**

Christopher Columbus

Fort of Castillo de San Marcos at St. Augustine

AMERICAN EVENTS

1492
Seeking a westward route from Europe to Asia, Christopher Columbus reaches the Caribbean. His voyage marks the start of regular contact between Europe and the Americas.

1519
Spanish warrior Hernando Cortés begins conquest of the Aztec empire.

1565
Spain builds a fort at St. Augustine. Today, St. Augustine, Florida, is the oldest city in the United States.

1475   1525   1575

WORLD EVENTS

1492 ▲
Christians expel Moors and Jews from Spain.

▲ **1500s**
Enslavement of Africans begins.

▲ **1517**
Protestant Reformation begins in Europe.

European Voyages of Exploration, 1487–1522

In the late 1400s, European explorers began to sail and chart the oceans of the world.

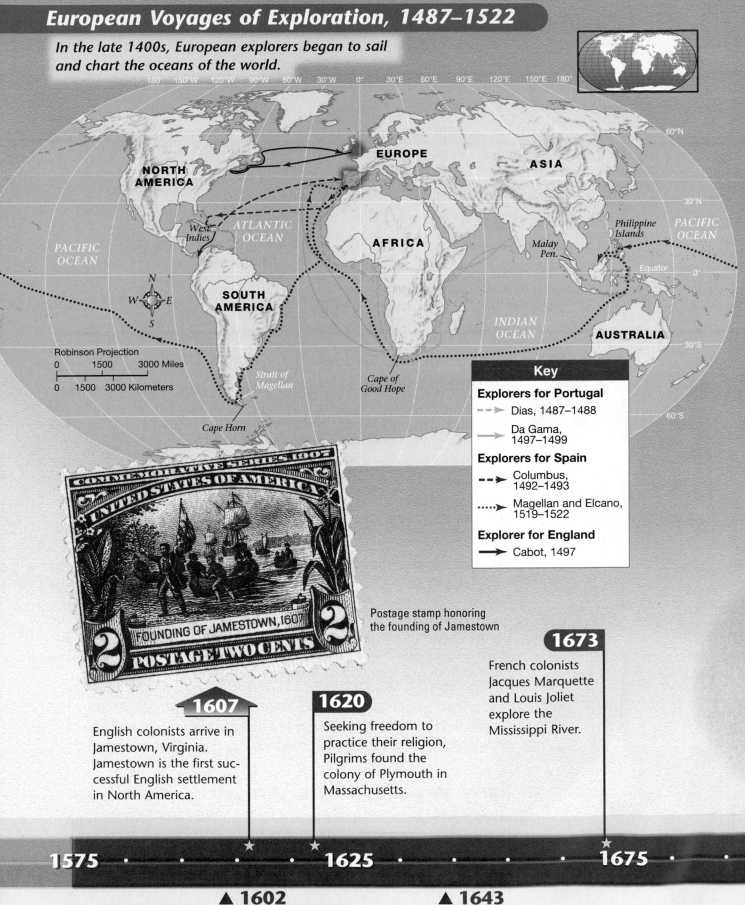

Key

Explorers for Portugal
- – – – Dias, 1487–1488
- ——→ Da Gama, 1497–1499

Explorers for Spain
- – – ▶ Columbus, 1492–1493
- ·····▶ Magellan and Elcano, 1519–1522

Explorer for England
- ——▶ Cabot, 1497

Postage stamp honoring the founding of Jamestown

1607
English colonists arrive in Jamestown, Virginia. Jamestown is the first successful English settlement in North America.

1620
Seeking freedom to practice their religion, Pilgrims found the colony of Plymouth in Massachusetts.

1673
French colonists Jacques Marquette and Louis Joliet explore the Mississippi River.

1575 · · · · · · **1625** · · · · · · **1675** · · ·

▲ **1602**
Dutch East India Company is formed to trade in Asia.

▲ **1643**
Louis XIV becomes king of France.

1 An Era of Exploration

Prepare to Read

Objectives

In this section, you will
- Identify the impact of Columbus's voyage.
- Describe how Spanish explorers found a route across the Pacific Ocean.
- Explain how exploration set off a global exchange of goods and services.

Key Terms

colony

turning point

circumnavigate

Columbian Exchange

 **Target Reading Skill**

Cause and Effect Copy the chart below. As you read, complete the chart to show some of the effects of the journey of Christopher Columbus. Add as many boxes as you need.

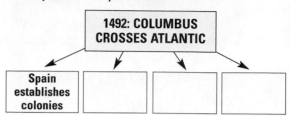

1492: COLUMBUS CROSSES ATLANTIC

| Spain establishes colonies | | | |

Main Idea Despite some earlier contacts, Europeans began to explore the Americas fully only after Columbus reached the West Indies in 1492.

Viking warriors

Setting the Scene

A band of seafarers sailed across the Atlantic to settle at a place they called Vinland. To their surprise, a multitude of kayaks came paddling by one morning—"so many that the bay looked as though it was sown with charcoal." One settler recalled:

66 As soon as [the two peoples] met they began trading together. Most of all, these people wanted to buy red cloth, in return for which they had furs to offer and gray [seal] skins. 99

—*Saga of Erik the Red*

Trading continued until a large bull that the seafarers had brought with them "ran out of the forest bellowing loudly." The natives, who had never seen such an animal, ran to their kayaks and paddled away.

This meeting took place about 1,000 years ago. It was one of the earliest encounters between Native Americans and Europeans. The people in kayaks were Inuits. The settlers were Vikings, seafaring people from Scandinavia in Northern Europe.

The Vikings abandoned the settlement after only a few years. Nearly 500 years later, an expedition from Spain sailed into the Caribbean Sea. This time, the arrival of Europeans launched an era of exploration that dramatically affected both the Americas and Europe.

Early Voyages to the Americas

Many stories exist about early people from Europe or Asia sailing to the Americas. Yet, real evidence has been hard to find. Most experts agree that such voyages were rare, if they occurred at all.

The Vikings left behind the most detailed record of their voyages. In 1001, Viking sailors led by Leif Ericson reached the northern tip of North America. Today, many archaeologists believe that the Viking settlement of Vinland was located in present-day Newfoundland. The Vikings did not stay in Vinland long and no one is sure why they left. However, Viking stories describe fierce battles with Skraelings, the Viking name for the Inuits.

Some historians suggest that Asians continued to cross the Bering Sea into North America after the last ice age ended. Others believe that ancient seafarers from Polynesia may have traveled to the Americas using their knowledge of the stars and winds. Modern Polynesians have sailed canoes thousands of miles in this way. Still others claim that fishing boats from China and Japan blew off course and landed on the western coast of South America.

Perhaps such voyages occurred. If so, they were long forgotten. The peoples of Asia and Europe had no knowledge of the Americas and their remarkable civilizations.

Columbus Reaches the Americas

As you read, Portuguese sailors pioneered new routes around Africa toward Asia in the late 1400s. Spain, too, wanted a share of the Asian spice trade. King Ferdinand and Queen Isabella agreed to finance a voyage of exploration by Christopher Columbus. Columbus, an Italian sea captain, planned to reach the East Indies by sailing west across the Atlantic.

The Atlantic Crossing In August 1492, Columbus set out with three ships and a crew of about 90 sailors. As captain, he commanded the largest vessel, the *Santa María*. The other ships were the *Niña* and the *Pinta*.

After a brief stop at the Canary Islands, the little fleet continued west into unknown seas. Fair winds sped them along, but a month passed without the sight of land. Some sailors began to grumble. They had never been away from land for so long. Still, Columbus sailed on.

On October 7, sailors saw flocks of birds flying southwest. Columbus changed course to follow the birds. A few days later, crew members spotted tree branches and flowers floating in the water. At 2 A.M. on October 12, the lookout on the *Pinta* spotted white cliffs shining in the moonlight. *"Tierra! Tierra!"* he shouted. "Land! Land!"

At dawn, Columbus rowed ashore and planted the banner of Spain on the beach. He was convinced that he had reached the East Indies in Asia. In fact, he had reached islands off the coasts of North America and South America in the Caribbean Sea. These islands later became known as the West Indies.

For three months, Columbus explored the West Indies. To his delight, he found signs of gold on the islands. Eager to report his success, he returned to Spain.

Spain Authorizes Colonies In Spain, Columbus presented Queen Isabella and King

Viewing History

The *Santa María* Columbus's report on his first voyage included this picture of the *Santa María*. Improved navigational equipment, such as the astrolabe (inset), enabled Columbus to cross the Atlantic. **Evaluating Information** *The artist who made this drawing never saw the Santa María. Would you consider it a reliable piece of historical evidence? Why or why not?*

Oceanica Classis

Columbus Meets the Tainos

In his journals, Christopher Columbus recorded his first meeting with the Tainos:

"All whom I saw were young, not above thirty years of age, well made, with fine shapes and faces; their hair short, and coarse like that of a horse's tail, combed toward the forehead. . . . It appears to me that the people are ingenious, and would be good servants and I am of opinion that they would very readily become Christians, as they appear to have no religion. They very quickly learn such words as are spoken to them. If it please our Lord, I intend at my return to carry home six of them to your Highnesses, that they may learn our language."

—Christopher Columbus, *Journal*

Analyzing Primary Sources
How would you describe Columbus's attitude toward the Tainos?

Ferdinand with gifts of pink pearls and brilliantly colored parrots. The royal couple listened intently as Columbus described many things that Europeans had never seen before: tobacco, pineapples, and hammocks used for sleeping. Columbus also described the "Indians" he had met, the Tainos (TI nohz). The Tainos, he promised, could easily be converted to Christianity and could also be used as slaves.

The Spanish monarchs were impressed. They gave Columbus the title Admiral of the Ocean Sea. They also agreed to finance future voyages.

Columbus made three more voyages across the Atlantic. In 1493, he founded the first Spanish colony in the Americas, on an island he called Hispaniola (present-day Haiti and the Dominican Republic). A **colony** is a group of people who settle in a distant land but are still ruled by the government of their native land. Columbus also explored present-day Cuba and Jamaica and sailed along the coasts of Central America and northern South America. He claimed all these lands for Spain.

Columbus proved to be a better explorer than a governor. During his third expedition, settlers at Hispaniola complained of his harsh rule. Queen Isabella appointed an investigator, who sent Columbus back to Spain in chains. In the end, the queen pardoned Columbus, but he never regained the honors he had won earlier. He died in 1506, still convinced that he had reached Asia.

A Lasting Impact

Columbus has long been honored as the bold sea captain who "discovered America." Today, we recognize that Native Americans had "discovered" and settled these lands long before 1492. Still, in at least one sense, Columbus deserves the honors history has given him. Europeans knew nothing of the Americas until Columbus told them about this "new world." His daring voyages marked the beginning of lasting contact among the peoples of Europe, Africa, and the Americas.

For a great many Native Americans, contact had tragic results. Columbus and those who followed were convinced that European culture was superior to that of the Indians. The Spanish claimed Taino lands and forced Tainos to work in gold mines, on ranches, or in Spanish households. Many Tainos died from harsh conditions or European diseases. Within 100 years of Columbus's arrival, the Taino population was virtually wiped out.

For better or worse, the voyages of Columbus signaled a turning point for the Americas. A **turning point** is a moment in history that marks a decisive change. Curious Europeans saw the new lands as a place where they could settle, trade, and grow rich.

The Spanish Cross the Pacific

After Columbus, the Spanish explored and settled other Caribbean islands. By 1511, they had conquered Puerto Rico, Jamaica, and Cuba. They also explored the eastern coasts of North America and South America in search of a western route to Asia.

In 1513, Vasco Núñez de Balboa (bal BOH uh) plunged into the jungles of the Isthmus of Panama. Native Americans had told him that a large body of water lay to the west. With a party of Spanish soldiers and Indians, Balboa reached the Pacific Ocean after about 25 days. He stood in the crashing surf and claimed the ocean for Spain.

The Spanish had no idea how wide the Pacific was until a sea captain named Ferdinand Magellan (muh JEHL uhn) sailed across it. The expedition—made up of five ships and about 250 crew members—left Spain in 1519. Fifteen months later, it rounded the stormy southern tip of South America and entered the Pacific Ocean. Crossing the Pacific, the sailors ran out of food. One sailor recalled:

> 66 We remained 3 months and 20 days without taking in provisions or other refreshments and ate only old biscuit reduced to powder, full of grubs and stinking from the dirt which rats had made on it. We drank water that was yellow and stinking. 99
> —Antoñio Pigafetta, *The Diary of Antoñio Pigafetta*

Magellan himself was killed in a battle with the local people of the Philippine Islands off the coast of Asia.

In 1522, only one ship and 18 sailors returned to Spain. They were the first people to **circumnavigate,** or sail completely around, the world. In doing so, they had found an all-water western route to Asia. Their voyage made Europeans aware of the true size of the Earth.

A Global Cultural Exchange

The encounter between the peoples of the Eastern and Western hemispheres sparked a global exchange of goods and ideas. Because it started with the voyages of Columbus, this transfer is known as the **Columbian Exchange.** The Columbian Exchange covered a wide range of areas, including food, medicine, government, technology, the arts, and language.

The exchange went in both directions. Europeans learned much from Native Americans. At the same time, Europeans contributed in many ways to the culture of the Americas.

European Influences Europeans introduced domestic animals such as chickens from Europe and Africa. European pigs, cattle, and horses often escaped into the wild and multiplied rapidly. As horses spread through North America, Indians learned to ride them and used them to carry heavy loads.

Plants from Europe and Africa changed the way Native Americans lived. The first bananas came from the Canary Islands. By

---

The Columbian Exchange

From the Americas to Europe, Africa, and Asia	From Europe, Africa, and Asia to the Americas
maize	wheat
potato	sugar
sweet potato	banana
beans	rice
peanut	grape (wine)
squash	olive oil
pumpkin	dandelion
peppers	horse
pineapple	pig
tomato	cow
cocoa	goat
	chicken
	smallpox
	typhus

CHART Skills

The four voyages of Christopher Columbus set off a worldwide exchange of goods and ideas.

1. **Comprehension**
   (a) Identify two kinds of livestock that Europeans brought to the Americas.
   (b) Identify two food crops that Europeans carried from the Americas.

2. **Critical Thinking Identifying Causes and Effects** What elements shown here led to a decline in Native American population?

Economics $

1520, one Spaniard reported that banana trees had spread "so greatly that it is marvelous to see the great abundance of them." Oranges, lemons, and figs were also new to the Americas. In North America, explorers also brought such plants as bluegrass, the daisy, and the dandelion. These plants spread quickly in American soil.

Tragically, Europeans also brought new diseases, such as small-pox and influenza. Native Americans had no resistance to these diseases. Historians estimate that within 75 years, diseases from Europe had killed almost 90 percent of the people in the Caribbean islands and in Mexico.

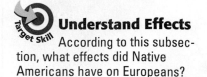

Understand Effects
Target Skill According to this subsection, what effects did Native Americans have on Europeans? Add this information to your chart.

Native American Influences For their part, Native Americans introduced Europeans to new customs and ideas. After 1492, elements of Native American ways of life gradually spread around the world.

Native Americans introduced Europeans to valuable food crops such as corn, potatoes, beans, tomatoes, manioc, squash, peanuts, pineapples, and blueberries. Today, almost half the world's food crops come from plants that were first grown in the Americas.

Europeans carried the new foods with them as they sailed around the world. Everywhere, people's diets changed and populations increased. In South Asia, people used American hot peppers and chilis to spice stews. Chinese peasants began growing sweet potatoes. Italians made sauces from tomatoes. People in West Africa grew manioc and maize.

European settlers often adopted Native American skills. In the North, Indians showed Europeans how to use snowshoes and trap beavers and other fur-bearing animals. European explorers learned how to paddle Indian canoes. Some leaders studied Native American political structures. Benjamin Franklin admired the League of the Iroquois and urged colonists to unite in a similar way.

★ ★ ★ Section 1 Assessment ★ ★ ★

Recall
1. **Identify** Explain the significance of **(a)** Leif Ericson, **(b)** Ferdinand and Isabella, **(c)** Christopher Columbus, **(d)** Vasco Núñez de Balboa, **(e)** Ferdinand Magellan, **(f)** Columbian Exchange.
2. **Define (a)** colony, **(b)** turning point, **(c)** circumnavigate.

Comprehension
3. Describe two effects of Columbus's voyage.
4. What route did Magellan's expedition take?
5. **(a)** Identify two European influences on the Americas. **(b)** Identify two Native American influences on the rest of the world.

Critical Thinking and Writing
6. **Exploring the Main Idea** Review the Main Idea statement at the beginning of this section. Then, write a paragraph explaining why historians consider Columbus to be more important than Leif Ericson.
7. **Supporting a Point of View** Today, Columbus Day is a national holiday. Yet, some Americans oppose the celebration. List one reason to support each point of view.

ACTIVITY

Go Online
PHSchool.com

Connecting to Today
Use the Internet to find English words that were borrowed from Indian languages. Create fact cards for three words. State what language each word came from, what it originally meant, and what it means today. For help in completing the activity, visit PHSchool.com, **Web Code mfd-0301.**

Sequencing

When learning about past events, such as Columbus's voyage, you must first understand sequence. In what order did various events take place? How was one event related to another? To start this lesson, read the excerpt and study the timetable below.

The following excerpts are from the log that Columbus kept on his first voyage:

Sunday, 9 September 1492 This day we completely lost sight of land, and many men sighed and wept for fear they would not see it again for a long time. I comforted them with great promises of lands and riches.

Saturday, 15 September 1492 I sailed to the west day and night for 81 miles, or more. Early this morning I saw a marvelous meteorite fall into the sea 12 to 15 miles away to the SW. This was taken by some people as a bad omen . . .

Sunday, 7 October 1492 This morning we saw what appeared to be land to the west . . . the *Niña* . . . ran ahead and fired a cannon and ran up a flag on her mast to indicate that land had been sighted. Joy turned to dismay as the day progressed, for by evening we had found no land . . .

Thursday, 11 October 1492 Then, at two hours after midnight, the *Pinta* fired a cannon, my prearranged signal for the sighting of land.

1492: First Voyage of Columbus

Date	Event
August 3	Sets sail from Palos
August 9	Stops for repairs in Canary Islands
September 6	Sets sail from Canary Islands
September 15	Sees a meteorite
September 24	Writes of trouble with crew
October 7	Alters course to follow birds
October 12	Goes ashore

Learn the Skill *To sequence information, use the following steps:*

1. **Identify the order in which events happen.** Applying absolute and relative chronology gives you a clearer picture of events.

2. **Identify time-order words.** Words such as first, next, and last give helpful time signals. Pay attention to other words such as later, now, then, while, this evening, before, and after.

3. **Figure out time intervals.** Understand how much time takes place between events.

4. **Make connections.** Ask: Are the events related? How does one event lead to the next?

Practice the Skill *Use the log entries and timetable to answer the following questions:*

1. **(a)** On what date did Columbus first set sail? **(b)** On what date did Columbus leave the Canary Islands? **(c)** Did Columbus see a meteorite before or after he changed course?

2. Identify two time words or phrases that Columbus used in his log.

3. **(a)** How much time passed between the false sighting of land and the true one? **(b)** About how much time did Columbus spend in the Canary Islands?

4. **(a)** On September 24, Columbus wrote of trouble with the crew. What earlier event might have contributed to this? **(b)** How might the events of October 7 and October 11 be related?

Apply the Skill *See the Chapter Review and Assessment.*

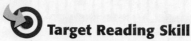

2 Spain Builds an Empire

Prepare to Read

Objectives

In this section, you will

- Describe how conquistadors defeated two Indian empires.
- Name the areas the Spanish explored.
- Explain how Spain settled its colonies.
- Summarize what life was like for Native Americans under Spanish rule.

Key Terms

conquistador
pueblo
presidio
mission
peninsulare
creole
mestizo
encomienda
plantation

Target Reading Skill

Main Idea Copy the concept web below. As you read, fill in the blank ovals with important facts about Spain's American empire. Add as many ovals as you need.

Main Idea Spain's conquest, exploration, and colonization of the Americas brought wealth to some and tragedy to others.

Spanish coin found in Florida

Setting the Scene

"What a troublesome thing it is to discover new lands. The risks we took, it is hardly possible to exaggerate." Thus spoke Bernal Díaz del Castillo, one of the many Spanish **conquistadors** (kahn KWIS tuh dorz), or conquerors, who marched into the Americas in the 1500s. When asked why they traveled to the Americas, Díaz responded, "We came here to serve God and the king and also to get rich."

In their search for glory and gold, the conquistadors made Spain one of the richest nations in Europe. Spanish colonists followed the conquistadors and created a vast new empire in the Americas.

Spanish Conquistadors

The rulers of Spain gave conquistadors permission to establish settlements in the Americas. In return, conquistadors agreed to give Spain one fifth of any gold or treasure they captured.

Like other conquistadors, Hernando Cortés was eager to win riches and glory. He had heard rumors of a fabulously wealthy Native American empire in Mexico. With only about 600 soldiers and 16 horses, Cortés set sail for Mexico in 1519 in search of gold.

Conquest of the Aztecs Moctezuma (mokt uh ZOO muh), the Aztec emperor who ruled over much of Mexico, heard disturbing reports of a large house floating on the sea. It was filled with white men with long, thick beards. Aztec sacred writings predicted that a powerful white-skinned god would come from the east to rule the Aztecs. As the strangers neared Tenochtitlán, the Aztec capital, Moctezuma decided to welcome them as his guests.

Cortés took advantage of Moctezuma's invitation. Shrewdly, Cortés had already begun to win the support of other Indians who resented Aztec rule. One of his trusted advisors was an Indian

woman the Spanish called Doña Marina. She gave Cortés valuable information about the Aztecs and acted as a translator and negotiator.

On November 8, 1519, Cortés marched into Tenochtitlán. Thousands upon thousands of Aztecs turned out to see the astonishing newcomers riding horses. Díaz recalled:

> 66 Who could count the multitude of men, women and children which had come out on the roofs, in their boats on the canals, or in the streets, to see us? 99
> —Bernal Díaz del Castillo, *True History of the Conquest of New Spain*

At first, Cortés was friendly to Moctezuma. Soon, however, he made the emperor a prisoner in his own city. Tensions mounted in Tenochtitlán over the next half year.

Finally, the Aztecs drove out the Spanish. Their victory, however, was brief. Aided by people whom the Aztecs had conquered, Cortés recaptured the city. In the end, the Spanish killed Moctezuma and destroyed Tenochtitlán. The Aztec empire had fallen.

Conquest of the Incas Another bold conquistador, Francisco Pizarro (pee SAR oh), set his sights on the Incan empire. Pizarro sailed down the Pacific coast of South America with fewer than 200 Spanish soldiers. In 1532, he captured the Incan emperor Atahualpa (ah tuh WAHL puh) and later executed him. Without the leadership of Atahualpa, Incan resistance collapsed. By 1535, Pizarro controlled much of the Incan empire.

Reasons for Spanish Victories How were the Spanish able to conquer two great empires with only a handful of soldiers? First, the Spanish had superior military equipment. They were protected by steel armor and had guns. The Aztecs and Incas relied on clubs, bows and arrows, and spears. Also, the Native Americans had never seen horses. They were frightened by mounted Spanish soldiers.

In addition, the Native Americans did not fight as hard as they might have. The Aztecs hesitated to attack at first because they

Viewing History

Spanish and Aztecs Meet

This Aztec drawing depicts a meeting between Spanish conquistadors (left) and Aztecs (right). Not all encounters between the two sides were as peaceful as this one. **Analyzing Information** *What elements shown here might have seemed unfamiliar to the Aztecs? To the Spanish?*

thought the Spanish might be gods. The Incas were weak from fighting among themselves over control of their government.

Finally, many Indians died from European diseases, such as chickenpox, measles, and influenza. Some historians believe that disease alone would have ensured Spanish victory over the Indians.

Exploring the Spanish Borderlands

The Spanish search for treasure reached beyond the lands of the Aztecs and Incas. Moving north, conquistadors explored the area known as the Spanish borderlands. The borderlands spanned the present-day United States from Florida to California.

Juan Ponce de León (PAWN suh day LAY awn) traveled through parts of Florida in 1513, looking for a legendary fountain of youth. Indians claimed that anyone who bathed in its magical water would remain young forever. Ponce de León found no such fountain.

An Ill-Fated Journey Another explorer, Pánfilo Narváez (nar vah EHS), led an expedition that ended in disaster. In 1528, a storm struck his fleet in the Gulf of Mexico. Narváez and many others were lost at sea. The rest landed on an island near present-day Texas. Indians captured the few survivors and held them prisoner. Álvar Núñez Cabeza de Vaca assumed leadership of the small group.

Cabeza de Vaca, an enslaved African named Estevanico, and two others finally escaped their captors in 1533. The four walked across the plains of Texas, searching for a Spanish settlement. Finally, in 1536, they reached a town in Mexico. They had traveled by foot more than 1,000 miles through the Southwest.

GEOGRAPHY Skills

In the 1500s, the Spanish explored and settled North American lands from Florida to California.

1. **Location** On the maps, locate (a) Ponce de León's route, (b) De Soto's route, (c) St. Augustine, (d) San Antonio, (e) Santa Fe, (f) San Francisco.

2. **Movement** Which Spanish explorers crossed the Rio Grande?

3. **Critical Thinking Linking Past and Present** Compare these maps to a map of the modern United States. Identify three states in which you would expect Spanish influence to be strong.

Spanish Explorers/Spanish Settlements

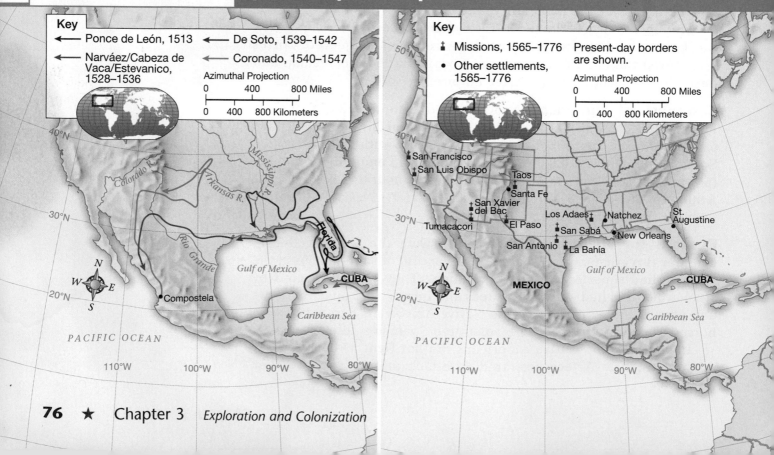

Key
← Ponce de León, 1513   ← De Soto, 1539–1542
← Narváez/Cabeza de Vaca/Estevanico, 1528–1536   ← Coronado, 1540–1547
Azimuthal Projection
0   400   800 Miles
0   400   800 Kilometers

Colorado R.   Arkansas R.   Mississippi R.   Rio Grande   Florida   Gulf of Mexico   CUBA   Compostela   Caribbean Sea   PACIFIC OCEAN

Key
⚑ Missions, 1565–1776   Present-day borders are shown.
• Other settlements, 1565–1776
Azimuthal Projection
0   400   800 Miles
0   400   800 Kilometers

San Francisco   San Luis Obispo   Taos   Santa Fe   San Xavier del Bac   Los Adaes   Natchez   St. Augustine   Tumacacori   El Paso   San Sabá   New Orleans   San Antonio   La Bahía   MEXICO   Gulf of Mexico   CUBA   Caribbean Sea   PACIFIC OCEAN

De Soto and Coronado From 1539 to 1542, Hernando De Soto explored Florida and other parts of the Southeast. In his search for gold, he reached the Mississippi River. De Soto died along the riverbank, without finding the riches he sought.

The conquistador Francisco Coronado (koh roh NAH doh) heard legends about "seven cities of gold." In 1540, he led an expedition into the southwestern borderlands. He traveled to present-day Arizona and New Mexico. Some of his party went as far as the Grand Canyon. Still, the Zuñi villages he visited had no golden streets.

The Spanish expeditions into the borderlands met with little success. Faced with strong Indian resistance in the north, Spain focused instead on bringing order to its empire in the south.

Settling New Spain

At first, Spain let the conquistadors govern the lands they conquered. When the conquistadors proved to be poor rulers, the Spanish king took away their authority. He then set up a strong system of government to rule his growing empire. In 1535, he divided his American lands into New Spain and Peru. The borderlands were part of New Spain. The king put a viceroy in charge of each region to rule in his name.

A code called the Laws of the Indies stated how the colonies should be organized and ruled. The code provided for three kinds of settlements in New Spain: pueblos, presidios (prih SIHD ee ohz), and missions. Some large communities included all three.

Pueblos and Presidios The pueblos, or towns, were centers of farming and trade. In the middle of the town was a plaza, or public square. Here, townspeople and farmers came to do business or worship at the church. Shops and homes lined the four sides of the plaza.

The Spanish took control of Indian pueblos and built new towns as well. In 1598, Juan de Oñate (oh NYAH tay) founded the colony of New Mexico among the adobe villages of the Pueblo Indians. He used brutal force to conquer the Native Americans of the region. Don Pedro de Paralta later founded Santa Fe as the Spanish capital of New Mexico.

Presidios were forts where soldiers lived. Inside the high, thick walls were shops, stables, and storehouses for food. Soldiers protected the farmers who settled nearby. The first presidio in the borderlands was built in 1565 at St. Augustine, Florida.

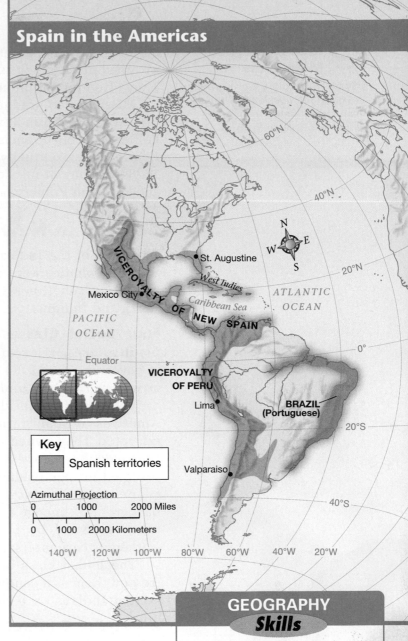

Spain in the Americas

GEOGRAPHY
Skills

In 1535, the king of Spain divided his American colonies into New Spain and Peru.

1. **Location** On the map, locate **(a)** New Spain, **(b)** Peru, **(c)** West Indies, **(d)** Mexico City.

2. **Region (a)** Which viceroyalty included Florida? **(b)** What other European power colonized part of South America?

3. **Critical Thinking Drawing Conclusions** Why was control of the Caribbean Sea important to Spain?

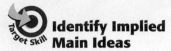
Missions Like other Europeans in the Americas, the Spanish believed they had a duty to convert Indians to Christianity. They set up **missions,** religious settlements run by Catholic priests and friars. They often forced Indians to live and work on the missions.

Missionaries gradually spread across the Spanish borderlands. The first mission in Texas was founded in 1659 at El Paso. In 1691, Father Eusebio Francisco Kino (KEE noh) crossed into present-day Arizona. He eventually set up 24 missions in the area. By the late 1700s, a string of missions also dotted the California coast from San Diego to San Francisco.

Society in New Spain

The Laws of the Indies also set up a strict social system. People in Spanish colonies were divided into four social classes: peninsulares (puh NIHN suh LAH rayz), creoles (KREE ohlz), mestizos (mehs TEE zohz), and Indians.

Four Social Classes At the top of the social scale were the **peninsulares.** Born in Spain, peninsulares held the highest jobs in government and the Church. They also owned large tracts of land as well as rich gold and silver mines.

Below the peninsulares were the **creoles,** people born in the Americas to Spanish parents. Many creoles were wealthy and well educated. They owned farms and ranches, taught at universities, and practiced law. However, they could not hold the jobs that were reserved for peninsulares.

Below the creoles were people of mixed Spanish and Indian background, known as **mestizos.** Mestizos worked on farms and ranches owned by peninsulares and creoles. In the cities, they worked as carpenters, shoemakers, tailors, and bakers.

The lowest class in the colonies was the Indians. The Spanish treated them as a conquered people. Under New Spain's strict social system, Indians were kept in poverty for hundreds of years.

A Blend of Cultures A new way of life took shape in New Spain that blended Spanish and Indian ways. Spanish settlers brought their own culture to the colonies. They introduced their language, laws, religion, and learning. In 1551, the Spanish founded the University of Mexico.

Native Americans also influenced the culture of New Spain. As you have read, colonists adopted Indian foods and items of Indian clothing, such as the poncho and moccasins. Indian workers used materials they knew well, such as adobe bricks, to build fine libraries, theaters, and churches. Sometimes, Indian artists decorated church walls with paintings of local traditions.

Harsh Life for Native Americans

Spanish colonists needed workers for their ranches, farms, and mines. To help them, the Spanish government gave settlers **encomiendas** (ehn koh mee EHN dahz), land grants that included the right to demand labor or taxes from Native Americans.

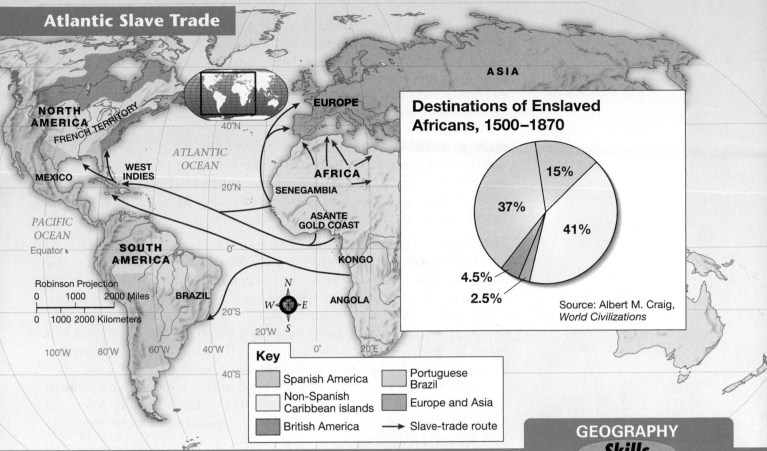

Destinations of Enslaved
Africans, 1500–1870

15%

37%

41%

4.5%

2.5%

Source: Albert M. Craig,
World Civilizations

Key

Spanish America

Non-Spanish
Caribbean islands

British America

Portuguese
Brazil

Europe and Asia

→ Slave-trade route

Hard Labor Mines in Mexico, Peru, and other parts of the Americas made Spain rich. Treasure ships laden with thousands of tons of gold and silver sailed regularly across the Atlantic.

The Spanish forced Native Americans to work in the gold and silver mines. In flickering light, Indians hacked out rich ores in narrow dark tunnels. Many died when tunnels caved in.

These harsh conditions led one priest, Bartolomé de Las Casas (day lahs KAH sahs), to seek reform. Traveling through New Spain, Las Casas witnessed firsthand the deaths of Indians due to hunger, disease, and mistreatment. What he saw horrified him:

66 The Indians were totally deprived of their freedom. . . . Even beasts enjoy more freedom when they are allowed to graze in the field. 99

—Bartolomé de Las Casas, *Tears of the Indians*

Las Casas journeyed to Europe and asked the king of Spain to protect the Indians. In the 1540s, the royal government did pass laws prohibiting the enslavement of Native Americans. The laws also allowed Indians to own cattle and grow crops. However, few officials in New Spain enforced the new laws.

Slave Trade Between Africa and the Americas Begins The death toll among Native Americans continued to rise. Faced with a severe shortage of workers, Spanish colonists looked across the Atlantic Ocean for a new source of labor.

GEOGRAPHY
Skills

Destinations of Enslaved Africans

The Atlantic slave trade began with Spain's efforts to supply labor for its American empire.

1. **Comprehension** Which two regions of the Americas received the largest number of enslaved Africans?

2. **Critical Thinking Drawing Conclusions** Why do you think the growth of the slave trade had relatively little effect on eastern Africa?

Still seeking to protect Native Americans, Bartolomé de Las Casas made a suggestion that had a lasting, tragic impact. His idea was that Africans be brought as slaves to replace forced Indian laborers. Las Casas argued that Africans were less likely to die from European diseases. He also claimed that Africans would suffer less because they were used to doing hard farm work in their homelands.

Las Casas's arguments led to the Atlantic slave trade, or the trade of enslaved Africans across the Atlantic to the Americas. By the time he died, Las Casas had come to regret his suggestion. He saw that enslaved Africans suffered as much as the Indians. By that time, however, it was too late to undo the damage. Slavery had become a key part of the colonial economy.

The Slave Trade Spreads The European demand for African labor grew rapidly, not only in New Spain, but elsewhere in the Americas. Enslaved Africans were especially valued on sugar plantations on Caribbean islands and in the Portuguese colony of Brazil. A **plantation** is a large estate farmed by many workers. Sugar could not be grown on small estates because it required too much land and labor. Enslaved Africans often worked all through the night cutting sugar, which was then sold in Europe for a large profit.

Some scholars estimate that Europeans transported more than 10 million enslaved Africans across the Atlantic Ocean to the Americas between the 1500s and the 1800s. (See the map and chart on page 79.) The vast majority came from West Africa.

Most of the enslaved Africans were sent to Brazil or the Caribbean. However, a total of more than 500,000 enslaved Africans would eventually arrive in the British colonies of North America. (You will read more about the effects of the Atlantic slave trade on the Americas and Africa in the next chapter.)

★ ★ ★ Section 2 Assessment ★ ★ ★

Recall

1. **Identify** Explain the significance of **(a)** Hernando Cortés, **(b)** Moctezuma, **(c)** Francisco Pizarro, **(d)** Juan Ponce de León, **(e)** Bartolomé de Las Casas.

2. **Define** **(a)** conquistador, **(b)** pueblo, **(c)** presidio, **(d)** mission, **(e)** peninsulare, **(f)** creole, **(g)** mestizo, **(h)** encomienda, **(i)** plantation.

Comprehension

3. Why were the Spanish able to conquer the Americas?

4. What areas of North America did the Spanish explore?

5. How did the Laws of the Indies regulate life in New Spain?

6. **(a)** What was life like for Native Americans under Spanish rule? **(b)** Why did Spain bring Africans to the Americas?

Critical Thinking and Writing

7. **Exploring the Main Idea** Review the Main Idea statement at the beginning of this section. Then, write two generalizations about Spanish rule, from the viewpoints of a peninsulare and of an Indian.

8. **Drawing Inferences** Why do you think Spain reserved the most powerful positions for Spanish-born officials?

ACTIVITY

Writing an Obituary Based on what you have read, write an obituary for one of the figures discussed in this section, such as Hernando Cortés, Estevanico, or Bartolomé de Las Casas. Briefly summarize that person's most notable achievement and express a point of view about him or her.

3 Colonizing North America

Prepare to Read

Objectives

In this section, you will
- Explain why European powers sought a new route to Asia.
- Identify how the Protestant Reformation affected rivalries among European nations.
- Describe how a rivalry developed between New France and New Netherland.

Main Idea Following Spain's example, England, France, and the Netherlands set out to establish colonies in North America.

Key Terms

northwest passage

Protestant Reformation

coureur de bois

alliance

Target Reading Skill

Compare and Contrast Copy this incomplete Venn diagram. As you read, fill in key facts about French and Dutch settlements in North America. Write common characteristics in the overlapping section.

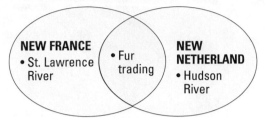

NEW FRANCE
- St. Lawrence River

- Fur trading

NEW NETHERLAND
- Hudson River

Setting the Scene The court of King Henry VII of England buzzed with excitement in August 1497. Italian sea captain Giovanni Caboto and a crew of English sailors had just returned from a 79-day Atlantic voyage.

Caboto, called John Cabot by the English, cut a swaggering figure on the streets of London. He dressed himself in fine silks and made such a stir that ordinary Londoners "[ran] after him like madmen," reported one observer. Cabot appeared before King Henry to announce that he had reached a "new-found island" in Asia where fish were plentiful.

Cabot was one of many Europeans who explored North America between the 1400s and 1600s. England, France, and the Netherlands all envied Spain's new empire. They wanted American colonies of their own.

John Cabot

Search for a Northwest Passage

Throughout the 1500s, European nations continued to look for new ways to reach the riches of Asia. Magellan's route around South America seemed long and difficult. They wanted to discover a shorter **northwest passage,** or waterway through or around North America.

Although John Cabot was confident he had found such a passage, he was mistaken. His "new-found island" off the Asian coast in fact lay off the coast of North America. Today, Newfoundland is the easternmost province of Canada.

Exploring for France The French sent another Italian captain, Giovanni da Verrazano (vehr rah TSAH noh), in search of a northwest passage. Verrazano journeyed along the North American coast from the Carolinas to Canada. During the 1530s, Jacques Cartier (kar tee YAY), also sailing for the French, traveled more than halfway up the river now known as the St. Lawrence.

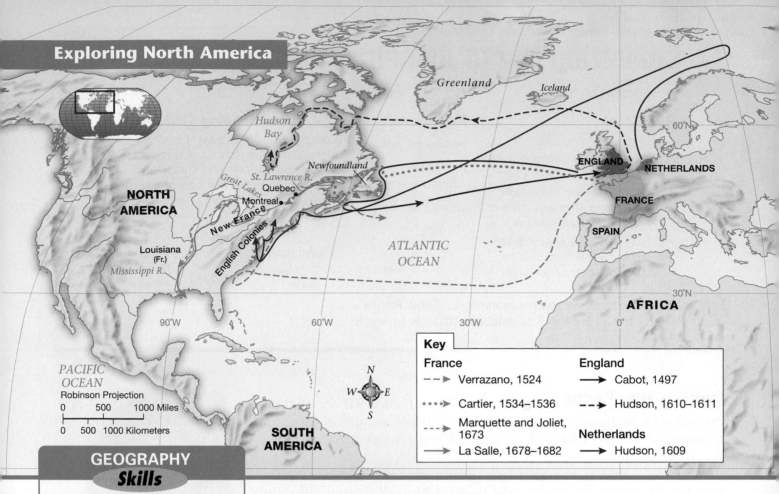

Exploring North America

Greenland

Iceland

Hudson Bay

Newfoundland

NORTH AMERICA

Great Lakes

St. Lawrence R.

Quebec

Montreal

New France

Louisiana (Fr.)

Mississippi R.

English Colonies

ATLANTIC OCEAN

ENGLAND

NETHERLANDS

FRANCE

SPAIN

AFRICA

60°N

30°N

PACIFIC OCEAN

Robinson Projection

0 500 1000 Miles

0 500 1000 Kilometers

90°W 60°W 30°W 0°

SOUTH AMERICA

N W E S

Key

France
- - - ► Verrazano, 1524
• • • ► Cartier, 1534–1536
- - - ► Marquette and Joliet, 1673
——► La Salle, 1678–1682

England
——► Cabot, 1497
- - ► Hudson, 1610–1611

Netherlands
——► Hudson, 1609

GEOGRAPHY
Skills

Explorers from England, France, and the Netherlands competed to find a northwest passage to Asia.

1. **Location** On the map, locate **(a)** New France, **(b)** Newfoundland, **(c)** St. Lawrence River, **(d)** Hudson Bay, **(e)** Mississippi River.

2. **Movement** Describe the route taken by Henry Hudson when he explored for the Netherlands.

3. **Critical Thinking Making Predictions** Based on this map, why might you expect conflict to develop between the English and French in North America?

Henry Hudson In 1609, the English explorer Henry Hudson sailed for the Dutch. His ship, the *Half Moon*, entered present-day New York harbor. Hudson continued to sail some 150 miles up the river that now bears his name.

The following year, Hudson made a voyage into the far north—this time for the English. After spending a harsh winter in present-day Hudson Bay, his crew rebelled. They set Hudson, his son, and seven loyal sailors adrift in a small boat. The boat and its crew were never seen again.

Failure and Success None of these explorers found a northwest passage to Asia. However, they did map and explore many parts of North America. The rulers of Western Europe began thinking about how to profit from the region's rich resources.

Rivalries Among European Nations

European nations began to compete for riches around the world. Religious differences heightened their rivalry. Until the 1500s, the Roman Catholic Church was the only church in Western Europe. That unity ended when a major religious reform movement sharply divided Christians.

Religious Divisions In 1517, a German monk named Martin Luther publicly challenged many practices of the Catholic Church. Soon after, he split with the Church entirely. Luther believed that the Church had become too worldly. He opposed the power of popes. He also objected to the Catholic teaching that believers could gain eternal life by performing good works. Luther argued that people could be saved only by faith in God.

Because of their protests against the church, Luther's supporters became known as Protestants. The **Protestant Reformation,** as the new movement was known, divided Europe. Soon, the Protestants themselves split, forming many different churches.

By the late 1500s, religion divided the states of Western Europe. Roman Catholic monarchs ruled Spain and France. A Protestant queen, Elizabeth I, ruled England. In the Netherlands, the Dutch people were mostly Protestant.

Rivalries in the Americas As Europeans settled in the Americas, they brought their religious conflicts with them. Queen Elizabeth encouraged English adventurers to raid Spanish colonies and capture Spanish treasure fleets. Protestant England also competed with Catholic France for lands in North America.

Not all rivalries were religious. Both the Netherlands and England were Protestant. Still, they competed for control of land in North America and for economic markets all over the world.

Viewing History

Fur Trapper in New France
Coureurs de bois, like the one shown here, depended on beaver furs for a living. By 1675, trappers and traders in New France were exporting nearly 90,000 pounds of beaver pelts a year. **Applying Information** *Based on what you have read, how does this picture show that* **coureurs de bois** *made use of Native American technology?*

New France

Samuel de Champlain (sham PLAYN) founded Port Royal, the first permanent French settlement in North America, in 1605. Three years later, he led another group of settlers along the route Cartier had pioneered. On a rocky cliff high above the St. Lawrence River, Champlain built a trading post known as Quebec (kwi BEHK).

Economy of New France Unlike Spain's American empire, New France had little gold or silver. Instead, the French profited from fishing, trapping, and trading.

French colonists who lived and worked in the woods became known as *coureurs de bois* (koo RYOOR duh BWAH), or "runners of the woods." The French brought knives, kettles, cloth, and other items for trade with Native Americans. In return, the Indians gave them beaver skins and other furs that sold for high prices in Europe.

Coureurs de bois established friendly relations with the Native Americans. Unlike the Spanish, the French did not attempt to conquer the Indians. Also, because *coureurs de bois* did not build farms, they did not interfere with Indian

lands. Indians taught the French trapping and survival skills, such as how to make snowshoes and canoes. Many coureurs married Indian women.

Missionary Work Catholic missionaries often traveled with fur traders. A missionary is a person who goes to another land to win converts for a religion. French missionaries worked to teach Native Americans about Christianity. They also drew maps and wrote about the lands they explored.

Life was difficult, especially in winter. One French priest recalled traveling on foot through deep snow:

> 66 If a thaw came, dear Lord, what pain! . . . I was marching on an icy path that broke with every step I took; as the snow softened . . . we often sunk in it up to our . . . waist. 99
>
> —Paul Le Jeune, quoted in *The Jesuits in North America* (Parkman)

Expansion to the Mississippi French trappers followed the St. Lawrence deep into the heart of North America. Led by Indian guides, they reached the Great Lakes. Here, Indians spoke of a mighty river, which they called Mississippi, or "Father of the Waters."

A French missionary, Father Jacques Marquette (mar KEHT), and a fur trader, Louis Joliet (joh lee EHT), set out to reach the Mississippi in 1673. Led by Indian guides, they followed the river for more than 700 miles before turning back. Nine years later, Robert de La Salle completed the journey to the Gulf of Mexico. La Salle named the region Louisiana in honor of the French king, Louis XIV.

To keep Spain and England out of Louisiana, the French built forts in the north along the Great Lakes. Among them was Fort Detroit, built by Antoine Cadillac near Lake Erie. The French also built New Orleans, a fort at the mouth of the river. New Orleans grew into a busy trading center.

French colonists imported thousands of Africans to work as slaves on nearby plantations. Some slaves, however, joined with the Natchez Indians in a revolt against the French. The French put down the Natchez Revolt in 1729. Some slaves who fought on the side of the French received their freedom. In Louisiana, free and enslaved Africans together made up the majority of settlers.

Government of New France New France was governed much like New Spain. The French king controlled the government directly, and people had little freedom. A council appointed by the king made all decisions.

Viewing History

Joliet and Marquette

Route of Joliet and Marquette

The journey of Joliet and Marquette to the Mississippi was often difficult. This engraving from the 1900s shows the French explorers portaging, or carrying, their canoe over a waterfall. **Evaluating Information** *Do you think this is a realistic picture of Joliet and Marquette? Explain.*

Identify Contrasts

Target Skill As you read about New France, note the missionary work, slavery, and economy. On the following pages, you will contrast these with conditions in New Netherland.

Louis XIV worried that too few French were moving to New France. In the 1660s, therefore, he sent about a thousand farmers to the colony, including many young women. Despite the king's efforts to increase the population, New France grew slowly. Only about 10,000 settlers lived in the colony by 1680. Of those, one third lived on farms along the St. Lawrence. Many more chose to become *coureurs de bois,* living largely free of government control.

New Netherland

Like the French, the Dutch hoped to profit from their discoveries in the Americas. In 1626, Peter Minuit (MIHN yoo wiht) led a group of Dutch settlers to the mouth of the Hudson River. There, he bought Manhattan Island from local Indians. Minuit called his settlement New Amsterdam. Other Dutch colonists settled farther up the Hudson River. The entire colony was known as New Netherland (now known as New York).

From a tiny group of 30 houses, New Amsterdam grew into a busy port. The Dutch welcomed people of many nations and religions to their colony. A Roman Catholic priest who visited New Netherland in 1643 reported:

66 On the island of Manhattan, and in its environs, there may well be four or five hundred men of different sects and nations: the Director General told me that there were men of eighteen different languages; they are scattered here and there on the river, above and below, as the beauty and convenience of the spot has invited each to settle. 99

—Father Isaac Jogues, quoted in *Narratives of New Netherland, 1609–1664* (Jameson)

The Dutch also built trading posts along the Hudson River. The most important one was Fort Orange, today known as Albany. Dutch merchants became known for their good business sense.

The Dutch enlarged New Netherland in 1655 by taking over the colony of New Sweden. The Swedes had established New Sweden along the Delaware River some 15 years earlier.

Rivalry Over Furs Dutch traders sent furs to the Netherlands. The packing list for the first shipment included "the skins of 7,246 beaver, 853 otter, 81 mink, 36 cat lynx, and 34 small rats."

The Dutch and French became rivals in the fur trade. Both sought alliances with Native Americans. An **alliance** is an agreement between nations to aid and protect one another. The Dutch

---

Cause *and* Effect

Causes

- Europeans want more goods from Asia
- Muslims gain control of trade between Europe and Asia
- Rulers of European nations seek ways to increase their wealth
- European nations look for a sea route to Asia
- Columbus reaches the Americas

EXPLORATION OF THE AMERICAS

Effects

- Spain builds an empire in the Americas
- English, French, and Dutch set up colonies in North America
- Millions of Native Americans die from "European" diseases
- Slave traders bring enslaved Africans to the Americas
- Foods from the Americas are introduced into Europe

Effects Today

- The United States is a multicultural society
- American foods, such as corn and potatoes, are important to people's diets around the world

GRAPHIC ORGANIZER
Skills

Exploration had a dramatic impact on the Americas, Europe, Africa, and Asia.

1. **Comprehension** Identify two economic causes of European exploration.

2. **Critical Thinking Linking Past and Present** Based on the chart, what cultures may have helped shape American culture today?

Connecting to Today

From Wall to Wall Street

"How can we protect ourselves from attack?" That was the problem New Amsterdam town leaders met to discuss in March 1653. They decided to build a wall on the northern edge of the city. Less than a mile long, the wooden wall never faced the test of battle. Much of it was dismantled over the years by people needing wood. Dutch colonists later built a road in its place: Wall Street.

Today, Wall Street is the center of banking and business in the United States. It is home to the New York Stock Exchange and many great commercial businesses. The little Dutch road is now a symbol of finance throughout the world.

What streets or other places in your community get their name from their location?

made friends with the Iroquois. The Hurons (HYOO rahnz) helped the French. Fighting raged for years among the Europeans and their Native American allies.

Dutch Ways in North America The Dutch brought many of their customs from Europe to New Netherland. They liked to ice-skate, and in winter, the frozen rivers and ponds filled with skaters. Every year on Saint Nicholas's birthday, Dutch children put out their shoes to be filled with all sorts of presents. Later, "Saint Nick" came to be called Santa Claus.

Some Dutch words entered the English language. A Dutch master was a *boss*. The people of New Amsterdam sailed in *yachts*. Dutch children munched on *cookies* and rode through the snow on *sleighs*.

Impact on Native Americans European settlement of North America brought major changes to Native Americans. As in New Spain, European diseases killed thousands of Indians. Rivalry over the fur trade increased Indian warfare as European settlers encouraged their Native American allies to attack one another. The scramble for furs also led to overtrapping. By 1640, trappers had almost wiped out the beavers on Iroquois lands in upstate New York.

The arrival of Europeans affected Native Americans in other ways. Missionaries tried to convert Indians to Christianity. Indians eagerly adopted European trade goods, such as copper kettles and knives. They also bought muskets and gunpowder for hunting and warfare. Alcohol sold by European traders had a harsh effect on Native American life.

The French, Dutch, and English all waged warfare to seize Indian lands. As Indians were forced off their lands, they moved westward onto lands of other Indians. The conflict between Native Americans and Europeans would continue for many years.

★ ★ ★ Section 3 Assessment ★ ★ ★

Recall

1. **Identify** Explain the significance of **(a)** John Cabot, **(b)** Jacques Cartier, **(c)** Protestant Reformation, **(d)** Samuel de Champlain, **(e)** Marquette and Joliet, **(f)** Peter Minuit.
2. **Define** **(a)** northwest passage, **(b)** *coureur de bois*, **(c)** missionary, **(d)** alliance.

Comprehension

3. Why did Europeans seek a northern route to Asia?
4. **(a)** What religious differences divided Europe? **(b)** How did these differences affect the race for American colonies?

5. How did the rivalry between French and Dutch colonists affect Native Americans?

Critical Thinking and Writing

6. **Exploring the Main Idea** Review the Main Idea statement at the beginning of this section. Then, write a paragraph explaining whether you think the French and Dutch achieved their goals.
7. **Making Decisions** Both *coureurs de bois* and missionaries endured great hardships in New France. For each of them, list two reasons they might have decided to come to North America.

ACTIVITY

Making a Map Suppose you could send a map back through time to Joliet and Marquette or to La Salle. Create a map showing how they could travel by land and water from Newfoundland through New France to the mouth of the Mississippi. Include a list of supplies they might need to complete the journey.

4 Building the Jamestown Colony

Prepare to Read

Objectives

In this section, you will
- Identify challenges faced by the first English colonies.
- Describe how Virginia began a tradition of representative government.
- Name the groups of people who made up the new arrivals in Virginia after 1619.

Key Terms

charter

burgess

House of Burgesses

representative government

Magna Carta

Parliament

Target Reading Skill

Clarifying Meaning As you read, prepare an outline of this section. Use roman numerals to indicate the major headings, capital letters for the subheadings, and numbers for the supporting details. The sample at right will help you get started.

> I. The First English Colony
>   A. England seeks riches
>   B.
> II. Challenge and Survival
>   A. Setting up Jamestown
>   1. King grants charter
>   2.
>   B. Early problems
>   1. Geography
>   2.

Main Idea Founded in 1607, England's Jamestown colony survived hard times and set up a representative government.

Setting the Scene

Thomas Gates was full of plans as he sailed from England to help run the Jamestown Colony in Virginia. The colony had been founded three years earlier, in 1607. Since then, nearly 700 English colonists had crossed the Atlantic Ocean to settle in Jamestown.

Gates was hardly prepared for the sight that greeted him. Of the 700 colonists, only 60 remained. They came staggering out to the shore, he reported, "so lean that they looked like [skeletons], crying out, 'We are starved, we are starved.'" Many had resorted to eating turtles, poisonous snakes, or their own horses.

Discouraged, Gates loaded everyone onto his ships and turned to sail for home. By chance, however, a new fleet from England arrived that day, bringing supplies and more settlers. The colony survived. Yet, it would take more than ten years before the English colony in Virginia put down permanent roots.

Tortoise shell found in Jamestown

The First English Colony

England watched with envy as Spain gained riches from its American colonies. Several ambitious English gentlemen proposed that England settle the Americas as well. With Queen Elizabeth's permission, Sir Walter Raleigh raised money to outfit a colony in North America. In 1585, about 100 men set sail across the Atlantic.

The colonists landed on Roanoke (ROH uh nohk), an island off the coast of present-day North Carolina. Within a year, however, the colonists had run short of food and were quarreling with neighboring Indians. When an English ship stopped in the harbor, the weary settlers sailed home.

In 1587, Raleigh sent John White, one of the original colonists, back to Roanoke with a new group of settlers, including women and children. When supplies ran low, White returned to England, leaving behind 117 colonists. He planned to return in a few months. When he

got back to England, however, he found the country was then preparing for war with Spain. It was three years before he was able to sail back to Roanoke.

When White arrived, he found the settlement strangely quiet. Houses stood empty. Vines twined through the windows and pumpkins sprouted from the earthen floors. On a tree, someone had carved the word CROATOAN, the name of a nearby island. No other trace of the colonists remained.

White was eager to investigate, but a storm was blowing up and his crew refused to make the trip. To this day, the fate of the "Lost Colony" remains a mystery.

Challenge and Survival in Jamestown

After the failure of Roanoke, nearly 20 years passed before England again tried to establish a colony in North America. In 1606, the Virginia Company of London received a charter from King James I. A **charter** is a legal document giving certain rights to a person or company.

The royal charter gave the Virginia Company the right to settle lands between present-day North Carolina and the Potomac River. The charter also guaranteed that colonists of this land, called Virginia, would have the same rights as English citizens.

A Disastrous Start In the spring of 1607, a group of 105 colonists arrived in Virginia. They sailed into Chesapeake Bay and began building homes along the James River. They named their tiny outpost Jamestown after their king.

The colonists soon discovered that Jamestown was located in a swampy area. The water was unhealthy, and mosquitoes spread malaria. Many settlers suffered or died from disease.

Governing the colony also proved difficult. The Virginia Company had chosen a council of 13 men to rule the settlement. Members of the council quarreled with one another and did little to plan for the colony's future. By the summer of 1608, the colony was near failure.

Starvation and Recovery Another major problem the Jamestown colonists faced was starvation. Captain John Smith, a young soldier and explorer, observed that the colonists were not planting enough crops. He complained that people wanted only to "dig gold, wash gold, refine gold, load gold." As they searched in vain for gold, the colony ran out of food.

Smith helped to save the colony. He set up stern rules that forced colonists to work if they wished to eat. He also visited nearby Indian villages. Powhatan (pow uh TAN), the most powerful chief in the area, agreed to supply corn to the English.

Peaceful relations with Native Americans did not last, however. Whenever the Indians refused to supply food, the colonists used force to seize what they needed. Once, Smith aimed a gun at Powhatan's brother until the Indians provided corn to buy his freedom. Such incidents led to frequent and bloody warfare. Peace was restored briefly when the colonist John Rolfe married Pocahontas, daughter of Powhatan.

Even in times of peace, Jamestown did not prosper. Problems arose soon after John Smith returned to England in 1609. As you read, the colony suffered terribly for the next few years. Desperate settlers cooked "dogs, cats, snakes, [and] toadstools" to survive. To keep warm, they broke up houses to burn as firewood.

A Profitable Crop Jamestown's economy finally improved after 1612, when colonists began growing tobacco. Europeans had learned about tobacco from Native Americans.

King James called pipe smoking "a vile custom." Still, the new fad caught on quickly. By 1620, England was importing more than 30,000 pounds of tobacco a year. At last, Virginians had found a way to make their colony succeed.

Representative Government

For a time, the governors sent by the Virginia Company ran the colony like a military outpost. Each morning, a drumbeat summoned settlers to work at assigned tasks. Harsh laws imposed the death penalty even for small offenses, like stealing an ear of corn. Such conditions were unlikely to attract new colonists. As John Smith commented after his return to England, "No Man will go . . . to have less freedom there than here."

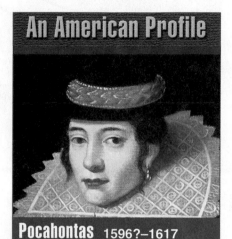

An American Profile

Pocahontas 1596?–1617

As a young woman, Pocahontas, whose name means "playful one," captured the affections of John Rolfe, a Jamestown tobacco planter. They were married in 1614.

In 1616, when she was about twenty years old, Pocahontas accompanied her husband and infant son, Thomas, to England. The English were fascinated by this "Indian princess." She was invited to the court of King James I. A painting shows her dressed as an English noblewoman in velvet and lace. In 1617, as she prepared to return to Virginia, Pocahontas became ill. She died and was buried in England.

Why do you think the English wanted to meet Pocahontas?

The First English Settlements

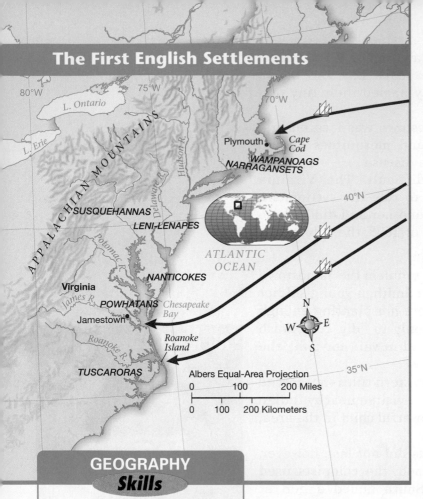

GEOGRAPHY
Skills

After a difficult start, England finally established successful colonies in North America.

1. **Location** On the map, locate **(a)** Roanoke, **(b)** James River, **(c)** Jamestown, **(d)** Cape Cod, **(e)** Plymouth.

2. **Region** What Native American groups lived near the Jamestown Colony?

3. **Critical Thinking Comparing** What did the first three English colonies in North America have in common? Why?

Reforms of 1619 To attract more settlers, the Virginia Company took steps to establish a more stable government. In 1619, it sent a new governor with orders to consult settlers on all important matters. Male settlers were allowed to elect **burgesses,** or representatives to the government.

The burgesses met in an assembly called the **House of Burgesses.** Together with the governor and his council, they made laws for the colony. The first session met in the Jamestown church in July and August 1619. In steamy weather, the burgesses sat in the church pews, while the governor and council took their places in the choir stalls.

The House of Burgesses marked the beginning of representative government in the English colonies. In a **representative government,** voters elect representatives to make laws for them.

English Traditions The idea that people had political rights was deeply rooted in English history. In 1215, English nobles had forced King John to sign the **Magna Carta,** or Great Charter. This document said that the king could not raise taxes without first consulting a Great Council of nobles and church leaders.

Over time, the rights won by nobles were extended to other people. The Great Council grew into a representative assembly, called **Parliament.** Parliament was divided into the House of Lords, made up of nobles, and an elected House of Commons. Only a few rich men had the right to vote. Still, the English had established the principle that even monarchs had to obey the law.

Virginia's Representative Tradition At first, free Virginians had even greater rights than citizens in England. They did not have to own property in order to vote. In 1670, however, the colony restricted the vote to free, white, male property owners.

Despite these limits, representative government remained important. The idea took root that settlers should have a say in the affairs of the colony. Colonists came to refer to the Virginia Company's 1619 frame of government as their own "Great Charter."

New Arrivals

During the early years of the Jamestown Colony, only a few women chose to make the journey from England. Nor did enough workers come to raise tobacco and other crops.

Women in Virginia The colony's first women arrived in 1608—a "Mistress Forrest" and her maid, Anne Burras. Few others followed until 1619, when the Virginia Company sent about 100 women to help "make the men more settled." This shipload of women quickly found husbands. The Virginia Company profited from the marriages because it charged each man who found a wife 150 pounds of tobacco.

Women survived the hardships of Virginia better than men. One colonist commented that women "escape better than men, either that their work lies chiefly [inside] or because they are of a colder temper." In fact, men were almost twice as likely as women to die from diseases or other causes.

Still, life for women remained a daily struggle. Women had to make everything from scratch—food, clothing, even medicines. Many died young from hard work or childbirth. By 1624, there were still fewer than 300 women in the Jamestown colony, compared to over a thousand men.

The First Africans Africans came to Virginia early on. Recently discovered records show that at least 15 black men and 17 black women were already living there by 1619. That same year, a Dutch ship arrived with about 20 Africans. The Dutch sold the Africans to Virginians who needed laborers to grow tobacco. The colonists valued the agricultural skills that the Africans brought with them.

About 300 Africans lived in Virginia by 1644. Some were slaves for life. Others worked as servants and expected one day to own their own farms. Some Africans did become free planters. Anthony Johnson owned 250 acres of land and employed five servants to help him work it. For a time, free Africans in Virginia also had the right to vote.

In the late 1600s, Virginia set up a system of laws allowing white colonists to enslave Africans for life. As slavery expanded, free Africans lost rights. By the early 1700s, free African property owners could not vote.

 **Summarize**
When you summarize, you review and state in the correct order the main points you have read. Write two or three sentences summarizing the impact of the "new arrivals" to the Jamestown Colony in 1619.

★ ★ ★ Section 4 Assessment ★ ★ ★

Recall
1. **Identify** Explain the significance of (a) Walter Raleigh, (b) John Smith, (c) Powhatan, (d) House of Burgesses, (e) Magna Carta, (f) Parliament.
2. **Define** (a) charter, (b) burgess, (c) representative government.

Comprehension
3. (a) Describe three problems the Jamestown Colony faced after 1607. (b) Why was the colony finally able to survive?
4. What were the origins of representative government in the English colonies?

5. What new arrivals helped the Jamestown Colony thrive?

Critical Thinking and Writing
6. **Exploring the Main Idea** Review the Main Idea statement at the beginning of this section. Then, list what you would consider to be the four most important milestones in the growth of Jamestown.
7. **Linking Past and Present** Name three important features of Jamestown's government. For each item, write a sentence explaining how it is also an element of American representative government today.

ACTIVITY
Creating an Advertisement You are an investor in the Virginia Company. In order to make a profit, you must encourage people to leave England and move to Jamestown. Create an advertisement describing the advantages of living in Virginia. If possible, include an illustration.

The House of Burgesses

The House of Burgesses first met in Jamestown, Virginia, on July 30, 1619. That hot day marks the beginning of representative government in what became the United States.

The first session passed a variety of laws. The burgesses decreed:

- that colonists plant mulberry trees and grape vines.
- that penalties be imposed for drunkenness, idleness, and gambling.
- that colonists attend church twice on Sunday—and that they bring their guns and swords with them.
- that "no injury or oppression be [committed] by the English against the Indians."
- that each town and plantation had to educate a number of Indian children.

The first burgesses wore multiple layers of velvets and silks, like upper-class members of the British Parliament (left). But Jamestown's hot, humid July climate proved deadly. Several burgesses got sick, and one died.

The 22 elected burgesses gathered in the Jamestown church. Parson Buck opened the meeting with a prayer. As each burgess heard his name called, he took his seat before the governor.

ACTIVITY

Choose one of the laws listed above. With a partner, enact a discussion in the House of Burgesses about that law. Explain why you think such a law is necessary for the well-being of the colony.

5 Seeking Religious Freedom

Prepare to Read

Objectives

In this section, you will
- Describe how European states controlled or regulated religion.
- Explain why the colonists at Plymouth wanted the Mayflower Compact.
- Identify how the Pilgrims survived early hardships.

Key Terms

Pilgrims

established church

persecution

Mayflower Compact

precedent

Thanksgiving

Target Reading Skill

Sequence Copy this flowchart. As you read, fill in the boxes with the major events and developments relating to the founding of the Plymouth Colony. The first and last boxes have been completed to help you get started. Add as many boxes as you need.

England persecutes Separatists
↓
↓
↓
↓
First successful harvest in Plymouth

Main Idea The Pilgrims founded Plymouth Colony in 1620 in order to practice their religion freely.

Setting the Scene

The small sailing ship had been tossed by so many storms that leaks had sprung in the ship's hull. After two hard months at sea, the colonists on board were relieved to see the shores of New England. Still, there were no European colonies for hundreds of miles. Worse, it was already November of 1620, much too late for crops to be planted. One of the voyagers, William Bradford, vividly remembered the situation:

> 66 Being thus passed the vast ocean . . . they had now no friends to welcome them nor inns to entertain or refresh their weatherbeaten bodies; no houses or much less towns to repair to . . . And for the season it was winter, and they that know the winters of that country know them to be sharp and violent. 99
>
> —William Bradford, *Of Plymouth Plantation*

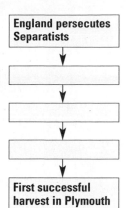

Cradle carried on the Mayflower

Despite many hardships, the newcomers made their new colony succeed. Unlike the Jamestown colonists or the Spanish, they sought neither gold nor silver nor great riches. What they wanted most was to practice their religion freely. Years later, the founders of Plymouth became known to history as the Pilgrims.*

European States and Religion

It was not easy for people to practice religion freely in Europe during the 1500s. As you have read, after the Protestant Reformation, European Christians were divided into Protestants and Roman Catholics. This division led to fierce religious wars. In France, for example, Protestants and Catholics fought each other for nearly 40

---

*The founders of the Plymouth Colony did not call themselves Pilgrims. However, William Bradford once wrote that they were "pilgrims . . . [who] lifted up their eyes to the heavens, their dearest country." A pilgrim is anyone who makes a long journey for religious reasons.

years. Thousands upon thousands of people were killed because of their religious beliefs.

Most European rulers believed that they could not maintain order unless the state supported a particular religion. The chosen religion was known as the **established church.** In England, for example, the established church was the Anglican church, or Church of England. In the 1530s, Parliament passed laws making the English monarch the head of the Church of England.

In England and other nations, people who did not follow the established religion were often persecuted. **Persecution** is the mistreatment or punishment of certain people because of their beliefs. Sometimes, members of persecuted groups had to worship secretly. If they were discovered, they might be imprisoned or even executed by being burned at the stake.

Separatists Seek Religious Freedom One religious group in England that faced persecution were the people we now call the Pilgrims. At the time, they were known as Separatists. They were called that because, although they were Protestant, they wanted to separate from the Church of England.

The English government bitterly opposed the Separatists. William Bradford remembered what some Separatists suffered:

66 They . . . were hunted and persecuted on every side. . . . For some were taken and clapped up in prison, others had their houses beset and watched night and day . . . and the most were [glad] to flee and leave their houses. 99

—William Bradford, *Of Plymouth Plantation*

In the early 1600s, a group of Separatists left England for Leyden, a city in the Netherlands. The Dutch allowed the newcomers to worship freely. Still, the Pilgrims missed their English way of life. They were also worried that their children were growing up more Dutch than English.

The Pilgrim Colony at Plymouth

A group of Separatists decided to return to England. Along with some other English people who were not Separatists, they won a charter to set up a colony in Virginia. In September 1620, more than 100 men, women, and children set sail aboard a small ship called the *Mayflower.* As you have read, the journey was long and difficult.

At last, in November 1620, the *Mayflower* landed on the cold, bleak shore of Cape Cod, in present-day Massachusetts. The passengers had planned to settle farther south along the Hudson River, but the difficult sea voyage exhausted them. The colonists decided to travel no further. They called their new settlement Plimoth, or Plymouth, because the *Mayflower* had sailed from the port of Plymouth, England.

The Mayflower Compact Before going ashore, the Pilgrims realized that they would not be settling within the boundaries of Virginia. As a result, the terms of their charter would not apply to their new colony. In that case, who would govern them? The question

---

Primary Source

The Mayflower Compact

On November 11, 1620, the 41 male passengers on the Mayflower *signed a binding agreement for self-government:*
"We, whose names are underwritten. . . . Having undertaken for the Glory of God, and Advancement of the Christian Faith and honor of our King and country, a voyage to plant the first colony in the northern parts of Virginia, do . . . solemnly and mutually in the presence of God, and one of another, covenant and combine ourselves into a civil body politic . . . to enact, constitute, and frame, such just and equal Laws . . . as shall be thought most [fitting] and convenient for the general Good of the Colony; unto which we promise all due submission and obedience."
—Mayflower Compact

Analyzing Primary Sources
Identify two promises the signers of the Mayflower Compact made with regard to laws for their colony.

was important because not all colonists on the Mayflower were Pilgrims. Some of these "strangers," as the Pilgrims called them, said they were not bound to obey the Pilgrims, "for none had power to command them."

In response, the Pilgrims joined together to write a framework for governing their colony. On November 11, 1620, the 41 male passengers—both Pilgrims and non-Pilgrims—signed the **Mayflower Compact.** They pledged themselves to unite into a "civil body politic," or government. They agreed to make and abide by laws that insured "the general Good of the Colony." (See the Primary Source on the preceding page.)

The Mayflower Compact established an important tradition. When the Pilgrims found themselves without a government, they banded together themselves to make laws. In time, they set up a government in which adult male colonists elected a governor and council. Thus, like Virginia's Great Charter, the Mayflower Compact strengthened the English tradition of governing through elected representatives.

Tradition of Religious Freedom The Pilgrims were the first of many English settlers who came to North America in order to worship as they pleased. Still, as you will read in the next chapter, that did not mean that religious freedom spread quickly through England's colonies. Many settlers who wished to worship as they

Before the *Mayflower* anchored in what is now Provincetown Harbor off Cape Cod, the male passengers signed the Mayflower Compact. This painting depicts the event. **Drawing Inferences** *What does this painting suggest about the women aboard the* Mayflower?

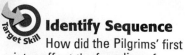
Plymouth

Plimoth Plantation

By 1627, Plymouth was a stable settlement. Using records from that year, historians carefully re-created Plimoth Plantation on the grounds of the old village in Massacusetts. Plimoth is a "living museum," where people in authentic costumes tend crops, make tools, and tell you about their lives. Even the animals at Plimoth are all breeds that were raised by the Pilgrims.

Go Online
PHSchool.com

Virtual Field Trip For an interactive look at the Plimouth Plantation, visit PHSchool.com, **Web Code mfd-0302.**

pleased still believed that only their own religious beliefs should be observed. Most of the later English colonies set up their own established churches.

Still, the Pilgrims' desire to worship freely set an important **precedent, or** example for others to follow in the future. Plymouth's leaders announced "that any honest men may live with them, that will carry themselves peaceably and seek the common good." In time, the idea of religious freedom for all would become a cornerstone of American democracy.

Early Hardships

The Pilgrims built their settlement on the site of a Native American village that had been abandoned because of disease. The colonists even found baskets filled with corn that they were able to eat.

First Winter in Plymouth However, the corn was not enough to get the Pilgrims through their first winter. The Pilgrims had failed to bring enough food with them, and it was too late in the season to plant new crops.

The harsh season was also difficult to survive because the Pilgrims had not had enough time to build proper shelters. Most threw together crude houses of sod, or clumps of earth. Some dug themselves into pits in the ground, covered by branches to protect themselves from the weather. Nearly half the settlers perished of disease or starvation.

Identify Sequence
Target Skill How did the Pilgrims' first winter affect the founding of Plymouth Colony? Add this information to your flowchart.

Among those who died that winter was the colony's first governor. William Bradford was chosen to take his place. Bradford's able leadership helped the colony survive. Reelected many times, he would lead Plymouth for most of the next 36 years.

Despite the great suffering of the "Starving Time," the Pilgrims' religious faith remained strong. They believed that it was God's will for them to remain in Plymouth. "What could now sustain them," wrote Bradford, "but the Spirit of God and His grace?"

Help From Native Americans In the spring, the Pilgrims began to clear land and plant crops. They also received help from neighboring Native Americans. A Pemaquid Indian, Samoset, had learned English from earlier explorers sailing along the coast. He introduced the Pilgrims to Massasoit (MAS uh soit), chief of the local Wampanoag (wahm puh NOH ahg) Indians.

The Wampanoag who helped the Pilgrims most was named Squanto. As a young man, Squanto had been captured by an English expedition led by John Smith. Squanto lived for a time in England, where he learned to speak the language. As a result, he could communicate easily with the Pilgrims.

Squanto brought the Pilgrims seeds of native plants—corn, beans, and pumpkins—and showed them how to plant them. He also taught the settlers how to catch eels from nearby rivers. By treading water, he stirred up eels from the mud at the river bottom and then snatched them up with his hands. The grateful Pilgrims called Squanto "a special instrument sent of God."

In the fall, the Pilgrims had a very good harvest. Because they believed that God had given them this harvest, they set aside a day for giving thanks. In later years, the Pilgrims celebrated after each harvest season with a day of thanksgiving. Americans today celebrate Thanksgiving as a national holiday.

★ ★ ★ Section 5 Assessment ★ ★ ★

Recall
1. **Identify** Explain the significance of (a) William Bradford, (b) Pilgrims, (c) Mayflower Compact, (d) Squanto, (e) Thanksgiving.
2. **Define** (a) established church, (b) persecution, (c) precedent.

Comprehension
3. Why did many religious groups in Europe face persecution?
4. (a) How did the Mayflower Compact resolve a conflict among the Plymouth settlers? (b) Why is this document important?

5. How did Native Americans help the Pilgrims survive?

Critical Thinking and Writing
6. **Exploring the Main Idea** Review the Main Idea statement at the beginning of this section. Then, write a letter from one Separatist in England to another explaining why you have decided to sail on the *Mayflower.*
7. **Comparing** Write a list of three ways the founding of Plymouth was different from or similar to the founding of Jamestown.

Review and Assessment

Section 1
Christopher Columbus did not discover a route to Asia, but his voyage had a lasting impact. Explorers who came after Columbus opened a cultural exchange between Europe and the Americas.

Section 2
Conquistadors created a Spanish empire in the Americas when they conquered the Aztecs and Incas. Native American deaths in the Spanish colonies led to the introduction of the slave trade.

Section 3
The French, English, and Dutch competed for the fertile land that they discovered in North America. Native Americans suffered as a result of their encounters with Europeans.

Section 4
Jamestown, in Virginia, became the first permanent English colony in North America. The colonists in Virginia brought their English traditions with them, including the practice of representative government.

Section 5
Religious persecution brought the Pilgrims to North America. They established a colony in Plymouth. After barely surviving their first winter, the Pilgrims planted crops with the help of Native Americans.

Building Vocabulary

Write sentences, using the chapter vocabulary words listed below, leaving blanks where the vocabulary words would go. Exchange your sentences with another student and fill in the blanks.

1. colony
2. circumnavigate
3. conquistador
4. presidio
5. mission
6. peninsulare
7. northwest passage
8. charter
9. representative government
10. established church

Reviewing Key Facts

11. Identify one reason Spain financed Columbus's voyage in 1492. (Section 1)

For additional review and enrichment activities, see the interactive version of *The American Nation,* available on the Web and on CD-ROM.

Chapter Self-Test For practice test questions for Chapter 3, visit PHSchool.com, **Web Code mfa-0304.**

12. How were European and Native American cultures blended in New Spain? (Section 2)
13. How did Dutch ways help shape American culture? (Section 3)
14. Describe two English political traditions of the Jamestown Colony. (Section 4)
15. Why did the Pilgrims decide to start a colony? (Section 5)

Critical Thinking and Writing

16. **Recognizing Points of View** For each of the following, write one sentence describing the person's feelings about Bartolomé de Las Casas: **(a)** a Native American working on a Caribbean plantation; **(b)** a Spanish plantation owner; **(c)** a slave trader in East Africa; **(d)** an African sent to the Americas as a slave.

17. **Connecting to Geography: Movement** Look at a world map or a map of North America. **(a)** Write a description of a possible northern sea route around the Americas to Asia. **(b)** Based on what you know of this part of the world, why do you think the British, French, or Dutch never found a northwest passage?

18. **Comparing (a)** List one similarity and one difference between Jamestown's "Great Charter" of 1619 and the Mayflower Compact. **(b)** Write a paragraph evaluating the importance of these documents.

Analyzing Primary Sources

Read the following excerpt from Jacques Marquette's journal and answer the questions that follow:

66 We slept in the chief's cabin, and on the following day we took leave of him, promising to pass again by his village, within four moons. He conducted us to our canoes, with nearly 600 persons who witnessed our embarkation, giving us every possible sign of the joy that our visit had caused them. For my own part, I promised . . . that I would come the following year, and reside with them to instruct them. **99**

—Jacques Marquette, quoted in *The Jesuit Relations and Allied Documents* (Thwaites)

19. When Marquette wrote that he would return "within four moons," he probably meant that he would be back in about four
   A. days.   C. months.
   B. weeks.   D. years.

20. Upon his return to the village, Marquette probably intended to teach the Indians about
   A. the art of making canoes.
   B. Christianity.
   C. how to tell time using a watch or clock.
   D. the shortest route to the Mississippi.

Sequencing

Below are some key events relating to the first English colonies. The events are not listed in correct time sequence. Look at the events and answer the questions that follow.

I.	House of Burgesses is formed
II.	Pilgrims leave England
III.	Jamestown Colony is founded
IV.	Mayflower Compact is signed
V.	Roanoke colonists disappear
VI.	Squanto teaches Pilgrims
VII.	Colonists begin to grow tobacco

21. In which set below are the events listed in the correct sequence?
   A. VII, IV, II
   B. V, I, VI
   C. III, VI, IV
   D. II, VII, VI

22. Choose two events from the list above. Identify the correct time sequence and explain how the two events are related.

ACTIVITIES

Connecting With . . . Geography

Creating a Thematic Map With the class, create a map of the Era of Exploration and Colonization. Use the information found on the various maps in this chapter. (Your teacher may suggest that you look at additional maps as well.) Draw a large base map of the world. Label important continents, countries, oceans, and rivers. Create a color key for the major European powers discussed in the chapter. Choose who you consider to be the 10 most important explorers and show their routes on the map. Then, color in the areas of the Americas that were colonized by European nations. Use the same color key to show a nation, its explorers, and its colonies.

Exploring Historical Scholarship

Summarizing Use the Internet to find one theory about the disappearance of the colony at Roanoke. In a one-minute talk, summarize the theory and the evidence for it. For help in starting this activity, visit PHSchool.com, **Web Code mfd-0306.**

The Thirteen English Colonies

1630–1750

Puritan settlers building homes

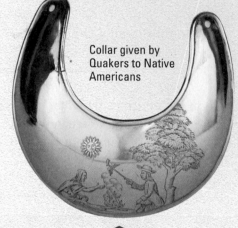

Collar given by Quakers to Native Americans

AMERICAN EVENTS

1630
Puritans from England set up the Massachusetts Bay Colony.

1675
Metacom leads fight against settlers in New England.

1682
William Penn founds the colony of Pennsylvania.

1630 · · · **1660** · · **1690**

WORLD EVENTS

1660 ▲
English Parliament passes a stronger version of the Navigation Act.

1689 ▲
William and Mary sign the English Bill of Rights.

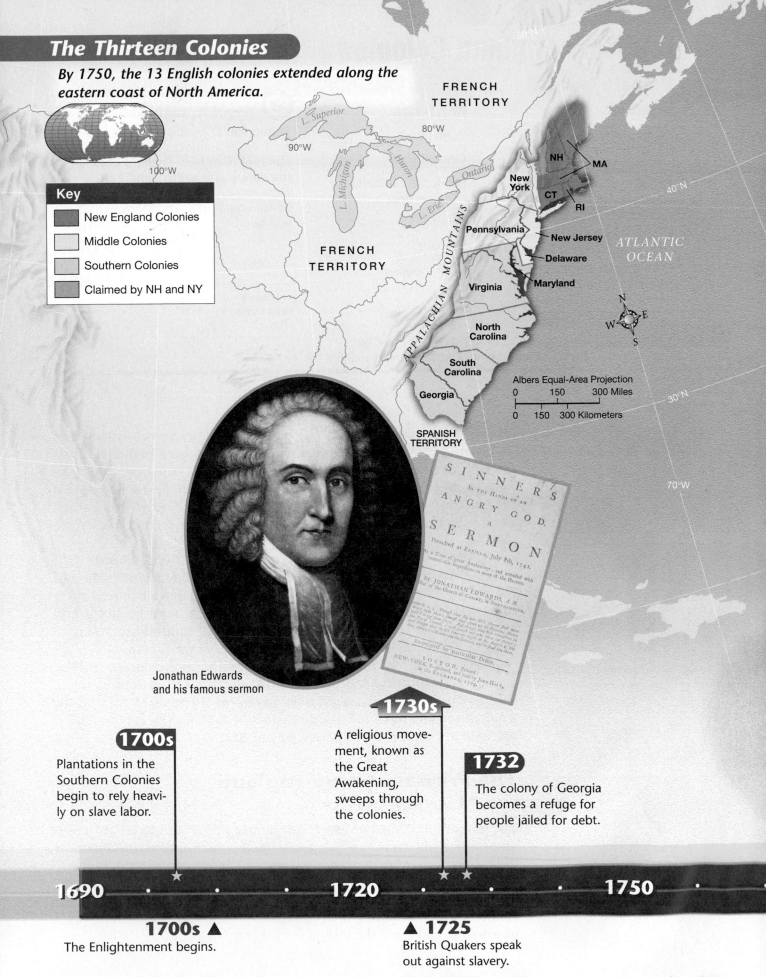

The Thirteen Colonies

By 1750, the 13 English colonies extended along the eastern coast of North America.

Key
- New England Colonies
- Middle Colonies
- Southern Colonies
- Claimed by NH and NY

FRENCH TERRITORY

FRENCH TERRITORY

SPANISH TERRITORY

ATLANTIC OCEAN

L. Superior
L. Michigan
L. Huron
L. Ontario
L. Erie

APPALACHIAN MOUNTAINS

NH
MA
New York
CT
RI
Pennsylvania
New Jersey
Delaware
Maryland
Virginia
North Carolina
South Carolina
Georgia

Albers Equal-Area Projection
0   150   300 Miles
0   150   300 Kilometers

Jonathan Edwards and his famous sermon

SINNERS IN THE HANDS OF AN ANGRY GOD. A SERMON
Preached at ENFIELD, July 8th, 1741.
BY JONATHAN EDWARDS, A.M.

1700s
Plantations in the Southern Colonies begin to rely heavily on slave labor.

1730s
A religious movement, known as the Great Awakening, sweeps through the colonies.

1732
The colony of Georgia becomes a refuge for people jailed for debt.

1690   •   •   1720   •   •   •   1750

1700s ▲
The Enlightenment begins.

▲ 1725
British Quakers speak out against slavery.

1 The New England Colonies

Prepare to Read

Objectives

In this section, you will

- List the reasons the Puritans decided to leave England.
- Identify problems in the Massachusetts colony that caused people to leave.
- Explain why the Puritans and Native Americans fought.
- Summarize why towns and villages were important in New England.

Key Terms

Puritans

General Court

Fundamental Orders of Connecticut

religious tolerance

Sabbath

town meeting

 **Target Reading Skill**

Sequence Copy this chart. As you read, fill in the boxes with the name of each New England Colony, the date it was settled, and why. The first two boxes have been started for you. Add as many lines as you need.

COLONY	DATE SETTLED	REASONS FOR SETTLEMENT
• Plymouth • Massachusetts Bay	• 1620 • 1630	• •

Main Idea The New England Colonies were founded by reformers and developed around tightly knit towns and villages.

Powdered wig from the 1700s

Setting the Scene Boston merchant Samuel Sewall frowned as he greeted Mr. Hayward, an acquaintance. Hayward had cut off his long gray hair and was wearing a full wig of dark hair that made him look younger! Sewall protested that in the Bible, Jesus had said a person cannot "make one's Hair white or black." Hayward gulped nervously. He claimed that his doctors had advised him to wear the wig.

By the time Sewall recorded this story in 1685, Boston had become the busiest town in the Massachusetts Bay Colony. Most of the colony's founders were no longer living. Yet, Sewall shared their ideals. He looked to the Bible to guide him in matters large and small—even the treatment of one's hair. Sewall wanted his colony to be a "holy commonwealth" that followed the laws of God.

Religion played a large part in the founding of colonies in New England. During the 1630s, thousands of English settlers came to live around Massachusetts Bay, north of Plymouth. Gradually, English settlers built towns and farms throughout the region. These settlements shared a distinctive way of life.

The Puritans Leave England for Massachusetts

The migration to Massachusetts Bay during the 1630s was led by a religious group known as the **Puritans.** Unlike the Pilgrims, the Puritans did not want to separate entirely from the Church of England. Instead, they hoped to reform the church by introducing simpler forms of worship. They wanted to do away with many practices inherited from the Roman Catholic Church, such as organ music, finely decorated houses of worship, and special clothing for priests.

Leaving England During "Evil Times"

The Puritans were a powerful group in England. Although some were small farmers, many were well-educated and successful merchants or landowners.

Charles I, who became king in 1625, disapproved of the Puritans and their ideas. He canceled Puritan business charters and even had a few Puritans jailed.

By 1629, some Puritan leaders were convinced that England had fallen on "evil and declining times." They persuaded royal officials to grant them a charter to form the Massachusetts Bay Company. The company's bold plan was to build a new society based on biblical laws and teachings. John Winthrop, a lawyer and a devout Puritan, believed that the new colony would set an example to the world.

Some settlers joined the Massachusetts colonists for economic rather than religious reasons. In wealthy English families, the oldest son usually inherited his father's estate. With little hope of owning land, younger sons sought opportunity elsewhere. They were attracted to Massachusetts Bay because it offered cheap land or a chance to start a business.

Governing the Colony In 1629, the Puritans sent a small advance party to North America. John Winthrop and a party of more than 1,000 arrived the following year. Winthrop was chosen first governor of the Massachusetts Bay Colony.

Once ashore, Winthrop set an example for others. Although he was governor, he worked hard to build a home, clear land, and plant crops.

There was discontent among some colonists, though. Under the charter, only stockholders who had invested money in the Massachusetts Bay Company had the right to vote. Most settlers, however, were not stockholders. They resented taxes and laws passed by a government in which they had no say.

Winthrop and other stockholders saw that the colony would run more smoothly if a greater number of settlers could take part. At the same time, Puritan leaders wished to keep non-Puritans out of the government. As a result, they granted the right to vote for governor to all men who were church members. Later, male church members also elected representatives to an assembly called the General Court.

Under the leadership of Winthrop and other Puritans, the Massachusetts Bay Colony prospered. Between 1629 and 1640, some 15,000 men, women, and children journeyed from England to Massachusetts. This movement of people is known as the Great Migration. Many of the newcomers settled in Boston, which grew into the colony's largest town.

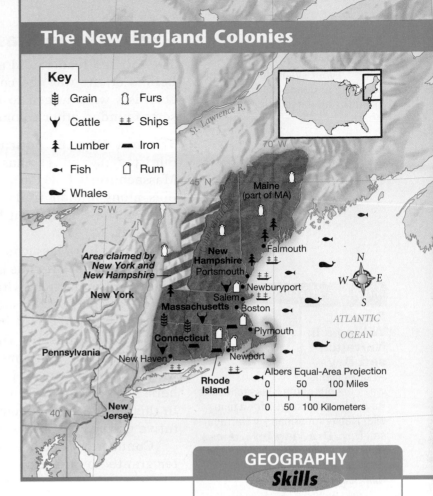

The New England Colonies

Key

- 🌾 Grain
- 🐂 Cattle
- 🌲 Lumber
- 🐟 Fish
- 🐋 Whales
- 🦫 Furs
- ⚓ Ships
- ⚒ Iron
- 🍶 Rum

St. Lawrence R.

70° W

45° N

75° W

Area claimed by New York and New Hampshire

New York

Pennsylvania

40° N

New Jersey

Maine (part of MA)

New Hampshire
Portsmouth

Falmouth

Newburyport

Salem

Massachusetts Boston

Plymouth

Connecticut

New Haven

Newport

Rhode Island

ATLANTIC OCEAN

N
W E
S

Albers Equal-Area Projection
0   50   100 Miles
0   50   100 Kilometers

GEOGRAPHY
Skills

The New England colonies were among the first English settlements in North America. Major economic activities in the region included shipbuilding, fishing, and fur trapping.

1. **Location** On the map, locate: **(a)** Massachusetts, **(b)** Connecticut, **(c)** Rhode Island, **(d)** New Hampshire, **(e)** Boston, **(f)** Plymouth.

2. **Interaction** In which colonies did settlers mine iron ore?

3. **Critical Thinking Analyzing Information** How did New England's geography encourage the growth of shipbuilding?

Problems in Massachusetts Bay

The Puritan leaders did not like anyone to question their religious beliefs or the way the colony was governed. Usually, discontented colonists were forced to leave. Some colonists who left Massachusetts founded other colonies in New England.

Thomas Hooker Founds Connecticut In May 1636, a Puritan minister named Thomas Hooker led about 100 settlers out of Massachusetts Bay. Pushing west, they drove their cattle, goats, and pigs along Indian trails that cut through the forests. When they reached the Connecticut River, they built a town, which they called Hartford.

Hooker left Massachusetts Bay because he believed that the governor and other officials had too much power. He wanted to set up a colony in Connecticut with strict limits on government.

The settlers wrote a plan of government called the **Fundamental Orders of Connecticut** in 1639. It created a government much like that of Massachusetts. There were, however, two important differences. First, the Fundamental Orders gave the vote to all men who were property owners, including those who were not church members. Second, the Fundamental Orders limited the governor's power. In this way, the Fundamental Orders expanded the idea of representative government in the English colonies.

Connecticut became a separate colony in 1662, with a new charter granted by the king of England. By then, 15 towns were thriving along the Connecticut River.

Viewing History

Roger Williams in Narragansett Bay

Rhode Island

After Williams was cast out of the Massachusetts Bay Colony, he stayed for a time with Native Americans in Narragansett Bay. **Drawing Inferences** *How would you describe Williams's relationship with the Native Americans?*

Roger Williams Settles Rhode Island Another Puritan who challenged the leaders of Massachusetts Bay was Roger Williams. A young minister in the village of Salem, Williams was gentle and good-natured. William Bradford described him as "zealous but very unsettled in judgment." Some Puritan leaders probably agreed with this. Most people, including Governor Winthrop, liked him. Williams's ideas, however, alarmed Puritan leaders.

Williams believed that the Puritan church in Massachusetts had too much power. In Williams's view, the business of church and state should be completely separate since concern with political affairs would corrupt the church. The role of the state, said Williams, was to maintain order and peace. It should not support a particular church. Finally, Williams did not believe that the Puritan leaders had the right to force people to attend religious services.

Williams also believed in religious tolerance. **Religious tolerance** means a willingness to let others practice their own beliefs.

In Puritan Massachusetts, non-Puritans were not allowed to worship freely.

Puritan leaders viewed Williams as a dangerous troublemaker. In 1635, the General Court ordered him to leave Massachusetts. Fearing that the court would send him back to England, Williams fled to Narragansett Bay, where he spent the winter with Indians. In the spring of 1636, the Indians sold him land for a settlement. After a few years, the settlement became the English colony of Rhode Island.

In Rhode Island, Williams put into practice his ideas about tolerance. He allowed complete freedom of religion for all Protestants, Jews, and Catholics.* He did not set up a state church or require settlers to attend church services. He also gave all white men the right to vote. Before long, settlers who disliked the strict Puritan rule of Massachusetts flocked to Providence and other towns in Rhode Island.

Anne Hutchinson Speaks Out Among those who fled to Rhode Island was Anne Hutchinson. A devout Puritan, Hutchinson regularly attended church services in Boston, where she first lived. After church, she and her friends gathered at her home to discuss the minister's sermon. Often, she seemed to question some of the minister's teachings. Hutchinson was very persuasive and neighbors flocked to hear her.

Puritan leaders grew angry. They believed that Hutchinson's opinions were full of religious errors. Even worse, they said, a woman did not have the right to explain God's law. In November 1637, Hutchinson was ordered to appear before the Massachusetts General Court.

At her trial, Hutchinson answered the questions put to her by Governor Winthrop and other members of the court. Each time, her answers revealed weaknesses in their arguments. They could not prove that she had broken any Puritan laws or that she had disobeyed any religious teachings.

Then, after two long days of hostile questioning, Hutchinson made a serious mistake. She told the court that God spoke directly to her, "By the voice of His own spirit to my soul." Members of the court were shocked. Puritans believed that God spoke only through the Bible, not directly to individuals. The court ordered her out of the colony.

In 1638, Hutchinson, along with her family and some friends, went to Rhode Island. The Puritan leaders had won their case. For later Americans, however, Hutchinson became an important symbol of the struggle for religious freedom.

Viewing History

Anne Hutchinson Known in the colony as a "woman of ready wit with a bold spirit," Hutchinson won the respect of Puritan leaders at first. However, they soon saw her as a troublemaker. Here, she defends herself before the General Court. **Making Decisions** *Do you think Hutchinson was a "bold spirit"? Explain.*

---

*In 1763, Jewish settlers in Rhode Island built Touro Synagogue, the first Jewish house of worship in North America. It still stands today.

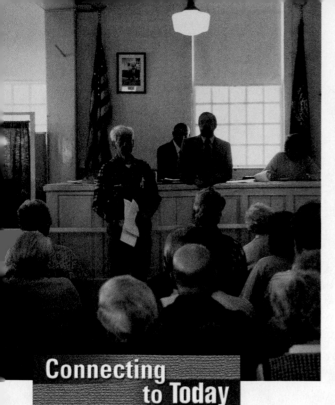

Puritans at War With Native Americans

From Massachusetts Bay, settlers fanned out across New England. Some built trading and fishing villages along the coast north of Boston. In 1680, the king made these coastal settlements into a separate colony called New Hampshire.

The first meetings between English settlers and Native Americans did not foreshadow the conflict that would eventually occur between them. Some colonial leaders such as William Penn and Roger Williams tried to treat Native Americans fairly.

As more colonists settled in New England, they began to take over more Native American lands. By 1670, nearly 45,000 English settlers were living in the towns in New England. As a result, fighting broke out between white settlers and Indian nations of the region.

The largest conflict came in 1675. Metacom, also known by his English name, King Phillip, was chief of the Wampanoag Indians. He watched for years as English towns were built on Wampanoag lands. "I am resolved not to see the day when I have no country," he told an English friend. Metacom's people attacked villages throughout New England. Other Indian groups, from Rhode Island to Maine, soon allied themselves with the Wampanoags. They were determined to drive the English settlers off their land. Metacom and his allies destroyed 12 towns and killed more than 600 European settlers.

After more than a year of fighting, however, Metacom was captured and killed. The English sold his family and about 1,000 other Indians into slavery in the West Indies. Other Indians were forced from their homelands.

The pattern of English expansion followed by war was repeated between colonists and Indians throughout the colonies. It would continue for many years to come.

Life in New England Towns and Villages

Puritans believed that people should worship and tend to local matters as a community. As a result, New England became a land of tightly knit towns and villages.

At the center of each village was the common, an open field where cattle grazed. Nearby stood the meetinghouse, where Puritans worshiped and held town meetings.

Religion and Family The Puritans took their **Sabbath,** or holy day of rest, very seriously. On Sundays, no one was allowed to play games or visit taverns to joke, talk, and drink. The law required all citizens to attend Sunday church services, which would last all day.

Connecting to Today

Democracy in Action

In New England and some other states, town meetings still occur. Citizens discuss and vote on important issues, such as town laws or how to use the town's money.

Today, new technology is giving a whole new meaning to town meetings. In "electronic town meetings" (ETM), televisions, telephones, or computers link people from distant locations and provide instant voting results. Experts give background talks on an issue. Citizens ask questions, speak their minds, and then vote. The way in which citizens conduct their meetings is different from the way it was in colonial times. However, the citizens' desire to make their voices heard is the same.

What issues might you like to see addressed by a town meeting in your community?

During the 1600s, women sat on one side of the church and men on the other. Blacks and Indians stood in a balcony at the back. Children had separate pews, where an adult watched over them.

Government At **town meetings,** settlers discussed and voted on many issues. What roads should be built? How much should the schoolmaster be paid? Town meetings gave New Englanders a chance to speak their minds. This early experience encouraged the growth of democratic ideas in New England.

Puritan laws were strict. About 15 crimes carried the death penalty. One crime punishable by death was witchcraft. In 1692, Puritans in Salem Village executed 20 men and women as witches.

Economy New England was a difficult land for colonists. The rocky soil was poor for farming. After a time, however, Native Americans taught English settlers how to grow many crops, such as Indian corn, pumpkins, squash, and beans.

Although the soil was poor, the forests were full of riches. Settlers hunted wild turkey and deer. Settlers also cut down trees and floated them to sawmills near ports such as Boston, Massachusetts, or Portsmouth, New Hampshire. These cities grew into major shipbuilding centers.

Other New Englanders fished for cod and halibut. In the 1600s, people began to hunt whales. Whales supplied oil for lamps and other products. In the 1700s and 1800s, whaling grew into a big business.

Decline of the Puritans During the 1700s, the Puritan tradition declined. Fewer families left England for religious reasons. Ministers had less influence on the way colonies were governed. Nevertheless, the Puritans had stamped New England with their distinctive customs and their dream of a religious society.

★ ★ ★ Section 1 Assessment ★ ★ ★

Recall

1. **Identify** Explain the significance of (a) Puritans, (b) John Winthrop, (c) General Court, (d) Thomas Hooker, (e) Fundamental Orders of Connecticut, (f) Roger Williams, (g) Anne Hutchinson, (h) Metacom.
2. **Define** (a) religious tolerance, (b) Sabbath, (c) town meeting.

Comprehension

3. Why did the Puritans settle the Massachusetts Bay Colony?
4. Why did Thomas Hooker leave the colony?
5. Discuss how the settlement affected Native Americans.
6. What was the purpose of the town meeting?

Critical Thinking and Writing

7. **Exploring the Main Idea** Review the Main Idea statement at the beginning of this section. Then, write a paragraph about how religion and politics affected the development of the New England Colonies.
8. **Drawing Conclusions** The way in which the Puritans governed the Massachusetts Bay Colony led to its success. List arguments to support this viewpoint. Then, list arguments that do not support this statement.

ACTIVITY

Writing a Persuasive Letter You have followed Roger Williams to Rhode Island. Write a letter persuading some friends from Massachusetts to join you.

2 The Middle Colonies

Prepare to Read

Objectives

In this section, you will
- Explain why the colony of New Netherland became the colony of New York.
- Identify why New Jersey separated from New York.
- Describe how Pennsylvania was founded.
- Summarize life in the Middle Colonies.

Key Terms

patroon

proprietary colony

royal colony

Quakers

Pennsylvania Dutch

cash crop

Target Reading Skill

Main Idea Copy the concept web below. As you read, fill in the blank ovals with important facts about the settlement of the Middle Colonies. Add as many ovals as you need.

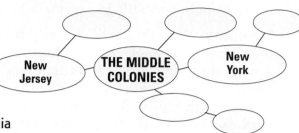

Main Idea The Middle Colonies attracted a wide variety of immigrants who settled on farms and in the cities of Philadelphia and New York.

A chair from colonial Philadelphia

Setting the Scene A doctor from the colony of Maryland traveled north to Philadelphia in the summer of 1744. Dr. Hamilton kept his eyes open to see how the customs in that city differed from those of Maryland. Merchants opened for business much earlier, he discovered: at five in the morning. For dinner at a tavern, Hamilton sat around a single large table with 24 other diners. Unfortunately, the "great hall [was] well stocked with flies," he complained.

However, what most surprised Hamilton was the variety of people at the table:

> ❝ I dined at a tavern with a very mixed company of different nations and religions. There were Scots, English, Dutch, Germans, and Irish. There were Roman Catholics, Church [of England] men, Presbyterians, Quakers, . . . Moravians . . . and one Jew. ❞
> —Alexander Hamilton, *Itinerarium*, 1744

By 1700, England had four colonies in the region south of New England. These colonies became known as the Middle Colonies because they were located between New England and the Southern Colonies. As Dr. Hamilton observed, the Middle Colonies had a much greater mix of people than either New England or the Southern Colonies.

New Netherland Becomes New York

As you have read, the Dutch set up the colony of New Netherland along the Hudson River. In the colony's early years, settlers traded with Indians for furs and built the settlement of New Amsterdam into a thriving port. Since beaver skins were very valuable, most people came to the colonies to trade furs.

To encourage farming in New Netherland, Dutch officials granted large parcels of land to a few rich families. A single land grant could stretch for miles. Indeed, one grant was as big as Rhode Island! Owners of these huge estates were called **patroons.** In return for the grant, each patroon promised to settle at least 50 European farm families on the land. Few farmers wanted to work for the patroons, however. Patroons had great power and could charge whatever rents they pleased.

Most settlers lived in the trading center of New Amsterdam. They came from all over Europe. Many were attracted by the chance to practice their religion freely. African slaves were in demand as well. In the early years they made up more than a quarter of the population of the town.

Dutch colonists were mainly Protestants who belonged to the Dutch Reformed Church. Still, they permitted members of other religions—including Roman Catholics, French Protestants, and Jews—to buy land. "People do not seem concerned what religion their neighbor is," wrote a shocked visitor from Virginia. "Indeed, they do not seem to care if he has any religion at all."

By 1664, the rivalry between England and the Netherlands for trade and colonies was at its height. In August of that year, English warships entered New Amsterdam's harbor. Peter Stuyvesant (STI vuh sehnt), the governor of New Netherland, swore to defend the city. However, he had few weapons and little gunpowder. Also, Stuyvesant had made himself so unpopular with his harsh rule and heavy taxes that the colonists refused to help him. In the end, he surrendered without firing a shot.

King Charles II of England then gave New Netherland to his brother, the Duke of York. He renamed the colony New York in the duke's honor.

New Jersey Separates From New York

At the time of the English takeover, New York stretched as far south as the Delaware River. The Duke of York decided that the colony was too big to govern easily. He gave some of the land to friends, Lord Berkeley and Sir George Carteret. They set up a proprietary (proh PRI uh tehr ee) colony, which they called New Jersey, in 1664.

In setting up a **proprietary colony,** the king gave land to one or more people in return for a yearly payment. These proprietors were free to divide the land and rent it to others. They made laws for the colony but had to respect the rights of colonists under English law.

Like New York, New Jersey had fertile farmland and a wealth of other resources that attracted people from many lands. Settlers came from Finland, Ireland, Scotland, Germany, and Sweden. There were also English and Dutch settlers who moved there from the colony of New York. In addition, some New England colonists, hoping to find better farmland, chose to relocate to New Jersey.

In 1702, New Jersey became a **royal colony,** which is a colony under the direct control of the English crown. The colony's charter protected religious freedom and the rights of an assembly that voted on local matters.

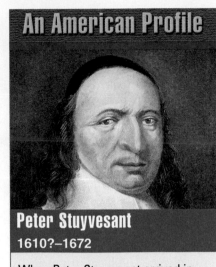

An American Profile

Peter Stuyvesant
1610?–1672

When Peter Stuyvesant arrived in New Amsterdam in 1647, the town was in chaos. "I shall govern you as a father his children," he told the colonists. On his orders, roaming pigs were fenced in. Outdoor toilets were removed from public streets. A new police force patrolled the town after dark. With his big sword, heavy mustache, and silver-tipped wooden leg, Stuyvesant was a commanding sight. Many colonists disliked him. They said he dressed like a one-legged peacock and that he ruled them like the czar of Russia. Even so, Stuyvesant restored law and order in New Amsterdam.

How does your town or county protect the health and safety of its citizens?

Identify Supporting Details

List the subheads under "The Founding of Pennsylvania." As you read, list one or two facts about each subhead.

The Founding of Pennsylvania

West of New Jersey, William Penn founded the colony of Pennsylvania in 1681. Penn came from a wealthy English family and was a personal friend of King Charles II. At age 22, however, Penn shocked family and friends by joining the **Quakers,** one of the most despised religious groups in England.

The Quakers Like Pilgrims and Puritans, Quakers were Protestant reformers. Their reforms went further than those of other groups, however. Quakers believed that all people—men and women, nobles and commoners—were equal in God's sight. They allowed women to preach in public and refused to bow or remove their hats in the presence of nobles. Quakers spoke out against all war and refused to serve in the army.

To most English people, Quaker beliefs seemed wicked. In both England and New England, Quakers were arrested, fined, or even hanged for their ideas. Penn became convinced that the Quakers must leave England. He turned to the king for help.

Charles II issued a royal charter naming Penn proprietor of a large tract of land in North America. The king named the new colony Pennsylvania, or Penn's woodlands.

A Policy of Fairness Penn thought of his colony as a "holy experiment." He wanted it to be a model of religious freedom, peace, and Christian living. Protestants, Catholics, and Jews went to Pennsylvania to escape persecution. Later, English officials forced Penn to turn away Catholic and Jewish settlers.

Penn's Quaker beliefs led him to speak out for fair treatment of Native Americans. Penn believed that the land in North America belonged to the Indians. He insisted that settlers should pay for the land. Native Americans respected him for this policy. As a result, Pennsylvania colonists enjoyed many years of peace with their Indian neighbors. One settler remarked, "as Penn treated the Indians with extraordinary humanity, they became civil and loving to us."

The Colony Grows Penn sent pamphlets describing his colony all over Europe. Soon, settlers from England, Scotland, Wales, the Netherlands, France, and Germany began to cross the Atlantic Ocean to Pennsylvania.

Among the new arrivals were large numbers of German-speaking Protestants. They became known as **Pennsylvania Dutch** because people could not pronounce the word Deutsch (DOICH), which means German. African slaves were also brought to Pennsylvania. They made up about one third of all new arrivals to the colony between 1730 and 1750. Most stayed in Philadelphia, working as laborers.

Penn carefully planned a capital city along the Delaware River. He named it Philadelphia, a Greek word meaning "brotherly love." Philadelphia grew quickly. By 1710, a visitor wrote that it was "the most noble, large, and well-built city I have seen."

Delaware For a time, Pennsylvania included some lands along the lower Delaware River. The region was known as Pennsylvania's Lower Counties.

Primary Source

A Letter to the Native Americans

Before he would allow people to settle his colony, William Penn insisted on establishing good relations with the Native Americans. He wrote this letter:

"The king of the country where I live hath given me a great province, but I desire to enjoy it with your love and consent, that we may always live together as neighbors and friends, else what would the great God say to us, who hath made us not to devour and destroy one another, but live soberly and kindly together in the world. . . ."

—William Penn, Letter to the Indians, 1681

Analyzing Primary Sources
How does Penn explain his belief about living peacefully with Native Americans?

Settlers in the Lower Counties did not want to send delegates to a distant assembly in Philadelphia. In 1701, Penn allowed them to elect their own assembly. Later, in 1704, the Lower Counties would break away to form the colony of Delaware.

Life in the Middle Colonies

The majority of the people made their living by farming. Farmers found more favorable conditions in the Middle Colonies than in New England. The broad Hudson and Delaware river valleys were rich and fertile. Winters were milder than in New England, and the growing season lasted longer.

A Thriving Economy in the Eastern Counties On such promising land, farmers in the eastern counties of the Middle Colonies cleared their fields. They raised wheat, barley, and rye. These were **cash crops,** or crops that are sold for money at market. In fact, the Middle Colonies exported so much grain that they became known as the Breadbasket Colonies.

Farmers of the Middle Colonies also raised herds of cattle and pigs. Every year, they sent tons of beef, pork, and butter to the ports of New York and Philadelphia. From there, the goods went by ship to New England and the South or to the West Indies, England, and other parts of Europe.

Farms in the Middle Colonies were generally larger than those in New England. Landowners hired workers to help with the planting, harvesting, and other tasks. Enslaved African Americans worked on a few large farms. However, most workers were farmhands who worked alongside the families that owned the land.

Aside from farmers, there were also skilled artisans in the Middle Colonies. Encouraged by William Penn, skilled German craftsworkers set up shop in Pennsylvania. In time, the colony became a center of manufacturing and crafts. One visitor reported that workshops turned out "hardware, clocks, watches, locks, guns, flints, glass, stoneware, nails, [and] paper."

Settlers in the Delaware River valley profited from the region's rich deposits of iron ore. Heating the ore in furnaces, they purified it and then hammered it into nails, tools, and parts for guns.

Middle Colony Homes Because houses tended to be far apart in the Middle Colonies, towns were less important than in New England. Counties, rather than villages, became centers of local government.

The different groups who settled the Middle Colonies had their own favorite ways of building. Swedish settlers introduced log cabins to the Americas. The Dutch used red bricks to build narrow, high-walled

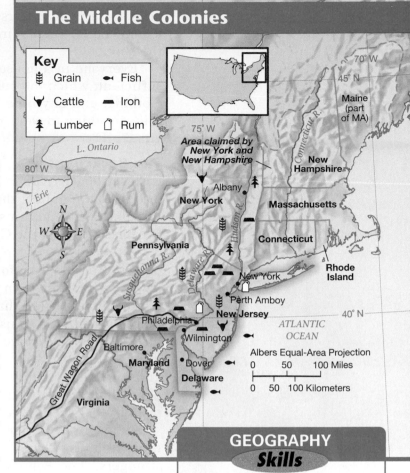

The Middle Colonies

Key
- Grain
- Cattle
- Lumber
- Fish
- Iron
- Rum

GEOGRAPHY
Skills

The Middle Colonies were located to the south and west of New England and north of the Southern Colonies.

1. **Location** On the map, locate: **(a)** New York, **(b)** New Jersey, **(c)** Pennsylvania, **(d)** Delaware, **(e)** Hudson River, **(f)** Philadelphia, **(g)** Great Wagon Road.

2. **Movement** Identify two ways settlers could have traveled inland from the Atlantic coast.

3. **Critical Thinking Analyzing Information** Based on the map, why do you think Philadelphia would become a major trading center?

houses. German settlers developed a wood-burning stove that heated a home better than a fireplace, which let blasts of cold air leak down the chimney.

Everyone in a household had a job to do. Households were self-sufficient, which meant that everything needed for survival—food, clothing, and any other items—was made at home. As one farmer said, "Nothing to wear, eat, or drink was purchased, as my farm provided all."

The Backcountry In the 1700s, thousands of German and Scotch-Irish settlers arrived in Philadelphia. From there, they traveled west into the backcountry, the area of land along the eastern slopes of the Appalachian Mountains. Settlers followed an old Iroquois trail that became known as the Great Wagon Road.

Although settlers planned to follow farming methods they had used in Europe, they found the challenge of farming the backcountry more difficult than they had thought it would be. To farm the backcountry, settlers had to clear thick forests. From Indians, settlers learned how to use knots from pine trees as candles to light their homes. They made wooden dishes from logs, gathered honey from hollows in trees, and hunted wild animals for food. German gunsmiths developed a lightweight rifle for use in forests. Sharpshooters boasted that the "Pennsylvania rifle" could hit a rattlesnake between the eyes at 100 yards.

Many of the settlers who arrived in the backcountry moved onto Indian lands. "The Indians . . . are alarmed at the swarm of strangers," one Pennsylvania official reported. "We are afraid of a [fight] between them for the [colonists] are very rough to them." On more than one occasion, disputes between settlers and Indians resulted in violence.

★ ★ ★ Section 2 Assessment ★ ★ ★

Recall

1. **Identify** Explain the significance of **(a)** Peter Stuyvesant, **(b)** William Penn, **(c)** Quakers, **(d)** Pennsylvania Dutch.
2. **Define** **(a)** patroon, **(b)** proprietary colony, **(c)** royal colony, **(d)** cash crop.

Comprehension

3. How did New Netherland become New York?
4. Why did New Jersey become a proprietary colony?
5. Why did the Quakers settle Pennsylvania?
6. How did life in the Middle Colonies differ from life in the backcountry?

Critical Thinking and Writing

7. **Exploring the Main Idea** Review the Main Idea statement at the beginning of this section. Then, write a paragraph explaining why settlers were attracted to the Middle Colonies.
8. **Comparing** **(a)** How was Penn's "holy experiment" like the Puritan idea of setting an example for the world? **(b)** How was it different?

ACTIVITY

Go Online
PHSchool.com

Connecting to Today
Descendants of the Pennsylvania Dutch still live in Pennsylvania today. Use the Internet to find out about the Pennsylvania Dutch. Write a brief report or create a short Powerpoint presentation describing how and where they live. For help in completing the activity, visit PHSchool.com, **Web Code mfd-0401.**

3 The Southern Colonies

Prepare to Read

Objectives

In this section, you will
- Explain Maryland's religious beginnings.
- Describe how the Carolinas and Georgia were founded.
- Identify two ways of life that developed in the Southern Colonies.
- Summarize slave trade growth in the 1700s.

Key Terms

Mason-Dixon Line

Act of Toleration

Bacon's Rebellion

indigo

debtor

slave code

racism

Target Reading Skill

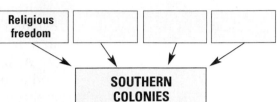

Cause and Effect Copy the chart below. As you read, complete the chart to show the causes that led to the founding of the Southern Colonies. Add as many boxes as you need.

```
[Religious freedom]  [       ]  [       ]  [       ]
           ↓            ↓          ↓          ↓
              [SOUTHERN COLONIES]
```

Main Idea The large tobacco and rice plantations of the Tidewater region contrasted with the settlements of hunters and farmers in the backcountry.

Setting the Scene In 1763, two English surveyors, Charles Mason and Jeremiah Dixon, began a remarkable journey that lasted nearly four years. Their mission was to survey the 244-mile boundary between Pennsylvania and Maryland.

Mason and Dixon used surveyors' instruments and long chains to map their line. As they went, they carefully laid stone markers on the border between the two colonies. If the line crossed a river, they stretched chains across to measure. If the line went up hills or through swamps, Mason and Dixon followed. More than once, fierce thunderstorms swirled around them:

> 66 The Lightning . . . continued [in] streams or streaks, from the Cloud to the ground all round us; about 5 minutes before the hurricane of wind and Rain; the Cloud from the Western part of the Mountain put on the most Dreadful appearance I ever saw . . . 99
>
> —Charles Mason *Journal*, August 4, 1766

Charles Mason and Jeremiah Dixon

The **Mason-Dixon Line** was more than just the boundary between Pennsylvania and Maryland. It also divided the Middle Colonies from the Southern Colonies. South of the Mason-Dixon Line, the Southern Colonies developed a way of life different in many ways from that of the other English colonies.

Lord Baltimore's Colony of Maryland

In 1632, Sir George Calvert persuaded King Charles I to grant him land for a colony in the Americas. Calvert had ruined his career in Protestant England by becoming a Roman Catholic. Now, he planned to build a colony where Catholics could practice their religion freely.

He named the colony Maryland in honor of Queen Henrietta Maria, the king's wife.

Calvert died before his colony could get underway. His son Cecil, Lord Baltimore, pushed on with the project.

Settling the Colony In the spring of 1634, about 200 colonists landed along the upper Chesapeake Bay, across from England's first southern colony, Virginia. Maryland was truly a land of plenty. Chesapeake Bay was full of fish, oysters, and crabs. Across the bay, Virginians were already growing tobacco for profit. Maryland's new settlers hoped to do the same.

Remembering the early problems at Jamestown, the newcomers avoided the swampy lowlands. They built their first town, St. Mary's, in a drier location.

As proprietor of the colony, Lord Baltimore appointed a governor and a council of advisers. He gave colonists a role in government by creating an elected assembly. Eager to attract settlers to Maryland, Lord Baltimore made generous land grants to anyone who brought over servants, women, and children.

A few women took advantage of Lord Baltimore's offer of land. Two sisters, Margaret and Mary Brent, arrived in Maryland in 1638 with nine male servants. In time, they set up two plantations of about 1,000 acres each. Later, Margaret Brent helped prevent a rebellion among the governor's soldiers. The Maryland assembly praised her efforts, saying that "the colony's safety at any time [was better] in her hands than in any man's."

Religious Tolerance To make sure Maryland continued to grow, Lord Baltimore welcomed Protestants as well as Catholics to the colony.

Later, Lord Baltimore came to fear that Protestants might try to deprive Catholics of their right to worship freely. In 1649, he asked the assembly to pass an **Act of Toleration**. The law provided religious freedom for all Christians. As in many colonies, this freedom did not extend to Jews.

Bacon's Rebellion Meanwhile, English settlers continued to arrive in Virginia, attracted by the promise of profits from tobacco. Wealthy planters, however, controlled the best lands near the coast. Newcomers had to push farther inland, onto Indian lands.

As in New England, conflicts over land led to fighting between some white settlers and Indians. After several bloody clashes, settlers called on the governor to take action against Native Americans. The governor refused. He was unwilling to act, in part because he profited from his own fur trade with Indians. Frontier settlers were furious.

Finally, in 1676, Nathaniel Bacon, an ambitious young planter, organized angry men and women on the frontier. He raided Native American villages, regardless of whether the Indians there had been friendly to the colonists or not. Then, he led his followers to Jamestown and burned the capital.

The uprising, known as **Bacon's Rebellion,** lasted only a short time. When Bacon died suddenly, the revolt fell apart. The governor hanged 23 of Bacon's followers. Still, he could not stop English settlers from moving onto Indian lands along the frontier.

The Carolinas

South of Virginia and Maryland, English colonists settled in a region which they called the Carolinas. In 1663, a group of eight English nobles received a grant of land from King Charles II. Settlement took place in two separate areas, one in the north and the other in the south.

In the northern part of the Carolinas, settlers were mostly poor tobacco farmers who had drifted south from Virginia. They tended to have small farms. Eventually, in 1712, the colony became known as North Carolina.

Farther south, the group of eight English nobles set up a larger colony. The largest settlement, Charles Town, sprang up where the Ashley and Cooper rivers met. Later, Charles Town's name was shortened to Charleston. The colony became known as South Carolina in 1719.

Most early settlers in Charleston were English people who had been living in Barbados, a British colony in the Caribbean. Later, other immigrants arrived, including Germans, Swiss, French Protestants, and Spanish Jews.

Rise of Plantation Slavery Around 1685, a few planters discovered that rice grew well in the swampy lowlands along the coast. However, they were unable to grow rich crops until Africans from rice-growing areas of Africa arrived in the colony. Before long, Carolina rice was a profitable crop traded around the world. Settlers in southern Carolina later learned to raise **indigo,** a plant used to make a valuable blue dye.

Carolina planters needed large numbers of workers to grow rice. At first, they tried to enslave local Indians; however, many Indians died of disease or mistreatment, while others escaped into the forests.

Planters then turned to Africa for slave labor. By 1700, most people coming to Charleston were African men and women brought against their will. Soon, enslaved Africans in South Carolina outnumbered Europeans by more than two to one. On the mainland of North America, South Carolina was the only English colony where enslaved Africans made up the majority of the population.

Georgia

The last of England's 13 colonies was carved out of the southern part of South Carolina. James Oglethorpe, a respected English soldier and energetic reformer, founded Georgia in 1732. He wanted the new colony to be a

GEOGRAPHY Skills

The five Southern Colonies stretched along the Atlantic coast from Maryland to Georgia. Farm products and lumber were important to the economy of the region.

1. **Location** On the map, locate: **(a)** Maryland, **(b)** Virginia, **(c)** North Carolina, **(d)** South Carolina, **(e)** Georgia, **(f)** Chesapeake Bay, **(g)** Charles Town.

2. **Place** Describe the area where cattle herding took place.

3. **Critical Thinking Comparing** Compare this map to the maps on pages 103 and 111. **(a)** What crops were grown only in the Southern Colonies? **(b)** Why do you think such products were not grown farther north?

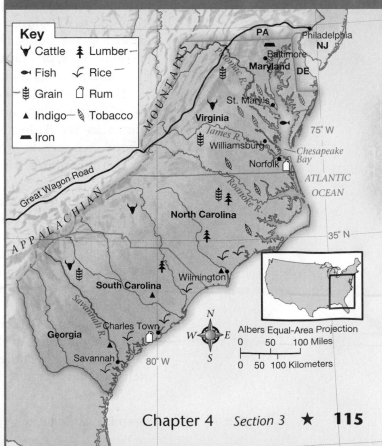

The Southern Colonies

Key
- Cattle
- Fish
- Grain
- Indigo
- Iron
- Lumber
- Rice
- Rum
- Tobacco

Recognizing Multiple Causes

A cause makes something happen. Why did James Oglethorpe found Georgia?

place where **debtors,** or people who owed money they could not pay back, could make a fresh start.

Under English law, the government could imprison debtors until they paid what they owed. If they ever got out of jail, debtors often had no money and no place to live. Oglethorpe offered to pay for debtors and other poor people to travel to Georgia. "In America," he said, "there are enough fertile lands to feed all the poor of England."

In 1733, Oglethorpe and 120 colonists built the colony's first settlement at Savannah, above the Savannah River. Oglethorpe set strict rules for the colony. Farms could be no bigger than 500 acres, and slavery was forbidden.

At first, Georgia grew slowly. Later, however, Oglethorpe changed the rules to allow large plantations and slave labor. After that, the colony grew more quickly.

Two Ways of Life

Today, we often think of the colonial South as a land where wealthy planters lived in elegant homes, with large numbers of enslaved Africans toiling in the fields or serving in the planter's house. In fact, this picture is only partly true. As the Southern Colonies grew, two distinct ways of life emerged—one along the Atlantic coast and another in the backcountry.

Tidewater Plantations The Southern Colonies enjoyed warmer weather and a longer growing season than the colonies to the north. Virginia, Maryland, and parts of North Carolina all became major tobacco-growing areas. Settlers in South Carolina and Georgia raised rice and indigo.

Colonists soon found that it was most profitable to raise tobacco and rice on large plantations. As you recall, a plantation is a large estate farmed by many workers. On these southern plantations, anywhere from 20 to 100 slaves did most of the work. Most enslaved Africans worked in the fields. Others were skilled workers, such as carpenters, barrel makers, or blacksmiths. Still other enslaved Africans worked in the main house as cooks, servants, or housekeepers.

The earliest planters settled along rivers and creeks of the coastal plain. Because the land was washed by ocean tides, the region was known as the Tidewater. The Tidewater's gentle slopes and rivers offered rich farmland for plantations.

Farther inland, planters settled along rivers. Rivers provided an easy way to move goods to market. Planters loaded crops onto ships bound for the West Indies and Europe. On the return trip, the ships carried English manufactured goods and other luxuries for planters and their families.

Most Tidewater plantations had their own docks along the river, and merchant ships picked up crops and delivered goods directly to them. For this reason, few large seaport cities developed in the Southern Colonies.

Only a small percentage of white southerners owned large plantations. Yet, planters set the style of southern living. Life centered around the Great House. There, the planter's family lived in elegant quarters, including a parlor for visitors, a dining room, and guest bedrooms.

Charleston,
South Carolina

Drayton Hall

By the 1700s, there were plantations in South Carolina that produced cash crops such as rice, tobacco, and indigo. One plantation in Charleston, South Carolina, was Drayton Hall. Completed in 1742, it is one of the oldest surviving plantation houses in the South.

Go **Online**
PHSchool.com

Virtual Field Trip For an interactive look at the Drayton Hall, visit PHSchool.com, **Web Code mfd-0402.**

During the growing season, planters decided which fields to plant, what crops to grow, and when to harvest the crops. Planters' wives kept the household running smoothly. They directed house slaves and made sure daily tasks were done, such as milking cows.

Enslaved Africans played a crucial role on many plantations. They used farming skills they had brought from West Africa. With their help, English settlers learned how to grow rice. Africans also knew how to use wild plants unfamiliar to the English. They made water buckets out of gourds, and they used palmetto leaves to make fans, brooms, and baskets.

The Backcountry South West of the Tidewater, life was very different. Here, at the base of the Appalachians, rolling hills and thick forests covered the land. As in the Middle Colonies, this inland area was called the backcountry. Attracted by rich soil, settlers followed the Great Wagon Road into the backcountry of Maryland, Virginia, and the Carolinas.

The backcountry was more democratic than the Tidewater. Settlers there were more likely to treat one another as equals. Men tended smaller fields of tobacco or garden crops such as beans, corn, or peas. They also hunted game. Largely self-sufficient, these farmers provided all the food they needed. Surplus goods were sold at local markets. Women cooked meals and fashioned simple, rugged clothing out of wool or deerskins. Another major difference between the backcountry and the Tidewater was slavery. Few enslaved Africans worked on the smaller farms in the backcountry.

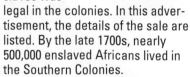
The hardships of backcountry life brought settlers closer together. Families gathered to husk corn or help one another build barns. Spread out along the edge of the Appalachians, these hardy settlers felled trees, grew crops, and changed the face of the land.

Growth of Slavery and the Slave Trade

In the early years, Africans in the English colonies included free people and servants as well as enslaved persons. Indeed, during the 1600s, even Africans who were enslaved enjoyed some privileges. The first enslaved Africans arrived in Virginia in 1619. However, for the next fifty years, since the African population was small, the status of Africans in the colony was not clearly established. Some Africans were enslaved and some became servants. There were instances where enslaved Africans could purchase their freedom. Several Africans during the 1600s, such as Anthony Johnson, became successful property owners. In South Carolina some enslaved Africans worked without supervision as cowboys, herding cattle to market.

By 1700, plantations in the Southern Colonies had come to rely on slave labor. After a time, enslaved Africans made up the majority of the population in South Carolina and Georgia. They cleared the land, worked the crops, and tended the livestock. In order to maintain the supply of slaves, southern planters relied on a system of slave trading that stretched halfway across the globe.

Slavery in Africa In Africa, as elsewhere around the world, slavery had been part of the social and economic system since ancient times. Usually, slaves were people who had been captured in war. Slaves were part of a community and were treated as servants. Most were enslaved for a specific period of time, and then they became free again. Traders often transported and sold slaves as laborers. Muslim merchants also carried enslaved Africans into Europe and the Middle East.

Over a period of less than 400 years, as the transatlantic slave trade grew, millions of Africans were enslaved. Slave traders from European nations set up posts along the West African coast. They offered guns and other goods in exchange for Africans. As the demand for cheap labor increased, Africans who lived along the coast made raids into the interior, seeking captives to sell to the Europeans. They marched their captives to the coast. There, the Africans were loaded aboard European ships headed for the Americas.

The Middle Passage In the 1700s, English sailors began referring to the passage of slave-trading ships west across the Atlantic Ocean as the Middle Passage. Below the decks of these ships, enslaved

Africans were crammed tightly together on shelves. One observer noted that they were "chained to each other hand and foot, and stowed so close, that they were not allowed above a foot and a half for each in breadth." The captives were allowed above deck to eat and exercise in the fresh air only once or twice a day.

Many enslaved Africans resisted, but only a few escaped. Some fought for their freedom during the trip. They would stage a mutiny or revolt. The slave traders lived in fear of this and were heavily armed. Other slaves resisted by refusing to eat or by committing suicide by jumping overboard to avoid a life of enslavement.

Records of slave-trading ships show that about 10 percent of Africans loaded aboard a ship for passage to the Americas died during the voyage. Many died of illnesses that spread rapidly in the filthy, crowded conditions inside a ship's hold. Others died of mistreatment. This slave trade lasted about 400 years. During that time, it may have caused the deaths of as many as 2 to 3 million Africans.

Limiting Rights As the importance of slavery increased, greater limits were placed on the rights of slaves. Colonists passed laws that set out rules for slaves' behavior and denied slaves basic human rights. These **slave codes** treated enslaved Africans not as human beings but as property.

Most English colonists did not question the justice of owning slaves. They believed that black Africans were inferior to white Europeans. The belief that one race is superior to another is called **racism.** Some colonists believed that they were helping enslaved Africans by teaching them Christianity.

A handful of colonists spoke out against the evils of slavery. In 1688, Quakers in Germantown, Pennsylvania, became the first group of colonists to call for an end to slavery.

★ ★ ★ Section 3 Assessment ★ ★ ★

Recall

1. **Identify** Explain the significance of **(a)** Mason-Dixon Line, **(b)** Lord Baltimore, **(c)** Act of Toleration, **(d)** Bacon's Rebellion, **(e)** James Oglethorpe.
2. **Define** **(a)** indigo, **(b)** debtor, **(c)** slave code, **(d)** racism.

Comprehension

3. Why did Lord Baltimore set up the colony of Maryland?
4. Why was Georgia called a "haven for debtors"?
5. How was life in the Tidewater different from life in the backcountry South?

6. What role did Africans play in the economy of the Southern Colonies by 1700?

Critical Thinking and Writing

7. **Exploring the Main Idea** Review the Main Idea statement at the beginning of this section. List the reasons why you think tensions might have developed between the backcountry and the Tidewater.
8. **Analyzing Information** Review the discussion of religious tolerance. Did Maryland's Act of Toleration provide true religious tolerance? Write your answer in a paragraph.

ACTIVITY

Creating Flashcards Do you get confused about the 13 English colonies? Use the text, including the maps and charts, to create 13 flashcards. On one side, write the name of a colony. On the other, write three facts about that colony. You may later use these cards for review.

4 Roots of Self-Government

Prepare to Read

Objectives

In this section, you will
- Summarize why England wanted to regulate colonial trade.
- Describe colonial governments.
- Explain how the liberties of the colonists were limited.

Key Terms

mercantilism

export

import

Navigation Acts

Yankee

triangular trade

legislature

Glorious Revolution

bill of rights

English Bill of Rights

Target Reading Skill

Clarifying Meaning As you read, prepare an outline of this section. Use roman numerals to indicate the major headings, capital letters for subheadings, and numbers for the supporting details. The sample below will help you get started.

```
I.  England Regulates Trade
    A.
        1.
        2.
II. Trade in Rum and Slaves
    A.
    B.
    C.
III. Colonial Government
```

Main Idea During the late 1600s and 1700s, England regulated colonial trade, while colonial legislatures passed laws.

Horse-drawn carriage

Setting the Scene

Young Stephen Lamb hardly had time to look up before it was too late. A horse-drawn cart raced by, and the next instant Stephen was pulled beneath the wheels. One of Boston's newspapers reported the sad news: "A Child of about Five Years old, at the South End of the Town, was run over by a Cart, and died immediately after."

The streets in colonial cities like Boston had become busy—and sometimes dangerous—by the early 1700s. Farmers drove cattle, pigs, and sheep to market along narrow cobblestone streets. New York merchants complained that "Mischievous Mastiffs, Bull Doggs and Other Useless Dogs" chased their cattle and horses. Philadelphia spaced wooden posts along both sides of its main streets. The posts protected pedestrians from the "excessive Galloping, Trotting & Pacing of Horses."

Colonial city streets were becoming hazardous because there was so much activity. By the 1700s, trade flourished all along the Atlantic coast. As trade increased, England began to take a new interest in its colonies.

England Regulates Trade

Like other European nations at the time, England believed that its colonies should benefit the home country. This belief was part of an economic theory known as mercantilism (MER kuhn tihl ihz uhm). According to this theory, a nation became strong by keeping strict control over its trade. As one English gentleman put it, "Whosoever commands the trade of the world commands the riches of the world."

Mercantilists thought that a country should export more than it imported. **Exports** are goods sent to markets outside a country. **Imports** are goods brought into a country. If England sold more goods abroad, gold would flow into the home country as payment for those exports.

Beginning in the 1650s, the English Parliament passed a series of Navigation Acts that regulated trade between England and its colonies. The purpose of these laws was to ensure that only England benefited from colonial trade.

Under the new laws, only colonial or English ships could carry goods to and from the colonies. The Navigation Acts also listed certain products, such as tobacco and cotton, that colonial merchants could ship only to England. In this way, Parliament created jobs for English workers who cut and rolled tobacco or spun cotton into cloth.

The Navigation Acts helped the colonies as well as England. For example, the law encouraged colonists to build their own ships. As a result, New England became a prosperous shipbuilding center. Also, because of the acts, colonial merchants did not have to compete with foreign merchants because they were sure of having a market for their goods in England.

Still, many colonists resented the Navigation Acts. In their view, the laws favored English merchants. Colonial merchants often ignored the Navigation Acts or found ways to get around them.

Trade in Rum and Slaves

The colonies produced a wide variety of goods, and merchant ships sailed up and down the Atlantic coast. Merchants from New England dominated colonial trade. They were known as Yankees, a nickname that implied they were clever and hardworking. Yankee traders earned a reputation for profiting from any deal.

Colonial merchants developed many trade routes. One route was known as the triangular trade because the three legs of the route formed a triangle. On the first leg, ships from New England carried fish, lumber, and other goods to the West Indies. There, Yankee traders bought molasses—a dark-brown syrup made from sugar cane—and sugar. The ships then sailed back to New England, where colonists used the molasses and sugar to make rum.

On the second leg of the journey, ships carried rum, guns, gunpowder, cloth, and tools from New England to West Africa. In Africa, Yankee merchants traded these goods for slaves. On the final leg, ships carried enslaved Africans to the West Indies. With the profits from selling the enslaved Africans, traders bought more molasses.

Viewing History

A Yankee Trader Some colonial merchants, such as wealthy New England trader Moses Marcy, benefited from the Navigation Acts. **Drawing Inferences** *How can you tell that Moses Marcy is successful?*

New England Colonies

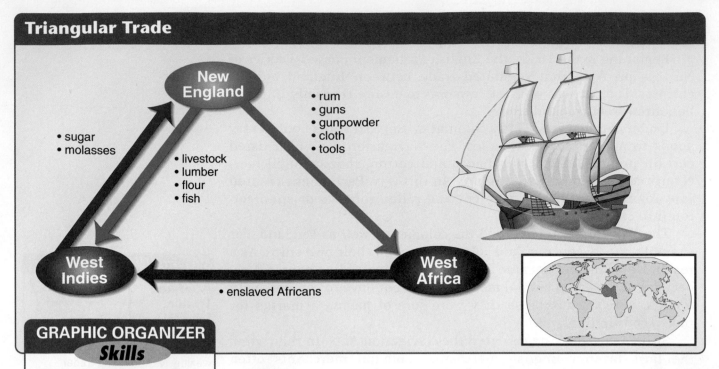

Triangular Trade

New England

• sugar
• molasses

• livestock
• lumber
• flour
• fish

• rum
• guns
• gunpowder
• cloth
• tools

West Indies

West Africa

• enslaved Africans

GRAPHIC ORGANIZER
Skills

Colonists traded with the West Indies, Africa, and Europe in a route known as the triangular trade.

1. **Comprehension**
   (a) What did American ships bring to Africa?
   (b) Where were enslaved Africans traded for molasses?

2. **Critical Thinking Making Decisions**
   How did New England benefit from the slave trade?

Economics $

Many New England merchants grew wealthy from the triangular trade. In doing so, they often disobeyed the Navigation Acts. Traders were supposed to buy sugar and molasses only from English colonies in the West Indies. However, the demand for molasses was so high that New Englanders smuggled in cargoes from the Dutch, French, and Spanish West Indies, too. Bribes made customs officials look the other way.

Colonial Government

Although each colony developed its own government, the governments had much in common. A governor directed the colony's affairs and enforced the laws. Most governors were appointed, either by the king or by the colony's proprietor. In Rhode Island and Connecticut, however, colonists elected their own governors.

Elected Assemblies Each colony also had a legislature. A legislature is a group of people who have the power to make laws. In most colonies, the legislature had an upper house and a lower house. The upper house was made up of advisers appointed by the governor.

The lower house was an elected assembly. It approved laws and protected the rights of citizens. Just as important, it had the right to approve any taxes the governor asked for. This "power of the purse," or right to raise or spend money, was an important check on the governor's power. Any governor who ignored the assembly risked losing his salary.

The Right to Vote Each colony had its own rules about who could vote. By the 1720s, however, all the colonies had laws that restricted the right to vote to white Christian men over the age of 21. In some colonies, only Protestants or members of a particular church could vote. All voters had to own property. Colonial leaders believed that only property owners knew what was best for a colony.

A Bill of Rights Colonists took great pride in their elected assemblies. They also valued the rights that the Magna Carta gave them as English subjects.

Colonists won still more rights as a result of the Glorious Revolution of 1688. Parliament removed King James II from the throne and asked William and Mary of the Netherlands to rule. In return for Parliament's support, William and Mary signed the English Bill of Rights in 1689. A **bill of rights** is a written list of freedoms the government promises to protect.

The **English Bill of Rights** protected the rights of individuals and gave anyone accused of a crime the right to a trial by jury. Just as important, the English Bill of Rights said that a ruler could not raise taxes or an army without the approval of Parliament.

Limits on Liberties

English colonists in the Americas enjoyed more freedoms than did the English themselves. However, the rights of English citizens did not extend to all colonists. Women had more rights in the colonies but far fewer rights than did free, white males. A woman's father or husband was supposed to protect her. A married woman could not start her own business or sign a contract unless her husband approved it.

In most colonies, unmarried women and widows had more rights than married women. They could make contracts and sue in court. In Maryland and the Carolinas, women settlers who headed families could buy land on the same terms as men.

Africans and Native Americans in the colonies had almost no rights. While so many colonists enjoyed English liberties, most Africans were bound in slavery. The conflict between liberty and slavery would not be resolved until the 1860s.

Summarize
Summarize the paragraphs under "Limits on Liberties." Add this information to your outline.

★ ★ ★ **Section 4 Assessment** ★ ★ ★

Recall

1. **Identify** Explain the significance of **(a)** Navigation Acts, **(b)** Yankee, **(c)** Glorious Revolution, **(d)** English Bill of Rights.
2. **Define** **(a)** mercantilism, **(b)** export, **(c)** import, **(d)** triangular trade, **(e)** legislature, **(f)** bill of rights.

Comprehension

3. List two ways in which the Navigation Acts benefited **(a)** England **(b)** the colonies.
4. How were colonial governments organized?
5. Which colonists had the right to vote?

Critical Thinking and Writing

6. **Exploring the Main Idea** Review the Main Idea statement at the beginning of this section. Then, write a paragraph in which you analyze how colonial legislatures reflected the tradition of self-rule.
7. **Making Predictions** How do you think the Navigation Acts might affect future relations between England and the colonies? Write your answer in a paragraph.

ACTIVITY

Start a Dialogue You are a New England merchant who meets with another colonial merchant. Write a conversation you might have about trade in the colonies. Consider the Navigation Acts and triangular trade.

Summarizing

What were the sources of the English colonists' ideas about self-government? As you read different references to learn about these roots, you'll find it helpful to summarize information.

A document deeply rooted in the English concept of representative government is the Magna Carta signed by King John in 1215. These excerpts are from this important document.

(12) No [tax] may be levied in our kingdom without its general consent, unless it is for the ransom of our person, to make our eldest son a knight, and (once) to marry our eldest daughter. For these purposes only a reasonable [tax] may be levied.

(14) To obtain the general consent of the realm for the assessment of a [tax]—except in the three cases specified above—we will cause the archbishops, bishops, abbots, earls, and greater barons to be summoned individually by letter. To those who hold lands directly of us we will cause a general summons to be issued, through the sheriffs and other officials, to come together on a fixed day (of which at least forty days notice shall be given) and at a fixed place. In all letters of summons, the cause of the summons will be stated. When a summons has been issued, the business appointed for the day shall go forward in accordance with the resolution of those present, even if not all those who were summoned have appeared.

—The Magna Carta, 1215

King John signing the Magna Carta

Learn the Skill *To summarize information, use the following steps:*

1. **Identify the main idea.** The main idea of a passage explains its purpose. Usually, the main idea is presented in the first sentence of the passage.

2. **Look for details.** These include facts, reasons, explanations, examples, and descriptions that expand the main idea.

3. **Restate the main idea.** Put the main idea in your own words.

4. **Choose important details.** Select the most significant details to include in your summary. Remember, a summary should be brief and to the point.

Practice the Skill *Answer the following questions about the passages above:*

1. Which sentence contains the main point of these passages?

2. **(a)** What three exceptions are given? **(b)** Who has to approve the assessment of a tax? **(c)** Identify another detail about approving taxes.

3. Restate the main idea in your own words.

4. Complete your summary by adding two important details to go with your main idea statement.

Apply the Skill *See the Chapter Review and Assessment.*

5 Life in the Colonies

Prepare to Read

Objectives

In this section, you will
- List the class differences that existed in colonial society.
- Summarize how the Great Awakening affected the colonies.
- Describe education for colonial children.
- Explain how the colonies were affected by the spread of new ideas.

Key Terms

gentry
middle class
indentured servant
Great Awakening
public school
tutor
apprentice
dame school
Enlightenment
libel

Target Reading Skill

Cause and Effect Copy the cause-and-effect chart at right. As you read, complete the chart to show the effect of different factors in shaping life in the colonies. Add as many entries as you need.

> **CAUSES**
>
> I. Puritan belief in education
> 2.
> 3.
>
> **LIFE IN THE COLONIES**
>
> **EFFECTS**
>
> I. Public school system in New England
> 2.
> 3.

Main Idea During the 1700s, England's 13 colonies became societies with their own ideas and traditions.

Setting the Scene On a warm May day in the 1750s, a parade made its way down a main street in Newport, Rhode Island. Most of the city's Africans had turned out for a holiday known as Negro Election Day. Dressed in their finest clothes, enslaved and free Africans alike sang and marched. One resident recalled:

> 66 All the various languages of Africa, mixed with broken . . . English, filled the air, accompanied with the music of the fiddle, tambourine, the banjo [and African] drum. 99
>
> —Henry Bull, *Memoir of Rhode Island,* 1837

African drum

Similar parades took place throughout New England. Each year, at about the time white New Englanders voted for their colonial government, Africans elected a leader of their community. The winner's job was to settle disputes that arose among black townspeople during the year.

Negro Election Day was a truly American custom, blending traditions from Africa and England. As the American colonies grew in the 1700s, they became more than rough settlements. Gradually, old customs and ideas were being shaped into a new culture that was distinctly American.

Colonial Society

For the most part, colonists enjoyed more social equality than people in England, where a person's opportunities in life were largely determined by birth. Still, class differences existed. Like Europeans, colonial Americans thought it was only natural that some people rank more highly than others. A person's birth and wealth still determined his or her social status.

The Gentry and the Middle Class

At the top of society stood the **gentry.** The gentry included wealthy planters, merchants, ministers, successful lawyers, and royal officials. They could afford to dress in the latest fashions from London.

Below the gentry were the **middle class.** The middle class included farmers who worked their own land, skilled craftsworkers, and some tradespeople. Nearly three quarters of all white colonists belonged to the middle class. They prospered because land in the colonies was plentiful and easy to buy.

Indentured Servants

The lowest social class included hired farmhands, indentured servants, and slaves. **Indentured servants** signed contracts to work without wages for a period of four to seven years for anyone who would pay their ocean passage to the Americas. When their term of service was completed, indentured servants received "freedom dues": a set of clothes, tools, and 50 acres of land. Because there were so few European women in the colonies, female indentured servants often shortened their terms of service by marrying.

Thousands of men, women, and children came to North America as indentured servants. After completing their terms, some became successful and rose into the middle class.

Women's Work in the Colonies

From New Hampshire to Georgia, colonial women performed many of the same tasks. A wife took care of her household, husband, and family. By the kitchen fire, she cooked the family's meals. She milked cows, watched the children, and made clothing.

In the backcountry, wives and husbands often worked side by side in the fields at harvest time. With so much to be done, no one worried whether harvesting was proper "woman's work." One surprised visitor described a backcountry woman's activities: "She will carry a gunn in the woods and kill deer, turkeys &c., shoot down wild cattle, catch and tye hoggs, knock down [cattle] with an ax, and perform the most manfull Exercises as well as most men."

In cities, women sometimes worked outside the home. A young single woman from a poorer family might work for one of the gentry as a maid, a cook, or a nurse. Other women were midwives, who delivered babies. Still others sewed fine hats or dresses to be sold to women who could afford them. Learning such skills often required years of training.

Some women learned trades from their fathers, brothers, or husbands. They worked as butchers, shoemakers, or silversmiths. Quite a few women became printers. A woman might take over her husband's business when he died.

African Cultural Influences

By the mid-1700s, the culture of Africans in the colonies varied greatly. On rice plantations in South Carolina, enslaved Africans used methods from West Africa for growing and harvesting rice. For example, flat baskets holding the grains were waved in the wind to separate the grains from leaves and other particles. Then a wooden mortar and pestle were used to clean the grains.

Primary Source

An Indentured Servant

This is a contract Richard Garfford entered into with Thomas Workman. Garfford wanted to become an indentured servant: "The Condition of this obligation is such that . . . Richard Garfford . . . shall well and truly deliver or cause to be delivered [to] . . . Thomas Workman . . . in Virginia a sound and able man servant between Eighteen and 25 years of age that shall have [four] years to serve at the least, and that [when] the first second or third ship . . . [arrives] in the Port of James Ariver in Virginia from London, that then the bond above [will] be [void] . . ."

—Richard Garfford, 1654

Analyzing Primary Sources

What kind of worker is Thomas Workman looking for?

Identify Causes and Effects

What influence did African culture have on colonial society? Add this information to your chart.

Language is another area where African influences were strong. In some coastal areas, enslaved Africans spoke a distinctive combination of English and West African languages known as **Gullah**. Parents often chose African names for their children, such as Quosh or Juba or Cuff.

In Charleston and other South Carolina port towns, some Africans worked along the dock, making rope or barrels or helping to build ships. Skilled craftsworkers made fine wooden cabinets or silver plates and utensils. Many of their designs reflected African artistic styles. Although most Africans in these towns were enslaved, many opened their own shops or stalls in the market. Some used their earnings to buy their own and their family's freedom.

In the Middle Colonies and New England, the African population increased during the 1700s. As you have read, customs like Negro Election Day became a part of colonial life, especially in cities.

The Great Awakening

In the 1730s and 1740s, a religious movement known as the **Great Awakening** swept through the colonies. Its drama and emotion touched women and men of all backgrounds and classes.

Powerful Preachers A New England preacher, Jonathan Edwards, helped set off the Great Awakening. In powerful sermons, Edwards called on colonists, especially young people, to examine their lives. He preached of the sweetness and beauty of God. At the same time, he warned listeners to heed the Bible's teachings. Otherwise, they would be "sinners in the hands of an angry God," headed for the fiery torments of hell.

In 1739, when an English minister named George Whitefield arrived in the colonies, the movement spread like wildfire. Whitefield drew huge crowds to outdoor meetings. An enthusiastic and energetic preacher, his voice would ring with feeling as he called on sinners to repent. After hearing Whitefield speak, Jonathan Edwards's wife reported, "I have seen upwards of a thousand people hang on his words with breathless silence, broken only by an occasional half-suppressed sob."

Impact of the Great Awakening The Great Awakening aroused bitter debate. People who supported the movement often split away from their old churches to form new ones. Opponents warned that the movement was too emotional. Still, the growth of so many new churches forced colonists to become more tolerant of people with different beliefs.

The Great Awakening contributed in another way to the spread of democratic feelings in the colonies. Many of the new preachers were not as well educated as most ministers. They argued that formal training was less important than a heart filled with the holy spirit. Such teachings encouraged a spirit of independence. Many believers felt more free to challenge authority when their liberties were at stake. People began to think differently about their political rights and their governments. They felt if they could figure out how to worship on their own, then they could govern themselves. Eventually, many of these colonists would challenge British authority.

Viewing History

George Whitefield
George Whitefield was the most popular preacher of the Great Awakening. Nathan Cole, who attended one of Whitefield's sermons said "[he] appeared almost angelical before thousands of people with a bold, [fearless] countenance."
Synthesizing Information
Why did some American preachers oppose preachers like Whitefield?

Education in the Colonies

Among the colonists, New Englanders were the most concerned about education. Puritans taught that all people had a duty to study the Bible. If colonists did not learn to read, how would they fulfill this duty?

New England In 1642, the Massachusetts assembly passed a law ordering all parents to teach their children "to read and understand the principles of religion." They also required all towns with 50 or more families to hire a schoolteacher. Towns with 100 or more families also had to set up a grammar school to prepare boys for college.

In this way, Massachusetts set up the first public schools, or schools supported by taxes. Public schools allowed both rich and poor children to receive an education.

The first New England schools had only one room for students of all ages. Parents paid the schoolteacher with corn, peas, or other foods. Each child was expected to bring a share of wood to burn in the stove. Students who forgot would find themselves seated in the coldest corner of the room!

Middle and Southern Colonies In the Middle Colonies, churches and individual families set up private schools. Because pupils paid to attend, only wealthy families could afford to educate their children.

In the Southern Colonies, people lived too far from one another to bring children together in one school building. Some planters engaged tutors, or private teachers. The wealthiest planters sent their sons to school in England. As a rule, slaves were denied education of any kind.

Apprenticeships and Dame Schools Boys whose parents wished them to learn a trade or craft served as apprentices (uh PREHN tihs ehz). An apprentice worked for a master to learn a trade or a craft. For example, when a boy reached the age of 12 or 13, his parents might apprentice him to a master glassmaker. The young apprentice lived in the glassmaker's home for six or seven years while learning the craft. The glassmaker gave the boy food and clothing. He was also supposed to teach his apprentice how to read and write and provide him with religious training.

In return, the apprentice worked without pay in the glassmaker's shop and learned the skills he needed to set up his own shop. Boys were apprenticed in many trades, including papermaking and printing, and tanning (making leather).

In New England, most schools accepted only boys. However, some girls attended dame schools, or private schools run by women in their own homes. Other girls, though, usually learned skills from their mothers, who taught them to spin wool, weave, and embroider. A few learned to read and write.

Spread of Ideas

During the 1600s, European scientists began to use reason and logic instead of superstition to understand the world. They developed theories, and then performed experiments to test them. In doing so,

▲ **Past**

▲ **Present**

they discovered many of the laws of nature. The English scientist Isaac Newton, for example, explained the law of gravity.

The Enlightenment Spreads European thinkers of the late 1600s and 1700s believed that reason and scientific methods could be applied to the study of society. They tried to discover the natural laws that governed human behavior. Because these thinkers believed in the light of human reason, the movement that they started is known as the Enlightenment. John Locke, an English philosopher, wrote works that were widely read in the colonies. He said people could gain knowledge of the world by observing and by experimenting.

In the 13 colonies, the Enlightenment spread among better educated colonists. They included wealthy merchants, lawyers, ministers, and others who had the leisure to read the latest books from Europe. Urban craftsmen also heard and discussed these ideas.

Benjamin Franklin The best example of the Enlightenment spirit in the 13 colonies was Benjamin Franklin. Franklin was born in 1706, the son of a poor Boston soap and candle maker. Although he had only two years of formal schooling, he used his spare time to study literature, mathematics, and foreign languages.

At age 17, Franklin made his way to Philadelphia. There, he built up a successful printing business. His most popular publication was *Poor Richard's Almanack*. Published yearly, it contained useful information and clever quotes, such as "Early to bed, early to rise, makes a man healthy, wealthy, and wise."

Viewing History

School Days

Students in colonial times attended one-room schools. Usually, they studied subjects that would help them in their daily lives. Today, students attend schools that offer many subjects and the latest technology. Sometimes, students study in special classrooms, such as computer rooms like the one shown here.

Applying Information
(a) How has public education changed since colonial times?
(b) How is it the same?

Like other Enlightenment thinkers, Franklin wanted to use reason to improve the world around him. He invented practical devices such as a lightning rod, a smokeless fireplace, and bifocal glasses. As a community leader, Franklin persuaded Philadelphia officials to pave streets, organize a fire company, and set up the first lending library in the Americas. Franklin's inventions and his public service earned him worldwide fame.

Colonial Cities While most colonists lived on farms, towns and cities strongly influenced colonial life. Through the great ports of Philadelphia, New York, Boston, and Charleston, merchants shipped products overseas. Towns and cities also served as the center of a busy trade between the coast and the growing backcountry.

Culture flourished in the cities. By the mid-1700s, many colonial cities had their own theaters. City dwellers found entertainment at singing societies, traveling circuses, carnivals, and horse races.

In 1704, John Campbell founded the *Boston News-Letter,* the first regular weekly newspaper in the English colonies. Within 50 years, each of the colonies, except New Jersey and Delaware, had at least one weekly paper.

The Trial of John Peter Zenger The growth of colonial newspapers led to a dispute over freedom of the press. John Peter Zenger published the *Weekly Journal* in New York City. In 1734, he was arrested for publishing stories that criticized the governor. Zenger was put on trial for libel—the act of publishing a statement that may unjustly damage a person's reputation. Zenger's lawyer argued that, since the stories were true, his client had not committed libel. The jury agreed and freed Zenger. At the time, the case did not attract a great deal of attention. However, freedom of the press would become recognized as a basic American right.

★ ★ ★ **Section 5 Assessment** ★ ★ ★

Recall

1. **Identify** Explain the significance of **(a)** Great Awakening, **(b)** Jonathan Edwards, **(c)** George Whitefield, **(d)** Enlightenment, **(e)** Benjamin Franklin, **(f)** John Peter Zenger.
2. **Define** **(a)** gentry, **(b)** middle class, **(c)** indentured servant, **(d)** public school, **(e)** tutor, **(f)** apprentice, **(g)** dame school, **(h)** libel.

Comprehension

3. What social classes existed in the colonies?
4. How did the Great Awakening affect religion in the colonies?

5. Why did the Puritans support public education?
6. In what ways did Benjamin Franklin's ideas reflect the ideas of the Enlightenment?

Critical Thinking and Writing

7. **Exploring the Main Idea** Review the Main Idea statement at the beginning of this section. Then, make a list of five statements that support the main idea.
8. **Drawing Inferences** Why do you think there was greater social equality in the colonies than in England?

ACTIVITY

Go Online
PHSchool.com

Preparing a Skit
Use the Internet to find out more about the John Peter Zenger trial. Then, prepare a class skit of the trial. For help in completing the activity, visit PHSchool.com, **Web Code mfd-0403.**

Benjamin Franklin,
Scientist and Inventor

In his day, Benjamin Franklin was a well-known journalist and diplomat. He was also well known for his scientific experiments and inventions.

Benjamin Franklin

Bifocals

After he turned forty, the nearsighted Franklin needed a second pair of glasses for reading. He invented bifocals. Now, he could see objects far away and read—all without changing glasses. Every major optical store still sells bifocals.

Odometer

When he was postmaster, Franklin had to map the mailing routes for surrounding towns. He came up with a simple odometer for his carriage. It counted the number of times the wheels of his wagon rotated on a trip. Today, odometers are used in cars to measure mileage.

Electricity Experiments

Franklin was curious about electricity. In some of his experiments, he used a vacuum pump (shown here). An experiment he tried in 1752 gave him the idea for a lightning rod. Variations of this device protect homes and buildings from lightning to this day.

ACTIVITY

Make a list of at least three inventions that you think would make people's lives easier, healthier, or just more fun. For each of your ideas, explain how you think it might work, whom it would benefit, and if you think it will ever be used.

Review and Assessment

CHAPTER SUMMARY

Section 1
Political and religious reformers settled the New England colonies. Life in the region centered around small towns and villages. Tensions between settlers and Native Americans led to war.

Section 2
A variety of immigrants populated the five Middle Colonies. Skilled artisans and farmers contributed to a thriving economy in this region.

Section 3
The Southern Colonies developed two ways of life—one along the Atlantic coast and one in the backcountry. Slavery became part of the fabric of the economy of the Southern Colonies.

Section 4
Although England controlled the economy of its colonies, self-government emerged over time in the English settlements. Legislatures, the right to vote, and a bill of rights were features of many colonies.

Section 5
The 13 colonies developed their own ideas and traditions during the eighteenth century. Both the Great Awakening and the Enlightenment had a profound impact on the English colonies.

For additional review and enrichment activities, see the interactive version of *The American Nation,* available on the Web and on CD-ROM.

Chapter Self-Test For practice test questions for Chapter 4, visit PHSchool.com, **Web Code mfa-0404.**

Reviewing Key Facts

11. What caused conflicts between the New England colonists and the Native Americans? (Section 1)
12. What policies did William Penn follow in the Pennsylvania Colony? (Section 2)
13. What events caused Nathaniel Bacon and his followers to rebel in 1676? (Section 3)
14. How did England's belief in mercantilism affect the colonies? (Section 4)
15. How did cities influence colonial life? (Section 5)

Building Vocabulary

Review the chapter vocabulary words listed below. Then, use the words and their definitions to create a matching quiz. Exchange quizzes with another student. Check each other's answers when you are finished.

1. religious tolerance
2. town meeting
3. royal colony
4. cash crop
5. indigo
6. mercantilism
7. import
8. bill of rights
9. apprentice
10. libel

Critical Thinking and Writing

16. **Connecting to Geography: Location** Analyze how location influenced a colony's economy.
17. **Comparing** Discuss the differences between the Southern plantations and the farms in the Middle and New England Colonies.
18. **Analyzing Information** Explain how each of the following individuals contributed to the growth of self-government: **(a)** John Winthrop, **(b)** Thomas Hooker, **(c)** Lord Baltimore.
19. **Synthesizing Information** Why do you think the colonists were open to the ideas of the Enlightenment?
20. **Linking Past and Present** What rights and freedoms enjoyed by Americans today had their beginnings in colonial times?

In the trial of John Peter Zenger, his lawyer Andrew Hamilton gave a speech to the jury defending Zenger. Read the excerpt, and then answer the questions.

> **66** . . . the question before the court and you gentlemen of the jury, is not of small nor private concern. It is not the cause of the poor printer . . . it may in its consequence affect every freeman that lives under a British Government on the main of America. It is the best cause. It is the cause of liberty; and I make no doubt but your upright conduct, this day, will . . . entitle you to the love and esteem of your fellow citizens. . . . **99**
>
> —Andrew Hamilton, speech before the jury in the Zenger trial, New York, 1735

21. According to Hamilton, what is the main issue in the Zenger case?
    A. the cause of liberty
    B. the power of the British government
    C. the cause of printers
    D. the importance of "upright conduct"
22. Hamilton probably feels that the jury's verdict
    A. will have very little impact on society.
    B. can be ignored.
    C. will be overturned on appeal.
    D. is very important.

Read the following passage about river trade in colonial Virginia. Answer the questions.

An early Tye River Scottish tobacco planter, Parson Robert Rose, was one of the first to use the Indian dugout canoe to carry his hogsheads [of tobacco] to the Richmond market, but found them neither large enough nor stable enough to carry much cargo. By the mid 1740s, Parson Rose . . . devised a method of lashing two canoes together with a sawn board platform in between which enabled him to carry up to nine hogshead at a time down the James . . . Hogsheads could now be transported downriver . . . to the market in Richmond.

> —Dian McNaught, "The Early Virginia River Trade of the 1700s"

23. What is the main idea of this passage?
    A. Indian dugout canoes are sturdy.
    B. Hogsheads are durable holding devices.
    C. Double dugout canoes are best for carrying goods.
    D. Parson Rose was a wealthy planter.
24. (a) What details in the passage support the main idea? (b) Write a summary of the paragraph.

ACTIVITIES

Connecting With... Culture

Making a Chart Make a chart that describes the lifestyle in the colonies. Write the names of the colonial regions—New England, Middle Colonies, and Southern Colonies—at the top of the chart. The left column should include: Geography, Economy, Government, Education, Region, Population Density. You may add other categories.

Go Online
PHSchool.com

Connecting to Today

A Comparison Report Use the Internet to research facts about past and present-day immigration. Compare the challenges faced by immigrants coming to the United States today with those of the English colonists in the 1600s and early 1700s. Work with a partner to complete your report. For help in starting this activity, visit PHSchool.com, **Web Code mfd-0405.**

TEST PREPARATION

1. Which of the following is not an example of a primary source?

   A   An entry from Christopher Columbus's journal

   B   The cargo list of a colonial slave ship

   C   A modern biography of Benjamin Franklin

   D   The Fundamental Orders of Connecticut

Use the map _and_ your knowledge of social studies to answer the following question.

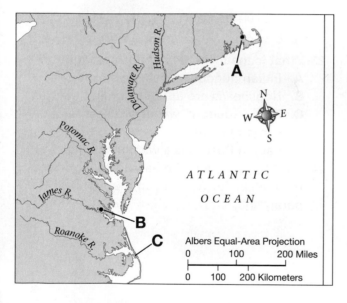

2. In what sequence were the three English colonies shown on the map settled?

   A   A, B, C

   B   C, B, A

   C   B, A, C

   D   B, C, A

3. The Navigation Acts were linked to which economic system?

   A   Mercantilism

   B   Feudalism

   C   Encomienda system

   D   Free enterprise

4. "Nomadic bands learned to make the most of limited resources." This statement best applies to Native Americans living in which region?

   A   Eastern Woodlands

   B   Arctic

   C   Southeast

   D   Pacific Northwest

Use the quotation _and_ your knowledge of social studies to answer the following question.

"There has been a great lasting change in this town in many respects. There has been vastly more religion kept up. . . . There has also been an evident change with respect to a charitable spirit to the poor."

5. What event or development is described in this passage?

   A   The founding of Pennsylvania

   B   The signing of the Mayflower Compact

   C   The Enlightenment

   D   The Great Awakening

6 How was the founding of the Virginia House of Burgesses similar to the signing of the Mayflower Compact?

A Both strengthened the English Parliament's control over the colonies.

B Both gave settlers the right to establish colonies.

C Both contributed to the development of representative democracy.

D Both created elected legislatures.

7 Which kind of thematic map would you use to find out how much of your state is made up of farmland?

A A political map

B A climate map

C A land use map

D A population density map

8 Which of the following individuals is best known for helping the spread of new ideas in Europe?

A Prince Henry of Portugal

B Johannes Gutenberg

C Augustus Caesar

D Martin Luther

Use the chart _and_ your knowledge of social studies to answer the following question.

Ethnic Division of Colonial Population, 1775

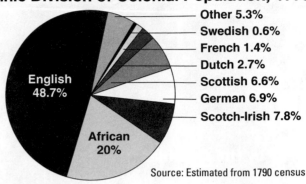

English 48.7%

Other 5.3%
Swedish 0.6%
French 1.4%
Dutch 2.7%
Scottish 6.6%
German 6.9%
Scotch-Irish 7.8%

African 20%

Source: Estimated from 1790 census

9 What valid conclusion about the colonial population can you draw from this pie chart?

A More people in the colonies were of English descent than all other European nationalities combined.

B Slaves made up 20 percent of the colonial population.

C The Dutch population lived entirely in New York.

D One out of every ten colonists was of either German or French background.

Writing Practice

10 **(a)** What are the major elements of the free enterprise system? **(b)** Describe some of the benefits of free enterprise. Use at least one example from modern life.

11 Trace the development of religious freedom in the 13 colonies. Describe at least three milestones. Then, make two generalizations about the roots of religious freedom.

Unit 2
The Revolutionary Era

Revolutionary Turning Point
General George Washington looks determined to win an American victory as he leads troops across the Delaware River.

"If we separate from Britain, what code of laws will be established? How shall we be governed so as to retain our liberties?"

—Abigail Adams, wife of John Adams (1775)

Crisis in the Colonies

1745–1775

1 The French and Indian War
2 Turmoil Over Taxation
3 From Protest to Revolution

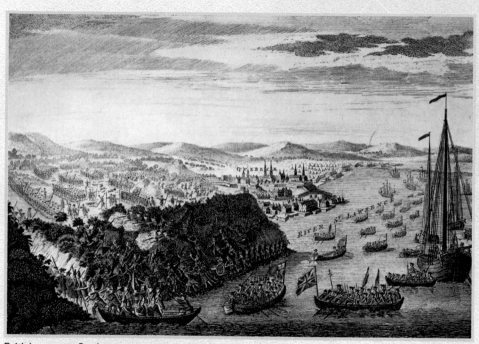

British capture Quebec

AMERICAN EVENTS

1740s
The first migration of settlers across the Appalachian Mountains sets off conflicts with the Indians of the Ohio River Valley.

1754
The Albany Congress proposes to unite the British colonies. However, the proposal is rejected by all the colonies.

1759
British forces climb to the Plains of Abraham and capture Quebec, the capital of New France.

1740 · · · **1750** · · · **1760**

WORLD EVENTS

▲ **1748**
Britain and France fight for control of trade in India.

▲ **1756**
Seven Years' War begins in Europe between France and Britain.

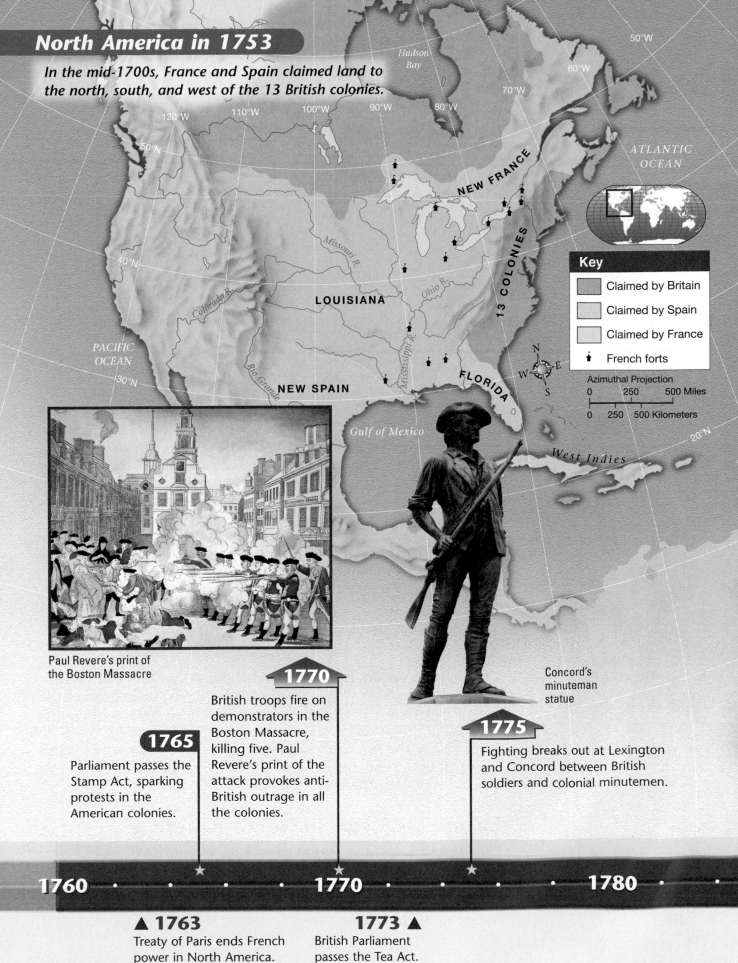

North America in 1753

In the mid-1700s, France and Spain claimed land to the north, south, and west of the 13 British colonies.

Hudson Bay

50°W

60°W

70°W

ATLANTIC OCEAN

120°W   110°W   100°W   90°W   80°W

50°N

NEW FRANCE

40°N

Missouri R.

13 COLONIES

PACIFIC OCEAN

LOUISIANA

Ohio R.

30°N

Colorado R.

Rio Grande

NEW SPAIN

Mississippi R.

FLORIDA

Key

Claimed by Britain

Claimed by Spain

Claimed by France

French forts

N W E S

Azimuthal Projection

0   250   500 Miles

0   250   500 Kilometers

20°N

Gulf of Mexico

West Indies

Paul Revere's print of the Boston Massacre

Concord's minuteman statue

1770

British troops fire on demonstrators in the Boston Massacre, killing five. Paul Revere's print of the attack provokes anti-British outrage in all the colonies.

1765

Parliament passes the Stamp Act, sparking protests in the American colonies.

1775

Fighting breaks out at Lexington and Concord between British soldiers and colonial minutemen.

1760 · · · · 1770 · · · · 1780 · · ·

▲ **1763**
Treaty of Paris ends French power in North America.

1773 ▲
British Parliament passes the Tea Act.

1 The French and Indian War

Prepare to Read

Objectives

In this section, you will
- Explain why war began in North America.
- Describe how mistakes led to British defeats early in the war.
- Identify what turned the tide of war in Britain's favor.
- Explain how British troops defeated French troops.

Key Terms

French and Indian War

Albany Plan of Union

Plains of Abraham

Treaty of Paris

Target Reading Skill

Reading Process As you read, prepare an outline of this section. Use roman numerals to indicate major headings, capital letters for subheadings, and numbers for supporting details. The sample below will get you started.

> I. European Rivals in North America
> A.
> B.
> II. The French and Indian War Begins
> III. The Albany Congress

Main Idea Britain's victory in the French and Indian War marked the end of the French empire in North America.

George Washington as a young officer

Setting the Scene When Captain Daniel Joncaire sat down to dinner on December 4, 1753, he wasn't expecting company. The weather was cold, rainy, and miserable at the French fort near Lake Erie. To Joncaire's surprise, a tall young stranger strode into the room. He introduced himself as Major George Washington. Washington had traveled several hundred miles from Virginia to deliver a letter to the French.

Joncaire politely invited Washington to dine. As they ate, the captain boasted that France was determined to control the Ohio River Valley. Washington reported:

> 66 He told me, That it was their absolute Design to take possession of the Ohio [River], and by God they would do it. 99
>
> —George Washington, in his journal

Joncaire's remark made Washington pause. The letter he was carrying from Virginia's governor warned the French to get out of the Ohio River Valley! For years, tensions had been building between France and England. At stake was more than control of the Ohio River Valley. The two rivals wanted to drive each other out of North America. In the end, the issue was decided by war. And Washington was the man who struck the first blow.

European Rivals in North America

By the mid-1700s, the major powers of Europe were locked in a worldwide struggle for empire. England, France, Spain, and the Netherlands competed for trade and colonies in far-flung corners of the globe. The English colonies in North America soon became caught up in the contest.

The most serious threat came from France. It claimed a vast area that stretched from the St. Lawrence River west to the Great Lakes and south to the Gulf of Mexico. To protect their land claims, the French built an extensive system of forts. These forts blocked the English colonies from expanding to the west.

Conflict in the Ohio Valley At first, most English settlers were content to remain along the Atlantic coast. By the 1740s, however, traders were crossing the Appalachian Mountains in search of furs. Pushing into the Ohio Valley, they tried to take over the profitable French trade with the Indians.

France was determined to stop the English from expanding westward. The Ohio River was especially important to the French because it provided a vital link between their lands in Canada and their settlements along the Mississippi River.

Native Americans Choose Sides Native Americans had hunted animals and grown crops in the Ohio Valley for centuries. They did not want to give up the land to European settlers, French or English. One Native American protested to an English trader, "You and the French are like the two edges of a pair of shears. And we are the cloth which is to be cut to pieces between them."

Still, the growing conflict between England and France was too dangerous to ignore. Some Native Americans decided that the only way to protect their way of life was to take sides in the struggle.

The French expected the Indians to side with them. Most French in North America were trappers and traders. Generally, they did not destroy Indian hunting grounds by clearing forests for farms. Also, many French trappers married Native American women and adopted their ways. As a result, France had built strong alliances with such Native American groups as the Algonquins and the Hurons.

Many English settlers were farmers. These settlers usually ignored Indian rights by felling trees and clearing land for crops. In the end, though, Britain managed to convince the powerful Iroquois nations to join with them. The British alliance was attractive to the Iroquois because they were old enemies of the Algonquin and the Huron peoples.

An English trader and official, William Johnson, helped gain Iroquois support for England. The Iroquois respected Johnson. He was one of the few English settlers who had an Indian wife, Molly Brant. She was the sister of the Mohawk chief Thayendanegea, known to the English as Joseph Brant. Both Joseph and Molly Brant became valuable allies for the English. The English also won Native American allies in the Ohio Valley by charging lower prices than the French for trade goods.

Viewing History

A Pioneer Home
After clearing the woods, pioneer families built their log cabins and set out to harvest the riches of the land. This romantic view of a pioneer homestead was created more than 100 years after pioneers started crossing the Appalachian Mountains.
Identifying Points of View *Do you think the artist admired the early pioneers? Explain your answer. How does he show his point of view?*

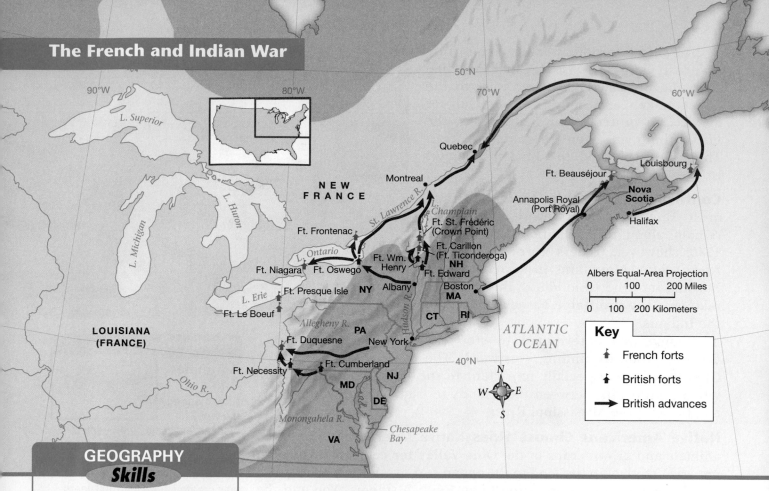

NEW FRANCE

LOUISIANA (FRANCE)

Quebec
Montreal
Ft. Beauséjour
Louisbourg
Annapolis Royal (Port Royal)
Nova Scotia
Halifax
Ft. Frontenac
L. Champlain
Ft. St. Frédéric (Crown Point)
Ft. Carillon (Ft. Ticonderoga)
Ft. Niagara
Ft. Oswego
Ft. Wm. Henry
NH
Ft. Edward
Ft. Presque Isle
NY
Albany
Boston
MA
Ft. Le Boeuf
RI
L. Erie
Allegheny R.
PA
CT
Ft. Duquesne
New York
ATLANTIC OCEAN
Ft. Necessity
Ft. Cumberland
NJ
Ohio R.
MD
DE
Monongahela R.
Chesapeake Bay
VA

L. Superior
L. Huron
L. Michigan
L. Ontario
St. Lawrence R.
Hudson R.

Albers Equal-Area Projection
0   100   200 Miles
0   100   200 Kilometers

Key
† French forts
† British forts
→ British advances

GEOGRAPHY *Skills*

During the French and Indian War, Britain and France battled for control of North America. The conflict began in the Ohio River Valley.

1. **Location** On the map locate **(a)** Fort Necessity, **(b)** Fort Duquesne, **(c)** Louisbourg, **(d)** Albany.

2. **Movement** About how many miles did advancing British forces travel from Louisbourg to Quebec?

3. **Critical Thinking Analyzing Information** How were the causes of the French and Indian War related to events during the Age of Exploration?

The French and Indian War Begins

Three times between 1689 and 1748, France and Great Britain* fought for power in Europe and North America. Each war ended with an uneasy peace.

In 1754, fighting broke out for a fourth time. English settlers called the conflict the **French and Indian War** because it pitted them against France and its Native American allies. Once again, the Ohio River Valley was at the center of the dispute. There, the opening shots of the war were fired by soldiers led by George Washington.

A Bold Young Leader Washington was only 22 years old in 1754. He had grown up on a plantation in Virginia, the son of wealthy parents. Gifted at mathematics, he began working as a land surveyor at the age of 15. His job took him to frontier lands in western Virginia.

After Washington returned from his first visit to the French, the governor of Virginia sent him west again. This time Washington's assignment was to build a fort where the Monongahela and Allegheny rivers meet to form the Ohio River.

Washington led 150 men into the Ohio country in April 1754. Along the way, he heard that the French had just completed Fort

---

*In 1707, England and Scotland were officially joined into the United Kingdom of Great Britain. After that date, the terms *Great Britain* and *British* were used to describe the country and its people. However, the terms *England* and *English* were still used throughout much of the 1700s.

Duquesne (doo KAYN) at the very spot where Washington hoped to build his fort.

Conflict at Fort Necessity Determined to carry out his orders, Washington hurried on. Indian allies revealed that French scouts were camped in the woods ahead. Marching quietly through the night, Washington launched a surprise attack and scattered the French.

His success was brief, however. Hearing that the French were about to counterattack, Washington and his men quickly threw up a makeshift stockade. They named it Fort Necessity. A force of 700 French and Indians surrounded the fort. Badly outnumbered, the Virginians surrendered. The French then released Washington, and he returned home.

British officials recognized the significance of Washington's skirmish. "The volley fired by this young Virginian in the forests of America," a British writer noted, "has set the world in flames."

The Albany Congress

While Washington was defending Fort Necessity, delegates from seven colonies gathered in Albany, New York. One purpose of the meeting was to cement the alliance with the Iroquois. Another goal was to plan a united colonial defense.

The delegates in Albany knew that the colonists had to work together to defeat the French. Benjamin Franklin, the delegate from Pennsylvania, proposed the **Albany Plan of Union.** The plan was an attempt to create "one general government" for the 13 colonies. It called for a Grand Council made up of representatives from each colony. The council would make laws, raise taxes, and set up the defense of the colonies.

The delegates voted to accept the Plan of Union. However, when the plan was submitted to the colonial assemblies, not one approved it. None of the colonies wanted to give up any of its powers to a central council. A disappointed Benjamin Franklin expressed his frustration at the failure of his plan:

> 66 Everyone cries a union is necessary. But when they come to the manner and form of the union, their weak noodles are perfectly distracted. 99
>
> —Benjamin Franklin, in a letter to Governor William Shirley, 1755

A String of British Defeats

In 1755, General Edward Braddock led British and colonial troops in an attack against Fort Duquesne. Braddock was a stubborn man who had little experience at fighting in the forests of North America. Still, the general boasted that he would sweep the French from the Ohio Valley.

Disaster for Braddock Braddock's men moved slowly and noisily through the forests. Although warned of danger by Washington and by Indian scouts, Braddock pushed ahead.

As the British neared Fort Duquesne, the French and their Indian allies launched a surprise attack. Sharpshooters hid in the

Set a Purpose for Reading

When you set a purpose for reading, you give yourself a focus. As you read about Washington and Fort Necessity, think about the meaning of the British writer's comment. Why did he say that Washington had "set the world in flames"?

Primary Source

Battle in the Wilderness

Early in the war, a small force of Native Americans and French routed an army led by Edward Braddock. George Washington later wrote of the defeat:
"The Virginia troops showed a good deal of bravery, and were near all killed. For I believe out of three companies that were there, there are scarce 30 men left alive. . . . The general [Braddock] was wounded; of which he died three days after. Sir Peter Halket was killed in the field, where died many other brave officers. I luckily escaped without a wound, though I had four bullets through my coat and two horses shot under me."

—George Washington in a letter to his mother, July 18, 1755

Analyzing Primary Sources
How did the battle build Washington's reputation among his fellow colonists?

forest and picked off British soldiers, whose bright red uniforms made easy targets.

Braddock himself had five horses shot out from under him before he fell, fatally wounded. Almost half the British were killed or wounded. Washington, too, was nearly killed.

Further British Setbacks During the next two years, the war continued to go badly for the British. British attacks against several French forts failed. Meanwhile, the French won important victories, capturing Fort Oswego on Lake Ontario and Fort William Henry on Lake George. All these defeats put a serious strain on the alliances with Native Americans who had been counting on the British to protect them from the French.

The Tide of Battle Turns

In 1757, William Pitt became the new head of the British government. Pitt made it his first job to win the war in North America. Once that goal was achieved, he argued, the British would be free to focus on victory in other parts of the world. So Pitt sent Britain's best generals to North America. To encourage the colonists to support the war, he promised large payments for military services and supplies.

Under Pitt's leadership, the tide of battle turned. In 1758, Major General Jeffrey Amherst captured Louisbourg, the most important fort in French Canada. That year, the British also seized Fort Duquesne, which they renamed Fort Pitt after the British leader. The city of Pittsburgh later grew up on the site of Fort Pitt.

The Fall of New France

The British enjoyed even greater success in 1759. By summer, they had pushed the French from Fort Niagara, Crown Point, and Fort Ticonderoga (ty kahn duh ROH guh). Next, Pitt sent General James Wolfe to take Quebec, capital of New France.

Battle for Quebec Quebec was vital to the defense of New France. Without Quebec, the French could not supply their forts farther up the St. Lawrence River. Quebec was well defended, though. The city sat on the edge of the **Plains of Abraham,** on top of a steep cliff high above the St. Lawrence. An able French general, the Marquis de Montcalm, was prepared to fight off any British attack.

General Wolfe devised a bold plan to capture Quebec. He knew that Montcalm had only a few soldiers guarding the cliff because the French thought that it was too steep to climb. Late at night, Wolfe ordered

GEOGRAPHY
Skills

The Treaty of Paris ended the French and Indian War and greatly changed the map of North America.

1. **Location** On the map, locate **(a)** the 13 colonies, **(b)** Louisiana, **(c)** New Spain.

2. **Region** Which countries shared control of North America after 1763?

3. **Critical Thinking Comparing** Compare this map to the map at the beginning of the chapter. What effect did the Treaty of Paris have on French power in North America?

North America in 1763

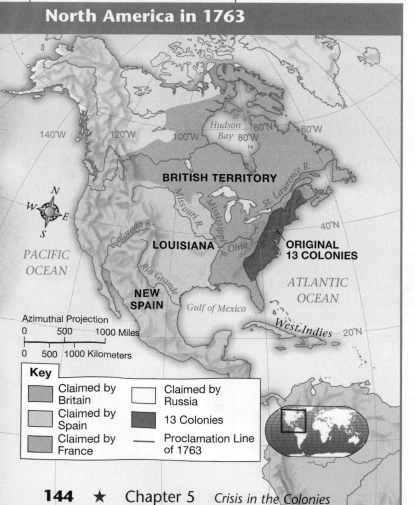

Key

- Claimed by Britain
- Claimed by Spain
- Claimed by France
- Claimed by Russia
- 13 Colonies
- Proclamation Line of 1763

British troops to row quietly in small boats to the foot of the cliff. In the dark, the soldiers swarmed ashore, climbed up the cliff, and assembled at the top.

The next morning, Montcalm awakened to a surprise. A force of 4,000 British troops was drawn up and ready for battle on the Plains of Abraham.

Quickly, Montcalm marched his own troops out to join in battle. By the time the fierce fighting was over, both Montcalm and Wolfe lay dead. Moments before Wolfe died, a soldier gave him the news that the British had won. Wolfe is said to have whispered, "Now, God be praised, I will die in peace." On September 18, 1759, Quebec surrendered to the British.

Treaty of Paris The fall of Quebec sealed the fate of New France, though fighting dragged on in Europe for several more years. Finally, in 1763, Britain and France signed the Treaty of Paris, bringing the long conflict to an end.

The Treaty of Paris marked the end of French power in North America. By its terms, Britain gained Canada and all French lands east of the Mississippi River except New Orleans. France was allowed to keep only two islands in the Gulf of St. Lawrence and its prosperous sugar-growing islands in the West Indies. Spain, which had entered the war on the French side in 1762, gave up Florida to Britain. In return, Spain received all French land west of the Mississippi. In addition, Spain gained the vital port city of New Orleans. Spain retained control of its vast empire in Central America and South America.

After years of fighting, peace returned to North America. Yet, in a few short years, a new conflict would break out. This time, the struggle would pit Britain against its own 13 colonies.

★ ★ ★ Section 1 Assessment ★ ★ ★

Recall

1. **Identify** Explain the significance of **(a)** George Washington, **(b)** Joseph Brant, **(c)** French and Indian War, **(d)** Benjamin Franklin, **(e)** Albany Plan of Union, **(f)** Edward Braddock, **(g)** William Pitt, **(h)** Plains of Abraham, **(i)** Treaty of Paris.

Comprehension

2. Why did France and Britain go to war in 1754?
3. How did defeat and disunity hurt the early British war effort?
4. What events turned the tide of battle after William Pitt became head of the British government?

5. How did the battle of Quebec lead to the fall of New France to the British?

Critical Thinking and Writing

6. **Exploring the Main Idea** Review the Main Idea statement at the beginning of this section. Write a paragraph explaining how Britain's victory in the French and Indian War made it the most powerful force in North America.

7. **Analyzing Ideas (a)** List two ways in which the Albany Plan of Union would have helped the colonies fight the French. **(b)** Why did the colonists reject the Plan of Union?

ACTIVITY

Writing a Skit
Use the Internet to find resources describing the strategies of Generals Wolfe and Montcalm at Quebec. Then, prepare a five-minute skit about an imaginary meeting between the two generals. For help in completing the activity, visit PHSchool.com, **Web Code mfd-0501.**

2 Turmoil Over Taxation

Prepare to Read

Objectives

In this section, you will
- Describe how Britain tried to ease growing tensions on the American frontier.
- List the ways colonists reacted to new taxes imposed by Parliament.
- Identify new colonial leaders.
- Explain the events that led to the Boston Massacre.

Key Terms

Pontiac's War
Proclamation of 1763
Stamp Act
petition
boycott
repeal
Townshend Acts
writ of assistance
Boston Massacre
committee of
   correspondence

Target Reading Skill

Main Idea Copy the concept web below. As you read the section, fill in the blank ovals with important facts that led to the conflict between Britain and its American colonies. Add as many ovals as you need.

Main Idea Many colonists opposed Parliament's attempts to tighten control over Britain's North American empire.

A tax stamp

Setting the Scene

The lieutenant governor of Massachusetts, Thomas Hutchinson, was at supper with his children in Boston when an out-of-breath messenger arrived. A mob was coming for Hutchinson, he warned. "I directed my children to fly to a secure place," Hutchinson recalled. Then, he fled to a neighbor's house.

> 66 I had been there but a few minutes before the hellish crew fell upon my house with the Rage of devils and in a moment with axes split down the doors and entered. . . . 99
>
> —Thomas Hutchinson, lieutenant governor of Massachusetts, 1765

The furious mob went to work. It smashed windows and broke down walls. It ripped up Hutchinson's garden and chopped down his trees. The entire house would have been demolished except that daylight came before the job could be finished. "Such ruins were never seen in America," Hutchinson mourned.

How could such a riot take place? Only two years earlier, in 1763, British colonists had celebrated Britain's victory over France. They lit bonfires and set church bells ringing. Now, some of these same people were destroying the homes of royal officials. In truth, the riots of 1765 were only the beginning of a growing dispute.

New Troubles on the Frontier

By 1760, the British and their Indian allies had driven France from the Ohio Valley. Their troubles in the region were not over, however. For many years, fur traders had sent back glowing reports of the land beyond the Appalachian Mountains. With the French gone, British colonists eagerly headed west to claim the lands for themselves.

Clashes With Native Americans Many Native American nations lived in the Ohio Valley. They included the Senecas, Delawares, Shawnees, Ottawas, Miamis, and Hurons. As British settlers moved into the valley, they often clashed with these Native Americans.

In 1762, the British sent Lord Jeffrey Amherst to the frontier to keep order. French traders had always treated Native Americans as friends, holding feasts for them and giving them presents. Amherst refused to do this. Instead, he raised the price of goods traded to Indians. Also, unlike the French, Amherst allowed settlers to build farms and forts on Indian lands.

Angry Native Americans found a leader in Pontiac, an Ottawa chief who had fought on the French side. An English trader remarked that Pontiac "commands more respect amongst these nations than any Indian I ever saw." In April 1763, Pontiac spoke out against the British, calling them "dogs dressed in red, who have come to rob [us] of [our] hunting grounds and drive away the game."

War on the Frontier Soon after, Pontiac led an attack on British troops at Fort Detroit. A number of other Indian nations joined him. In a few short months, they captured most British forts in the Ohio country. British and colonial troops then struck back and regained much of what they had lost.

Pontiac's War, as it came to be called, did not last long. In October 1763, the French told Pontiac that they had signed the Treaty of Paris. Because the treaty marked the end of French power in North America, the Indians could no longer hope for French aid against the British. One by one, the Indian nations stopped fighting and returned home.

Proclamation of 1763

Pontiac's War convinced British officials that they should stop British subjects from settling on the western frontier. To do this, the government issued the Proclamation of 1763. The proclamation drew an imaginary line along the crest of the Appalachian Mountains. Colonists were forbidden to settle west of the line. All settlers already west of the line were "to remove themselves" at once.

The proclamation was meant to protect Indians in the western lands. To enforce it, Britain sent 10,000 troops to the colonies. Few troops went to the frontier, however. Most stayed in cities along the Atlantic coast.

The proclamation angered colonists. Some colonies, including New York, Pennsylvania, and Virginia, claimed lands in the west. Also, colonists now had to pay for the additional British troops that had been sent to enforce the proclamation. In the end, many settlers simply ignored the proclamation and moved west anyway.

Crisis on the Frontier

```
┌─────────────────┐      ┌─────────────────┐      ┌─────────────────┐
│  Colonists settle│ ──▶  │  Pontiac's War  │ ──▶  │ Proclamation of │
│  on Indian lands │      │  breaks out on  │      │    1763 stops   │
│   in the west    │      │   the frontier  │      │  settlement in  │
│                  │      │                 │      │    the west     │
└─────────────────┘      └─────────────────┘      └─────────────────┘
                                                            │
┌─────────────────┐      ┌─────────────────┐      ┌─────────────────┐
│  Sugar and Stamp│ ◀──  │British government│ ◀── │ Stationing British│
│   Acts burden   │      │  decides American│     │ troops in the    │
│  colonists with │      │  colonists should│     │  colonies        │
│    new taxes    │      │  help pay for    │     │  proves costly   │
│                 │      │     troops       │     │                  │
└─────────────────┘      └─────────────────┘      └─────────────────┘
        │
        ▼
┌───────────────────────────────────────────────┐
│  Stormy protests break out in many colonies    │
└───────────────────────────────────────────────┘
```

One colonist who defied the Proclamation of 1763 was Daniel Boone. In 1767, Boone visited Kentucky, west of the Appalachians. In 1769, he began what became a two-year journey of exploration through Kentucky. He traveled as far as the Falls of the Ohio, the site of the present-day city of Louisville. Later, he led settlers through the Cumberland Gap along an old Indian path. During his travels, Boone fought a number of battles against the Indians and was taken captive for a short period.

Britain Imposes New Taxes

The French and Indian War plunged Britain deeply into debt. As a result, the taxes paid by citizens in Britain rose sharply. The British prime minister, George Grenville, decided that colonists in North America should help share the burden. In a mercantilist system, colonies were expected to serve the colonial power. Grenville reasoned that the colonists would not oppose small tax increases.

Sugar Act In 1764, Grenville asked Parliament to approve the Sugar Act, which put a new tax on molasses. Molasses, you will recall, was a valuable item in the triangular trade.

The Sugar Act replaced an earlier tax, which had been so high that any merchant who paid it would have been driven out of business. As a result, most colonial merchants simply avoided the tax by smuggling molasses into the colonies. Often, they bribed tax collectors to look the other way. The Sugar Act of 1764 lowered the tax. At the same time, the law made it easier for British officials to bring colonial smugglers to trial. Grenville made it clear that he expected the new tax to be paid.

Stamp Act Grenville also persuaded Parliament to pass the Stamp Act of 1765. The act placed new duties on legal documents such as wills, diplomas, and marriage papers. It also taxed newspapers, almanacs, playing cards, and even dice.

All items named in the law had to carry a stamp showing that the tax had been paid. Stamp taxes were used in Britain and other countries to raise money. However, Britain had never required American colonists to pay such a tax.

Protesting the Stamp Act

When British officials tried to enforce the Stamp Act, they met with stormy protests from colonists. Lieutenant Governor Hutchinson in Massachusetts was not the only official to feel the anger of a mob. Some colonists threw rocks at agents trying to collect the unpopular tax. Others tarred and feathered the agents. In addition to riots in Boston, other disturbances broke out in New York City, Newport, and Charleston. In New York City, rioters destroyed the home of a British official who had said he would "cram the stamps down American throats" at the point of his sword.

The fury of the colonists shocked the British. After all, Britain had spent a great deal of money to protect the colonies against the French. The British at home were paying much higher taxes than the colonists. Why, British officials asked, were colonists so angry about the Stamp Act? As one English letter-writer commented,

> **66** Our Colonies must be the biggest Beggars in the World, if such small Duties appear to be intolerable Burdens in their Eyes. **99**
>
> —"Pacificus," Maryland *Gazette*, March 20, 1766

"No Taxation Without Representation!" Colonists replied that the Stamp Act taxes were unjust. The taxes, they claimed, went against the principle that there should be no taxation without representation. That principle was rooted in English traditions dating back to the Magna Carta.

Colonists insisted that only they or their elected representatives had the right to pass taxes. Since the colonists did not elect representatives to Parliament, Parliament had no right to tax them. The colonists were willing to pay taxes—but only if the taxes were passed by their own colonial legislatures.

Uniting in Peaceful Protest The Stamp Act crisis united colonists from New Hampshire to Georgia. Critics of the law called for delegates from every colony to meet in New York City. There, a congress would form to consider actions against the hated Stamp Act.

In October 1765, nine colonies sent delegates to what became known as the Stamp Act Congress. The delegates drew up petitions to King George III and to Parliament. A **petition** is a formal written request to someone in authority, signed by a group of people. In these petitions, the delegates rejected the Stamp Act and asserted that Parliament had no right to tax the colonies. Parliament paid little attention.

Viewing History

Protesting the Stamp Act

The Stamp Act created a storm of opposition in the colonies. Colonists expressed their opposition to the tax in many ways, including this message on a teapot. **Linking Past and Present** *How do people today display their support or opposition to a political issue?*

The colonists took other steps to change the law. They joined together to boycott British goods. To **boycott** means to refuse to buy certain goods and services. The boycott of British goods took its toll. Trade fell off by 14 percent. British merchants complained that they were facing ruin. So, too, did British workers who made goods for the colonies.

Finally, in 1766, Parliament **repealed,** or canceled, the Stamp Act. At the same time, however, it passed a law asserting that Parliament had the right to raise taxes in "all cases whatsoever."

The Townshend Acts

Identify Supporting Details

What details in the subsection "The Townshend Acts" tell you about the conflict between Britain and the colonies? Add these details to your concept web.

In May 1767, Parliament reopened the debate over taxing the colonies. In a fierce exchange, George Grenville, now a member of Parliament, clashed with Charles Townshend, the official in charge of the British treasury. "You are cowards, you are afraid of the Americans, you dare not tax America!" Grenville shouted.

"Fear? Cowards?" Townshend snapped back. "I dare tax America!"

The next month, Parliament passed the Townshend Acts, which taxed goods such as glass, paper, paint, lead, and tea. The taxes were low, but colonists still objected. The principle was the same: Parliament did not have the right to tax them without their consent.

Searching Without a Reason The Townshend Acts also set up new ways to collect taxes. Customs officials were sent to American ports with orders to stop smuggling. Using legal documents known as **writs of assistance,** the officers would be allowed to inspect a ship's cargo without giving a reason.

Colonists protested that the writs of assistance violated their rights as British citizens. Under British law, a government official could not search a person's property without a good reason for suspecting that the person had committed a crime. Colonists angrily cited the words of James Otis of Massachusetts. Arguing against a British attempt to impose writs of assistance six years earlier, he had said:

> 66 Now, one of the most essential branches of English liberty is the freedom of one's house. A man's house is his castle; and while he is quiet, he is as well guarded as a prince in his castle. This writ, if it should be declared legal, would totally destroy this privilege. Customhouse officers may enter our houses when they please . . . break locks, bars, and everything in their way. . . . 99
>
> —James Otis, February 24, 1761

Colonial Protests Widen Colonists responded swiftly and strongly to the Townshend Acts. From north to south, colonial merchants and planters signed agreements promising to stop importing goods taxed by the Townshend Acts. The colonists hoped that the new boycott would win repeal of the Townshend Acts.

To protest British policies, some angry colonists formed the Sons of Liberty. From Boston to Charleston, Sons of Liberty staged mock hangings of cloth or straw effigies, or likenesses, dressed as British

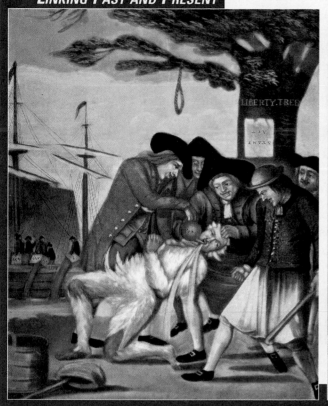

▲ Past

▲ Present

officials. The hangings were meant to show tax collectors what might happen to them if they tried to collect the unpopular taxes.

Some women joined the Daughters of Liberty. They paraded, signed petitions, and organized a boycott of fine British cloth. They urged colonial women to raise more sheep, prepare more wool, and spin and weave their own cloth. A slogan of the Daughters of Liberty declared, "It is better to wear a Homespun coat than to lose our Liberty."

Some Sons and Daughters of Liberty also used other methods to support their cause. They visited merchants and urged them to boycott British imports. A few even threatened people who continued to buy British goods.

New Colonial Leaders

As the struggle over taxes continued, new leaders emerged in all the colonies. Men and women in New England and Virginia were especially active in the colonial cause.

In Massachusetts Samuel Adams of Boston stood firmly against Britain. Sam Adams seemed an unlikely leader. He was a failure in business and a poor public speaker. Often, he wore a red suit and a cheap gray wig for which people poked fun at him. Still, Adams loved politics. He always attended Boston town meetings and Sons of Liberty rallies. Adams's real talent was organizing people. He worked behind the scenes, arranging protests and stirring public support.

Viewing History

Demonstrations Then and Now

Colonial demonstrations over taxes imposed by the British could get pretty nasty, as when protestors tarred and feathered a tax collector and poured tea down his throat. The recent demonstration at right is more peaceful, but also deals with a controversial issue. **Drawing Inferences** *Why do issues such as taxes and gas prices bring out strong emotions?*

Sam's cousin John was another important Massachusetts leader. John Adams had been a schoolteacher before becoming a skilled lawyer. Adams longed for fame and could often be difficult. Still, he was more cautious than his cousin Sam. He weighed evidence carefully before taking any actions. His knowledge of British law earned him much respect.

Mercy Otis Warren also aided the colonial cause. Warren wrote plays that made fun of British officials. The plays were published in newspapers and widely read in the colonies. Warren formed a close friendship with Abigail Adams, the wife of John Adams. The two women used their pens to spur the colonists to action. They also called for greater rights for women in the colonies.

In Virginia Virginia contributed many leaders to the struggle against taxes. In the House of Burgesses, George Washington joined other Virginians to protest the Townshend Acts.

A young lawyer, Patrick Henry, became well known as a vocal critic of British policies. His speeches in the House of Burgesses moved listeners to both tears and anger. Once, Henry attacked Britain with such fury that some listeners cried out, "Treason!" Henry boldly replied, "If this be treason, make the most of it!" Henry's words moved a young listener, Thomas Jefferson. At the time, Jefferson was a 22-year-old law student.

The Boston Massacre

Port cities like Boston and New York were centers of protest. In New York, a dispute arose over the Quartering Act. Under that law, colonists had to provide housing, candles, bedding, and beverages to soldiers stationed in the colonies. When the New York assembly refused to obey the law, Britain dismissed the assembly in 1767.

Britain also sent two regiments to Boston to protect customs officers from local citizens. To many Bostonians, the soldiers were a daily reminder that Britain was trying to bully them into paying unjust taxes. When British soldiers walked along the streets of Boston, they risked insults or even beatings. A serious clash was not long in coming.

A Bloody Night On the night of March 5, 1770, a crowd gathered outside the Boston customs house. Colonists shouted insults at the "lobsterbacks," as they called the redcoated British who guarded the building. Then the Boston crowd began to throw snowballs, oyster shells, and chunks of ice at the soldiers.

The crowd grew larger and rowdier. Suddenly, the soldiers panicked. They fired into the crowd. When the smoke from the musket volley cleared, five people lay dead or dying. Among the first to die were Samuel Maverick, a 17-year-old white youth, and Crispus Attucks, a free black sailor.

Colonists were quick to protest the incident, which they called the Boston Massacre. A Boston silversmith named Paul Revere fanned anti-British feeling with an engraving that showed British soldiers firing on unarmed colonists. Sam Adams wrote letters to other colonists to build outrage about the shooting.

An American Profile

Mercy Otis Warren
1728–1814

Like most young women in the American colonies, Mercy Otis Warren received no formal schooling. She managed to educate herself, however, and like her brother, James Otis, became dedicated to the cause of freedom.

She was infuriated when James Otis was struck on the head by a British officer and suffered permanent brain damage. Warren used her writing skills to stir feelings against the British. In plays like *The Blockheads,* she ridiculed British officials. Her home became a meeting place for colonists who opposed British policies.

How do writers influence public opinion today?

The soldiers were arrested and tried in court. John Adams agreed to defend them, saying that they deserved a fair trial. He wanted to show the world that the colonists believed in justice, even if the British government did not. At the trial, Adams argued that the crowd had provoked the soldiers. His arguments convinced the jury. In the end, the heaviest punishment any soldier received was a branding on the hand.

Samuel Adams later expanded on the idea of a letter-writing campaign by forming a **committee of correspondence.** Members of the committee regularly wrote letters and pamphlets reporting to other colonies on events in Massachusetts. Within three months, there were 80 committees organized in Massachusetts. Before long, committees of correspondence became a major tool of protest in every colony.

A Temporary Calm By chance, on the very day of the Boston Massacre, a bill was introduced into Parliament to repeal most of the Townshend Acts. British merchants, harmed by the American boycott of British goods, had again pressured Parliament to end the taxes. The Quartering Act was repealed and most of the taxes that had angered the Americans were ended. However, King George III asked Parliament to retain the tax on tea. "There must always be one tax to keep up the right [to tax]," he argued. Parliament agreed.

News of the repeal delighted the colonists. Most people dismissed the remaining tax on tea as unimportant and ended their boycott of British goods. For a few years, calm returned. Yet the basic issue—Britain's power to tax the colonies—remained unsettled. The debate over taxes had forced the colonists to begin thinking more carefully about their political rights.

★ ★ ★ Section 2 Assessment ★ ★ ★

Recall

1. **Identify** Explain the significance of (a) Pontiac's War, (b) Proclamation of 1763, (c) Stamp Act, (d) Townshend Acts, (e) writ of assistance, (f) Boston Massacre, (g) committee of correspondence.
2. **Define** (a) petition, (b) boycott, (c) repeal.

Comprehension

3. How did Pontiac's War and the Proclamation of 1763 grow out of the migration of colonists?
4. Why did colonists oppose the Stamp Act and the Townshend Acts?

5. Name some of the new leaders who protested British policy.
6. What role did the Townshend Acts play in the events that led to the Boston Massacre?

Critical Thinking and Writing

7. **Exploring the Main Idea** Review the Main Idea statement at the beginning of this section. Then, write a letter to a newspaper explaining why colonists object to the new taxes.
8. **Supporting a Point of View** Write a position paper explaining how British policies spurred the growth of representative government during the colonial period.

The Economic Effects of the Stamp Act

Much of the opposition to the Stamp Act in the colonies focused on whether Americans could be taxed by a parliament in which they were not represented. Yet, the Stamp Act also stirred opposition because of its economic effects.

Fast Facts

1. Britain believed that the tax would cover 20 percent of the cost of keeping an army in North America.
2. Samuel Adams, one of the most outspoken opponents of the Stamp Act, had once been a tax collector.

Fighting Back

The Stamp Act placed a tax on almost every business record, such as invoices, bills, and receipts. It took effect at a time when economies were slumping following the French and Indian War. Businesses were hurt when the British Army stopped buying food and clothing in the colonies.

Not surprisingly, the opposition to the Stamp Act was led by the very people who were most affected by it—shippers, manufacturers, merchants, lawyers, journalists, and clergy. They faced a major loss of income because they expected many Americans to resist buying stamps.

To protest, many American merchants stopped trading with Britain. This led British business leaders to voice serious opposition to the Stamp Act. As a result, Parliament repealed the Stamp Act in March 1766.

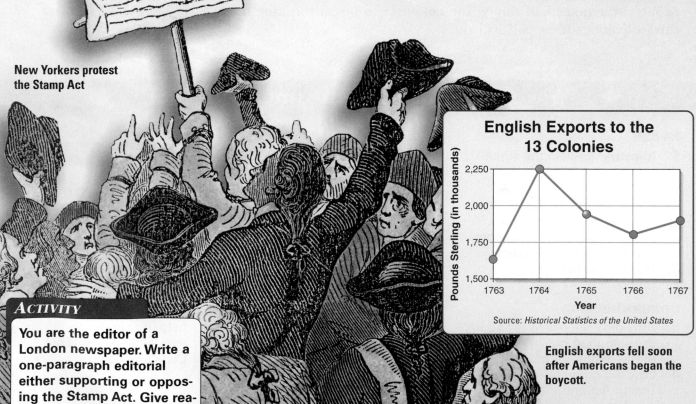

New Yorkers protest the Stamp Act

English Exports to the 13 Colonies

Pounds Sterling (in thousands)

Year

Source: *Historical Statistics of the United States*

English exports fell soon after Americans began the boycott.

ACTIVITY

You are the editor of a London newspaper. Write a one-paragraph editorial either supporting or opposing the Stamp Act. Give reasons for your point of view.

3 From Protest to Revolution

Prepare to Read

Objectives

In this section, you will
- Explain how a dispute over tea led to tension between the colonists and Britain.
- Describe how Parliament struck back at Boston.
- Identify the reasons fighting broke out at Lexington and Concord.

Key Terms

Tea Act
Boston Tea Party
Intolerable Acts
Quebec Act
First Continental Congress
militia
minuteman
battles of Lexington and Concord

Target Reading Skill

Sequence Copy this flowchart. As you read, fill in the boxes with some of the major events described in this section that led from the dispute over taxes on tea to fighting at Lexington and Concord.

British East India Company has millions of pounds of unsold tea in its warehouses.
↓
↓
Fighting breaks out at Lexington and Concord.

 **Main Idea** Crises such as the Boston Tea Party and the Intolerable Acts led to the outbreak of fighting between Britain and the colonies.

Setting the Scene

All day, the men collected burnt cork and coal dust. As dusk approached, they began to gather in small groups. In twos and threes, they met in homes across Boston. It was December 16, 1773. Outside, a cold drizzle was falling. Inside, by warm fires, the men were smearing coal dust and cork on their faces. Then, they threw blankets over their shoulders, trying to disguise themselves as Indians.

George Hewes, a shoemaker, waited with some of the others for a signal from a packed town meeting. By the time the signal came, the rain had stopped and night had fallen. As Hewes recalled:

66 When I first appeared in the street after being disguised, I fell in with many who were dressed, equipped and painted as I was, and . . . marched in order to the place of our destination. 99

—George Hewes, *Recollections,* 1834

Colonial tea jar

That place was Griffin's Wharf, and the painted "Indians" were after tea. By 1773, the quarrel between Britain and the 13 colonies had erupted again over taxes. Only, this time colonists began to think the unthinkable. Perhaps the time had come to reject British rule and declare independence.

A Dispute Over Tea

Tea was tremendously popular in the colonies. By 1770, at least one million Americans brewed tea twice a day. People "would rather go without their dinners than without a dish of tea," a visitor to the colonies noted.

Parliament Passes the Tea Act Most of the tea was brought to the colonies by the British East India Company. The company bought tea in southern Asia, shipped it to the colonies, and then sold it to colonial tea merchants. The merchants then sold the tea to the colonists. To make a profit, the merchants sold the tea at a higher price than they had paid for it.

In the 1770s, however, the British East India Company found itself in deep financial trouble. The British Parliament had kept a tax on tea as a symbol of its right to tax the colonies. The tax was a small one, but colonists resented it. Many of them refused to buy British tea. As a result, more than 15 million pounds of tea sat unsold in British warehouses.

Parliament tried to help the British East India Company by passing the Tea Act of 1773. The act let the company bypass the tea merchants and sell directly to colonists. Although colonists would still have to pay the tea tax, they would not have to pay the higher price charged by tea merchants. As a result, the tea itself would cost less than ever before. Parliament hoped this would encourage Americans to buy more British tea.

To the surprise of Parliament, colonists protested the Tea Act. American tea merchants were angry because they had been cut out of the tea trade. They believed that forcing Americans to buy tea through the British East India Company violated the Americans right to conduct free enterprise.

Even tea drinkers, who would have benefited from the law, scorned the Tea Act. They believed that it was a British trick to make them accept Parliament's right to tax the colonies.

A New Boycott Once again, colonists responded to the new tax with a boycott. A Philadelphia poet, Hannah Griffitts, urged American women to:

> 66 Stand firmly resolved and bid Grenville to see
> That rather than freedom we part with our tea,
> And well as we love the dear drink when a-dry,
> As American patriots our taste we deny. 99
>
> —Hannah Griffitts in Milcah Martha Moore, *Commonplace Book,* 1773

Daughters of Liberty and women like Griffitts led the boycott. They served coffee or made "liberty tea" from raspberry leaves. At some ports, Sons of Liberty enforced the boycott by keeping the British East India Company from unloading cargoes of tea.

Boston Tea Party Three ships loaded with tea reached Boston harbor in late November 1773. The colonial governor of Massachusetts, Thomas Hutchinson, insisted that they unload their cargo as usual.

Sam Adams and the Sons of Liberty had other plans. On the night of December 16, they met in Old South Meetinghouse. They sent a message to the governor, demanding that the ships leave the harbor. When the governor rejected the demand, Adams stood up and declared, "This meeting can do nothing further to save the country."

Adams's words seemed to be a signal. As if on cue, a group of men in Indian disguises burst into the meetinghouse. From the gallery above, voices cried, "Boston harbor a teapot tonight! The Mohawks are come!"

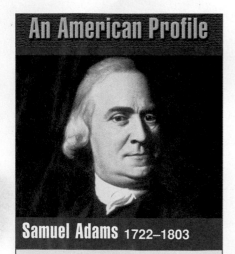

An American Profile

Samuel Adams 1722–1803

Sam Adams was not afraid of a little controversy. For example, when he was a student at Harvard University, Sam read his graduation paper to a large audience that included the governor of Massachusetts. Sam's subject, disobeying the law, deeply disturbed the governor. Sam argued that when a law was morally wrong, a person was entitled to break the law. This belief paved the way for his challenge to British authority.

Why might Sam Adams's graduation paper have disturbed many people in his audience?

The disguised colonists left the meetinghouse and headed for the harbor. Others joined them along the way. Under a nearly full moon, the men boarded the ships, split open the tea chests, and dumped the tea into the harbor. By 10 P.M., the Boston Tea Party, as it was later called, was over. The contents of 342 chests of tea floated in Boston harbor. The next day, John Adams wrote about the event in his diary.

> 66 This destruction of the tea is so bold, so daring, so firm . . . it must have such important and lasting results that I can't help considering it a turning point in history. 99

—Diary of John Adams, December 17, 1773

Parliament Strikes Back

Colonists had mixed reactions to the Boston Tea Party. Some cheered it as a firm protest against unfair British laws. Others worried that it would encourage lawlessness in the colonies. Even those who condemned the Boston Tea Party, though, were shocked at Britain's harsh response to it.

Punishing Massachusetts The British were outraged by what they saw as Boston's lawless behavior. In 1774, Parliament, encouraged by King George III, acted to punish Massachusetts. Colonists called the four laws they passed the Intolerable Acts because they were so harsh.

Viewing History

Boston Tea Party

Disguised as Indians, some 50 or 60 Bostonians attacked British tea ships. A crowd watched as the colonists dumped tea into Boston harbor. British officials called the Boston Tea Party "the most wanton and unprovoked insult offered to the civil power that is recorded in history." At lower right is a tea chest. **Drawing Conclusions** *Why did the colonists disguise themselves as Indians?*

Recognize Words That Signal Sequence

Signal words point out relationships among ideas or events. What words signal sequence in the first four paragraphs on this page? Can you find other signal words on this page?

First, Parliament shut down the port of Boston. No ship could enter or leave the harbor—not even a small boat. The harbor would remain closed until the colonists paid for the tea they had destroyed in the Boston Tea Party and repaid British officials, such as Thomas Hutchinson, for damage to personal property.

Second, Parliament forbade Massachusetts colonists to hold town meetings more than once a year without the governor's permission. In the past, colonists had called town meetings whenever they wished. All juries would now be selected by the king's officials, rather than be elected by citizens.

Third, Parliament allowed customs officers and other officials who might be charged with major crimes to be tried in Britain or Canada instead of in Massachusetts. Colonists protested. They argued that a dishonest official could break the law in the colonies and avoid punishment by being tried before a sympathetic jury.

Fourth, Parliament passed a new Quartering Act. No longer would redcoats camp in tents on Boston Common. Instead, colonists would have to house British soldiers in their homes when no other housing was available.

Quebec Act About the same time, Parliament also passed the Quebec Act. It set up a government for Canada and gave complete religious freedom to French Catholics. The Quebec Act also extended the borders of Quebec to include the landing between the Ohio and Missouri rivers. The act pleased French Canadians. But it angered the American colonists, because some of the colonies claimed ownership of these lands.

Other Colonies Support Boston The committees of correspondence spread news of the Intolerable Acts to other colonies. They warned that the people of Boston faced hunger while their port was closed. People from other colonies responded quickly. Carts rolled into the city with rice from South Carolina, corn from Virginia, and flour from Pennsylvania.

In the Virginia assembly, Thomas Jefferson suggested that a day be set aside to mark the shame of the Intolerable Acts. The royal governor of Virginia rejected the idea. The colonists went ahead anyway. On June 1, 1774, church bells tolled slowly. Merchants closed their shops. Many colonists prayed and fasted all day.

In September 1774, colonial leaders called a meeting in Philadelphia. Delegates from 12 colonies gathered in what became known as the First Continental Congress. Only Georgia did not send delegates.

After much debate, the delegates passed a resolution backing Massachusetts in its struggle. They agreed to boycott all British goods and to stop exporting goods to Britain until the Intolerable Acts were repealed. The delegates also urged each colony to set up and train its own militia (muh LIHSH uh). A militia is an army of citizens who serve as soldiers during an emergency.

Before leaving Philadelphia, the delegates agreed to meet again in May 1775. Little did they suspect that before then, an incident in Massachusetts would change the fate of the colonies forever.

Concord, Massachusetts

Minute Man National Park

The battles at Lexington and Concord began the long struggle for independence of the 13 American colonies against Britain. Today, Minute Man National Historical Park in Massachusetts preserves the historic sites. Here, present-day Americans re-create the battle at the Concord Bridge.

Go Online
PHSchool.com

Virtual Field Trip For an interactive look at Minute Man National Park, visit PHSchool.com, **Web Code mfd-0503.**

Lexington and Concord

In Massachusetts, colonists were already preparing to resist. Newspapers called on citizens to prevent what they called "the Massacre of American Liberty." Volunteers known as **minutemen** trained regularly. Minutemen got their name because they kept their muskets at hand and were prepared to fight at a minute's notice. In towns near Boston, minutemen collected weapons and gunpowder. Meanwhile, Britain built up its forces. More troops arrived in Boston, bringing the total number of British soldiers in that city to 4,000.

Early in 1775, General Thomas Gage, the British commander, sent scouts to towns near Boston. They reported that minutemen had a large store of arms in Concord, a village about 18 miles from Boston. Gage planned a surprise march to Concord to seize the arms.

Sounding the Alarm On April 18, about 700 British troops quietly left Boston in the darkness. Their goal was to seize the colonial arms. The Sons of Liberty were watching. As soon as the British set out, the Americans hung two lamps from the Old North Church in Boston. This signal meant that the redcoats were crossing the Charles River.

Colonists who were waiting across the Charles River saw the signal. Messengers mounted their horses and galloped through the night toward Concord. One midnight rider was Paul Revere. "The redcoats are coming! The redcoats are coming!" shouted Revere as he passed through each sleepy village along the way.

"The Shot Heard Round the World" At daybreak on April 19, the redcoats reached Lexington, a town near Concord. On the village green, some 70 minutemen were waiting, commanded by Captain John Parker. The British ordered the minutemen to go home.

Outnumbered, the colonists began to leave. Suddenly, a shot rang out through the chill morning air. No one knows who fired it. In the brief struggle that followed, eight colonists were killed.

The British pushed on to Concord. Finding no arms in the village, they turned back to Boston. On a bridge outside Concord, they met 300 minutemen. Again, fighting broke out. This time, the British were forced to retreat. As the redcoats withdrew, colonial sharp-shooters took deadly aim at them from the woods and fields. Local women also fired at the British from their windows. By the time they reached Boston, the redcoats had lost 73 men. Another 200 British soldiers were wounded or missing.

News of the battles of Lexington and Concord spread swiftly. To many colonists, the fighting ended all hope of a peaceful settlement. Only war would decide the future of the 13 colonies.

More than 60 years after the battles of Lexington and Concord, a well-known New England writer, Ralph Waldo Emerson, wrote a poem honoring the minutemen. Emerson's "Concord Hymn" created a vivid picture of the clash at Concord. It begins:

> **❝** By the rude bridge that arched the flood,
> Their flag to April's breeze unfurled,
> Here once the embattled farmers stood,
> And fired the shot heard round the world. **❞**
>
> —Ralph Waldo Emerson, "Concord Hymn," 1837

The "embattled farmers" faced six long years of fighting. At war's end, though, the 13 colonies would be a new, independent nation.

★ ★ ★ Section 3 Assessment ★ ★ ★

Recall

1. **Identify** Explain the significance of (a) Tea Act, (b) Samuel Adams, (c) Boston Tea Party, (d) Intolerable Acts, (e) Quebec Act, (f) First Continental Congress, (g) minuteman, (h) Lexington and Concord.
2. **Define** militia.

Comprehension

3. Why did the Tea Act anger many people in the colonies?
4. Describe two of the Intolerable Acts.
5. Explain why fighting broke out at Lexington and Concord in 1775.

Critical Thinking and Writing

6. **Exploring the Main Idea** Review the Main Idea statement at the beginning of this section. Then, draw a flowchart showing the connection between the Boston Tea Party and the fighting at Lexington and Concord.
7. **Analyzing Information** You are a concerned citizen of Boston in 1775. Write a letter to the editor of your newspaper analyzing the political and economic causes of the American Revolution.

ACTIVITY

Composing a Catchy Tune You are a colonist in Boston in 1773. You are so angry at British actions that you are composing a ditty—a catchy tune—to encourage other colonists to boycott British goods. Take any tune you know and write eight lines of lyrics that will support a boycott.

The events that shape history don't just happen. They are related to earlier events. To understand historical events, it is important to recognize their causes. It also is important to recognize the effects of the events—what resulted because the event happened.

Cause *and* Effect

Causes

- Parliament passes the Townshend Acts
- Parliament repeals the Townshend Acts but later passes a new tax, the Tea Act
- The colonies oppose the tax by boycotting tea
- The British ship tea to Boston harbor

THE BOSTON TEA PARTY

Effects

- Parliament passes the Intolerable Acts to punish Massachusetts
- Other colonies back Massachusetts in its struggle against Britain
- Massachusetts minutemen clash with British soldiers at Lexington and Concord

Learn the Skill *To learn to analyze a cause-and-effect chart, use the following steps:*

1. **Look at the headings.** The headings on the chart indicate which statements are the causes of an event and which statements are the results of it.

2. **Read the causes.** These statements give reasons why a particular event occurred. Some events have one cause. Others have many.

3. **Identify the effects.** These statements tell what happened because of the event. Very important events may have effects in many different areas.

4. **Make connections.** Think about why certain causes led to the event and why the event in turn had the results it did. Remember that an event will be both cause and effect. It may flow out of a previous event while itself creating many results.

Practice the Skill *Answer the following questions about the chart above.*

1. **(a)** What event do the causes on this chart lead to? **(b)** If you could add to the chart, under which heading would you put the outbreak of the French and Indian War?

2. Give two reasons for the Boston Tea Party.

3. Give two effects of the Boston Tea Party.

4. **(a)** Why did the tea shipped to Boston harbor lead to the Boston Tea Party? **(b)** How was the clash at Lexington and Concord a result of the Boston Tea Party?

Apply the Skill *See the Chapter Review and Assessment.*

Review and Assessment

CHAPTER SUMMARY

Section 1
The French and Indian War marked the end of the French empire in North America. In the treaty that ended the war, Britain gained control of Canada and lands east of the Mississippi River, except New Orleans.

Section 2
Many colonists opposed Parliament's attempts to tighten control over the colonies. Colonists met Britain's efforts to tax the colonies with protests. Rising tensions resulted in the Boston Massacre in March 1770.

Section 3
Crises such as the Boston Tea Party and the Intolerable Acts increased the gulf between Britain and the colonies. Unified against Britain, the colonies sent delegates to the First Continental Congress. In 1775, fighting broke out in Lexington and Concord.

For additional review and enrichment activities, see the interactive version of *The American Nation,* available on the Web and on CD-ROM.

Chapter Self-Test For practice test questions for Chapter 5, visit PHSchool.com, **Web Code mfa-0504.**

Building Vocabulary

Write sentences using the vocabulary words below. Leave blanks where the vocabulary words go. Exchange your sentences with a classmate, and fill in the blanks in each other's sentences.

1. petition
2. boycott
3. repeal
4. militia
5. minuteman
6. **French and Indian War**
7. **Albany Plan of Union**
8. **Pontiac's War**
9. **Proclamation of 1763**
10. **writ of assistance**

Reviewing Key Facts

11. What were the main results of the Treaty of Paris of 1763? (Section 1)
12. What role did Sam Adams play in aiding the colonial cause? (Section 2)
13. How did the Intolerable Acts unite people in the American colonies? (Section 3)

Critical Thinking and Writing

14. **Analyzing Primary Sources** Review the statement made by a Native American to an English trader: "You and the French are like the two edges of a pair of shears. And we are the cloth which is to be cut to pieces between them." **(a)** Write a paragraph explaining what the speaker meant by these words. **(b)** Do you think he believed that Native Americans could hold out against the British and French? Write a paragraph explaining your answer.
15. **Drawing Conclusions** List three ways your life might be different if France, not Britain, had won the French and Indian War.
16. **Ranking** List the events described in Sections 2 and 3. Then, rank them in the order of their importance in bringing about war between the American colonies and Britain. Put the most important event at the top of the list and the least important event at the bottom.
17. **Connecting to Geography: Place** Describe how the geographic setting influenced the way the battles of Lexington and Concord were fought.

Read this selection from Patrick Henry's speech and answer the questions that follow:

> 66 . . . The war is inevitable—and let it come! I repeat, sir, let it come. . . . The next gale that sweeps from the north will bring to our ears the clash of resounding arms! Our brethren are already in the field! Why stand we here idle? What is it that gentlemen wish? What would they have? Is life so dear, or peace so sweet, as to be purchased at the price of liberty and slavery? Forbid it, Almighty God! I know not what course others may take; but as for me, give me liberty or give me death. 99
>
> —From a speech by Patrick Henry, March 23, 1775

18. When Henry says, " . . . let it come! I repeat, sir, let it come," to what is he referring?
   A. the Boston Massacre
   B. the French and Indian War
   C. war with Britain
   D. war with Spain

19. Who are the "brethren . . . already in the field"?
   A. British soldiers
   B. minutemen
   C. Native American allies
   D. French soldiers

The French and Indian War

Causes
- British colonists settle on lands claimed by France
- France and Britain involved in a worldwide struggle for empire

THE FRENCH AND INDIAN WAR

Effects
- Britain left with a large debt
- Colonists begin settling in Ohio River Valley

20. What was Britain's financial situation after the French and Indian War?
   A. It was in debt.
   B. It was extremely prosperous.
   C. It had so much money it was able to lend some to hard-pressed colonies.
   D. It had to pay large amounts of money to France.

21. How did the French and Indian War lead to the Proclamation of 1763?

ACTIVITIES

Connecting With . . . Culture

Write a Poem At the end of this chapter, you read a portion of Emerson's "Concord Hymn," which celebrates the minutemen at Concord Bridge. Another famous poem about this period is Henry Wadsworth Longfellow's "Paul Revere's Ride." It begins "Listen, my children, and you shall hear / Of the midnight ride of Paul Revere." Pick another event covered in this chapter and write a short poem about it. The poem should convey a sense of the emotions of the time. It need not be longer than eight lines.

Go Online PHSchool.com

Creating a Database
Collecting Information About Colonial Leaders
Use the Internet to research the colonial leaders mentioned in this chapter. Find the following information: date of birth, date of death, home state/colony, major event involved in. Use the computer to list the information on a chart. Then, sort the information by (1) alphabetized last name, (2) date of birth, and (3) home state/colony. For help in starting this activity, visit PHSchool.com, **Web Code mfd-0506.**

History Through Literature

Johnny Tremain
Esther Forbes

Introduction *Johnny Tremain* is a work of historical fiction, a novel that uses actual people, places, and events to tell a fictional story. The author, Esther Forbes, wrote both real histories and historical fiction. The selection below begins as Boston is facing punishment by Britain for the Boston Tea Party.

Vocabulary Before you read the selection, find the meanings of these words in a dictionary: **paroxysm, indifferent, submission, gesticulating, wharfingers, tethered, flintlocks, impartially, filching, misdemeanor.**

Esther Forbes (1891–1967)

When that bill [for the Tea Party] came . . . , it was so much heavier than anyone expected, Boston was thrown into a paroxysm of anger and despair. There had been many a moderate man who had thought the Tea Party a bit lawless and was now ready to vote payment for the tea. But when these men heard how cruelly the Town was to be punished, they swore it would never be paid for. And those other thirteen colonies. Up to this time many of them had had little interest in Boston's struggles. Now they were united as never before. The punishment united the often jealous, often indifferent, separate colonies, as the Tea Party itself had not.

Sam Adams was so happy his hands shook worse than ever.

For it had been voted in far-off London that the port of Boston should be closed—not one ship might enter, not one ship might leave the port, except only His Majesty's warships and transports, until the tea was paid for. Boston was to be starved into submission.

On that day, that first of June, 1774, Johnny and Rab, like almost all the other citizens, did no work, but wandered from place to place over the town. People were standing in angry knots talking, gesticulating, swearing that yes, they would starve, they would go down to ruin rather than give in now. Even many of the Tories were talking like that, for the punishment fell equally heavily upon the King's most loyal subjects in Boston and the very "Indians" who had tossed the tea overboard. This closing of the port of Boston was indeed tyranny; this was oppression; this was the last straw upon the back of many a moderate man.

The boys strolled the waterfront. Here, on Long Wharf, merchants' counting houses were closed and shuttered, sail lofts deserted, the riggers and porters stood idle. Overnight, hundreds of such, and sailors and ropemakers, wharfingers and dock hands, had been thrown out of work. The great ships of Boston, which had been bringing wealth for over a hundred years, were idle at their berths. No one might come and go. . . .

June was ending and the boys stood about the Common watching the soldiers of the First Brigade camped there under Earl Percy. Row upon row of identical tents, cook fires, tethered horses of officers, camp followers, stacked muskets, the quick, smart pacing of sentries. All was neat and orderly.

Muskets. It was the muskets which interested Rab the most. Already on every village green throughout New England, men and boys were drilling in defiance of the King's orders. They said they were afraid of an attack from the French. These men had no uniforms. They came from the fields and farms in the very clothes they used for plowing. That was all right. But the weapons they brought to their drilling were not. Many had ancient flintlocks, old squirrel guns, handed down for generations. Rab, for instance, all that spring had been going to Lexington once or twice a week to drill with his fellow townsmen. But he could not beg nor buy a decent gun. . . .

Rab, so concerned over a gun as he was, did an uncharacteristic, foolish thing. The two boys were standing close to a stack of muskets. As Rab explained to Johnny their good points, he put out a hand and touched the lock on one.

Without even showing bad temper, almost impartially, a mounted officer sitting on his horse close by [and] chatting with a couple of Boston's Tory girls, swung about and struck Rab a heavy blow on the side of his head with the flat of his sword. Then he went on flirting with the girls as though nothing had happened. Rab never knew what hit him. . . .

A gray, older man, a medical officer, approached, called for water, sponged Rab's face for him, and said he was coming to. Johnny was not to worry.

"What was he doing?"

"Just looking at a gun."

"Touching it?"

"Well. . . yes."

British soldiers entering Boston

"And only got hit over the head? He got off easy. Filching a soldier's arms is a serious misdemeanor. Wonder Lieutenant Bragg didn't kill him."

Rab said thickly, "I hadn't thought to filch it! Not a bad idea. Guess I'll. . . guess I'll. . ." He was still groggy from the blow. "If ever I get a chance I'll. . . ."

The medical man only laughed at him.

Analyzing Literature

1. When Johnny and Rab strolled along the waterfront, they found that people were
   A ready to give in to the British.
   B saying they would starve rather than give in to the British.
   C so busy with their jobs they took little notice of British actions.
   D agreeing with the British.

2. How would you describe the attitude of the British medical officer toward Rab and Johnny?
   A Angry
   B Uncaring
   C Sympathetic
   D Nervous

3. **Critical Thinking and Writing Drawing Inferences** (a) What do the actions of the British officer, Lieutenant Bragg, suggest about his attitude toward the colonists? (b) In what ways do you think the medical officer agreed with Lieutenant Bragg? In what ways do you think he disagreed with Bragg?

CHAPTER 6 The American Revolution

1775–1783

1. **Fighting Begins in the North**
2. **The Colonies Declare Independence**
3. **Struggles in the Middle States**
4. **Fighting for Liberty on Many Fronts**
5. **Winning the War in the South**

The Battle of Bunker Hill

Drum carried at the battle

AMERICAN EVENTS

1775
In the first major battle of the American Revolution, the colonists face the British at Bunker Hill.

1777
The American victory at the Battle of Saratoga is the turning point of the war. After this victory, the French decide to join the Americans in their fight against the British.

★ 1775 • 1777 • 1779

WORLD EVENTS

1778 ▲
France recognizes American independence.

1779 ▲
Spain enters the war against Britain.

Turning Points in the Revolution

In spite of early defeats in the war, the Americans scored victories that renewed their hopes for winning independence.

Key

- ⚔ American victories
- ⚔ British victories
- 🏳 Forts
- (1777) Date of battle

Albers Equal-Area Projection

0 — 150 — 300 Miles

0 — 150 — 300 Kilometers

BRITISH TERRITORY

Quebec

Maine (part of MA)

Montreal

Ft. Ticonderoga

Saratoga (1777)

NH

Ft. Oswego
Ft. Stanwix

Albany

Boston

Bunker Hill (1775)

MA

L. Superior

L. Huron

L. Michigan

L. Ontario

L. Erie

Mississippi R.

90°W

Ft. Detroit

Ft. Miami

Ft. Pitt

Trenton (1776)

Pennsylvania

Valley Forge

Brandywine (1777)

Philadelphia

NY

CT

RI

NJ

New York

Princeton (1777)

MD

DE

Wabash R.

Ohio R.

Cahokia (1778)

Kaskaskia (1778)

Vincennes (1779)

Virginia

Richmond

James R.

Potomac R.

Roanoke R.

Chesapeake Bay

Yorktown (1781)

Guilford Courthouse (1781)

North Carolina

Kings Mt. (1780)

Camden (1780)

Wilmington

APPALACHIAN MOUNTAINS

Mississippi R.

Savannah R.

South Carolina

Charles Town

Georgia

Savannah

ATLANTIC OCEAN

70°W

80°W

30°N

40°N

St. Lawrence R.

Champlain

Hudson R.

Delaware R.

Marquis de Lafayette, Major General, American army

Flag of a new nation

1781

The British surrender to the Americans at Yorktown.

1783

Great Britain recognizes American independence in the Treaty of Paris.

1779 · **1781** · **1783**

▲ **1780**

Tupac Armaru, a descendant of the Incas, leads a revolt against Spain.

1 Fighting Begins in the North

Prepare to Read

Objectives

In this section, you will
- Describe how Congress struggled between peace and war with Britain.
- List the advantages each side had as it entered the war.
- Explain how the Continental Army gained control of Boston.

Key Terms

Olive Branch Petition
Green Mountain Boys
Continental Army
Patriot
Loyalist
Battle of Bunker Hill
blockade
mercenary

Target Reading Skill

Comparison and Contrast Copy the chart. As you read, add facts to show how Americans struggled between keeping peace and waging war.

PEACE	WAR
• **Many colonists hope to avoid final break with Britain**	• **Green Mountain Boys capture Fort Ticonderoga**
•	•
•	•

Main Idea Even while Congress tried to make peace with Britain, fighting began in New England.

Uniform of a colonial soldier

Setting the Scene News of the fighting at Lexington and Concord spread like wildfire. Riders galloped off carrying hurriedly scrawled messages about the battles. The messengers were urged to "ride day and night" and spread the news "without the least delay." Within a few days, between 10,000 and 15,000 militia rushed to Boston. They surrounded the city and the British troops stationed there.

The sudden arrival of rebellious colonists was a clear sign that the quarrel between Britain and its American colonies was about to blaze into war. Still, many colonists hoped for a peaceful solution. Was there no way to heal relations with Britain?

Peace or War?

Just a few weeks after the battles at Lexington and Concord, on May 10, 1775, colonial delegates met at the Second Continental Congress in Philadelphia. Most of the delegates still hoped to avoid a final break with Britain. However, while they were meeting, the fighting spread.

A Peace Petition After much debate, the delegates sent a petition to King George. In the Olive Branch Petition, they declared their loyalty to the king and asked him to repeal the Intolerable Acts.

George III was furious when he heard about the petition. The colonists, he raged, were trying to begin a war "for the purpose of establishing an independent empire!" The king vowed to bring the rebels to justice. He ordered 20,000 more troops to the colonies to crush the revolt.

Congress did not learn of the king's response until months later. But even before the petition was sent, leaders like John and Sam Adams were convinced that war could not be avoided.

Rebels Take Ticonderoga Ethan Allen, a Vermont blacksmith, did not wait for Congress to act. Allen decided to lead a band of Vermonters, known as the Green Mountain Boys, in a surprise attack on Fort Ticonderoga, located at the southern tip of Lake Champlain. (See the map on page 170.) Allen knew that the fort held cannons that the colonists could use.

In early May, the Green Mountain Boys crept quietly through the morning mists to Fort Ticonderoga. They quickly overpowered the guard on duty and entered the fort. Allen rushed to the room where the British commander slept. "Come out, you old rat!" he shouted. The commander demanded to know by whose authority Allen acted. "In the name of the Great Jehovah and the Continental Congress!" Allen replied.

The British commander surrendered Ticonderoga. With the fort, the Green Mountain Boys won a valuable supply of cannons and gunpowder. Allen's success also gave Americans control of a key route into Canada.

Setting Up an Army In the meantime, the Second Continental Congress had to decide what to do about the makeshift army gathering around Boston. In June, delegates took the bold step of setting up the Continental Army. They appointed George Washington of Virginia as commander.

Washington knew that he would be fighting against one of the world's toughest armies. Still, he was willing to do his best. He set off at once to take charge of the forces around Boston.

Advantages of the Opposing Sides

The colonists who favored war against Britain called themselves Patriots. They thought British rule was harsh and unjust. About one third of the colonists were Patriots, one third were Loyalists, and one third did not take sides.

Patriots The Patriots entered the war with many disadvantages. Colonial forces were poorly organized and untrained. They had few cannons, little gunpowder, and no navy. Also, few colonists were willing to enlist in the Continental Army for long terms of service. They preferred to fight near home, as part of a local militia.

Yet, the Patriots also had advantages. Many Patriots owned rifles and were good shots. Their leader, George Washington, developed into a brilliant commander. Furthermore, Patriots were determined to fight to defend their homes and property. Reuben Stebbins of Massachusetts was

Identify Contrasts
How did the Green Mountain Boys differ from the delegates who signed the Olive Branch Petition? In which categories on your chart would you place each group?

Viewing History

Rebels Take Fort Ticonderoga

In May 1775, Ethan Allen and the Green Mountain Boys made a bold attack on Fort Ticonderoga. In this painting, Allen demands that the British commander surrender the fort. **Applying Information** *Why was Fort Ticonderoga an important prize?*

The War for Independence Begins

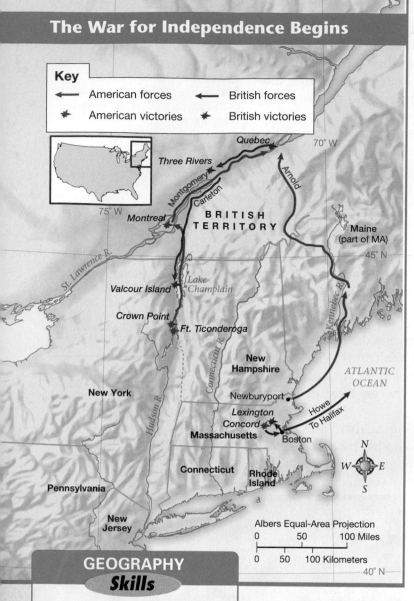

Key
← American forces ← British forces
✶ American victories ✶ British victories

Quebec
Three Rivers
70° W
Montgomery
Arnold
Carleton
Montreal
BRITISH TERRITORY
75° W
St. Lawrence R.
Maine (part of MA)
45° N
Valcour Island
Lake Champlain
Kennebec R.
Crown Point
Ft. Ticonderoga
Connecticut R.
New Hampshire
New York
Hudson R.
ATLANTIC OCEAN
Newburyport
Lexington
Howe To Halifax
Concord
Massachusetts
Boston
N
W—E
S
Connecticut
Rhode Island
Pennsylvania

Albers Equal-Area Projection
0   50   100 Miles
0   50   100 Kilometers
40° N

New Jersey

GEOGRAPHY Skills

At the beginning of the War for Independence, most of the fighting took place in the northern colonies and in Canada.

1. **Location** On the map, locate **(a)** Lexington, **(b)** Concord, **(c)** Boston, **(d)** Fort Ticonderoga, **(e)** Quebec.

2. **Movement** **(a)** Describe Arnold's route to Canada. **(b)** Describe Montgomery's route from Crown Point to Quebec.

3. **Critical Thinking Making Decisions** Based on the map, which American commander would have a harder time reaching Quebec? Explain.

typical of many patriotic farmers. When the British approached, he rode off to battle. "We'll see who's going t'own this farm!" he cried.

The British The British were a powerful foe. They had highly trained, experienced troops. Their navy was the best in the world. In addition, many colonists supported the British.

Still, Britain faced problems. Its armies were 3,000 miles from home. News and supplies took months to travel from Britain to North America. Also, British soldiers risked attacks by colonists once they marched out of the cities into the countryside.

Loyalists American colonists who remained loyal to Britain were known as **Loyalists**. They included wealthy merchants and former officials of the royal government. However, some farmers and craftsworkers were also Loyalists. There were more Loyalists in the Middle Colonies and the South than in New England.

Loyalists faced hard times during the war. Patriots tarred and feathered people known to favor the British. Many Loyalists fled to England or Canada. Others found shelter in cities controlled by the British. Those who fled lost their homes, stores, and farms.

The Fight for Boston

During the first year of conflict, much of the fighting centered around Boston. About 6,000 British troops were stationed there. Colonial militia surrounded the city and prevented the British from marching out.

Battle of Bunker Hill Even before Washington reached Boston, the Patriots took action. On June 16, 1775, Colonel William Prescott led 1,200 minutemen up Bunker Hill, across the river from Boston. From there, they could fire on British ships in Boston harbor. Prescott, however, noticed that nearby Breed's Hill was an even better position. He ordered his men to move there.

At sunrise, the British general, William Howe, spotted the Americans. He ferried about 2,400 redcoats across the harbor to attack the rebels' position. As the British approached, the Patriots held their fire.

When the Americans finally fired, the British were forced to retreat. A second British attack was also turned back. On the third try, the British pushed over the top. They took both Bunker Hill and Breed's Hill, but they paid a high price for their victory. More than

1,000 redcoats lay dead or wounded. American losses numbered only about 400.

The **Battle of Bunker Hill** was the first major battle of the Revolution. It proved that the Americans could fight bravely. It also showed that the British would not be easy to defeat.

The British Leave Boston When Washington reached Boston a few weeks after the Battle of Bunker Hill, he found about 16,000 troops camped in huts and tents at the edge of the city.

General Washington quickly began to turn raw recruits into a trained army. His job was especially difficult because soldiers from different colonies mistrusted one another. "Connecticut wants no Massachusetts men in her corps," he wrote. And "Massachusetts thinks there is no necessity for a Rhode Islander to be introduced into her [ranks]." However, Washington won the loyalty of his troops. They, in turn, learned to take orders and work together.

In January 1776, Washington had a stroke of good fortune. The cannons that the Green Mountain Boys had captured at Fort Ticonderoga arrived in Boston. Soldiers had dragged them across the mountains from Fort Ticonderoga. Washington had the cannons placed on Dorchester Heights, overlooking the harbor.

Once General Howe saw the American cannons in place, he knew that he could not hold Boston. In March 1776, he and his troops sailed from Boston to Halifax, Canada. About 1,000 American Loyalists went with them.

Although the British left New England, they did not give up. King George III ordered a blockade of all colonial ports. A **blockade** is the shutting of a port to keep people or supplies from moving in or out. The king also used **mercenaries,** or troops for hire, from Germany to help fight the colonists.

★ ★ ★ Section 1 Assessment ★ ★ ★

Recall
1. **Identify** Explain the significance of **(a)** King George III, **(b)** Olive Branch Petition, **(c)** Green Mountain Boys, **(d)** Continental Army, **(e)** George Washington, **(f)** Patriot, **(g)** Loyalist, **(h)** Battle of Bunker Hill.
2. **Define** **(a)** blockade, **(b)** mercenary.

Comprehension
3. **(a)** What steps did the Continental Congress take to pursue peace with Britain? **(b)** What steps did the Congress take to pursue war with Britain?

4. **(a)** What advantages did the Patriots have as the war began? **(b)** What advantages did the British have?
5. How did Washington force the British to leave Boston?

Critical Thinking and Writing
6. **Exploring the Main Idea** Review the Main Idea statement at the beginning of this section. Then, write a letter to Congress explaining why you think war can or cannot be avoided.
7. **Drawing Inferences** Why did some Loyalists feel they had to go with the British to Canada?

ACTIVITY

Writing a Diary Entry
You have George Washington's job at the beginning of the war. Write several diary entries describing the task you face as commander of the Continental Army.

When reading about a historical event, it is important to keep in mind that people wrote about an event from different points of view.

Ann Hulton was a Loyalist who lived with her brother in Boston just before the Revolution. His job was to collect taxes for the British. In this letter, Hulton describes an attack by a mob:

This engraving shows boys laughing at a Loyalist.

❝ You will be surprised to hear how we were obliged to take refuge on board the *Romney* man of war lying in Boston Harbor. Mrs. Burch at whose house I was, had frequently been alarmed with the Sons of Liberty surrounding her house with most hideous howlings. . . . She had been exposed since her arrival and threatened with greater violence. She had removed her most valuable [possessions] and held herself in readiness to depart at an hour's notice. The occasion soon happened . . . we soon found that the mobs here are very different from those in Old England . . . these Sons of Violence after attacking houses, breaking windows, beating, stoning and bruising several gentlemen belonging to the Customs, the Collector mortally and burning his boat. . . . All was ended with a speech from one of the leaders, concluding thus, 'We will defend our Liberties and property, by the Strength of our Arm and the Help of our God. . . .' This is a specimen of the Sons of Liberty, of whom no doubt you have heard, and will hear more. . . . ❞

—Ann Hulton, in a letter written June 30, 1768

Learn the Skill *Use these steps to identify points of view:*

1. **Identify the source.** If you know the background of the writer, you can evaluate that person's attitude.

2. **Note the frame of reference.** The place, time, and circumstances can make a difference.

3. **Find main ideas.** What is the main point that the writer or speaker is making?

4. **Look for emotionally charged words.** How information is presented affects the point of view.

5. **Identify points of view.** How does the writer or speaker feel?

Practice the Skill *Use the introduction and the letter to answer the following questions:*

1. How do you know that Ann Hulton was writing to a Loyalist?

2. **(a)** Where did the event described take place? **(b)** How would you characterize the event?

3. Restate the main point of the letter.

4. Identify three emotionally charged words used in the letter.

5. **(a)** What is the writer's point of view? **(b)** Explain how you can tell.

Apply the Skill *See the Chapter Review and Assessment.*

2 The Colonies Declare Independence

Prepare to Read

Objectives

In this section, you will
- Describe the impact of *Common Sense*.
- List the steps Congress took to declare independence.
- Summarize the main ideas of the Declaration of Independence.

Key Terms

Common Sense
traitor
Declaration of Independence
preamble
natural rights

Target Reading Skill

Clarifying Meaning Copy the concept web. As you read, fill in the blank ovals with information about the creation and contents of the Declaration of Independence. Add as many ovals as you need.

(Concept web:) Thomas Jefferson writes the Declaration — Preamble — Part 1 — DECLARATION OF INDEPENDENCE

Main Idea In July 1776, the colonies declared independence from Britain.

Setting the Scene
Dr. Benjamin Rush of Philadelphia looked down at the manuscript in his hand. A line referring to King George as "the royal brute of Great Britain" seemed to leap off the page. Apparently, that was only the beginning! Would any printer dare to publish such a document?

Rush had asked his friend Thomas Paine to write an essay urging the colonies to declare independence. By the winter of 1775, the Patriots had been fighting Britain for months. Yet, many colonists were still reluctant to cut their ties with Britain. In a fiery pamphlet, Paine told these colonists that it was time to make the break. He called the pamphlet *Common Sense.*

When *Common Sense* appeared in January 1776, curious readers snatched up copies. In six months, more than 500,000 were sold. "*Common Sense* is working a powerful change in the minds of men," George Washington observed.

Urged on by Paine and other radicals—people who want to make drastic changes in society—the colonists were beginning to think the unthinkable. They were thinking of creating a nation of their own.

Thomas Paine

Common Sense

By 1776, many colonists had come to believe that Parliament did not have the right to make laws for the 13 colonies. After all, they argued, the colonists had their own elected legislatures. At the same time, however, most colonists still felt a bond of loyalty to Britain. They especially felt that they owed allegiance to the king.

In *Common Sense,* Thomas Paine set out to change the colonists' attitudes toward Britain and the king. Colonists, he said, did not owe loyalty to George III or any other monarch. The very idea of having kings and queens was wrong, he said.

> ❝ In England a King hath little more to do than to make war and give away [jobs]; which in plain terms, is

Viewing History

Signing the Declaration

Thomas Jefferson labored many hours perfecting the Declaration of Independence. In this painting, Jefferson and other committee members present the Declaration to the Continental Congress. **Evaluating Information** *How does the artist show the significance of the meeting?*

to impoverish the nation. . . . Of more worth is one honest man to society and in the sight of God, than all the crowned ruffians that ever lived. **99**

—Thomas Paine, *Common Sense,* 1776

The colonists did not owe anything to Britain, either, Paine went on. If the British had helped the colonists, they had done so for their own profit. It could only hurt the colonists to remain under British rule. "Everything that is right or reasonable pleads for separation," he concluded. " 'Tis time to part."

Congress Votes for Independence

Common Sense sold many colonists on the idea of independence. It also deeply impressed many members of the Continental Congress. Richard Henry Lee of Virginia wrote to Washington, "I am now convinced . . . of the necessity for separation." In June 1776, Lee arose in Congress to introduce a resolution in favor of independence:

66 *Resolved,* That these United Colonies are and of right ought to be, free and independent States, that they are absolved from all allegiance to the British Crown, and that all political connection between them and the State of Great Britain is, and ought to be, totally dissolved. **99**

—Richard Henry Lee, Resolution at the Second Continental Congress, June 7, 1776

Making the Break The delegates faced a difficult decision. There could be no turning back once they declared independence. If they fell into British hands, they would be hanged as traitors. A **traitor** is a person who betrays his or her country.

After long debate, the Congress took a fateful step. They appointed a committee to draw up a formal declaration of independence. The committee included John Adams, Benjamin Franklin, Thomas Jefferson, Robert Livingston, and Roger Sherman. Their job was to tell the world why the colonies were breaking away from Britain.

The committee asked Thomas Jefferson to write the document. Jefferson was one of the youngest delegates. He was a quiet man who spoke little at formal meetings. Among friends, however, he liked to sprawl in a chair with his long legs stretched out and talk for hours. His ability to write clearly and gracefully had earned him great respect.

Signing the Document In late June, Jefferson completed the declaration, and it was read to the Congress. On July 2, the Continental Congress voted that the 13 colonies were "free and independent States." After polishing Jefferson's language, the delegates adopted the document on the night of July 4, 1776. They then ordered the **Declaration of Independence** to be printed.

John Hancock, president of the Continental Congress, signed the Declaration first. He penned his signature boldly, in large, clear letters. "There," he said, "I guess King George will be able to read that."

Copies of the Declaration were distributed throughout the colonies. Patriots greeted the news of independence with joyous— and sometimes rowdy—celebrations. In New York, colonists tore down a statue of King George III. In Boston, the sound of cannons could be heard for hours.

The Declaration of Independence

The Declaration of Independence consists of a **preamble,** or introduction, followed by three main parts.*

Natural Rights The first section of the Declaration stresses the idea of **natural rights,** or rights that belong to all people from birth. In bold, ringing words, Jefferson wrote:

> 66 We hold these truths to be self-evident, that all men are created equal; that they are endowed by their Creator with certain unalienable rights; that among these are life, liberty, and the pursuit of happiness. 99

According to the Declaration of Independence, people form governments in order to protect their natural rights and liberties. Governments can exist only if they have the "consent of the governed." If a government fails to protect the rights of its citizens, then it is the people's "right [and] duty, to throw off such government, and to provide new guards for their future security."

---

*The complete Declaration of Independence is printed at the end of this section on pages 177–180.

Primary Source

"Remember the Ladies"

While John Adams served as a delegate in the second Continental Congress, his wife, Abigail, wrote him the following letter:
"I long to hear that you have independence. And . . . in the new Code of Laws which I suppose it will be necessary for you to make I desire you would Remember the Ladies, and be more generous and favourable to them than your ancestors. Do not put such unlimited power into the hands of the Husbands. . . . If particular care and attention is not paid to the Ladies we are determined to foment a Rebellion, and will not hold ourselves bound by any Laws in which we have no voice, or Representation."
—Abigail Adams, letter to John Adams, March 31, 1776

Analyzing Primary Sources
How did Abigail Adams use arguments for independence made by Patriots to promote greater rights for women?

British Wrongs The second part of the Declaration lists the wrongs that led the Americans to break away from Britain. Jefferson condemned King George III for disbanding colonial legislatures and for sending troops to the colonies in peacetime. He complained about limits on trade and about taxes imposed without the consent of the people.

Jefferson listed many other wrongs to show why the colonists had the right to rebel. He also pointed out that the colonies had petitioned the king to correct these injustices. Yet, the injustices remained. A ruler who treated his subjects in this manner, he boldly concluded, is a tyrant and not fit to rule:

> 66 In every state of these oppressions, we have petitioned for redress in the most humble terms; our repeated petitions have been answered only by repeated injury. A prince whose character is thus marked by every act which may define a tyrant is unfit to be the ruler of a free people. 99

Independence The last part of the Declaration announces that the colonies are the United States of America. All political ties with Britain have been cut. As a free and independent nation, the United States has the full power to "levy war, conclude peace, contract alliances, establish commerce, and to do all other acts and things which independent states may of right do."

The signers close the declaration with a solemn pledge:

> 66 And, for the support of this declaration, with a firm reliance on the protection of Divine Providence, we mutually pledge to each other our lives, our fortunes, and our sacred honor. 99

Summarize
Write a paragraph that summarizes the three major parts of the Declaration of Independence.

★ ★ ★ Section 2 Assessment ★ ★ ★

Recall

1. **Identify** Explain the significance of (a) Thomas Paine, (b) *Common Sense*, (c) Richard Henry Lee, (d) Thomas Jefferson, (e) Declaration of Independence.

2. **Define** (a) traitor, (b) preamble, (c) natural rights.

Comprehension

3. What arguments did Thomas Paine use in *Common Sense* to persuade the colonists to declare independence?

4. What actions did Congress take to make the final break with Britain?

5. Describe the main parts of the Declaration of Independence.

Critical Thinking and Writing

6. **Exploring the Main Idea** Review the Main Idea statement at the beginning of this section. Explain the arguments that the colonies used for declaring independence from Britain.

7. **Analyzing Primary Sources** Review the excerpt from Thomas Paine's *Common Sense* that appears on pages 173–174. Explain the meaning of this excerpt in your own words.

ACTIVITY

Connecting to Today
Use the Internet to visit the exhibition of the original Declaration of Independence in Washington, D.C. Prepare a guided tour of the exhibit. Include information about the meaning of the document to Americans today. For help in completing the activity, visit PHSchool.com, **Web Code mfd-0601.**

The Declaration of Independence

On June 7, 1776, the Continental Congress approved the resolution that "these United Colonies are, and of right ought to be, free and independent States." Congress then appointed a committee to write a declaration of independence. The committee members were John Adams, Benjamin Franklin, Robert Livingston, Roger Sherman, and Thomas Jefferson.

Jefferson actually wrote the Declaration, but he got advice from the others. On July 2, Congress discussed the Declaration and made some changes. On July 4, 1776, it adopted the Declaration of Independence in its final form.

The Declaration is printed in black. The headings have been added to show the parts of the Declaration. They are not part of the original text. Annotations, or explanations, are on the white side of the page. Difficult words are defined.

When in the course of human events it becomes necessary for one people to dissolve the political bands which have connected them with another and to assume, among the powers of the earth, the separate and equal station to which the laws of nature and of nature's God entitle them, a decent respect to the opinions of mankind requires that they should declare the causes which impel them to the separation.

dissolve: break **powers of the earth:** other nations **station:** place **impel:** force

The colonists feel that they must explain to the world the reasons why they are breaking away from England.

The Purpose of Government Is to Protect Basic Rights

We hold these truths to be self-evident, that all men are created equal; that they are endowed by their Creator with certain unalienable rights; that among these are life, liberty, and the pursuit of happiness. That, to secure these rights, governments are instituted among men, deriving their just powers from the consent of the governed; that, whenever any form of government becomes destructive of these ends, it is the right of the people to alter or to abolish it, and to institute a new government, laying its foundation on such principles and organizing its powers in such form, as to them shall seem most likely to effect their safety and happiness. Prudence, indeed, will dictate that governments long established should not be changed for light and transient causes; and, accordingly, all experience hath shown that mankind are more disposed to suffer, while evils are sufferable, than to right themselves by abolishing the forms to which they are accustomed. But when a long train of abuses and usurpations, pursuing invariably the same object, evinces a design to reduce them under absolute despotism, it is their right, it is their duty, to throw off such government and to provide new guards for their future security. Such has been the patient sufferance of these colonies, and such is now the necessity which constrains them to alter their former systems of government. The history of the present King of Great Britain is a history of repeated injuries and usurpations, all having, in direct object, the establishment of an absolute tyranny over these States. To prove this, let facts be submitted to a candid world:

endowed: given **unalienable rights:** so basic that they cannot be taken away **secure:** protect **instituted:** set up **deriving:** getting **alter:** change **effect:** bring about

People set up governments to protect their basic rights. Governments get their power from the consent of the governed. If a government takes away the basic rights of the people, the people have the right to change the government.

prudence: wisdom **transient:** temporary, passing **disposed:** likely

usurpations: taking and using powers that do not belong to a person **invariably:** always **evinces a design to reduce them under absolute despotism:** makes a clear plan to put them under complete and unjust control **sufferance:** endurance

constrains: forces **absolute tyranny:** harsh and unjust government **candid:** free from prejudice

People do not readily change governments. But they are forced to do so when a government becomes tyrannical. King George III has a long record of abusing his power.

Wrongs Done by the King

assent: approval **relinquish:** give up **inestimable:** too great a value to be measured **formidable:** causing fear

This part of the Declaration spells out three sets of wrongs that led the colonists to break with Britain.

The first set of wrongs is the king's unjust use of power. The king refused to approve laws that are needed. He has tried to control the colonial legislatures.

depository: storehouse **fatiguing:** tiring out **compliance:** giving in **dissolved:** broken up **annihilation:** total destruction **convulsions:** disturbances

The king has tried to force colonial legislatures into doing his will by wearing them out. He has dissolved legislatures (such as those of Massachusetts).

endeavored: tried **obstructing:** blocking **naturalization:** process of becoming a citizen **migration:** moving **hither:** here **appropriations:** grants **obstructed the administration of justice:** prevented justice from being done **judiciary powers:** system of law courts **tenure:** term (of office) **erected:** set up **multitude:** large number **swarms:** huge crowds **harass:** cause trouble **render:** make

Among other wrongs, he has refused to let settlers move west to take up new land. He has prevented justice from being done. Also, he has sent large numbers of customs officials to cause problems for the colonists.

jurisdiction: authority **quartering:** housing **mock:** false

The king has joined with others, meaning Parliament, to make laws for the colonies. The Declaration then lists the second set of wrongs—unjust acts of Parliament.

He has refused his assent to laws the most wholesome and necessary for the public good.

He has forbidden his governors to pass laws of immediate and pressing importance, unless suspended in their operation till his assent should be obtained; and, when so suspended, he has utterly neglected to attend to them.

He has refused to pass other laws for the accommodation of the large districts of people, unless those people would relinquish the right of representation in the legislature; a right inestimable to them and formidable to tyrants only.

He has called together legislative bodies at places unusual, uncomfortable, and distant from the depository of their public records, for the sole purpose of fatiguing them into compliance with his measures.

He has dissolved representative houses, repeatedly for opposing, with manly firmness, his invasions on the rights of the people.

He has refused, for a long time after such dissolutions, to cause others to be elected: whereby the legislative powers, incapable of annihilation, have returned to the people at large for their exercise; the state remaining, in the meantime, exposed to all the danger of invasion from without and convulsions within.

He has endeavored to prevent the population of these States; for that purpose, obstructing the laws for naturalization of foreigners, refusing to pass others to encourage their migration hither, and raising the conditions of new appropriations of lands.

He has obstructed the administration of justice by refusing his assent to laws for establishing judiciary powers.

He has made judges dependent on his will alone for the tenure of their offices and the amount and payment of their salaries.

He has erected a multitude of new offices and sent hither swarms of officers to harass our people and eat out their substance.

He has kept among us, in time of peace, standing armies, without the consent of our legislatures.

He has affected to render the military independent of, and superior to, the civil power.

He has combined with others to subject us to a jurisdiction foreign to our Constitution and unacknowledged by our laws, giving his assent to their acts of pretended legislation:

For quartering large bodies of armed troops among us;

For protecting them by a mock trial from punishment for any murders which they should commit on the inhabitants of these States;

For cutting off our trade with all parts of the world;

For imposing taxes on us without our consent;

For depriving us, in many cases, of the benefit of trial by jury;

For transporting us beyond seas to be tried for pretended offences;

For abolishing the free system of English laws in a neighboring province, establishing therein an arbitrary government, and enlarging its boundaries, so as to render it at once an example and fit instrument for introducing the same absolute rule into these colonies;

For taking away our charters, abolishing our most valuable laws, and altering, fundamentally, the powers of our governments;

For suspending our own legislatures and declaring themselves invested with power to legislate for us in all cases whatsoever.

He has abdicated government here by declaring us out of his protection and waging war against us.

He has plundered our seas, ravaged our coasts, burnt our towns, and destroyed the lives of our people.

He is, at this time, transporting large armies of foreign mercenaries to complete the works of death, desolation, and tyranny already begun with circumstances of cruelty and perfidy scarcely paralleled in the most barbarous ages, and totally unworthy the head of a civilized nation.

He has constrained our fellow citizens, taken captive on the high seas, to bear arms against their country, to become the executioners of their friends and brethren, or to fall themselves by their hands.

He has excited domestic insurrections amongst us and has endeavored to bring on the inhabitants of our frontiers, the merciless Indian savages, whose known rule of warfare is an undistinguished destruction of all ages, sexes, and conditions.

In every state of these oppressions, we have petitioned for redress in the most humble terms; our repeated petitions have been answered only by repeated injury. A prince whose character is thus marked by every act which may define a tyrant is unfit to be the ruler of a free people.

Nor have we been wanting in attention to our British brethren. We have warned them, from time to time, of attempts made by their legislature to extend an unwarrantable jurisdiction over us. We have reminded them of the circumstances of our emigration and settlement here. We have appealed to their native justice and magnanimity, and we have conjured them, by the ties of our common kindred, to disavow these usurpations, which would inevitably interrupt our connections and correspondence. They, too, have been deaf to the voice of justice and consanguinity. We must, therefore, acquiesce in the necessity which denounces our separation, and hold them, as we hold the rest of mankind, enemies in war, in peace, friends.

imposing: forcing *depriving:* taking away *transporting us beyond seas:* sending colonists to England for trial *neighboring province:* Quebec *arbitrary government:* unjust rule *fit instrument:* suitable tool *invested with power:* having the power

During the years leading up to 1776, the colonists claimed that Parliament had no right to make laws for them because they were not represented in Parliament. Here, the colonists object to recent laws of Parliament, such as the Quartering Act and the blockade of colonial ports, which cut off their trade. They also object to Parliament's claim that it had the right to tax them without their consent.

abdicated: given up *plundered:* robbed *ravaged:* attacked *mercenaries:* hired soldiers *desolation:* misery *perfidy:* falseness *barbarous:* uncivilized *constrained:* forced *brethren:* brothers *domestic insurrections:* internal revolts

Here, the Declaration lists the third set of wrongs—warlike acts of the king. Instead of listening to the colonists, the king has made war on them. He has hired soldiers to fight in America.

oppressions: harsh rule *petitioned:* asked *redress:* relief *unwarrantable jurisdiction over:* unfair authority *magnanimity:* generosity *conjured:* called upon *common kindred:* relatives *disavow:* turn away from *consanguinity:* blood relationships, kinship *acquiesce:* agree *denounces:* speaks out against

During this time, colonists have repeatedly asked for relief. But their requests have brought only more suffering. They have appealed to the British people but received no help. So they are forced to separate.

Colonies Declare Independence

We, therefore, the representatives of the United States of America, in general Congress assembled, appealing to the Supreme Judge of the world for the rectitude of our intentions, do, in the name and by the authority of the good people of these colonies, solemnly publish and declare, that these united colonies are, and of right ought to be, free and independent states: that they are absolved from all allegiance to the British Crown, and that all political connection between them and the state of Great Britain is, and ought to be, totally dissolved; and that, as free and independent states, they have full power to levy war, conclude peace, contract alliances, establish commerce, and to do all other acts and things which independent states may of right do. And, for the support of this declaration, with a firm reliance on the protection of Divine Providence, we mutually pledge to each other our lives, our fortunes, and our sacred honor.

Signers of the Declaration of Independence

John Hancock, President

Charles Thomson, Secretary

New Hampshire
Josiah Bartlett
William Whipple
Matthew Thornton

Massachusetts
Samuel Adams
John Adams
Robert Treat Paine
Elbridge Gerry

Rhode Island
Stephen Hopkins
William Ellery

Connecticut
Roger Sherman
Samuel Huntington
William Williams
Oliver Wolcott

Delaware
Caesar Rodney
George Read
Thomas McKean

New York
William Floyd
Philip Livingston
Francis Lewis
Lewis Morris

New Jersey
Richard Stockton
John Witherspoon
Francis Hopkinson
John Hart
Abraham Clark

Georgia
Button Gwinnett
Lyman Hall
George Walton

Maryland
Samuel Chase
William Paca
Thomas Stone
Charles Carroll

North Carolina
William Hooper
Joseph Hewes
John Penn

Virginia
George Wythe
Richard Henry Lee
Thomas Jefferson
Benjamin Harrison
Thomas Nelson, Jr.
Francis Lightfoot Lee
Carter Braxton

South Carolina
Edward Rutledge
Thomas Heyward, Jr.
Thomas Lynch, Jr.
Arthur Middleton

Pennsylvania
Robert Morris
Benjamin Rush
Benjamin Franklin
John Morton
George Clymer
James Smith
George Taylor
James Wilson
George Ross

3 Struggles in the Middle States

Prepare to Read

Objectives

In this section, you will
- List the battles fought in New York and New Jersey.
- Explain how the Battle of Saratoga marked a turning point in the war.
- Describe the conditions at Valley Forge.

Key Terms

Battle of Long Island

Battle of Trenton

Battle of Saratoga

ally

cavalry

Valley Forge

Target Reading Skill

Sequence Copy the flow-chart. As you read, fill in the boxes with the major events of the struggles in the Middle States.

August, 1776 Defeat at Long Island forces Washington to retreat
↓
↓
↓
Winter, 1777–1778 Washington's troops suffer hardships at Valley Forge

Main Idea After a series of Patriot defeats, an American victory at Saratoga marked a major turning point in the Revolution.

Setting the Scene

Early one morning in June 1776, Daniel McCurtin glanced out his window at New York harbor. He was amazed to see "something resembling a wood of pine trees trimmed." He watched the forest move across the water. Then, he understood. The trees were the masts of ships!

> 66 I could not believe my eyes . . . the whole bay was full of shipping as ever it could be. I declare that I thought all London was afloat. 99
>
> —George F. Scheer and Hugh F. Rankin, *Rebels and Redcoats*

McCurtin had witnessed the arrival of a large British fleet in New York. Aboard the ships were General Howe and thousands of redcoats. Thus began a new stage in the war. Previously, most of the fighting of the American Revolution had taken place in New England. In mid-1776, the heavy fighting shifted to the Middle States. There, the Continental Army suffered through the worst days of the war.

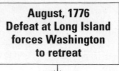

A British redcoat

The British Take New York

Washington, expecting Howe's attack, had led his forces south from Boston to New York City. His army, however, was no match for the British. Howe had about 34,000 troops and 10,000 sailors. He also had ships to ferry them ashore. Washington had fewer than 20,000 poorly trained troops. Worse, he had no navy.

In August, Howe's army landed on Long Island. In the **Battle of Long Island,** more than 1,400 Americans were killed, wounded, or captured. The rest retreated to Manhattan. The British pursued. To avoid capture, Washington hurried north.

Throughout the autumn, Washington fought a series of battles with Howe's army. In November, he crossed the Hudson River into

The Revolutionary War, 1776–1777

Albers Equal-Area Projection

0   100   200 Miles

0   100   200 Kilometers

GEOGRAPHY
Skills

In 1776 and 1777, the Americans and British battled over a large area. The American victory at Saratoga marked a major turning point in the war.

1. **Location** On the map, locate **(a)** Long Island, **(b)** New York City, **(c)** Trenton, **(d)** Hudson River, **(e)** Saratoga, **(f)** Valley Forge.

2. **Movement** How did the British use sea power to help them capture Philadelphia?

3. **Critical Thinking Applying Information** How did Burgoyne and St. Leger use geography to help move their armies quickly toward Albany?

New Jersey. Chased by the British, the Americans retreated across the Delaware River into Pennsylvania.

During the campaign for New York, Washington needed information about Howe's forces. Nathan Hale, a young Connecticut officer, volunteered to go behind British lines. On his way back with the information, Hale was seized by the British and searched. Hidden in the soles of his shoes was information about British troop movements.

There was no trial. Howe ordered Hale to be hanged the next morning. As Hale walked to the gallows, he is said to have declared: "I only regret that I have but one life to lose for my country."

Washington Turns Retreat Into Victory in New Jersey

Months of hard campaigning took a toll on the Continental Army. In December 1776, Washington described his troops as sick, dirty, and "so thinly clad as to be unfit for service." Every day, soldiers deserted. Washington wrote to his brother: "I am wearied to death. I think the game is pretty near up."

Washington decided on a bold move: a surprise attack on Trenton. On Christmas night, he secretly led his troops across the icy Delaware River. Soldiers shivered as spray from the river froze on their faces. Once ashore, they marched through swirling snow. Some had no shoes. They tied rags around their feet. "Soldiers, keep by your officers," Washington urged.

Early on December 26, the Americans surprised the Hessian troops guarding Trenton and took most of them prisoner. The Hessians were soldiers from Germany. An American summed up the Battle of Trenton: "Hessian population of Trenton at 8 A.M.—1,408 men and 39 officers; Hessian population at 9 A.M.—0."

British General Charles Cornwallis set out at once to retake Trenton and to capture Washington. Late on January 2, 1777, he saw the lights of Washington's campfires. "At last we have run down the old fox," he said, "and we will bag him in the morning."

Washington fooled Cornwallis. He left the fires burning and slipped behind British lines to attack a British force that was marching toward Princeton. There, the Continental Army won another victory. From Princeton, Washington moved to Morristown, where the army would spend the winter. The victories at Trenton and Princeton gave the Americans new hope.

A Turning Point in the War

In London, British officials were dismayed by the army's failure to crush the rebels. Early in 1777, General John Burgoyne (buhr GOIN) presented a new plan for victory. If British troops cut off New England from the other colonies, he argued, the war would soon be over.

Burgoyne's Plan Burgoyne wanted three British armies to march on Albany, New York, from different directions. They would crush American forces there. Once they controlled the Hudson River, the British could stop the flow of soldiers and supplies from New England to Washington's army.

Burgoyne's plan called for General Howe to march on Albany from New York City. George III, however, wanted Howe to capture Philadelphia first.

In July 1777, Howe sailed from New York to Chesapeake Bay, where he began his march on Philadelphia. Howe captured Philadelphia, defeating the Americans at the battles of Brandywine and Germantown. But instead of moving toward Albany to meet Burgoyne as planned, he retired to comfortable quarters in Philadelphia for the winter. For his part, Washington retreated to Valley Forge, Pennsylvania.

Meanwhile, British armies under Burgoyne and Barry St. Leger (lay ZHAIR) marched from Canada toward Albany. St. Leger tried to take Fort Stanwix. However, a strong American army, led by Benedict Arnold, drove him back.

Victory at Saratoga Only Burgoyne was left to march on Albany. His army moved slowly because it had many heavy baggage carts to drag through the woods. To slow Burgoyne further, Patriots cut down trees and dammed up streams to block the route.

Despite these obstacles, Burgoyne recaptured Fort Ticonderoga. He then sent troops into Vermont to find food and horses. There, Patriots attacked the redcoats. At the Battle of Bennington, they wounded or captured nearly 1,000 British.

Burgoyne's troubles grew. The Green Mountain Boys hurried into New York to help American forces there. At the village of Saratoga, the Americans surrounded the British. When Burgoyne tried to break free, the Americans beat him back. Realizing that he was trapped, Burgoyne surrendered his entire army to the Americans on October 17, 1777.

The American victory at the Battle of Saratoga was a major turning point in the war. It ended the British threat to New England. It boosted American spirits at a time when Washington's army was suffering defeats. Most important, it convinced France to become an ally of the United States. Nations that are allies work together to achieve a common goal.

Aid From Europe The Continental Congress had long hoped for French aid. In 1776, the Congress had sent Benjamin Franklin to Paris to persuade Louis XVI, the French king, to give the Americans weapons and other badly needed supplies. In addition, the Congress wanted France to declare war on Britain.

Identifying Sequence

Read the paragraphs that appear below "A Turning Point in the War." Identify the important events and note them on your flowchart.

France Enters the War

France and Britain in conflict for many years

→ Conflict between France and Britain increases after the French and Indian War

→ Americans appeal to France for support during the Revolutionary War

→ France gives American rebels money and supplies but stays neutral

→ Americans defeat British at Saratoga

→ Victory at Saratoga proves to France that Americans can win

→ **France gives military and naval support to American forces**

GRAPHIC ORGANIZER
Skills

The American defeat of the British at Saratoga was a turning point in the war.

1. **Comprehension** What happened between France and Britain after the French and Indian War?

2. **Critical Thinking Making Decisions** What do you think France hoped to gain by helping the Americans?

The French were eager to defeat Britain, but they were also cautious. France was still angry about its defeat at British hands in the French and Indian War. However, Louis XVI did not want to help the Americans openly unless he was sure that they could win.

The American victory at Saratoga convinced France that the United States could stand up to Britain. In February 1778, France became the first nation to sign a treaty with the United States. It recognized the new nation and agreed to provide military aid. Later, the Netherlands and Spain also joined in the war against Britain. France, the Netherlands, and Spain all provided loans to the United States.

Even before European nations agreed to help the United States, individual volunteers had been coming from Europe to join the American cause. Some became leading officers in the American army.

The Marquis de Lafayette (lah fee EHT), a young French noble, brought trained soldiers to help the Patriot cause. Lafayette, who fought at Brandywine, became one of Washington's most trusted friends.

From the German state of Prussia came Friedrich von Steuben (STOO buhn), who helped train Washington's troops to march and drill. Von Steuben had served in the Prussian army, which was considered the best in Europe.

Two Polish officers also joined the Americans. Thaddeus Kosciusko (kahs ee UHS koh), an engineer, helped build forts and other defenses. Casimir Pulaski trained **cavalry,** or troops on horseback.

The Hardships of Valley Forge

The victory at Saratoga and the promise of help from Europe boosted American morale. Even so, Washington's Continental Army had to face hard times as it suffered through the long, cold winter of 1777–1778 at a makeshift camp at **Valley Forge.**

Conditions at Valley Forge were terrible. Soldiers shivered in damp, drafty huts. Many slept on the frozen ground. Some soldiers stood guard wrapped only in blankets. Others had no shoes, so they wrapped bits of cloth around their feet. As the bitter winter wore on, soldiers suffered from frostbite and disease. An army surgeon from Connecticut wrote about his hardships:

> **66** I am sick—discontented—and out of humor. Poor food—hard lodging—cold weather—fatigue—nasty clothes—nasty cookery . . . a pox on my bad luck! There comes a bowl of beef soup, full of burnt leaves and dirt. . . . Away with it, boys!—I'll live like the chameleon upon air. **99**
>
> —Albigence Waldo, *Diary,* December 14, 1777

As news of the suffering at Valley Forge spread, Patriots from around the nation sent help. Women collected food, medicine, warm clothes, and ammunition for the army. Some women, like Martha Washington, wife of the commander, went to Valley Forge to help the sick and wounded.

The arrival of desperately needed supplies was soon followed by warmer weather. The drills of Baron von Steuben helped the Continentals to march and fight with a new skill. By the spring of 1778, the army at Valley Forge was more hopeful. Washington could not know it at the time, but the Patriots' bleakest hour had passed.

★ ★ ★ Section 3 Assessment ★ ★ ★

Recall

1. **Identify** Explain the significance of **(a)** Battle of Long Island, **(b)** Nathan Hale, **(c)** Battle of Trenton, **(d)** General John Burgoyne, **(e)** Battle of Saratoga, **(f)** Marquis de Lafayette, **(g)** Friedrich von Steuben, **(h)** Thaddeus Kosciusko, **(i)** Valley Forge.
2. **Define** **(a)** ally, **(b)** cavalry.

Comprehension

3. How did Washington turn retreat into victory in New Jersey?
4. Explain the results of the Battle of Saratoga.
5. How did the Continental Army come through the terrible winter at Valley Forge with new hope?

Critical Thinking and Writing

6. **Exploring the Main Idea** Review the Main Idea statement at the beginning of this section. Then, write a newspaper article celebrating the victory at Saratoga. Why was it a turning point?
7. **Analyzing Information** Why do you think people from other lands, such as Lafayette and Pulaski, were willing to risk their lives to help the American cause?

> **ACTIVITY**
>
> **Creating a Dramatic Scene** Write a scene in which Benjamin Franklin meets with the French King Louis XVI to convince him to support the Continental Army. Focus on how France and the Continental Army would benefit from such an alliance.

4 Fighting for Liberty on Many Fronts

Prepare to Read

Objectives

In this section, you will
- Describe the role of women in the war.
- List the choices African Americans had during the American Revolution.
- Explain how the war was fought on the frontier and at sea.

Main Idea During the Revolution, Americans fought for liberty on many fronts and in many ways.

Target Reading Skill

Cause and Effect Copy the cause chart below. As you read, fill in the chart to show how the cause of fighting for independence united different groups of colonists. Add as many boxes as you need.

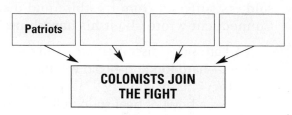

Patriots

COLONISTS JOIN THE FIGHT

Setting the Scene Ten years before the Revolution, white colonists in Charleston protested the Stamp Act. "Liberty! Liberty and stamped paper!" they cried as they paraded around the homes of British officials. Shortly after, a group of enslaved Africans held their own parade. To the amazement of white colonists, the marchers chanted the same cry: "Liberty! Liberty!"

Many enslaved Africans believed that the ideal of liberty applied to them just as it did to whites. In Massachusetts, a group of slaves presented petitions to the governor, asking for their freedom. One slave compared the situation of whites and enslaved Africans:

> 66 You [white colonists] are taxed without your consent, because you are not represented in parliament. I grant that [is] a grievance . . . [But] pray, sir, . . . are not your hearts also hard, when you hold [Africans] in slavery who are entitled to liberty by the law of nature, equal as yourselves? 99
>
> —Letter to a Boston newspaper *The Massachusetts Spy*, February 10, 1774

As the fighting continued, Americans worked for liberty in many ways and on many fronts. Sailors, as well as soldiers, fought in the various battles of the war. Women, free blacks, and enslaved Africans took part too.

Women Take Part in the War

When men went off to fight in the Revolution, women took on added work at home. Some planted and harvested the crops. Others made shoes and wove cloth for blankets and uniforms. One woman, called "Handy Betsy the Blacksmith," was known for making cannons and guns for the army.

Helping the Army Many women joined their husbands at the front. They cared for the wounded, washed clothes, and cooked. Martha Washington joined her husband whenever she could.

Some women achieved lasting fame for their wartime service. Betsy Ross of Philadelphia sewed flags for Washington's army. Legend claims that she made the first American flag of stars and stripes.

A few women even took part in battle. During the Battle of Monmouth in 1778, Mary Ludwig Hays carried water to her husband and other soldiers. The soldiers called her Molly Pitcher. When her husband was wounded, she took his place, loading and firing the cannon.

New Attitudes As women participated in the war, they began to think differently about their rights. Those women who had taken charge of farms or their husbands' businesses became more confident and willing to speak out.

Most men in Congress did not agree that women should be treated equally. Still, the Revolution established important ideals of liberty and equality. In later years, these ideals of the Revolution would encourage women to campaign for equal treatment—and eventually to win it.

African Americans Face Hard Choices

By 1776, more than a half million African Americans lived in the colonies. At first, the Continental Congress refused to let African Americans, whether free or enslaved, join the army. Some members doubted the loyalty of armed African Americans. The British, however, offered freedom to some male slaves who would serve the king. Washington feared that this would greatly increase the ranks of the British army. In response, Washington changed his policy and asked Congress to allow free African Americans to enlist.

Joining the Fight About 5,000 African Americans from all the colonies, except South Carolina, served in the army. Another 2,000 served in the navy which, from the start, allowed African Americans to join. At least nine black minutemen saw action at Lexington and Concord. One of them, Prince Estabrook, was wounded. Two others, Peter Salem and Salem Poor, went on to fight bravely at Bunker Hill.

Some African Americans formed special regiments. Others served in white regiments as drummers, fifers, spies, and guides. Saul Matthews and James Armistead were among those African Americans who served as spies. Whites recognized the courage of their African American comrades. As one eyewitness recalled, "Three times in succession, [African Americans] were attacked . . . by [British troops] and three times did they successfully repel the assault and . . . preserve our army from capture. . . ."

Viewing History

James Armistead

Though enslaved, James Armistead served the Patriot cause as a spy. Under the direction of General Lafayette, Armistead was a volunteer in British army camps. The information he gained contributed to the American victory at Yorktown. **Drawing Inferences** *Why do you think Armistead later decided to change his name to Lafayette?*

Enslaved African Americans faced difficult choices. If they joined the American army or continued to work on Patriot plantations, the British might capture and sell them. If they tried to flee to the British army to gain freedom, they risked being hanged by angry Patriots.

Hoping for Freedom Yet, many slaves did flee their masters, especially those who lived near the coast, where the British navy patrolled. One British captain reported that "near 500" runaway slaves offered their services to him. Toward the end of the war, several thousand slaves sought freedom by following British troops through the Carolinas.

Black Patriots hoped that the Revolution would bring an end to slavery. After all, the Declaration of Independence proclaimed that "all men are created equal." Some white leaders also hoped the war would end slavery. James Otis wrote that "the colonists are by the law of nature free born, as indeed all men are, white or black." Quakers in particular spoke out strongly against slavery.

By the 1770s, slavery was declining in the North, where a number of free African Americans lived. During the American Revolution, several states moved to make slavery illegal, including Massachusetts, New Hampshire, and Pennsylvania. Other states also began to debate the slavery issue.

The War on the Western Frontier

As the war spread to Indian lands in the West, the Americans and British both tried to win the support of Indian tribes. In the end, the British were more successful. They convinced many Native Americans that a Patriot victory would mean more white settlers crossing the Appalachians and taking Indian lands.

Indian Allies of the British In the South, the British gained the support of the Cherokees, Creeks, Choctaws, and Chickasaws. The British encouraged the Cherokees to attack dozens of settlements on the southern frontier. Only after hard fighting were Patriot militia able to drive the Native Americans into the mountains.

Fighting was equally fierce on the northern frontier. In 1778, Iroquois forces led by the Mohawk leader Joseph Brant joined with Loyalists in raiding settlements in Pennsylvania and New York. The next year, Patriots struck back by destroying dozens of Iroquois villages.

Victory at Vincennes Farther west, in 1778, George Rogers Clark led Virginia frontier fighters against the British in the

GEOGRAPHY Skills

American, British, and Native American forces fought for control of lands in the West.

1. **Location** On the map, locate (a) Kaskaskia, (b) Vincennes, (c) Ohio River, (d) Fort Detroit.

2. **Place** What was the importance of the place where Fort Pitt was built?

3. **Critical Thinking**
Applying Information Why did many Native Americans ally themselves with the British?

The War in the West

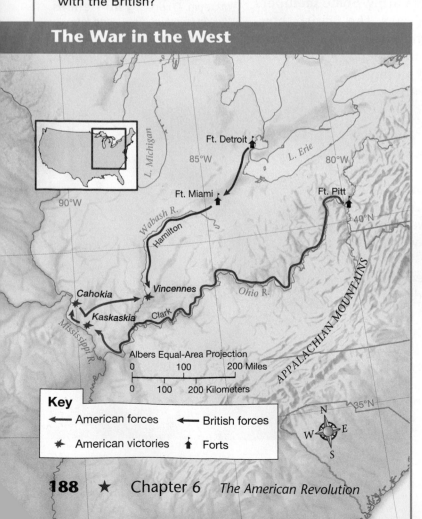

Key
← American forces
← British forces
✦ American victories
↟ Forts

Ohio Valley. With help from Miami Indians, Clark captured the British forts at Kaskaskia and Cahokia.

Clark then plotted a surprise attack on the British fort at Vincennes. When Clark's small force reached the fort, they spread out through the woods to make their numbers appear greater than they really were. The British commander thought it was useless to fight so many Americans. He surrendered Vincennes in February 1779.

Spanish Aid On the southwestern frontier, Americans received help from New Spain. In the early years of the war, Spain was neutral. However, Bernardo de Gálvez, governor of Spanish Louisiana, favored the Patriots. He secretly supplied medicine, cloth, muskets, and gunpowder to the Americans.

When Spain entered the war against Britain in 1779, Gálvez took a more active role. He seized British forts along the Mississippi River and the Gulf of Mexico. He also drove the British out of West Florida. The city of Galveston, in Texas, is named after this courageous leader.

Fighting at Sea

At sea, the Americans could do little against the powerful British navy. British ships blockaded American ports. From time to time, however, a bold American captain captured a British ship.

The greatest American sea victory took place in September 1779 in Britain's backyard, on the North Sea. After a hard-fought battle, Captain John Paul Jones, captured the powerful British warship *Serapis.*

Raids on the high seas and along the frontiers kept many Americans on the alert. However, the war between the Americans and Great Britain would be settled by battles in the South.

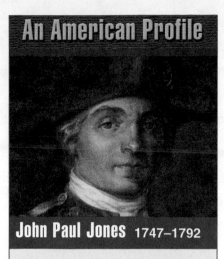

An American Profile

John Paul Jones 1747–1792

John Paul Jones was the first lieutenant commissioned in the Continental Navy. He showed his daring by sailing into British waters to raid enemy merchant ships. On September 23, 1779, Jones, at the helm of *Bonhomme Richard*, attacked the clearly superior British warship *Serapis* in the North Sea. The *Richard* was badly damaged in the first few minutes of battle. With their ship sinking beneath them, Jones and his men fought on. But the *Serapis* was also hurt. At last, the British captain of the *Serapis* lowered his flag and surrendered.

How did John Paul Jones help the Patriot cause?

★ ★ ★ **Section 4 Assessment** ★ ★ ★

Recall

1. **Identify** Explain the significance of **(a)** Mary Ludwig Hays, **(b)** Peter Salem, **(c)** George Rogers Clark, **(d)** Bernardo de Gálvez, **(e)** John Paul Jones.

Comprehension

2. How did the war change many women's attitudes?
3. **(a)** Why did some slaves escape to the British? **(b)** Why did African American Patriots hope that the Revolution would end slavery?
4. Why was John Paul Jones a hero to Americans?

Critical Thinking and Writing

5. **Exploring the Main Idea** Review the Main Idea statement at the beginning of this section. List three ways in which Americans fought for liberty during the Revolution.
6. **Identifying Causes and Effects** Read the following two statements. Decide which is the cause and which is the effect: **(a)** Many Native Americans sided with the British. **(b)** During the Revolution, settlers continued to push west of the Appalachians. Write a paragraph explaining the importance of the effect on the war.

ACTIVITY

Go Online
PHSchool.com

Making an Almanac
Use the Internet to research women who took part in the Revolution. Among the women you might research are Margaret Corbin and Deborah Sampson. Use what you find to draw up a Who's Who of Women During the Revolution. For help in completing the activity, visit PHSchool.com, **Web Code mfd-0602.**

Women in the Revolution

Many women patriots of the Revolution performed courageous deeds. They were spies and couriers, and disguised as men, enlisted in the army. Many women, just as courageous, fought for the cause on the home front.

Deborah Sampson When young Robert Shurtleff was wounded, he deliberately concealed his leg wound. But when he came down with yellow fever and was taken to a hospital, the truth was discovered: "He" was really Deborah Sampson, a woman in disguise! Instead of being punished for her deception, Deborah earned respect from her comrades. She received an honorable discharge.

Sybil Ludington Sometimes called the "female Paul Revere," Sybil Ludington was just 16 years old when on a chilly April night in 1777 she mounted her horse, Star, to gallop through the countryside and call the militia to report. The British were attacking, and there was no one to call the men to arms but Sybil.

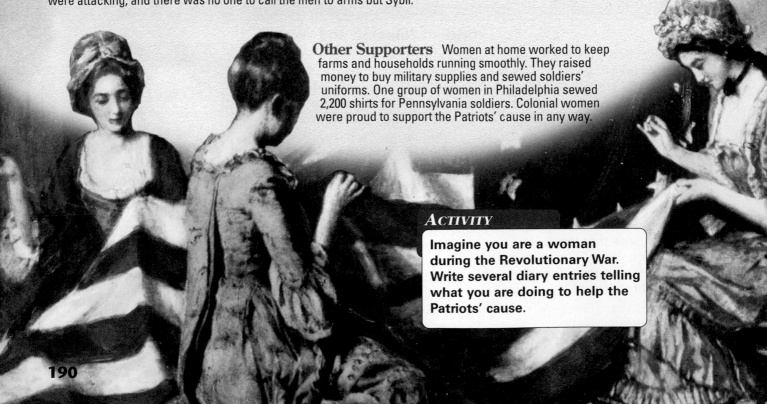

Other Supporters Women at home worked to keep farms and households running smoothly. They raised money to buy military supplies and sewed soldiers' uniforms. One group of women in Philadelphia sewed 2,200 shirts for Pennsylvania soldiers. Colonial women were proud to support the Patriots' cause in any way.

ACTIVITY

Imagine you are a woman during the Revolutionary War. Write several diary entries telling what you are doing to help the Patriots' cause.

5 Winning the War in the South

Prepare to Read

Objectives

In this section, you will
- Explain why Britain decided to start fighting in the South.
- Describe the British defeat at Yorktown.
- List the terms of the Treaty of Paris.
- Explain why the Americans won the war.

Key Terms

Battle of Cowpens
guerrilla
siege
Battle of Yorktown
Treaty of Paris
ratify

🎯 Target Reading Skill

Main Idea As you read, prepare an outline of the section. Use roman numerals to indicate major headings, capital letters for subheadings, and numbers for supporting details.

> I. Fighting in the South
>   A. Patriots versus Loyalists
>   1. Patriots and Loyalists launch raids
>   2.
>   B. Green and Morgan help turn the tide
>   1.
>   2.
>   C.
> II. Victory at Yorktown
>   A.
>   B.

Main Idea After the British surrendered at Yorktown, Britain recognized the United States as an independent country.

Setting the Scene When he was only 16 years old, Thomas Young set out with about 900 other Patriots to capture Kings Mountain in South Carolina. Although they were barefoot, they moved quickly up the wooded hillside, shouldering their old muskets. They were determined to take the mountain from the Loyalists who were dug in at the top.

Whooping and shouting, Young and his comrades dashed from tree to tree, dodging bullets as they fired back. Suddenly, Thomas heard the frantic cry, "Colonel Williams is shot!"

> 66 I ran to his assistance for I loved him as a father. . . . He revived, and his first words were, 'For God's sake boys, don't give up the hill!' 99

—Thomas Young, Memoir, *The Orion*

Colonial soldiers received badges of honor for acts of bravery

The Patriots captured Kings Mountain on October 7, 1780. The victory was an important sign. Britain had decided to make the South the key to winning the war. The American victory at Kings Mountain showed that Britain's new strategy might not work.

Fighting in the South

The South became the main battleground of the war in 1778. Sir Henry Clinton, the new British commander-in-chief, knew that many Loyalists lived in the southern backcountry. He hoped that if British troops marched through the South, Loyalists would join them.

At first, Clinton's plan seemed to work. In short order, beginning in December 1778, the British seized Savannah in Georgia and Charleston and Camden in South Carolina. "I have almost ceased to hope," wrote Washington when he learned of the defeats.

Patriots versus Loyalists In the Carolina backcountry, Patriots and Loyalists launched violent raids against one another. Both sides

The War Ends in the South

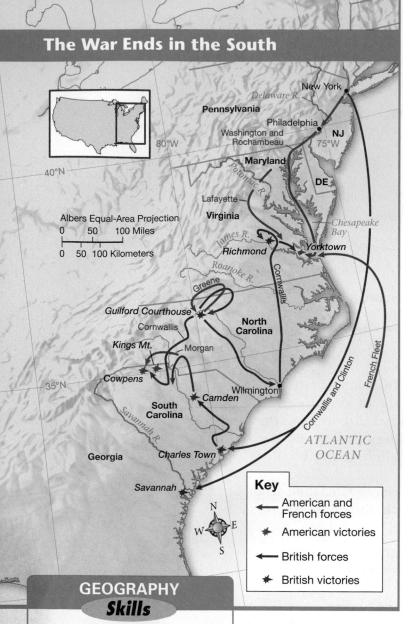

The war ended in the South. After a string of defeats, the Americans gradually gained the upper hand. The last major battle was the American victory at Yorktown.

1. **Location** On the map, locate **(a)** Savannah, **(b)** Kings Mountain, **(c)** Guilford Courthouse, **(d)** Chesapeake Bay, **(e)** Yorktown.

2. **Region** Did the British have greater control over coastal or inland regions of the South?

3. **Critical Thinking Drawing Conclusions** Why was it a mistake for Cornwallis to retreat to the Yorktown peninsula?

burned farms, killed civilians, and sometimes even tortured prisoners.

After 1780, attacks by British troops and Loyalist militia became especially cruel. As a result, more settlers began to side with the Patriots. As one Loyalist admitted, "Great Britain has now a hundred enemies, where it had one before."

Greene and Morgan Help Turn the Tide After the victory at Kings Mountain, two able American generals helped turn the tide against the main British army, led by General Charles Cornwallis. They were Nathanael Greene of Rhode Island and Daniel Morgan of Virginia.

General Greene's ability as a military leader was perhaps second only to Washington's. In 1780, Greene took command of the Continental Army in the South. Using his knowledge of local geography, Greene engaged the British only on ground that put them at a disadvantage. General Cornwallis wore out his soldiers trying to catch Greene's army.

In January 1781, General Morgan won an important victory at Cowpens, South Carolina. Morgan used a clever tactic to defeat the British. He divided his soldiers into a front line and a rear line. He ordered the front line to retreat after firing just two volleys. The British, thinking the Americans were retreating, charged forward—straight into the fire of Morgan's second rank. In this way, the Americans won the Battle of Cowpens.

Greene and Morgan combined their armies when they fought Cornwallis at Guilford Courthouse, near present-day Greensboro, North Carolina. The battle was one of the bloodiest of the war. Although the Americans retreated, the British sustained great losses.

Hit and Run Known as the Swamp Fox, Francis Marion of South Carolina added to British frustrations. He led a small band of militia, who often slept by day and traveled by night. His soldiers used **guerrilla,** or hit-and-run, tactics to harass the British. Marion's band appeared suddenly out of the swamps, attacked quickly, and retreated swiftly back into the swamps.

Victory at Yorktown

Cornwallis abandoned his plan to take the Carolinas. In the spring of 1781, he moved his troops north into Virginia. He planned to conquer Virginia and cut off the Americans' supply routes to the South.

An American Traitor The British had achieved some success in Virginia, even before the arrival of Cornwallis. Benedict Arnold, formerly one of the Americans' best generals, was now leading British troops. Arnold captured and burned the capital city of Richmond. His forces also raided and burned other towns.

Arnold had turned traitor to the American cause in September 1780, while commanding West Point, a key fort in New York. The ambitious general was angry because he felt that he had not received enough credit for his victories. He also needed money. Arnold secretly agreed to turn over West Point to the British. The plot was uncovered by a Patriot patrol, but Arnold escaped to join the British.

Arnold's treason and his raids on towns in Connecticut and Virginia enraged the Patriots. Thomas Jefferson, governor of Virginia, offered a sizable reward for his capture. Washington ordered Arnold to be hanged. However, he was never captured.

Battle at Yorktown Cornwallis hoped to meet with the same kind of success in Virginia that Arnold had achieved. At first, things went well. Cornwallis sent Loyalist troops to attack Charlottesville, where the Virginia legislature was meeting. Governor Thomas Jefferson and other officials had to flee.

American troops under Lafayette fought back by staging raids against the British. Lafayette did not have enough troops to fight a major battle. Still, his strategy kept Cornwallis at bay.

Then, Cornwallis made a mistake. He disregarded an order from Sir Henry Clinton to send part of his army to New York. Instead, he retreated to Yorktown peninsula, a strip of land jutting into Chesapeake Bay. He felt confident that British ships could supply his army from the sea.

Washington saw an opportunity to trap Cornwallis on the Yorktown peninsula. He marched his Continental troops south from New York. With the Americans were French soldiers under the Comte de Rochambeau (roh shahm BOH). The combined army rushed to join Lafayette in Virginia.

Meanwhile, a French fleet under Admiral de Grasse was also heading toward Virginia. Once in Chesapeake Bay, De Grasse's fleet closed the trap. Cornwallis was cut off. He could not get supplies. He could not escape by land or by sea.

The British Surrender By the end of September, more than 16,000 American and French troops laid siege to Cornwallis's army of fewer than 8,000. A **siege** occurs when an army surrounds and blockades an enemy position in an attempt to capture it. Day after day, American and French artillery pounded the British.

For several weeks, Cornwallis held out. Finally, with casualties mounting and his supplies running low, the general decided that the situation was hopeless. The British had lost the **Battle of Yorktown.**

On October 19, 1781, the British surrendered their weapons. The French and the Americans lined up in two facing columns. As the defeated redcoats marched between the victorious troops, a British army band played the tune "The World Turned Upside Down."

Geography and History

Britain's Dilemma

Because they controlled the seas, the British could land and establish bases almost anywhere along the American coast. The navigable rivers that flowed inland from the coast provided convenient invasion routes into the interior. To win the war, the British Army had to move away from these coastal bases and rivers. Yet when it did so, it opened its lines of communications and supply to constant attack. British armies nearly always met defeat when they moved away from the areas where they could be supplied by ships from the homeland. These problems, a British colonel noted in 1777, had "absolutely prevented us this whole war from going fifteen miles from a navigable river."

 Why did the British face problems when they moved away from the coast?

Yorktown, Virginia

Yorktown

October 17, 1781, marked the end of a long battle between the American army and powerful Great Britain. The Yorktown victory led to peace talks, which began in Paris in 1782. The next year, the representatives from the new nation and Great Britain signed the Treaty of Paris. The battle site of Yorktown is part of the Colonial National Historic Park.

Go Online PHSchool.com

Virtual Field Trip For an interactive look at Yorktown, visit PHSchool.com, **Web Code mfd-0603.**

The Peace Treaty

In London, the defeat shocked the British. "It is all over," cried the British prime minister, Lord North. Discouraged, he agreed to peace talks.

The talks began in Paris in 1782. Congress sent Benjamin Franklin and John Adams, along with John Jay of New York and Henry Laurens of South Carolina, to work out a treaty. Because Britain was eager to end the war, the Americans got most of what they wanted.

Under the Treaty of Paris, the British recognized the United States as an independent nation. It extended from the Atlantic Ocean to the Mississippi River. The northern border of the United States stopped at the Great Lakes. The southern border stopped at Florida, which was returned to Spain.

For their part, the Americans agreed to ask the state legislatures to pay Loyalists for property they had lost in the war. In the end, however, most states ignored Loyalist claims.

On April 15, 1783, Congress ratified, or approved, the Treaty of Paris. It was almost eight years to the day since the battles of Lexington and Concord.

Why the Americans Won

Geography played an important role in the American victory. The British had to send soldiers and supplies to a war that was several thousand miles from home. They also had to fight an enemy that was spread over a wide area. For their part, the Americans were familiar with the local geography. They knew the best routes and the best places to fight.

Foreign Help Help from other nations was crucial to the American cause. Spanish forces attacked the British along the Gulf of Mexico and in the Mississippi Valley. French money helped pay for supplies, and French military aid provided vital support to American troops. Without French soldiers and warships, for example, the Americans might not have won the Battle of Yorktown.

Americans' Growing Patriotism The Americans' patriotic spirit and fighting skills were another key to their victory. Despite early setbacks, the Patriots battled on. Gradually, Washington's inexperienced troops learned how to drill, how to march, and how to fight. Perhaps most important was Washington himself. By the end of the war, the general's leadership and military skills were respected by Americans and British alike.

Washington's Farewell In December 1783, General Washington bid farewell to his officers at Fraunces Tavern in New York City. Colonel Benjamin Tallmadge recalled the event:

> 66 Such a scene of sorrow and weeping I had never before witnessed. . . . We were then about to part from the man who had conducted us through a long and bloody war, and under whose conduct the glory and independence of our country had been achieved. 99
>
> —Benjamin Tallmadge, *Memoir*

All along Washington's route home to Virginia, crowds cheered their hero. The new nation faced difficult days ahead. In time, Americans would call on Washington to lead them once again.

Identify Supporting Details

What details in this paragraph tell why the Americans won the war? Add these details to your outline.

★ ★ ★ Section 5 Assessment ★ ★ ★

Recall

1. **Identify** Explain the significance of (a) Henry Clinton, (b) Charles Cornwallis, (c) Nathanael Greene, (d) Daniel Morgan, (e) Battle of Cowpens, (f) Francis Marion, (g) Benedict Arnold, (h) Comte de Rochambeau, (i) Battle of Yorktown, (j) Treaty of Paris.
2. **Define** (a) guerrilla, (b) siege, (c) ratify.

Comprehension

3. Why did the South become the main battleground of the war in 1778?
4. Why was Cornwallis forced to surrender at Yorktown?

5. Describe the major points of the Treaty of Paris.
6. Give three reasons why the Americans defeated the British in the Revolution.

Critical Thinking and Writing

7. **Exploring the Main Idea** Review the Main Idea statement at the beginning of this section. Then, create a timeline of the major events at the end of the war, beginning with the Battle of Kings Mountain and ending with the Treaty of Paris.
8. **Making Predictions** Suppose that Britain had won the war. What might have been the effects of a British victory?

ACTIVITY

Writing a Letter You are General Cornwallis. In a letter to George III, describe the events at Yorktown.

CHAPTER SUMMARY

Section 1
Fighting broke out in New England even while Congress tried to make peace with Britain. The opening battles indicated that the war would not be easily won by either side.

Section 2
Thomas Paine's *Common Sense* persuaded many colonists to support independence. In July 1776, the colonies declared independence from Britain.

Section 3
After a series of defeats, an American victory at Saratoga marked a major turning point in the Revolution. The victory convinced several European nations to aid the Americans.

Section 4
During the Revolution, women such as Martha Washington and Mary Ludwig Hays contributed to the American war effort. Free and enslaved African Americans made decisions to join American or British forces.

Section 5
In October 1781, the British surrendered at Yorktown. In the 1783 Treaty of Paris, Britain recognized United States independence.

Building Vocabulary

Use the chapter vocabulary words listed below to create a crossword puzzle. Exchange puzzles with a classmate. Complete the puzzles, and then check each other's answers.

1. blockade
2. mercenary
3. traitor
4. preamble
5. natural rights
6. ally
7. cavalry
8. guerrilla
9. siege
10. ratify

Reviewing Key Facts

11. What did the Battle of Bunker Hill show about each side in the conflict? (Section 1)

For additional review and enrichment activities, see the interactive version of *The American Nation*, available on the Web and on CD-ROM.

Chapter Self-Test For practice test questions for Chapter 6, visit PHSchool.com, **Web Code mfa-0604.**

12. Describe three ideas contained in the Declaration of Independence. (Section 2)
13. When did France decide to help the Americans? (Section 3)
14. How did African Americans support the Patriot cause? (Section 4)
15. List the terms of the Treaty of Paris. (Section 5)

Critical Thinking and Writing

16. **Analyzing Primary Sources** According to the Declaration of Independence, when do people have a right and duty to rebel against their government?

17. **Identifying Causes and Effects (a)** Apply absolute chronology by placing the following events in order: **(1)** British defeat at Yorktown, **(2)** American victory at Saratoga, **(3)** French entry into the war against Britain, **(4)** signing of the Treaty of Paris. **(b)** Explain how each event caused the following event.

18. **Connecting to Geography: Place** How did the Patriots' knowledge of local geography help them to defeat the British?

19. **Synthesizing Information** What were the three biggest mistakes of British political and military leaders between 1775 and 1783? Explain.

20. **Linking Past and Present** Today, the United States and Britain are close allies. Why do you think the two nations now have close ties?

Analyzing Primary Sources

Thomas Paine had retreated with Washington's army through New Jersey. Seated by a campfire and using a drum for a desk, he wrote *The Crisis*. Read the following excerpt. Then, answer the questions:

> 66 These are the times that try men's souls. The summer soldier and the sunshine patriot will, in this crisis, shrink from the service of his country; but he that stands it now deserves the love and thanks of man and woman. Tyranny . . . is not easily conquered; yet we have this consolation with us . . . the harder the conflict, the more glorious the triumph. 99

Thomas Paine, *The Crisis,* 1776

21. The terms "summer soldier" and "sunshine patriot" refer to people who
    A. support the Revolution in all times.
    B. support the Revolution in good times but refuse to support it in hard times.
    C. fought at Princeton and Trenton.
    D. fought only in warm weather.

22. Based on the excerpt, what tyranny is Paine speaking of?
    A. American generals' treatment of their troops
    B. the treatment of African Americans
    C. the terms of the Treaty of Paris
    D. Britain's harsh rule over the colonies

Identifying Points of View

THE HORSE AMERICA, *throwing his Master.*

This cartoon was published in 1779. Read the caption. Then, answer the questions.

23. How would you describe the event shown?
    A. The colonies are at peace with Britain.
    B. The colonies want independence.
    C. Britain won the war.
    D. The colonies are at war with France.

24. How does the cartoonist feel about the Patriot cause? Explain.

ACTIVITIES

Connecting With . . . Geography

On a large sheet of paper, draw an outline map of the United States. On the map, show the sites of major battles of the American Revolution. Mark each site with a symbol to show who won. For each battle, include a text box giving one or two important facts about it.

Go Online
PHSchool.com

Connecting to Today

Conducting an Interview During the Revolution, African Americans fought in special regiments. Use the Internet to research significant contributions of African Americans to the United States military since then. Prepare a short fictional interview with the group or person that you have researched. For help in starting this activity, visit PHSchool.com, **Web Code mfd-0605.**

Creating a Republic

1776–1790

1 **A Loose Confederation**
2 **The Constitutional Convention**
3 **Ideas Behind the Constitution**
4 **Ratification and the Bill of Rights**

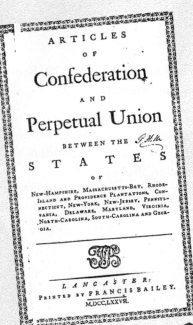

Articles of
Confederation

Surveyors (right) and
surveying compass (left)

**AMERICAN
EVENTS**

1777
The Continental Congress
approves the Articles of
Confederation. The
Articles create a loose
association of states.

1785
Congress passes the Land Ordinance of
1785. It sets up a system for surveying
and settling the Northwest Territory
between the Mississippi and Ohio
Rivers.

1781
The Articles of Confederation
take effect.

Presidential Terms:

1775   1780   1785

**WORLD
EVENTS**

▲ **1776**
Adam Smith publishes
The Wealth of Nations.

▲ **1781**
The Emperor of Austria
grants religious toleration.

Ratifying the Constitution

A new, united nation took shape as each of the 13 original states in turn ratified, or approved, the Constitution.

BRITISH TERRITORY

Claimed by Great Britain and the United States

Maine (part of Mass.)

New Hampshire (June 21, 1788)

Massachusetts (Feb. 6, 1788)

(claimed by NY & NH)

New York (July 26, 1788)

Rhode Island (May 29, 1790)

Connecticut (Jan. 9, 1788)

Pennsylvania (Dec. 12, 1787)

New Jersey (Dec. 18, 1787)

Delaware (Dec. 7, 1787)

Maryland (Apr. 28, 1788)

NORTHWEST TERRITORY

Virginia (June 25, 1788)

Chesapeake Bay

ATLANTIC OCEAN

SPANISH LOUISIANA

North Carolina (Nov. 21, 1789)

South Carolina (May 23, 1788)

Georgia (Jan. 2, 1788)

SPANISH FLORIDA

Key

(Dec. 7, 1787) Date of ratification

Albers Equal-Area Projection

0   150   300 Miles

0   150   300 Kilometers

Writing of the Constitution

1787
The Constitutional Convention meets in Philadelphia. The new Constitution creates a stronger central government.

1789
The first election under the new Constitution takes place.

1791
The Bill of Rights is added to the Constitution to protect individual liberties.

George Washington 1789–1797

1785 · · · ★ · · · ★ · · · 1790 · · · ★ · · · · · · 1795

1789 ▲
The French Revolution begins.

1793 ▲
The Emperor of China rejects British trade.

1 A Loose Confederation

Prepare to Read

Objectives

In this section, you will
- Explain why state governments wrote constitutions.
- List the weaknesses of the Articles of Confederation.
- Describe the process the Articles created for admitting new states.
- Explain why many Americans called for changes in the Articles.

Key Terms

constitution
bill of rights
Articles of Confederation
cede
currency
Land Ordinance of 1785
Northwest Ordinance
depression
Shays' Rebellion

Target Reading Skill

Reading Process As you read, prepare an outline of this section. Use roman numerals to indicate the major headings, capital letters for the subheadings, and numbers for the supporting details. The sample at right will help you get started.

> I. The States Write Constitutions
>   A. Type of government
>   1. Legislature
>   2.
>   B.
> II. The Articles of Confederation
>   A. Limited power
>   1.
>   2.
>   B.

Main Idea The Articles of Confederation created a weak central government and a loose alliance of independent states.

Thomas Jefferson

Setting the Scene In 1775, Thomas Jefferson rode 300 miles from Virginia to attend the Continental Congress in Philadelphia. The roads were so poorly marked that Jefferson got lost twice. The only way he could get back on the path was to hire guides.

The ties uniting the 13 states often seemed as hard to find as the roads linking them. The Declaration of Independence had created a new nation. But the former colonies had little experience working together. Many Americans wondered if they could create a central government that would unite the states effectively.

The States Write Constitutions

In forming a government, most states wrote constitutions. A **constitution** is a document that sets out the laws, principles, organization, and processes of a government. States wrote constitutions for two reasons. First, a written constitution would spell out the rights of all citizens. Second, it would limit the power of government.

Virginia's constitution included a **bill of rights,** or list of freedoms that the government promises to protect. Virginia's bill of rights guaranteed trial by jury, freedom of religion, and freedom of the press. Several other states followed Virginia's lead. For example, the Massachusetts state constitution guaranteed people:

> 66 . . . the right of enjoying and defending their lives and liberties; that of acquiring, possessing, and protecting property; in [short], that of seeking and obtaining their safety and happiness. 99
>
> —Massachusetts Constitution of 1780

The new state governments were somewhat similar to the colonial governments in structure. The states divided power between an executive and a legislature. The legislature was elected by the voters to pass laws. Every state but Pennsylvania had a governor to execute, or carry out, the laws.

Under the state constitutions, more people had the right to vote than in colonial times. To vote, a citizen had to be white, male, and over age 21. He had to own a certain amount of property or pay a certain amount of taxes. For a time, some women in New Jersey could vote. In a few states, free African American men who owned property could vote.

The Articles of Confederation

As citizens formed state governments, the Continental Congress was drafting a plan for the nation as a whole. Delegates believed that the colonies needed to be united by a national government in order to win independence.

It was hard to write a constitution that all states would approve. They were reluctant to give up power to a central government. Few Americans saw themselves as citizens of one nation. Instead, they felt loyal to their own states. Also, people feared replacing the "tyranny" of British rule with another strong government.

After much debate, the Continental Congress approved the first American constitution in 1777. The Articles of Confederation created a very loose alliance of 13 independent states.

Limited Powers Under the Articles of Confederation, the states sent delegates to Congress. Each state had one vote. Congress could declare war, appoint military officers, and coin money. It was also responsible for foreign affairs.

Still, compared to the states, Congress had very limited powers. Congress could pass laws, but nine states had to approve a law before it could go into effect. Congress could not regulate trade between states or between states and foreign countries. Nor did it have the power to tax. To raise money, Congress had to ask the states for it or borrow it. No state could be forced to contribute funds.

The Articles included no president to execute laws. It was up to the states to enforce the laws passed by Congress. There was also no system of courts to settle conflicts between states.

Dispute Over Western Lands A dispute arose even before the Articles of Confederation went into effect. Maryland refused to ratify

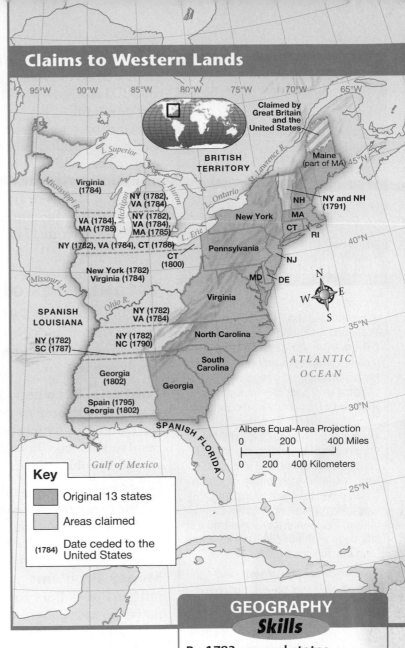

Claims to Western Lands

Key

Original 13 states

Areas claimed

(1784) Date ceded to the United States

GEOGRAPHY
Skills

By 1783, several states claimed land west of the Appalachians.

1. **Location** On the map, locate western lands claimed by **(a)** Virginia, **(b)** New York, **(c)** Massachusetts, **(d)** Spain.

2. **Region** Which states had no western land claims?

3. **Critical Thinking Making Predictions** Based on this map, how might western land claims threaten national unity?

Set a Purpose

When you set a purpose for reading, you give yourself a focus. If your purpose is to learn about the Articles of Confederation, how do the paragraphs under "Weaknesses of the Confederation" help you meet your goal? Add this information to your outline.

the Articles unless Virginia and other states **ceded,** or gave up, their claims to lands west of the Appalachian Mountains. Like other small states, Maryland feared that "landed" states would become too powerful.

One by one, the states agreed to cede their western claims to Congress. Finally, only Virginia held out. However, Thomas Jefferson and other leading Virginians recognized the great need to form a central government. They persuaded state lawmakers to give up Virginia's claims in the West.

With its demands met, Maryland ratified the Articles of Confederation in 1781. The new American government could at last go into effect.

Weaknesses of the Confederation

By 1783, the United States had won its independence. Yet, the end of the American Revolution did not solve the confederation's troubles. Americans had reason to doubt whether "these United States" could survive.

Conflicts Between States Disputes continued to arise among states. For example, both New Hampshire and New York claimed Vermont. The Articles did not give the central government power to resolve such conflicts. Noah Webster, a teacher from New England, saw the problem clearly:

66 So long as any individual state has power to defeat the measures of the other twelve, our pretended union is but a name, and our confederation, a cobweb. 99

—Noah Webster, *Sketches of American Policy*

Money Problems After the Revolution, the United States owed millions of dollars to individuals and foreign nations. Without the power to tax, Congress had no way to repay these debts. It asked the states for money, but the states often refused.

During the Revolution, the Continental Congress had solved the problem of raising funds by printing paper **currency,** or money. However, the Continental dollar had little value because it was not backed by gold or silver.* Before long, Americans began to describe any useless thing as "not worth a Continental."

As Continental dollars became nearly worthless, states printed their own currency. This caused confusion. How much was a North Carolina dollar worth? Was a Virginia dollar as valuable as a Maryland dollar? Most states refused to accept the money of others. As a result, trade became very difficult.

Other Nations Take Advantage Foreign countries took advantage of the confederation's weakness. Ignoring the Treaty of Paris, Britain refused to withdraw its troops from the Ohio Valley. Spain

*In a stable economy, currency has value because the government keeps reserves of gold or silver. Coins and paper money represent a portion of this reserve. Today, the United States government keeps its gold reserves in underground vaults at Fort Knox, Kentucky.

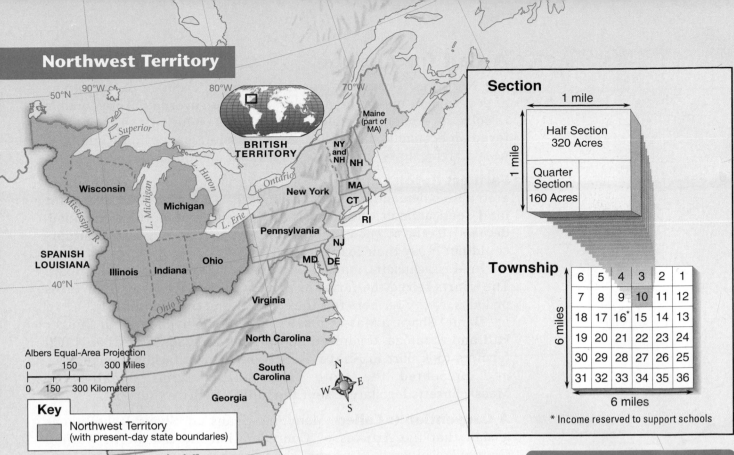

Northwest Territory

50°N 90°W 80°W 70°W

BRITISH TERRITORY

Maine (part of MA)

Wisconsin

Michigan

SPANISH LOUISIANA

Illinois Indiana Ohio

40°N

NY and NH NH

New York MA CT RI

Pennsylvania

NJ

MD DE

Virginia

North Carolina

South Carolina

Georgia

L. Superior L. Huron L. Michigan L. Erie Ontario Mississippi R. Ohio R.

Albers Equal-Area Projection

0   150   300 Miles

0   150   300 Kilometers

N E S W

Key

Northwest Territory
(with present-day state boundaries)

Section

1 mile

1 mile

Half Section
320 Acres

Quarter
Section
160 Acres

Township

6	5	4	3	2	1
7	8	9	10	11	12
18	17	16*	15	14	13
19	20	21	22	23	24
30	29	28	27	26	25
31	32	33	34	35	36

6 miles

6 miles

* Income reserved to support schools

closed its port in New Orleans to American shipping. This was a serious blow to western farmers, who depended on the port to ship their products to the East.

Admitting New States

Despite its troubles, Congress did pass important laws about how to govern the Northwest Territory. These lands lay north of the Ohio River and east of the Mississippi. The laws established how territories would be governed and how they could become states.

The Land Ordinance of 1785 set up a system for settling the Northwest Territory. The law called for the territory to be surveyed and divided into townships. Each township would then be further divided into 36 sections of 1 square mile each. Congress planned to sell sections to settlers for $640 apiece. One section in every township was set aside to support public schools.

In 1787, Congress passed the Northwest Ordinance. It set up a government for the Northwest Territory, guaranteed basic rights to settlers, and outlawed slavery there. It also provided for the vast region to be divided into separate territories in the future.

The Northwest Ordinance provided a way to admit new states to the nation. Once a territory had a population of 60,000 free settlers, it could ask Congress to be admitted as a new state. Each new state would be "on an equal footing with the original states in all respects whatsoever." In time, the states of Ohio, Indiana, Illinois, Michigan, and Wisconsin were created from the Northwest Territory.

GEOGRAPHY Skills

Under the Articles of Confederation, Congress set up a system for settling and governing the Northwest Territory.

1. **Location** On the map, locate (a) Ohio, (b) Michigan, (c) Indiana, (d) Illinois, (e) Wisconsin.

2. **Place** What was the size of a township? A section?

3. **Critical Thinking Synthesizing Information** Did Indiana have public education when it became a state in 1816? Explain.

A Call for Change

The Northwest Ordinance was the finest achievement of the national government under the Articles. Still, the government was unable to solve its economic problems. After the Revolution, the nation suffered an economic depression. A **depression** is a period when business activity slows, prices and wages fall, and unemployment rises.

Farmers Revolt The depression hit farmers hard. The war had created a high demand for farm products. Farmers borrowed money for land, seed, animals, and tools. However, when the Revolution ended, demand for farm goods went down. As prices fell, many farmers could not repay their loans.

In Massachusetts, matters worsened when the state raised taxes. The courts seized the farms of those who could not pay their taxes or loans. Angry farmers felt they were being treated unfairly.

Daniel Shays, a Massachusetts farmer who had fought at Bunker Hill and Saratoga, organized an uprising in 1786. More than 1,000 farmers took part in **Shays' Rebellion.** They attacked courthouses and prevented the state from seizing farms. Finally, the Massachusetts legislature sent the militia to drive them off.

A Convention Is Called Many Americans saw Shays' Rebellion as a sign that the Articles of Confederation did not work. Warned George Washington, "I predict the worst consequences from a half-starved, limping government, always moving upon crutches and tottering at every step."

To avert a crisis, leaders from several states called for a convention to revise the Articles of Confederation. They met in Philadelphia in May 1787. In the end, however, this convention would create an entirely new framework of government.

★ ★ ★ **Section 1 Assessment** ★ ★ ★

Recall

1. **Identify** Explain the significance of (a) Articles of Confederation, (b) Land Ordinance of 1785, (c) Northwest Ordinance, (d) Shays' Rebellion.
2. **Define** (a) constitution, (b) bill of rights, (c) execute, (d) cede, (e) currency, (f) depression.

Comprehension

3. What kind of governments did state constitutions create?
4. Describe two weaknesses of the Articles of Confederation.
5. Explain the process by which a territory became a state.

6. How did many Americans react to Shays' Rebellion?

Critical Thinking and Writing

7. **Exploring the Main Idea** Review the Main Idea statement at the beginning of this section. Then, list two arguments in favor of creating a stronger central government.
8. **Solving Problems** Choose one of the problems the nation faced in 1787. Then, write a letter to a delegate to the upcoming Philadelphia Convention. Suggest one idea to solve that problem.

Settling the Western Frontier

Migration into the Northwest Territory was slow at first. Clarksville, the first American town to be set up in the territory, had only 40 settlers in 1793. In time, more and more Americans endured hardship and danger to make the journey west.

Why did people go west? Reports like this one certainly attracted eager and adventurous Americans:

> 66 The toils of agriculture will here be rewarded with a greater variety of valuable productions, than in any part of America. The advantages of almost every climate are here blended together; every considerable commodity that is [grown] in any part of the United States is here produced in the greatest plenty and perfection. The high and dry lands are of a deep, rich soil—producing, in abundance, wheat, rye, Indian corn, buck wheat, oats, barley, flax. . . . 99
> —Manasseh Cutler, *The First Map and Description of Ohio*, 1787

After 1780, pioneers from the east floated down the Ohio River in large, flat-bottomed rafts such as these. Settlers sweated and strained as they propelled the boats with long barge poles. Down river, families dismantled the rafts, using the planks to build wilderness homes.

All settlers did their part to clear land and build homes in the thick forest. Families then outfitted their log cabins with the necessities they had brought on their raft—from rifles and seed to pots and the family Bible.

ACTIVITY

Based on the pictures and reading here, write a letter from a settler in the Northwest Territory to a friend back east. Explain how you feel about living on the frontier and what you hope the future will bring.

2 The Constitutional Convention

Prepare to Read

Objectives

In this section, you will
- Identify the leaders of the Constitutional Convention.
- Explain the main differences between the two rival plans for the new Constitution.
- Describe the compromises the delegates had to reach before the Constitution could be signed.

Key Terms

Constitutional Convention
Virginia Plan
legislative branch
executive branch
judicial branch
New Jersey Plan
compromise
Great Compromise
Three-Fifths Compromise

Target Reading Skill

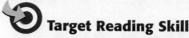

Comparison and Contrast Copy the table below. As you read, complete the table with information about rival plans proposed at the Constitutional Convention.

VIRGINIA PLAN	NEW JERSEY PLAN	GREAT COMPROMISE
•	• Proposed by Paterson	• Proposed by Sherman
• Favored large states	•	•
•	•	•
•	•	•

Main Idea Delegates to the Constitutional Convention of 1787 had to compromise on key issues in order to complete a new constitution.

The Liberty Bell at the State House

Setting the Scene An air of mystery hung over the State House in Philadelphia. All through the hot summer of 1787, the nation's great leaders passed in and out of the doors. Guards allowed only the delegates to enter. The windows remained closed, to keep passersby from overhearing any debates.

Like other Philadelphians, Susannah Dillwyn was curious and excited. She wrote to her father, "There is now sitting in this city a grand convention, who are to form some new system of government or mend the old one."

What would the convention decide? Rumors buzzed. Wrote Dillwyn, "They say it depends entirely upon their pleasure whether we shall in the future have a congress." For almost four months, Americans waited to learn the fate of their infant republic.

The Delegates to the Convention

The Constitutional Convention opened on May 25, 1787. Its goal was to revise the Articles of Confederation. Every state except Rhode Island sent representatives.

An Amazing Assembly The convention's 55 delegates were a remarkable group. Eight of them had signed the Declaration of Independence, including the oldest, Benjamin Franklin. At age 81, Franklin was wise in the ways of government and human nature. George Washington was a representative from Virginia. Washington was so well respected that the delegates at once elected him president of the Convention.

Still, most of the delegates represented a new generation of American leaders. Nearly half were young men in their thirties, including Alexander Hamilton of New York. During the Revolution,

Philadelphia

Independence Hall

To many, the birthplace of the United States is the old Pennsylvania State House in Philadelphia, known today as Independence Hall. Here, independence was declared, the Articles of Confederation were approved, and the Constitution was debated and signed. Enter the chamber today and you can almost see patriots like Washington, Madison, Franklin, and Hamilton forging a new nation.

Go Online
PHSchool.com

Virtual Field Trip For an interactive look at Independence Hall, visit PHSchool.com, **Web Code mfd-0702.**

Hamilton had served for a time as Washington's private secretary. Hamilton despised the Articles of Confederation. "The nation," he wrote, "is sick and wants powerful remedies." The powerful remedy he prescribed was a strong central government.

James Madison Perhaps the best-prepared delegate was 36-year-old James Madison of Virginia. For months, he had been reading books on history, politics, and commerce. He arrived in Philadelphia with a case bulging with volumes of research.

Madison was quiet and rather shy. Still, his keen intelligence and his ideas about how to structure a democratic government strongly influenced the other delegates. Today, Madison is often called the "Father of the Constitution."

Secret Debates When the Convention began, the delegates decided to keep their talks secret. They wanted to speak their minds freely and be able to explore issues without pressures from outside.

The closed windows helped keep the debates secret, but they made the room very hot. New Englanders in their woolen suits suffered terribly in the summer heat. Southerners, with clothing more suited to warm temperatures, were less bothered.

Two Rival Plans

Soon after the meeting began, the delegates realized they would have to do more than simply revise the Articles of Confederation. They chose instead to write an entirely new constitution for the

Compare and Contrast

How did the Virginia Plan differ from the New Jersey Plan? How were the plans similar?

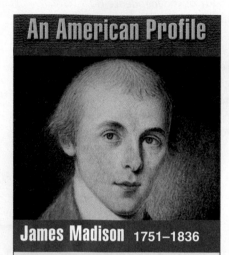

An American Profile

James Madison 1751–1836

Someone once said that James Madison looked "no bigger than a half a piece of soap." If so, looks were deceiving. By the age of 25, Madison was a skilled politician and a learned scholar.

Madison kept a close record of the debates at the Constitutional Convention. He chose a seat directly in front of the president's chair. "I was not absent a single day," he said. Unpublished for more than 50 years, Madison's notebooks are now our main source of information about the birth of the Constitution.

Why do you think Madison did not publish his notebooks immediately?

nation. They disagreed, however, about what form the new national government should take.

The Virginia Plan Edmund Randolph and James Madison, both from Virginia, proposed a plan for the new government. This Virginia Plan called for a strong national government with three branches. The legislative branch would pass the laws. The executive branch would carry out the laws. The judicial branch, or system of courts, would decide if laws were carried out fairly.

According to the Virginia Plan, the legislature would consist of two houses. Seats would be awarded on the basis of population. Thus, in both houses, larger states would have more representatives than smaller ones. Under the Articles of Confederation, each state, regardless of population, only had one vote in Congress.

The New Jersey Plan Small states opposed the Virginia Plan. They feared that the large states could easily outvote them in Congress. Supporters of the Virginia Plan replied that it was only fair for a state with more people to have more representatives.

After two weeks of debate, William Paterson of New Jersey presented a plan that had the support of the small states. Like the Virginia Plan, the New Jersey Plan called for three branches of government. However, it provided for a legislature that had only one house. Each state, regardless of its population, would have one vote in the legislature.

The Great Compromise

For a while, no agreement could be reached. With tempers flaring, it seemed that the Convention would fall apart without adopting any plan. Finally, Roger Sherman of Connecticut worked out a compromise that he hoped would satisfy both the large and small states. A compromise is a settlement in which each side gives up some of its demands in order to reach an agreement.

Sherman's compromise called for the creation of a two-house legislature. Members of the lower house, known as the House of Representatives, would be elected by popular vote. As the larger states wished, seats in the lower house would be awarded to each state according to its population.

Members of the upper house, called the Senate, would be chosen by state legislatures. Each state, no matter what its size, would have two senators. This part of Sherman's compromise appealed to the smaller states.

On July 16, the delegates narrowly approved Sherman's plan. It became known as the Great Compromise. Each side gave up some demands to achieve unity.

Northern and Southern States Compromise

Just as there were disagreements between large states and small states, there were also disagreements between northern states and southern states. The most serious disagreements concerned the issue of slavery. Would slaves be counted as part of a state's population?

Would the slave trade continue to bring enslaved Africans into the United States?

The Three-Fifths Compromise Southerners wanted to include slaves in the population count even though they would not let slaves vote. If slaves were counted, southern states would have more representatives in the House of Representatives. Northerners objected. They argued that, since slaves could not vote, they should not be counted when assigning representatives.

Once again, the delegates compromised. They agreed that three fifths of the slaves in any state would be counted. In other words, if a state had 5,000 slaves, 3,000 of them would be included in the state's population count. This agreement became known as the **Three-Fifths Compromise.**

The Slave Trade There was another disagreement over slavery. By 1787, some northern states had banned the slave trade within their borders. Delegates from these states urged that the slave trade be banned in the entire nation. Southerners warned that such a ban would ruin their economy.

In the end, northern and southern states compromised once more. Northerners agreed that Congress could not outlaw the slave trade for at least 20 years. After that, Congress could regulate the slave trade if it wished. Northerners also agreed that no state could stop a fugitive slave from being returned to an owner who claimed that slave.

Viewing History

Signing the Constitution
This painting by Howard Chandler Christy shows the signing of the Constitution on September 17, 1787. Some of the same men had signed the Declaration of Independence 11 years earlier.
Evaluating Information *How would you describe the way Washington is portrayed? Why do you think Christy painted him this way?*

Roger Sherman

James Madison

Benjamin Franklin

George Washington

Signing the Constitution

As the long, hot summer drew to a close, the weary delegates struggled with one difficult question after another. How many years should the President, head of the executive branch, serve? How should the system of federal courts be organized? Would members of Congress be paid?

Finally, on September 17, 1787, the Constitution was ready to be signed. Its opening lines, or Preamble, expressed the goals of the framers: "We the People of the United States, in order to form a more perfect union . . . "

Gathering for the last time, delegates listened quietly as Benjamin Franklin rose to speak. He pleaded that the document be accepted:

> 66 I doubt . . . whether any other Convention . . . may be able to make a better Constitution. . . . I cannot help expressing a wish, that every member of the Convention who may still have objections to it, would with me, on this occasion, doubt a little of his own infallibility, and . . . put his name to this instrument. 99
>
> —Benjamin Franklin, *Records of the Federal Convention of 1787*

One by one, delegates came forward to sign the document. All but three of the delegates remaining in Philadelphia did so. Edmund Randolph and George Mason of Virginia, along with Elbridge Gerry of Massachusetts, refused to sign. They feared that the new Constitution gave too much power to the national government.

The Constitution called upon each state to hold a convention to approve or reject the plan for the new government. Once nine states endorsed it, the Constitution would go into effect.

★ ★ ★ Section 2 Assessment ★ ★ ★

Recall

1. **Identify** Explain the significance of **(a)** Constitutional Convention, **(b)** James Madison, **(c)** Virginia Plan, **(d)** New Jersey Plan, **(e)** Roger Sherman, **(f)** Great Compromise, **(g)** Three-Fifths Compromise.

2. **Define** **(a)** legislative branch, **(b)** executive branch, **(c)** judicial branch, **(d)** compromise.

Comprehension

3. In what way did the delegates to the 1787 Convention represent a new generation of American leaders?

4. **(a)** Why did small states oppose the Virginia Plan? **(b)** How was this conflict resolved?

5. What compromises did the North and South reach?

Critical Thinking and Writing

6. **Exploring the Main Idea** Review the Main Idea statement at the beginning of this section. Then, list two or three things you think might have happened if the delegates had been unable to compromise.

7. **Drawing Inferences** Some historians call slavery the "unfinished business" of the 1787 Convention. Write a paragraph explaining why.

ACTIVITY

Drawing a Political Cartoon Draw a political cartoon analyzing the conflict between the large and small states at the Constitutional Convention. Identify in which state your cartoon might have appeared. Select a viewpoint, either in favor of the larger states, in favor of the smaller states, or in favor of compromise.

3 Ideas Behind the Constitution

Prepare to Read

Objectives

In this section, you will
- Explain what American leaders learned from studying ancient Rome.
- Identify the traditions of freedom that Americans inherited from Great Britain and from their own colonial past.
- Explain how Enlightenment ideas shaped the development of the Constitution.

Key Terms

Founding Fathers

republic

dictatorship

Magna Carta

English Bill of Rights

habeas corpus

separation of powers

Target Reading Skill

Main Idea Copy the concept web below. As you read, add ovals and fill them in with ideas that influenced the Constitution.

Main Idea The Constitution reflects ancient traditions, Enlightenment ideas, and Americans' experience.

Setting the Scene Serving as the ambassador to France, Thomas Jefferson did not attend the Constitutional Convention. James Madison, however, kept in touch with his friend in Paris. As Madison prepared for the convention, he asked Jefferson to send whatever books "may throw light" on various governments.

Jefferson sent not five or ten books but hundreds. Some discussed the laws of nations. Others were biographies of important leaders. A French encyclopedia alone came to 37 volumes. In gratitude, Madison shipped Jefferson unusual American plants to show the French. (Jefferson had also asked for a live opossum, but that, alas, Madison could not manage!)

Today, we often refer to Madison, Jefferson, and other leaders who laid the groundwork for the United States as the Founding Fathers. These patriots were well aware that their nation was embarking on a bold experiment. Still, they did not have to invent a government from scratch.

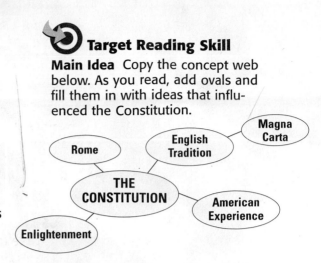

French encyclopedia

The Lessons of Rome's Republic

Long before the Revolution, John Adams called on Americans to investigate how governments worked:

> 66 Let us . . . search into the spirit of the British constitution; read the histories of ancient ages; contemplate the great examples of Greece and Rome; [and] set before us the conduct of our own British ancestors. . . . 99
>
> —John Adams, *Dissertation on the Canon and Feudal Law*

The delegates to the Constitutional Convention followed this advice. They wanted to create a **republic,** a government in which citizens rule themselves through elected representatives. Few

Viewing History

Respect for the Ancient World

United States

Even the arts reflected the respect that Americans felt for ancient Greece and Rome. Roman domes and Greek pillars influenced Thomas Jefferson's design for his home, Monticello (above). The bust (left) shows Benjamin Franklin dressed in a Roman toga. **Linking Past and Present** *What kinds of buildings today have similarities to Monticello?*

republics in the history of the world had survived very long. In order to create one that would last, American leaders looked first to the ancient examples of Greece and, especially, Rome.

The Roman Example Americans greatly admired the Roman Republic. General Charles Lee, one of George Washington's commanders, commented, "I used to regret not being thrown into the World in the glorious [era] of the Romans."

Independence and public service were virtues that the Founding Fathers saw in the citizens of Rome. Roman citizens were willing to serve in public office, not for money, but because they were devoted to their republic. American colonists admired Rome so much that when they debated politics in the newspapers, they often signed their opinions with Roman names like Cincinnatus or Cicero.

The Roman Warning At the same time, the Founding Fathers saw the collapse of Rome's republic as a warning to the United States. No republic could survive unless its citizens remained independent and devoted to public service. Under the ruler Caesar Augustus, Rome eventually became a **dictatorship,** a government in which one person or a small group holds complete authority. The leaders of the American Revolution believed that Romans stumbled once they began to value luxury and comfort more than independence.

Historians today admit that the Founding Fathers somewhat exaggerated the virtues of Rome's republic. Yet, the lessons they learned still have force. Republics do not always die because they are invaded from outside. Without educated and dedicated citizens, republics can decay from within.

Britain's Traditions of Freedom

Greece and Rome were not the only examples of democratic government. Despite their quarrel with Great Britain, leaders of the Revolution valued British traditions of freedom.

Magna Carta As you learned in Chapter 3, King John of England signed the Magna Carta in 1215. The Magna Carta contained two basic ideas that helped to shape both British and American government. First, it made it clear that English monarchs themselves had to obey the law. King John agreed not to raise taxes without first consulting the Great Council of nobles and church officials. Eventually, the Great Council grew into the British Parliament.

Just as important, the Magna Carta stated that English nobles had certain rights—rights that were later extended to other classes of people as well. These included rights to private property and the right to trial by jury.

English Bill of Rights In 1689, the English Bill of Rights went further in protecting the rights of citizens. The document said that parliamentary elections should be held regularly. It upheld the right to a trial by jury and allowed citizens to bear arms. It also affirmed the right of **habeas corpus,** the idea that no person could be held in prison without first being charged with a specific crime.

The American Experience

Americans enjoyed a long tradition of representative government. The Virginia colonists set up the House of Burgesses. Eventually, each British colony elected its own legislature.

A Constitutional Tradition Americans were also used to relying on written documents that clearly identified the powers and limits of government. The Mayflower Compact, written in 1620, was the first document of self-government in North America. Each of the 13 colonies had a written charter granted by the monarch or by Parliament.

The Revolutionary Era The framers of the Constitution also drew on their own experiences. The Founding Fathers bitterly remembered their grievances against the English king. In writing the Constitution, they sought to prevent such abuses.

For example, the Declaration of Independence accused the king of placing military power above civilian authority. The Constitution made the elected President "Commander in Chief of the Army and Navy . . . and of the militia of the several states." The Declaration protested that the king had made judges "dependent on his will alone." The Constitution set up a court system independent of the President and legislature.

The framers were very familiar with the workings of the Second Continental Congress, the Articles of Confederation, and their own state governments. Much that went into the Constitution came either from the Articles or from the state constitutions.

Teachings of the Enlightenment

The Constitution was also based on the ideas of the European Enlightenment. As you read in Chapter 4, Enlightenment thinkers believed that people could improve society through the use of reason. Many of the Constitution's framers had read the works of Enlightenment thinkers.

Identify Supporting Details

What details in the first two paragraphs on this page tell which English traditions influenced the Constitution? Add these details to your concept web.

The Spirit of the Laws

Baron de Montesquieu's ideas about government had a strong influence on American thinkers. Here, Montesquieu discusses separation of powers:

"There is no liberty, if the judiciary power be not separated from the legislative and executive. Were it joined . . . to the executive power, the judge might behave with violence and oppression. There would be an end of everything, were the same man or the same body, whether of the nobles or of the people, to exercise those three powers, that of enacting laws, that of executing the public laws, and of trying the causes of individuals."

—Baron de Montesquieu,
The Spirit of the Laws

Analyzing Primary Sources
What does Montesquieu say would result if judges also had the power to make and carry out laws?

Locke and Natural Rights The English writer John Locke published *Two Treatises of Government* in 1690. In it, he stated two important ideas. First, Locke declared that all people had natural rights to life, liberty, and property. Second, he suggested that government is an agreement between the ruler and the ruled. The ruler must enforce the laws and protect the people. If a ruler violates the people's natural rights, the people have a right to rebel.

Locke's ideas were popular among Americans. The framers of the Constitution wanted to protect people's natural rights and limit the power of government. They saw the Constitution as a contract between the people and their government.

Montesquieu and the Separation of Powers The French Enlightenment thinker Baron de Montesquieu (MOHN tehs kyoo) influenced American ideas of how a government should be constructed. In his 1748 book *The Spirit of the Laws*, Montesquieu stressed the importance of the rule of law. The powers of government, he said, should be clearly defined and divided up. He suggested that three separate branches be created: the legislative, executive, and judicial. This idea, known as the **separation of powers,** was designed to keep any person or group from gaining too much power. In the next chapter, you will see how the Constitution established separation of powers in the United States government.

From Out of the Old, the New The Founding Fathers drew on many traditions. In the end, though, the new system of government was not quite like anything that came before it.

When John Adams received the news from Philadelphia, he wrote, "As we say at sea, huzza for the new world and farewell to the old one!" He called the Constitution "the greatest single effort of national deliberation that the world has ever seen."

★ ★ ★ Section 3 Assessment ★ ★ ★

Recall

1. **Identify** Explain the significance of **(a)** Founding Fathers, **(b)** Magna Carta, **(c)** English Bill of Rights, **(d)** John Locke, **(e)** Baron de Montesquieu.

2. **Define** **(a)** republic, **(b)** dictatorship, **(c)** habeas corpus, **(d)** separation of powers.

Comprehension

3. How did the Roman republic provide both an example and a warning to Americans?

4. Identify two ways the Constitution addressed grievances listed in the Declaration of Independence.

5. What ideas did Americans adopt from John Locke?

Critical Thinking and Writing

6. **Exploring the Main Idea** Review the Main Idea statement at the beginning of this section. Then, write a letter from Madison to Jefferson discussing why American leaders looked to the past.

7. **Applying Information** The Magna Carta states, "Neither we nor our [representatives] shall take . . . wood which is not ours, against the will of the owner of that wood." Write a paragraph explaining how this principle applies to the United States.

ACTIVITY

Go Online
PHSchool.com

Giving a Talk
Use the Internet to find quotations from an Enlightenment writer such as Locke, Montesquieu, or Voltaire. Choose one quotation and give a one-minute talk explaining how it relates to American ideals and principles. For help in completing the activity, visit PHSchool.com, **Web Code mfd-0703.**

4 Ratification and the Bill of Rights

Prepare to Read

Objectives

In this section, you will
- List the key issues in the constitutional debate.
- Explain how the Constitution was finally ratified.
- Describe how the Bill of Rights was added to the Constitution.

Key Terms

Federalists

Antifederalists

The Federalist Papers

amend

Bill of Rights

Target Reading Skill

Sequence Copy this flow-chart. As you read, fill in the boxes with the major events relating to the ratification of the Constitution. The first and last boxes have been completed to help you get started. Add as many boxes as you need.

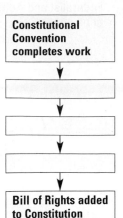

Constitutional Convention completes work
↓
↓
↓
↓
Bill of Rights added to Constitution

Main Idea After heated debates, the 13 states voted one by one to approve the new Constitution.

Setting the Scene

Across the nation, Americans discussed the new Constitution. The Boston *Daily Advertiser* called for citizens to debate the new plan in the pages of its newspaper:

> 66 Come on brother scribblers, 'tis idle to lag!
> The Convention has let the cat out of the bag. 99
> —quoted in *Miracle at Philadelphia* (Bowen)

The Constitutional Convention had done its work. Now, in the fall of 1787, the debates began. Each state had to decide whether or not to ratify the new framework of government.

Federalists Debate Antifederalists

The framers of the Constitution sent the document to Congress, along with a letter from George Washington. Washington warmly approved the document, predicting that the Constitution would "promote the lasting welfare of that country so dear to us all."

The framers had set up a process for the states to approve the new government. At least 9 of the 13 states had to ratify the Constitution before it could go into effect. In 1787 and 1788, voters in each state elected delegates to special state conventions. These delegates would decide whether or not to ratify the Constitution.

The Federalist Position In every state, heated debates took place. Supporters of the Constitution called themselves Federalists because they favored a strong federal, or national, government. They called people who opposed the Constitution Antifederalists.

Federalists argued that the Articles of Confederation left too much power with the individual states. This imbalance produced a dangerously weak central government. Disputes among the states, Federalists said, made it too difficult for the government to function.

Federalists believed that the Constitution gave the national government the authority it needed to function effectively. At the same

Printing press

Understand Sequence

Where on the flowchart will the Federalist and Antifederalist positions appear?

Connecting to Today

A Coin for Every State

Delaware, the second smallest state in the nation, enjoys one big honor no other state can match. It has the right to call itself "The First State." On December 7, 1787, Delaware became the first state to ratify the Constitution.

Delaware again led the way more than 200 years later. The United States mint began to issue a series of special quarters honoring the 50 states. The "heads" side of each coin carries the familiar image of George Washington. The "tails" side displays a different design for each state, in the order they ratified the Constitution or joined the Union. The Delaware quarter was issued on January 1, 1999. The final coins—honoring Alaska and Hawaii—are scheduled to be released in 2008.

Why do you think many people are eager to collect all 50 state quarters?

time, they said, the Constitution still protected the rights and powers of the individual states.

Federalists James Madison, Alexander Hamilton, and John Jay wrote a series of essays, known today as the *Federalist Papers.* Their purpose was to explain and defend the Constitution. They used pen names, but most people knew who they were. Today, the *Federalist Papers* remains one of the best discussions of the political theory behind the American system of government.

The Antifederalist Position Antifederalists felt that the Constitution made the national government too strong and left the states too weak. They also thought that the Constitution gave the President too much power. Patrick Henry of Virginia protested:

> 66 This Constitution is said to have beautiful features, but . . . they appear to me horribly frightful. . . . Your President may become king . . . If your American chief be a man of ambition and abilities, how easy is it for him to render himself absolute! 99
>
> —Patrick Henry, Speech to the Virginia Convention, June 1788

Most people expected George Washington to be elected President. Antifederalists admired Washington, but they warned that future Presidents might lack Washington's honor and skill. For this reason, they said, the office should not be too powerful.

Key Issue: Need for a Bill of Rights

The chief objection of Antifederalists was that the Constitution had no bill of rights. Americans, they said, had just fought a revolution to protect their freedoms. A bill of rights was needed to protect such basic liberties as freedom of speech and religion.

One of the strongest supporters of a bill of rights was George Mason of Virginia. In 1776, Mason had written the bill of rights for Virginia's constitution. After the Constitutional Convention refused to include a bill of rights, Mason joined the Antifederalists.

Federalists replied that it was impossible to list all the natural rights of people. Besides, they said, the Constitution protected citizens well enough as it was. Antifederalists responded that unless rights were spelled out, they could be too easily ignored.

The States Vote to Ratify

One by one, the states voted. Delaware led the way, ratifying on December 7, 1787. Pennsylvania and New Jersey soon followed.

New England Approves Massachusetts was the first key battleground. There, the old patriots Sam Adams and John Hancock held back their support. The delay seemed "very ominous," wrote Madison. Finally, Adams and Hancock convinced the state convention to recommend adding a bill of rights to the Constitution.

Still the debate continued. "Some gentlemen say, don't be in a hurry . . . don't take a leap in the dark," a Federalist farmer told his fellow delegates. "I say . . . gather fruit when it is ripe." In February 1788, Massachusetts became the sixth state to ratify.

In June, New Hampshire joined ranks as the ninth state. The new government could now go into effect. Still, the nation's unity remained in doubt. New York and Virginia, two of the largest states, had not yet ratified the plan. In both states, Federalists and Antifederalists were closely matched.

Last Holdouts In Virginia, Patrick Henry, George Mason, and Governor Edmund Randolph led the opposition. Still a spellbinding speaker, Henry at one point spoke for seven hours. Soft-spoken, James Madison could not match Henry's dramatic style. Yet his arguments in favor of the Constitution were always clear, patient, and to the point.

The tide finally turned when Governor Randolph changed his mind. He gave his support when the Federalists promised to support a bill of rights. Virginia voted to ratify in late June.

In New York, the struggle went on for another month. In July 1788, the state convention voted to ratify. North Carolina followed in November 1789. Only Rhode Island, which had refused to send delegates to the Constitutional Convention, remained. On May 29, 1790, Rhode Island became the last state to ratify.

The Nation Celebrates Throughout the land, Americans celebrated the news that the Constitution was ratified. The city of Philadelphia set its festival for July 4, 1788.

A festive parade filed along Market Street, led by soldiers who had fought in the Revolution. Thousands cheered as six colorfully outfitted horses pulled a blue carriage shaped like an eagle. Thirteen stars and stripes were painted on the front, and the Constitution was raised proudly above it. Benjamin Rush, a Philadelphia doctor and strong supporter of the Constitution, wrote to a friend, "'Tis done. We have become a nation."

Adding a Bill of Rights

Americans voted in the first election under the Constitution in January 1789. As expected, George Washington was elected President, while John Adams was chosen as Vice President.

The first Congress met in New York City, which was chosen as the nation's first capital. Congress quickly turned its attention to adding a bill of rights to the Constitution. As you have read, several states had agreed to ratify the Constitution only on the condition that a bill of rights be added.

Cause *and* Effect

Causes

- Articles of Confederation creates weak national government
- Trade and money problems arise between states
- Foreign nations take advantage of weak government
- Shays' Rebellion breaks out
- Convention meets to revise Articles of Confederation

THE WRITING OF THE CONSTITUTION

Effects

- New government includes President and two-house legislature
- Power is divided between national and state governments
- Compromises allow slavery to continue
- States debate and ratify Constitution
- Bill of Rights is added

Effects Today

- United States is world's oldest continuing constitutional democracy
- Debate about federal versus state power continues
- Amendments extend rights to more citizens
- New democracies look to the Constitution as a model

GRAPHIC ORGANIZER
Skills

The long-term impact of the Constitutional Convention reached far beyond its original goals.

1. **Comprehension** Why is Shays' Rebellion listed as a cause?

2. **Critical Thinking Linking Past and Present** Why do you think new nations see the United States Constitution as a model?

Civics

Proposed and Ratified The framers had established a way to amend, or change, the Constitution. They did not want people to make changes lightly, however. Thus, they made the process of amending the Constitution fairly difficult. (You will read more about the amendment process in Chapter 8.)

In 1789, the first Congress proposed a set of twelve amendments, written by James Madison. As required by the Constitution, the amendments then went to the states. By December 1791, three fourths of the states had ratified 10 of the 12 amendments. These 10 amendments became known as the Bill of Rights.

The Bill of Rights James Madison insisted that the Bill of Rights does not give Americans any rights. The rights listed, he said, are natural rights that belong to all human beings. The Bill of Rights simply prevents the government from taking these rights away.

Some of the first 10 amendments were intended to prevent the kind of abuse Americans had suffered under English rule. For example, the Declaration of Independence had condemned the king for forcing colonists to quarter troops in their homes and for suspending trial by jury. The Third Amendment forbids the government to quarter troops in citizens' homes without their consent. The Sixth and Seventh Amendments guarantee the right to trial by jury.

Other amendments protected individual rights as many states had already done. In 1786, the Virginia Statute of Religious Freedom stated that "No man shall be compelled to frequent or support any religious worship . . . or otherwise suffer, on account of his religious opinions or belief." Religious freedom became the very first right listed in the First Amendment. (You will read more about the freedoms protected by the Bill of Rights in Chapter 8.)

With the Bill of Rights in place, the new framework of government was complete. Over time, the Constitution became a living document that grew and changed along with the nation.

★ ★ ★ Section 4 Assessment ★ ★ ★

Recall
1. **Identify** Explain the significance of (a) Federalists, (b) Antifederalists, (c) *The Federalist Papers,* (d) George Mason, (e) Bill of Rights.
2. **Define** amend.

Comprehension
3. (a) Why did Federalists support the Constitution? (b) Why did Antifederalists oppose it?
4. Describe the ratification debate in one battleground state.
5. Why did the new government quickly take steps to amend the Constitution?

Critical Thinking and Writing
6. **Exploring the Main Idea** Review the Main Idea statement at the beginning of this section. Then, write a paragraph explaining what you think was the single most important reason in favor of ratifying the Constitution.
7. **Drawing Conclusions** Analyze the views of George Mason and Alexander Hamilton about the Bill of Rights. Explain how the influence of both shaped the Bill of Rights as it now exists.

ACTIVITY

Planning a Celebration You are an official in an American city or village in 1789. With a group of classmates, create a plan for your own celebration of the ratification of the Constitution. Make a list of activities you would include. If you like, you may also design a banner, prepare a short speech, or select music.

Why did the Antifederalists oppose the new Constitution? To gain an accurate understanding of past events, it is often helpful to analyze the words of those who were present when the events took place.

Patrick Henry, a fiery patriot and a firm Antifederalist, spoke against the ratification of the Constitution to the delegates at the Virginia state convention:

Patrick Henry

❝ You ought to be extremely cautious, watchful, jealous of your liberty; for instead of securing your rights, you may lose them forever. If a wrong step be now made, the republic may be lost forever. If this new government will not come up to the expectation of the people, and they shall be disappointed, their liberty will be lost, and tyranny must and will arise. I repeat it again, and I beg gentlemen to consider that a wrong step made now will plunge us into misery, and our republic will be lost. . . .

And here I would make this inquiry of those worthy characters who composed a part of the late federal Convention. . . . I have the highest veneration for those gentlemen; but, sir, give me leave to demand: What right had they to say, 'We, the people'? My political curiosity, exclusive of my anxious [concern] for the public welfare, leads me to ask: Who authorized them to speak the language of, 'We, the people,' instead of, 'We, the states'? ❞

—Patrick Henry, Speech at the Virginia Convention, June 1788

Learn the Skill *To analyze a primary source, use the following steps:*

1. **Identify the writer.** Knowing the source of a document helps you evaluate the writer's information and point of view.

2. **Identify the context.** When was the document written? What was its purpose?

3. **Identify the main idea.** What is the main idea of the document?

4. **Look for words that indicate the point of view.** Emotional words can be a clue to the writer's feelings about the subject matter.

5. **Analyze.** What conclusions can you reach about the writer and the information given?

Practice the Skill *Answer the following questions about the document above:*

1. What do you know about Patrick Henry and his political views?

2. What was Henry's purpose in giving the speech?

3. In this excerpt, what are Henry's main objections to the new Constitution?

4. **(a)** What words indicate that Henry has strong feelings about the Constitution? **(b)** Describe his attitude toward the framers.

5. Analyze Henry's view of the relationship of the central government to the states.

Apply the Skill *See the Chapter Review and Assessment.*

Review and Assessment

CHAPTER SUMMARY

Section 1
The Articles of Confederation created a weak central government and loose alliance of independent states. These weaknesses and an economic depression led to calls for change.

Section 2
Delegates to the Constitutional Convention had to compromise to create a new constitution. After compromising on a number of key issues, delegates signed the Constitution.

Section 3
The U.S. Constitution draws on many ideas. These include Greek and Roman traditions, British traditions, Enlightenment ideas, and the unique American experience.

Section 4
After heated debates, the 13 states voted to approve the new Constitution. The first ten amendments to the Constitution make up the Bill of Rights. These amendments protect personal liberties and the natural rights of citizens.

Building Vocabulary

Review the meaning of the chapter vocabulary words listed below. Then, write a sentence for each word in which you define the word and describe its relation to the writing of the Constitution.

1. **constitution**
2. **bill of rights**
3. **depression**
4. **legislative branch**
5. **executive branch**
6. **judicial branch**
7. **compromise**
8. **republic**
9. **habeas corpus**
10. **separation of powers**

Reviewing Key Facts

11. Summarize the strengths and weaknesses of the Articles of Confederation. (Section 1)
12. What kind of legislature did the Constitution create? Why? (Section 2)

For additional review and enrichment activities, see the interactive version of *The American Nation,* available on the Web and on CD-ROM.

Chapter Self-Test For practice test questions for Chapter 7, visit PHSchool.com, **Web Code mfa-0704.**

13. How did the Constitution build on the earlier experience of Americans? (Section 3)
14. Identify one way Antifederalists influenced the Constitution. (Section 4)

Critical Thinking and Writing

15. **Connecting to Geography: Regions** Review the map Claims to Western Lands in Section 1. **(a)** Describe the region that was considered "the West" in the 1780s. **(b)** Write a paragraph describing what would have happened if Virginia had won all of its land claims.
16. **Analyzing Information** Choose one issue at the Philadelphia Convention of 1787. Describe what each side won and gave up. Was the issue resolved successfully? Explain.
17. **Applying Information** Review the opening lines of the Declaration of Independence in Chapter 6. Copy two sentences or phrases that reflect the ideas of John Locke. Explain how they show that Locke influenced Jefferson.
18. **Supporting a Point of View** When the Constitution was ratified, Benjamin Rush commented, "We have become a nation." List three reasons to support Rush's comment. Explain in what way the United States was not a "nation" before the Constitution.

Analyzing Primary Sources

The cartoon below appeared in an American newspaper in 1788. Look at the cartoon and answer the questions that follow:

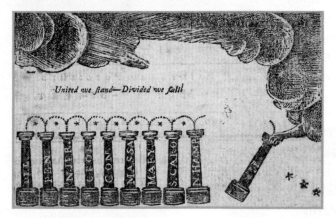

United we stand—Divided we fall!

19. The subject of this cartoon is the
   A. American Revolution.
   B. Great Compromise.
   C. great power of state governments.
   D. ratification of the Constitution.
20. What do the pillars represent?
   A. the states
   B. articles of the Constitution
   C. U.S. expansion west
   D. presidential candidates

Analyzing a Primary Source

In this letter, George Washington discusses the weaknesses of the early government. Read the excerpt and answer the questions that follow:

66 I am told that even respectable characters speak of a monarchical form of government without horror. . . . What a triumph for the advocates of [tyranny] to find that we are incapable of governing ourselves, and that systems founded on the basis of equal liberty are merely ideal and [false]! Would to God that wise measures be taken in time to avert the consequences. 99
   —George Washington, Letter to John Jay, August 1, 1786

21. Washington is disturbed because
   A. the Constitution has no bill of rights.
   B. the Articles of Confederation have no executive.
   C. some Americans want a monarchy.
   D. a government based on equal liberty can never succeed.
22. How does this letter help explain why Washington agreed to serve as president of the Constitutional Convention?

ACTIVITIES

Connecting With . . .
Government and Citizenship

Making a Chart With a partner, review the Declaration of Independence printed in Chapter 6. Identify the list of grievances against the king of England. Then, skim the Constitution and Bill of Rights, which appear at the end of this chapter. Make a chart showing how specific grievances in the Declaration were addressed in the Constitution. Include at least five grievances.

Go Online
PHSchool.com

Connecting to Today

Exploring American Symbols In 1782, Congress declared the bald eagle to be an official symbol of the new nation. Use the Internet to find out more about another familiar American symbol. Prepare a three-minute report on the meaning of that symbol. For help in starting this activity, visit PHSchool.com, **Web Code mfd-0705.**

Creating a Database

A Constitutional Convention Information Bank With the class, create an information bank on the delegates to the Constitutional Convention. Use the Internet to find information about one delegate. Prepare a fact sheet showing his background, the state he represented, and his position on a key issue. Combine your fact sheet with those of the rest of the class. For help in starting this activity, visit PHSchool.com, **Web Code mfd-0706.**

The Constitution at a Glance

Original Constitution

Preamble

Article

Amendments

Bill of Rights

Additional Amendments

The Constitution of the United States of America

The Constitution is printed in black. The titles of articles, sections, and clauses are not part of the original document. They have been added here to help you find information in the Constitution. Some words or lines are crossed out because they have been changed by amendments or no longer apply. Annotations, or explanations, are on the tan side of the page. Difficult words are defined.

Preamble

We the people of the United States, in order to form a more perfect Union, establish justice, insure domestic tranquillity, provide for the common defense, promote the general welfare, and secure the blessings of liberty to ourselves and our posterity, do ordain and establish this Constitution for the United States of America.

The Preamble describes the purpose of the government set up by the Constitution. Americans expect their government to defend justice and liberty and provide peace and safety from foreign enemies.

Article 1. The Legislative Branch

Section 1. A Two-House Legislature

All legislative powers herein granted shall be vested in a Congress of the United States, which shall consist of a Senate and House of Representatives.

The Constitution gives Congress the power to make laws. Congress is divided into the Senate and the House of Representatives.

Section 2. House of Representatives

1. **Election of Members**   The House of Representatives shall be composed of members chosen every second year by the people of the several states, and the electors in each state shall have the qualifications requisite for electors of the most numerous branch of the state legislature.

    Clause 1 *Electors* refers to voters. Members of the House of Representatives are elected every two years. Any citizen allowed to vote for members of the larger house of the state legislature can also vote for members of the House.

2. **Qualifications**   No person shall be a Representative who shall not have attained to the age of twenty-five years, and been seven years a citizen of the United States, and who shall not, when elected, be an inhabitant of that state in which he shall be chosen.

    Clause 2 A member of the House of Representatives must be at least 25 years old, an American citizen for 7 years, and a resident of the state he or she represents.

3. **Determining Representation**   Representatives ~~and direct taxes~~ shall be apportioned among the several states which may be included within this Union, according to their respective numbers ~~which shall be determined by adding to the whole number of free persons, including those bound to service for a term of years, and excluding Indians not taxed, three fifths of all other persons.~~ The actual enumeration shall be made within three years after the first meeting of the Congress of the United States, and within every subsequent term of ten years, in such manner as they shall by law direct. The number of Representatives shall not exceed one for every 30,000, but each state shall have at least one Representative; ~~and until such enumeration shall be made, the state of New Hampshire shall be entitled to choose three; Massachusetts, eight; Rhode Island and Providence Plantations, one; Connecticut, five; New York, six; New Jersey, four; Pennsylvania, eight; Delaware, one; Maryland, six; Virginia, ten; North Carolina, five; South Carolina, five; and Georgia, three.~~

    Clause 3 The number of representatives each state elects is based on its population. An *enumeration,* or census, must be taken every 10 years to determine population. Today, the number of representatives in the House is fixed at 435.
    This is the famous Three-Fifths Compromise worked out at the Constitutional Convention. *Persons bound to service* meant indentured servants. *All other persons* meant slaves. All free people in a state were counted. However, only three fifths of the slaves were included in the population count. This three-fifths clause became meaningless when slaves were freed in 1865 by the Thirteenth Amendment.

Clause 4 *Executive authority* means the governor of a state. If a member of the House leaves office before his or her term ends, the governor must call a special election to fill the seat.

Clause 5 The House elects a speaker. Today, the speaker is usually chosen by the party that has a majority in the House. Also, only the House has the power to *impeach,* or accuse, a federal official of wrongdoing.

Clause 1 Each state has two senators, who serve for six-year terms. The Seventeenth Amendment changed the way senators were elected.

Clause 2 Every two years, one third of the senators run for reelection. Thus, the makeup of the Senate is never totally changed by any one election. The Seventeenth Amendment changed the way that *vacancies,* or empty seats, are filled. Today, the governor of a state must choose a senator to fill a vacancy that occurs between elections.

Clause 3 A senator must be at least 30 years old, an American citizen for 9 years, and a resident of the state he or she represents.

Clause 4 The Vice President presides over Senate meetings, but he or she can vote only to break a tie.

Clause 5 *Pro tempore* means "temporary." The Senate chooses a member to serve as president *pro tempore* when the Vice President is absent.

Clause 6 The Senate acts as a jury if the House impeaches a federal official. The Chief Justice of the Supreme Court presides if the President is on trial. Two thirds of all senators present must vote for *conviction,* or a finding of guilty. No President has ever been convicted, though the House impeached President Andrew Johnson in 1868 and President Bill Clinton in 1998. In 1974, President Richard Nixon resigned before he could be impeached.

Clause 7 If an official is found guilty by the Senate, he or she can be removed from office and barred from holding federal office in the future. These are the only punishments the Senate can impose. However, the convicted official can still be tried in a criminal court.

4. **Filling Vacancies** When vacancies happen in the representation from any state, the executive authority thereof shall issue writs of election to fill such vacancies.

5. **Selection of Officers; Power of Impeachment** The House of Representatives shall choose their Speaker and other officers; and shall have the sole power of impeachment.

Section 3. The Senate

1. **Selection of Members** The Senate of the United States shall be composed of two Senators from each state ~~chosen by the legislature thereof~~, for six years, and each Senator shall have one vote.

2. **Alternating Terms; Filling Vacancies** Immediately after they shall be assembled in consequence of the first election, they shall be divided as equally as may be into three classes. ~~The seats of the Senators of the first class shall be vacated at the expiration of the second year, of the second class at the expiration of the fourth year, and of the third class at the expiration of the sixth year,~~ so that one-third may be chosen every second year; ~~and if vacancies happen by resignation, or otherwise, during the recess of the legislature of any state, the executive thereof may make temporary appointments until the next meeting of the legislature, which shall then fill such vacancies.~~

3. **Qualifications** No person shall be a Senator who shall not have attained to the age of thirty years, and been nine years a citizen of the United States, and who shall not, when elected, be an inhabitant of that state for which he shall be chosen.

4. **President of the Senate** The Vice-President of the United States shall be president of the Senate, but shall have no vote, unless they be equally divided.

5. **Election of Senate Officers** The Senate shall choose their other officers, and also a president *pro tempore,* in the absence of the Vice-President, or when he shall exercise the office of the President of the United States.

6. **Impeachment Trials** The Senate shall have the sole power to try all impeachments. When sitting for that purpose, they shall be on oath or affirmation. When the President of the United States is tried, the Chief Justice shall preside; and no person shall be convicted without the concurrence of two-thirds of the members present.

7. **Penalties Upon Conviction** Judgment in cases of impeachment shall not extend further than to removal from office, and disqualification to hold and enjoy any office of honor, trust, or profit under the United States; but the party convicted shall nevertheless be liable and subject to indictment, trial, judgment, and punishment, according to law.

Section 4. Elections and Meetings

1. **Election of Congress** The times, places, and manner of holding elections for Senators and Representatives shall be prescribed in each state by the legislature thereof; but the Congress may at any time by law make or alter such regulations, except as to the places of choosing Senators.

2. **Annual Sessions** The Congress shall assemble at least once in every year, ~~and such meeting shall be on the first Monday in December, unless they shall by law appoint a different day.~~

Section 5. Rules for the Conduct of Business

1. **Organization** Each house shall be the judge of the elections, returns, and qualifications of its own members, and a majority of each shall constitute a quorum to do business; but a smaller number may adjourn from day to day, and may be authorized to compel the attendance of absent members, in such manner, and under such penalties, as each house may provide.

2. **Procedures** Each house may determine the rules of its proceedings, punish its members for disorderly behavior, and with the concurrence of two-thirds, expel a member.

3. **A Written Record** Each house shall keep a journal of its proceedings, and from time to time publish the same, excepting such parts as may in their judgment require secrecy; and the yeas and nays of the members of either house on any question shall, at the desire of one-fifth of those present, be entered on the journal.

4. **Rules for Adjournment** Neither house, during the session of Congress, shall, without the consent of the other, adjourn for more than three days, nor to any other place than that in which the two houses shall be sitting.

Section 6. Privileges and Restrictions

1. **Salaries and Immunities** The Senators and Representatives shall receive a compensation for their services, to be ascertained by law and paid out of the Treasury of the United States. They shall in all cases, except treason, felony, and breach of the peace, be privileged from arrest during their attendance at the session of their respective houses, and in going to and returning from the same; and for any speech or debate in either house, they shall not be questioned in any other place.

2. **Restrictions on Other Employment** No Senator or Representative shall, during the time for which he was elected, be appointed to any civil office under the authority of the United States, which shall have been created, or the emoluments whereof shall have been increased, during such time; and no person holding any office under the United States shall be a member of either house during his continuance in office.

Clause 1 Each state legislature can decide when and how congressional elections take place, but Congress can overrule these decisions. In 1842, Congress required each state to set up congressional districts with one representative elected from each district. In 1872, Congress decided that congressional elections must be held in every state on the same date in even-numbered years.

Clause 2 Congress must meet at least once a year. The Twentieth Amendment moved the opening date of Congress to January 3.

Clause 1 Each house decides whether a member has the qualifications for office set by the Constitution. A *quorum* is the smallest number of members who must be present for business to be conducted. Each house can set its own rules about absent members.

Clause 2 Each house can make rules for the conduct of members. It can only expel a member by a two-thirds vote.

Clause 3 Each house keeps a record of its meetings. *The Congressional Record* is published every day with excerpts from speeches made in each house. It also records the votes of each member.

Clause 4 Neither house can *adjourn*, or stop meeting, for more than three days unless the other house approves. Both houses of Congress must meet in the same city.

Clause 1 *Compensation* means "salary." Congress decides the salary for its members. While Congress is in session, a member is free from arrest in civil cases and cannot be sued for anything he or she says on the floor of Congress. This allows for freedom of debate. However, a member can be arrested for a criminal offense.

Clause 2 *Emolument* also means "salary." A member of Congress cannot hold another federal office during his or her term. A former member of Congress cannot hold an office created while he or she was in Congress. An official in another branch of government cannot serve at the same time in Congress. This strengthens the separation of powers.

Clause 1 *Revenue* is money raised by the government through taxes. Tax bills must be introduced in the House. The Senate, however, can make changes in tax bills. This clause protects the principle that people can be taxed only with their consent.

Clause 2 A *bill,* or proposed law, that is passed by a majority of the House and Senate is sent to the President. If the President signs the bill, it becomes law.

A bill can also become law without the President's signature. The President can refuse to act on a bill. If Congress is in session at the time, the bill becomes law 10 days after the President receives it.

The President can *veto,* or reject, a bill by sending it back to the house where it was introduced. Or if the President refuses to act on a bill and Congress adjourns within 10 days, then the bill dies. This way of killing a bill without taking action is called the *pocket veto.*

Congress can override the President's veto if each house of Congress passes the bill again by a two-thirds vote. This clause is an important part of the system of checks and balances.

Section 7. Law-Making Process

1. **Tax Bills**   All bills for raising revenue shall originate in the House of Representatives; but the Senate may propose or concur with amendments as on other bills.

2. **How a Bill Becomes a Law**   Every bill which shall have passed the House of Representatives and the Senate shall, before it become a law, be presented to the President of the United States; if he approve, he shall sign it, but if not, he shall return it, with his objections, to that house in which it shall have originated, who shall enter the objections at large on their journal, and proceed to reconsider it. If after such reconsideration two-thirds of that house shall agree to pass the bill, it shall be sent, together with the objections, to the other house, by which it shall likewise be reconsidered, and, if approved by two-thirds of that house, it shall become a law. But in all such cases the votes of both houses shall be determined by yeas and nays, and the names of the persons voting for and against the bill shall be entered on the journal of each house respectively. If any bill shall not be returned by the President within ten days (Sundays excepted) after it shall have been presented to him, the same bill shall be a law, in like manner as if he had signed it, unless the Congress by their adjournment prevent its return, in which case it shall not be a law.

How a Bill Becomes a Law

GRAPHIC ORGANIZER
Skills

The House of Representatives, the Senate, and the President all play a role in the law-making process.

1. **Comprehension**
   (a) Where can a bill be introduced? **(b)** At what point do members of the House and Senate come together? **(c)** What can the President do?

2. **Critical Thinking**
   Drawing Inferences
   Every year thousands of bills are introduced. Why do you think committees hold hearings on bills?

Civics

Introduction	Committee Action	Floor Action		Enactment Into Law	
Introduced in House	Referred to House committee	House debates and passes its form of bill	House and Senate members confer, reach compromise on single form of bill	President signs bill into law	The bill becomes law
Introduced in Senate	Referred to Senate committee	Senate debates and passes its form of bill			With a two-thirds majority vote of Congress, the bill is passed over the President's veto
			House and Senate approve compromise	President vetoes bill	
Most bills begin as similar proposals in House and Senate	Committee holds hearings, makes changes, recommends passage	All bills must go through both House and Senate before reaching President			Congress does not override the President's veto
					The bill fails to become law

3. **Resolutions Passed by Congress** Every order, resolution, or vote to which the concurrence of the Senate and House of Representatives may be necessary (except on a question of adjournment) shall be presented to the President of the United States; and before the same shall take effect, shall be approved by him, or being disapproved by him, shall be repassed by two-thirds of the Senate and House of Representatives, according to the rules and limitations prescribed in the case of a bill.

Clause 3 Congress can pass resolutions or orders that have the same force as laws. Any such resolution or order must be signed by the President (except on questions of adjournment). This clause prevents Congress from bypassing the President simply by calling a bill by another name.

Section 8. Powers Delegated to Congress

The Congress shall have the power

1. **Taxes** To lay and collect taxes, duties, imposts, and excises, to pay the debts and provide for the common defense and general welfare of the United States; but all duties, imposts, and excises shall be uniform throughout the United States;

Clause 1 *Duties* are tariffs. *Imposts* are taxes in general. *Excises* are taxes on the production or sale of certain goods. Congress has the power to tax and spend tax money. Taxes must be the same in all parts of the country.

2. **Borrowing** To borrow money on the credit of the United States;

Clause 2 Congress can borrow money for the United States. The government often borrows money by selling *bonds,* or certificates that promise to pay the holder a certain sum of money on a certain date.

3. **Commerce** To regulate commerce with foreign nations, and among the several states, and with the Indian tribes;

Clause 3 Only Congress has the power to regulate foreign and *interstate trade,* or trade between states. The Constitution recognizes four sovereign governments: the federal government, state governments, American Indian Tribal governments, and foreign nations.

4. **Naturalization; Bankruptcy** To establish a uniform rule of naturalization, and uniform laws on the subject of bankruptcies throughout the United States;

Clause 4 *Naturalization* is the process whereby a foreigner becomes a citizen. *Bankruptcy* is the condition in which a person or business cannot pay its debts. Congress has the power to pass laws on these two issues.

5. **Coins; Weights; Measures** To coin money, regulate the value thereof, and of foreign coin, and fix the standard of weights and measures;

Clause 5 Congress has the power to coin money and set its value. Congress has set up the National Bureau of Standards to regulate weights and measures.

6. **Counterfeiting** To provide for the punishment of counterfeiting the securities and current coin of the United States;

Clause 6 *Counterfeiting* is the making of imitation money. *Securities* are bonds. Congress can make laws to punish counterfeiters.

7. **Post Offices** To establish post offices and post roads;

Clause 7 Congress has the power to set up and control the delivery of mail.

8. **Copyrights; Patents** To promote the progress of science and useful arts by securing for limited times to authors and inventors the exclusive right to their respective writings and discoveries;

Clause 8 Congress may pass copyright and patent laws. A *copyright* protects an author. A *patent* makes an inventor the sole owner of his or her work for a limited time.

9. **Federal Courts** To constitute tribunals inferior to the Supreme Court;

Clause 9 Congress has the power to set up *inferior,* or lower, federal courts under the Supreme Court.

10. **Piracy** To define and punish piracies and felonies committed on the high seas and offenses against the law of nations;

Clause 10 Congress can punish *piracy,* or the robbing of ships at sea.

Clause 11 Only Congress can declare war. Declarations of war are granted at the request of the President. *Letters of marque and reprisal* were documents allowing merchant ships to arm themselves. They are no longer issued.

Clauses 12, 13, 14 These clauses place the army and navy under the control of Congress. Congress decides on the size of, and the amount of money to spend on, the armed forces. It also has the power to write rules governing the armed forces.

Clauses 15, 16 The *militia* is a body of citizen soldiers. Congress can call up the militia to put down rebellions or fight foreign invaders. Each state has its own militia, today called the National Guard. Normally, the militia is under the command of a state's governor. However, it can be placed under the command of the President.

Clause 17 Congress controls the district around the national capital. In 1790, Congress made Washington, D.C., the nation's capital. In 1973, it gave residents of the District the right to elect local officials.

Clause 18 Clauses 1–17 list the powers delegated to Congress. The framers added Clause 18 so that Congress could make laws as needed to carry out the first 17 clauses. Clause 18 is sometimes called the elastic clause because it lets Congress stretch the meaning of its power.

Clause 1 *Such persons* refers to slaves. This clause resulted from a compromise between the supporters and the opponents of the slave trade. In 1808, as soon as Congress was permitted to abolish the slave trade, it did so. The import tax was never imposed.

Clause 2 A *writ of habeas corpus* is a court order requiring government officials to bring a prisoner to court and explain why he or she is being held. A writ of habeas corpus protects people from unlawful imprisonment. This right cannot be suspended except in times of rebellion or invasion.

11. **Declarations of War** To declare war, ~~grant letters of marque and reprisal,~~ and make rules concerning captures on land and water;

12. **Army** To raise and support armies, but no appropriation of money to that use shall be for a longer term than two years;

13. **Navy** To provide and maintain a navy;

14. **Rules for the Military** To make rules for the government and regulation of the land and naval forces;

15. **Militia** To provide for calling forth the militia to execute the laws of the Union, suppress insurrections, and repel invasions;

16. **Rules for the Militia** To provide for organizing, arming, and disciplining the militia, and for governing such part of them as may be employed in the service of the United States, reserving to the states, respectively, the appointment of the officers, and the authority of training the militia according to the discipline prescribed by Congress;

17. **National Capital** To exercise exclusive legislation in all cases whatsoever, over such district (not exceeding ten miles square) as may, by cession of particular states, and the acceptance of Congress, become the seat of government of the United States, and to exercise like authority over all places purchased by the consent of the legislature of the state in which the same shall be, for the erection of forts, magazines, arsenals, dock-yards, and other needful buildings;—and

18. **Necessary Laws** To make all laws which shall be necessary and proper for carrying into execution the foregoing powers, and all other powers vested by this Constitution in the government of the United States, or in any department or officer thereof.

Section 9. Powers Denied to the Federal Government

1. **The Slave Trade** ~~The migration or importation of such persons as any of the states now existing shall think proper to admit shall not be prohibited by the Congress prior to the year 1808; but a tax or duty may be imposed on such importation, not exceeding $10 for each person.~~

2. **Writ of Habeas Corpus** The privilege of the writ of habeas corpus shall not be suspended, unless when in cases of rebellion or invasion the public safety may require it.

3. **Bills of Attainder and _Ex Post Facto_ Laws**   No bill of attainder or _ex post facto_ law shall be passed.

4. **Apportionment of Direct Taxes**   ~~No capitation or other direct tax shall be laid, unless in proportion to the census or enumeration herein before directed to be taken.~~

5. **Taxes on Exports**   No tax or duty shall be laid on articles exported from any state.

6. **Special Preference for Trade**   No preference shall be given any regulation of commerce or revenue to the ports of one state over those of another; nor shall vessels bound to, or from, one state, be obliged to enter, clear, or pay duties in another.

7. **Spending**   No money shall be drawn from the Treasury, but in consequence of appropriations made by law; and a regular statement and account of the receipts and expenditures of all public money shall be published from time to time.

8. **Creation of Titles of Nobility**   No title of nobility shall be granted by the United States; and no person holding any office of profit or trust under them, shall, without the consent of the Congress, accept of any present, emolument, office, or title, of any kind whatever, from any king, prince, or foreign state.

Section 10. Powers Denied to the States

1. **Unconditional Prohibitions**   No state shall enter into any treaty, alliance, or confederation; grant letters of marque and reprisal; coin money; emit bills of credit; make anything but gold and silver coin a tender in payment of debts; pass any bill of attainder, _ex post facto_ law, or law impairing the obligation of contracts, or grant any title of nobility.

2. **Powers Conditionally Denied**   No state shall, without the consent of the Congress, lay any imposts or duties on imports or exports, except what may be absolutely necessary for executing its inspection laws; and the net produce of all duties and imposts, laid by any state on imports or exports, shall be for the use of the Treasury of the United States; and all such laws shall be subject to the revision and control of the Congress.

3. **Other Denied Powers**   No state shall, without the consent of Congress, lay any duty of tonnage, keep troops, or ships of war in time of peace, enter into any agreement or compact with another state, or with a foreign power, or engage in war, unless actually invaded, or in such imminent danger as will not admit of delay.

Clause 3 A _bill of attainder_ is a law declaring that a person is guilty of a particular crime. An _ex post facto law_ punishes an act which was not illegal when it was committed. Congress cannot pass such laws.

Clause 4 A _capitation tax_ is a tax placed directly on each person. _Direct taxes_ are taxes on people or on land. They can be passed only if they are divided among the states according to population. The Sixteenth Amendment allowed Congress to tax income without regard to the population of the states.

Clause 5 This clause forbids Congress to tax exports. Southerners insisted on this clause because their economy depended on exports.

Clause 6 Congress cannot make laws that favor one state over another in commerce. Also, states cannot place tariffs on interstate trade.

Clause 7 The federal government cannot spend money unless Congress _appropriates_ it, or passes a law allowing it. The government must publish a statement showing how it spends public funds.

Clause 8 The government cannot award titles of nobility, such as Duke or Duchess. Americans cannot accept titles of nobility from foreign governments without the consent of Congress.

Clause 1 The writers of the Constitution did not want the states to act like separate nations. So, they prohibited states from making treaties or coining money. Some powers denied to the federal government are also denied to the states. For example, states cannot pass _ex post facto laws_.

Clauses 2, 3 Powers listed here are forbidden to the states, but Congress can lift these prohibitions by passing laws that give these powers to the states.
Clause 2 forbids states from taxing imports and exports without the consent of Congress. States may charge inspection fees on goods entering the states. Any profit from these fees must be turned over to the United States Treasury.
Clause 3 forbids states from keeping an army or navy without the consent of Congress. States cannot make treaties or declare war unless an enemy invades or is about to invade.

Article 2. The Executive Branch

Section 1. President and Vice-President

Clause 1 The President is responsible for *executing*, or carrying out, laws passed by Congress.

Clauses 2, 3 Some writers of the Constitution were afraid to allow the people to elect the President directly. Therefore, the Constitutional Convention set up the electoral college. Clause 2 directs each state to choose electors, or delegates to the electoral college, to vote for President. A state's electoral vote is equal to the combined number of senators and representatives. Each state may decide how to choose its electors. Members of Congress and federal officeholders may not serve as electors. This much of the original electoral college system is still in effect.

Clause 3 called upon each elector to vote for two candidates. The candidate who received a majority of the electoral votes would become President. The runner-up would become Vice President. If no candidate won a majority, the House would choose the President. The Senate would choose the Vice President.

The election of 1800 showed a problem with the original electoral college system. Thomas Jefferson was the Republican candidate for President, and Aaron Burr was the Republican candidate for Vice President. In the electoral college, the vote ended in a tie. The election was finally decided in the House, where Jefferson was chosen President. The Twelfth Amendment changed the electoral college system so that this could not happen again.

Clause 4 By a law passed in 1792, electors are chosen on the Tuesday after the first Monday of November every four years. Electors from each state meet to vote in December.

Today, voters in each state choose *slates*, or groups, of electors who are pledged to a candidate for President. The candidate for President who wins the popular vote in each state wins that state's electoral vote.

1. **Chief Executive** The executive power shall be vested in a President of the United States of America. He shall hold his office during the term of four years, and together with the Vice-President, chosen for the same term, be elected as follows:

2. **Selection of Electors** Each state shall appoint, in such manner as the legislature thereof may direct, a number of electors, equal to the whole number of Senators and Representatives to which the state may be entitled in the Congress; but no Senator or Representative, or person holding an office or trust or profit under the United States, shall be appointed an elector.

3. **Electoral College Procedures** ~~The electors shall meet in their respective states, and vote by ballot for two persons, of whom one at least shall not be an inhabitant of the same state with themselves. And they shall make a list of all the persons voted for, and of the number of votes for each; which list they shall sign and certify, and transmit sealed to the seat of the government of the United States, directed to the president of the Senate. The president of the Senate shall, in the presence of the Senate and House of Representatives, open all the certificates, and the votes shall then be counted. The person having the greatest number of votes shall be President, if such number be a majority of the whole number of electors appointed; and if there be more than one who have such majority, and have an equal number of votes, then the House of Representatives shall immediately choose by ballot one of them for President; and if no person have a majority, then from the five highest on the list the said House shall in like manner choose the President. But in choosing the President the votes shall be taken by states, the representation from each state having one vote. A quorum for this purpose shall consist of a member or members from two thirds of the states, and a majority of all the states shall be necessary to a choice. In every case, after the choice of the President, the person having the greatest number of votes of the electors shall be the Vice President. But if there should remain two or more who have equal votes, the Senate shall choose from them by ballot the Vice President.~~

4. **Time of Elections** The Congress may determine the time of choosing the electors, and the day on which they shall give their votes; which day shall be the same throughout the United States.

5. **Qualifications for President**   No person except a natural-born citizen ~~or a citizen of the United States, at the time of the adoption of this Constitution,~~ shall be eligible to the office of the President; neither shall any person be eligible to that office who shall not have attained to the age of thirty-five years, and been fourteen years a resident within the United States.

6. **Presidential Succession**   In case of the removal of the President from office, or of his death, resignation, or inability to discharge the powers and duties of the said office, the same shall devolve on the Vice-President, and the Congress may by law provide for the case of removal, death, resignation, or inability, both of the President and Vice-President, declaring what officer shall then act as President, and such officer shall act accordingly, until the disability be removed, or a President shall be elected.

7. **Salary**   The President shall, at stated times, receive for his services, a compensation, which shall neither be increased nor diminished during the period for which he shall have been elected, and he shall not receive within that period any other emolument from the United States, or any of them.

8. **Oath of Office**   Before he enter on the execution of his office, he shall take the following oath or affirmation:—"I do solemnly swear (or affirm) that I will faithfully execute the office of President of the United States, and will to the best of my ability, preserve, protect, and defend the Constitution of the United States."

Section 2. Powers of the President

1. **Commander in Chief of the Armed Forces**   The President shall be Commander in Chief of the Army and Navy of the United States, and of the militia of the several states, when called into the actual service of the United States; he may require the opinion, in writing, of the principal officer in each of the executive departments, upon any subject relating to the duties of their respective offices, and he shall have power to grant reprieves and pardons for offenses against the United States, except in cases of impeachment.

Clause 5   The President must be a citizen of the United States from birth, at least 35 years old, and a resident of the country for 14 years. The first seven Presidents of the United States were born under British rule, but they were allowed to hold office because they were citizens at the time the Constitution was adopted.

Clause 6   The powers of the President pass to the Vice President if the President leaves office or cannot discharge his or her duties. The wording of this clause caused confusion the first time a President died in office. When President William Henry Harrison died, it was uncertain whether Vice President John Tyler should remain Vice President and act as President or whether he should be sworn in as President. Tyler persuaded a federal judge to swear him in. So he set the precedent that the Vice President assumes the office of President when it becomes vacant. The Twenty-fifth Amendment clarified this clause.

Clause 7   The President is paid a salary. It cannot be raised or lowered during his or her term of office. The President is not allowed to hold any other federal or state position while in office. Today, the President's salary is $400,000 a year.

Clause 8   Before taking office, the President must promise to protect and defend the Constitution. Usually, the Chief Justice of the Supreme Court gives the oath of office to the President.

Clause 1   The President is head of the armed forces and the state militias when they are called into national service. So, the military is under *civilian*, or nonmilitary, control.
The President can get advice from the heads of executive departments. In most cases, the President has the power to grant a reprieve or pardon. A *reprieve* suspends punishment ordered by law. A *pardon* prevents prosecution for a crime or overrides the judgment of a court.

Clause 2 The President has the power to make treaties with other nations. Under the system of checks and balances, all treaties must be approved by two thirds of the Senate. Today, the President also makes agreements with foreign governments. These executive agreements do not need Senate approval.

The President has the power to appoint ambassadors to foreign countries and to appoint other high officials. The Senate must **confirm**, or approve, these appointments.

Clause 3 If the Senate is in **recess**, or not meeting, the President may fill vacant government posts by making temporary appointments.

The President must give Congress a report on the condition of the nation every year. This report is now called the State of the Union Address. Since 1913, the President has given this speech in person each January.

The President can call a special session of Congress and can adjourn Congress if necessary. The President has the power to receive, or recognize, foreign ambassadors.

The President must carry out the laws. Today, many government agencies oversee the execution of laws.

Civil officers include federal judges and members of the Cabinet. **High crimes** are major crimes. **Misdemeanors** are lesser crimes. The President, Vice President, and others can be forced out of office if impeached and found guilty of certain crimes.

Judicial power is the right of the courts to decide legal cases. The Constitution creates the Supreme Court but lets Congress decide the size of the Supreme Court. Congress has the power to set up inferior, or lower, courts. The Judiciary Act of 1789 set up district and circuit courts, or courts of appeal. Today, there are 94 district courts and 13 courts of appeal. All federal judges serve for life.

2. **Making Treaties and Nominations** He shall have power, by and with the advice and consent of the Senate, to make treaties, provided two-thirds of the Senators present concur; and he shall nominate, and by and with the advice and consent of the Senate, shall appoint ambassadors, other public ministers and consuls, judges of the Supreme Court, and all other officers of the United States, whose appointments are not herein otherwise provided for, and which shall be established by law; but the Congress may by law vest the appointment of such inferior officers, as they think proper, in the President alone, in the courts of law, or in the heads of departments.

3. **Temporary Appointments** The President shall have power to fill up all vacancies that may happen during the recess of the Senate, by granting commissions which shall expire at the end of their next session.

Section 3. Duties

He shall from time to time give to the Congress information of the state of the Union, and recommend to their consideration such measures as he shall judge necessary and expedient; he may, on extraordinary occasions, convene both houses, or either of them, and in case of disagreement between them, with respect to the time of adjournment, he may adjourn them to such time as he shall think proper; he shall receive ambassadors and other public ministers; he shall take care that the laws be faithfully executed, and shall commission all the officers of the United States.

Section 4. Impeachment and Removal From Office

The President, Vice-President, and all civil officers of the United States, shall be removed from office on impeachment for, and conviction of, treason, bribery, or other high crimes or misdemeanors.

Article 3. *The Judicial Branch*

Section 1. Federal Courts

The judicial power of the United States shall be vested in one Supreme Court, and in such inferior courts as the Congress may from time to time ordain and establish. The judges, both of the Supreme and inferior courts, shall hold their offices during good behavior, and shall, at stated times, receive for their services a compensation, which shall not be diminished during their continuance in office.

Separation of Powers

Legislative Branch (Congress)	Executive Branch (President)	Judicial Branch (Supreme Court and Other Federal Courts)

Passes Laws	**Carries Out Laws**	**Interprets Laws**
• Can override President's veto • Approves treaties and presidential appointments • Can impeach and remove President and other high officials • Creates lower federal courts • Appropriates money • Prints and coins money • Raises and supports the armed forces • Can declare war • Regulates foreign and interstate trade	• Proposes laws • Can veto laws • Negotiates foreign treaties • Serves as commander in chief of the armed forces • Appoints federal judges, ambassadors, and other high officials • Can grant pardons to federal offenders	• Can declare laws unconstitutional • Can declare executive actions unconstitutional

GRAPHIC ORGANIZER
Skills

The Constitution set up three branches of government. Each branch has its own powers.

1. **Comprehension**
   (a) Who heads the executive branch? **(b)** What is the role of the legislative branch?

2. **Critical Thinking**
   Analyzing Information
   Based on this chart, what is the relationship between the judicial branch and the legislative branch?

Civics

Section 2. Jurisdiction of Federal Courts

1. **Scope of Judicial Power** The judicial power shall extend to all cases, in law and equity, arising under this Constitution, the laws of the United States, and treaties made or which shall be made, under their authority; to all cases affecting ambassadors, other public ministers and consuls; to all cases of admiralty and maritime jurisdiction; to controversies to which the United States shall be a party; to controversies between two or more states; ~~between a state and citizens of another state;~~ between citizens of the same state claiming lands under grants of different states, and between a state or the citizens thereof, and foreign states, citizens, or subjects.

2. **The Supreme Court** In all cases affecting ambassadors, other public ministers and consuls, and those in which a state shall be a party, the Supreme Court shall have original jurisdiction. In all the other cases before mentioned, the Supreme Court shall have appellate jurisdiction, both as to law and fact, with such exceptions, and under such regulations as the Congress shall make.

Clause 1 *Jurisdiction* refers to the right of a court to hear a case. Federal courts have jurisdiction over cases that involve the Constitution, federal laws, treaties, foreign ambassadors and diplomats, naval and maritime laws, disagreements between states or between citizens from different states, and disputes between a state or citizen and a foreign state or citizen.

In *Marbury* v. *Madison,* the Supreme Court established the right to judge whether or not a law is constitutional.

Clause 2 *Original jurisdiction* means the power of a court to hear a case where it first arises. The Supreme Court has original jurisdiction over only a few cases, such as those involving foreign diplomats. More often, the Supreme Court acts as an appellate court. An *appellate court* does not decide guilt. It decides whether the lower court trial was properly conducted and reviews the lower court's decision.

Clause 3 This clause guarantees the right to a jury trial for anyone accused of a federal crime. The only exceptions are impeachment cases. The trial must be held in the state where the crime was committed.

Clause 1 Treason is clearly defined. An *overt act* is an actual action. A person cannot be convicted of treason for what he or she thinks. A person can be convicted of treason only if he or she confesses or two witnesses testify to it.

Clause 2 Congress has the power to set the punishment for traitors. Congress may not punish the children of convicted traitors by taking away their civil rights or property.

Each state must recognize the official acts and records of any other state. For example, each state must recognize marriage certificates issued by another state. Congress can pass laws to ensure this.

Clause 1 All states must treat citizens of another state in the same way it treats its own citizens. However, the courts have allowed states to give residents certain privileges, such as lower tuition rates.

Clause 2 *Extradition* means the act of returning a suspected criminal or escaped prisoner to a state where he or she is wanted. State governors must return a suspect. However, the Supreme Court has ruled that governors cannot be forced to do so if they feel that justice will not be done.

Clause 3 *Persons held to service or labor* refers to slaves or indentured servants. This clause required states to return runaway slaves to their owners. The Thirteenth Amendment replaces this clause.

Clause 1 Congress has the power to admit new states to the Union. Existing states cannot be split up or joined together to form new states unless both Congress and the state legislatures approve. New states are equal to all other states.

Clause 2 Congress can make rules for managing and governing land owned by the United States. This includes territories not organized into states, such as Puerto Rico, and federal lands within a state.

3. **Trial by Jury** The trial of all crimes, except in cases of impeachment, shall be by jury; and such trial shall be held in the state where the said crimes shall have been committed; but when not committed within any state, the trial shall be at such place or places as the Congress may by law have directed.

Section 3. Treason

1. **Definition** Treason against the United States shall consist only in levying war against them, or in adhering to their enemies, giving them aid and comfort. No person shall be convicted of treason unless on the testimony of two witnesses to the same overt act, or on confession in open court.

2. **Punishment** The Congress shall have power to declare the punishment of treason, but no attainder of treason shall work corruption of blood or forfeiture except during the life of the person attainted.

Article 4. Relations Among the States

Section 1. Official Records and Acts

Full faith and credit shall be given in each state to the public acts, records, and judicial proceedings of every other state. And the Congress may by general laws prescribe the manner in which such acts, records, and proceedings shall be proved, and the effect thereof.

Section 2. Privileges of Citizens

1. **Privileges** The citizens of each state shall be entitled to all privileges and immunities of citizens in the several states.

2. **Extradition** A person charged in any state with treason, felony, or other crime, who shall flee from justice, and be found in another state, shall on demand of the executive authority of the state from which he fled, be delivered up, to be removed to the state having jurisdiction of the crime.

3. **Return of Fugitive Slaves** ~~No person held to service or labor in one state, under the laws thereof, escaping into another, shall in consequence of any law or regulation therein, be discharged from such service or labor, but shall be delivered up on claim of the party to whom such service or labor may be due.~~

Section 3. New States and Territories

1. **New States** New states may be admitted by the Congress into this Union; but no new state shall be formed or erected within the jurisdiction of any other state; nor any state be formed by the junction of two of more states, or parts of states, without the consent of the legislatures of the states concerned as well as of the Congress.

2. **Federal Lands** The Congress shall have power to dispose of and make all needful rules and regulations respecting the territory or other property belonging to the United States; and nothing in this Constitution shall be so construed as to prejudice any claims of the United States, or of any particular state.

The Federal System

Powers Delegated to the National Government
- Regulate interstate and foreign trade
- Set standard weights and measures
- Create and maintain armed forces
- Make copyright and patent laws
- Establish postal offices
- Establish foreign policy
- Create federal courts
- Coin money
- Declare war
- Admit new states

Shared Powers
- Provide for public welfare
- Administer criminal justice
- Charter banks
- Raise taxes
- Borrow money

Powers Reserved to the States
- Create corporation laws
- Regulate trade within state
- Establish and maintain schools
- Establish local governments
- Make laws about marriage and divorce
- Conduct elections
- Provide for public safety

GRAPHIC ORGANIZER
Skills

Federalism is the distribution of power between the national government and the state governments.

1. **Comprehension**
   (a) Name two powers reserved to the states.
   (b) Name two powers shared by the national and state governments.

2. **Critical Thinking**
   Applying Information
   Why do you think the power to create and maintain the armed forces was delegated to the national government?

Civics

Section 4. Guarantees to the States

The United States shall guarantee to every state in this Union a republican form of government, and shall protect each of them against invasion; and on application of the legislature, or of the executive (when the legislature cannot be convened) against domestic violence.

In a **republic**, voters choose representatives to govern them. The federal government must protect the states from foreign invasion and from **domestic**, or internal, disorder if asked to do so by a state.

Article 5. Amending the Constitution

The Congress, whenever two-thirds of both houses shall deem it necessary, shall propose amendments to this Constitution, or, on the application of the legislatures of two-thirds of the several states, shall call a convention for proposing amendments, which, in either case, shall be valid to all intents and purposes, as part of this Constitution, when ratified by the legislatures of three-fourths of the several states, or by conventions in three-fourths thereof, as the one or the other mode of ratification may be proposed by the Congress; provided that ~~no amendments which may be made prior to the year 1808 shall in any manner affect the first and fourth clauses in the Ninth Section of the First Article; and that~~ no state, without its consent, shall be deprived of its equal suffrage in the Senate.

The Constitution can be **amended**, or changed, if necessary. An amendment can be proposed by (1) a two-thirds vote of both houses of Congress or (2) a national convention called by Congress at the request of two thirds of the state legislatures. (This second method has never been used.) An amendment must be **ratified**, or approved, by (1) three fourths of the state legislatures or (2) special conventions in three fourths of the states. Congress decides which method will be used.

Article 6. National Supremacy

Section 1. Prior Public Debts

The United States government promised to pay all debts and honor all agreements made under the Articles of Confederation.

All debts contracted and engagements entered into, before the adoption of this Constitution, shall be as valid against the United States under this Constitution, as under the Confederation.

Section 2. Supreme Law of the Land

The Constitution, federal laws, and treaties that the Senate has ratified are the supreme, or highest, law of the land. Thus, they outweigh state laws. A state judge must overturn a state law that conflicts with the Constitution or with a federal law.

This Constitution, and the laws of the United States which shall be made in pursuance thereof, and all treaties made, or which shall be made, under the authority of the United States, shall be the supreme law of the land; and the judges in every state shall be bound thereby, anything in the constitution or laws of any state to the contrary notwithstanding.

Section 3. Oaths of Office

State and federal officeholders take an oath, or solemn promise, to support the Constitution. However, this clause forbids the use of religious tests for officeholders. During the colonial period, every colony except Rhode Island required a religious test for officeholders.

The Senators and Representatives before mentioned, and the members of the several state legislatures, and all executive and judicial officers, both of the United States and of the several states, shall be bound by oath or affirmation, to support this Constitution; but no religious test shall ever be required as a qualification to any office or public trust under the United States.

Article 7. Ratification

During 1787 and 1788, states held special conventions. By October 1788, the required nine states had ratified the Constitution.

The ratification of the conventions of nine states shall be sufficient for the establishment of the Constitution between the states so ratifying the same.

Done in convention, by the unanimous consent of the states present, the seventeenth day of September, in the year of our Lord one thousand seven hundred and eighty-seven, and of the independence of the United States of America the twelfth. In Witness *whereof, we have hereunto subscribed our names.*

Attest: William Jackson
Secretary

George Washington
President and deputy from Virginia

New Hampshire
John Langdon
Nicholas Gilman

Massachussetts
Nathaniel Gorham
Rufus King

Connecticut
William Samuel
  Johnson
Roger Sherman

New York
Alexander Hamilton

New Jersey
William Livingston
David Brearley
William Paterson
Jonathan Dayton

Pennsylvania
Benjamin Franklin
Thomas Mifflin
Robert Morris
George Clymer
Thomas FitzSimons
Jared Ingersoll
James Wilson
Gouverneur Morris

Delaware
George Read
Gunning Bedford, Jr.
John Dickinson
Richard Bassett
Jacob Broom

Maryland
James McHenry
Dan of St. Thomas
  Jennifer
Daniel Carroll

Virginia
John Blair
James Madison, Jr.

North Carolina
William Blount
Richard Dobbs Spaight
Hugh Williamson

South Carolina
John Rutledge
Charles Cotesworth
  Pinckney
Charles Pinckney
Pierce Butler

Georgia
William Few
Abraham Baldwin

Amendments to the Constitution

Amendment 1

Freedoms of Religion, Speech, Press, Assembly, and Petition

Congress shall make no law respecting an establishment of religion, or prohibiting the free exercise thereof; or abridging the freedom of speech, or of the press; or the right of the people peaceably to assemble, and to petition the government for a redress of grievances.

Congress cannot set up an established, or official, church or religion for the nation. During the colonial period, most colonies had established churches. However, the authors of the First Amendment wanted to keep government and religion separate.

Congress may not *abridge*, or limit, the freedom to speak and write freely. The government may not censor, or review, books and newspapers before they are printed. This amendment also protects the right to assemble, or hold public meetings. *Petition* means "ask." *Redress* means "to correct." *Grievances* are wrongs. The people have the right to ask the government for wrongs to be corrected.

Amendment 2

Right to Bear Arms

A well-regulated militia, being necessary to the security of a free state, the right of the people to keep and bear arms shall not be infringed.

Each state has the right to maintain a *militia,* an armed force for its own protection. Today, the militia is the National Guard. The national government and the states can and do regulate the private ownership and use of firearms.

Amendment 3

Lodging Troops in Private Homes

No soldier shall, in time of peace, be quartered in any house, without the consent of the owner; nor in time of war, but in a manner to be prescribed by law.

During the colonial period, the British quartered, or housed, soldiers in private homes without the permission of the owners. This amendment limits the government's right to use private homes to house soldiers.

Amendment 4

Search and Seizure

The right of the people to be secure in their persons, houses, papers, and effects, against unreasonable searches and seizures, shall not be violated; and no warrants shall issue but upon probable cause, supported by oath or affirmation, and particularly describing the place to be searched, and the persons or things to be seized.

This amendment protects Americans from unreasonable searches and seizures. Search and seizure are permitted only if a judge has issued a *warrant,* or written court order. A warrant is issued only if there is probable cause. This means an officer must show that it is probable, or likely, that the search will produce evidence of a crime. A search warrant must name the exact place to be searched and the things to be seized. In some cases, courts have ruled that searches can take place without a warrant. For example, police may search a person who is under arrest. However, evidence found during an unlawful search cannot be used in a trial.

This amendment protects the rights of the accused. **Capital crimes** are those that can be punished with death. **Infamous crimes** are those that can be punished with prison or loss of rights. The federal government must obtain an **indictment,** or formal accusation, from a **grand jury** to prosecute anyone for such crimes. A grand jury is a panel of between 12 and 23 citizens who decide if the government has enough evidence to justify a trial. This procedure prevents prosecution with little or no evidence of guilt. (Soldiers and the militia in wartime are not covered by this rule.)

Double jeopardy is forbidden. This means that a person cannot be tried twice for the same crime—unless a court sets aside a conviction because of a legal error. A person on trial cannot be forced to testify, or give evidence, against himself or herself. A person accused of a crime is entitled to **due process of law,** or a fair hearing or trial. Finally, the government cannot seize private property for public use without paying the owner a fair price for it.

In criminal cases, the jury must be **impartial,** or not favor either side. The accused is guaranteed the right to a trial by jury. The trial must be speedy. If the government purposely postpones the trial so that it becomes hard for the person to get a fair hearing, the charge may be dismissed. The accused must be told the charges against him or her and be allowed to question prosecution witnesses. Witnesses who can help the accused can be ordered to appear in court.

The accused must be allowed a lawyer. Since 1942, the federal government has been required to provide a lawyer if the accused cannot afford one. In 1963, the Supreme Court decided that states must also provide lawyers for a defendant too poor to pay for one.

Common law refers to rules of law established by judges in past cases. This amendment guarantees the right to a jury trial in lawsuits where the sum of money at stake is more than $20. An appeals court cannot change a verdict because it disagrees with the decision of the jury. It can set aside a verdict only if legal errors made the trial unfair.

Bail is money the accused leaves with the court as a pledge to appear for trial. If the accused does not appear for trial, the court keeps the money. **Excessive** means too high. This amendment forbids courts to set unreasonably high bail. The amount of bail usually depends on the seriousness of the charge and whether the accused is likely to appear for the trial. The amendment also forbids cruel and unusual punishments such as mental and physical abuse.

Amendment 5

Rights of the Accused

No person shall be held to answer for a capital, or otherwise infamous, crime, unless on a presentment or indictment of a grand jury, except in cases arising in the land or naval forces, or in the militia, when in actual service in time of war or public danger; nor shall any person be subject for the same offense to be twice put in jeopardy of life and limb; nor shall be compelled, in any criminal case, to be a witness against himself; nor be deprived of life, liberty, or property, without due process of law; nor shall private property be taken for public use, without just compensation.

Amendment 6

Right to Speedy Trial by Jury

In all criminal prosecutions, the accused shall enjoy the right to a speedy and public trial, by an impartial jury of the state and district wherein the crime shall have been committed, which district shall have been previously ascertained by law, and to be informed of the nature and cause of the accusation; to be confronted with the witnesses against him; to have compulsory process for obtaining witnesses in his favor, and to have the assistance of counsel for his defense.

Amendment 7

Jury Trial in Civil Cases

In suits at common law, where the value in controversy shall exceed $20, the right of trial by jury shall be preserved, and no fact tried by a jury shall be otherwise re-examined in any court of the United States than according to the rules of the common law.

Amendment 8

Bail and Punishment

Excessive bail shall not be required, nor excessive fines imposed, nor cruel and unusual punishments inflicted.

Amendment 9

Powers Reserved to the People

The enumeration in the Constitution, of certain rights, shall not be construed to deny or disparage others retained by the people.

People have rights not listed in the Constitution. This amendment was added because some people feared that the Bill of Rights would be used to limit rights to those actually listed.

Amendment 10

Powers Reserved to the States

The powers not delegated to the United States by the Constitution, nor prohibited by it to the states, are reserved to the states respectively, or to the people.

This amendment limits the power of the federal government. Powers that are not given to the federal government belong to the states. The powers reserved to the states are not listed in the Constitution.

Amendment 11

Suits Against States

Passed by Congress on March 4, 1794. Ratified on January 23, 1795.

The judicial power of the United States shall not be construed to extend to any suit in law or equity, commenced or prosecuted against one of the United States, by citizens of another state, or by citizens or subjects of any foreign state.

This amendment changed part of Article 3, Section 2, Clause 1. As a result, a private citizen from one state cannot sue the government of another state in federal court. However, a citizen can sue a state government in a state court.

Amendment 12

Election of President and Vice-President

Passed by Congress on December 9, 1803. Ratified on June 15, 1804.

The electors shall meet in their respective states, and vote by ballot for President and Vice-President, one of whom, at least, shall not be an inhabitant of the same state with themselves; they shall name in their ballots the person voted for as President, and in distinct ballots the person voted for as Vice-President, and they shall make distinct lists of all persons voted for as President, and of all persons voted for as Vice-President, and of the number of votes for each, which lists they shall sign and certify, and transmit, sealed, to the seat of government of the United States, directed to the President of the Senate; the President of the Senate shall, in the presence of the Senate and House of Representatives, open all the certificates and the votes shall then be counted; the person having the greatest number of votes for President shall be the President, if such number be a majority of the whole number of electors appointed; and if no person have such majority, then from the persons having the highest numbers not exceeding three on the list of those voted for as President, the House of Representatives shall choose immediately, by ballot, the President. But in choosing the President, the votes shall be taken by the states, the representation from each state having one vote; a quorum for this purpose shall consist of a member or members from two-thirds of the states, and a majority of all the states shall be necessary to a choice. And if the House of Representatives shall not choose a President whenever the right of choice shall devolve upon them, before the fourth day of March next following, then the Vice-President shall act as President, as in the case of the death or other constitutional disability of the President. The person having the greatest number of votes as Vice-President, shall be the Vice-President, if such number be a majority of the whole

This amendment changed the way the electoral college voted. Before the amendment was adopted, each elector simply voted for two people. The candidate with the most votes became President. The runner-up became Vice President. In the election of 1800, however, a tie vote resulted between Thomas Jefferson and Aaron Burr.

In such a case, the Constitution required the House of Representatives to elect the President. Federalists had a majority in the House. They tried to keep Jefferson out of office by voting for Burr. It took 35 ballots in the House before Jefferson was elected President.

To keep this from happening again, the Twelfth Amendment was passed and ratified in time for the election of 1804.

This amendment provides that each elector choose one candidate for President and one candidate for Vice President. If no candidate for President receives a majority of electoral votes, the House of Representatives chooses the President. If no candidate for Vice President receives a majority, the Senate elects the Vice President. The Vice President must be a person who is eligible to be President.

This system is still in use today. However, it is possible for a candidate to win the popular vote and lose in the electoral college. This happened in 1876 and again in 2000.

number of electors appointed, and if no person have a majority, then, from the two highest numbers on the list, the Senate shall choose the Vice-President; a quorum for the purpose shall consist of two-thirds of the whole number of Senators, and a majority of the whole number shall be necessary to a choice. But no person constitutionally ineligible to the office of President shall be eligible to that of Vice-President of the United States.

Amendment 13

Abolition of Slavery

Passed by Congress on January 31, 1865. Ratified on December 6, 1865.

Section 1. Neither slavery nor involuntary servitude, except as a punishment for crime whereof the party shall have been duly convicted, shall exist within the United States, or any place subject to their jurisdiction.

Section 2. Congress shall have power to enforce this article by appropriate legislation.

The Emancipation Proclamation (1863) freed slaves only in areas controlled by the Confederacy. This amendment freed all slaves. It also forbids *involuntary servitude,* or labor done against one's will. However, it does not prevent prison wardens from making prisoners work.
  Section 2 says that Congress can pass laws to carry out this amendment.

Amendment 14

Rights of Citizens

Passed by Congress on June 13, 1866. Ratified on July 9, 1868.

Section 1. Citizenship All persons born or naturalized in the United States and subject to the jurisdiction thereof, are citizens of the United States and of the state wherein they reside. No state shall make or enforce any law which shall abridge the privileges or immunities of citizens of the United States; nor shall any state deprive any person of life, liberty, or property, without due process of law; nor deny to any person within its jurisdiction the equal protection of the laws.

Section 1 defines citizenship for the first time in the Constitution, and it extends citizenship to blacks. It also prohibits states from denying the rights and privileges of citizenship to any citizen. This section also forbids states to deny due process of law.
  Section 1 guarantees all citizens "equal protection under the law." For a long time, however, the Fourteenth Amendment did not protect blacks from discrimination. After Reconstruction, separate facilities for blacks and whites sprang up. In 1954, the Supreme Court ruled that separate facilities for blacks and whites were by their nature unequal. This ruling, in the case of *Brown* v. *Board of Education,* made school segregation illegal.

Section 2. Apportionment of Representatives Representatives shall be apportioned among the several states according to their respective numbers, counting the whole number of persons in each state, excluding Indians not taxed. But when the right to vote at any election for the choice of electors for President and Vice-President of the United States, Representatives in Congress, the executive and judicial officers of a state, or the members of the legislature thereof, is denied to any of the male inhabitants of such state, being twenty-one years of age and citizens of the United States, or in any way abridged, except for participation in rebellion, or other crime, the basis of representation therein shall be reduced in the proportion which the number of such male citizens shall bear to the whole number of male citizens twenty-one years of age in such state.

Section 2 replaced the three-fifths clause. It provides that representation in the House of Representatives is decided on the basis of the number of people in the state. It also provides that states which deny the vote to male citizens over age 21 will be punished by losing part of their representation in the House. This provision has never been enforced.
  Despite this clause, black citizens were often prevented from voting. In the 1960s, federal laws were passed to end voting discrimination.

Section 3. Former Confederate Officials No person shall be a Senator or Representative in Congress, or elector of President and Vice-President, or hold any office, civil or military, under the United States, or under any state, who, having previously taken an oath, as a member of Congress, or as an officer of the United

This section prohibited people who had been federal or state officials before the Civil War and joined the Confederate cause from serving again as government officials. In 1872, Congress restored the rights of former Confederate officials.

States, or as a member of any state legislature, or as an executive or judicial officer of any state, to support the Constitution of the United States, shall have engaged in insurrection or rebellion against the same, or given aid or comfort to the enemies thereof. But Congress may, by vote of two-thirds of each house, remove such disability.

Section 4. Government Debt The validity of the public debt of the United States, authorized by law, including debts incurred for payment of pensions and bounties for services in suppressing insurrection or rebellion, shall not be questioned. But neither the United States nor any state shall assume or pay any debt or obligation incurred in aid of insurrection or rebellion against the United States or any claim for the loss or emancipation of any slave; but all such debts, obligations, and claims shall be held illegal and void.

This section recognized that the United States must repay its debts from the Civil War. However, it forbade the repayment of debts of the Confederacy. This meant that people who had loaned money to the Confederacy would not be repaid. Also, states were not allowed to pay former slave owners for the loss of slaves.

Section 5. Enforcement The Congress shall have power to enforce, by appropriate legislation, the provisions of this article.

Congress can pass laws to carry out this amendment.

Amendment 15

Voting Rights

Passed by Congress on February 26, 1869. Ratified on February 2, 1870.

Section 1. Extending the Right to Vote The right of citizens of the United States to vote shall not be denied or abridged by the United States or any state on account of race, color, or previous condition of servitude.

Previous condition of servitude refers to slavery. This amendment gave blacks, both former slaves and free blacks, the right to vote. In the late 1800s, southern states used grandfather clauses, literacy tests, and poll taxes to keep blacks from voting.

Section 2. Enforcement The Congress shall have power to enforce this article by appropriate legislation.

Congress can pass laws to carry out this amendment. The Twenty-fourth Amendment barred the use of poll taxes in national elections. The Voting Rights Act of 1965 gave federal officials the power to register voters in places where there was voting discrimination.

Amendment 16

The Income Tax

Passed by Congress on July 12, 1909. Ratified on February 3, 1913.

The Congress shall have power to lay and collect taxes on incomes, from whatever source derived, without apportionment among the several states, and without regard to any census or enumeration.

Congress has the power to collect taxes on people's income. An income tax can be collected without regard to a state's population. This amendment changed Article 1, Section 9, Clause 4.

Amendment 17

Direct Election of Senators

Passed by Congress on May 13, 1912. Ratified on April 8, 1913.

Section 1. Method of Election The Senate of the United States shall be composed of two Senators from each state, elected by the people thereof, for six years; and each Senator shall have one vote. The electors in each state shall have the qualifications requisite for electors of the most numerous branch of the state legislatures.

This amendment replaced Article 1, Section 3, Clause 1. Before it was adopted, state legislatures chose senators. This amendment provides that senators are directly elected by the people of each state.

Section 2. Vacancies When vacancies happen in the representation of any state in the Senate, the executive authority of such state shall issue writs of election to fill such vacancies: *Provided* that the legislature of any state may empower the executive thereof to make temporary appointments until the people fill the vacancies by election as the legislature may direct.

When a Senate seat becomes vacant, the governor of the state must order an election to fill the seat. The state legislature can give the governor power to fill the seat until an election is held.

Senators who had already been elected by the state legislatures were not affected by this amendment.

This amendment, known as *Prohibition,* banned the making, selling, or transporting of alcoholic beverages in the United States. Later, the Twenty-first Amendment *repealed,* or canceled, this amendment.

Both the states and the federal government had the power to pass laws to enforce this amendment.

This amendment had to be approved within seven years. The Eighteenth Amendment was the first amendment to include a time limit for ratification.

Neither the federal government nor state governments can deny the right to vote on account of sex. Thus, women won *suffrage,* or the right to vote. Before 1920, some states had allowed women to vote in state elections.

Congress can pass laws to carry out this amendment.

The date for the President and Vice President to take office is January 20. Members of Congress begin their terms of office on January 3. Before this amendment was adopted, these terms of office began on March 4.

Congress must meet at least once a year. The new session of Congress begins on January 3. Before this amendment, members of Congress who had been defeated in November continued to hold office until the following March. Such members were known as *lame ducks.*

By Section 3, if the President-elect dies before taking office, the Vice President–elect becomes President. If no President has been chosen by January 20 or if the elected candidate fails to qualify for office, the Vice President–elect acts as President, but only until a qualified President is chosen.

Section 3. Exception   ~~This amendment shall not be so construed as to affect the election or term of any Senator chosen before it becomes valid as part of the Constitution.~~

Amendment 18

Prohibition of Alcoholic Beverages

Passed by Congress on December 18, 1917. Ratified on January 16, 1919.

Section 1. Ban on Alcohol   ~~After one year from the ratification of this article the manufacture, sale, or transportation of intoxicating liquors within, the importation thereof into, or the exportation thereof from, the United States and all territory subject to the jurisdiction thereof for beverage purposes is hereby prohibited.~~

Section 2. Enforcement   ~~The Congress and the several states shall have concurrent power to enforce this article by appropriate legislation.~~

Section 3. Method of Ratification   ~~This article shall be inoperative unless it shall have been ratified as an amendment to the Constitution by the legislatures of the several states, as provided in the Constitution, within seven years from the date of the submission hereof to the states by the Congress.~~

Amendment 19

Women's Suffrage

Passed by Congress on June 4, 1919. Ratified on August 18, 1920.

Section 1. The Right to Vote   The right of citizens of the United States to vote shall not be denied or abridged by the United States or by any state on account of sex.

Section 2. Enforcement   Congress shall have power to enforce this article by appropriate legislation.

Amendment 20

Presidential Terms; Sessions of Congress

Passed by Congress on March 2, 1932. Ratified on January 23, 1933.

Section 1. Beginning of Term   The terms of the President and Vice-President shall end at noon on the 20th day of January, and the terms of Senators and Representatives at noon on the 3rd day of January, of the years in which such terms would have ended if this article had not been ratified; and the terms of their successors shall then begin.

Section 2. Congressional Sessions   The Congress shall assemble at least once in every year, and such meeting shall begin at noon on the 3rd day of January, unless they shall by law appoint a different day.

Section 3. Presidential Succession   If at the time fixed for the beginning of the term of the President, the President-elect shall have died, the Vice-President-elect shall become President. If a President shall not have been chosen before the time fixed for the beginning of his term, or if the President-elect shall have failed to qualify, then the Vice-President-elect shall act as President until a President shall have qualified; and the Congress may by law provide for the case wherein neither a President-elect nor a Vice-President-elect shall have qualified, declaring who shall then act as President, or the manner in which one who is to act shall be selected, and such person shall act accordingly until a President or Vice-President shall have qualified.

Finally, Congress can choose a person to act as President if neither the President-elect nor Vice President-elect is qualified to take office.

Section 4. Elections Decided by Congress The Congress may by law provide for the case of the death of any of the persons from whom the House of Representatives may choose a President whenever the right of choice shall have devolved upon them, and for the case of the death of any of the persons from whom the Senate may choose a Vice-President whenever the right of choice shall have devolved upon them.

Congress can pass laws in cases where a presidential candidate dies while an election is being decided in the House. Congress has similar power in cases where a candidate for Vice President dies while an election is being decided in the Senate.

Section 5. Date of Effect ~~Sections 1 and 2 shall take effect on the 15th day of October following the ratification of this article.~~

Section 5 sets the date for the amendment to become effective.

Section 6. Ratification Period ~~This article shall be inoperative unless it shall have been ratified as an amendment to the Constitution by the legislatures of three-fourths of the several states within seven years from the date of its submission.~~

Section 6 sets a time limit for ratification.

Amendment 21

Repeal of Prohibition

Passed by Congress on February 20, 1933. Ratified on December 5, 1933.

Section 1. Repeal of National Prohibition The eighteenth article of amendment to the Constitution of the United States is hereby repealed.

The Eighteenth Amendment is repealed, making it legal to make and sell alcoholic beverages. Prohibition ended December 5, 1933.

Section 2. State Laws The transportation or importation into any state, territory, or possession of the United States for delivery or use therein of intoxicating liquors, in violation of the laws thereof, is hereby prohibited.

Each state was free to ban the making and selling of alcoholic drink within its borders. This section makes bringing liquor into a "dry" state a federal offense.

Section 3. Ratification Period ~~This article shall be inoperative unless it shall have been ratified as an amendment to the Constitution by conventions in the several states, as provided in the Constitution, within seven years from the date of the submission hereof to the states by the Congress.~~

Special state conventions were called to ratify this amendment. This is the only time an amendment was ratified by state conventions rather than state legislatures.

Amendment 22

Limit on Number of President's Terms

Passed by Congress on March 12, 1947. Ratified on March 1, 1951.

Section 1. Two-Term Limit No person shall be elected to the office of the President more than twice, and no person who has held the office of President, or acted as President, for more than two years of a term to which some other person was elected President shall be elected to the office of the President more than once. ~~But this Article shall not apply to any person holding the office of President when this Article was proposed by the Congress, and shall not prevent any person who may be holding the office of President, or acting as President, during the term within which this Article becomes operative from holding the office of President or acting as President during the remainder of such term.~~

Before Franklin Roosevelt became President, no President served more than two terms in office. Roosevelt broke with this custom and was elected to four terms. This amendment provides that no President may serve more than two terms. A President who has already served more than half of someone else's term can serve only one more full term. However, the amendment did not apply to Harry Truman, who had become President after Franklin Roosevelt's death in 1945.

A seven-year time limit is set for ratification.

This amendment gives residents of Washington, D.C., the right to vote in presidential elections. Until this amendment was adopted, people living in Washington, D.C., could not vote for President because the Constitution had made no provision for choosing electors from the nation's capital. Washington, D.C., has three electoral votes.

Congress can pass laws to carry out this amendment.

A *poll tax* is a tax on voters. This amendment bans poll taxes in national elections. Some states used poll taxes to keep blacks from voting. In 1966, the Supreme Court struck down poll taxes in state elections, also.

Congress can pass laws to carry out this amendment.

If the President dies or resigns, the Vice President becomes President. This section clarifies Article 2, Section 1, Clause 6.

When a Vice President takes over the office of President, he or she appoints a Vice President who must be approved by a majority vote of both houses of Congress. This section was first applied after Vice President Spiro Agnew resigned in 1973. President Richard Nixon appointed Gerald Ford as Vice President.

Section 2. Ratification Period ~~This Article shall be inoperative unless it shall have been ratified as an amendment to the Constitution by the legislatures of three fourths of the several states within seven years from the date of its submission to the states by the Congress.~~

Amendment 23

Presidential Electors for District of Columbia

Passed by Congress on June 16, 1960. Ratified on April 3, 1961.

Section 1. Determining the Number of Electors The District constituting the seat of Government of the United States shall appoint in such manner as the Congress may direct: A number of electors of President and Vice-President equal to the whole number of Senators and Representatives in Congress to which the District would be entitled if it were a State, but in no event more than the least populous State; they shall be in addition to those appointed by the States, but they shall be considered, for the purposes of the election of President and Vice-President, to be electors appointed by a State; and they shall meet in the District and perform such duties as provided by the twelfth article of amendment.

Section 2. Enforcement The Congress shall have power to enforce this article by appropriate legislation.

Amendment 24

Abolition of Poll Tax in National Elections

Passed by Congress on August 27, 1962. Ratified on January 23, 1964.

Section 1. Poll Tax Banned The right of citizens of the United States to vote in any primary or other election for President or Vice-President, for electors for President or Vice-President, or for Senator or Representative in Congress, shall not be denied or abridged by the United States or any state by reason of failure to pay any poll tax or other tax.

Section 2. Enforcement The Congress shall have the power to enforce this article by appropriate legislation.

Amendment 25

Presidential Succession and Disability

Passed by Congress on July 6, 1965. Ratified on February 11, 1967.

Section 1. President's Death or Resignation In case of the removal of the President from office or his death or resignation, the Vice-President shall become President.

Section 2. Vacancies in Vice-Presidency Whenever there is a vacancy in the office of the Vice-President, the President shall nominate a Vice-President who shall take the office upon confirmation by a majority vote of both houses of Congress.

Section 3. Disability of the President Whenever the President transmits to the President *pro tempore* of the Senate and the Speaker of the House of Representatives his written declaration that he is unable to discharge the powers and duties of his office, and until he transmits to them a written declaration to the contrary, such powers and duties shall be discharged by the Vice-President as Acting President.

If the President declares in writing that he or she is unable to perform the duties of office, the Vice President serves as Acting President until the President recovers.

Section 4. Whenever the Vice-President and a majority of either the principal officers of the executive departments or of such other body as Congress may by law provide, transmit to the President *pro tempore* of the Senate and the Speaker of the House of Representatives their written declaration that the President is unable to discharge the powers and duties of his office, the Vice-President shall immediately assume the powers and duties of the office as Acting President.

Thereafter, when the President transmits to the President *pro tempore* of the Senate and the Speaker of the House of Representatives his written declaration that no inability exists, he shall resume the powers and duties of his office unless the Vice-President and a majority of either the principal officers of the executive department or of such other body as Congress may by law provide, transmit within four days to the President *as* of the Senate and the Speaker of the House of Representatives their written declaration that the President is unable to discharge the powers and duties of his office. Thereupon Congress shall decide the issue, assembling within 48 hours for that purpose if not in session. If the Congress, within 21 days after receipt of the latter written declaration, or, if Congress is not in session, within 21 days after Congress is required to assemble, determines by two-thirds vote of both houses that the President is unable to discharge the powers and duties of his office, the Vice-President shall continue to discharge the same as Acting President; otherwise, the President shall assume the powers and duties of his office.

Two Presidents, Woodrow Wilson and Dwight Eisenhower, have fallen gravely ill while in office. The Constitution contained no provision for this kind of emergency.

Section 3 provided that the President can inform Congress that he or she is too sick to perform the duties of office. However, if the President is unconscious or refuses to admit to a disabling illness, Section 4 provides that the Vice President and Cabinet may declare the President disabled. The Vice President becomes Acting President until the President can return to the duties of office. In case of a disagreement between the President and the Vice President and Cabinet over the President's ability to perform the duties of office, Congress must decide the issue. A two-thirds vote of both houses is needed to decide that the President is disabled or unable to fulfill the duties of office.

Amendment 26

Voting Age

Passed by Congress on March 23, 1971. Ratified on July 1, 1971.

Section 1. Lowering of Voting Age The right of citizens of the United States, who are 18 years of age or older, to vote shall not be denied or abridged by the United States or any state on account of age.

In 1970, Congress passed a law allowing 18-year-olds to vote. However, the Supreme Court decided that Congress could not set a minimum age for state elections. So this amendment was passed and ratified.

Section 2. Enforcement The Congress shall have the power to enforce this article by appropriate legislation.

Congress can pass laws to carry out this amendment.

Amendment 27

Congressional Pay Increases

Proposed by Congress on September 25, 1789. Ratified on May 7, 1992.

No law varying the compensation for the services of the Senators and Representatives shall take effect, until an election of Representatives shall have intervened.

If members of Congress vote themselves a pay increase, it cannot go into effect until after the next congressional election.

Government, Citizenship, and the Constitution

1787–PRESENT

1 Goals and Principles of the Constitution
2 How the Federal Government Works
3 Changing the Constitution
4 State and Local Governments
5 Rights and Responsibilities of Citizenship

Constitution of the United States

African American man voting for the first time

AMERICAN EVENTS

1787
The Constitution is written. It will serve as the framework of the United States government up to the present.

1830
In most states, white men over 21 can vote.

1870
As a result of the Fifteenth Amendment, African American men win the vote.

1780 • • • 1840 • • 1900

WORLD EVENTS

▲ **1791**
French constitution sets up a limited monarchy.

▲ **1821**
Mexico wins independence from Spain.

1893 ▲
New Zealand extends the vote to women.

The Electoral College

To become President, a candidate must win the majority of electoral votes.

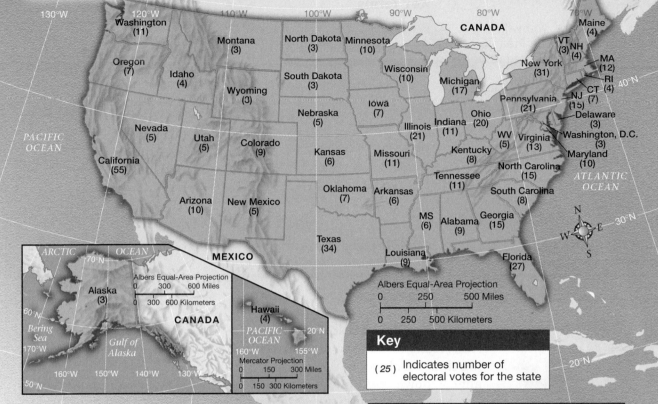

Washington (11)
Montana (3)
North Dakota (3)
Minnesota (10)
CANADA
Maine (4)
VT (3)
NH (4)
Oregon (7)
Idaho (4)
Wyoming (3)
South Dakota (3)
Wisconsin (10)
Michigan (17)
New York (31)
MA (12)
RI (4)
CT (7)
Nebraska (5)
Iowa (7)
Pennsylvania (21)
NJ (15)
Nevada (5)
Utah (5)
Colorado (9)
Illinois (21)
Indiana (11)
Ohio (20)
WV (5)
Virginia (13)
Delaware (3)
Washington, D.C. (3)
California (55)
Kansas (6)
Missouri (11)
Kentucky (8)
North Carolina (15)
Maryland (10)
Arizona (10)
New Mexico (5)
Oklahoma (7)
Arkansas (6)
Tennessee (11)
South Carolina (8)
Texas (34)
MS (6)
Alabama (9)
Georgia (15)
Louisiana (9)
Florida (27)

PACIFIC OCEAN
ATLANTIC OCEAN

Alaska (3)
ARCTIC OCEAN
Bering Sea
Gulf of Alaska
CANADA

Albers Equal-Area Projection
0   300   600 Miles
0   300   600 Kilometers

MEXICO

Hawaii (4)
PACIFIC OCEAN
Mercator Projection
0   150   300 Miles
0   150   300 Kilometers

Albers Equal-Area Projection
0   250   500 Miles
0   250   500 Kilometers

Key

(25) Indicates number of electoral votes for the state

Women's suffrage banner

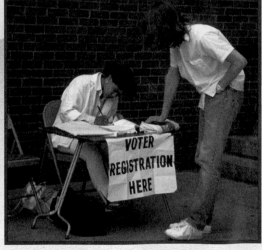

Voter registration drive

1920
The Nineteenth Amendment guarantees the right to vote to women.

1951
The Twenty-second Amendment limits the President to two terms.

1971
The Twenty-sixth Amendment extends the right to vote to Americans 18–21 years of age.

1900 · · · · · · 1960 · · · · · PRESENT · · · ·

1947 ▲
Japan adopts a democratic constitution.

1994 ▲
South Africa holds free multiracial elections.

1 Goals and Principles of the Constitution

Prepare to Read

Objectives

In this section, you will
- Explain how the Preamble defines the basic goals of the Constitution.
- Identify the framework of government established by the Constitution.
- Name the seven basic principles of American government.

Key Terms

Preamble
domestic tranquillity
civilian
general welfare
liberty
Articles
popular sovereignty
limited government
checks and balances
federalism

Target Reading Skill

Reading Process Copy the concept web below. As you read, add ovals and fill them in with goals and principles of the Constitution.

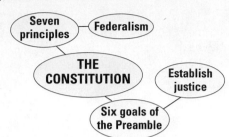

Main Idea The goals and principles of the Constitution have guided the United States for more than 200 years.

2000 election magazine cover

Setting the Scene

On Election Day, 2000, some 100 million Americans voted for a new President. But they learned the next morning that the election was not over. Across the nation, the vote was split almost down the middle. Neither the Democratic candidate, Albert Gore, nor the Republican candidate, George W. Bush, had the 270 electoral votes needed to become President. The result would depend on the vote in Florida—a race that was too close to call!

For 36 days, Americans watched and argued as the candidates battled for Florida's 25 electoral votes. Teams of lawyers, local election officials, state legislators, and state and federal judges all became involved in the battle. At last, a ruling by the Supreme Court of the United States allowed Bush to claim victory. Gore offered his opponent best wishes for a successful presidency.

The election of 2000 raised some troubling issues. In the end, though, the election showed the strength of our constitutional system. The electoral battle was fierce but not violent. The candidates fought bitterly to win, but they fought in the courts, not in the streets. As in the past, in a time of crisis Americans relied on the system established by their Constitution.

The Preamble Sets Goals

The Constitution is divided into three main parts: the **Preamble,** or opening statement, the Articles, and the Amendments. The Preamble defines six goals:

> **“** We the people of the United States, in order to form a more perfect Union, establish justice, insure domestic tranquillity, provide for the common defense, promote the general welfare, and secure the blessings of liberty to

ourselves and our posterity, do ordain and establish this
Constitution for the United States of America. **99**

—Preamble to the Constitution

To Form a More Perfect Union When the Constitution was written, the states saw themselves almost as separate nations. The framers wanted to work together as a unified nation. Fortunately for us, they achieved this goal. Think of what it would be like if you had to exchange your money every time you visited another state!

To Establish Justice The framers knew the nation needed a uniform system to settle legal disputes. Today, the American justice system requires that the law be applied fairly to every American, regardless of race, religion, gender, or country of origin.

To Insure Domestic Tranquillity Under the Constitution, the national government has the power to insure domestic tranquillity, or peace and order at home. Have you seen reports of the National Guard providing assistance in a disaster area? By such actions, the government works to insure domestic tranquillity.

To Provide for the Common Defense Every country has a duty to protect its citizens against foreign attack. The framers of the Constitution gave the national government the power to raise armies and navies. At the same time, they placed the military under civilian, or nonmilitary, control.

To Promote the General Welfare The Constitution set out to give the national government the means to promote the general welfare, or the well-being of all its citizens. For example, today the National Institutes of Health leads the fight against many diseases.

To Secure the Blessings of Liberty During the Revolution, the colonists fought and died for liberty, or freedom. It is no surprise that the framers made liberty a major goal of the Constitution. Over the years, amendments to the Constitution have extended the "blessings of liberty" to more and more Americans.

Viewing History

Working to Fulfill the Constitution

Every day, hundreds of Americans like these work to fulfill the goals set out in the Constitution.
Applying Information *Which of the goals set out in the Preamble is associated with each of the people shown here?*

Articles and Amendments

The main body of the Constitution is a short document, divided into seven sections called Articles. Together, they establish the framework for our government.

The Articles The first three Articles describe the three branches of the national government: legislative, executive, and judicial. Article I establishes the powers of and limits on Congress. Articles II and III do the same for the President and the courts.

Article IV deals with relations between the states. It requires states to honor one another's laws and legal decisions. It also sets out a system for admitting new states. Article V provides a process to amend the Constitution.

Article VI states that the Constitution is the "supreme law of the land." This means that states may not make laws that violate the Constitution. If a state law conflicts with a federal law, the federal

System of Checks and Balances

Executive Branch (President carries out laws) 	Checks on the Legislative Branch	Checks on the Judicial Branch
	• Can propose laws • Can veto laws • Can call special sessions of Congress • Makes appointments • Negotiates foreign treaties	• Appoints federal judges • Can grant pardons to federal offenders

Legislative Branch (Congress makes laws)	Checks on the Executive Branch	Checks on the Judicial Branch
	• Can override President's veto • Confirms executive appointments • Ratifies treaties • Can declare war • Appropriates money • Can impeach and remove President	• Creates lower federal courts • Can impeach and remove judges • Can propose amendments to overrule judicial decisions • Approves appointments of federal judges

Judicial Branch (Supreme Court interprets laws)	Check on the Executive Branch	Check on the Legislative Branch
	• Can declare executive actions unconstitutional	• Can declare acts of Congress unconstitutional

CHART Skills

Through checks and balances, each branch of the government limits the power of the other two.

1. **Comprehension** Identify two ways in which the President can check Congress.

2. **Critical Thinking Ranking** What do you think is the most important check Congress has on the President? Explain.

Civics 🏛

Set a Purpose Check to see whether you understand how the ideas of popular sovereignty and limited government differ from monarchy.

law prevails. The final article, Article VII, sets up a procedure for the states to ratify the Constitution.

Amendments In more than 200 years, only 27 formal changes have been made to the Constitution. The first ten amendments, known as the Bill of Rights, were added in 1791. In Section 3, you will read how other amendments have changed the working of the government or extended rights to more Americans.

Seven Basic Principles

The Constitution rests on seven basic principles. They are popular sovereignty, limited government, separation of powers, federalism, checks and balances, republicanism, and individual rights.

Popular Sovereignty The framers of the Constitution lived at a time when monarchs claimed that their power came from God. The Preamble, with its talk of "We the people," reflects a revolutionary new idea: that a government gets its authority from the people. This principle, known as **popular sovereignty,** states that the people have the right to alter or abolish their government.

Limited Government The colonists had lived under the harsh rule of a king. To avoid such tyranny in their new government, the framers made limited government a principle of the Constitution. In a **limited government,** the government has only the powers that the Constitution gives it. Just as important, everyone from you to the President must obey the law.

Separation of Powers To further limit government power, the framers provided for separation of powers. The Constitution divides the government into three branches. Congress, or the legislative branch, makes the laws. The executive branch, headed by the President, carries out the laws. The judicial branch, composed of the courts, explains and interprets the laws.

Checks and Balances A system of checks and balances safeguards against abuse of power. Each branch of government has the power to check, or limit, the actions of the other two. (You will read more about checks and balances in Section Two.)

Federalism The Constitution also establishes the principle of federalism, or division of power between the federal government and the states. Among the powers the Constitution gives the federal government are the power to coin money, declare war, and regulate trade between the states. States regulate trade within their own borders, make rules for state elections, and establish schools. Some powers are shared between the federal government and the states. (See the chart on page 235.) Powers not clearly given to the federal government belong to the states.

Republicanism The Constitution provides for a republican form of government. Instead of taking part directly in government, citizens elect representatives to carry out their will. Once in office, representatives vote according to their own judgment. However, they must remain open to the opinions of the people they represent. For that reason, members of Congress maintain offices in their home districts, and often Web sites as well.

Individual Rights The Constitution protects individual rights, such as freedom of speech, freedom of religion, and the right to trial by jury. You will read more about the rights protected by the Constitution later in this chapter.

Primary Source

Limits on Individual Rights

Although the Constitution protects individual rights, these rights are not unlimited. Here, Oliver Wendell Holmes, Jr., a justice of the Supreme Court, talks about the limits on free speech:

"The character of every act depends upon the circumstances in which it is done. The most [strict] protection of free speech would not protect a man in falsely shouting fire in a theatre and causing a panic. . . . The question in every case is whether the words used are used in such circumstances and are of such a nature as to create a clear and present danger that they will bring about the [real] evils that Congress has a right to prevent."

—Oliver Wendell Holmes, Jr.,
Schenck v. *United States,* 1919

Analyzing Primary Sources
What do you think Holmes meant by "a clear and present danger"?

★ ★ ★ **Section 1 Assessment** ★ ★ ★

Recall

1. **Identify** Explain the significance of (a) Preamble, (b) Articles.
2. **Define** (a) domestic tranquility, (b) civilian, (c) general welfare, (d) liberty, (e) popular sovereignty, (f) limited government, (g) checks and balances, (h) federalism.

Comprehension

3. Identify the six goals of the Constitution.
4. What system is established in Articles I, II, and III?

5. List the seven basic principles behind the Constitution.

Critical Thinking and Writing

6. **Exploring the Main Idea** Review the Main Idea statement at the beginning of this section. Then, choose three principles of the Constitution. Analyze the meaning of each, and list two ways in which you can see that principle at work today.
7. **Ranking** Which of the goals set out in the Preamble do you think is most important? Write a paragraph explaining why.

ACTIVITY

Designing a Poster
With a partner, design a poster as part of a display celebrating the Constitution. The poster should highlight one of the six goals or seven principles described in this section. Use a combination of words and pictures to create your poster.

Prepare to Read

Objectives

In this section, you will
- List the powers of the legislative branch.
- Identify the roles the President fills as head of the executive branch.
- Describe how the judicial branch is organized.
- Explain how each branch of government can check the powers of the others.

Key Terms

House of Representatives

Senate

bill

electoral college

Supreme Court

appeal

unconstitutional

veto

override

impeach

 Target Reading Skill

Main Idea Copy the table below. As you read, complete the table with information about the three branches of the federal government.

LEGISLATIVE	EXECUTIVE	JUDICIAL
• Congress • Makes laws	• President •	• •

Main Idea The United States government is divided into three branches with separate roles and responsibilities.

Great Seal of the United States

Setting the Scene Tonight, the vast chamber of the House of Representatives is packed to capacity. Applause begins as the President of the United States enters the room and steps to the podium. Behind the President sit the Vice President and the Speaker of the House. In the audience are many of the most powerful people in the nation—members of Congress, justices of the Supreme Court, Cabinet secretaries. At home, millions of Americans tune in on their television sets. The State of the Union Address is about to begin.

In delivering this speech each January, the President fulfills a duty spelled out in the Constitution: "He shall from time to time give to the Congress information of the state of the Union, and recommend to their consideration such measures as he shall judge necessary and expedient." The State of the Union Address also gives Americans a rare chance to see leaders of the legislative, executive, and judicial branches in one place at one time. Our government depends on these three branches working together.

The Legislative Branch

The first and longest article of the Constitution deals with the legislative, or lawmaking, branch. Article I sets up the Congress to make the nation's laws. Congress is made up of two bodies: the House of Representatives and the Senate.

House of Representatives The larger of the two bodies is the House of Representatives, which currently has 435 members. Representation in the House is based on population, with larger states having more representatives than smaller states. Every state has at least one representative.

Federal Officeholders

Office	Number	Term	Selection	Requirements
Representative	At least 1 per state; based on population	2 years	Elected by voters of congressional district	Age 25 or over Citizen for 7 years Resident of state in which elected
Senator	2 per state	6 years	Original Constitution—elected by state legislature Amendment 17—elected by voters	Age 30 or over Citizen for 9 years Resident of state in which elected
President and Vice President	1	4 years	Elected by electoral college	Age 35 or over Natural-born citizen Resident of United States for 14 years
Supreme Court Justice	9	Life	Appointed by President Approved by Senate	No requirements in Constitution

CHART
Skills

The Constitution details the length of term, method of selection, and requirements for officeholders in the three branches of government.

1. **Comprehension**
   (a) At what age can you be elected to the Senate? The House of Representatives? **(b)** How long may a Supreme Court Justice remain in office?

2. **Critical Thinking**
   Drawing Inferences
   Why are the requirements for President and Vice President the same?

Civics

Representatives are elected by the people of their district for two-year terms. As a result, the entire House is up for election every other year. Representatives may run for reelection as many times as they want.

The leader of the House is called the Speaker. The Speaker of the House is one of the most powerful people in the federal government. The Speaker regulates debates and controls the agenda. If the President dies or leaves office, the Speaker of the House is next in line after the Vice President to become President.

The Senate Unlike the House, the Senate is based on equal representation, with two senators for each state. Senators are elected to six-year terms. Their terms overlap, however, so that one third of the members come up for election every two years. This way, there is always a majority of experienced senators.

Not all of the Founding Fathers trusted the judgment of the common people. As a result, they called for senators to be chosen by state legislatures. Over the years, the nation slowly became more democratic. The Seventeenth Amendment, ratified in 1913, provided that senators be directly elected by the people, like members of the House.

The Vice President of the United States is president of the Senate. The Vice President presides over the Senate and casts a vote when there is a tie. The Vice President cannot, however, take part in Senate debates. When the Vice President is absent, the president pro tempore, or temporary president, presides.

Powers of Congress The most important power of Congress is the power to make the nation's laws. All laws start as proposals called bills. A new bill may be introduced in either the House or the Senate. However, an appropriations bill, which is a bill designed to raise money for the government, must be introduced in the House. After a bill is introduced, it is debated. If both houses vote to approve the bill, it is then sent to the President, who must sign it before it becomes a law. (See the chart on page 226 to see the steps a bill must follow in order to become a law.)

The Constitution gives Congress many other powers besides law-making. Article I, Section 8, lists most of the powers of Congress. They include the power to levy, or collect, taxes and to borrow money. Congress also has the power to coin money, to establish post offices, to fix standard weights and measures, and to declare war.

The Elastic Clause Not all the powers of Congress are specifically listed. Article I, Section 8, Clause 18, states that Congress can "make all laws which shall be necessary and proper" for carrying out its specific duties. This clause is known as the elastic clause because it enables Congress to stretch its powers to deal with the changing needs of the nation.

Americans have long debated the true meaning of the elastic clause. What did the framers mean by the words *necessary* and *proper?* For example, early leaders debated whether the elastic clause gave Congress the right to set up a national bank, even though the Constitution does not specifically give Congress that power. Today, some Americans still worry that Congress might use the clause to abuse its powers.

Committees The first Congress, meeting from 1789 to 1791, considered a total of 31 new bills. Today, more than 10,000 bills are introduced in Congress each year. Clearly, it would be impossible for every member of Congress to give each new bill careful study. To deal with this problem, Congress relies on committees.

Both the House and the Senate have permanent, or standing, committees. Each committee deals with a specific topic, such as agriculture, banking, business, defense, education, science, or transportation. Members who have served in Congress the longest are usually appointed to the most important committees.

Congress may sometimes create joint committees made up of both Senate and House members. One of the most important kinds of joint committees is the conference committee. Its task is to settle differences between House and Senate versions of the same bill.

The Executive Branch

Article II of the Constitution sets up an executive branch to carry out the laws and run the affairs of the national government. The President is the head of the executive branch. Other members include the Vice President, the Cabinet, and the many departments and agencies that help them in their work.

Roles of the President You are probably more familiar with the President than with any other government leader. You see him on television climbing in and out of airplanes, greeting foreign leaders, or making speeches. Yet, many Americans do not know exactly what the President does.

Washington, D.C.

The White House

No building is more a symbol of the United States than the White House, official home of the President. Originally called the "Presidential Palace," it got its white coat of paint after being burned during the War of 1812. Here, Presidents meet with leaders of Congress and host grand dinners for foreign leaders. The front lawn is also the site of an annual Easter egg roll for local children!

Go Online
PHSchool.com

Virtual Field Trip For an interactive look at the White House, visit PHSchool.com, **Web Code mfd-0801**.

The framers thought that Congress would be the most important branch of government. Thus, while the Constitution is very specific about the role of the legislature, it offers fewer details about the powers of the President. Beginning with George Washington, Presidents have often taken those actions they thought necessary to carry out the job. In this way, they have shaped the job of President to meet the nation's changing needs.

The President is our highest elected official and, along with the Vice President, the only one who represents all Americans. As head of the executive branch, the President has the duty to carry out the nation's laws. The President directs foreign policy and has the power to make treaties with other nations and to appoint ambassadors.

The President is Commander in Chief of the armed forces. (Only Congress, however, has the power to declare war.) As the nation's chief legislator, the President suggests new laws and works for their passage. The President can grant pardons and call special sessions of Congress. The President is also the living symbol of the nation. Presidents welcome foreign leaders, make speeches to commemorate national holidays, and give medals to national heroes.

Electing the President The President is elected for a four-year term. As a result of the Twenty-second Amendment, adopted in 1951, no President may be elected to more than two complete terms.

The framers set up a complex system for electing the President, known as the **electoral college.** When Americans vote for President, they do not vote directly for the candidate of their choice. Rather, they

Identify Supporting Details

Why do you think the framers of the Constitution set a specific term of office for the President? Add information about the President's term of office to your chart.

Federal Court System

United States Supreme Court

- Nation's highest court
- Reviews the decisions of lower courts
- Decides cases involving United States Constitution and federal laws

State Route

State Supreme Court
- Highest state court
- Hears appeals of appellate court cases

Appellate Court
- Hears appeals of trial court cases

Trial Court
- Handles civil and criminal cases
- Juries render verdicts based on evidence
- Judges enforce rules of procedure

Federal Route

Court of Appeals
- Hears appeals of cases originating in United States District Courts
- Can review decisions by federal administrative agencies

District Court
- Federal trial court
- Handles civil and criminal cases
- Juries render verdicts based on evidence
- Judges ensure fair trial

CHART Skills

Cases may come before the Supreme Court either through federal courts or through state courts.

1. **Comprehension** Describe the steps by which a case might travel from a state trial court to the Supreme Court.

2. **Critical Thinking Drawing Conclusions** Why do you think relatively few cases come before the Supreme Court?

Civics

---

vote for a group of electors who are pledged to the candidate. The number of a state's electors depends on the number of its Senators and Representatives. No state has fewer than three electors.

A few weeks after Election Day, the electors meet in each state to cast their votes for President. In most states, the candidate with the majority of the popular vote receives all that state's electoral votes. The candidate who receives a majority of the electoral votes nationwide becomes President.

Because of the "winner-take-all" nature of the electoral college, a candidate can lose the popular vote nationwide but still be elected President. This has happened four times. Today, some people favor replacing the electoral college with a system that directly elects the President by popular vote. Others oppose any change, pointing out that the system has served the nation well for over 200 years.

The Judicial Branch

The Constitution establishes a **Supreme Court** and authorizes Congress to establish any other courts that are needed. Under the Judiciary Act of 1789, Congress set up the system of federal courts that is still in place today.

Lower Courts Most federal cases begin in district courts. Evidence is presented during trials, and a jury or a judge decides the facts of the case. A party that disagrees with the decision of the judge or jury may **appeal** it, that is, ask that the decision be reviewed by a higher court. The next level of courts is the appellate court, or court of appeal. Appellate court judges review decisions of district courts to decide whether the lower court judges interpreted and applied the law correctly.

Supreme Court At the top of the American judicial system is the Supreme Court. The Court is made up of a Chief Justice and eight Associate Justices. The President appoints the justices, but Congress must approve the appointments. Justices serve for life.

The main job of the Supreme Court is to serve as the nation's final court of appeals. It hears cases that have been tried and appealed in lower courts. Because its decisions are final, the Supreme Court is called "the court of last resort."

The Supreme Court hears and decides fewer than 100 cases each year. Most of the cases are appeals from lower courts that involve federal laws. After hearing oral arguments, the justices vote. Decisions rest on a majority vote of at least five justices.

The greatest power of the Supreme Court is the power to decide what the Constitution means. In the words of Chief Justice Charles Evans Hughes, "The Constitution is what the judges say it is." Early on, the Court asserted the right to declare whether acts of the President or laws passed by Congress are **unconstitutional,** that is, not allowed under the Constitution.

Checks and Balances

The framers hoped that the separation of powers among three branches would prevent the rise of an all-powerful leader who would rob the people of their liberty. But how could the framers prevent one of the branches from abusing its power? To answer this problem, they set up a system of checks and balances.

The system of checks and balances allows each of the three branches of government to check, or limit, the power of the other two. The President, for example, can check the actions of Congress by **vetoing,** or rejecting, bills that Congress has passed. Congress can check the President by **overriding,** or overruling, the veto. Congress must also approve presidential appointments and ratify treaties made by the President. The Supreme Court can check both the President and Congress by declaring laws unconstitutional.

Congress's most extreme check on the President is its power to remove the President from office. To do this, the House of Representatives must **impeach,** or bring charges of serious wrongdoing against, the President. The Senate then conducts a trial. If two thirds of the senators vote to convict, the President must leave office. Throughout our history, only two Presidents—Andrew Johnson and Bill Clinton—have been impeached by the House. Neither was convicted by the Senate.

An American Profile

Sandra Day O'Connor
born 1930

Sandra Day O'Connor graduated with honors from law school but then had trouble finding work at a leading law firm. "None had ever hired a woman as a lawyer," she recalled, "and they were not prepared to do so." Still, she worked her way up to the top. In 1981, she became the first woman to serve on the Supreme Court.

As a justice, O'Connor earned a reputation for sticking closely to the facts and the law in making her decisions. She received many letters from young girls saying they wanted to be just like her.

Why do you think many girls have admired O'Connor?

★ ★ ★ **Section 2 Assessment** ★ ★ ★

Recall
1. **Identify** Explain the significance of **(a)** House of Representatives, **(b)** Senate, **(c)** electoral college, **(d)** Supreme Court.
2. **Define** **(a)** bill, **(b)** appeal, **(c)** unconstitutional, **(d)** veto, **(e)** override, **(f)** impeach.

Comprehension
3. What is the most important power given to Congress?
4. Describe two powers or roles of the President.
5. What is the main job of the Supreme Court?
6. **(a)** Describe one way the President can check the power of Congress. **(b)** Describe one way Congress can check the power of the President.

Critical Thinking and Writing
7. **Exploring the Main Idea** Review the Main Idea statement at the beginning of this section. Then, write a paragraph summarizing the reasons that the Constitution separated the government into branches.
8. **Supporting a Point of View** Write a letter to the editor of your local newspaper explaining whether or not you think the electoral college should be retained.

ACTIVITY

Go Online
PHSchool.com

Reviewing a Web Site
Use the Internet to find the Web site of your own Senator or Representative. Write a review of the Web site describing the kind of information that is available and how useful it is. For help in completing the activity, visit PHSchool.com, **Web Code mfd-0802.**

Chapter 8   Section 2   ★   **257**

Interpreting Bar and Line Graphs

Graphs are visual presentations of data organized so that you can see information at a glance. Two types of graphs that show changes over time are bar graphs and line graphs.

A bar graph shows statistics in the form of bars at regular time intervals.

A line graph shows statistics as connected points. The line that connects the points shows a pattern over time.

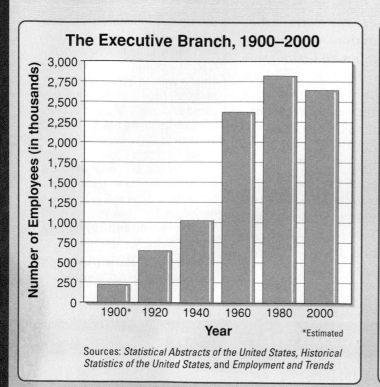

The Executive Branch, 1900–2000

Number of Employees (in thousands)

Year

*Estimated

Sources: *Statistical Abstracts of the United States, Historical Statistics of the United States,* and *Employment and Trends*

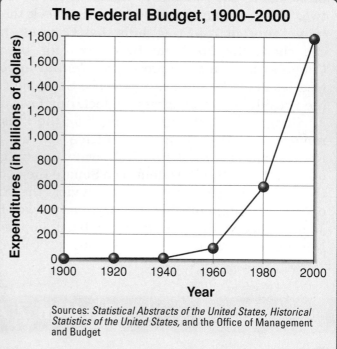

The Federal Budget, 1900–2000

Expenditures (in billions of dollars)

Year

Sources: *Statistical Abstracts of the United States, Historical Statistics of the United States,* and the Office of Management and Budget

Learn the Skill *To review how to read line and bar graphs, use the following steps:*

1. **Read the title.** The title identifies the basic information shown on a graph.

2. **Read the graph labels.** Both the horizontal axis and the vertical axis of a graph have labels that give more specific information about the data. When you read a graph, check the intervals between the dates or other statistics.

3. **Read the statistics on the graph.** Find the points where the horizontal axis meets the vertical axis.

4. **Interpret the statistics.** Draw conclusions or make predictions about the data given on the graph.

Practice the Skill *Use the graphs above to answer the following questions:*

1. **(a)** What is the subject of the bar graph? **(b)** What does the line graph show?

2. **(a)** What years do both graphs show? **(b)** Which graph shows the number of employees?

3. **(a)** In what year were there about one million employees in the executive branch? **(b)** What was the federal budget in 1960? **(c)** During what years did the budget increase the most?

4. Make one generalization about the federal government based on these two graphs.

Apply the Skill *See the Chapter Review and Assessment.*

3 Changing the Constitution

Prepare to Read

Objectives

In this section, you will
- Describe how to amend the Constitution.
- Name the rights that the Bill of Rights protects.
- Explain how later amendments expanded democratic rights.

Key Terms

First Amendment

Second Amendment

incriminate

civil

Civil War Amendments

Nineteenth Amendment

Twenty-sixth Amendment

Target Reading Skill

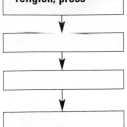

Sequence Copy this chart. As you read, fill in the boxes with information about constitutional amendments discussed in this section.

FIRST AMENDMENT
• Part of Bill of Rights • Freedom of speech, religion, press

↓

| |

↓

| |

↓

| |

Main Idea The amendment process has made the Constitution a living document that reflects changing times.

Setting the Scene

"My faith in the Constitution is whole, it is complete, it is total." The speaker was Barbara Jordan, the first African American elected to Congress from Texas. In her rich voice, Jordan reminded her listeners of the first words of the Constitution:

❝ When that document was completed, on the seventeenth of September in 1787, I was not included in that *We, the people.* . . . But through the process of amendment, interpretation, and court decision I have finally been included in *We, the people.* ❞

—Barbara Jordan, testimony before the House Judiciary Committee, July 25, 1974

Barbara Jordan

Jordan lived in a different world from that of the framers of the Constitution. They did not know *how* the nation would change. But they knew it *would* change and that the Constitution would have to change with it. The formal amendment process that they designed has helped make the Constitution a living document.

The Amendment Process

The framers did not want to make it too easy for Americans to change the Constitution. As a result, they created a complex amendment process. (See the chart on the next page.) The process may take months, or even years, to complete.

Article V outlines two ways to propose an amendment. An amendment may be proposed by two thirds of both the House and the Senate, or by a national convention called by Congress at the request of two thirds of the state legislatures. The second method has never been used.

An amendment may also be ratified in one of two ways. An amendment may be approved by the legislatures of three fourths of

Methods of Amending the Constitution

Proposed by CONGRESS by two-thirds vote of each house

or

Proposed by NATIONAL CONVENTION called by Congress at request of two thirds of state legislatures

Ratified by Legislatures in three fourths of states

or

Ratified by Conventions in three fourths of states

GRAPHIC ORGANIZER Skills

The amendment process requires two steps: proposal and ratification.

1. **Comprehension** (a) Can an amendment proposed by Congress be ratified by state conventions? (b) Can an amendment proposed by a national convention be ratified by state legislatures?

2. **Critical Thinking Evaluating Information** Which method of proposing an amendment seems more difficult? Explain.

the states. Every amendment but the Twenty-first was ratified using this method. In the second method, an amendment may be approved by special conventions in three fourths of the states.

The Bill of Rights

As one of its first acts, the new Congress drafted a series of amendments in 1789 and sent them to the states for approval. In 1791, the Bill of Rights, the first ten amendments, became part of the Constitution.

Protecting Individual Liberties The First Amendment safeguards basic individual liberties. It protects freedom of religion, speech, and the press. It also guarantees the right to assemble peacefully and to petition the government to change its policies.

Because of the First Amendment, you cannot be arrested for criticizing a government official. You can attend the house of worship of your choice or none at all. You can read newspapers that do not represent the views of an official party. Still, there are limits on the First Amendment. For example, the government can limit free speech if there is "a clear and present danger," such as in time of war.

Protecting Against Abuse of Power The next three amendments reflect the colonists' experiences under British rule. (See Chapter 5.) The Second Amendment states, "A well-regulated militia being necessary to the security of a free state, the right of the people to keep and bear arms shall not be infringed." The Third Amendment says that Congress may not force citizens to put up troops in their homes. The Fourth Amendment protects Americans from unlawful searches of home or property.

Since early times, Americans have debated the exact meaning of the Second Amendment. Some experts believe that it guarantees individuals a basic right to bear arms. Others argue that it simply guarantees the individual states the right to maintain a militia. Gun control is one of the most complex and controversial constitutional issues facing Americans today.

Protecting Rights of the Accused The Fifth through Eighth amendments deal with the rights of people accused of crimes. The Fifth Amendment states that people cannot be forced to incriminate, or give evidence against, themselves. The Sixth Amendment guarantees the right to a speedy and public trial by an impartial, or fair, jury. It also states that people accused of crimes have the right to know the charges against them, as well as the right to confront the person making the charges.

The Seventh Amendment provides for juries for civil, or non-criminal, trials. The Eighth Amendment forbids judges from ordering excessive bail or fines or "cruel and unusual punishments."

Amendments Nine and Ten Some Americans had opposed adding a Bill of Rights. They argued that, if specific rights were listed in the Constitution, Americans might lose other rights that were not listed. The Ninth Amendment solved that problem. It makes clear that a citizen's rights are not limited to those listed in the Constitution.

The Tenth Amendment reaffirmed the framers' plan to create a limited federal government. It states that all powers not given to the national government or denied to the states are reserved for the states or for the people.

Later Amendments

Since the addition of the Bill of Rights, the Constitution has been amended only 17 times. Many later amendments reflect changing attitudes about equality and the expansion of democracy.

The Thirteenth, Fourteenth, and Fifteenth amendments are known as the Civil War Amendments. The Thirteenth Amendment abolished slavery. The Fourteenth Amendment guaranteed citizenship to former slaves. The Fifteenth Amendment declared that states may not deny the vote to any citizen on the basis of "race, color, or previous condition of servitude." This guaranteed African American men the right to vote.

Other amendments further expanded voting rights. The Nineteenth Amendment, ratified in 1920, gave women the right to vote. Women achieved this victory after more than 70 years of struggle. In 1971, changing attitudes toward the rights and responsibilities of young people gave birth to the Twenty-sixth Amendment. It lowered the minimum voting age from 21 to 18.

Identify Sequence
When did the amendments discussed in this subsection take place? Where should you place them on your chart?

★ ★ ★ Section 3 Assessment ★ ★ ★

Recall
1. **Identify** Explain the significance of (a) First Amendment, (b) Second Amendment, (c) Civil War Amendments, (d) Nineteenth Amendment, (e) Twenty-sixth Amendment.
2. **Define** (a) incriminate, (b) civil.

Comprehension
3. How can an amendment to the Constitution be ratified?
4. Summarize the rights protected by the Bill of Rights.

5. How did later amendments reflect changing ideas about equality?

Critical Thinking and Writing
6. **Exploring the Main Idea** Review the Main Idea statement at the beginning of this section. Then, write a sentence giving your own definition of the term "living document."
7. **Drawing Conclusions** Why do you think the Bill of Rights carefully spells out the rights of people accused of crimes?

ACTIVITY

Prepare a Dialogue
With a partner, act out a scene between two students. One of you is an American. The other has fled from a country that does not protect freedom of speech, the press, or religion. Discuss the importance of these freedoms to Americans.

4 State and Local Governments

Prepare to Read

Objectives

In this section, you will
- Compare state constitutions to the national Constitution.
- Summarize the services that state governments provide.
- Describe how local governments affect our daily lives.

Main Idea State and local governments often play a more direct role in our daily lives than does the federal government.

Key Terms

constitutional initiative

infrastructure

local government

 Target Reading Skill

Comparison and Contrast Copy this incomplete Venn diagram. As you read, write key services provided by state and local governments. Include shared services in the overlapping section.

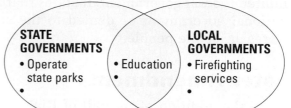

STATE GOVERNMENTS
- Operate state parks
-

• Education
•

LOCAL GOVERNMENTS
- Firefighting services
-

Visitors at the Bronx Zoo

Setting the Scene In the Bronx, New York, more families wanted to enjoy the area's most popular attraction: the Bronx Zoo, the largest zoo in the United States. A state senator introduced a law allowing local families free admission to the zoo one day a week.

In Oxnard, California, the Police Commissioner learned that 20 percent of all 9-1-1 emergency calls—many of them false alarms—were being made by children. To solve the problem, he got together with state education officials to create "9-1-1 for Kids." This program educates young children on what to do in a real emergency.

In Bexar County, Texas, parents needed help getting their children to school. Local officials banded together to start a program called SchoolPool. It identifies parents who live near one another and provides information about driving duties. Besides helping busy parents, the program reduced the number of cars on local roads.

When we hear the word *government,* most of us think first of the national government in Washington, D.C. Yet, day to day, state and local governments often have a more direct impact on our lives.

State Constitutions

The Constitution divides power between the federal government and the states. The federal government deals with national issues. The states have the power to meet more local needs.

A Frame of Government Each of the 50 states has a constitution that sets forth the principles and framework of its government. Although constitutions vary from state to state, they must all conform to the Constitution of the United States. If a conflict arises, the national Constitution—the "supreme law of the land"—prevails.

Most state constitutions resemble the national Constitution in form. They start with a preamble stating their goals and include a bill of rights guaranteeing individual liberties. State constitutions tend to be longer and more detailed than the national Constitution. Many include provisions on finance, education, and other matters.

State constitutions set up a government with three branches. The powers of the legislative, executive, and judicial branches on the state level are similar to those of the national government.

Changing Constitutions State constitutions can be changed in several ways. In the most common method, amendments are proposed by the state legislature and approved by the people in an election.

In almost one half of the states, citizens can act directly to change the constitution. In a process known as the **constitutional initiative,** sponsors of an amendment gather signatures on a petition. When the required number of signatures is attained, the petition goes to the legislature or to the voters for approval.

Finally, a state can rewrite its constitution. With the approval of the legislature or the people, the state may call a constitutional convention. The new constitution is then submitted to the people.

States Provide Services

State governments provide a wide range of services. They maintain law and order, enforce criminal law, protect property, and regulate business. They also supervise public education, provide public health and welfare programs, build and maintain highways, operate state parks and forests, and regulate use of state-owned land.

The states, not the federal government, have the main responsibility for public education in the United States. Most students attend schools paid for and overseen by the state. The state sets general standards for schools and establishes a recommended course of study. It also sets requirements for promotion and graduation.

Each state must build and maintain its own **infrastructure,** or system of roads, bridges, and tunnels. State departments or agencies manage more than 3,000 state parks and recreation areas. To help maintain high standards, state governments license the professionals who serve you, such as doctors, lawyers, and teachers. When you are old enough to drive, the state will test you and, if you pass, give you a license. State police keep highways safe and protect us against criminal acts.

Local Governments

The Constitution defines the powers of the federal and state governments. But it does not mention **local government,** that is, government on the county, parish, city, town, village, or district level. Local governments are created

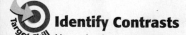
entirely by the states and have only those powers and functions that states give them.

Local governments have perhaps the greatest impact on our daily lives. At the same time, it is on the local level that citizens have the greatest opportunity to influence government.

Local Governments and Education The service that local governments spend the most money on is education. While state governments set standards for schools, it is the cities or school districts that actually run them. Local school boards build schools and hire teachers and staff. They also have a strong say in which courses will be taught. However, school officials must make all decisions within the guidelines set by state law.

Education is one area of local government where citizens exert a great deal of control. Local residents may give up part of their time to serve on local school boards. In most communities, voters have the right to approve or turn down the annual school budget.

Other Services Local governments provide a variety of other services. They hire or support firefighters, police, and garbage collectors. Local governments provide sewers and water, maintain local roads and hospitals, and conduct safety inspections of buildings and restaurants. In many cases, water and sewage treatment plants are owned and run by local governments. Other communities hire private companies to supply local needs.

Over the years, Americans have looked to local government for more than basic services. Today, most local governments provide libraries and parks and other cultural and recreational facilities. In larger cities, citizens expect their local governments to support airports, sports arenas, and civic centers. San Francisco, for example, maintains a busy airport, a major-league baseball stadium, several major museums, a world-class zoo, and a leading convention center.

★ ★ ★ Section 4 Assessment ★ ★ ★

Recall

1. **Define** (a) constitutional initiative, (b) infrastructure, (c) local government.

Comprehension

2. (a) Describe one way in which state constitutions are similar to the United States Constitution. (b) Describe one way in which they are different.
3. Identify two services performed by state governments.
4. How do local governments support education?

Critical Thinking and Writing

5. **Exploring the Main Idea** Review the Main Idea statement at the beginning of this section. Then, rank in order what you consider to be the five most important services you get from your state and local governments.
6. **Drawing Inferences** Why do you think state constitutions tend to be longer than the United States Constitution?

5 Rights and Responsibilities of Citizenship

Prepare to Read

Objectives

In this section, you will
- Explain what makes a person a citizen of the United States.
- Identify how Americans can develop democratic values.
- Describe the responsibilities of citizenship.

Key Terms

citizen
naturalize
immigrant
resident alien
civic virtue
patriotism
jury duty

Target Reading Skill

Clarifying Meaning As you read, prepare an outline of this section. Use roman numerals to indicate the major headings, capital letters for the subheadings, and numbers for the supporting details.

> I. What Is a Citizen?
>   A. Definition of citizenship
>   1. Born in United States
>   2.
>   B. Becoming a citizen
>   1.
>   2.
>   C.
> II. Civic Virtue and Democratic Values
>   A.
>   B.

Main Idea Being an American citizen brings both rights and responsibilities.

Setting the Scene

While he was in middle school, David Levitt of Seminole, Florida, read about an organization that collected left-over food from restaurants and donated it to the needy. This gave Levitt an idea. Why not start a similar program in his community?

He started by asking his principal if the school could donate left-over cafeteria food. Levitt went on to present his idea to the school board. A year later, at his bar mitzvah, he collected 500 pounds of canned goods from his guests. In time, the food program expanded across Florida and led to passage of a new state law.

Florida governor Jeb Bush called David Levitt a "big-hearted . . . young man blessed with a strong desire to help others." But Levitt insisted that all young people had the power to get things done:

David Levitt

> 66 You have to use your age as an advantage. In government, adults face people who complain and ask for things. It's such a change of pace to hear someone say, 'We can do this.' 99
>
> —David Levitt, quoted in *American Profile* (Schantz-Feld)

The framers of the Constitution planned our government carefully. Yet, a good constitution alone is not enough. To safeguard our democracy, each of us must exercise our rights and fulfill our responsibilities as citizens.

What Is a Citizen?

A **citizen** is a person who owes loyalty to a particular nation and is entitled to all its rights and protections. To be a citizen of the United States, you must fulfill one of three requirements:

- You were born in the United States (or at least one parent is a citizen of the United States).

- You were **naturalized,** that is, you have completed the official legal process for becoming a citizen.

- You were 18 or younger when your parents were naturalized.

Becoming a Citizen Throughout American history, many millions of immigrants have become naturalized citizens. An **immigrant** is a person who enters another country in order to settle there. To illustrate the naturalization process, we will look at one immigrant's story.

At age 15, Carla Rojas came to the United States from Argentina. Her mother returned home two years later, but Rojas decided to remain. After submitting numerous documents and photographs and attending several interviews, she received permission to remain in the country as a **resident alien,** or noncitizen living in the country.

After a required five-year waiting period, Carla submitted an application for citizenship. She had to take a test to show that she was comfortable with the English language and that she was familiar with American history and government. She also had to show that she was of "good moral character." Then, a naturalization examiner interviewed her about her reasons for becoming a citizen.

At last, Rojas stood before a judge and took the oath that confirmed her as an American citizen:

> 66 I hereby declare, on oath, that . . . I will support and defend the Constitution and laws of the United States against all enemies . . . that I will bear true faith and allegiance to the same . . . so help me God. 99
>
> —Oath of Allegiance to the United States

A naturalized citizen enjoys every right of a natural-born citizen except one. Only natural-born citizens may serve as President or Vice President.

Rights and Responsibilities All American citizens have equal rights under the law. As Americans, you have the right to speak freely, to worship as you choose, to vote, and to serve on juries. These rights are not based on inherited wealth or family connections. They are yours because you are a citizen.

Still, nothing is free. As you will see, if we want to enjoy the rights of citizenship, we must also accept its responsibilities.

Civic Virtue and Democratic Values

The Founding Fathers admired **civic virtue,** that is, the willingness to work for the good of the nation or community even at great sacrifice. They looked to Roman models such as Cincinnatus, who, it was said, gave up a peaceful life on his farm when called upon to lead Rome. Again and again, leaders such as Washington and Jefferson put the common good ahead of their own wishes.

Still, you do not have to go to such lengths to be a good citizen. At home, at school, and in the community, you can work to develop the values that are the foundation of our democratic system. Among these basic values are honesty and compassion. Others include patriotism, respect, responsibility, and courage.

A key democratic value is **patriotism,** or a feeling of love and devotion toward one's country. A sense of patriotism inspires

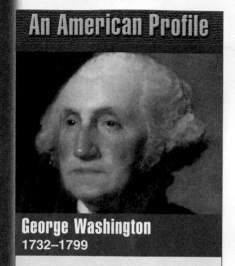

An American Profile

George Washington
1732–1799

Several times in his life, George Washington set aside his hopes for a quiet life to serve his country.

After winning the battle of Yorktown in 1781, Washington ached to return home. Still, he led the army until a peace treaty was signed two years later. In 1787, though ill, he yielded to friends who urged him to attend the Constitutional Convention. After his first term as President, Washington sought to retire. Once again, Washington was persuaded to stay on to keep the young republic stable. After his second term, Washington finally retired. He died two years later.

Why do many people point to Washington as an example of civic virtue?

"Maybe I ought to listen. This is the year I start voting."

POLITICAL CARTOON
Skills

Young Voters
Voting is one of the main responsibilities of citizenship. This cartoon appeared in 1960, a presidential election year.

1. **Comprehension** Describe what is going on in this cartoon.

2. **Understanding Main Ideas** What point does the cartoon make about staying informed?

3. **Critical Thinking Supporting a Point of View** Based on this cartoon, would you call this young man a good citizen? Explain.

Civics

Americans to serve their nation. It also encourages us to fulfill the ideals set forth in the Declaration of Independence, the Constitution, and the Bill of Rights.

As citizens, we must respect ourselves, our families, our neighbors, and the other members of our community. Respect may also involve objects or ideas. For example, a good citizen respects the property of others and the laws of the nation.

Responsibility may be both personal and public. We must accept responsibility for ourselves and the consequences of our actions. For example, parents have a duty to support their families and teach their children. As a student, you have a responsibility to learn.

Courage may be either physical or moral. Soldiers, police, or firefighters display physical courage when they risk their lives for the good of others. Moral courage enables us to do the right thing even when it is unpopular, difficult, or dangerous. Americans such as George Washington, Abraham Lincoln, Susan B. Anthony, and Martin Luther King, Jr., faced risks in order to defend their democratic values.

Responsibilities of a Citizen

As citizens, we must accept our own civic responsibilities. Only if government and citizens work together can we meet our needs as a democratic society.

Voting As citizens of a republic, we have the right to select the people who will represent us in government. But if that right is to have any meaning, then we must fulfill our responsibility to vote. A good citizen studies the candidates and the issues in order to make responsible choices.

Paraphrase
Target Skill When you paraphrase, you restate what you have read in your own words. Paraphrase the information about the responsibilities of a citizen. Add this information to your outline.

Obeying the Laws In the Constitution, "we the people" give the government the power to make laws for us. Thus, we have a duty to obey the nation's laws. We have thousands of laws that keep us from hurting one another, regulate contracts, or protect citizens' rights. No one can know them all, but you must know and obey the laws that affect your life and actions.

Defending the Nation Americans have the duty to help defend the nation against threats to its peace or security. At age 18, all men must register for the draft. In time of war, the government may call them to serve in the armed forces. Many young citizens feel the duty to enlist in the military without being called.

Serving on a Jury The Bill of Rights guarantees the right to trial by jury. In turn, every citizen has the responsibility to serve on a jury when called. **Jury duty** is a serious matter. Jurors must take time out from their work and personal lives to decide the fate of others.

Serving the Community Many Americans use their time and skills to improve their communities or to help others. As you read, David Levitt was in middle school when he started a program to help the needy in his Florida community. Many young people participate in walk-a-thons or bike-a-thons for charity. Others volunteer in hospitals or fire departments. When terrorist attacks hit New York City and Washington, D.C., in September 2001, millions of citizens aided in rescue efforts, donated blood, or contributed money and supplies.

Being Informed Thomas Jefferson observed, "If a nation expects to be ignorant and free . . . it expects what never was and never will be." You cannot protect your rights as a citizen unless you know what they are. It is your responsibility to be informed. You can watch television news programs and read newspapers, magazines, or government pamphlets. Your work in school will help you become educated about our history, our government, and the workings of our society.

★ ★ ★ Section 5 Assessment ★ ★ ★

Recall

1. **Define** (a) citizen, (b) naturalize, (c) immigrant, (d) resident alien, (e) civic virtue, (f) patriotism, (g) jury duty.

Comprehension

2. How may a person become an American citizen?
3. List four values that citizens in a democratic society need.
4. Describe two responsibilities of citizenship.

Critical Thinking and Writing

5. **Exploring the Main Idea** Review the Main Idea statement at the beginning of this section. Then, write a paragraph analyzing how rights and responsibilities help define our identity as Americans.
6. **Making Decisions** You are a resident alien who has decided to apply for citizenship. Write a letter to a family member in your native country explaining why you reached that decision.

Becoming an American Citizen

Becoming an American citizen is not easy. But for many immigrants, the benefits of freedom and opportunity make it worth the effort.

Steps to Citizenship

 Establish five-year residency.

 Apply for citizenship.
- Submit application and fee
- Get fingerprinted for background check

3 Go through the interview process.
- Take English and civics tests
- Answer questions about background and character

 Take Oath of Allegiance

Could you pass the citizenship test? See how many of the following typical test questions you can answer correctly.

1. How many stripes are there on our flag?
2. What country did we fight during the Revolutionary War?
3. Who elects the President of the United States?
4. What are the duties of the Supreme Court?
5. What are the three branches of our government?
6. How many Senators are there in Congress?
7. For how long do we elect each senator?
8. Who said, "Give me liberty or give me death"?
9. How many terms can the President serve?
10. Who is the Commander in Chief of the United States military?

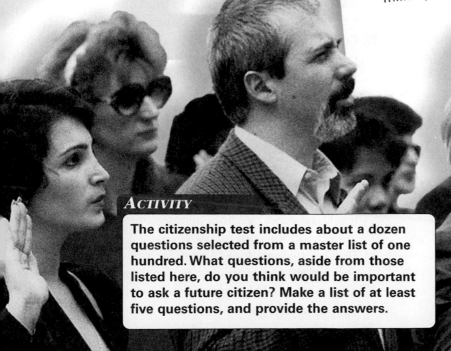

ACTIVITY

The citizenship test includes about a dozen questions selected from a master list of one hundred. What questions, aside from those listed here, do you think would be important to ask a future citizen? Make a list of at least five questions, and provide the answers.

Review and Assessment

CHAPTER SUMMARY

Section 1
The ideals expressed in the U.S. Constitution have guided the nation for more than 200 years. The Preamble sets goals, while the first three articles set up the framework for government.

Section 2
The U.S. government is divided into three branches: the legislative, executive, and judicial branches. Each branch has separate roles and responsibilities.

Section 3
The U.S. Constitution can be amended. The first ten amendments are the Bill of Rights. There have been 27 amendments to the Constitution.

Section 4
State and local governments provide many services on which we rely. In fact, state and local governments often play a more direct role in our daily lives than does the federal government.

Section 5
Being a U.S. citizen brings both rights and responsibilities. These include voting, obeying laws, and defending the country.

Building Vocabulary

Use the chapter vocabulary words listed below to create a crossword puzzle. Exchange puzzles with a classmate. Complete the puzzles, and then check each other's answers.

1. liberty
2. popular sovereignty
3. checks and balances
4. federalism
5. bill
6. veto
7. citizen
8. naturalize
9. civic virtue
10. patriotism

Reviewing Key Facts

11. What is limited government? (Section 1)
12. How does the electoral college work? (Section 2)

For additional review and enrichment activities, see the interactive version of *The American Nation,* available on the Web and on CD-ROM.

Chapter Self-Test For practice test questions for Chapter 8, visit PHSchool.com, **Web Code mfa-0804.**

13. In what two ways can a constitutional amendment be proposed? (Section 3)
14. How are local governments created? (Section 4)
15. Summarize the steps of the naturalization process. (Section 5)

Critical Thinking and Writing

16. **Contrasting (a)** How does our republican system differ from a system where all citizens participate directly in government? **(b)** Write a sentence explaining why you think the framers chose a republican system.
17. **Supporting a Point of View** Your local newspaper has printed an editorial arguing that the process of amending the Constitution should be simplified. Write a letter to the editor agreeing or disagreeing with this position.
18. **Connecting to Geography: Movement** Locate the Mississippi River on a map of the United States. Do you think the federal government or the state governments would be primarily responsible for laws regarding shipping along the Mississippi? Write a paragraph explaining the reason for your answer.
19. **Finding the Main Idea** A popular saying states, "Your right to swing your fist ends where my nose begins." Write a sentence restating the main idea of this saying in your own words.

General John A. Wickham, Jr., served as Chief of Staff for the United States Army. Here, he talks about what military service means to him:

66 The history of the Army is intertwined with the history of our Constitution. Before our young nation could even be in a position to draft a constitution, her freedom had to be won. It was won with the courage and blood of the first American soldiers. Once our liberty was secured, these same soldiers became the citizens upon whose commitment and hard work a great nation would be built. 99

—John A. Wickham, Jr., in *Collected Works of the Thirtieth Chief of Staff,* United States Army

20. According to Wickham, which of the following qualities do soldiers and citizens need?
   A. courage and commitment
   B. popular sovereignty
   C. patriotism and naturalization
   D. pacifism and liberty
21. Which of the following statements accurately reflects Wickham's point of view?
   A. No Army was needed after the Revolution.
   B. Before the Constitution could be written, American soldiers had to win the war.
   C. Soldiers do not make good citizens.
   D. Only soldiers should be naturalized.

Look at the bar graph below, and answer the questions that follow.

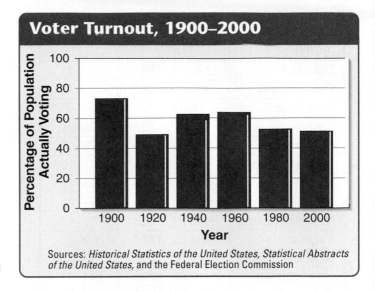

Voter Turnout, 1900–2000

Sources: *Historical Statistics of the United States, Statistical Abstracts of the United States,* and the Federal Election Commission

22. Which statement about voter turnout does this graph support?
   A. Voter turnout steadily declined after 1900.
   B. Voter turnout steadily rose after 1920.
   C. Voter turnout varied in the 1900s.
   D. Most Americans do not vote.
23. List three factors that you think might lead to an increase in voter turnout.

ACTIVITIES

Connecting With . . .
Government and Citizenship

Creating an Election Chart Look at the electoral college map at the beginning of this chapter. Suppose there is a presidential election between Smith and Jones. Smith wins 18 states: Alabama, Arizona, Arkansas, California, Florida, Georgia, Illinois, Kentucky, Louisiana, Michigan, Missouri, New Mexico, North Carolina, South Carolina, Tennessee, Texas, Virginia, and Wyoming. Jones wins the other 32 states plus the District of Columbia. Create a two-column chart showing the electoral votes for each candidate. Then, determine the winner of the election.

Go Online
PHSchool.com

Connecting to Today
Giving a News Report Use the Internet to find a recent court case that involves the freedoms protected by the Bill of Rights. Deliver to the class a one- to two-minute summary of that case. For help in starting this activity, visit PHSchool.com, **Web Code mfd-0805.**

TEST PREPARATION

Use the table **and** your knowledge of social studies to answer the following question.

Ratification of the Constitution

STATE	DATE	VOTE
Delaware	Dec. 7, 1787	30–9
Pennsylvania	Dec. 12, 1787	46–23
New Jersey	Dec. 18, 1787	38–0
Georgia	Jan. 2, 1788	26–0
Connecticut	Jan. 9, 1788	128–40
Massachusetts	Feb. 6, 1788	187–168
Maryland	Apr. 28, 1788	63–11
South Carolina	May 23, 1788	149–73
New Hampshire	June 21, 1788	57–47
Virginia	June 25, 1788	89–79
New York	July 26, 1788	30–27
North Carolina	Nov. 21, 1789	194–77
Rhode Island	May 29, 1790	34–32

1 Which conclusion about the ratification of the Constitution is supported by this table?

A Antifederalist influence was strong in Georgia.

B Federalists faced little opposition in New England.

C Antifederalist influence was stronger in New York than in New Jersey.

D The Constitution could go into effect by June 1, 1788.

2 Which statement best summarizes the main idea of Thomas Paine's *Common Sense*?

A The colonists must make one last effort to reconcile with the king.

B The best strategy for winning the war would be for Americans to seek help from France.

C At this time, Washington and the army need the full support of all Patriots.

D Separation from England is the most logical course for the American colonies.

3 How did the French and Indian War lead to the American Revolution?

A The British king encouraged colonists to settle on lands won from France.

B The British government taxed the colonists to help pay for the war.

C The French encouraged American colonists to seek independence from Britain.

D After the war, more British troops were permanently stationed in the colonies.

4 Which is not a power of Congress under the Constitution?

A Declaring war

B Ratifying constitutional amendments

C Removing a President from office

D Regulating foreign trade

Use the quotation **and** your knowledge of social studies to answer the following question.

> ### Constitution of the United States, Article I, Section 1
>
> "The House of Representatives shall be composed of members chosen every second year by the people of the several states. . . ."

5 Which principle of the Constitution is primarily reflected in the passage above?

A Republicanism

B Federalism

C Checks and balances

D Individual rights

6 In which of the following pairs was the first event an immediate cause of the second?

A Intolerable Acts; Boston Tea Party

B Battle of Saratoga; French aid to colonies

C Declaration of Independence; Battle of Lexington

D Stamp Act; Shays' Rebellion

Use the map _and_ your knowledge of social studies to answer the following question.

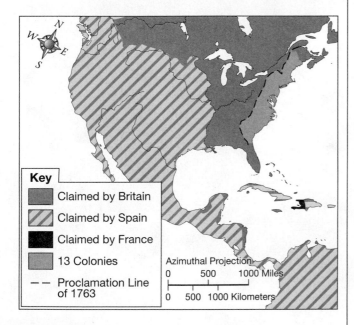

Key
- Claimed by Britain
- Claimed by Spain
- Claimed by France
- 13 Colonies
- – – Proclamation Line of 1763

Azimuthal Projection
0   500   1000 Miles
0 500 1000 Kilometers

7 How would a map showing the same area 10 years earlier have looked different?

A The original 13 colonies would have taken up a larger area.

B British land claims would have taken up a larger area.

C French land claims would have taken up a larger area.

D The map would have looked about the same.

8 Which of these grievances against England listed in the Declaration of Independence was later addressed in the Bill of Rights?

A "... imposing taxes on us without our consent"

B "... depriving us, in many cases, of the benefit of trial by jury"

C "... cutting off our trade with all parts of the world"

D "... suspending our own legislatures"

9 The dispute between large states and small states at the Constitutional Convention largely concerned what subject?

A Legislative branch of government

B Executive branch of government

C Judicial branch of government

D Checks and balances among the three branches of government

Writing Practice

10 Compare the advantages and disadvantages of the Americans and the British during the American Revolution. Then, explain why the United States won the war.

11 Choose one of the following principles of the Constitution: republicanism, checks and balances, federalism, separation of powers, popular sovereignty, or individual rights. Explain its meaning, why the framers valued that principle, and how it affects American government and society.

Unit 3 The Early Republic

Life on the Canals
The building of canals like the one shown in *Junction of the Erie and Northern (Champlain) Canals* by John Hill helped spur economic growth during the early 1800s.

> **❝***We have learned to love our country . . . because the sweat of our fathers' brows has subdued its soil . . . because it embraces our fathers and mothers.***❞**
> —John Thornton Kirkland, Boston minister (1798)

Launching the New Government

1789–1800

1 **Washington Takes Office**
2 **Creating a Foreign Policy**
3 **Political Parties Emerge**
4 **The Second President**

Washington's inaugural flag, 1789

Benjamin Banneker

Map of the new capital city

AMERICAN EVENTS

1789
George Washington is inaugurated as the first President of the United States.

1791
Benjamin Banneker helps lay out the District of Columbia, the nation's new capital.

1793
Washington issues the Neutrality Proclamation to prevent the United States from being dragged into a European war.

Presidential Terms: George Washington   1789–1797

1788   •   **1791**   •   **1794**

WORLD EVENTS

▲ **1789**
The French Revolution begins.

1793 ▲
French radicals execute the king and queen of France.

Where Americans Lived, 1800

In the early years of the United States, most Americans lived along the eastern coastal plain.

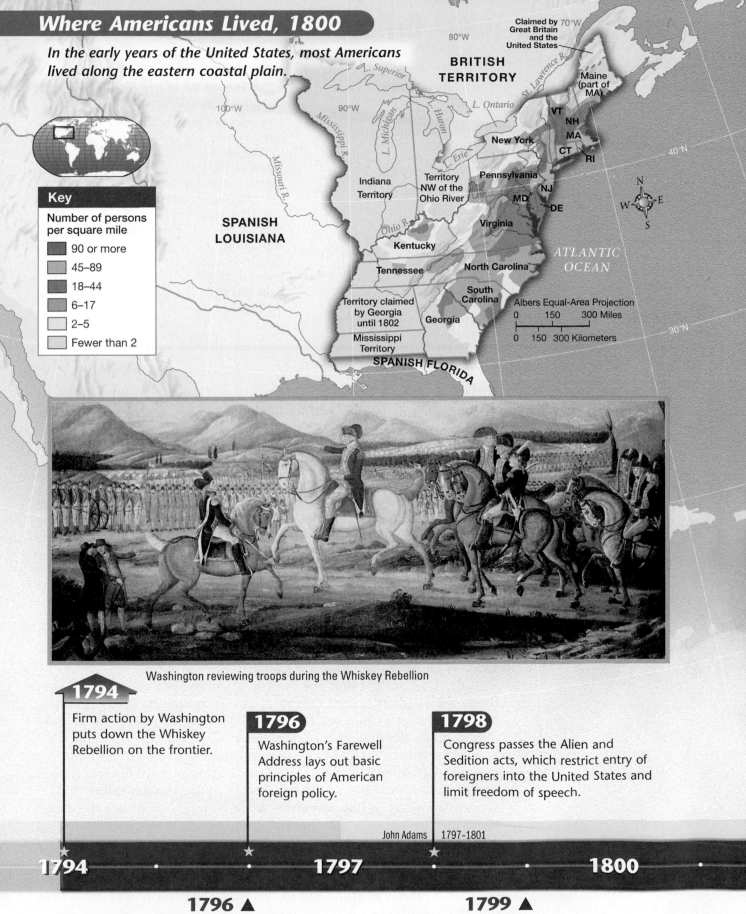

Key

Number of persons per square mile

- 90 or more
- 45–89
- 18–44
- 6–17
- 2–5
- Fewer than 2

Claimed by Great Britain and the United States

BRITISH TERRITORY

Maine (part of MA)

L. Superior

L. Michigan

L. Huron

L. Ontario

L. Erie

St. Lawrence R.

VT

NH

MA

New York

CT

RI

Indiana Territory

Territory NW of the Ohio River

Pennsylvania

NJ

MD

DE

SPANISH LOUISIANA

Mississippi R.

Missouri R.

Ohio R.

Virginia

Kentucky

ATLANTIC OCEAN

Tennessee

North Carolina

South Carolina

Territory claimed by Georgia until 1802

Georgia

Mississippi Territory

SPANISH FLORIDA

Albers Equal-Area Projection

0 150 300 Miles

0 150 300 Kilometers

Washington reviewing troops during the Whiskey Rebellion

1794

Firm action by Washington puts down the Whiskey Rebellion on the frontier.

1796

Washington's Farewell Address lays out basic principles of American foreign policy.

1798

Congress passes the Alien and Sedition acts, which restrict entry of foreigners into the United States and limit freedom of speech.

John Adams 1797–1801

1794 • **1797** • **1800**

1796 ▲
Emperor Qianlong ends his 60-year reign in China by resigning from office.

1799 ▲
Napoleon Bonaparte seizes power in France.

Chapter 9 ★ 277

1 Washington Takes Office

Prepare to Read

Objectives

In this section, you will
- Describe the steps Washington took to make the new government work.
- Explain Hamilton's plan to reduce the nation's debt and build the economy.
- List the causes and results of the Whiskey Rebellion.

Key Terms

inauguration

precedent

Cabinet

Judiciary Act

national debt

bond

speculator

Bank of the United States

tariff

Whiskey Rebellion

Target Reading Skill

Main Idea As you read, prepare an outline of this section. Use roman numerals to indicate the major headings, capital letters for the subheadings, and numbers for the supporting details. The sample at right will help you get started.

> I. Washington's First Steps
>   A. The first Cabinet
>   B.
> II. Reducing the Nation's Debt
>   A. Hamilton's plan
>   1.
>   2.
>   B.
>   C.
> III. Plans to Build the Economy
> IV.

Main Idea As the nation's first President, George Washington faced many economic and political challenges.

Washington's first inaugural

Setting the Scene When the new Congress met in 1789, it debated a curious question. How should people address the President? Some members of Congress favored the simple title "President Washington." Others urged a more dignified title, such as "His Highness the President of the United States and Protector of the Rights of the Same."

Washington soon let Congress know that he preferred "President of the United States." By choosing that simple title, he rejected the grandeur and power linked to European monarchs. With that decision, as with many others, Washington set an example for later Presidents.

Washington's First Steps

George Washington was inaugurated in New York City on April 30, 1789. A presidential **inauguration** is the ceremony in which the President officially takes the oath of office. A witness reported that the new President looked "grave, almost to sadness." Washington, no doubt, felt a great burden. He knew that Americans were looking to him to make the new government work.

As the first President, Washington was setting an example for future generations. Although the Constitution provided a framework for the new government, it did not explain how the President should govern from day to day. "There is scarcely any part of my conduct," he said, "which may not hereafter be drawn into precedent." A **precedent** (PREHS uh dehnt) is an act or a decision that sets an example for others to follow.

Washington set an important precedent at the end of his second term. In 1796, he decided not to run for a third term. Not until 1940 did any President seek a third term.

Mount Vernon

Mount Vernon was George Washington's home for more than 45 years. He had a deep affection for the place. "I can truly say I had rather be at home at Mount Vernon with a friend or two about me than to be attended at the seat of the government by the officers of State and the representatives of every power in Europe." Today, more than a million people a year visit the estate.

Go Online
PHSchool.com

Virtual Field Trip For an interactive look at Mount Vernon, visit PHSchool.com, **Web Code mfd-0901.**

The First Cabinet The Constitution said little about how the executive branch should be organized. It was clear, however, that the President needed talented people to help him carry out his duties.

In 1789, the first Congress created five executive departments. They were the departments of State, Treasury, and War and the offices of Attorney General and Postmaster General. The heads of these departments made up the President's Cabinet. Members of the Cabinet gave Washington advice and were responsible for directing their departments.

Washington set a precedent by choosing well-known leaders to serve in his Cabinet. The two most influential were the Secretary of State, Thomas Jefferson, and the Secretary of the Treasury, Alexander Hamilton.

The Federal Court System The Constitution called for a Supreme Court. Congress, however, had to set up the federal court system. In 1789, Congress passed the Judiciary Act. It called for the Supreme Court to consist of one Chief Justice and five Associate Justices.* Washington named John Jay the first Chief Justice of the United States.

The Judiciary Act also set up a system of district courts and circuit courts across the nation. Decisions made in these lower courts could be appealed to the Supreme Court, the highest court in the land.

---

* Today, the Supreme Court has a Chief Justice and eight Associate Justices.

Money Problems of the New Nation, 1789–1791

Amount of Money It Cost to Run the Government, 1789–1791	Amount of Money the United States Owed	Total Income United States Received, 1789–1791
$4,269,000	$77,228,000	$4,419,000

Total Debt: $81,497,000

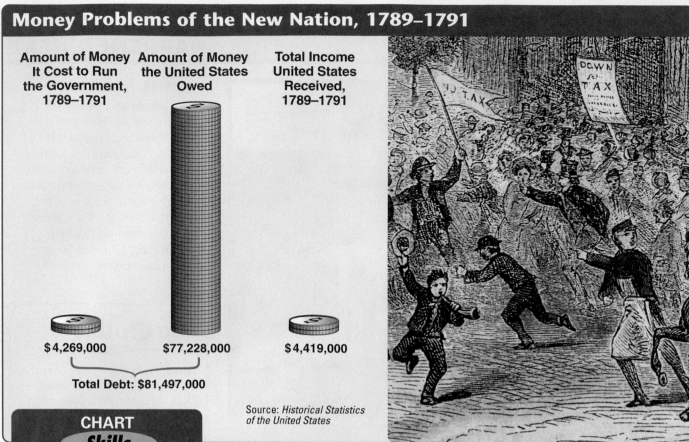

Source: *Historical Statistics of the United States*

Reducing the Nation's Debt

As Secretary of the Treasury, Alexander Hamilton faced many problems. Among the most pressing was the large national debt. The **national debt** is the total amount of money that a government owes to others.

During the Revolution, both the national government and individual states had desperately needed money. They had borrowed heavily from foreign countries and ordinary citizens to pay soldiers and buy supplies. Then, as now, governments borrowed money by issuing bonds. A **bond** is a certificate that promises to repay the money loaned, plus interest, on a certain date. For example, if a person pays $100 for a bond, the government agrees to pay back $100 plus interest by a certain time.

Hamilton's Plan Hamilton called for the government to repay both federal and state debts. He wanted the government to buy up all the bonds issued by both the national and state governments before 1789. He then planned to issue new bonds to pay off the old debts. As the economy improved, the government would then be able to pay off the new bonds. Many people, including bankers and investors, welcomed Hamilton's plan. Others attacked it.

Debating Hamilton's Plan James Madison led the opposition. Madison argued that Hamilton's plan would reward speculators. A **speculator** is someone who invests in a risky venture in the hope of making a large profit.

During the Revolution, the government had issued bonds to soldiers and citizens who supplied goods. Many of these bondholders needed cash to survive. So, they sold their bonds to speculators. Speculators bought bonds worth one dollar for only 10 or 15 cents. If the government paid off the old bonds in full, speculators stood to make fortunes. Madison thought that speculators did not deserve to make such profits.

Hamilton replied that the United States must repay its debts in full. Otherwise, he said, it risked losing the trust of investors in the future. The support of investors, he argued, was crucial to building the new nation's economy. After much debate, Congress approved full repayment of the national debt.

As a southerner, James Madison also led the fight against the other part of Hamilton's plan, the repaying of state debts. By 1789, most southern states had paid off their debts from the Revolution. They thought that other states should do the same. As a result, they bitterly opposed Hamilton's plan.

Hamilton's Compromise In the end, Hamilton proposed a compromise. Many southerners wanted the nation's capital to be located in the South. Hamilton offered to support that goal if southerners agreed to his plan to repay state debts.

Madison and others accepted the compromise. In July 1790, Congress voted to repay state debts and to build a new capital city. The new capital would not be part of any state. Instead, it would be built on land along the Potomac River between Virginia and Maryland. Congress called the area the District of Columbia. Today, it is known as Washington, D.C. Plans called for the new capital to be ready by 1800. Meanwhile, the nation's capital was moved from New York to Philadelphia.

Plans to Build the Economy

Hamilton's next challenge was to strengthen the faltering national economy. His economic plan was designed to help both agriculture and industry.

Hamilton called on Congress to set up a national bank. In 1791, Congress created the Bank of the United States. The government deposited money from taxes in the Bank. In turn, the Bank issued paper money to pay the government's bills and to make loans to farmers and businesses. Through these loans, the Bank encouraged economic growth.

To help American manufacturers, Hamilton asked Congress to pass a tariff, or tax, on foreign goods brought into the country. He wanted a high tariff, to make imported goods more expensive than American-made goods. A tariff meant to protect local industry from foreign competition is called a protective tariff.

In the North, where there were more and more factories, many people supported Hamilton's plan. Southern farmers, however, bought many imported goods. They opposed a protective tariff that would make imports more expensive.

In the end, Congress did pass a tariff, but it was much lower than the protective tariff Hamilton wanted.

Identify Supporting Details

Which details in the first two paragraphs on this page describe the debate over Hamilton's plan to reduce the national debt? Add these details to your outline.

Geography and History

Building the Nation's New Capital

The location of the nation's new capital was at a crossroads between the North and the South. Pierre L'Enfant, the city's first designer, drew up ambitious plans for the new capital. L'Enfant's assistant, Benjamin Banneker, then helped lay out the wide streets and the mile-long avenue—today's Pennsylvania Avenue. The city was built on tobacco fields, marshes, woodlands, and pastures. For years, residents faced severe problems from mud, insects, and malaria. Even after John Adams moved into the White House in 1800, a nearby creek often flooded Pennsylvania Avenue, and pigs roamed among the half-finished buildings and tree stumps.

 What geographic challenges did planners face in building Washington, D.C.?

The Whiskey Rebellion

To raise money for the Treasury, Congress approved a tax on all liquor made and sold in the United States. Hamilton wanted this tax to raise money for the Treasury. Instead, the new tax sparked a rebellion that tested the strength of the new government.

A Hated Tax Like many Americans, backcountry farmers grew corn. However, corn was bulky and hard to haul over rough roads. Instead, farmers converted their corn into whiskey. Barrels of whiskey could be shipped more easily to markets in the East.

Backcountry farmers hated the tax on whiskey. Many refused to pay it. They compared it to the taxes Britain had forced on the colonies.

In 1794, when officials in western Pennsylvania tried to collect the tax, farmers rebelled. Thousands marched in protest through the streets of Pittsburgh. They sang Revolutionary songs and tarred and feathered the tax collectors.

A Show of Strength Washington responded quickly. He called up the militia and dispatched them to Pennsylvania. When the rebels heard that thousands of troops were marching against them, they fled back to their farms. Hamilton wanted the leaders of the rebellion executed, but Washington disagreed and pardoned them. He believed that the government had shown its strength to all. Now, it was time to show mercy.

The Whiskey Rebellion tested the will of the new government. Washington's quick response proved to Americans that their new government would act firmly in times of crisis. The President also showed those who disagreed with the government that violence would not be tolerated.

★ ★ ★ Section 1 Assessment ★ ★ ★

Recall
1. **Identify** Explain the significance of **(a)** Judiciary Act, **(b)** Bank of the United States, **(c)** Whiskey Rebellion.
2. **Define** **(a)** inauguration, **(b)** precedent, **(c)** Cabinet, **(d)** national debt, **(e)** bond, **(f)** speculator, **(g)** tariff.

Comprehension
3. Describe two steps that George Washington took as President to organize the new government.
4. What were three features of Alexander Hamilton's plan to lower the national debt and strengthen the economy?

5. How did the Whiskey Rebellion reveal George Washington's concern with national security?

Critical Thinking and Writing
6. **Exploring the Main Idea** Review the Main Idea statement at the beginning of this section. Then, write five statements of fact that support the main idea.
7. **Supporting a Point of View** Hamilton and Madison disagreed about paying off bonds issued during the Revolution. Suppose that you had to defend one side. Write a statement explaining which side you support in that debate and why.

ACTIVITY

Go Online
PHSchool.com

Connecting to Today
Use the Internet to find the names of the current Cabinet departments and the person who runs each today. Make a chart listing each department and its head. Then, summarize its main functions. For help in completing the activity, visit PHSchool.com, **Web Code mfd-0902.**

EARLY AMERICAN *Folk Art*

Early American folk artists were rarely trained in art. They were usually house painters, carpenters, cabinetmakers, blacksmiths, sailors, farmers, and homemakers. They believed that what they were creating would be used, not left to sit in museums.

Whirligigs, or wind toys, were made as outdoor decorations, usually carved of wood. The wind caused the arms of a whirligig, such as those of this swordsman from the 1800s, to turn.

This 1730 painting of a child named Susanna Truax was created by an unknown artist who painted it on a mattress cover.

Shipping was an important industry in the new nation, and ship carvers created figureheads and other parts of a ship. This figurehead was carved in the early 1800s, probably for a small ship.

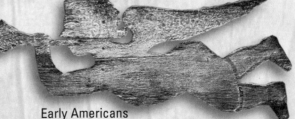

Early Americans used much imagination in creating weather vanes. This "trumpeting angel" weather vane was made of sheet iron around 1800.

ACTIVITY

Design your own piece of folk art. Think of an object that you see or use every day—a storage chest, a pencil sharpener, a tablecloth, or some other object. Then, sketch a design for it that expresses some emotion or patriotic feeling.

2 Creating a Foreign Policy

Prepare to Read

Objectives

In this section, you will
- Describe American opinions of the French Revolution.
- Explain why Washington wanted the nation to remain neutral in foreign affairs.
- Describe why it was difficult for the United States to remain neutral.

Key Terms

French Revolution

foreign policy

neutral

Neutrality Proclamation

Jay's Treaty

Farewell Address

Target Reading Skill

Clarifying Meaning Copy the concept web below. As you read, fill in each blank oval with events and developments that affected President Washington's foreign policy. Add as many ovals as you need.

French Revolution — Old treaty with France — WASHINGTON'S FOREIGN POLICY — Neutrality Proclamation

Main Idea As the French Revolution and wars raged in Europe, President Washington steered a neutral course in foreign affairs.

The guillotine: death machine of the French Revolution

Setting the Scene Late in 1789, French ships arrived in American ports with startling news. On July 14, an angry mob in Paris, France, had destroyed the Bastille (bahs TEEL), an ancient fort that was used as a prison. The attack on the Bastille was an early event in the French Revolution. Before long, the revolution would topple the monarch and lead to the execution of thousands of ordinary French citizens.

The French Revolution broke out a few years after Americans had won their independence. Like Americans, the French fought for liberty and equality. As the French Revolution grew more violent, however, it deepened political divisions within the United States.

Responses to the French Revolution

The French had many reasons to rebel against their king, Louis XVI. The peasants and the middle class paid heavy taxes, while nobles paid none. Reformers wanted a constitution to limit the king's power and protect basic rights, as the American Constitution did.

American Support At first, most Americans supported the French Revolution. They knew what it meant to struggle for liberty. Then, too, France had been their first ally. Also, many Americans admired the Marquis de Lafayette, a leading French reformer, who had fought with them in the American Revolution.

In 1793, however, the French Revolution turned more and more violent. Radical reformers gained power. They beheaded the king and later the queen. During the Reign of Terror, tens of thousands of ordinary French citizens were executed.

Violence Stirs Division The violence in France divided Americans. Some, like Thomas Jefferson, continued to support the French. He condemned the executions of the king and queen. Still, he felt that the French had the right to use violence to win freedom.

Alexander Hamilton, John Adams, and others strongly disagreed. One could no more create democracy through widespread violence, claimed Adams, "than a snowball can exist in the streets of Philadelphia under a burning sun."

The United States Remains Neutral

The French Revolution frightened most European rulers and nobles. They wanted to prevent revolutionary ideas from spreading to their lands. Europe was soon plunged into a string of wars that lasted on and off for more than 20 years.

A Difficult Decision Faced with war in Europe, President Washington had to decide on a foreign policy. **Foreign policy** refers to the actions that a nation takes in relation to other nations. During the American Revolution, the United States and France had signed a treaty that made the two countries allies. Now, France wanted to use American ports to supply its ships and launch attacks on British ships. Washington worried that the United States could not honor its treaty with France and still remain neutral in the European conflict. **Neutral** means not taking sides in a conflict.

Divisions in the Cabinet The issue of the treaty deepened the divisions within Washington's Cabinet. Hamilton pointed out that the United States had signed the treaty with Louis XVI. With the king dead, he argued, the treaty was no longer valid. Jefferson, a supporter of France, urged strict acceptance of the treaty.

After much debate, Washington issued the **Neutrality Proclamation** in April 1793. It stated that the United States would not support either side in the war. Further, it forbade Americans from aiding either Britain or France.

The Neutrality Proclamation was a defeat for Jefferson. This and other defeats eventually led Jefferson to leave the Cabinet.

Viewing History

On the March

At the start of the French Revolution, famine gripped Paris. Thousands of angry women marched on the palace of the king shouting "Bread, Bread." **Drawing Conclusions** *Why might women such as these expect Americans to support their revolution?*

Paraphrase
Paraphrase the information about Jay's Treaty. Add this information to your concept web.

Struggling to Remain Neutral

Declaring neutrality was easier than enforcing it. Americans wanted to trade with both Britain and France. However, those warring nations seized American cargoes headed for each other's ports.

Jay's Treaty In 1793, the British captured more than 250 American ships trading in the French West Indies. Some Americans called for war. Washington, however, knew that the United States was too weak to fight. He sent Chief Justice John Jay to Britain for talks.

Jay negotiated an agreement that called for Britain to pay damages for the seized American ships. Britain also agreed to give up the forts it still held in the West. Meanwhile, Americans had to pay debts long owed to British merchants.

Jay's Treaty sparked loud protests because it did nothing to protect the rights of neutral American ships. After furious debate, the Senate finally approved the treaty in 1795.

Washington Retires Before retiring in 1796, George Washington published his Farewell Address. In it, he advised Americans against becoming involved in European affairs:

> 66 Tis our true policy to steer clear of permanent Alliances, with any portion of the foreign World. . . . The great rule of conduct for us, in regard to foreign nations is . . . to have with them as little political connection as possible. 99
>
> —George Washington, Farewell Address, 1796

Washington did not oppose foreign trade, but he did reject alliances that could drag the country into war. His advice guided American foreign policy for many years.

★ ★ ★ Section 2 Assessment ★ ★ ★

Recall

1. **Identify** Explain the significance of **(a)** French Revolution, **(b)** Neutrality Proclamation, **(c)** Jay's Treaty, **(d)** Farewell Address.
2. **Define (a)** foreign policy, **(b)** neutral.

Comprehension

3. Why did the French Revolution divide Americans?
4. Describe two actions that Washington took to avoid war.
5. What problems did the United States have remaining neutral when France and Britain went to war?

Critical Thinking and Writing

6. **Finding the Main Idea** Review the Main Idea statement at the beginning of this section. Then, list two threats to American neutrality during the 1790s. Explain how Washington responded to each.
7. **Identifying Points of View** Writing about the French Revolution, Thomas Jefferson said that he was willing to see "half the earth devastated" in order to win the "liberty of the whole." **(a)** Restate Jefferson's main idea in your own words. **(b)** What does this idea tell you about Jefferson's values?

ACTIVITY

Giving an Introduction
President Washington has decided to give his Farewell Address in your school auditorium. You have been asked to introduce him. Prepare a two-minute introduction, mentioning what you consider to be Washington's greatest achievements.

3 Political Parties Emerge

Prepare to Read

Objectives

In this section, you will
- Explain why many Americans distrusted the idea of political parties.
- Contrast the views of Hamilton and Jefferson.
- Explain why political parties developed.
- Describe how the election of 1796 increased political tensions.

Main Idea During the 1790s, two political parties were formed: the Federalists and the Republicans.

Key Terms

faction

unconstitutional

Democratic Republican

Federalist

Target Reading Skill

Comparison and Contrast Copy the table below. As you read, fill in each column with the views of Hamilton and Jefferson. Add as many rows as you need.

HAMILTON'S VIEWS	JEFFERSON'S VIEWS
• Admired British economy; favored manufacturing, trade, cities	•
•	• Wanted to keep federal government small
•	•

Setting the Scene

When George Washington took office in 1789, the United States had no political parties. In fact, most American leaders disliked even the idea of parties. "If I could not go to heaven but with a party," said Thomas Jefferson, "I would not go at all."

Early on, though, political disagreements divided Americans. "Men who have been [friends] all their lives," noted Jefferson, "cross streets to avoid meeting, and turn their heads another way, lest they should be obliged to touch their hats." Before Washington left office in 1797, two rival political parties had emerged to compete for power.

E pluribus unum

A Distrust of Political Parties

Americans had reason to distrust political parties. They had seen how **factions,** or opposing groups within parties, worked in Britain. There, members of factions often plotted to win government favors and bribes. Many were more interested in personal gain than in the public good.

Americans also saw political parties as a threat to national unity. They agreed with George Washington, who warned Americans that parties would lead to "jealousies and false alarms."

Despite the President's warning, factions grew up around two members of his Cabinet, Alexander Hamilton and Thomas Jefferson. The two men differed in background, looks, and personality as well as in politics. Born in the West Indies, Hamilton had worked his way up from poverty. He dressed in fine clothes and spoke forcefully. Energetic, brilliant, and restless, Hamilton enjoyed political debate.

Jefferson was tall and lanky. Although he was a wealthy Virginia planter, he dressed and spoke informally. One senator recalled:

66 His clothes seem too small for him. He sits in a lounging manner, on one hip commonly, and with one of his shoulders elevated much above the other. His face has a sunny aspect. His whole figure has a loose, shackling air. . . . [His conversation] was loose and rambling; and yet he scattered information wherever he went. 99

—The Diary of William Maclay and Other Notes on Senate Debates

Differing Views

Hamilton and Jefferson disagreed on many issues. Their quarrels were rooted in their different views about what was best for the new nation.

Manufacturing or Farming The two leaders differed on economic policy. Hamilton wanted the United States to model itself on Britain. The government, he thought, should encourage manufacturing and trade. He also favored the growth of cities and the merchant class.

Jefferson thought that farmers, rather than merchants, were the backbone of the new nation. "Cultivators of the earth," he wrote, "are the most valuable citizens." He feared that a manufacturing economy would corrupt the United States by concentrating power in the hands of a small group of wealthy Americans.

Federal or State Power Hamilton and Jefferson also disagreed about the power of the federal government. Hamilton wanted the federal government to have greater power than state governments. A strong federal government, he argued, was needed to increase commerce. It would also be able to restrain mob violence like that of the Whiskey Rebellion.

In contrast, Jefferson wanted as small a federal government as possible, in order to protect individual freedom. He feared that a strong federal government might take over powers that the Constitution gave to the states.

Strict or Loose Interpretation of the Constitution Jefferson and Hamilton also clashed over the Bank of the United States. Jefferson worried that a national bank would give too much power to wealthy investors who would help run it and to the government.

Jefferson opposed the law setting up the bank. He claimed that it was **unconstitutional,** or not permitted by the Constitution. Nowhere did the Constitution give Congress the power to create a Bank, he argued. For Jefferson, any power not specifically given to the federal government belonged to the states.

Hamilton did not agree with Jefferson's strict interpretation of the Constitution. He preferred a looser interpretation. The Constitution gave Congress the power to make all laws "necessary and proper" to carry out its duties. Hamilton argued that the Bank was necessary for the government to collect taxes and pay its bills.

An American Profile

Alexander Hamilton
1757–1804

When Alexander Hamilton was about eight years old, his father abandoned his family. A few years later, Alexander's mother died. Despite these early losses, the boy worked hard to succeed. He studied his mother's books. At the age of 11, Alexander became an apprentice to a local merchant. He quickly rose to become manager. Impressed by his talents, his employer paid for Alexander to be educated in New York. There the 19-year-old college student wrote three pamphlets supporting the Patriot cause. Readers were startled to learn that the author was such a young man.

How might Hamilton's early life have helped prepare him for government service?

Federalists vs. Republicans

FEDERALISTS

1 Were led by Alexander Hamilton
2 Believed wealthy and well educated should lead nation
3 Favored strong central government
4 Emphasized manufacturing, shipping, and trade
5 Favored loose interpretation of Constitution
6 Were pro-British
7 Favored national bank
8 Favored protective tariff

VS.

REPUBLICANS

1 Were led by Thomas Jefferson
2 Believed people should have political power
3 Favored strong state governments
4 Emphasized agriculture
5 Favored strict interpretation of Constitution
6 Were pro-French
7 Opposed national bank
8 Opposed protective tariff

GRAPHIC ORGANIZER
Skills

By the late 1790s, there were two political parties in the United States: the Federalist party and the Republican party.

1. **Comprehension** Describe two ways in which the Republicans and the Federalists differed on economic issues.

2. **Critical Thinking Analyzing Primary Sources** "The average person is far too ignorant to make wise political decisions." Do you think a Republican or a Federalist would be more likely to agree with this statement? Explain your answer.

Civics

Britain or France Finally, the two leaders disagreed over foreign policy. Hamilton wanted close ties with Britain, a major trading partner. Jefferson favored France, the first ally of the United States.

Development of Political Parties

At first, Hamilton and Jefferson clashed in private. Then, as Congress began to pass many of Hamilton's programs, Jefferson and James Madison decided to organize supporters of their views.

The two men moved cautiously at first. In 1791, they went to New York, telling people that they wanted to study its wildlife. In fact, Jefferson was interested in nature. Their main goal, though, was to meet with leading New York politicians like Governor George Clinton and Aaron Burr, a fierce critic of Hamilton. Jefferson asked them to help defeat Hamilton's program by convincing New Yorkers to vote for Jefferson's supporters.

Republicans and Federalists Soon, leaders in other states were organizing to support either Hamilton or Jefferson. Jefferson's supporters called themselves Democratic Republicans, often shortened to Republicans.* This group included small farmers, artisans, and some wealthy planters.

Hamilton and his supporters were called Federalists because they wanted a strong federal government. Federalists drew support mainly from merchants and manufacturers in such cities as Boston and New York. They also had the backing of some southern planters.

Newspapers Take Sides In the late 1700s, the number of American newspapers more than doubled. This growth met a

Identify Contrasts As you read, check to see if you understand the major differences between the Republicans and the Federalists.

---

*Jefferson's Republican party was not the same as today's Republican party. In fact, his party later grew into the Democratic party.

demand for information. A European visitor was surprised that so many Americans could read. "The common people . . . all read and write, and understand arithmetic," he reported, and "almost every little town now furnishes a circulating library."

As party rivalry grew, newspapers took sides. In the *Gazette of the United States*, publisher John Fenno backed Hamilton and the Federalists. Jefferson's friend Philip Freneau (frih NOH) started a rival paper, the *National Gazette*, which supported Republicans.

Newspapers had great influence on public opinion. In stinging language, they raged against political opponents. Often, articles mixed rumor and opinion with facts. Emotional attacks and counterattacks fanned the flames of party rivalry.

Election of 1796

Political parties played a large role in the election of George Washington's successor. In 1796, Republicans backed Thomas Jefferson for President and Aaron Burr for Vice President. Federalists supported John Adams for President and Thomas Pinckney for Vice President.

The election had an unexpected outcome. Under the Constitution, the person with the most electoral votes became President. The candidate with the next highest total was made Vice President. John Adams, a Federalist, won office as President. The leader of the Republicans, Thomas Jefferson, came in second and became Vice President.

Having the President and Vice President from opposing parties further increased political tensions. John Adams took office in March 1797 as the nation's second President. Events soon deepened the distrust between him and Jefferson.

★ ★ ★ Section 3 Assessment ★ ★ ★

Recall
1. **Identify** Explain the significance of (a) Democratic Republican, (b) Federalist.
2. **Define** (a) faction, (b) unconstitutional.

Comprehension
3. What reasons did Americans have to distrust political parties?
4. List two issues on which Thomas Jefferson and Alexander Hamilton disagreed and describe their points of view.
5. Explain why political parties emerged in the 1790s.
6. What role did political parties play in the election of 1796?

Critical Thinking and Writing
7. **Exploring the Main Idea** Review the Main Idea statement at the beginning of this section. Then, write a letter to the editor supporting either the Republicans or the Federalists in the election of 1796.
8. **Supporting a Point of View** Whose political ideas do you favor, Jefferson's or Hamilton's? Explain your answer.

ACTIVITY

Writing Newspaper Headlines You are the publisher of either the *Gazette of the United States* or the *National Gazette.* Write three headlines about the election of 1796. Be sure that your headlines express the point of view of your newspaper.

4 The Second President

Prepare to Read

Objectives

In this section, you will
- Summarize how John Adams handled the conflict with France.
- Explain why the Federalist party split.
- Describe how the Alien and Sedition acts raised the issue of the rights of states.
- Identify the role Congress played in the election of 1800.

Key Terms

XYZ Affair

frigate

Alien and Sedition acts

sedition

nullify

Kentucky and Virginia resolutions

states' rights

Target Reading Skill

Sequence As you read, complete this table describing the major events of John Adams's presidency. Add as many rows as needed to complete the table.

CONFLICT WITH FRANCE	ALIEN AND SEDITION ACTS	ELECTION OF 1800
• French seize U.S. ships	•	•

Main Idea As President, John Adams pursued policies that made the Federalists increasingly unpopular.

Setting the Scene John Adams was very different from George Washington. Washington was tall and dignified. Adams was short and a bit pudgy. Washington spoke little and chose his words carefully. Adams was outspoken. He said what he believed, and he held strong beliefs. Jefferson recalled how Adams sometimes became so angry during an argument that he ended up "dashing and trampling his wig on the floor."

Despite his temper, Adams was an honest and able leader. As President, he tried to act in the best interests of the nation, even when he knew his actions could hurt him politically. More than once, Adams stood up to public opinion or the leaders of his party.

Adams as President

Conflict With France

No sooner had Adams taken office than he faced a crisis with France. The French objected to Jay's Treaty because they felt that it favored Britain. In 1797, French ships began to seize American ships in the West Indies, as the British had done.

Once again, Americans called for war, this time against France. To avoid war, Adams sent diplomats to Paris to discuss the rights of neutral nations.

The French foreign minister, Charles Maurice de Talleyrand, did not deal directly with the Americans. Instead, he sent three agents to offer the Americans a deal. Before Talleyrand would even begin talks, the agents said, he wanted $250,000 for himself and a $10 million loan to France. "Not a sixpence!" replied one of the Americans angrily.

The diplomats informed Adams about the offer. He then told Congress. Adams did not reveal the names of the French agents, referring to them only as X, Y, and Z.

The XYZ Affair
The French demand for tribute outraged Americans. In the cartoon, a five-headed monster demands a bribe from three Americans. They respond: "Cease bawling, Monster. We will not give you sixpence!"

1. **Comprehension**
   (a) Who does the monster represent? **(b)** Who are the three people at left?

2. **Understanding Main Ideas** How does the cartoonist show that the XYZ Affair stirred strong feelings?

3. **Critical Thinking Identifying Points of View** What details in the cartoon show the cartoonist's dislike of the French Revolution?

Civics

Many Americans were outraged when they heard about the XYZ Affair in 1798. They took up the slogan, "Millions for defense, but not one cent for tribute!" They were willing to spend money to defend their country, but they would not pay a bribe to another nation.

The XYZ Affair ignited war fever in the United States. Despite strong pressure, Adams refused to ask Congress to declare war on France. Like Washington, he wanted to keep the country out of European affairs. However, he could not ignore French attacks on American ships, so he strengthened the navy by building frigates, fast-sailing ships with many guns. That move helped convince France to stop attacking American ships.

The Federalist Party Splits

Led by Hamilton, many Federalists criticized Adams. They hoped a war would weaken the Republicans, who supported France. War would also force the nation to build its military forces. A strong military would increase federal power, a key Federalist goal.

Although Adams was a Federalist, he resisted Hamilton's pressure for war. Their disagreement created a split in the Federalist party.

Over Hamilton's opposition, Adams again sent diplomats to France. When they arrived, they found an ambitious young army officer, Napoleon Bonaparte, in charge. Napoleon was planning for war against several European powers. Thus, he had no time for a war with the United States. He signed an agreement to stop seizing American ships.

Like Washington, Adams kept the nation out of war. His success, however, cost him the support of many Federalists and weakened the party for the election of 1800.

Alien and Sedition Acts

In 1798, during the crisis with France, Federalists pushed several laws through Congress. These laws were known as the Alien and Sedition acts.

Under the Alien Act, the President could expel any alien, or foreigner, thought to be dangerous to the country. Another law made it harder for immigrants to become citizens. Before 1798, white immigrants could become citizens after living in the United States for five years. The new law made immigrants wait 14 years. The Federalists passed this act because many recent immigrants supported Jefferson and the Republicans. The act would keep these immigrants from voting for years.

Republicans grew even angrier when Congress passed the Sedition Act. Sedition means stirring up rebellion against a government. Under this law, citizens could be fined or jailed if they criticized the government or its officials. In fact, several Republican newspaper editors, and even members of Congress, were fined and jailed for expressing their opinions.

Republicans protested that the Sedition Act violated the Constitution. The First Amendment, they argued, protected freedom of speech and of the press. Jefferson warned that the new laws threatened American liberties:

> **❝** They have brought into the lower house a sedition bill, which . . . undertakes to make printing certain matters criminal . . . Indeed this bill & the alien bill both are so [against] the Constitution as to show they mean to pay no respect to it. **❞**
>
> —*The Writings of Thomas Jefferson*, 1798

The Rights of States

Vice President Jefferson bitterly opposed the Alien and Sedition acts. He could not ask the courts for help because the Federalists controlled them. So, he urged the states to take strong action against the acts. He argued that the states had the right to nullify, or cancel, a law passed by the federal government. In this way, states could resist the power of the federal government.

With help from Jefferson and Madison, Kentucky and Virginia passed resolutions in 1798 and 1799. The Kentucky and Virginia resolutions claimed that each state "has an equal right to judge for itself" whether a law is constitutional. If a state decides a law is unconstitutional, said the resolutions, it has the power to nullify that law within its borders.

The Kentucky and Virginia resolutions raised the issue of states' rights. Did the federal government have only those powers that were listed in the Constitution? If so, the states possessed all other powers—for example, the power to declare a federal law unconstitutional? Within a few years, the Alien and Sedition acts were changed or dropped. Still, the issue of a state's right to nullify federal laws would come up again.

Identify Sequence
Target Skill What events resulted from the Alien and Sedition acts? Add this information to your chart.

Primary Source

The Virginia Resolution

The Virginia Resolution was a protest against the Alien and Sedition acts passed by Congress: "[Virginia protests] against the . . . alarming infractions of the Constitution, . . . the first of which exercises a power no where delegated to the federal government, . . . and the other of which acts, exercises in like manner, a power which . . . [violates] that right of freely examining public characters and measures, and of free communication among the people . . . which has ever been justly deemed, the only [effective] guardian of every other right."

Analyzing Primary Sources
What right is "the only [effective] guardian of every other right"?

Election of 1800

By 1800, the war cry against France was fading. As the election neared, Republicans focused on two issues. First, they attacked the Federalists for raising taxes to prepare for war. Second, they opposed the unpopular Alien and Sedition acts.

Republicans backed Thomas Jefferson for President and Aaron Burr for Vice President. Despite the bitter split in the Federalist party, John Adams was again named its candidate.

Deadlock In the race for the presidency, Republicans won the popular vote. However, when the electoral college voted, Jefferson and Burr each received 73 votes. At the time, the electoral college did not vote separately for President and Vice President. Each Republican elector cast one vote for Jefferson and one vote for Burr.

Under the Constitution, if no candidate wins the electoral vote, the House of Representatives decides the election. Only after four days and 36 votes was the tie finally broken. The House chose Jefferson as President. Burr became Vice President.

Soon after, Congress passed the Twelfth Amendment. It required electors to vote separately for President and Vice President. The states ratified the amendment in 1804.

The election of 1800 set an important precedent. From then until today, power has passed peacefully from one party to another.

The Federalist Era Ends After 1800, the Federalist party slowly declined. Federalists won fewer seats in Congress. In 1804, the party was greatly weakened after its leader, Alexander Hamilton, was killed in a duel with Aaron Burr. Despite its early decline, the Federalist party did help shape the new nation. Even Republican Presidents kept most of Hamilton's economic programs.

★ ★ ★ Section 4 Assessment ★ ★ ★

Recall
1. **Identify** Explain the significance of (a) XYZ Affair, (b) Alien and Sedition acts, (c) Kentucky and Virginia resolutions.
2. **Define** (a) frigate, (b) sedition, (c) nullify, (d) states' rights.

Comprehension
3. How did President Adams deal with the French seizure of American ships?
4. Why did Adams lose the support of many Federalists?
5. Why did Thomas Jefferson and the Republicans oppose the Alien and Sedition acts?

6. Why did Congress have to settle the election of 1800?

Critical Thinking and Writing
7. **Finding the Main Idea** Review the Main Idea statement at the beginning of this section. Then, write a paragraph explaining why the Federalists lost popular support during Adams's presidency.
8. **Applying Information** How did the Kentucky and Virginia resolutions reflect Jefferson's view of government?

As you study history, you are constantly interpreting what you read. Sometimes, you make *inferences*. This involves adding what you already know to ideas that are implied but not directly stated in the text. By making inferences, you can more fully understand what you read and can analyze different points of view.

Read this passage comparing John Adams with George Washington:

George Washington and John Adams were a study in contrasts. Washington was tall and dignified, and because he was a general, his officers addressed him as "Excellency." Adams was short and a bit pudgy. His rivals referred to him as "His Rotundity."

Washington spoke little and chose his words carefully, but John Adams could never do the same. He said what he believed, and he held strong beliefs. At times, his anger led him to trample his wig on the floor. Still, Adams was an honest and able leader who always tried to act in the nation's best interests.

Learn the Skill *To make inferences, use the following steps:*

1. **Identify main ideas.** What is the main point being made in the passage?

2. **Note stated facts and opinions.** What information is directly stated?

3. **Identify unstated ideas.** What ideas or information are suggested but not directly stated in the passage?

4. **Add what you know.** What details can you fill in from your own knowledge or experience to make inferences about the text?

5. **Identify the point of view.** Based on the inferences you made, what does the writer or speaker feel or believe about this topic?

Practice the Skill *Answer the following questions about the passage above:*

1. **(a)** How did his officers address Washington? **(b)** What did the rivals of Adams call him?

2. **(a)** Find a sentence that directly states a fact. **(b)** Find a sentence that directly states an opinion.

3. What does the passage suggest about how Adams was viewed by others?

4. How could always speaking one's mind create problems for a President?

5. What does the writer infer about Adams's leadership qualities?

Apply the Skill *See the Chapter Review and Assessment.*

CHAPTER SUMMARY

Section 1
George Washington was America's first President. He faced many challenges, including how to organize the new government and build a strong economy.

Section 2
As the French Revolution and wars raged in Europe, President Washington steered a neutral course in foreign affairs. In his Farewell Address, Washington advised Americans to remain neutral.

Section 3
During the 1790s, two political parties were formed: the Federalists and the Republicans. Alexander Hamilton led the Federalists. Thomas Jefferson led the Republicans.

Section 4
As President, John Adams pursued policies that made the Federalists increasingly unpopular. Some of Adams's decisions split the Federalist party. In 1800, Thomas Jefferson was elected President.

For additional review and enrichment activities, see the interactive version of *The American Nation,* available on the Web and on CD-ROM.

Chapter Self-Test For practice test questions for Chapter 9, visit PHSchool.com, **Web Code mfa-0904.**

Building Vocabulary

Use the chapter vocabulary words listed below to create a crossword puzzle. Exchange puzzles with a classmate. Complete the puzzles, and then check each other's answers.

1. inauguration
2. precedent
3. bond
4. tariff
5. foreign policy
6. faction
7. unconstitutional
8. frigate
9. sedition
10. nullify

Reviewing Key Facts

11. Describe how the Judiciary Act provided the framework for the nation's court system. (Section 1)
12. What advice did George Washington give in his Farewell Address? (Section 2)
13. Name three differences between the Federalists and the Republicans. (Section 3)
14. How was the Sedition Act used to silence Republicans? (Section 4)

Critical Thinking and Writing

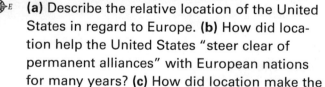

15. Connecting to Geography: **Location**
    (a) Describe the relative location of the United States in regard to Europe. **(b)** How did location help the United States "steer clear of permanent alliances" with European nations for many years? **(c)** How did location make the possession of a strong navy important to the United States?
16. **Summarizing** Summarize arguments for and against protective tariffs and a national banking system.
17. **Ranking (a)** List the disagreements that divided Jefferson and Hamilton. **(b)** In your opinion, which of these disagreements was the most serious? Explain.
18. **Analyzing Information** Write a paragraph explaining how the Twelfth Amendment helped prevent deadlocks like the one that took place in the election of 1800.

Read this passage from your textbook, and then answer the questions below:

> When George Washington took office in 1789, the United States had no political parties. . . . Early on, though, political disagreements divided Americans. "Men who have been [friends] all their lives," noted Jefferson, "cross streets to avoid meeting, and turn their heads another way, lest they should be obliged to touch their hats." Before Washington left office in 1797, two rival political parties had emerged. . . .

George Washington was the focus of attention when he arrived in New York in 1789 for his first inauguration.

19. In the painting, you can identify George Washington
  A. in the bow of the boat, tipping his hat.
  B. as the first person rowing the boat.
  C. on shore waiting to greet the boat.
  D. nearest the shelter on the boat.

20. The mood of the painting can be described as
  A. somber.   **C.** angry.
  B. joyful.   **D.** unpatriotic.

21. The author does not say why the men avoid meeting, but a reader can infer that
  A. the men have quarreled over finances.
  B. religion is starting to divide the nation.
  C. old wounds from the American Revolution are still open.
  D. the men support different political parties.

22. If the men were forced to meet, what do you think they would talk about? Explain your reasoning.

ACTIVITIES

Connecting With . . .
Government and Citizenship

Creating a Line Graph The chart below shows the change in the number of people serving in the navy. **(a)** Use the data to describe what happened to the United States Navy between 1798 and 1801. **(b)** Use the figures below to create a line graph.

YEAR	NUMBER OF PEOPLE
1798	1,856
1799	2,200
1800	5,400
1801	2,700

Source: *Historical Statistics of the United States*

Go Online
PHSchool.com

Connecting to Today

Making a Database Use the Internet to find information about the Federal Reserve Bank. Then, make a database that includes the main functions of the Federal Reserve Bank and the location of the 12 regional reserve banks. For help in starting this activity, visit PHSchool.com, **Web Code mfd-0905.**

History Through Literature

The Patriots
Sidney Kingsley

Introduction Sidney Kingsley was a leading American playwright of the first part of the twentieth century. Many of his plays dealt with serious social issues. His 1943 play, *The Patriots*, focuses on major problems facing the nation's first leaders. In this scene, Jefferson has just told Hamilton that he has accepted the position of secretary of state in President Washington's Cabinet.

Vocabulary Before you read the selection, find the meanings of these words in a dictionary: **in concert, chaos, galling, promissory, secede.**

Sidney Kingsley (1906–1995)

HAMILTON: My congratulations. We must work in concert.

JEFFERSON: I'm such a stranger here, I shall lean on you.

HAMILTON: No, I'm afraid—it's—I who need your help. [*Suddenly agitated, emotional*] Mr. Jefferson, it's enough to make any man who loves America want to cry. Forgive me! I really shouldn't burden you with this. It's a matter of my own department.

JEFFERSON: If I can be of any assistance . . . ?

HAMILTON: It's often been remarked that it's given to this country here to prove once and for all whether men can govern themselves by reason, or whether they must forever rely on the accident of tyranny. An interesting thought, Mr. Jefferson.

JEFFERSON: God, yes. We live in an era perhaps the most important in all history.

HAMILTON: An interesting thought! An awful thought! For if it is true, then we dare not fail.

JEFFERSON: No.

HAMILTON: But we are failing. The machinery is already breaking down. [*He snaps his fingers.*] We haven't that much foreign credit. The paper money issued by States is worthless. We are in financial chaos. [*He paces to and fro.*] The galling part is I have a remedy at hand. The solution is so simple. A nation's credit, like a merchant's, depends on paying its promissory notes in full. I propose to pay a hundred cents on the dollar for all the paper money issued by the States. Our credit would be restored instantaneously.

JEFFERSON: [*Worried*] Mr. Madison spoke to me very briefly of your bill last night. It seems there's been some speculation in this paper, and he fears . . .

HAMILTON: Madison! I loved that man. I thought so high of that man. I swear I wouldn't have taken this office—except I counted on his support. And now, he's turned against me.

JEFFERSON: Mr. Madison has a good opinion of your talents. But this speculation . . .

HAMILTON: I don't want his good opinion. I want his support. Will you use your influence?

JEFFERSON: You understand I've been away six years. I've gotten out of touch here. I'll need time to study the facts.

HAMILTON: There is no time.

JEFFERSON: Well, three or four weeks.

HAMILTON: Three or four . . . ? For God's sake, man, can't you understand what I'm trying to tell you? The North is about to secede!

JEFFERSON: Secede?

HAMILTON: Hasn't the President told you?

JEFFERSON: No.

HAMILTON: Unless my bill is passed there is every prospect the Union will dissolve.

JEFFERSON: I'm aware there's a great deal of tension here, but . . .

HAMILTON: Walk in on a session of Congress tomorrow.

JEFFERSON: I see evils on both sides. [*A long pause*] However, it seems to me—if the Union is at stake—reasonable men sitting about a table discussing this coolly should arrive at some compromise. [*He comes to a sudden decision.*] Have dinner with me tomorrow night.

HAMILTON: Delighted.

JEFFERSON: I'll invite a friend or two.

HAMILTON: Mr. Madison?

JEFFERSON: I can't promise anything. He's bitterly opposed to your plan.

HAMILTON: I have a way to sweeten the pill. The cost of living in New York has become so unreasonable there's talk of moving the capital.

JEFFERSON: Yes.

HAMILTON: It's already been promised temporarily to Philadelphia. Give me my bill and I can promise Madison the nation's capital will go to the South. Permanently. I was born in the West Indies—I have no local preference. However, for the sake of the Great Man, I'd like to see it go to Virginia.

JEFFERSON: [*Pause*] Well, I'll bring you together, and sit at the table to see you don't shoot each other.

Hamilton and Jefferson in a 1943 production of *The Patriots*

HAMILTON: [*Laughs*] Fair enough.

JEFFERSON [*Takes out his fan-shaped notebook, jots down the appointment*] You see, Colonel Hamilton, we must never permit ourselves to despair of the republic.

HAMILTON: My dear Jefferson, if I haven't despaired of this republic till now, it's because of my nature, not my judgment. [JEFFERSON *laughs.*]

Analyzing Literature

1. When Hamilton asks whether men "must forever rely on the accident of tyranny," he is referring to
  A breaking the traditions of the Roman Republic.
  B relying on rule by a hereditary monarch.
  C relying on accidents and assassination to replace unpopular government leaders.
  D a new emphasis on frontier democracy.

2. When Hamilton says "for the sake of the Great Man," he is referring to
  A George Washington.
  B King George III.
  C Thomas Jefferson.
  D James Madison.

3. Critical Thinking and Writing Making Predictions **(a)** Based on your reading of Chapter 9, what do you think will happen to the proposal to build the new nation's capital? **(b)** What do you think will happen to the working relationship between Hamilton and Jefferson?

CHAPTER 10

The Age of Jefferson

1801–1816

1 A Republican Takes Office
2 The Louisiana Purchase
3 New Threats From Overseas
4 The Road to War
5 The War of 1812

Lewis and Clark with Native American translator Sacagawea

Thomas Jefferson

1801

Thomas Jefferson becomes President. Jefferson seeks to reduce the power of the federal government.

1803

The United States purchases Louisiana from France. The next year, Jefferson sends Lewis and Clark to explore the Louisiana Purchase.

1807

The Embargo Act halts American overseas trade.

AMERICAN EVENTS

Presidential Terms:

Thomas Jefferson 1801–1809

1800   1804   1808

WORLD EVENTS

1804 ▲
Haiti declares independence from France.

▲ 1805
British and French navies clash at the Battle of Trafalgar.

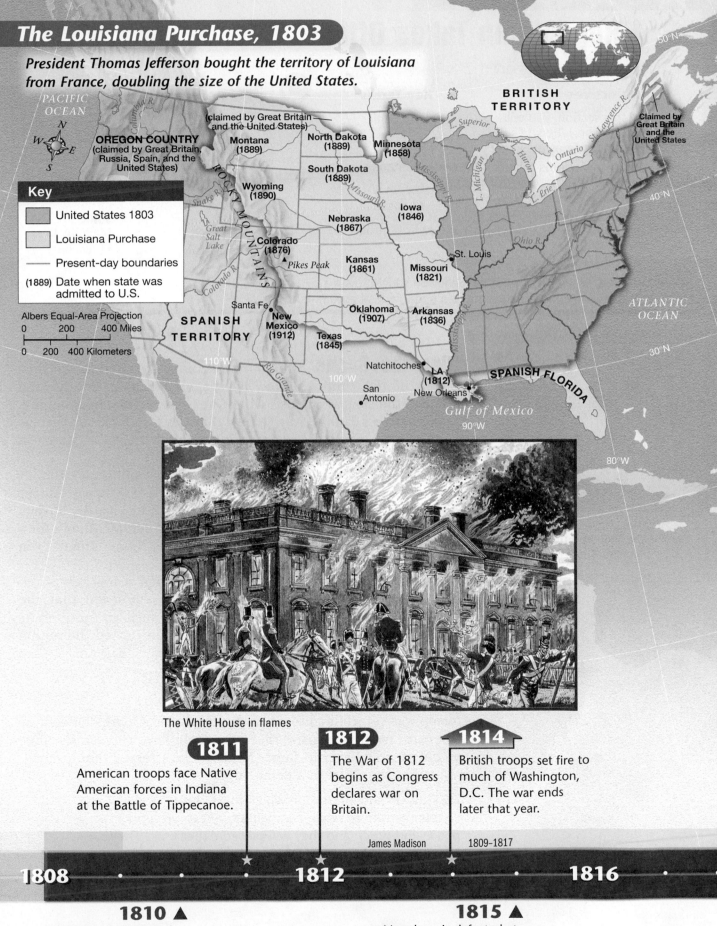

The Louisiana Purchase, 1803

President Thomas Jefferson bought the territory of Louisiana from France, doubling the size of the United States.

BRITISH TERRITORY

Claimed by Great Britain and the United States

PACIFIC OCEAN

(claimed by Great Britain and the United States)

OREGON COUNTRY
(claimed by Great Britain, Russia, Spain, and the United States)

Montana (1889)

North Dakota (1889)

Minnesota (1858)

South Dakota (1889)

Wyoming (1890)

Nebraska (1867)

Iowa (1846)

St. Louis

Colorado (1876)

Pikes Peak

Kansas (1861)

Missouri (1821)

Great Salt Lake

Santa Fe

New Mexico (1912)

Oklahoma (1907)

Arkansas (1836)

SPANISH TERRITORY

Texas (1845)

Natchitoches

LA (1812)

SPANISH FLORIDA

San Antonio

New Orleans

Gulf of Mexico

ATLANTIC OCEAN

Key

United States 1803

Louisiana Purchase

——— Present-day boundaries

(1889) Date when state was admitted to U.S.

Albers Equal-Area Projection

0   200   400 Miles

0   200   400 Kilometers

The White House in flames

1811
American troops face Native American forces in Indiana at the Battle of Tippecanoe.

1812
The War of 1812 begins as Congress declares war on Britain.

1814
British troops set fire to much of Washington, D.C. The war ends later that year.

James Madison   1809–1817

1808 · · · **1812** · · **1816** ·

1810 ▲
Mexico declares independence from Spain.

1815 ▲
Napoleon is defeated at the Battle of Waterloo.

1 A Republican Takes Office

Prepare to Read

Objectives

In this section, you will
- Describe Jefferson's democratic style as president.
- List the actions Jefferson took to reduce the power of the federal government.
- Explain how Chief Justice John Marshall strengthened the Supreme Court.

Key Terms

democratic

laissez faire

free market

Marbury v. *Madison*

judicial review

Target Reading Skill

Comparison and Contrast Copy this incomplete Venn diagram. As you read, fill in key facts about Thomas Jefferson and John Marshall. Write common characteristics in the overlapping section.

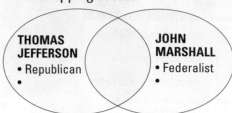

THOMAS JEFFERSON
- Republican
-

JOHN MARSHALL
- Federalist
-

Main Idea As President, Thomas Jefferson sought to set a democratic tone and to reduce the role of the federal government.

Banner celebrating Jefferson's inauguration

Setting the Scene The morning Thomas Jefferson became President of the United States, he ate breakfast at Conrad and McMunn's, the boardinghouse where he was staying. Washington, D.C., the nation's capital, was so new that the Capitol Building was still unfinished. Even so, Congress assembled there on March 4, 1801, to witness Jefferson's inauguration.

Jefferson wanted his inauguration to be simple, not showy. Rather than riding in a carriage to the Capitol, he walked. The new President gave a speech at the ceremony, but in a voice so low, hardly anyone could hear him. Then, he walked back to Conrad and McMunn's for a quiet dinner. When he entered, only one of his fellow diners even bothered to stand and offer Jefferson a chair.

Jefferson deliberately made his inauguration a low-key affair. Although he came from a wealthy family, he believed that the nation's strength came from ordinary people, such as farmers. As President, he rejected most Federalist ideas and turned the nation in a new direction.

Jefferson's Democratic Style

Jefferson was determined to make the government more democratic. **Democratic** means ensuring that all people have the same rights. Years before, in a letter to James Madison, he stressed that each citizen should play a part in a democracy:

> 66 Educate and inform the whole mass of the people. Enable them to see that it is their interest to preserve peace and order, and they will preserve them. . . . They are the only [ones to rely on] for the preservation of our liberty. 99
>
> —Thomas Jefferson, letter to James Madison, 1787

Jefferson's personal style matched his democratic beliefs. The new President preferred quiet dinners to the formal parties that George Washington and John Adams had given. He wore casual clothes and greeted people by shaking hands instead of bowing. With his informal manner, Jefferson showed that the President was an ordinary citizen.

Some Federalists were worried about Jefferson's democratic beliefs. They knew that he supported the French Revolution and they feared that he might bring revolutionary change to the United States. They were also afraid that he might punish Federalists who had used the Alien and Sedition acts to jail Republicans.

In his inaugural address, Jefferson tried to calm Federalists' fears. He promised that, although the Republicans were in the majority, he would not treat the Federalists harshly. "The minority possess their equal rights, which equal laws must protect," he told the nation. He called for an end to the political disputes of the past few years. "We are all Republicans, we are all Federalists," the President concluded.

A Smaller Role for the Federal Government

Jefferson had no plan to punish Federalists. He did, however, want to change their policies. In his view, the Federalists had made the national government too large and too powerful.

New Economic Policies One way Jefferson wanted to lessen government power was by reducing the federal budget. Such budget cuts would also keep the federal debt low. His Secretary of the Treasury, Albert Gallatin (GAHL uh tin), helped him achieve this goal. A financial wizard, Gallatin reduced government spending through careful management.

Jefferson believed in an economic idea known as **laissez faire** (lehs ay FAYR), a French term meaning "let alone." The idea of laissez faire was promoted by the Scottish economist Adam Smith. In his book *The Wealth of Nations*, Smith argued in favor of a **free market** where goods and services are exchanged with little regulation. Free competition, Smith said, would benefit everyone, not just the wealthy.

Laissez faire economists believed that government should play as small a role as possible in economic affairs. Laissez faire was very different from the Federalist idea of government. Alexander Hamilton, you recall, wanted government to promote trade and manufacturing.

Goals and Policies of Jefferson

Policies
- Tries to cut federal budget and reduce federal debt
- Promotes laissez-faire policies in economic affairs
- Decreases the size of government departments
- Reduces the size of the army and navy
- Asks Congress to repeal the whiskey tax

GOAL
Reduce size of government

Reconcile party differences

Policies
- Retains the Bank of the United States
- Continues to pay off state debts using federal moneys
- Allows many Federalists to keep their government jobs

GRAPHIC ORGANIZER
Skills

Jefferson set the nation in a new direction, but kept some existing policies.

1. **Comprehension** Identify two ways Jefferson continued Federalist policies.

2. **Critical Thinking Linking Past and Present** Which of the goals and policies shown here might still be issues today? Why?

A Less Active Government Jefferson believed that the government should protect the rights of its citizens. Beyond that, he wanted the federal government to take a less active role in governing the nation. He decreased the size of government departments and cut the federal budget. With the approval of Congress, he reduced the size of the army and navy. He also asked Congress to repeal the unpopular whiskey tax.

The Sedition Act expired the day before Jefferson took office. Jefferson hated the law, and he pardoned those who were in jail because of it. He also asked Congress to restore the law allowing foreign-born people to become citizens after only a five-year waiting period.

Federalist Policies Remain Jefferson did not discard all Federalist programs. On the advice of Albert Gallatin, he kept the Bank of the United States. The federal government also continued to pay off state debts, which it had taken over while Washington was President. In addition, Jefferson let many Federalists keep their government jobs.

Compare and Contrast

How was John Marshall different from Thomas Jefferson? What did they have in common? Add these observations to your Venn diagram.

Strengthening the Supreme Court

The election of 1800 gave Republicans control of Congress. Federalists, however, remained powerful in the courts.

Several months passed between Jefferson's election and his inauguration. In that time, Federalists in the old Congress passed a law increasing the number of federal judges. President Adams then appointed Federalists to fill these new judicial positions.

One of the judges that Adams appointed was John Marshall, the Chief Justice of the Supreme Court. Like Jefferson, Marshall was a rich Virginia planter with a brilliant mind. Unlike Jefferson, however, Marshall was a staunch Federalist. He wanted to make the federal government stronger.

The framers of the Constitution expected the courts to balance the powers of the President and Congress. However, John Marshall found the courts to be much weaker than the other branches of government. In his view, it was not clear what powers the federal courts had.

Marbury v. Madison In 1803, Marshall decided a case that increased the power of the Supreme Court. The case involved William Marbury, one of the judges appointed by Adams. Adams made the appointment on his last night as President. The Republicans refused to accept this "midnight judge." They accused Federalists of using unfair tactics to keep control of the courts. Jefferson ordered Secretary of State James Madison not to deliver the official papers confirming Marbury's appointment.

Marbury sued Madison. According to the Judiciary Act of 1789, only the Supreme Court could decide a case that was brought against a federal official. Therefore, the case of *Marbury* v. *Madison* was tried before the Supreme Court.

An Important Precedent The Supreme Court ruled against Marbury. Chief Justice Marshall wrote the decision, stating that the Judiciary Act was unconstitutional. The Constitution, Marshall argued, did not give the Supreme Court the right to decide cases brought against federal officials. Therefore, Congress could not give the Court that power simply by passing the Judiciary Act.

The Supreme Court's decision in *Marbury* v. *Madison* set an important precedent. It gave the Supreme Court the power to decide whether laws passed by Congress were constitutional and to reject laws that it considered to be unconstitutional. This power of the Court is called **judicial review.**

Jefferson was displeased with the decision. True, Marshall had ruled against Marbury, the Federalist judge. But Marshall's decision gave more power to the Supreme Court, where Federalists were still strong. Jefferson also argued that the decision upset the balance of power among the three branches of government:

> **66** The opinion which gives to the judges the right to decide what laws are constitutional and what not, not only for themselves . . . but for the Legislature and Executive also . . . would make the Judiciary a [tyrannical] branch. **99**
>
> —Thomas Jefferson, letter to Abigail Adams, 1804

In the end, the President and Congress accepted the right of the Court to overturn laws. Today, judicial review remains one of the most important powers of the Supreme Court.

Connecting to Today

The Supreme Court

Under the strong hand of John Marshall, the Supreme Court increased its power. Today, as in Marshall's time, the justices base their decisions on the Constitution, as well as on past decisions. They may overturn a law because it violates the Constitution. They may reverse decisions by lower courts that did not apply the Constitution correctly.

Today, the Court faces questions that Marshall could not have imagined. How does freedom of speech apply to the Internet? Can members of a school athletic team be required to submit to random drug tests? Can a state government release information contained in a driver's license? Such decisions reach into the lives of every American.

Why do Supreme Court decisions have a wider effect than decisions by state courts?

★ ★ ★ Section 1 Assessment ★ ★ ★

Recall

1. **Identify** Explain the significance of **(a)** Albert Gallatin, **(b)** John Marshall, **(c)** *Marbury* v. *Madison.*
2. **Define** **(a)** democratic, **(b)** laissez faire, **(c)** free market, **(d)** judicial review.

Comprehension

3. **(a)** How did Jefferson's actions as President reflect his democratic beliefs? **(b)** Why did his beliefs worry Federalists?
4. Describe three steps that Jefferson took to reduce the power of the federal government.

5. What important precedent did John Marshall set in the case of *Marbury* v. *Madison*?

Critical Thinking and Writing

6. **Exploring the Main Idea** Review the Main Idea statement at the beginning of this section. Then, write an outline for a speech Jefferson might have given to explain his goals.
7. **Supporting a Point of View** Write a paragraph explaining whether or not you think judicial review upsets the balance of power in the government.

ACTIVITY

Go Online PHSchool.com

Connecting to Today
Use the Internet to find out about a current law that affects the goods Americans buy. Summarize the law, and explain what a laissez faire economist would think of it. For help in completing the activity, visit PHSchool.com, **Web Code mfd-1001.**

2 The Louisiana Purchase

Prepare to Read

Objectives

In this section, you will
- Explain why control of the Mississippi River was important to the United States.
- Describe how the United States purchased Louisiana.
- List the results of the explorations of Lewis and Clark and of Zebulon Pike.

Key Terms

Pinckney Treaty

Louisiana Purchase

expedition

continental divide

Target Reading Skill

Sequence Copy this flow-chart. As you read, fill in the boxes with events that led up to the Lewis and Clark expedition. Two boxes have been completed to help you get started. Add as many boxes as you need.

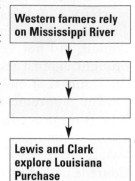

Western farmers rely on Mississippi River

↓

↓

↓

Lewis and Clark explore Louisiana Purchase

Main Idea In 1803, the United States purchased the territory of Louisiana from France, doubling the size of the nation.

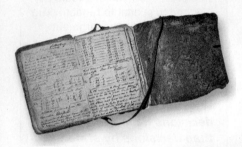

William Clark's journal

Setting the Scene In Jefferson's day, riders of the "post" usually traveled on horseback, carrying mail in saddlebags. But the parcels arriving at the White House this particular day must have required a whole cart. Jefferson eagerly opened package after package, to find a remarkable assortment of goods.

The smaller items included more than a hundred plants, a tin box full of insects, and mineral specimens. Skeletons of pronghorned antelope and the horns of a mountain ram took up more room. There was even live cargo—a prairie dog and a magpie!

Almost two years earlier, the United States had purchased from France vast lands west of the Mississippi River. Jefferson then sent Meriwether Lewis and William Clark to explore the territory. The President carefully examined their reports and packages, and later read their detailed journals. All this evidence confirmed Jefferson's belief that the new lands were a valuable addition to the nation.

Control of the Mississippi

By 1800, almost one million Americans lived between the Appalachian Mountains and the Mississippi River. Most were farmers. With few roads west of the Appalachians, western farmers relied on the Mississippi to ship their wheat and corn. First, they sent their produce down the river to the city of New Orleans. From there, ocean-going ships carried the produce to ports along the Atlantic coast.

Spain, which controlled New Orleans, sometimes threatened to close the port to Americans. In 1795, President Washington sent Thomas Pinckney to find a way to keep the vital port open. In the **Pinckney Treaty,** Spain agreed to let Americans ship their goods down the Mississippi and store them in New Orleans.

For a time, Americans shipped their goods through New Orleans peacefully. In 1800, however, Spain signed a treaty giving Louisiana back to France. President Jefferson was alarmed. He knew that the

Identify Sequence
When did the United States and Spain sign the Pinckney Treaty? What happened in 1800 to change the terms of the treaty? Add these events to your flowchart.

French ruler, Napoleon Bonaparte, had already set out to conquer Europe. Would he now try to build an empire in North America?

Jefferson had reason to worry. Napoleon wanted to grow food in Louisiana and ship it to French islands in the West Indies. However, events in Haiti, a French colony in the Caribbean, soon ruined Napoleon's plan. Inspired by the French Revolution, enslaved Africans in Haiti decided to fight for their liberty. Toussaint L'Ouverture (too SAN loo vehr TYOOR) led the revolt. By 1801, Toussaint and his followers had nearly forced the French out of Haiti.

Napoleon sent troops to retake Haiti. Although the French captured Toussaint, they did not regain control of the island. In 1804, Haitians declared their independence.

The United States Buys Louisiana

Meanwhile, Jefferson decided to try to buy New Orleans. He wanted to be sure that American farmers would always be able to ship their goods through the port. The President sent Robert Livingston and James Monroe to buy New Orleans and West Florida from Napoleon. Jefferson said they could offer as much as $10 million.

A Surprise Offer Livingston and Monroe negotiated with Talleyrand, the French foreign minister. At first, Talleyrand showed little interest in their offer. However, losing Haiti caused Napoleon to give up his plan for an empire in the Americas. He also needed money to pay for his costly wars in Europe. Suddenly, Talleyrand asked Livingston if the United States wanted to buy all of Louisiana, not just New Orleans.

The question surprised Livingston. He offered $4 million. "Too low," replied Talleyrand. "Reflect and see me tomorrow."

Livingston and Monroe carefully debated the matter. They had no authority to buy all of Louisiana. However, they knew that Jefferson wanted control of the Mississippi. They agreed to pay the French $15 million for Louisiana. "This is the noblest work of our whole lives," declared Livingston when he signed the treaty. "From this day the United States take their place among the powers of the first rank."

Was the Purchase Constitutional? Jefferson hailed the news from France. Still, he was not sure whether the President had the power to purchase Louisiana. He had always insisted that the federal government had only those powers spelled out in the Constitution. The document said nothing about a President having the power to buy land.

Viewing History

Celebrating the Louisiana Purchase This painting depicts a ceremony held in New Orleans on December 20, 1803. The French flag has been lowered and the American flag is being raised. **Evaluating Information** *What would you need to know to decide if this painting is accurate?*

Exploring the West, 1804–1807

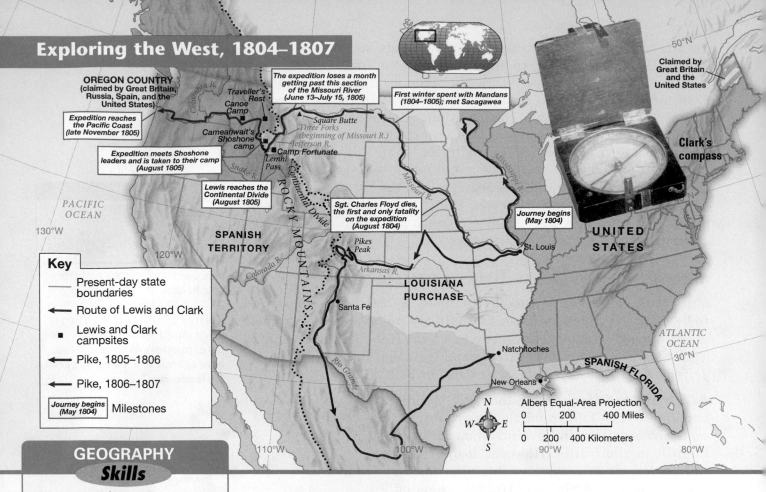

Key

— Present-day state boundaries

◄— Route of Lewis and Clark

■ Lewis and Clark campsites

◄— Pike, 1805–1806

◄— Pike, 1806–1807

| Journey begins (May 1804) | Milestones |

OREGON COUNTRY (claimed by Great Britain, Russia, Spain, and the United States)

Expedition reaches the Pacific Coast (late November 1805)

Expedition meets Shoshone leaders and is taken to their camp (August 1805)

Lewis reaches the Continental Divide (August 1805)

Traveller's Rest Canoe Camp

Cameahwait's Shoshone camp

Lemhi Pass

Camp Fortunate

The expedition loses a month getting past this section of the Missouri River (June 13–July 15, 1805)

Square Butte

Three Forks (beginning of Missouri R.)

Jefferson R.

First winter spent with Mandans (1804–1805); met Sacagawea

Sgt. Charles Floyd dies, the first and only fatality on the expedition (August 1804)

Journey begins (May 1804)

St. Louis

UNITED STATES

Clark's compass

Claimed by Great Britain and the United States

PACIFIC OCEAN

ROCKY MOUNTAINS

Continental Divide

Snake R.

Columbia R.

Missouri R.

Mississippi R.

SPANISH TERRITORY

Pikes Peak

Colorado R.

Arkansas R.

LOUISIANA PURCHASE

Santa Fe

Rio Grande

Natchitoches

New Orleans

SPANISH FLORIDA

ATLANTIC OCEAN

Albers Equal-Area Projection

0   200   400 Miles

0   200   400 Kilometers

130°W, 120°W, 110°W, 100°W, 90°W, 80°W, 50°N, 30°N

GEOGRAPHY Skills

The explorations of Lewis and Clark and of Zebulon Pike helped Americans learn more about the West.

1. **Location** On the map, locate **(a)** Louisiana Purchase, **(b)** Mississippi River, **(c)** St. Louis, **(d)** Rocky Mountains, **(e)** Pikes Peak.

2. **Movement** Along which rivers did Lewis and Clark travel in order to reach the Pacific Ocean?

3. **Critical Thinking Making Predictions** Based on this map, how might westward expansion lead to conflict with other nations?

In the end, Jefferson decided that he did have the authority to buy Louisiana. The Constitution, he reasoned, allowed the President to make treaties. At his request, the Senate approved the treaty, and the Louisiana Purchase went into effect. In 1803, the United States took control of the vast lands west of the Mississippi. With one stroke, the size of the nation had doubled.

Planning an Expedition Few Americans knew anything about the Louisiana territory. In 1803, Congress provided money for a team of explorers to study the new lands. Jefferson chose Meriwether Lewis, his private secretary, to head the expedition, or long voyage of exploration. Lewis asked William Clark to go with him.

Jefferson asked Lewis and Clark to map a route to the Pacific Ocean. He also told them to study the geography of the territory, including:

66 . . . climate as characterized by the thermometer, by the proportion of rainy, cloudy, and clear days, by lightning, hail, snow, ice . . . the dates at which particular plants put forth or lose their flower, or leaf, times of appearance of particular birds, reptiles or insects. 99

—Thomas Jefferson, letter to Meriwether Lewis, 1803

Jefferson also instructed Lewis and Clark to learn about the Indian nations who lived in the Louisiana Purchase. These Native Americans carried on a busy trade with English, French, and Spanish merchants. Jefferson hoped that the Indians might trade with American merchants instead. Therefore, he urged Lewis and Clark to tell the Indians of "our wish to be neighborly, friendly, and useful to them."

The Lewis and Clark Expedition

Dozens of adventurous young men eagerly competed to join the expedition. Lewis and Clark judged volunteers on the basis of their character, strength, hunting skills, and ability to survive in the wilderness. In the end, about 50 men made up the "Corps of Discovery." The party also included York, an enslaved African American who had been Clark's companion since boyhood.

In May 1804, Lewis and Clark started up the Missouri River from St. Louis. At first, the expedition's boats made slow progress against the Missouri's swift current. One night, the current tore away the riverbank where they were camping. The party had to scramble into the boats to avoid being swept downstream.

Across the Plains Lewis and Clark marveled at the broad, grassy plains that stretched "as far as the eye can reach." Everywhere, they saw "immense herds of buffalo, deer, elk, and antelope."

As they traveled across the plains, the expedition met people of various Indian nations. Lewis and Clark had brought many gifts for Native Americans. They carried "peace medals" stamped with the United States seal. They also brought mirrors, beads, knives, blankets, and thousands of sewing needles and fishhooks.

During the first winter, Lewis and Clark stayed with the Mandans in present-day North Dakota. The explorers planned to continue up the Missouri in the spring. However, they worried about how they would cross the steep Rocky Mountains.

Also staying with the Mandans was an Indian woman named Sacagawea (sahk uh guh WEE uh). Sacagawea belonged to the Shoshone (shoh SHOH nee) people, who lived in the Rockies. She and her French Canadian husband agreed to accompany Lewis and Clark as translators.

Over the Rockies In early spring, the party set out. In the foothills of the Rockies, the landscape and wildlife changed. Bighorn sheep ran along the high hills. The thorns of prickly pear cactus jabbed the explorers' moccasins. Once, a grizzly bear chased Lewis while he was exploring alone.

Finally, Lewis and Clark met some Shoshones. One of them was Sacagawea's brother, whom she had not seen for many years. Upon seeing her own people, wrote Clark, she began to "dance and show every mark of the most extravagant joy." The Shoshones supplied the expedition with food and horses. They also advised Lewis and Clark about the best route to take over the Rockies.

In the Rocky Mountains, Lewis and Clark crossed the Continental Divide. A **continental divide** is a mountain ridge that separates river systems flowing toward opposite sides of a continent. In North America, some rivers flow east from the Rockies into the Mississippi, which drains into the Gulf of Mexico. Other rivers flow west from the Rockies and empty into the Pacific Ocean.

An American Profile

Sacagawea 1790?–1812?

Sacagawea proved invaluable to the Lewis and Clark expedition. Because she knew about the healing qualities of plants and herbs, the expedition relied on her for medical help. The presence of Sacagawea and her baby showed Indians in the area that the party was friendly. As Clark noted, "a woman with a party of men is a token of peace." She helped win the needed gift of horses from her people, the Shoshone. After the journey was completed, Clark wrote that she "deserved a greater reward . . . than we had in our power to give her."

Why would the presence of a woman and baby be seen as a sign of peace?

To the Pacific After building canoes, Lewis and Clark's party floated toward the Columbia River into the Pacific Northwest. Finally, on November 7, 1805, Clark wrote in his journal, "Great joy in camp. We are in view of the ocean, this great Pacific Ocean which we have been so long anxious to see." Lewis and Clark had reached their goal.

The return trip to St. Louis took another year. In 1806, Americans celebrated the return of Lewis and Clark. The explorers brought back much useful information about the Louisiana Purchase.

Pike Explores the West

Before Lewis and Clark returned, another explorer set out from St. Louis. From 1805 to 1807, Zebulon Pike explored the upper Mississippi River, the Arkansas River, and parts of present-day Colorado and New Mexico. In November 1806, Pike viewed a mountain peak rising above the Colorado plains. Today, this mountain is known as Pikes Peak.

Continuing southward, Pike entered into Spanish territory. Spanish troops soon arrested Pike and his men and took them into Mexico. The Americans were later escorted through Texas back into the United States. The Spanish took Pike's maps and journals, but he was able to hide one map in the barrel of his gun. His report on the expedition greatly expanded Americans' knowledge about the Southwest.

The journeys of Pike and Lewis and Clark excited Americans. However, settlers did not move into the rugged western lands for a number of years. As you will read, they first settled the region closest to the Mississippi River. Soon, the territory around New Orleans had a large enough population of American citizens for the settlers to apply for statehood. In 1812, this territory entered the Union as the state of Louisiana.

★ ★ ★ **Section 2 Assessment** ★ ★ ★

Recall

1. **Identify** Explain the significance of **(a)** Pinckney Treaty, **(b)** Napoleon Bonaparte, **(c)** Toussaint L'Ouverture, **(d)** Louisiana Purchase, **(e)** Lewis and Clark, **(f)** Sacagawea, **(g)** Zebulon Pike.
2. **Define** **(a)** expedition, **(b)** continental divide.

Comprehension

3. Why did Jefferson seek to control the Mississippi River?
4. Why did the French offer to sell Louisiana to the United States?

5. Identify two goals and one result of the Lewis and Clark expedition.

Critical Thinking and Writing

6. **Exploring the Main Idea** Review the Main Idea statement at the beginning of this section. Then, list three ways in which the United States might be different today if Jefferson had not bought Louisiana in 1803.
7. **Making Decisions** If you had been a Shoshone or Mandan leader, would you have decided to help Lewis and Clark? Explain your reasons.

ACTIVITY

Writing a Journal You are a member of Lewis and Clark's "Corps of Discovery." Write three journal entries describing what you feel as you explore the territory and meet the Native Americans who live there.

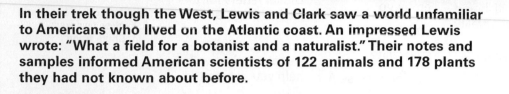

AMERICAN WILDLIFE

In their trek though the West, Lewis and Clark saw a world unfamiliar to Americans who lived on the Atlantic coast. An impressed Lewis wrote: "What a field for a botanist and a naturalist." Their notes and samples informed American scientists of 122 animals and 178 plants they had not known about before.

The only animals named for the explorers are this woodpecker (left) named for Lewis and this nutcracker (right) named for Clark.

At the expedition's winter quarters on the Pacific coast, Indians caught a 2-foot, 8-inch long coho salmon. Lewis sketched and described the fish in his journal.

In Nebraska, Lewis first saw these "barking squirrels." Another member of the expedition gave them the name they have today— prairie dogs.

ACTIVITY

With the class or in a small group, brainstorm a list of the wildlife native to your area. Choose one animal from the list. Prepare an entry for a visitor's guide describing that animal and how it reflects the local geography.

Native Americans had warned the explorers about the fierce grizzly bear. Lewis wrote that the explorers were "anxious to meet them." After being chased up a tree by a grizzly, Lewis wrote "I find the curiosity of our party is pretty well satisfied with respect to this animal."

3 New Threats From Overseas

Prepare to Read

Objectives

In this section, you will
- List the benefits and risks of overseas trade.
- Describe how the British and French violated the neutrality of American ships.
- Explain why Jefferson decided to impose an embargo.

Key Terms

tribute

impressment

embargo

Embargo Act

smuggling

Nonintercourse Act

Target Reading Skill

Clarifying Meaning As you read, prepare an outline of this section. Use roman numerals to indicate the major headings, capital letters for the subheadings, and numbers for the supporting details. The sample at right will help you get started.

> **I. Trading Around the World**
> A. Yankee traders
>   1. China trade
>   2.
> B.
>   1.
>   2.
> **II. American Neutrality Is Violated**
> A.
> B.

Main Idea As Great Britain went to war against France, both sides ignored the claim of the United States that American ships were neutral.

British seize American sailors

Setting the Scene It was along the coast of India that Jacob Nagle saw his chance to escape. An American sailor, Nagle had been forced to work on a British ship. He and three shipmates jumped into a small boat and rowed away as fast as they could.

The surf and wind made it difficult to reach shore before dark. Finally, Nagle and his mates rowed to another ship instead. Unfortunately, officers from their own ship were lying in wait. "Not suspecting, we asked for some water," Nagle later recalled:

> 66 The captain said if we would come up, he would give us some [drink]. . . . As soon as we got on the quarter deck they all surrounded us and the second mate clapped a pistol to my breast. 'If you move an inch, I will blow your brains out.' 99
>
> —Jacob Nagle, *The Nagle Journal: A Diary of the Life of Jacob Nagle, Sailor, From the Year 1775 to 1841*

In the early 1800s, the British navy forced thousands of American sailors to serve on their ships. This was only one of many dangers that Americans faced as their sea trade began to thrive.

Trading Around the World

After the Revolution, American overseas trade grew rapidly. Ships sailed from New England on voyages that sometimes lasted three years.

Yankee Traders Wherever they went, Yankee captains kept a sharp lookout for new goods and new markets. Clever traders sawed winter ice from New England ponds into blocks, packed it in sawdust, and carried it to India. There, they traded the ice for silk and spices. In 1784, the *Empress of China* became the first American ship to trade with China. New England merchants quickly built up a profitable China trade.

More than 10 years before Lewis and Clark, Yankee merchants sailed up the Pacific coast of North America. So many traders from Boston visited the Pacific Northwest that Indians there called every white man "Boston." Traders bought furs from Native Americans and sold them for large profits in China.

Conflict With the Barbary States Traders ran great risks, especially in the Mediterranean Sea. Pirates from the Barbary States, the nations along the coast of North Africa, attacked passing vessels. To protect American ships, the United States paid a yearly **tribute,** or **bribe,** to rulers of Barbary States such as Tripoli.

In 1801, Tripoli increased its demands. When Jefferson refused to pay, Tripoli declared war on the United States. Jefferson then ordered the navy to blockade the port of Tripoli.

During the blockade, the American ship *Philadelphia* ran aground near Tripoli. Pirates boarded the ship and hauled the crew off to prison. The pirates planned to use the *Philadelphia* to attack other ships. To prevent this, American naval officer Stephen Decatur and his crew quietly sailed into Tripoli harbor by night. They then set the captured American ship on fire.

In the meantime, American marines landed on the coast of North Africa. They marched 500 miles to launch a surprise attack on Tripoli. In 1805, the ruler of Tripoli signed a treaty promising not to interfere with American ships.

American Neutrality Is Violated

American ships faced another problem. Britain and France went to war again in 1803. At first, Americans profited from the conflict. British and French ships were too busy fighting to engage in trade. American merchants eagerly traded with both sides. As profits increased, Americans hurried to build new ships.

Neither Britain nor France wanted the United States to sell supplies to its enemy. As in the 1790s, they ignored American claims of neutrality. Napoleon seized American ships bound for England. At the same time, the British stopped Yankee traders on their way to France. Between 1805 and 1807, hundreds of American ships were captured.

Needing more sailors, the British navy stepped up **impressment,** the practice of forcing people into service. In Britain, impressment gangs raided English villages and took young men to serve in the navy. On the seas, British ships stopped American vessels, seizing any British sailors serving on American ships. Many American-born sailors were also impressed. Furious Americans clamored for war.

Viewing History

Trading in China

Chinese tea and fine dishes, or china, fetched high prices in the United States. Still, China permitted foreigners to trade in just a few ports, such as Canton (below). **Drawing Conclusions** *How would you describe the china shown here? Why do you think Americans were willing to pay high prices for such goods?*

Jefferson Tries an Embargo

Jefferson knew that the small American fleet was no match for the powerful British navy. Like Washington and Adams, he sought to avoid war.

A Total Ban Jefferson hoped that an American **embargo,** or ban on trade, would hurt France and Britain by cutting off needed supplies. "Our trade is the most powerful weapon we can use in our defense," one Republican newspaper wrote. In 1807, Jefferson persuaded Congress to impose a total embargo on foreign trade.

The **Embargo Act** did hurt Britain and France. But it hurt Americans even more. Supplies of imports such as sugar, tea, and molasses were cut off. Exports dropped by more than $80 million in one year. Docks in the South were piled high with cotton and tobacco. The Embargo Act hurt New England merchants most of all.

Merchants protested loudly against the embargo. Some turned to **smuggling,** importing or exporting goods in violation of trade laws. Jefferson began using the navy and federal troops to enforce the embargo. On the border between New York and Canada, some smugglers engaged in skirmishes with federal troops.

A Limited Ban In 1809, Jefferson admitted that the Embargo Act had failed. Congress replaced it with the milder **Nonintercourse Act.** It allowed Americans to carry on trade with all nations except Britain and France.

The embargo was the most unpopular measure of Jefferson's presidency. Still, Republicans remained strong. Following President Washington's precedent, Jefferson refused to run for a third term. Republican James Madison easily won the 1808 presidential election. Madison hoped that Britain and France would soon agree to respect American neutrality.

Summarize
Write two or three sentences explaining the purpose of the Embargo Act and its effects on Britain, France, and the United States. Add these details to your outline.

★ ★ ★ Section 3 Assessment ★ ★ ★

Recall

1. **Identify** Explain the significance of (a) *Empress of China,* (b) Stephen Decatur, (c) Embargo Act, (d) Nonintercourse Act.
2. **Define** (a) tribute, (b) impressment, (c) embargo, (d) smuggling.

Comprehension

3. How did increased overseas trade lead to conflict with the Barbary States?
4. Why did Britain and France begin to seize American ships after 1803?

5. (a) What was the goal of the Embargo Act? (b) Why did it fail?

Critical Thinking and Writing

6. **Exploring the Main Idea** Review the Main Idea statement at the beginning of this section. Then, list as many ways as you can think of that a war between two foreign powers can affect a neutral nation.
7. **Making Predictions** Write a paragraph explaining what you think President Madison might do if Britain and France continue to violate American neutrality.

Synthesizing Information

How did Jefferson's attempt to maintain American neutrality affect the nation's economy? As you learn about history, you will often use evidence from many types of sources. To get the most from these sources, you need to synthesize— that is, put different pieces of information together to form conclusions. To start this lesson, read the excerpt below and study the graph to the right.

A New Englander sent a letter to President Jefferson about the Embargo Act. It began with these words:

"You Infernal Villain:

How much longer are you going to keep this [cursed] Embargo on to starve us poor people? . . . One of my children has already starved to death of which I [am] ashamed and declared that it died of apoplexy. . . . I am a Federalist.**"**

—quoted in *A Diplomatic History of the American People* (Bailey)

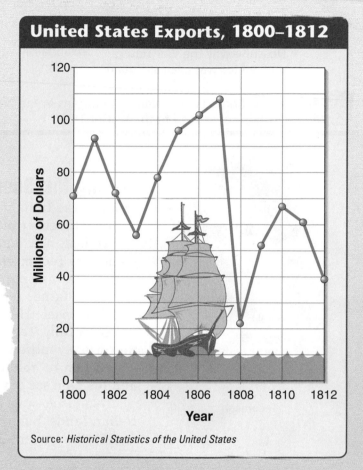

United States Exports, 1800–1812

Source: *Historical Statistics of the United States*

Learn the Skill *To synthesize information, use the following steps:*

1. **Identify the sources.** Knowing the background of a writer or the source of a graph helps you evaluate the information.

2. **Identify key facts and ideas.** What are the main points being made?

3. **Analyze the evidence.** Examine and compare the different kinds of evidence—graphs, pictures, text, primary sources—you are using.

4. **Draw conclusions.** Use the different pieces of evidence to form conclusions.

Practice the Skill *Use the letter, the graph, and what you have read in Section 3 to answer the following questions:*

1. **(a)** Who wrote the letter? **(b)** How did the writer feel about the embargo? **(c)** What is the source of the graph information?

2. **(a)** Restate the main point of the letter. **(b)** Describe the changes in the value of exports shown on the graph.

3. **(a)** Based on your reading, why did American exports fall sharply in 1807? **(b)** How does the graph explain the letter writer's point of view?

4. Based on the evidence, draw one conclusion about American trade in the early 1800s.

Apply the Skill *See the Chapter Review and Assessment.*

4 The Road to War

Prepare to Read

Objectives

In this section, you will
- Explain why conflicts between white settlers and Native Americans increased during the early 1800s.
- Identify the goal of Tecumseh's Native American confederation.
- Describe why the War Hawks pushed for war against Britain.

Key Terms

Treaty of Greenville

confederation

Battle of Tippecanoe

War Hawks

nationalism

Target Reading Skill

Cause and Effect Copy the chart below. As you read, complete the chart by filling in some of the causes that led Congress to declare war. Add as many boxes as you need.

British impressment of American sailors			

↓ ↓ ↓ ↓

CONGRESS DECLARES WAR

Main Idea Conflicts with Native Americans in the West and with the British at sea led to the War of 1812.

Tecumseh

Setting the Scene August 1810: William Henry Harrison, governor of the Indiana Territory, was ready to welcome an Indian delegation. Under a canopy, government officials sat and waited.

At last, the leader of the Indian delegation approached. His name was Tecumseh (tih KUHM suh). Behind him stood 30 members of the Shawnee nation.

"Your father requests you to sit by his side," Harrison's assistant told Tecumseh. He meant Harrison was a chief, a "white father."

Scornfully, Tecumseh pointed to the sky. "My father! The Great Spirit is my father! The earth is my mother. . . . Houses are made for white men to hold councils in. Indians hold theirs in open air." He and his men sat down where they were.

Tecumseh was determined to push back white settlers from Indian lands. Soon, the United States was fighting on two fronts—against Tecumseh's Indian allies and against Great Britain.

Conflict With Native Americans

About 900,000 white settlers moved west of the Appalachians between 1790 and 1810. Native Americans resented these newcomers, who built farms on Indian lands and hunted the animals Indians needed for food. The settlers ignored treaties that the United States had signed with Indian nations of the region.

Fighting often broke out between the Native Americans and settlers. Isolated acts of violence led to larger acts of revenge. As both sides killed innocent people, warfare spread. In Ohio, Little Turtle of the Miamis and Blue Jacket of the Shawnees organized Indian resistance in 1791. Armed with British muskets and gunpowder, the Indians drove white settlers from the area.

President Washington sent General Anthony Wayne into Ohio in 1794. Native American forces gathered at a place called Fallen Timbers. They thought that Wayne would have trouble fighting there because fallen trees covered the land. But Wayne's well-trained army pushed through the tangle of logs and defeated the Indians.

In 1795, leaders of the Miamis and other Indian nations signed the Treaty of Greenville. They gave up land that would later become part of Ohio. In return, they received $20,000 and the promise of more money if they kept the peace.

Tecumseh's Confederation

Ohio joined the Union in 1803. By then, white settlers were pushing beyond Ohio into the Indiana Territory. Angry Native Americans vowed to keep settlers from taking more Indian land. They included two Shawnee leaders: Tecumseh and his brother Tenskwatawa (tehn SKWAH tuh wuh), a religious leader also called the Prophet.

Unity and Old Ways The Prophet and Tecumseh taught that white customs corrupted the Indian way of life. They said that many Indians depended on white trade goods, such as muskets, cloth, cooking pots, and whiskey. They believed that by returning to the old ways, Indians could gain the power to resist white invaders.

In 1808, the Prophet built a village for his followers along Tippecanoe Creek in Indiana Territory. Indians from lands as far away as Missouri, Iowa, and Minnesota traveled to Prophetstown to hear his message.

Tecumseh worked to organize Indian nations into a confederation, or league. He called for unity against settlers:

> 66 The whites have driven us from the great salt water, forced us over the mountains. . . . The way, the only way, to check and stop this evil is for all red men to unite in claiming a common equal right in the land. 99
>
> —Tecumseh, quoted in *Tecumseh: Vision of Glory* (Tucker)

Tecumseh impressed white leaders. Governor William Henry Harrison grudgingly admitted, "He is one of those uncommon geniuses which spring up occasionally to produce revolutions and overturn the established order of things."

Showdown at Tippecanoe Rivalries among Native American nations kept Tecumseh from uniting all Indians east of the Mississippi River. Still, white settlers were alarmed at his success.

In 1811, Harrison marched 1,000 soldiers against Prophetstown on the Tippecanoe Creek. The Prophet was in charge because

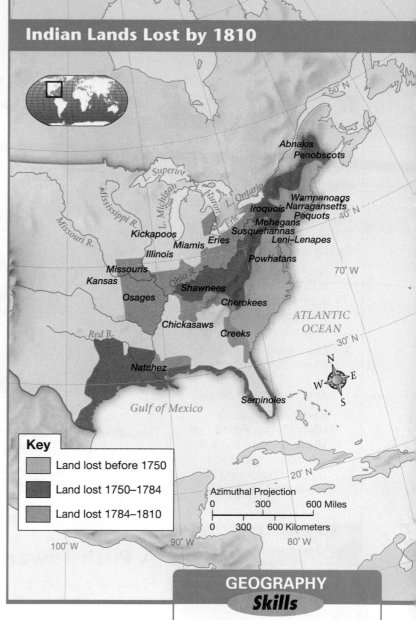

Indian Lands Lost by 1810

Key
- Land lost before 1750
- Land lost 1750–1784
- Land lost 1784–1810

Azimuthal Projection

0   300   600 Miles

0   300   600 Kilometers

GEOGRAPHY *Skills*

As settlers moved west, they settled on Native American lands.

1. **Location** On the map, locate the original lands of the **(a)** Iroquois, **(b)** Miamis, **(c)** Shawnees.

2. **Regions** When did Indian nations west of the Ohio River begin to lose land?

3. **Critical Thinking Drawing Inferences** Why do you think many of the lands lost by Indians were located along rivers?

POLITICAL CARTOON

Skills

The Embargo Continues
This famous political cartoon appeared in 1811, after Congress renewed the embargo against Britain. (The ship is flying a British flag.)

1. **Comprehension**
   (a) What is Ograbme spelled backward?
   (b) Describe the actions of the two speakers.

2. **Understanding Main Ideas** According to the cartoon, what is the effect of the embargo?

3. **Critical Thinking Identifying Points of View** Do you think that this cartoonist was in favor of enforcing the embargo? Explain.

Understanding Multiple Causes

As you read, look for the three main arguments that the War Hawks used to push for war against Britain. Add this information to your chart.

Tecumseh was away trying to organize Indians in the South. The Prophet led a surprise night attack on Harrison's troops. Both sides suffered heavy losses in the **Battle of Tippecanoe.** In the end, Harrison's troops defeated the Prophet's forces and destroyed Prophetstown. Whites celebrated the battle as a major victory. Still, Tecumseh and his followers continued to resist white settlement.

A Push Toward War

Fighting with Native Americans hurt relations between the United States and Britain. The British were supplying guns and ammunition to the Native Americans on the frontier. They also encouraged Indians to attack United States settlements.

Meanwhile, the continuing ban on trade with Britain and France was due to expire. Congress then authorized President Madison to make a tantalizing offer. If either the British or French stopped seizing American ships, the United States would halt trade with the other nation. Napoleon quickly announced that France would respect American neutrality. As promised, the United States continued trade with France, but stopped all shipments to Britain.

The War Hawks While Madison did not want war, other Americans were not as cautious. Except in New England, where many merchants wanted to restore trade with Britain, anti-British feeling ran strong. Members of Congress from the South and the West called for war. They were known as **War Hawks.**

War Hawks were stirred by a strong sense of **nationalism,** or devotion to one's country. War Hawks felt that Britain was treating the United States as if it were still a British colony. They were willing to fight a war to defend American rights.

The most outspoken War Hawk was Henry Clay of Kentucky. Clay wanted to punish Britain for seizing American ships. He also hoped to conquer Canada. "The militia of Kentucky are alone [able] to place Montreal and Upper Canada at your feet," Clay boasted to Congress.

War Hawks saw other advantages of war with Britain. If Americans went to war with Britain, War Hawks said, the United States could seize Florida from Britain's ally, Spain. They also pointed out that Britain was arming Native Americans on the frontier and encouraging them to attack settlers. The War Hawks felt that winning a war against Britain would bring lasting safety to settlers on the frontier.

Congress Declares War The United States and Britain drifted closer to war. The British continued to board American ships and impress American seamen. To cut off American trade with France, British warships blockaded some American ports. In May 1811, near New York Harbor, a brief battle broke out between an American frigate and a British warship. The Americans crippled the British ship and left 32 British sailors dead or wounded.

The War Hawks urged Congress to prepare for war. Others in Congress disagreed. John Randolph of Virginia warned that the people of the United States would "not submit to be taxed for this war of conquest and dominion." Representatives of New England were especially concerned. They feared that the British navy would attack New England seaports.

At last, President Madison gave in to war fever. In June 1812, he asked Congress to declare war on Britain. The House and Senate both voted in favor of war. Americans would soon learn, though, that declaring war was easier than winning.

Primary Source

A War Hawk Speaks

Felix Grundy of Tennessee was one of the most outspoken War Hawks in Congress. In December 1811, he gave an emotional speech on the benefits of war:

"This war, if carried on successfully, will have its advantages. We shall drive the British from our continent—they will no longer have an opportunity of intriguing with our Indian neighbors . . . . That nation will lose her Canadian trade, and by having no resting place in this country, her means of annoying us will be diminished. . . . I therefore feel anxious not only to add the Floridas to the South, but the Canadas to the North of this empire."

—Felix Grundy, *Annals of the Congress of the United States, 12th Congress, First Session*

Analyzing Primary Sources
How does Grundy's speech reflect a sense of nationalism?

★ ★ ★ **Section 4 Assessment** ★ ★ ★

Recall

1. **Identify** Explain the significance of **(a)** Treaty of Greenville, **(b)** Tecumseh, **(c)** the Prophet, **(d)** William Henry Harrison, **(e)** Battle of Tippecanoe, **(f)** War Hawks, **(g)** Henry Clay.
2. **Define** **(a)** confederation, **(b)** nationalism.

Comprehension

3. Why did war break out between Indians and white settlers in Ohio?
4. Why did Tecumseh want to unite Indian nations?
5. Identify three reasons why the War Hawks wanted Congress to declare war on Britain.

Critical Thinking and Writing

6. **Exploring the Main Idea** Review the Main Idea statement at the beginning of this section. Then, write a paragraph explaining how the Battle of Tippecanoe helped to pave the way for the coming war between Britain and the United States.
7. **Supporting a Point of View** Write an outline for a speech Tecumseh or the Prophet might have given to persuade Native Americans to join his league. Include at least two different reasons.

ACTIVITY

Drawing a Political Cartoon Draw a political cartoon that might have appeared in a War Hawk newspaper in 1812. Your cartoon should express one of the reasons that you favor a declaration of war against Britain. Use human figures to represent the United States and Britain.

5 The War of 1812

Prepare to Read

Objectives

In this section, you will
- Describe how the United States was not ready for war.
- List the successes Americans had in the West.
- Describe the progression of the final battles of the war.
- Explain why New Englanders protested the war.

Key Terms

Battle of Lake Erie

Battle of New Orleans

Hartford Convention

Treaty of Ghent

Target Reading Skill

Reading Process Copy the concept web below. As you read, fill in blank ovals with important facts about the War of 1812. Add as many ovals as you need.

Opposition to war — War in the West

WAR OF 1812 — Invasion of Canada

Main Idea Although neither nation won the War of 1812, Americans proved that their republic would remain independent.

Soldier's uniform of 1812

Setting the Scene Many Americans welcomed the news of war with Britain. In some cities, they fired cannons and guns and danced in the streets. A Republican newspaper published this poem:

> 66 Since war is the word, let us strain every nerve
> To save our America, her glory increase;
> So shoulder your firelock, your country preserve,
> For the hotter the war, boys, the quicker the peace. 99
>
> —War poem, quoted in *The Oxford History of the American People* (Morison)

Other Americans were less enthusiastic. New Englanders, especially, talked scornfully of "Mr. Madison's War." In fact, before the war ended, some New Englanders would threaten to leave the Union.

Early Days of the War

The American declaration of war took the British by surprise. They were locked in a bitter struggle with Napoleon and could not spare troops to fight the United States. As the war began, however, the United States faced difficulties of its own.

Unprepared for War The United States was not ready for war. Because Jefferson had reduced spending on defense, the navy had only 16 ships to meet the huge British fleet. The army was small and ill equipped, and many of the officers knew little about warfare."The state of the Army," said a member of Congress, "is enough to make any man who has the smallest love of country wish to get rid of it."

Since there were few regular troops, the government relied on volunteers. Congress voted to give them a bounty of cash and land. The money was equal to about a year's salary for most workers. Attracted by the high pay and the chance to own their own farms, young men eagerly enlisted. They were poorly trained, however, with little experience in battle. Many deserted after a few months.

Charlestown, Massachusetts

USS *Constitution*

The USS Constitution *is affectionately known as "Old Ironsides." During the War of 1812, British cannonballs bounced off her thick wooden hull. Later, a public outcry saved the old ship from being scrapped. Today, if you visit Boston, you can step aboard the restored "Old Ironsides." In the nearby museum, you can relive naval history by hoisting a sail or firing a cannon.*

Go **O**nline
PHSchool.com

Virtual Field Trip For an interactive look at the *Constitution*, visit PHSchool.com, **Web Code mfd-1003.**

Fighting at Sea The British navy blockaded American ports to stop American trade. Though unable to break the blockade, several American sea captains won stunning victories.

One famous battle took place early in the war, in August 1812. As he was sailing near Newfoundland, Isaac Hull, captain of the USS *Constitution,* spotted the British ship HMS *Guerrière* (gai ree AIR). For nearly an hour, the two ships jockeyed for position. At last, the guns of the *Constitution* roared into action. They tore holes in the sides of the *Guerrière* and shot off both masts. Stunned, the British captain had no choice but to surrender.

American sea captains won other victories at sea. These victories cheered Americans but did little to win the war.

War in the West

One goal of the War Hawks was to conquer Canada. They were convinced that Canadians would welcome the chance to throw off British rule and join the United States.

Invasion of Canada General William Hull moved American troops into Canada from Detroit. The Canadians had only a few untrained troops to ward off the invasion. However, they were led by a clever British general, Isaac Brock.

Brock paraded his soldiers in red coats to make it appear that experienced British troops were helping the Canadians. He also led Americans to think that a large number of Indians were fighting

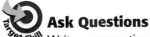 **Ask Questions**

Write one question relating to each subheading under the heading "War in the West." As you read, look for the answers to your questions. Add facts from the answers to your concept web.

alongside the Canadians. Brock's scare tactics worked. Hull retreated from Canada. Other attempts to invade Canada also failed.

Battle of Lake Erie In 1813, the Americans set out to win control of Lake Erie. Captain Oliver Hazard Perry had no fleet, so he designed and built his own ships. In September 1813, he sailed his tiny fleet against the British.

During the Battle of Lake Erie, the British battered Perry's own ship and left it helpless. Perry rowed over to another American ship and continued to fight. Finally, the Americans won the battle. Captain Perry wrote his message of victory on the back of an envelope: "We have met the enemy and they are ours."

Native American Losses After losing control of Lake Erie, the British and their ally Tecumseh retreated from Detroit into Canada. General William Henry Harrison, veteran of Tippecanoe, pursued them. The Americans won a decisive victory at the Battle of the Thames. Tecumseh died in the fighting. Without Tecumseh's leadership, the Indian confederation soon fell apart.

Still, the Creeks continued their fight against the settlers in the South. Andrew Jackson, a Tennessee officer, took command of American troops in the Creek War. In 1814, with the help of the Cherokees, Jackson won a crushing victory at the Battle of Horseshoe Bend. The leader of the Creeks walked alone into Jackson's camp to surrender. "Your people have destroyed my nation," he said.

Final Battles

In 1814, Britain and its allies defeated France. With the war in Europe over, Britain could send more troops and ships against the United States.

The British Burn Washington In August 1814, British ships sailed into Chesapeake Bay and landed an invasion force about 30 miles from Washington, D.C. American troops met the British at Bladensburg, Maryland. As President Madison watched, the battle-hardened British quickly scattered the untrained Americans. The British met little further resistance on their march to the capital.

In the White House, First Lady Dolley Madison waited for her husband to return. Hastily, she scrawled a note to her sister:

> 66 Will you believe it, my sister? We have had a battle or skirmish near Bladensburg and here I am still within sound of the cannon! Mr. Madison comes not. May God protect us. Two messengers covered with dust come bid me fly. But here I mean to wait for him. 99
>
> —Dolley Madison, *Memoirs and Letters of Dolley Madison*

Soon after, British troops marched into the capital. Dolley Madison gathered up important papers of the President and a portrait of George Washington. Then, she fled south. She was not there to see the British set fire to the White House and other buildings.

From Washington, the British marched north toward the city of Baltimore. The key to Baltimore's defense was Fort McHenry. From

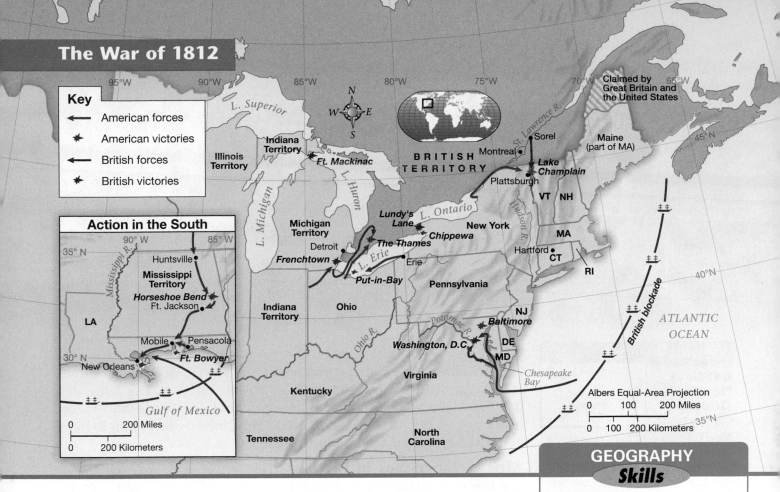

The War of 1812

Key
← American forces
✳ American victories
← British forces
✳ British victories

Action in the South

the evening of September 13 until dawn on September 14, British rockets bombarded the harbor.

When the early morning fog lifted, the "broad stripes and bright stars" of the American flag still waved over Fort McHenry. The British withdrew. Francis Scott Key, a young American lawyer who witnessed the battle, wrote a poem about it. Soon, "The Star-Spangled Banner" was published and set to music. Today, it is the national anthem of the United States.

Battle of New Orleans In late 1814, the British prepared to attack New Orleans. From there, they hoped to sail up the Mississippi. However, Andrew Jackson was waiting. Jackson had turned his frontier fighters into a strong army. He took Pensacola in Spanish Florida to keep the British from using it as a base. He then marched through Mobile and set up camp in New Orleans.

Jackson's force included thousands of frontiersmen and Choctaw Indians. The Choctaws were longtime rivals of the northern Indian nations who had been allied with the British. Many of Jackson's troops were expert riflemen. Citizens of New Orleans also joined the army to defend their city from the British. Among the volunteers were hundreds of African Americans.

The American soldiers dug trenches to defend themselves. On January 8, 1815, the British attacked. Again and again, British soldiers marched toward the American trenches. More than 2,000 British fell under the deadly fire of American sharpshooters and, especially, American cannons. Only seven Americans died.

GEOGRAPHY Skills

The War of 1812 was fought along several fronts.

1. **Location** On the map, locate the following:
   (a) Lake Erie,
   (b) Horseshoe Bend,
   (c) Baltimore, (d) New Orleans.

2. **Movement** Describe the American route from Huntsville to New Orleans.

3. **Critical Thinking Drawing Conclusions** Based on the map, do you think the British blockade had a serious impact on Americans? Explain.

Viewing History

Battle of New Orleans

The Battle of New Orleans was the single bloodiest engagement of the War of 1812. Here, Americans under the command of Andrew Jackson fire at advancing British soldiers.

Analyzing Information *How does this painting show the varied makeup of Jackson's troops?*

Americans cheered the victory at the Battle of New Orleans. Overnight, Andrew Jackson became a national hero. His fame did not dim even when Americans learned that the battle had taken place two weeks after the war ended. The United States and Britain had already signed a treaty in Europe.

African Americans in the War The Battle of New Orleans was not the only place where black and white soldiers fought side by side. Throughout the War of 1812, African Americans joined in defending the nation against the British.

Following the British attacks on Washington and Baltimore, African American volunteers helped defend Philadelphia against a possible British attack. Bishop Richard Allen and the Reverend Absalom Jones recruited more than 2,000 men to help build Philadelphia's fortifications. The state of New York organized two regiments of black volunteers to serve in the army.

African Americans also served with distinction in the United States Navy. They helped win the Battle of Lake Erie as well as other naval battles. Commander Nathaniel Shaler praised one particular black sailor who was killed in battle:

> 66 He fell near me, and several times requested to be thrown overboard, saying he was only in the way of others. When America has such [sailors], she has little to fear from the tyrants of the ocean. 99
> —Nathaniel Shaler, letter to his agent, January 1, 1813

Protest and Peace

In the early 1800s, news took weeks to cross the Atlantic Ocean. By late 1814, Americans knew that peace talks had begun, but they did not know if they would succeed or how long they would last. As Jackson was preparing to fight the British at New Orleans, New Englanders were meeting to protest "Mr. Madison's War."

New Englanders Protest The British blockade had hurt New England's sea trade. Also, many New Englanders feared that the United States might win land in Florida and Canada. If new states were carved out of these lands, the South and the West would become more influential than New England.

Delegates from around New England met in Hartford, Connecticut, in December 1814. Most were Federalists. They disliked the Republican President and the war. The delegates to the Hartford Convention threatened to leave the Union if the war continued.

Then, while the delegates debated what to do, news of the peace treaty arrived. The Hartford Convention ended quickly. With the war over, the protest was meaningless. In the end, the threat of secession further weakened the dying Federalist party.

"Nothing Was Settled" A peace treaty was signed in the city of Ghent, Belgium, on December 24, 1814. John Quincy Adams, one of the American delegates, summed up the Treaty of Ghent in one sentence: "Nothing was adjusted, nothing was settled."

Britain and the United States agreed to restore prewar conditions. The treaty said nothing about impressment or neutrality. These issues had faded due to the end of the wars in Europe. Other issues were settled later. In 1818, for example, the two nations settled a dispute over the border between Canada and the United States.

Looking back, some Americans felt that the War of 1812 had been a mistake. Others argued that Europe would now treat the young republic with more respect. The victories of heroes like Oliver Hazard Perry, William Henry Harrison, and Andrew Jackson gave Americans new pride in their country. As one Republican leader remarked, "The people are now more American. They feel and act more as a nation."

★ ★ ★ Section 5 Assessment ★ ★ ★

Recall

1. **Identify** Explain the significance of **(a)** Oliver Hazard Perry, **(b)** Battle of Lake Erie, **(c)** Andrew Jackson, **(d)** Dolley Madison, **(e)** Battle of New Orleans, **(f)** Hartford Convention, **(g)** Treaty of Ghent.

Comprehension

2. What military problems did the United States face at the start of the war?
3. How did the death of Tecumseh affect the war in the West?
4. How did Andrew Jackson achieve victory in the Battle of New Orleans?

5. Why did New Englanders threaten to leave the Union?

Critical Thinking and Writing

6. **Exploring the Main Idea** Review the Main Idea statement at the beginning of this section. Then, list two reasons supporting and two reasons opposing John Quincy Adams's statement, "Nothing was adjusted, nothing was settled."
7. **Drawing Conclusions** Both William Henry Harrison and Andrew Jackson later became President. Write a paragraph explaining why war heroes often make attractive political candidates.

> **ACTIVITY**
>
> **Writing a Song** Like Francis Scott Key, you are a witness to one of the major conflicts of the War of 1812. With a partner, write a song or poem describing your feelings about the events going on around you.

CHAPTER SUMMARY

Section 1
As President, Thomas Jefferson's goals included reducing the role of the federal government. *Marbury* v. *Madison* gave the Supreme Court the power of judicial review.

Section 2
In 1803, the United States purchased the Louisiana territory from France, doubling the size of the nation and giving it control of the Mississippi River. Lewis and Clark explored the Louisiana territory.

Section 3
As Great Britain went to war against France, both sides ignored U.S. neutrality. When France and Britain seized American ships, Jefferson imposed an embargo on the two nations.

Section 4
Tecumseh tried to unite several Indian nations to oppose the spread of white settlers west. Conflicts with Native Americans in the West and with the British at sea led to the War of 1812.

Section 5
Neither Great Britain nor the United States won the War of 1812. However, Americans proved that their republic would remain independent.

Building Vocabulary

Review the chapter vocabulary words listed below. Then, use the words and their definitions to create a matching quiz. Exchange quizzes with another student. Check each other's answers.

1. democratic	6. continental divide
2. laissez faire	7. impressment
3. free market	8. embargo
4. judicial review	9. confederation
5. expedition	10. nationalism

Reviewing Key Facts

11. Describe two ways that Jefferson reversed Federalist policies. (Section 1)

For additional review and enrichment activities, see the interactive version of *The American Nation,* available on the Web and on CD-ROM.

Chapter Self-Test For practice test questions for Chapter 10, visit PHSchool.com, **Web Code mfa-1004.**

12. Why did Jefferson decide that the Louisiana Purchase was constitutional? (Section 2)
13. How did Americans react to the British practice of impressment? (Section 3)
14. What were the results of the battles of Fallen Timbers and Tippecanoe? (Section 4)
15. What role did African American soldiers play in the War of 1812? (Section 5)

Critical Thinking and Writing

16. **Applying Information** In 1787, Jefferson stated, "The policy of the American government is to leave their citizens free, neither restraining nor aiding them in their pursuits." **(a)** Restate Jefferson's main point in your own words. **(b)** List two ways in which Jefferson's economic policies reflected this idea.

17. **Connecting to Geography: Place** Jefferson had Lewis and Clark take detailed notes about the Louisiana Purchase. Make a list of at least five geographic features, such as climate or plant life. For each item on your list, write a sentence explaining why information about this feature might be important for future settlers.

18. **Ranking** List the reasons the War Hawks wanted to go to war with Britain. Circle the reason you think is most valid, and underline the reason you think is least valid. Write a sentence explaining your ranking.

In 1812, a New York newspaper printed an editorial in favor of war with Britain. Nicholas Smyth of Boston wrote this reply. Read the excerpt and answer the questions that follow:

> 66 We hear from the halls of Congress the cry 'On to Canada!' It is the fur dealer and the land speculator who want war, but it is we of New England who will pay the price. If war comes, it is our seaports that will be blockaded; it is our cities that will be destroyed. The War Hawks of Tennessee and Kentucky are safe. I doubt if the English navy can reach them. 99

—Nicholas Smyth, Records of the House Foreign Affairs Committee

19. According to Smyth, who is in favor of conquering Canada?
    A. people from New England
    B. people from Great Britain
    C. shipbuilders and loggers
    D. fur dealers and land speculators
20. What does Smyth say will happen if war comes?
    A. New England's cities will be destroyed.
    B. America will conquer Canada.
    C. Tennessee and Kentucky will lose power in Congress.
    D. The western states will leave the Union.

War of 1812 Vote in House of Representatives

REGIONS	FOR WAR	AGAINST WAR
New England	12	20
Middle States	21	18
The South	37	11
The West	9	0
Total	79	49

Source: Thomas A. Bailey, *A Diplomatic History of the American People*

This table shows the war vote in the House of Representatives in 1812. Look at the table and compare it to the letter at left.

21. Based on the table, which is a true statement?
    A. New England was largely in favor of war.
    B. The West was largely in favor of war.
    C. The war had overwhelming support.
    D. Regional differences played no role.
22. How did the vote in Congress reflect the concerns expressed in Smyth's letter?

ACTIVITIES

Connecting With . . .
Government and Citizenship

Giving a Talk Give a one-minute talk based on one of the following quotations from Thomas Jefferson. Explain what Jefferson meant and how that idea still applies today.
• "The minority possess their equal rights, which equal laws must protect."
• "No government can continue good, but under the control of the people."
• "Whenever the people are well-informed, they can be trusted with their own government."

Go Online
PHSchool.com

Connecting to Today

Preparing a Report Use the Internet to find out about one of the Indian nations shown on the map in Section 4. Prepare a report showing where they live today and how they maintain their traditions. For help in starting this activity, visit PHSchool.com, **Web Code mfd-1005**.

11 The Nation Grows and Prospers

1790–1825

1 The Industrial Revolution
2 Americans Move Westward
3 Unity and Division
4 New Nations in the Americas

Slater's Mill

One of Fulton's early steamboats

1793

Samuel Slater builds a textile mill in Pawtucket, Rhode Island. It is the first successful textile mill in the United States.

1790s

The Lancaster Road improves travel between Philadelphia and central Pennsylvania.

Early 1800s

Development of the steam-powered boat creates a new age of steamboat travel on the major rivers of the United States.

AMERICAN EVENTS

George Washington
1789–1797

John Adams 1797–1801

Thomas Jefferson 1801–1809

James Madison
1809–1817

Presidential Terms:

★ 1790 · · · · ★ · · · ★ · · · · 1800 · · · ★ · · · · 1810

WORLD EVENTS

▲ **1791**
Enslaved plantation workers in Haiti revolt against their French masters.

▲ **1802**
Britain passes a law limiting child labor.

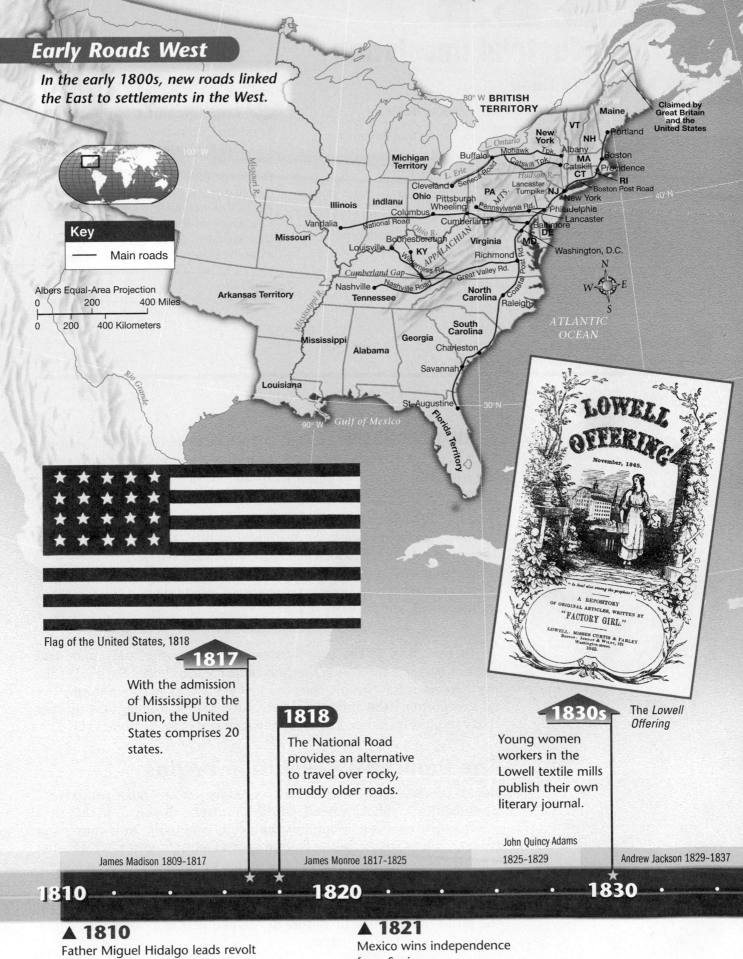

Early Roads West

In the early 1800s, new roads linked the East to settlements in the West.

Key

— Main roads

Albers Equal-Area Projection

0 ___ 200 ___ 400 Miles

0 ___ 200 ___ 400 Kilometers

BRITISH TERRITORY

Claimed by Great Britain and the United States

Maine

Portland

VT

NH

New York

Albany

Boston

MA

Providence

CT

RI

Boston Post Road

Michigan Territory

Buffalo

Mohawk Tpk.

Catskill Tpk.

Seneca Road

L. Ontario

L. Erie

Cleveland

Hudson R.

Lancaster Turnpike

New York

Ohio

Pittsburgh

PA

APPALACHIAN MTS.

Pennsylvania Rd.

Philadelphia

Illinois

Indiana

Columbus

Wheeling

Lancaster

Vandalia

National Road

Cumberland

Baltimore

DE

Ohio R.

MD

Missouri

Boonesborough

Virginia

Washington, D.C.

Louisville

KY

Richmond

Missouri R.

Nashville Road

Wilderness Rd.

Cumberland Gap

Great Valley Rd.

Coastal Post Rd.

Arkansas Territory

Nashville

Tennessee

North Carolina

Raleigh

Mississippi R.

South Carolina

Georgia

Charleston

Mississippi

Alabama

Savannah

ATLANTIC OCEAN

Louisiana

St. Augustine

Florida Territory

Gulf of Mexico

Rio Grande

N

W E

S

Flag of the United States, 1818

LOWELL OFFERING

November, 1845.

"Is Saul also among the prophets?"

A REPOSITORY OF ORIGINAL ARTICLES, WRITTEN BY "FACTORY GIRL."

LOWELL: MISSES CURTIS & FARLEY. BOSTON: JORDAN & WILEY, 121 Washington street. 1845.

The *Lowell Offering*

1817
With the admission of Mississippi to the Union, the United States comprises 20 states.

1818
The National Road provides an alternative to travel over rocky, muddy older roads.

1830s
Young women workers in the Lowell textile mills publish their own literary journal.

James Madison 1809-1817

James Monroe 1817-1825

John Quincy Adams 1825-1829

Andrew Jackson 1829-1837

1810 · · · · **1820** · · · · **1830** · · ·

▲ **1810**
Father Miguel Hidalgo leads revolt against Spanish rule in Mexico.

▲ **1821**
Mexico wins independence from Spain.

1 The Industrial Revolution

Prepare to Read

Objectives

In this section, you will
- Identify the Industrial Revolution and explain its effects on the United States.
- Explain why Lowell, Massachusetts, was called a model factory town.
- Describe life in early factories.
- Summarize the impact the Industrial Revolution had on American cities.

Key Terms

Industrial Revolution
spinning jenny
capital
capitalist
factory system
interchangeable parts
Lowell girl
urbanization

Target Reading Skill

Sequence Copy this flowchart. As you read the section, fill in the boxes with some of the major events described in it that led to the Industrial Revolution in the United States. Add as many boxes as you need to finish the flowchart.

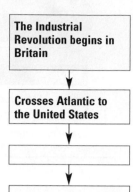

```
┌─────────────────────┐
│ The Industrial      │
│ Revolution begins in│
│ Britain             │
└─────────────────────┘
          │
          ▼
┌─────────────────────┐
│ Crosses Atlantic to │
│ the United States   │
└─────────────────────┘
          │
          ▼
┌─────────────────────┐
│                     │
└─────────────────────┘
          │
          ▼
┌─────────────────────┐
│                     │
└─────────────────────┘
```

 Main Idea During the early 1800s, the Industrial Revolution dramatically changed the American way of life.

Lucy Larcom

Setting the Scene At dawn, the factory bell woke 11-year-old Lucy Larcom. Rising quickly, she ate her breakfast and hurried to her job at a spinning mill in Lowell, Massachusetts. Years later, Larcom described her workplace:

> 66 The buzzing and hissing and whizzing of pulleys and rollers and spindles and flyers around me often grew tiresome. . . . I could look across the room and see girls moving backward and forward among the spinning frames, sometimes stooping, sometimes reaching up their arms, as their work required. 99
>
> —Lucy Larcom, *Among Lowell Mill-Girls: A Reminiscence,* 1881

In the early 1800s, busy factories and whirring machinery had become part of a revolution that was reaching the United States. Unlike the American Revolution, this one had no battles or fixed dates. The new revolution—the Industrial Revolution—was a long, slow process that completely changed the way in which goods were produced.

The Industrial Revolution Begins

Before the 1800s, most Americans were farmers and most goods were produced by hand. As a result of the Industrial Revolution, this situation slowly changed. Machines replaced hand tools. New sources of power, such as steam, replaced human and animal power. While most Americans continued to farm for a living, the economy began a gradual shift toward manufacturing.

New Technology The Industrial Revolution started in Britain in the mid-1700s. British inventors developed new machines that transformed the textile industry.

Viewing History

Changing Landscape New England

The Industrial Revolution changed the face of the nation. In this painting, the artist shows an early factory among the church spires and green fields of a New England town. **Identifying Points of View** *What do you think is the point of view of the artist toward the changing face of the village? Explain.*

Since the Middle Ages, workers had used spinning wheels to make thread. A spinning wheel, however, could spin only one thread at a time. In 1764, James Hargreaves developed the spinning jenny, a machine that could spin several threads at once. Other inventions speeded up the process of weaving thread into cloth. In the 1780s, Edmund Cartwright built a loom powered by water. It allowed a worker to produce a great deal more cloth in a day than was possible before.

The Factory System New inventions led to a new system of producing goods. Before the Industrial Revolution, most spinning and weaving took place in the home. Large machines however, had to be housed in large mills near rivers. Water flowing downstream or over a waterfall turned a wheel that produced the power to run the machines.

To set up and operate a spinning mill required large amounts of capital, or money. Capitalists supplied this money. A capitalist is a person who invests in a business in order to make a profit. Capitalists built factories and hired workers to run the machines.

The new factory system brought workers and machinery together in one place to produce goods. Factory workers earned daily or weekly wages. They had to work a set number of hours each day.

A Revolution Crosses the Atlantic

Britain wanted to keep its new technology secret. It did not want rival nations to copy the new machines. Therefore, the British Parliament passed a law forbidding anyone to take plans of the new machinery out of the country.

Slater Breaks the Law Samuel Slater soon proved that this law could not be enforced. Slater was a skilled mechanic in a British textile mill. When he heard that Americans were offering large rewards for plans of British factories, he decided to leave Britain. In 1789,

Identify Sequence
Target Skill What events noted on this page contributed to the rise of the Industrial Revolution in the United States? Add these events to your flowchart.

Slater boarded a ship bound for New York City. He knew that British officials searched the baggage of passengers sailing to the United States. To avoid getting caught, he memorized the design of the machines in the mill.

The First American Mill Slater soon visited Moses Brown, a Quaker capitalist who had a mill in Pawtucket, Rhode Island. The mill was not doing well because its machinery constantly broke down. Slater set to work on improving the machinery. By 1793, in Pawtucket, he built what became the first successful textile mill in the United States that was powered by water. Slater's wife, Hannah Slater, contributed to the success of the mill. She discovered how to make thread stronger so that it would not snap on the spindles.

Slater's factory was a huge success. Before long, other American manufacturers began using his ideas.

Interchangeable Parts American manufacturers benefited from the pioneering work of American inventor Eli Whitney. Earlier, skilled workers made goods by hand. For example, gunsmiths spent days making the barrel, stock, and trigger for a single musket. Because the parts were handmade, each musket differed a bit from every other musket. If a part broke, a gunsmith had to make a new part to fit that particular gun.

Whitney wanted to speed up the making of guns by having machines manufacture each part. All machine-made parts would be alike—for example, one trigger would be identical to another. Interchangeable parts would save time and money.

Because the government bought many guns, Whitney went to Washington, D.C., to try to sell his idea. At first, officials laughed at his plan. Carefully, Whitney sorted parts for 10 muskets into separate piles. He then asked an official to choose one part from each pile. In minutes, the first musket was assembled. Whitney repeated the process until 10 muskets were complete.

The idea of interchangeable parts spread rapidly. Inventors designed machines to produce interchangeable parts for clocks, locks, and many other goods. With such machines, small workshops grew into factories.

Lowell, Massachusetts: A Model Factory Town

The War of 1812 provided a boost to American industries. The British blockade cut Americans off from their supply of foreign goods. As a result, they had to produce more goods themselves.

The Lowell Mills During the war, Francis Cabot Lowell, a Boston merchant, found a way to improve on British textile mills. In Britain, one factory spun thread and a second factory wove it into cloth. Why not, Lowell wondered, combine spinning and weaving under one roof? The new mill that he built in Waltham, Massachusetts, had all the machines needed to turn raw cotton into finished cloth.

After Lowell's death, his partners took on a more ambitious project. They built an entire factory town and named it after him. In

1821, Lowell, Massachusetts, was a village of five farm families. By 1836, it boasted more than 10,000 people. Visitors to Lowell described it as a model community composed of "small wooden houses, painted white, with green blinds, very neat, very snug, very nicely carpeted."

"Lowell Girls" To work in their new mills, the company hired young women from nearby farms. The Lowell girls, as they came to be called, usually worked for a few years in the mills before returning home to marry. Most sent their wages home to their families.

At first, parents hesitated to let their daughters work in the mills. To reassure parents, the company built boardinghouses. The company also made rules to protect the young women.

Although factory work was often tedious and hard, many women valued the economic freedom they got from working in the mills. One worker wrote her sister Sarah back on a farm in New Hampshire:

> 66 Since I have wrote you, another pay day has come around. I earned 14 dollars and a half . . . I like it well as ever and Sarah don't I feel independent of everyone! 99
> — from *Lowell Offering: Writings by New England Mill Women*

Daily Life During the Industrial Revolution

In Lowell and elsewhere, mill owners hired mostly women and children. They did this because they could pay women and children half of what they would have had to pay men.

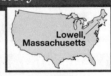

Viewing History

Inside a Textile Mill Work in the textile mills in the early 1800s was hard. Workers faced long hours on their feet amid the noisy machines. Yet, the mills were generally clean and orderly.
Analyzing Primary Sources
What clues does the picture give to conditions in this mill?

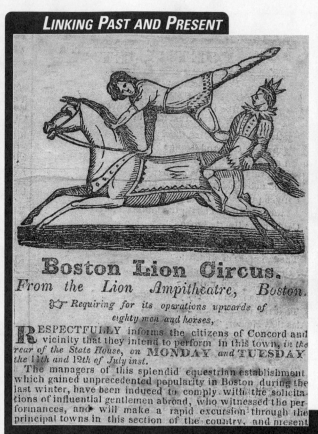

Boston Lion Circus.

From the Lion Ampitheatre, Boston.

☞ *Requiring for its operations upwards of eighty men and horses,*

RESPECTFULLY informs the citizens of Concord and vicinity that they intend to perform in this town, in the rear of the State House, on MONDAY and TUESDAY the 11th and 12th of July inst.

The managers of this splendid equestrian establishment which gained unprecedented popularity in Boston during the last winter, have been induced to comply with the solicitations of influential gentlemen abroad, who witnessed the performances, and will make a rapid excursion through the principal towns in this section of the country, and present

▲ **Past**

▲ **Present**

Viewing History

Circuses Then and Now

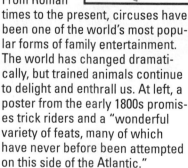

Concord, Massachusetts

From Roman times to the present, circuses have been one of the world's most popular forms of family entertainment. The world has changed dramatically, but trained animals continue to delight and enthrall us. At left, a poster from the early 1800s promises trick riders and a "wonderful variety of feats, many of which have never before been attempted on this side of the Atlantic."

Linking Past and Present
Why have circuses maintained their popularity for so many years?

Child Labor Boys and girls as young as seven worked in factories. Small children were especially useful in textile mills because they could squeeze around the large machines to change spindles.

Today, most Americans look upon child labor as cruel. Yet in the 1800s, farm children also worked hard. Most people did not see much difference between children working in a factory or on a farm. Often, a child's wages were needed to help support the family.

Long Hours Working hours in the mills were long—12 hours a day, 6 days a week. True, farmers also put in long hours. However, farmers worked shorter hours in winter. Mill workers, in contrast, worked nearly the same hours all year round.

In the early 1800s, conditions in American mills were generally much better than in most factories in Europe. As industries grew, however, competition increased and employers took less interest in the welfare of their workers. In later chapters, you will read how working conditions grew worse.

Changes in Home Life The Industrial Revolution had a great impact on home life. As the factory system spread, more family members left the home to earn a living.

These changes affected ideas about the role of women. In poorer families, women often had to go out to work. In wealthier families, husbands supported the family while wives stayed at home. For many husbands, having a wife who stayed at home became a sign of success.

Growing Cities

In 1800, the vast majority of Americans lived in rural areas. During the Industrial Revolution, many people left farms to work in factories. Older cities expanded rapidly, while new cities sprang up around factories. This movement of the population from farms to cities is called **urbanization.**

Urbanization was a steady but gradual process. In 1800, only 6 percent of the nation's population lived in urban areas. By 1850, the number had risen to 15 percent. Not until 1920 did more Americans live in cities than on farms.

By today's standards, these early cities were small. A person could walk from one end of any American city to the other in as little as 30 minutes. Buildings were only a few stories tall. As the factory system spread, the nation's cities grew.

Hazards Growing cities had many problems. Dirt and gravel streets turned into mudholes when it rained. Cities had no sewers, and people threw garbage into the streets. A visitor to New York reported that "The streets are filthy, and the stranger is not a little surprised to meet the hogs walking about in them, for the purpose of devouring the vegetables and trash thrown into the gutter."

Under these conditions, disease spread easily. Epidemics of influenza and cholera (KAHL er uh) raged through cities, killing hundreds.

Attractions Cities had attractions, too. Theaters, museums, and circuses created an air of excitement. In cities, people could shop in fine stores that sold the latest fashions from Europe. Some offered modern "ready-to-wear" clothing. While most women continued to sew their own clothes, many enjoyed visiting hat shops, china shops, shoe stores, and "fancy-goods" stores.

★ ★ ★ **Section 1 Assessment** ★ ★ ★

Recall

1. **Identify** Explain the significance of **(a)** Industrial Revolution, **(b)** Samuel Slater, **(c)** Eli Whitney, **(d)** Lowell girl.
2. **Define** **(a)** spinning jenny, **(b)** capital, **(c)** capitalist, **(d)** factory system, **(e)** interchangeable parts, **(f)** urbanization.

Comprehension

3. How did the Industrial Revolution begin in the United States?
4. What was unusual about the factory town of Lowell, Massachusetts?
5. What were conditions like for workers during the early Industrial Revolution?

6. Describe three ways in which American cities were changed by the early Industrial Revolution.

Critical Thinking and Writing

7. **Exploring the Main Idea** Review the Main Idea statement at the beginning of the section. Then, list three examples of changes in the way Americans lived and worked that were a result of the Industrial Revolution.
8. **Drawing Conclusions** Make a list of the reasons why both inventors and capitalists were needed to bring about the Industrial Revolution.

ACTIVITY

Go Online
PHSchool.com

Use the Internet to learn more about life for the "Lowell girls" of the early 1800s. Then, suppose that you are a worker at the mill, and compose a diary entry describing a typical day. For help in completing the activity, visit PHSchool.com, **Web Code mfd-1101.**

How a Textile Mill Worked

New technology, like that used by Samuel Slater's mill, helped spark the Industrial Revolution. The diagram shows how rapidly moving water turned a water wheel. The wheel produced the power to run the machines.

Samuel Slater

1 Wagons bring raw cotton to the mill to be spun into thread.

2 Fast-moving water causes the water wheel to turn.

3 The turning water wheel powers the mill's main shaft.

4 The main shaft drives pulleys, which turn belts that drive the mill machinery.

5 Carding machines comb the raw cotton fiber.

6 Drawing machines pull the combed cotton fibers into ropelike strands.

7 Spinning frames twist combed and drawn cotton strands into thread and wind them onto a bobbin.

8 Wagons carry spun thread to weavers, who use it to make cloth.

ACTIVITY

Make a drawing of the mill's water wheel and main mill shaft. Show how water power is transmitted through the water wheel to the mill's main shaft.

2 Americans Move Westward

Prepare to Read

Objectives

In this section, you will
- Describe how settlers traveled west.
- List the steps Americans took to improve their roads.
- Explain how steamboats and canals improved transportation for Americans.

Key Terms

flatboat
turnpike
Lancaster Turnpike
corduroy road
National Road
Clermont
Erie Canal

 Target Reading Skill

Reading Process As you read, complete this table listing important developments in transportation in the United States at the beginning of the 1800s. Add as many rows as you need.

TRAVELING WEST	IMPROVING ROAD TRANSPORTATION	NEW STEAMBOATS AND CANALS
• Roads to the West • Travel by flatboat	•	•

Main Idea Improvements in transportation in the first half of the 1800s helped make it easier to move people and goods in the expanding nation.

Setting the Scene The stagecoach was bogged down in the spring mud, its big wheels sunk up to the axles. The passengers stood by the side of the road while the stage driver urged his horses to pull the coach out of the mud. Suddenly, one traveler spotted a beautiful fur cap lying in the middle of a huge mudhole just ahead. He had to have that cap!

The traveler stepped through the mud until at last he snatched up the hat. To his surprise, he saw a man's head *underneath*—a man buried in the mud! "Come help pull this fellow out!" called the traveler to his friends. The man in the mud shook his head. "Just leave me alone, stranger," he said. "I have a good horse under me, and have just found bottom."

Americans during the 1830s loved to tell this tall tale. The story was so popular because travel in the United States was often difficult. As the young nation grew, Americans saw an urgent need to improve transportation, both on water and over land.

A necessary stop

Traveling West

Settlers had been moving steadily westward since the 1600s. In the early 1800s, the stream of pioneers turned into a flood. By 1820, so many people had moved west that the population in some of the original 13 states had actually declined!

Western Routes Settlers took a number of routes west. One well-traveled path was the Great Wagon Road across Pennsylvania. It dated back to colonial days. Some settlers then continued south and west along the trail opened by Daniel Boone before the Revolution. Known as the Wilderness Road, it led through the Cumberland Gap into Kentucky.

Other settlers pushed west to Pittsburgh. There, they loaded their animals and wagons onto **flatboats,** or flat-bottom boats, and journeyed down the Ohio River into Indiana, Kentucky, and Illinois.

Conner Prairie Village

Conner Prairie is a center for entertainment and education focusing on the lives and times of western settlers in the early 1800s. It consists of five historic areas, including the re-created 1836 village of Prairietown. Another site is the Lenape (luh-NAH-pay) Indian Camp and McKinnen's Trading Post, shown here. The historic areas are set on a 210-acre woodland site.

Conner Prairie Village, Indiana

Go Online
PHSchool.com

Virtual Field Trip For an interactive look at the Conner Prairie Village, visit PHSchool.com, **Web Code mfd-1102.**

Flatboats were well suited to the shallow waters of the Ohio. Even when carrying heavy cargoes, these barges rode high in the water.

Pioneers from Georgia and South Carolina followed other trails west to Alabama, Mississippi, and Louisiana. Enslaved African Americans helped to carve plantations in the rich, fertile soil of these territories.

People from New England, New York, and Pennsylvania pushed into the Northwest Territory. Some settlers traveled west from Albany, New York, along the Mohawk River and across the Appalachians. Many then sailed across Lake Erie into Ohio.

New States Before long, some western territories had populations large enough to apply for statehood. Between 1792 and 1819, eight states joined the Union: Kentucky (1792), Tennessee (1796), Ohio (1803), Louisiana (1812), Indiana (1816), Mississippi (1817), Illinois (1818), and Alabama (1819).

Improvements to Roads

Settlers faced difficult journeys to the West. Many roads were narrow trails, barely wide enough for a single wagon. Trails often plunged through muddy swamps. Tree stumps stuck up through the road and often broke the wagon axles of careless travelers. The nation badly needed better roads.

Turnpikes and Corduroy Roads In the United States, as in Europe, private companies built gravel and stone roads. To pay for

Ask Questions
As you read the next two sections, turn each blue heading into a question. Then, read to find the answers to these questions. Use the answers to fill in your table.

these roads, the companies collected tolls from travelers. At various points along the road, a pike, or pole, blocked the road. After a wagon driver had paid a toll, the pike keeper turned the pole aside to let the wagon pass. As a result, these toll roads were called **turnpikes.**

Probably the best road in the United States was the **Lancaster Turnpike.** Built in the 1790s by a private company, the road linked Philadelphia and Lancaster, Pennsylvania. Because the road was set on a bed of gravel, water drained off quickly. For a smooth ride, the road was topped with flat stones.

Other roads were more primitive. In swampy areas, roads were made of logs. These roads were known as **corduroy roads** because the lines of logs looked like corduroy cloth. Corduroy roads kept wagons from sinking into the mud, but they made for a very noisy and bumpy ride.

The National Road Some states set aside money to improve roads or build new ones. In 1806, for the first time, Congress approved funds for a national road-building project. The National Road was to run from Cumberland, Maryland, to Wheeling, in western Virginia.

Work on the National Road began in 1811. Because of the War of 1812, it was not completed until 1818. Later, the road was extended into Illinois. As each new section of road was built, settlers eagerly used it to drive their wagons west.

Steam Transport

Whenever possible, travelers and freight haulers used river transportation. Floating downstream on a flatboat was both faster and more comfortable than bumping along rutted roads. It also cost less.

Yet, river travel had its own problems. Moving upstream was difficult. People used paddles or long poles to push boats against the current. Sometimes, they hauled boats from the shore with ropes. Both methods were slow. A boat could travel downstream from Pittsburgh to New Orleans in about six weeks. However, the return trip upstream took at least 17 weeks!

Fitch and Fulton A new invention, the steam engine, opened a new era in river travel. In 1787, John Fitch showed members of the Constitutional Convention how a steam engine could power a boat. He then opened a ferry service on the Delaware River. However, few people used the ferry, and Fitch went out of business.

Inventor Robert Fulton may have seen Fitch's steamboat in Philadelphia. In 1807, Fulton launched his own steamboat, the *Clermont,* on the Hudson River. On its first run, the *Clermont* carried passengers from New York City to Albany and back. The 300-mile trip took just 62 hours—a record at the time.

The Age of Steamboats Fulton's success ushered in the age of steamboats. Soon, steamboats were ferrying passengers up and down the Atlantic coast. More important, steamboats revolutionized travel in the West. Besides carrying people, steamboats on the Mississippi, Ohio, and Missouri rivers gave farmers and merchants a cheap means of moving goods.

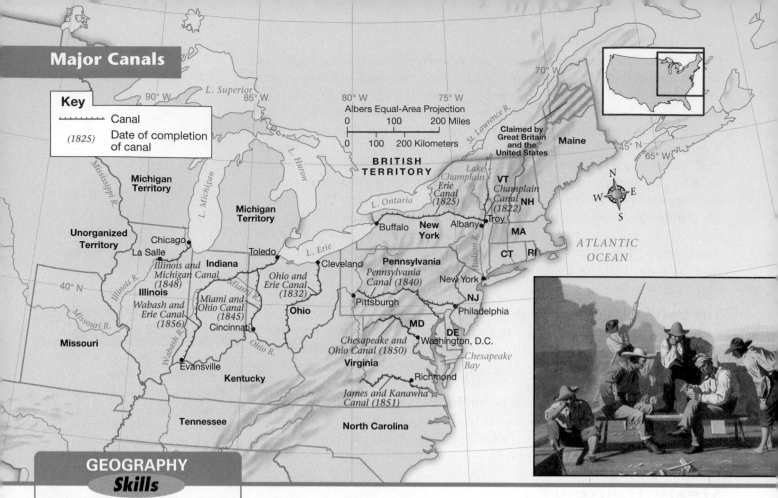

Major Canals

Key

╟─────╢ Canal

(1825) Date of completion of canal

Albers Equal-Area Projection
0 — 100 — 200 Miles
0 — 100 — 200 Kilometers

BRITISH TERRITORY

Claimed by Great Britain and the United States

Michigan Territory

Michigan Territory

Unorganized Territory

Chicago
La Salle

Illinois and Michigan Canal (1848)

Illinois

Wabash and Erie Canal (1856)

Missouri

Evansville

Kentucky

Tennessee

Indiana

Toledo

Ohio and Erie Canal (1832)

Miami and Ohio Canal (1845)

Cincinnati

Ohio

Cleveland

Pittsburgh

Virginia

Chesapeake and Ohio Canal (1850)

Richmond

James and Kanawha Canal (1851)

North Carolina

Lake Champlain

Erie Canal (1825)

Buffalo

New York

Albany

Troy

Champlain Canal (1822)

Pennsylvania Canal (1840)

New York

Maine

VT

NH

MA

CT RI

NJ

Philadelphia

MD

DE

Washington, D.C.

Chesapeake Bay

ATLANTIC OCEAN

Pennsylvania

GEOGRAPHY Skills

The success of the Erie Canal, completed in 1825, set off an age of canal building. The painting by George Caleb Bingham shows boatsmen relaxing after a long workday.

1. **Location** On the map, locate **(a)** New York City, **(b)** Troy, **(c)** Buffalo, **(d)** Lake Erie, **(e)** Erie Canal.

2. **Movement** What two bodies of water were linked by the Illinois and Michigan Canal?

3. **Critical Thinking Applying Information** Use the map to trace an all-water route from Evansville, Indiana, to New York City.

Because western rivers were shallow, Henry Shreve designed a flat-bottomed steamboat. It could carry heavy loads without getting stuck on sandbars.

Still, steamboat travel could be dangerous. Sparks from smokestacks could cause fires. As steamboat captains raced each other along the river, high-pressure boilers sometimes exploded. Between 1811 and 1851, 44 steamboats collided, 166 burned, and more than 200 exploded.

The Canal Boom

Steamboats and better roads brought many improvements. But they did not help western farmers get their goods directly to markets in the East. To meet this need, Americans dug canals. A canal is an artificial channel filled with water that allows boats to cross a stretch of land.

The earliest American canals were no more than a few miles long. Some provided routes around waterfalls on a river. Other canals linked rivers to nearby lakes. By the early 1800s, however, Americans were building longer canals.

Building the Erie Canal Some New Yorkers had a bold idea. They wanted to build a canal linking the Great Lakes with the Mohawk and Hudson rivers. The Erie Canal would let western farmers ship their goods to the port of New York. It would also bring business to towns along the route.

To many people, the idea of such a canal seemed far-fetched. When Thomas Jefferson heard of the plan, he exclaimed:

66 Why, sir, you talk of making a canal 350 miles through the wilderness—it is little short of madness to think of it at this day! 99
—Thomas Jefferson to Joshua Forman of New York, 1809

New York's governor DeWitt Clinton ignored such criticism. He persuaded state lawmakers to provide money for the Erie Canal. Scoffers referred to the project as "Clinton's Ditch."

Work on the Erie Canal began in 1817. At first, thousands of workers dug the waterway by hand. To speed up progress, inventors developed new equipment. One machine, a stump-puller, could pull out nearly 40 tree stumps a day. In two places, the canal had to cross over rivers. Workers built stone bridges to carry the canal over the rivers.

An Instant Success By 1825, the immense job was finished. On opening day of the Erie Canal, a cannon fired a volley in Buffalo, New York. When the sound got to the next town along the route, that town, too, fired a cannon. Town after town fired cannons—all the way to New York City. The thunderous salute took 80 minutes to complete.

The Erie Canal was an instant success. The cost of shipping goods dropped to about one tenth of what it had been before the canal was built. The canal also helped to make New York City a center of commerce.

The success of the Erie Canal led other states to build canals. These canals created vital economic links between western farms and eastern cities.

★ ★ ★ Section 2 Assessment ★ ★ ★

Recall
1. **Identify** Explain the significance of (a) Lancaster Turnpike, (b) National Road, (c) John Fitch, (d) Robert Fulton, (e) *Clermont,* (f) Henry Shreve, (g) DeWitt Clinton, (h) Erie Canal.
2. **Define** (a) flatboat, (b) turnpike, (c) corduroy road.

Comprehension
3. What routes did settlers use to reach the West in the early 1800s?
4. Describe two ways in which road transportation improved in the early 1800s.

5. What role did the steamboat play in the growing nation?

Critical Thinking and Writing
6. **Exploring the Main Idea** Review the Main Idea statement at the beginning of this section. Then, write an imaginary diary entry of a trip along the National Road that explains how the road has made travel easier.
7. **Identifying Alternatives** Examine the maps in this chapter. Then, describe two ways a farmer might have shipped a cargo of grain from Cleveland, Ohio, to New York City. Explain the advantages of each route.

ACTIVITY

Writing a Newspaper Story Review the chapter's description of opening day on the Erie Canal. Write a newspaper story reporting on that first day. Write a newspaper-style headline and a lead sentence that covers the *who, what, when, where,* and *why* of the event.

3 Unity and Division

Prepare to Read

Objectives

In this section, you will
- Discuss sectionalism's impact in the Era of Good Feelings.
- Explain how Congress helped industry after the war ended.
- Describe Henry Clay's American System.
- Explain how the Supreme Court gave more power to the federal government.

Key Terms

sectionalism

American System

internal improvements

McCulloch v. *Maryland*

Gibbons v. *Ogden*

interstate commerce

Target Reading Skill

Main Idea As you read, prepare an outline of this section. Use roman numerals to indicate the major headings of this section, capital letters for the subheadings, and numbers for the supporting details. The sample at right will help you get started.

> I. An Era of Good Feelings
> II. Three Sectional Leaders
>   A. Calhoun of the South
>   1.
>   2.
>   B. Webster of the North
>   1.
>   2.
>   C.
>   1.
>   2.
> III. Helping American Businesses Grow

Main Idea Despite some tensions between different sections, the nation enjoyed an "era of good feelings" after the War of 1812.

The Fourth of July in 1819

Setting the Scene In Charleston, a cook named Abigail Jones put her advertisement in the newspaper early. Turtle meat would be available for sale on July 4 only. When Americans celebrated the Fourth of July in the early 1800s, turtle soup was one of the two most popular holiday foods.

What was the other? For a hot summer holiday like the Fourth, Americans loved the rare treat of ice cream. In Boston, a Mr. Shindles advertised "iced creams, of the best quality" in four flavors. At Vauxhall Gardens in Charleston, sellers warned people to come early, before all the ice cream was eaten.

After the War of 1812, Fourth of July celebrations became more popular than ever. Americans were proud of their country. They were especially proud that the nation was growing rapidly. Improved transportation allowed the opening of new lands to settlers. New industries were appearing. In Congress, a new generation of political leaders sought to direct this expansion.

An Era of Good Feelings

In 1816, the Republican candidate for President, James Monroe, easily defeated the Federalist, Senator Rufus King of New York. The election showed how seriously the Federalist party had declined in popularity. Many Federalists had joined the Republican party and voted for Monroe.

Monroe was the last Revolutionary War officer to become President. He was almost 60 years old when he took office, and he still followed the fashions of the late 1700s. He wore a powdered wig at a time when young men were wearing their hair loose. While other Americans wore long trousers, he still wore breeches and long stockings.

Americans were fond of his old-fashioned ways. In 1817, he made a goodwill tour of the country. In Boston, crowds cheered Monroe enthusiastically. Boston newspapers expressed surprise at this warm welcome for a Republican from Virginia. After all, Boston had long been a Federalist stronghold.

Monroe hoped to create a new sense of national unity. One newspaper wrote that the United States was entering an "era of good feelings." By the time Monroe ran for a second term in 1820, no candidate opposed him. The Federalist party had disappeared.

Three Sectional Leaders

While conflict between political parties declined, disputes between different sections of the nation sharpened. In Congress, three ambitious young men took center stage. All three would play key roles in Congress for more than 30 years, as well as serving in other offices. Each represented a different section of the country.

Calhoun of the South John C. Calhoun spoke for the South. He had grown up on a frontier farm in South Carolina. Calhoun's immense energy and striking features earned him the nickname "young Hercules." He was slim and handsome, with deep-set eyes and a high forehead. His way of speaking was so intense that it sometimes made people uncomfortable to be in his presence.

Calhoun had supported the War of 1812. Like many southerners, he was a firm defender of slavery. In general, he opposed policies that would strengthen the power of the federal government.

Webster of the North Daniel Webster of New Hampshire was perhaps the most skillful public speaker of his time. With eyes flashing and shoulders thrown back, Webster was an impressive sight when he stood up to speak in Congress. An observer described him as a "great cannon loaded to the lips."

Like many New Englanders, Webster had opposed the War of 1812. He even refused to vote for taxes to pay for the war effort. After the war, he wanted the federal government to take a larger role in building the nation's economy. Unlike Calhoun, Webster thought that slavery was evil.

Clay of the West Henry Clay spoke for the West. You have already met Clay as a leader of the War Hawks, who pushed for war against Britain in 1812.

Clay was born in Virginia but moved to Kentucky when he was 20. As a young lawyer, he was once fined for brawling with an opponent. Usually, however, he charmed both friends and rivals. Supporters called him "Gallant Harry of the West." Like Webster, Clay strongly favored a more active role for the central government in promoting the country's growth.

Helping American Businesses Grow

After the War of 1812, leaders like Calhoun, Webster, and Clay had to deal with serious economic issues. Despite the nation's great physical growth and the soaring spirits of its people, the United States

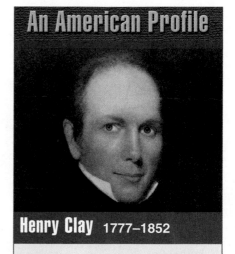

An American Profile

Henry Clay 1777–1852

During his long service to his country, Henry Clay was a firm defender of the Union. Clay helped to guide his country through some of its most difficult crises. Three times he helped resolve bitter disputes that threatened to tear the nation apart.

One office that eluded him was the presidency. He was defeated three times in efforts to become President. Yet, he was proud that he had held to his principles. Once, when asked if he was bitter about his failure to become President, he responded: "No. I had rather be right than be President."

Name two qualities that Clay demonstrated during his career in public service.

Identify Supporting Details

What details in this subsection explain the relationship between the money supply and the Bank of the United States? Add these details to your outline.

economy faced severe problems. This was due in part to the lack of a national bank.

The charter that had set up the Bank of the United States ran out in 1811. Without the Bank to lend money and regulate the nation's money supply, the economy suffered. State banks made loans and issued money. However, they often put too much money into circulation. With so much money available to spend, prices rose rapidly.

In the nation's early years, Republicans like Jefferson and Madison had opposed a national bank. By 1816, however, many Republicans believed that a bank was needed. They supported a law to charter the second Bank of the United States. By lending money and restoring order to the nation's money supply, the Bank helped American businesses grow.

Protection From Foreign Competition Another economic problem facing the nation was foreign competition, especially from Britain. In the early 1800s, the Embargo Act and then the War of 1812 kept most British goods out of the United States. In response, ambitious American business leaders like Francis Cabot Lowell established their own mills and factories. As a result, American industry grew quickly until 1815.

A Flood of British Goods With the end of the War of 1812, British goods again poured into the United States. Because the British had a head start in industrializing, they could make and sell goods more cheaply than Americans could. Most British factory buildings and machines were older and had already been paid for. In contrast, Americans still had to pay for their new factory buildings.

Sometimes, British manufacturers sold cloth in the United States for less than it cost to make. British manufacturers hoped to put American rivals out of business. Then, the British planned to raise prices.

Congress Passes a Protective Tariff The British plan caused dozens of New England businesses to fail. Angry owners asked Congress to place a protective tariff on all goods imported from Europe. As you have read, the purpose of a protective tariff is to protect a country's industries from foreign competition.

Viewing History

Cheapened Money

Without a national bank, the states began issuing money, like this one-dollar bank note issued by the state of Massachusetts. With so much money being issued, the value of the money declined. **Analyzing Primary Sources** *What do the illustrations on the money show about the changing nature of work at the time?*

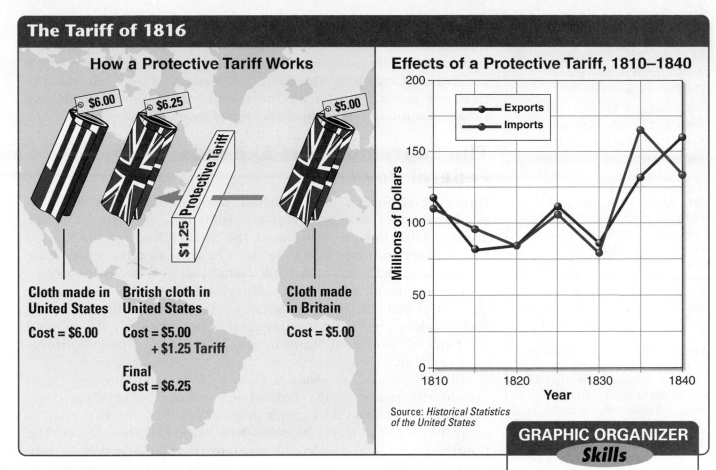

The Tariff of 1816

How a Protective Tariff Works

$6.00

$6.25

$1.25 Protective Tariff

$5.00

Cloth made in United States

Cost = $6.00

British cloth in United States

Cost = $5.00
+ $1.25 Tariff

Final
Cost = $6.25

Cloth made in Britain

Cost = $5.00

Effects of a Protective Tariff, 1810–1840

Exports
Imports

Millions of Dollars

Year

Source: *Historical Statistics of the United States*

Congress responded by passing the Tariff of 1816. It greatly raised tariffs on imports. This increase made imported goods far more expensive than similar American-made goods. Higher tariffs led to angry protests from southerners. Southerners had built few factories. As a result, they did not benefit from the tariff. Also, southerners bought many British goods. The new tariff drove up the price of British-made goods. Southerners complained that the tariff made northern manufacturers rich at the expense of the South.

Clay's American System

The bitter dispute over tariffs reflected the growth of sectionalism. **Sectionalism** is loyalty to one's state or section rather than to the nation as a whole. Americans identified themselves as southerners, northerners, or westerners. In Congress, representatives from different sections often clashed.

Henry Clay wanted to promote economic growth for all sections. His program, known as the **American System,** called for high tariffs on imports, which would help northern factories. With wealth from industry, Clay believed, northerners would have the money to buy farm products from the West and the South. High tariffs would also reduce American dependence on foreign goods.

Clay also urged Congress to use money from tariffs to build roads, bridges, and canals. A better transportation system, he believed, would make it easier and cheaper for farmers in the West and the South to ship goods to city markets.

Clay's American System never fully went into effect. While tariffs remained high, Congress spent little on internal improvements—improvements for roads, bridges, and canals. Southerners in particular disliked Clay's plan. The South had many fine rivers on which to transport goods. Many southerners opposed paying for roads and canals that brought them no direct benefits.

The Supreme Court Expands Federal Power

Under Chief Justice John Marshall, the Supreme Court strengthened the power of the federal government to promote economic growth. After Congress chartered the second Bank of the United States, Maryland tried to tax the Bank in order to drive it out of the state. James McCulloch, the Bank cashier, refused to pay the tax.

In the case of *McCulloch v. Maryland* (1819), the Court ruled that states had no right to interfere with federal institutions within their borders. The ruling strengthened federal power. It also allowed the Bank of the United States to continue, which helped the economy to expand.

In another case, *Gibbons v. Ogden* (1824), the Supreme Court upheld the power of the federal government to regulate trade between states. The Court struck down a New York law that tried to control steamboat travel between New York and New Jersey. The Court ruled that a state could regulate trade only within its own borders. Only the federal government had the power to regulate interstate commerce, or trade between different states. This decision helped the national economy by making it easier for the government to regulate trade.

★ ★ ★ Section 3 Assessment ★ ★ ★

Recall

1. **Identify** Explain the significance of (a) American System, (b) *McCulloch* v. *Maryland*, (c) *Gibbons* v. *Ogden*.
2. **Define** (a) sectionalism, (b) internal improvements, (c) interstate commerce.

Comprehension

3. How did Calhoun, Webster, and Clay each represent the views of his own section?
4. How did protective tariffs help American industry after the War of 1812?
5. Why did southerners oppose Clay's American System?

6. How did Supreme Court rulings give the federal government greater power?

Critical Thinking and Writing

7. **Exploring the Main Idea** Review the Main Idea statement at the beginning of this section. Then, describe one result of the Era of Good Feelings.
8. **Analyzing Primary Sources** In 1816, a member of Congress said, "It is unjust to aggravate the burdens of the people [to favor] the manufacturers." Do you think the speaker was from the North or the South? Explain.

ACTIVITY

Chairing a Debate It is 1825, and you are chairing a three-way debate between Calhoun, Webster, and Clay. Part of your responsibility is to introduce each debater. Write a one-paragraph introduction for each person. Then, work with a partner to practice giving the introduction.

Comparing and Contrasting

In what ways were the interests of Americans in the three regions of their country alike or different? As you learn about history, you often need to compare and contrast information to understand how the similarities and differences affected events. A graphic organizer is often helpful in comparing and contrasting information.

The Beginning of Sectionalism

Similarities
- Each region had a bright, young leader who represented its interests in the United States Congress.
- Each leader wanted to protect his region's economy.

North
- Economy: Textile mills and new factories
- Spokesperson: Daniel Webster
- Favored Tariff of 1816 because it kept Europeans from selling their goods at a lower price than that of American goods

South
- Economy: Agricultural with few factories
- Spokesperson: John C. Calhoun
- Opposed Tariff of 1816 because it raised prices on European goods that the South favored and forced Southerners to buy costly American-made goods

West
- Economy: Small farms
- Spokesperson: Henry Clay
- Wanted economic growth for all sections; supported tariff in belief that if North were protected, it would buy products from South and West and that the United States should reduce its dependence on foreign goods
- Wanted internal improvements such as better transportation in the United States

Learn the Skill *To compare and contrast information, use the following steps:*

1. **Read the title and headings.** These name the subject and tell what is being compared and contrasted.
2. **Identify similarities.** In what ways are the things being compared alike?
3. **Identify differences.** What contrasts or differences are given?
4. **Analyze the information.** What issues or problems might the differences cause?

Practice the Skill *Answer the following questions about the graphic organizer above:*

1. What are the three sections being compared?
2. What did all three regions of the nation have in common?
3. (a) How did the economy of the North differ from that of the South? (b) Why did southerners see the Tariff of 1816 as harmful to them? (c) What was Henry Clay's view of protective tariffs?
4. What issues do you think developed from these regional differences?

Apply the Skill *See the Chapter Review and Assessment.*

4 New Nations in the Americas

Prepare to Read

Objectives

In this section, you will
- Explain how Latin American nations won independence and became republics.
- Describe how the United States gained Florida.
- Explain the purpose of the Monroe Doctrine.

Key Terms

creole
Republic of Great Colombia
United Provinces of Central America
Negro Fort
Monroe Doctrine
intervention

Target Reading Skill

Cause and Effect As you read, complete the following chart to show some of the events that led to the Monroe Doctrine. Add as many boxes as you need.

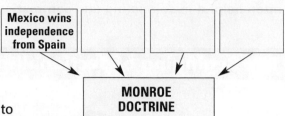

| Mexico wins independence from Spain | | | |

MONROE DOCTRINE

Main Idea The United States issued the Monroe Doctrine to discourage Europe from interfering in Latin America's affairs.

Father Hidalgo speaks

Setting the Scene On a quiet Sunday in September 1810, the church bell rang in the Mexican village of Dolores. In the square, Indians gathered around the village priest, Miguel Hidalgo (mee GEHL ee DAHL goh).

Hidalgo issued a bold call for Indians to join the struggle to make Mexico independent. No one knows the exact words Hidalgo used, but these are the words that have been passed down:

> 66 My children. . . . Will you be free? Will you recover the lands stolen 300 years ago from your forefathers by the hated Spaniards? We must act at once! 99
>
> —Father Miguel Hidalgo y Costilla, "Cry of Dolores" speech, September 16, 1810

Thousands of Mexicans rallied to Father Hidalgo's call for freedom.

Like Mexico, other Spanish colonies were reacting to the call for freedom from Spain. In most parts of Latin America,* people in the early 1800s fought wars for independence. As new nations emerged, President Monroe formed a bold new foreign policy. His goal was to keep Europeans from using the fighting as an excuse to create new colonies in the Americas.

Revolution in Latin America

By 1810, many people in Spain's American colonies were eager for independence. They had many reasons to be unhappy. Most people, even wealthy creoles, had little or no say in government. In Latin America, the term **creole** described people born to Spanish parents there. They demanded a role in government. Opposition to Spain was also growing among Indians. Harsh rules kept Indians forever in

---

* Latin America refers to the Western Hemisphere region in which Latin-based languages, such as Spanish, French, and Portuguese, are spoken. It includes Mexico, Central America, South America, and the West Indies.

debt. All over Latin America, people were eager to be free of the Spanish.

Mexican Independence As you have read, Miguel Hidalgo sounded the call for Mexican independence in 1810. Rebel forces won control of several provinces before Father Hidalgo was captured. In 1811, he was executed.

Another priest, José Morelos (hoh ZAY moh RAY lohs), took up the fight. Because he called for a program to give land to peasants, wealthy creoles opposed him. Before long, Morelos, too, was captured and killed by the Spanish.

Slowly, creoles began to join the revolutionary movement. In 1821, revolutionary forces led by creoles won control of Mexico. A few years later, Mexico became a republic with its own constitution.

The Liberator In South America, too, a series of revolutions freed colonies from Spanish rule. The best-known revolutionary leader was Simón Bolívar (see MOHN boh LEE vahr). He became known as The Liberator for his role in the Latin American wars of independence.

Bolívar came from a wealthy creole family in Venezuela. As a young man, he took up the cause of Venezuelan independence. Bolívar promised, "I will never allow my hands to be idle, nor my soul to rest until I have broken the shackles which chain us to Spain."

Bolívar rose to become a leader of the rebel forces. In a bold move, he led an army from Venezuela over the high Andes Mountains into Colombia. There, Bolívar took the Spanish forces by surprise and defeated them in 1819.

Soon after, Bolívar became president of the independent **Republic of Great Colombia.** It included the present-day nations of Venezuela, Colombia, Ecuador, and Panama.

Other New Nations Other independent nations emerged in Latin America. José de San Martín (san mahr TEEN) led Argentina to freedom in 1816. He then helped the people of Chile, Peru, and Ecuador win independence.

In 1821, the peoples of Central America declared independence from Spain. Two years later, they formed the **United Provinces of Central America.** It included the present-day nations of Nicaragua, Costa Rica, El Salvador, Honduras, and Guatemala. By 1825, Spain had lost all its colonies in Latin America except Puerto Rico and Cuba.

The Portuguese colony of Brazil won independence peacefully. When Brazilian revolutionaries demanded independence, Prince Pedro, son of the Portuguese king, joined their cause. He became emperor of the new independent nation of Brazil.

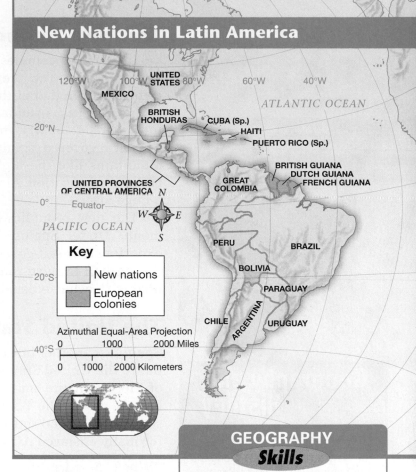

New Nations in Latin America

GEOGRAPHY Skills

Wars of independence led to the creation of many new countries in Latin America.

1. **Location** On the map, locate **(a)** Mexico, **(b)** Great Colombia, **(c)** United Provinces of Central America, **(d)** Brazil, **(e)** Argentina, **(f)** Chile, **(g)** Bolivia.

2. **Region** What parts of Latin America remained European colonies?

3. **Critical Thinking Applying Information** Use the world map in the Reference Section to identify the modern nations that were eventually carved out of Great Colombia.

The New Republics

Spain's former colonies modeled their constitutions on that of the United States. Yet, their experience after independence was very different from that of their neighbor to the north. Unlike the people of the 13 British colonies, the peoples of Latin America did not unite into a single country. In part, geography made unity difficult. Latin America covered a much larger area than the English colonies. Mountains like the high, rugged Andes acted as barriers to travel and communication. Also, the Spanish colonies were spread out over a huge area.

The new republics had a hard time setting up stable governments. Under Spanish rule, the colonists had gained little or no experience in self-government. Powerful leaders took advantage of the turmoil to seize control. As a result, the new nations were often unable to achieve democratic rule.

The United States Gains Florida

Spain lost another one of its colonies, Florida—not to independence, but to the United States. Many Americans wanted to gain possession of Florida. White southerners were especially worried about disturbances across the border. Creek and Seminole Indians in Florida sometimes raided settlements in Georgia. Also, Florida was a refuge for many enslaved Africans.

"Black Seminoles" Since the 1700s, Spanish officials had protected enslaved Africans who had fled from plantations in Georgia and South Carolina. Seminole Indians allowed Africans to live near their villages. In return, these "black Seminoles" gave the Indians a share of the crops they raised. The black Seminoles adopted many Indian customs.

One settlement on the Apalachicola River known as the Negro Fort contained about 1,000 black Seminoles. General Andrew Jackson demanded that Spain demolish the Negro Fort. (See Geography and History feature on this page.) When the Spanish governor refused, the United States invaded Florida and destroyed the fort.

Spain Gives Up Florida In 1818, Jackson again headed to Florida with a force of more than 3,000 soldiers. Spain protested but did little else. It was busy fighting rebels in Latin America and could not risk war with the United States.

In the end, Spain agreed to peace talks. Secretary of State John Quincy Adams worked out a treaty with Spain. In it, Spain agreed to give Florida to the United States in exchange for $5 million. The Adams-Onís (oh NEES) Treaty took effect in 1821.

The Monroe Doctrine

Americans cheered as Latin American nations won independence. The actions of European powers, however, worried Secretary Adams and President Monroe. In 1815, Prussia, France, Russia, and Austria formed an alliance aimed at crushing any revolution that sprang up

Geography and History

The Negro Fort

The Negro Fort was built along the Apalachicola River, in the Spanish territory of Florida, about 60 miles from Georgia. At its height, some 1,000 black Seminoles farmed along the river. They worried Georgia planters, who feared they would encourage enslaved Africans to revolt.

The fort sat on a hill surrounded on three sides by forests and swamps. The weak side lay along the river. In early skirmishes against the United States Army, the defenders beat their land forces. Then, the army launched an all-out attack by land and river. Gunboats bombarding the fort hit the room where gunpowder was stored. The explosion destroyed the fort, killing most of the inhabitants. The survivors were sold into slavery.

How might the defenders of the Negro Fort have inspired enslaved Africans in the United States?

in Europe. They seemed ready to help Spain regain its colonies in Latin America. In addition, Russia claimed lands on the Pacific coast of North America.

The British, too, worried about other European nations meddling in the Western Hemisphere. They feared that their profitable trade would be hurt if Spain regained control of its former colonies. Thus, they suggested that the United States and Britain issue a joint statement guaranteeing the freedom of the new nations of Latin America.

Monroe decided to act independently of Britain. In a message to Congress in 1823, he made a bold foreign policy statement, known as the Monroe Doctrine. Monroe declared that the United States would not interfere in the affairs of European nations or existing colonies of the European nations. At the same time, he warned European nations not to attempt to regain control of the newly independent nations of Latin America.

The Monroe Doctrine stated that the United States would oppose any attempt to build new colonies in the Americas. Monroe's message showed that the United States was determined to keep European powers out of the Western Hemisphere.

The United States did not have the military power to enforce the Monroe Doctrine. Britain, however, supported the statement. With its strong navy, it could stop Europeans from building new colonies in the Americas.

As the United States became stronger, the Monroe Doctrine grew in importance. On several occasions, the United States successfully challenged European intervention, or direct involvement, in Latin America. In the early 1900s, Presidents also used the Monroe Doctrine to justify sending troops to Caribbean nations. Thus, Monroe's bold statement helped shape United States foreign policy for more than 100 years.

Recognizing Multiple Causes

A cause makes something happen. What were some of the causes of the Monroe Doctrine? Add these causes to your chart.

★ ★ ★ Section 4 Assessment ★ ★ ★

Recall

1. **Identify** Explain the significance of (a) Republic of Great Colombia, (b) United Provinces of Central America, (c) Negro Fort, (d) Monroe Doctrine.
2. **Define** (a) creole, (b) intervention.

Comprehension

3. How did revolutions change Latin America?
4. How did the United States acquire Florida?
5. Why was the Monroe Doctrine issued?

Critical Thinking and Writing

6. **Exploring the Main Idea** Review the Main Idea statement at the beginning of this section. Then, list as many ways as you can think of in which the Western Hemisphere might be different today if the United States had not issued the Monroe Doctrine.
7. **Analyzing Information** What parts of the United States Constitution do you think most appealed to people in other nations?

CHAPTER SUMMARY

Section 1
The Industrial Revolution began in Great Britain but spread to the United States. It caused a great deal of change in how Americans worked and lived during the first half of the 1800s.

Section 2
Improvements in roads, the development of steam engines, and digging canals helped to move people and goods westward.

Section 3
Sectional tensions grew between the North, the South, and the West during the early 1800s. Congress began passing laws to help U.S. business grow.

Section 4
By 1825, most nations in Latin America had won independence. The United States issued the Monroe Doctrine to discourage Europe from intervening in the affairs of Latin American nations.

For additional review and enrichment activities, see the interactive version of *The American Nation,* available on the Web and on CD-ROM.

Chapter Self-Test For practice test questions for Chapter 11, visit PHSchool.com, **Web Code mfa-1104.**

Building Vocabulary

Write sentences using the chapter vocabulary words listed below, leaving blanks where the vocabulary words should go. Exchange your sentences with another student, and fill in the blanks in each other's sentences.

1. **spinning jenny**
2. **capital**
3. **capitalist**
4. **urbanization**
5. **flatboat**
6. **turnpike**
7. **corduroy road**
8. **sectionalism**
9. **creole**
10. **intervention**

Reviewing Key Facts

11. How did Samuel Slater bring the Industrial Revolution to the United States? (Section 1)
12. Describe three ways in which transportation improved in the early 1800s. (Section 2)
13. Why did southerners oppose the protective tariff while northern manufacturers supported it? (Section 3)

14. Why was British support of the Monroe Doctrine important to its success? (Section 4)

Critical Thinking and Writing

15. **Linking Past and Present (a)** Make a list of the ways in which the cities of today are like the cities of the early 1800s. **(b)** Make a list of the ways in which they are different.
16. **Connecting to Geography: Regions (a)** Make a list of the physical and economic differences between the North, South, and West. **(b)** Analyze how these differences affected the political views of people in the regions.
17. **Identifying Causes and Effects (a)** Which came first: the War of 1812 or the innovations of Francis Cabot Lowell? **(b)** Analyze the relationship between the War of 1812 and economic change in the United States.
18. **Analyzing Information** How did steam power help change the way goods were manufactured?

Analyzing Primary Sources

In 1831, a young Frenchman named Alexis de Tocqueville (TOHK vihl) made a nine-month tour of the United States. Tocqueville later described what he admired about the young nation.

66 Of all the countries in the world, America is that in which the spread of ideas and of human industry is most continual and most rapid. . . . The American . . . is less afraid than any other inhabitant of the globe to risk what he has gained in the hope of a better future. . . . There is not a country in the world where man . . . feels with more pride that he can fashion the universe to please himself. 99

—Alexis de Tocqueville, *Democracy in America,* 1835

19. According to Tocqueville, new ideas in the United States
    A. cannot thrive in the new country.
    B. do not exist because inventors copy European ideas.
    C. do not occur very often.
    D. are encouraged to flourish.
20. Based on this quote, what are the qualities Tocqueville admires about Americans?
    A. their willingness to take risks
    B. their willingness to expand their territory
    C. their ability to beat Britain in war
    D. their democratic government

Comparing and Contrasting

A Venn diagram is a useful way of showing similarities and differences between two people or groups. Study the Venn diagram below, and then answer the questions.

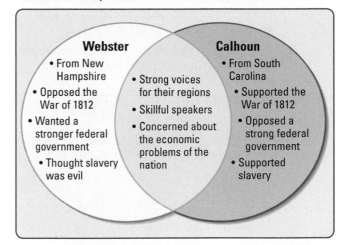

Webster
- From New Hampshire
- Opposed the War of 1812
- Wanted a stronger federal government
- Thought slavery was evil

- Strong voices for their regions
- Skillful speakers
- Concerned about the economic problems of the nation

Calhoun
- From South Carolina
- Supported the War of 1812
- Opposed a strong federal government
- Supported slavery

21. Which of the following characteristics did Webster and Calhoun share?
    A. They were both from South Carolina.
    B. They both supported the War of 1812.
    C. They were both concerned about the economic problems of the nation.
    D. They both hated slavery.
22. Based on this diagram, on what issues might you expect Calhoun to clash most seriously with Webster?

ACTIVITIES

Connecting With . . .

Science and Technology

Creating a Time Capsule It is December 31, 1825, and you are creating a time capsule to be buried on the lawn of the White House in Washington, D.C. The time capsule will celebrate the previous 35 years of change in the nation's transportation system. Write an imaginary news story with its own headline about one of the events discussed in this chapter. Use the library and Internet resources to write short biographies of some of the most important people who participated in this change.

Go Online
PHSchool.com

Creating a Database

Independence for Latin America Use the Internet to find sites relating to the struggles of Latin Americans for independence. Then, create a database that compares the road to independence of the various countries of Latin America. Include such categories as leaders and dates that independence was won. For help in starting this activity, visit PHSchool.com, **Web Code mfd-1106.**

TEST PREPARATION

1 Which of the following statements best reflects a key belief of the Democratic Republican Party?

   A "The Supreme Court must have the freedom to interpret the Constitution as it sees fit."

   B "Unless we take steps to encourage manufacturing, our national economy will fail."

   C "The United States must strengthen its economic bonds with Britain."

   D "The growing power of the central government is a threat to the rights of the states."

Use the quotation and your knowledge of social studies to answer the following question.

George Washington's Farewell Address, 1796

"The great rule of conduct for us, in regard to foreign nations, is . . . to have with them as little political connection as possible."

---

2 The statement above expresses Washington's support for what policy?

   A Imposing a trade embargo

   B Forming an alliance with France

   C Maintaining neutrality

   D Increasing the size of the navy

3 Which of the following did the most to establish the principle of judicial review?

   A The Bill of Rights

   B The Judiciary Act of 1789

   C *Marbury* v. *Madison*

   D *McCulloch* v. *Maryland*

4 Which of the following was not part of Alexander Hamilton's economic plan for the nation?

   A High tariffs

   B Payment of state debts

   C Laissez faire economics

   D A national bank

Use the map and your knowledge of social studies to answer the following question.

The Louisiana Purchase, 1803

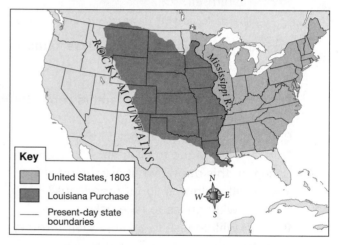

Key
- United States, 1803
- Louisiana Purchase
- Present-day state boundaries

5 Which statement is best supported by the map?

   A As a result of the Louisiana Purchase, the United States expanded to the Pacific Ocean.

   B Half of all current states were part of the Louisiana Purchase.

   C The Mississippi River formed most of the eastern border of the Louisiana Purchase.

   D The Louisiana Purchase gave the United States control of the Rocky Mountains.

6 Which of the following actions would President Monroe have viewed as a violation of the Monroe Doctrine?

A Spain invades Portugal.

B Spain retakes Mexico.

C Spain refuses to sell Florida.

D Simón Bolívar declares himself king of Venezuela.

Use the graph <u>and</u> your knowledge of social studies to answer the following question.

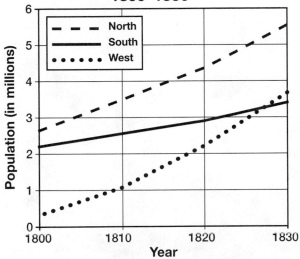

Population Growth and Distribution, 1800–1830

Source: *Historical Statistics of the United States*

7 Which generalization about the period from 1800–1830 is supported by the graph?

A The West had a larger population than the South.

B The population of the South declined.

C The West grew at a faster rate than the North.

D All three regions grew at an equal rate.

8 Which group would have been most likely to support the aims of the War Hawks?

A New England merchants

B Settlers on the western frontier

C Members of Tecumseh's federation

D Delegates to the Hartford Convention

9 Which of the following is the best example of the impact of geography on the Industrial Revolution?

A The location of the first American textile mill

B The invention of interchangeable parts

C The use of child labor

D The combination of spinning and weaving in a single factory

Writing Practice

10 "The first five Presidents provided models of bold leadership and creative thinking." Using at least two different Presidents, give three examples that support this statement.

11 Trace the development of American foreign policy from Washington to Monroe. Choose what you think were the three most important policies or events involving foreign nations. Describe the key issues and the course followed by the President. Then, make two generalizations about foreign policy in this period.

Unit 4
An Era of Expansion

The Nation Grows
In Oscar E. Berninghaus's *Westward Ho!*, a long line of wagons carries settlers west.

"Our population is rolling toward the shores of the Pacific. . . . It will soon . . . reach the Rocky Mountains and be ready to pour into the Oregon territory."

—John C. Calhoun, South Carolina Senator (1843)

CHAPTER 12

The Jacksonian Era

1824–1840

1 A New Era in Politics
2 Jackson in the White House
3 A New Crisis

Discussing politics

Cherokees on the Trail of Tears

1820s

A growing spirit of equality spreads through the nation. As President, Andrew Jackson supports the interests of the common people.

1830

Congress passes the Indian Removal Act, which forces Native Americans to move west of the Mississippi.

AMERICAN EVENTS

Presidential Terms:

John Quincy Adams 1825-1829   Andrew Jackson 1829-1837

1824 • • • **1828** • • • **1832**

WORLD EVENTS ▲ **1824**
Simón Bolívar becomes dictator of Peru.

▲ **1829**
The Swiss adopt universal male suffrage.

The Election of 1824

Andrew Jackson received the most popular votes in the 1824 election but not a majority of the electoral votes. The election was decided in the House of Representatives.

Claimed by Great Britain and the United States

BRITISH TERRITORY

Key

- Andrew Jackson
- John Quincy Adams
- William Crawford
- Henry Clay

States with more than one color divided their electoral votes among two or more candidates

Albers Equal-Area Projection

0   200   400 Miles

0   200   400 Kilometers

L. Superior

L. Michigan

L. Huron

L. Ontario

L. Erie

Michigan Territory

Unorganized Territory

MEXICO

Arkansas Territory

Missouri

Illinois   Indiana

Ohio

Kentucky

Tennessee

MS   Alabama

Louisiana

Maine

VT

NH

MA

New York

CT

RI

40°N

Pennsylvania

New Jersey

Delaware

Maryland

Virginia

North Carolina

South Carolina

Georgia

ATLANTIC OCEAN

70°W

30°N

Florida Territory

Gulf of Mexico

90°W   80°W

The Bank of the United States

Nicholas Biddle, President of the Bank of the United States

1832

President Jackson vetoes the bill to renew the charter of the Bank of the United States.

1836

The second Seminole War begins.

Martin Van Buren 1837–1841

1832 · · **1836** · · · **1840** · ·

▲ **1832**
The Reform Act doubles the number of eligible voters in Britain.

▲ **1837**
Canadian colonists revolt and demand democratic reform.

1 A New Era in Politics

Prepare to Read

Objectives

In this section, you will
- Summarize how more citizens gained suffrage in the 1820s.
- Explain the dispute over the 1824 election.
- Describe why President Adams was unpopular.
- List the new political parties.

Key Terms

suffrage

majority

Whigs

Democrats

caucus

nominating convention

Target Reading Skill

Cause and Effect Copy the chart below. As you read, complete the chart to show some of the developments that caused changes in political parties in the 1820s. Add as many boxes as you need.

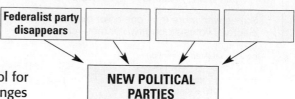

| Federalist party disappears | | | |

→ **NEW POLITICAL PARTIES**

Main Idea As President, Andrew Jackson became the symbol for the new democratic spirit that brought political and social changes to the nation.

Statue of Andrew Jackson

Setting the Scene Harry Ward, a New England teacher, made a visit to Cincinnati, Ohio, during the 1824 presidential election campaign. Writing to a friend, he described how Ohioans felt about Andrew Jackson, who was running for President. Jackson's supporters, he observed were "Strange! Wild! Infatuated! All for Jackson!"

On election day, more people voted for Andrew Jackson than for any of the other candidates. Oddly enough, Jackson did not become President that year.

Growing Spirit of Equality

The spirit of democracy, which was changing the political system, affected American ideas about social classes. Most Americans did not feel that the rich deserved special respect.

Wealthy European visitors to the United States were surprised that American servants expected to be treated as equals. Others were amazed that butlers and maids refused to be summoned with bells, as in Europe.

Alexis de Tocqueville A visitor from France, Alexis de Tocqueville (TOHK veel) became especially well known for his observations on American Democracy. He arrived in the United States in 1831. The French government had sent him to study the American prison system. For several months, Tocqueville toured much of the United States. However, he observed much more than prisons. He observed a society that was becoming more and more democratic.

After his return to France, Tocqueville recorded his experiences and observations in a book titled *Democracy in America*. In it, he admired the American democratic spirit and its goals of equality and freedom. He found the results of the "revolution taking place" in America while "still far from coming to an end" were "already incomparably greater than anything which has taken place in the world before."

More Voters During the 1820s, more people gained **suffrage,** or the right to vote. Others, however, were denied full participation in the growing democracy.

The United States was growing rapidly. New states were joining the Union, and there were many citizens eager to participate in elections. Some of the first states to give voting privileges to white males without property were in the West. In these states, any white man over age 21 could vote.

Reformers in the East worked to expand suffrage. By the 1830s, most eastern states dropped the requirement that voters own land. In this way, many craftsworkers and shopkeepers won the right to vote.

Throughout the country, growing numbers of Americans exercised their right to vote. Before 1828, the turnout of eligible voters was never more than 27 percent. That low percentage rose to nearly 58 percent in the election of 1828. By 1840, voter turnout was nearly 80 percent.

Limits on Suffrage Despite the nation's growing democratic spirit, a great many Americans did not have the right to vote. They included women, Native Americans, and the vast majority of African Americans. Slaves had no political rights at all.

As more white men were winning suffrage, free African Americans were losing it. In the early years of the nation, most northern states had allowed free African American men to vote. In the 1820s, many of these states took away that right. By 1830, only a few New England states permitted African American men to vote on equal terms with white men. In New York, African American men had to own property in order to vote. White men did not.

The Disputed Election of 1824

There were four candidates for President in 1824. All four were members of the old Republican party. However, each had support in different parts of the country. John Quincy Adams was strong in New England. Henry Clay and Andrew Jackson had support in the West. William Crawford was favored in the South. However, he became too ill to campaign.

The Candidates John Quincy Adams of Massachusetts was the son of Abigail and John Adams, the second President. A graduate of Harvard University, the younger Adams had served as Secretary of State and helped end the War of 1812. People admired Adams for his intelligence and high morals. Adams, however, was uncomfortable campaigning among the common people. In fact, to most people he seemed hard and cold.

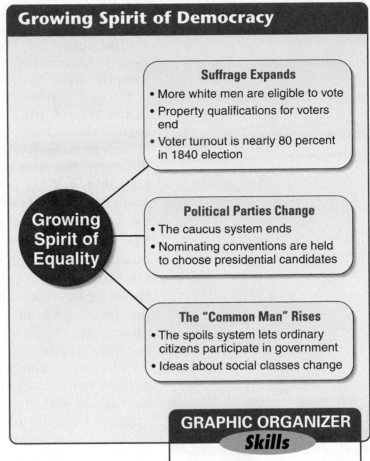

Growing Spirit of Democracy

Growing Spirit of Equality

Suffrage Expands
- More white men are eligible to vote
- Property qualifications for voters end
- Voter turnout is nearly 80 percent in 1840 election

Political Parties Change
- The caucus system ends
- Nominating conventions are held to choose presidential candidates

The "Common Man" Rises
- The spoils system lets ordinary citizens participate in government
- Ideas about social classes change

GRAPHIC ORGANIZER
Skills

The election of Andrew Jackson in 1828 marked a change in ideas about democracy.

1. **Comprehension** How were candidates chosen for office?

2. **Critical Thinking Supporting a Point of View** Do you think the growing spirit of democracy helped Jackson in the 1828 election? Explain.

Civics

A Kentuckian, Henry Clay was a shrewd politician who became Speaker of the House of Representatives. In Congress, Clay was a skillful negotiator. He worked out several important compromises. Despite his abilities, Clay was less popular than the other candidate from the West, Andrew Jackson.

Most Americans knew Andrew Jackson for his military victories in the War of 1812. He was the "Hero of New Orleans." He also earned the nickname "Old Hickory" after a soldier said that he was "tough as hickory." Although he was a landowner and a slave owner, many saw him as a man of the people. Jackson had been born in a log cabin, and his parents were poor farmers. He was admired by small farmers and others who felt left out of the growing economy in the United States.

The "Corrupt Bargain" No clear winner emerged from the election of 1824. Jackson won the popular vote, but no candidate won a **majority,** or more than half, of the electoral votes. As a result, the House of Representatives had to choose the President from among the top three candidates. Because he finished fourth, Clay was out of the running. As Speaker of the House, though, he was able to influence the results.

Clay urged members of the House to vote for Adams. After Adams became President, he named Clay his Secretary of State. Jackson and his backers were furious. They accused Adams and Clay of making a "corrupt bargain" and stealing the election from Jackson.

As Jackson was riding home to Tennessee, he met an old friend. "Well, General," said the friend, "we did all we could for you here, but the rascals at Washington cheated you out of it."

"Indeed, my old friend," replied Jackson, "there was cheating and corruption and bribery, too."

The charges were not true, however. The election was decided as the Constitution stated. Still, the anger of Jackson and his supporters seriously hampered President Adams's efforts to unify the nation.

An Unpopular President

Adams knew that the election had angered many Americans. To "bring the whole people together," he pushed for a program of economic growth through internal improvements. His plan backfired, however, and opposition to him grew.

Promoting Economic Growth Similar to Alexander Hamilton and Henry Clay, Adams thought that the federal government should promote economic growth. He called for the government to pay for new roads and canals. These internal improvements would help farmers to transport goods to market.

Adams also favored projects to promote the arts and the sciences. He suggested building a national university and an observatory from which astronomers could study the stars.

Most Americans objected to spending money on such programs. They feared that the federal government would become too powerful. Congress approved money for a national road and some canals but turned down most of Adams's other programs.

A Bitter Campaign In 1828, Adams faced an uphill battle for reelection. This time, Andrew Jackson was Adams's only opponent.

The campaign was a bitter contest. The focus was not on issues, but on the candidates' personalities. Jackson supporters, however, renewed charges that Adams made a "corrupt bargain" after the 1824 election. But they also attacked Adams as an aristocrat, or member of the upper class. Adams supporters replied with similar attacks. They called Jackson a dangerous "military chieftain." If Jackson became President, they warned, he could become a dictator like Napoleon Bonaparte of France.

Jackson won the election easily. His supporters cheered the outcome as a victory for common people. For the first time, the politics of the common people were important. By common people, they meant farmers in the West and South and city workers in the East.

Jacksonian Democracy Andrew Jackson's inauguration in 1829 reflected the growing spirit of democracy. The spread of political power to more people was part of what became known as Jacksonian democracy.

Jackson was also the first westerner to occupy the White House. His election represented the beginning of a shift of political power to the West.

As Jackson traveled to Washington to be inaugurated, large crowds cheered him along the way. For the first time, thousands of ordinary people flooded the capital to watch the President take the oath of office. After Jackson was sworn in, the crowd followed the new President to a reception at the White House. One onlooker described the scene with amazement:

> 66 Country men, farmers, gentlemen, mounted and dismounted, boys, women and children, black and white. Carriages, wagons, and carts all pursuing [Jackson] to the President's house. 99
>
> —Margaret Bayard Smith, *The First Forty Years of Washington Society*

The crowds were so huge, the observer continued, that the President was "almost suffocated and torn to pieces by the people in their eagerness to shake hands."

Jackson's critics said the scene showed that "King Mob" was ruling the nation. Amos Kendall, a loyal Jackson supporter, viewed the inauguration celebration in a more positive way: "It was a proud day for the people. General Jackson is their own President."

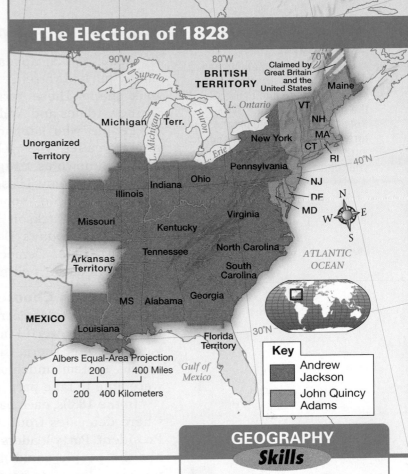

The Election of 1828

Key

- Andrew Jackson
- John Quincy Adams

GEOGRAPHY Skills

In the election of 1828, Andrew Jackson defeated John Quincy Adams. Unlike in the election of 1824, Jackson was a decisive winner in 1828.

1. **Location** On the map, locate **(a)** Massachusetts, **(b)** Kentucky, **(c)** Tennessee.

2. **Place** In which section of the country did Adams have the most support?

3. **Critical Thinking Applying Information** Which of the two candidates would probably have won Florida and Arkansas if they had been states in 1828? Explain.

New Political Parties

By 1820, the disappearance of the Federalist party temporarily ended party differences. In the 1830s, however, new political parties took shape. These parties grew out of the conflict between John Quincy Adams and Andrew Jackson.

People who supported Adams and his programs for national growth called themselves National Republicans. In 1834, they became known as **Whigs.** Whigs wanted the federal government to spur the economy. Those who supported the Whigs included eastern business people, some southern planters, and many former Federalists. Jackson and his supporters called themselves **Democrats.** Today's Democratic party traces its roots to Andrew Jackson's time. Democrats included frontier farmers, as well as workers in eastern cities.

New Ways to Choose Candidates The two new political parties developed more democratic ways to choose candidates for President. In the past, powerful members of each party held a **caucus,** or private meeting. There, they chose their candidate. Critics called the caucus system undemocratic because only a few powerful people were able to take part in it.

In the 1830s, each party began to hold a **nominating convention,** where delegates from all the states chose the party's candidate for President. Party leaders might still dominate a particular convention, but the people could now have some influence in the nominating process. Also, state nominating conventions encouraged citizen participation in elections. Once citizens learned about the events of the convention, they would work for their party's choices. Today, the major political parties still hold conventions.

★ ★ ★ Section 1 Assessment ★ ★ ★

Recall

1. **Identify** Explain the significance of
   (a) Alexis de Tocqueville,
   (b) John Quincy Adams,
   (c) Whigs, (d) Democrats.
2. **Define** (a) suffrage,
   (b) majority, (c) caucus,
   (d) nominating convention.

Comprehension

3. How did political parties reflect the growing spirit of equality?
4. Why did Andrew Jackson feel that the election of 1824 was unfair?
5. What programs did Adams propose that made him unpopular?

Critical Thinking and Writing

6. **Exploring the Main Idea** Review the Main Idea statement at the beginning of this section. Then, write a paragraph explaining how a Jackson supporter might respond to this question: "Does a man become wiser, stronger, or more virtuous and patriotic because he has a fine house?"
7. **Supporting a Point of View** Write a paragraph in which you agree or disagree with John Quincy Adams's position that government should spend money to support the arts and sciences. Explain your answer.

ACTIVITY

Writing a Dialogue
Write a dialogue in which John Quincy Adams and Andrew Jackson discuss the election of 1824.

2 Jackson in the White House

Prepare to Read

Objectives

In this section, you will
- List the qualities that helped Andrew Jackson succeed.
- Explain the spoils system.
- Summarize why President Jackson fought the Bank of the United States.

Key Terms

spoils system

"kitchen cabinet"

Target Reading Skill

Sequence Copy this flow-chart. As you read, fill in the boxes with the events that led to the closing of the Bank of the United States in 1836. The first and last boxes have been completed for you. Add as many boxes as you need.

```
┌─────────────────────────┐
│ Bank controls loans     │
│ made by state banks     │
└─────────────────────────┘
            ↓
┌─────────────────────────┐
│                         │
└─────────────────────────┘
            ↓
┌─────────────────────────┐
│                         │
└─────────────────────────┘
            ↓
┌─────────────────────────┐
│                         │
└─────────────────────────┘
            ↓
┌─────────────────────────┐
│  Bank closes in 1836    │
└─────────────────────────┘
```

Main Idea President Jackson showed the strength of his will in his fight with the Bank of the United States.

Setting the Scene During the 1828 election campaign, many stories about Andrew Jackson spread. One recalled his days as a judge in Tennessee. A frontiersman named Russell Bean was supposed to appear before Jackson's court, but he refused to come inside. Jackson came roaring out of the courthouse. "Surrender, you infernal villain," he shouted, "or I'll blow you through." Bean looked into Jackson's blazing eyes and quietly surrendered. The iron will that made Russell Bean surrender also made Jackson a powerful President.

Andrew Jackson confronts Russell Bean

Andrew Jackson

Like many who admired him, Jackson was born in a log cabin on the frontier. His parents had left Ireland to settle in the Carolinas. Both died before Jackson was 15. Young Andrew had to grow up quickly.

A Self-made Man Although he was lean, he was a strong fighter. A friend who wrestled with him recalled, "I could throw him three times out of four, but he would never stay throwed."

Always determined, Jackson showed his toughness at 13 when he joined the Patriots during the American Revolution. He was captured by the British. When a British officer ordered the young prisoner to clean his boots, Jackson refused. The officer took a sword and slashed the boy's hand and face. The memory of that attack stayed with Jackson for the rest of his life.

After the Revolution, Jackson studied law in North Carolina. Later, he moved to Tennessee and set up a successful law practice. He became very wealthy by buying and selling land in Georgia and Alabama. While still in his twenties, he was elected to Congress.

Jackson won national fame for his achievements during the War of 1812. He led American forces to a major victory over the British at the Battle of New Orleans. He also defeated the Creek Indians and forced them to give up vast amounts of land in Georgia and Alabama.

A Man of Many Qualities Andrew Jackson was a complex person. He had led a violent and adventurous life. He was quick to lose his temper, and he dealt with his enemies harshly. When he became President, his opponents sarcastically called him "King Andrew." Jackson intended to be a strong president by expanding the powers of the presidency.

At the same time, Jackson's supporters admired his ability to inspire and lead others. They considered him a man of his word and a champion of the common people.

To the Creek Indians, however, Jackson was an enemy who showed no mercy. After defeating them in battle during the War of 1812, Jackson threatened to kill their leaders if they did not give up lands guaranteed them by earlier treaties. As a result, the Creeks had no affection for Jackson. Their name for him was "Sharp Knife."

The Spoils System

In 1828, President Jackson knew that Americans wanted change. "The people expected reform," he said. "This was the cry from Maine to Louisiana."

Reward for Victory After taking office, Jackson fired many government employees. He replaced them with his own supporters. Most other Presidents had done the same, but Jackson did it on a larger scale. He dismissed more than 200 previous presidential appointees.

Critics accused Jackson of rewarding Democrats who had helped elect him instead of choosing qualified men. Jackson replied that he was serving democracy by letting more citizens take part in government. According to Jackson, this would prevent a small group of wealthy men from controlling the government. He felt that ordinary Americans could fill government jobs. "The duties of all public officers are . . . so plain and simple that men of intelligence may readily qualify themselves for their performance," he said.

A Jackson supporter explained the system another way. "To the victor belong the spoils," he declared. Spoils are profits or benefits. From then on, the practice of rewarding supporters with government jobs became known as the spoils system.

The "Kitchen Cabinet" Jackson rewarded a number of his supporters with Cabinet jobs. However, few of them were qualified for the positions. Only Secretary of State Martin Van Buren was truly qualified for his position.

As a result, Jackson seldom met with his official Cabinet. Instead, he relied on a group of unofficial advisers. They included Democratic leaders and newspaper editors. These men had a good sense of the nation's mood. Because Jackson met with them in the White House kitchen, the group became known as the "kitchen cabinet."

The Bank War

President Jackson waged war on the Bank of the United States. Like many westerners, he thought that it was too powerful.

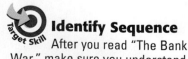

Identify Sequence
After you read "The Bank War," make sure you understand the issues involved in the Bank dispute. Add these issues to your chart in chronological order.

POLITICAL CARTOON
Skills

Andrew Jackson Battles the Bank of the United States In this cartoon, President Jackson battles the Bank of the United States and its branches (represented by the multiple heads).

1. **Comprehension** Read the cane Jackson is holding. What does it say?

2. **Understanding Main Ideas** How does Jackson fight the Bank?

3. **Critical Thinking Identifying Bias** How do you think the cartoonist felt about the Bank of the United States?

Civics

Mr. Biddle's Bank The Bank of the United States had been a subject of dispute since its early days. The Bank had great power because it controlled loans made by state banks. When the Bank's directors thought that state banks were making too many loans, they limited the amount these banks could lend. The cutbacks angered farmers and merchants who borrowed money to buy land or finance new businesses.

President Jackson and other leading Democrats saw the Bank as undemocratic. Although Congress created the Bank, it was run by private bankers. Jackson condemned these men as agents of "special privilege" who grew rich with public funds. He especially disliked Nicholas Biddle, president of the Bank since 1823.

Biddle came from a wealthy Philadelphia family. He was well qualified to run the bank, but he was also arrogant and vain. Jackson felt that Biddle used the Bank to benefit only the rich. He also resented Biddle's influence over certain members of Congress.

The War Begins Biddle and other Whigs worried that the President might try to destroy the Bank. Two Whig senators, Henry Clay and Daniel Webster, thought of a way to save the Bank and defeat Jackson at the same time.

The Bank's charter was not due for renewal by Congress until 1836. However, Clay and Webster wanted to make the Bank an issue in the 1832 election. They persuaded Biddle to apply for renewal early.

The Whigs believed that most Americans supported the Bank of the United States. If Jackson vetoed the bill to renew the charter, they felt sure that he would anger voters and lose the election. Clay pushed the charter renewal bill through Congress in 1832. Jackson was sick in bed when he heard that Congress had renewed the Bank's charter. "The Bank . . . is trying to kill me," Jackson fumed, "but I will kill it!"

Jackson's Veto In an angry message to Congress, Jackson vetoed the Bank bill. He gave two reasons for his veto. First, he declared the Bank unconstitutional, even though the Supreme Court had ruled in the Bank's favor. Jackson believed that only states, not the federal government, had the right to charter banks. Second, Jackson felt that the Bank helped aristocrats at the expense of the common people. He warned:

> ❝ When the laws undertake . . . to make the rich richer and the potent more powerful, the humble members of the society—the farmers, mechanics, and laborers—who have neither the time nor the means of [getting] like favors for themselves . . . have a right to complain of the injustice of their government. ❞
>
> —Andrew Jackson, Veto Message, July 10, 1832

As planned, the Whigs made the Bank a major issue in the election of 1832. They chose Henry Clay as their candidate to run against Andrew Jackson. The counted votes showed that Jackson had won a stunning election victory. The common people had surprised the Whigs by supporting Jackson and rejecting the Bank of the United States.

The Bank Closes Without a new charter, the Bank would have to close in 1836. Jackson refused to wait. He ordered Secretary of the Treasury Roger Taney to stop putting government money in the Bank. Instead, Taney deposited federal money in state banks. They became known as pet banks because Taney and his friends controlled many of them. The loss of federal money crippled the Bank of the United States. Its closing in 1836 contributed to an economic crisis.

★ ★ ★ **Section 2 Assessment** ★ ★ ★

Recall

1. **Identify** Explain the significance of (a) "King Andrew," (b) Nicholas Biddle.
2. **Define** (a) spoils system, (b) "kitchen cabinet."

Comprehension

3. Why was Andrew Jackson called a self-made man?
4. Explain the impact of Andrew Jackson's election on the spoils system.
5. Why did Jackson veto the bill to extend the charter of the Bank of the United States?

Critical Thinking and Writing

6. **Exploring the Main Idea** Review the Main Idea statement at the beginning of this section. Then, analyze the characteristics that made Andrew Jackson a strong leader.
7. **Evaluating Information** Why might one argue that Jackson was not serving democracy with the spoils system? Write your answer in a paragraph.

ACTIVITY

Go Online
PHSchool.com

Connecting to Today
In the 1800s, the Bank of the United States loaned money to banks and individuals. Today, the Federal Reserve Bank is the central bank of the United States. Use the Internet to find out how the Federal Reserve system works. Then, list four facts about it. For help in completing the activity, visit PHSchool.com, **Web Code mfd-1201.**

To understand history, it is important to be able to distinguish facts from opinions. A fact is something that can be proved or observed. An opinion is a judgment that reflects someone's feelings or beliefs. An opinion is not necessarily true.

In the following letter, Andrew Jackson writes about his political supporters:

> ❝ The most disagreeable duty I have to perform is the removals and appointments to office. It appears that all who possess office do so as a result of political reward. Thousands who are pressing for office do it upon the ground that they are starving, and say that their families will perish unless they can be relieved by receiving some political office.
>
> These hungry office-seekers, as well as those who are now in office, are dangerous contestants for the public purse. When it is so easy for men seeking these offices to get good recommendations, it requires the greatest skill and judgement to pick men of honesty and integrity.
>
> We have, as you shall see from the newspapers, begun to reform. We are trying to remove those with no ability from office and expose to view the corruption of some of the office-holders appointed by the previous administration. ❞
>
> —Andrew Jackson

Learn the Skill *To distinguish fact from opinion, use the following steps:*

1. **Identify the facts.** What information could be proved or observed in some way?

2. **Distinguish facts from opinions.** Look for phrases such as "I think," "I believe," or "I feel" and for emotion-packed words, which may signal opinions.

3. **Note how facts and opinions are mixed.** A combination of facts and opinions in a statement can be a clue to the writer's point of view. Are opinions supported by facts?

4. **Identify points of view.** How does the writer feel about this topic?

Practice the Skill *Use the letter to answer the following questions:*

1. **(a)** Identify one fact in this letter. **(b)** Explain how the fact could be proved.

2. **(a)** Identify two opinions in this letter. **(b)** Identify three emotion-packed words used by Jackson.

3. Reread the first sentence. **(a)** What part is fact? **(b)** What part is opinion?

4. How would you describe Jackson's point of view?

Apply the Skill *See the Chapter Review and Assessment.*

3 A New Crisis

Prepare to Read

Objectives

In this section, you will
- Explain how the tariff crisis led to the Nullification Act.
- Summarize why Native Americans were forced off their land.
- List the economic problems Martin Van Buren faced.
- Describe the campaigns of 1840.

Key Terms

states' rights
nullification
Nullification Act
Indian Removal Act
Trail of Tears
Seminole War
depression
mudslinging

Target Reading Skill

Main Idea Copy the concept web below. As you read, fill in the blank ovals with events that were influenced by the struggle over states' rights. Add as many ovals as you need.

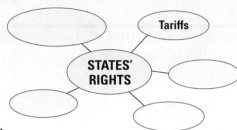

Tariffs

STATES' RIGHTS

Main Idea The states' rights issue led President Jackson to insist that a state cannot defy federal law, but Jackson defied federal law by removing Native Americans from their homes.

John C. Calhoun

Andrew Jackson

Setting the Scene

They had once been friends and allies. They were still the President and Vice President of the United States. Now, however, Andrew Jackson and John C. Calhoun were about to become fierce opponents. The issue that led them to quarrel was **states' rights,** or the right of states to limit the power of the federal government.

In 1830, the two men attended a dinner on the anniversary of Thomas Jefferson's birthday. Several guests made toasts in favor of states' rights. The room fell silent as the President rose. Old Hickory raised his glass, looked straight at the Vice President, and said "Our Federal Union—it must be preserved." Calhoun returned Jackson's stare. "The Union!" he returned, his glass trembling in his hand. "Next to our liberty, most dear."

During Andrew Jackson's presidency, the debate over states' rights affected two important issues. One was the tariff question. The second was the rights of Native Americans to lands they had been guaranteed in treaties.

A Crisis Over Tariffs

In 1828, Congress passed the highest tariff in the history of the nation. Southerners called it the Tariff of Abominations. An abomination is something that is hated.

Just like earlier tariffs, the new law, which was passed before Andrew Jackson's first term, protected manufacturers from foreign competition. Most manufacturers lived in the North. Southern planters, however, were hurt by the tariff. They sold their cotton in Europe and bought European goods in return. The high tariff meant that southerners had to pay more for these imports. Many people thought the tariff was unconstitutional.

Calhoun Versus Webster A leader in the South's fight against the tariff was Vice President John C. Calhoun. Calhoun claimed that a state had the right to nullify, or cancel, a federal law that it considered to be unconstitutional. This idea is called **nullification.** Calhoun supported states' rights. He argued that the states had final authority because they had created the national government.

Daniel Webster disagreed. He made a speech in 1830 before the Senate attacking the idea of nullification. The Constitution, he said, united the American people, not just the states. If states had the right to nullify federal laws, the nation would fall apart. Because Calhoun strongly disagreed with Jackson, he resigned from the office of Vice President. He was then elected as a senator from South Carolina. The debate over states' rights would continue for years.

The Nullification Crisis Anger against the tariff increased in the South. Congress passed a new tariff in 1832 that lowered the rate slightly. South Carolina was not satisfied. It passed the Nullification Act, declaring the new tariff illegal. It also threatened to secede, or withdraw, from the Union if challenged. Jackson was furious. He knew that nullification could lead to civil war.

Publicly, the President supported a lower compromise tariff proposed by Henry Clay. Jackson also asked Congress to pass the Force Bill. It allowed him to use the army, if necessary, to enforce the tariff.

Faced with Jackson's firm stand, no other state chose to support South Carolina. Calhoun supported the compromise tariff that Clay had proposed. South Carolina repealed the Nullification Act, and the Nullification Crisis passed. However, tensions between the North and South would increase in the years ahead.

Tragedy for Native Americans

Jackson took a firm stand on another key issue. It affected the fate of Native Americans. Since the early colonial era, white settlers had forced Native Americans off their land. Indian leaders like Pontiac and Tecumseh had failed to stop the invasion of white settlers.

Indian Nations in the Southeast The Creek, Choctaw, Chickasaw, Cherokee, and Seminole lived in the Southeast. Many hoped to live in peace with their white neighbors. However, their fertile land was attractive to white settlers because it was ideal for growing cotton.

At Jackson's urging, the government set aside lands beyond the Mississippi River and then persuaded or forced Indians to move there. Jackson believed that this policy would provide land for white settlers as well as protect Native Americans from destruction.

Few Indians wanted to move. Some tribes, like the Cherokee nation, had adapted customs in order to preserve their way of life. They created a legal system and government that blended European and Cherokee traditions. Others, like the Choctaw, believed they would be spared the move because they had sided with the United States during the War of 1812.

In 1821, Sequoyah (sih KWOY uh) created a written alphabet for his people. Using Sequoyah's letters, Cherokee children learned to read and write. The Cherokees also published a newspaper.

Identify Supporting Details

What details in this paragraph further explain the issue of states' rights? Add these details to your concept web.

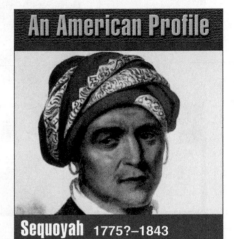

An American Profile

Sequoyah 1775?–1843

To the Cherokee Sequoyah, written words were power. He knew that white people collected and passed on knowledge with writing. Sequoyah wanted the same for his own people. In 1809 he began developing a writing system for the Cherokees. In his system, each symbol represented a syllable of the spoken Cherokee language.

Sequoyah's system was easy to learn, and it caught on quickly. Cherokees were soon writing and publishing books and newspapers in their own language and teaching the writing system in their schools.

Why do you think Sequoyah believed a writing system could help keep his people independent?

Kinderhook,
New York

Martin Van Buren Historic Site

While serving as President in 1839, Van Buren purchased the estate that would become his retirement home. Located near his birthplace, Kinderhook, the estate was named Lindenwald. During his stay there, the estate grew to 226 acres and became a profitable farm. Much of the estate remains as it was during Van Buren's lifetime.

Go Online
PHSchool.com

Virtual Field Trip For an interactive look at the Van Buren Historic Site, visit PHSchool.com, **Web Code mfd-1202.**

A Legal Battle Georgia claimed the right to make laws for the Cherokee nation in 1828. The Cherokees went to court pointing to treaties with the federal government that protected their rights and property. The Cherokee case reached the Supreme Court. In the 1832 case of *Worcester* v. *Georgia,* Chief Justice John Marshall declared Georgia's action unconstitutional and stated that Native Americans were protected by the U.S. Constitution.

However, President Jackson refused to enforce the Court's decision. In the Nullification Crisis, Jackson defended the power of the federal government. In the Cherokee case, he backed states' rights. He said that the federal government could not stop Georgia from extending its authority over Cherokee lands.

Forced to Leave Jackson supporters in Congress pushed through the Indian Removal Act in 1830. It forced many Native Americans to move west of the Mississippi. Whites did not mind turning land over to Indians that they thought was a vast desert. In 1838, the United States Army drove more than 15,000 Cherokees westward. The Cherokees trekked hundreds of miles over a period of several months. Thousands perished during the march, mostly children and the elderly. The Cherokees' long, sorrowful journey west became known as the Trail of Tears.

The Seminoles Resist In Florida, the Seminole Indians resisted removal. Led by Chief Osceola (ahs ee oh luh), they began fighting the United States Army in 1817. This conflict, known as the first

Seminole War, ended in 1818. The second Seminole War lasted from 1835 to 1842. It was the costliest war waged by the government to gain Indian lands.

In the end, after a third war ending in 1858, the Seminoles were defeated. The government forced the Seminole leaders and most of their people to leave Florida.

Indian Removal in the Old Northwest Further north, Native Americans were also facing pressure from expanding white settlements. As the white population expanded, groups of Sauk and Fox Indians were forced from their homes in Illinois across the Mississippi River. In 1832, a large band of Sauk and Fox returned to Illinois under the leadership of a warrior named Black Hawk.

Tensions rose sharply between Native Americans and settlers. In one confrontation, panicky settlers killed two Indians who had come to discuss peace. The Native Americans then defeated a band of settlers and retreated into what is today Wisconsin.

A force made up of U.S. Army troops and volunteer militia set out after the Indians. After months of searching, the Americans located the Native Americans and defeated them at the battle of Bad Axe. Many women and children were killed during the battle. Black Hawk soon surrendered, and the Native American resistance collapsed.

Martin Van Buren and Hard Times

Andrew Jackson left office after two terms. Americans then elected Martin Van Buren President. Although Van Buren did not have Jackson's popularity, he was clever and intelligent. As President, however, Van Buren needed more than sharp political instincts.

The Panic of 1837 Two months after taking office, Van Buren faced the worst economic crisis the nation had known. After the Bank of the United States closed, state banks could lend money without limit. To meet the demand for loans, state banks printed more and more paper money. Often, the paper money was not backed by gold or silver.

Before leaving office, Jackson was alarmed at the wild speculation in land. To slow it down, he ordered that anyone buying public land had to pay for it with gold or silver. Speculators and others rushed to state banks to exchange their paper money for gold and silver. Many banks did not have enough gold and silver and were forced to close.

Economic Depression The nation soon plunged into a deep economic **depression,** a period when business declines and many people lose their jobs. The depression lasted three years. In the worst days, 90 percent of the nation's factories were closed. Thousands of people were out of work.

Many Americans blamed Van Buren and his policies for the economic depression. Van Buren believed in laissez faire—the idea that government should play as small a role as possible in the economy. As the depression wore on, Van Buren became increasingly unpopular.

Campaigns of 1840

Although Van Buren lost support, the Democrats chose him to run for reelection in 1840. The Whigs chose William Henry Harrison of Ohio. Harrison was known as the hero of the Battle of Tippecanoe. To run for Vice President, the Whigs chose John Tyler.

To appeal to voters, the Whigs focused on Harrison's war record. "Tippecanoe and Tyler too" became their campaign slogan. The Whigs created an image for Harrison as a "man of the people." They presented him as a humble farmer and boasted that he had been born in a log cabin. Harrison was actually a wealthy, educated man who, at the time of the campaign, lived in a large mansion.

A New Sort of Politics The campaigns of 1840 reflected a new sort of politics. Harrison traveled across the land, making speeches and greeting voters. Both parties competed for votes with rallies, banquets, and entertainment.

In their campaigns, both Whigs and Democrats engaged in **mudslinging,** or the use of insults to attack an opponent's reputation. They used name-calling, half-truths, and lies to win votes.

Whigs in the White House Harrison won the election of 1840. The Whigs' program included creating a new Bank of the United States, improving roads and canals, and demanding a high tariff.

However, Whig hopes were dashed when, soon after taking office, President Harrison died of pneumonia. John Tyler became President.

President Tyler failed to live up to Whig expectations. A former Democrat, he opposed some Whig plans for developing the economy. When the Whigs in Congress passed a bill to recharter the Bank of the United States, Tyler vetoed it. In response, most of Tyler's Cabinet resigned. The Whigs threw Tyler out of their party.

★ ★ ★ Section 3 Assessment ★ ★ ★

Recall

1. **Identify** Explain the significance of **(a)** Nullification Act, **(b)** Indian Removal Act, **(c)** Trail of Tears, **(d)** Seminole War.
2. **Define (a)** states' rights, **(b)** nullification, **(c)** depression, **(d)** mudslinging.

Comprehension

3. Why did South Carolina pass the Nullification Act?
4. How did the Indian Removal Act affect Native Americans?
5. What hardships did citizens face during the Panic of 1837?

6. Describe some of the campaign tactics Democrats and Whigs used in the election of 1840.

Critical Thinking and Writing

7. **Exploring the Main Idea** Review the Main Idea statement at the beginning of this section. Then, answer the following question in a paragraph. Why do you think Andrew Jackson supported states' rights in the case of the Native Americans but not in the Nullification Crisis?
8. **Solving Problems** What do you think President Van Buren could have done to ease the economic crisis in 1837?

ACTIVITY

Go Online
PHSchool.com

The Banana Wars
Tariffs are still part of domestic and international trade. Use the Internet to find out about the recent banana wars between the United States and Europe. Prepare a brief oral report about the dispute. For help in completing the activity, visit PHSchool.com, **Web Code mfd-1203.**

The LOG CABIN Campaign

In *The Log Cabin Minstrel,* William Henry Harrison is portrayed as a poor farmer who "lives at his cabin, enjoying crackers, hard cider and cheese," while President Van Buren "drank up the milk of the Treasury Cow."

William Henry Harrison

Harrison Song

Tune: "Yankee Doodle"
When our frontiers were drench'd in tears,
Their cabins sack'd and gory,
He struck the blow, chastis'd the foe,
And conquer'd peace with glory.

Then join the throng and swell the song,
Extend the circle wider;
and let us on for HARRISON,
"Log Cabin and Hard Cider."

With HARRISON, our country's one,
No treachery can divide her,
The thing is done with "HARRISON,
Log Cabin and Hard Cider."

Come farmers all, attend the call,
'Tis working like a charmer,
Hitch on the team, and start for him,
For he's a *brother farmer.*

His cabin's fit, and snug and neat,
And full and free his larder,
And though his cider may be hard,
The times are vastly harder.

The South and West will stand the test,
In spite of every spoiler,
And we'll engage to seal the pledge
For HARRISON and TYLER.

—from *The Log Cabin Minstrel,* 1840

Fast Facts

• *The Log Cabin Minstrel* or *Tippecanoe Songster* was compiled in 1840 by the Roxbury, Massachusetts, Democratic Whig Association, and sold for 12 cents per copy.

• More people voted in 1840 than in any previous presidential election.

ACTIVITY

Prepare for a class discussion about the way in which political campaigns are conducted today. How can this affect voter turnout and the results of an election?

CHAPTER SUMMARY

Section 1
Andrew Jackson's victory in the presidential election signaled the birth of a democratic spirit that brought political and social changes to the nation. New political parties emerged during Jackson's presidency.

Section 2
Jackson was criticized for introducing the spoils system while serving as President. During his eight years in office, Jackson succeeded in closing the Bank of the United States.

Section 3
Jackson supported states in their attempts to relocate Native Americans, but he opposed states' rights during the Nullification Crisis. An economic crisis hit the country after Jackson left office.

For additional review and enrichment activities, see the interactive version of *The American Nation,* available on the Web and on CD-ROM.

Chapter Self-Test For practice test questions for Chapter 12, visit PHSchool.com, **Web Code mfa-1204.**

Building Vocabulary

Use the chapter vocabulary words listed below to create a crossword puzzle. Exchange puzzles with a classmate. Complete the puzzles, and then check each other's answers.

1. suffrage
2. Whigs
3. caucus
4. spoils system
5. "kitchen cabinet"
6. states' rights
7. nullification
8. Indian Removal Act
9. depression
10. mudslinging

Reviewing Key Facts

11. How was a winner selected in the election of 1824? Explain. [Section 1]
12. What role did each of the following play in the struggle over the Bank of the United States? **(a)** Nicholas Biddle **(b)** Henry Clay **(c)** Andrew Jackson [Section 2]
13. What were the causes of the Panic of 1837? [Section 3]

Critical Thinking and Writing

14. **Supporting a Point of View** Andrew Jackson said "The President is the direct representative of the people." During his time in office, did Jackson's actions uphold his statement? Write a paragraph in which you agree or disagree.
15. **Analyzing Information** The new voter group in the 1820s consisted of white men who did not own property. Consider the elections of 1828 and 1840. **(a)** How did Jackson appeal to this group in 1828? **(b)** How did the campaign of 1840 appeal to this group?
16. **Connecting to Geography: Regions** Analyze how the different economic interests of the North and the South influenced their views on the tariff of 1828.
17. **Evaluating Information** Do election campaigns today resemble the election campaign of 1840? Why or why not?

Davy Crockett, the frontiersman from Tennessee, served as a member of the Tennessee State legislature from 1821 to 1825. In the following excerpt, he offers advice to those seeking public office.

> 66 Get up on all occasions, and sometimes on no occasion at all, and make long-winded speeches, though composed of nothing else than wind. Talk of your devotion to your country, your modesty . . . or on any such fanciful subject. Rail against taxes of all kinds, officeholders, and bad harvest weather. . . . To be sure, you run the risk of being considered . . . an empty barrel. But never mind that; you will find enough of the same [company] to keep you in favor. 99

—Davy Crockett, *Advice to Politicians*, 1833

18. What advice does Crockett give to a person seeking public office?
   A. Do not talk in public.
   B. Worry about your image.
   C. Criticize taxes.
   D. Become a farmer.
19. What opinion might some people have after listening to a politician?
   A. They have no strong opinion.
   B. Some politicians say nothing of substance.
   C. Politicians are always well informed.
   D. Politicians tend to be shy.

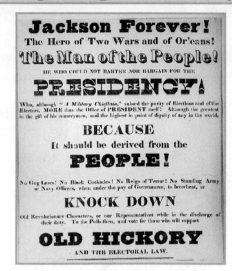

This is an 1828 election poster that praises Jackson's conduct during the election of 1824. Read the poster. Then, answer the following questions:

20. One fact stated on the poster is
   A. Jackson is a man of the people.
   B. An election should be derived from the people.
   C. Jackson was a hero of two wars.
   D. Jackson supports electoral law.
21. What point of view do Jackson's supporters want the public to have?

ACTIVITIES

Connecting With . . .
Government and Citizenship

Researching a Campaign Symbol The use of a donkey as the official campaign symbol for the Democratic party began during Andrew Jackson's campaign for election in 1828. Use the Internet to research the history of this campaign symbol and symbols of other political parties. Present the information you find in an illustrated chart.

PHSchool.com

An Illustrated Report

Researching de Tocqueville Use the Internet to find out more about Alexis de Tocqueville and his visit to the United States in 1831. Choose an event he wrote about. Describe how it reflected American life at that time. Add illustrations to your report. For help in starting this activity, visit PHSchool.com, **Web Code mfd-1206.**

CHAPTER 13 Westward Expansion

1820–1860

1 Oregon Country
2 The Republic of Texas
3 California and the Southwest
4 The Mexican War
5 Americans Rush West

Mountain man
Jim Beckwourth

Defending the Alamo

1820s

The era of the mountain men is at its height. Mountain men such as Jim Beckwourth open trails through the Rockies into Oregon and California.

1830

Joseph Smith founds the Mormon Church in Fayette, New York.

1836

Texans defend the Alamo during the Texas War of Independence.

AMERICAN EVENTS

John Quincy Adams

Martin Van Buren

Presidential Terms: James Monroe 1817–1825   1825–1829   Andrew Jackson 1829–1837   1837–1841

1820   1830   1840

WORLD EVENTS

▲ **1821**
Mexico wins independence from Spain.

▲ **1830**
Mexico bars any additional emigration from the United States to Texas.

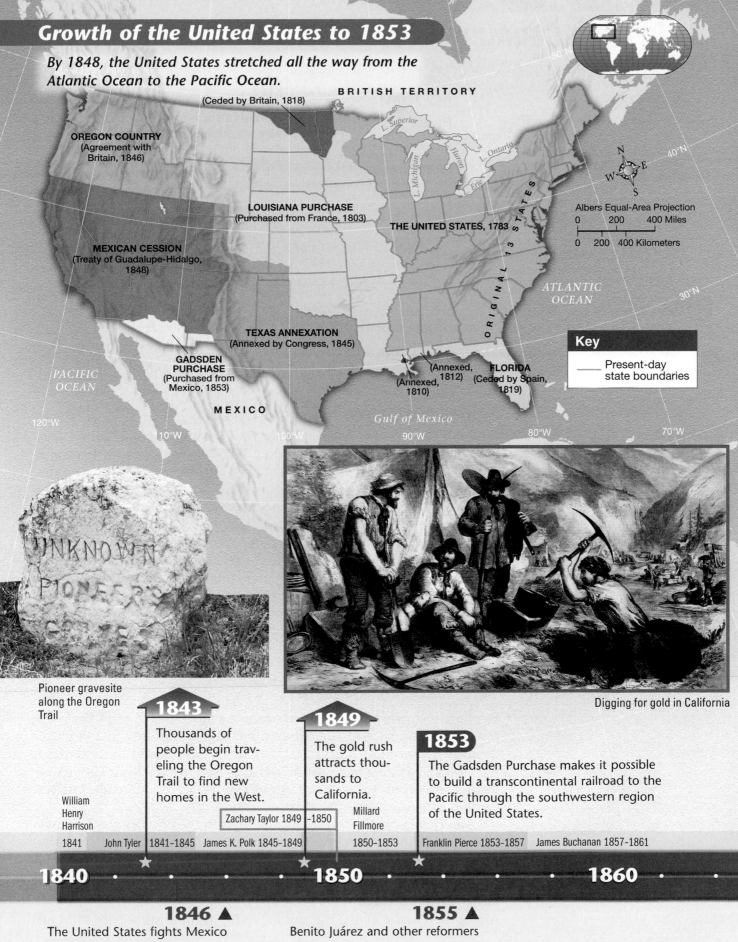

Growth of the United States to 1853

By 1848, the United States stretched all the way from the Atlantic Ocean to the Pacific Ocean.

BRITISH TERRITORY

(Ceded by Britain, 1818)

OREGON COUNTRY
(Agreement with Britain, 1846)

LOUISIANA PURCHASE
(Purchased from France, 1803)

THE UNITED STATES, 1783

L. Superior
L. Michigan
L. Huron
L. Erie
L. Ontario

ORIGINAL 13 STATES

MEXICAN CESSION
(Treaty of Guadalupe-Hidalgo, 1848)

Albers Equal-Area Projection
0   200   400 Miles
0   200   400 Kilometers

ATLANTIC OCEAN

TEXAS ANNEXATION
(Annexed by Congress, 1845)

PACIFIC OCEAN

GADSDEN PURCHASE
(Purchased from Mexico, 1853)

(Annexed, 1810)
(Annexed, 1812)
FLORIDA
(Ceded by Spain, 1819)

MEXICO

Gulf of Mexico

120°W   110°W   100°W   90°W   80°W   70°W

Key

Present-day state boundaries

Pioneer gravesite along the Oregon Trail

UNKNOWN PIONEER'S GRAVE

Digging for gold in California

1843
Thousands of people begin traveling the Oregon Trail to find new homes in the West.

1849
The gold rush attracts thousands to California.

1853
The Gadsden Purchase makes it possible to build a transcontinental railroad to the Pacific through the southwestern region of the United States.

William Henry Harrison 1841   John Tyler 1841–1845   James K. Polk 1845–1849   Zachary Taylor 1849–1850   Millard Fillmore 1850–1853   Franklin Pierce 1853–1857   James Buchanan 1857–1861

1840 · · · · **1850** · · · **1860** · ·

1846 ▲
The United States fights Mexico during the Mexican War.

1855 ▲
Benito Juárez and other reformers seize power in Mexico.

Chapter 13 ★ **379**

1 Oregon Country

Prepare to Read

Objectives

In this section, you will
- Explain the appeal of Oregon and the Far West.
- Summarize how mountain men helped explore the Far West.
- Describe the role missionaries played in Oregon.
- Identify the hardships faced on wagon trains to the West.

Key Terms

Oregon Country

mountain man

rugged individualist

rendezvous

Oregon Trail

Target Reading Skill

Reading Process As you read, prepare an outline of this section. Use roman numerals to indicate the major headings, capital letters for the subheadings, and numbers for the supporting details.

> I. The Lure of Oregon
>   A. Land and climate
>   1.
>   2.
>   B. Competing claims
>   1.
>   2.
> II. Fur Trappers in the Far West
>   A. Lives filled with danger
>   1.
>   2.
>   B.

Main Idea By the 1840s, thousands of pioneers were following in the footsteps of fur traders and missionaries to settle in Oregon Country.

Traveling the trail

Setting the Scene Young John Johnson and Jane Jones fell in love as their families were moving west by wagon train. John's parents did not like the match, so they left the wagon train. John and Jane, though, secretly promised to leave letters for each other on the buffalo skulls that dotted the trail. They signed their letters "Laurie." For the next month, Jane later told John "not a day passed . . . but what I have found a letter signed by Laurie so I knew just where you were and was sure we would overtake you."

The Johnson and Jones families were among thousands of people who traveled to Oregon in the mid-1800s. In 1820, Oregon had seemed a distant and dangerous place. Yet, by the early 1850s, large numbers of pioneers were heading across the Great Plains to the Far West. Their presence would support the claims of the United States to Oregon and put the nation into conflict with Great Britain.

The Lure of Oregon

By the 1820s, white settlers had occupied much of the land between the Appalachians and the Mississippi River. Families in search of good farmland kept moving farther west. Few, however, settled on the Great Plains between the Mississippi and the Rockies. The plains were considered too dry to support settlement. Instead, settlers headed to lands in the Far West.

Americans first heard about the area known as Oregon Country in the early 1800s. **Oregon Country** was a huge region west of the Rocky Mountains. Today, it includes Oregon, Washington, Idaho, and parts of Wyoming, Montana, and western Canada.

Land and Climate The geography of Oregon Country is varied. Along the Pacific coast, the soil is fertile. Temperatures are mild all year round, and rainfall is plentiful. Early white settlers found fine farmland in the valley of the Willamette River and the lowlands around Puget Sound.

Farther inland, dense forests covered the coastal mountain range. Beavers and other fur-bearing animals roamed these forests and the Rocky Mountains to the east. For this reason, fur trappers were the first whites to head into Oregon Country.

Not all of Oregon Country attracted Americans. Between the coastal mountains and the Rockies is a barren and dry plateau. This region was home to neither fur trappers nor farmers.

Competing Claims In the early 1800s, four countries claimed Oregon. They were the United States, Great Britain, Spain, and Russia. Of course, Native American groups had lived there for centuries. However, the United States and European nations gave little thought to Indian rights.

In 1818, the United States and Britain agreed to occupy Oregon jointly. Citizens of each nation would have equal rights in Oregon. Spain and Russia had few settlers there, so they withdrew their claims to Oregon Country.

Fur Trappers in the Far West

At first, only a handful of Europeans or Americans traveled to Oregon Country. Most were fur traders. Since furs could be sold for huge profits in China, merchants from New England stopped along the Oregon coast before crossing the Pacific. In fact, so many Yankee traders visited Oregon to buy furs that, in some areas, the Indian name for a white man was "Boston."

Only a few hardy trappers actually settled in Oregon. These adventurous men hiked through the region's vast forests, trapping animals and living off the land. They were known as **mountain men.**

Mountain men were admired as **rugged individualists,** people who follow their own independent course in life. Even their colorful appearance set them apart from ordinary society. Their shirts and trousers were made of animal hides and decorated with porcupine quills. Their hair reached to their shoulders. Pistols and tomahawks hung from their belts.

Lives Filled With Danger Mountain men could make fine profits selling their furs. They led dangerous lives, however. The long, cold winters demanded special survival skills. In the forests, mountain men had to watch out for bears, wildcats, or other animals that might attack.

Oregon Country

Key
Area settled by 1845
Oregon Trail
Forts

Albers Equal-Area Projection
0   200   400 Miles
0   200   400 Kilometers

GEOGRAPHY Skills

Oregon Country was the first area in the far west to draw settlers from the United States.

1. **Location** On the map, locate **(a)** Oregon Country, **(b)** British territory, **(c)** Willamette River, **(d)** South Pass.

2. **Region** What line of latitude marked the northern boundary of Oregon Country after 1846?

3. **Critical Thinking Drawing Inferences** Why do you think the Oregon Trail often followed the course of a river?

In winter, food was scarce. Faced with starvation, a hungry trapper would eat almost anything. "I have held my hands in an anthill until they were covered with ants, then greedily licked them off," one mountain man recalled.

Trappers often spent winters in Native American villages. They learned trapping and hunting skills from Indians. Some mountain men married Indian women who helped the newcomers survive in the harsh mountains.

Trading Furs During the fall and spring, mountain men tended their traps. Then in July, they tramped out of the wilderness to meet with fur traders. They headed to a place chosen the year before, called the rendezvous (RAHN day voo). **Rendezvous** is a French word meaning "get-together."

The first day of the rendezvous was a time for entertainment. A visitor to one rendezvous captured the excitement:

❝ [The mountain men] engaged in contests of skill at running, jumping, wrestling, shooting with the rifle, and running horses. . . . They sang, they laughed, they whooped; they tried to out-brag and out-lie each other in stories of their adventures. ❞

—Washington Irving, *The Adventures of Captain Bonneville, U.S.A., in the Rocky Mountains and the Far West,* 1837

Soon enough, trappers and traders settled down to bargain. As long as beaver hats were in demand in the East and in Europe, mountain men got a good price for their furs.

By the late 1830s, however, the fur trade was dying. Trappers had killed too many beavers, and the animals had become scarce. Also, beaver hats went out of style. Even so, the mountain men found new uses for their skills. Some began to lead settlers across rugged mountain trails into Oregon.

Exploring New Lands

In their search for furs, mountain men explored many parts of the West. They followed Indian trails through passes in the Rocky Mountains. Later, they showed these trails to settlers heading west.

Jedediah Smith led settlers across the Rockies through South Pass, in present-day Wyoming. Manuel Lisa, a Latino fur trader, led a trip up the Missouri River in 1807. He founded Fort Manuel, the first outpost on the upper Missouri.

James Beckwourth, an African American, traveled west from Virginia to escape slavery. He was accepted as a chief by the Crow Indians. As a guide, Beckwourth discovered a mountain pass through the Sierra Nevadas that later became a major route to California.

Missionaries in Oregon

The first white Americans to settle permanently in Oregon Country were missionaries. Among them were Marcus and Narcissa Whitman. The couple married in 1836 and set out for Oregon, where they planned to convert local Native Americans to Christianity.

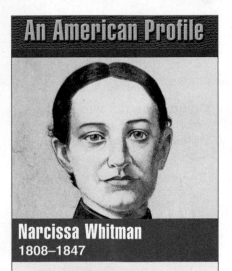

The Whitmans built their mission near the Columbia River and began to work with Cayuse (KI oos) Indians, setting up a mission school and a clinic. Soon, other missionaries and settlers joined them.

Missionaries like the Whitmans helped stir up interest in Oregon Country. Eager to have others join them, the missionaries sent back glowing reports about the land. People throughout the nation read these reports. By 1840, more and more Americans were making the long and difficult journey to Oregon.

As settlers spread onto Cayuse lands, conflicts arose. Worse, the newcomers carried diseases that often killed the Indians.

In 1847, tragedy struck. A measles outbreak among the settlers spread to the Cayuses. Many Cayuse children died. Blaming the settlers, a band of angry Indians attacked the mission, killing the Whitmans and 12 others.

Wagon Trains West

Despite the killings, other pioneers boldly set out for Oregon. They were attracted by tales of wheat that grew taller than a man and turnips five feet around. Stories like these touched off a race to get to Oregon. Americans called it "Oregon fever."

As Oregon fever spread, pioneers clogged the trails west. Beginning in 1843, wagon trains left every spring for Oregon. They followed a route called the Oregon Trail.

Families planning to go west met at Independence, Missouri, in the early spring. By mid-April, the prairie outside Independence was packed with people and wagons. Somehow, the pioneers formed themselves into wagon trains. Each group elected leaders to make decisions along the way.

The Oregon-bound pioneers hurried to leave Independence in May. Timing was important. Travelers had to reach Oregon by early October before the snow fell in the mountains. This meant that pioneers had to cover 2,000 miles in five months. In the 1840s, traveling 15 miles a day was considered making good time!

Life on the Trail On the trail, families woke at dawn to a bugle blast. Everyone had a job to do. Girls helped their mothers prepare food. Men and boys harnessed the horses and oxen. By 6 A.M., the cry of "Wagons Ho!" rang across the plains.

The wagon train stopped for a brief noonday meal. Then, it returned to the trail until 6 or 7 P.M. At night, wagons drew up into a circle to keep the cattle from wandering.

Viewing History

On the Trail

People and wagon trains crowded the trails to the West in the 1840s. Here, families struggle to drive their animals just a few miles farther before darkness. At the bottom of the picture is a trunk that one woman used to get her precious china to the West. **Making Generalizations** *Based on these pictures, make a generalization about the character of the people who journeyed along the Oregon Trail.*

Most pioneer families started the journey with a large amount of gear. As they crossed rivers and scaled mountains, they discarded belongings to lighten their wagons.

The trail west held many dangers. During the spring, travelers risked drowning as they floated their wagons across rain-swollen rivers. In summer, they faced blistering heat on the treeless plains. Early snows could block passes through the mountains. Getting the heavy wagons past these obstacles was hard work.

The biggest threat was sickness. Cholera and other diseases could wipe out whole wagon trains. Because the travelers lived so close together, diseases spread quickly.

Trading With Native Americans As they moved toward the Rockies, pioneers often saw Indians. Many Native Americans traded with the wagon trains. Hungry pioneers were grateful for the food that the Indians sold in return for clothing and tools. A traveler noted:

Use Prior Knowledge As you read this quotation, think about how the description of pioneers and Native Americans differs from what has often been portrayed in movies.

66 Whenever we camp near any Indian village, we are no sooner stopped than a whole crowd may be seen coming galloping into our camp. The [women] do all the swapping. 99

—John S. Unruh, quoted in *The Plains Across: The Overland Emigrants and the Trans-Mississippi West, 1840–1860*

Oregon at Last! Despite the many hardships, more than 50,000 people reached Oregon between 1840 and 1860. Their wagon wheels cut so deeply into the plains that the ruts can still be seen today.

By the 1840s, Americans outnumbered the British in Oregon. As you have read, the two nations had agreed to occupy Oregon jointly. Now, many Americans wanted Oregon for the United States alone.

★ ★ ★ Section 1 Assessment ★ ★ ★

Recall

1. **Identify** Explain the significance of (a) Oregon Country, (b) James Beckwourth, (c) Oregon Trail.
2. **Define** (a) mountain man, (b) rugged individualist, (c) rendezvous.

Comprehension

3. Why were trappers and settlers attracted to Oregon Country?
4. How did mountain men contribute to the settlement of the Far West?
5. How did missionaries like the Whitmans attract other people to settle in Oregon?

6. Describe two difficulties that settlers faced on the Oregon Trail.

Critical Thinking and Writing

7. **Exploring the Main Idea** Review the Main Idea statement at the beginning of this section. Then, write a letter that a missionary might have sent East encouraging people to settle in the Oregon Country.
8. **Linking Past and Present** (a) What qualities helped the settlers survive the Oregon Trail? (b) Do you think such qualities are still important today? Write a paragraph explaining your answers.

ACTIVITY

Go Online
PHSchool.com

Writing a Diary
Use the Internet to find out more about the life of the mountain men. Then, use the information to write two or three diary entries describing the way of life of an imaginary mountain man. For help in completing the activity, visit PHSchool.com, **Web Code mfd-1301.**

2 The Republic of Texas

Prepare to Read

Objectives

In this section, you will
- Summarize why Americans in Texas conflicted with Mexico.
- Explain how Texas gained independence.
- Describe how the Alamo affected Texans.
- Identify the challenges the Lone Star Republic faced.

Key Terms

dictator

Tejano

Alamo

siege

Battle of San Jacinto

Lone Star Republic

annex

Target Reading Skill

Cause and Effect As you read, complete the following chart to show some of the causes that led Texans to declare independence from Mexico.

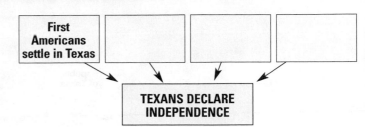

First Americans settle in Texas

TEXANS DECLARE INDEPENDENCE

Main Idea In 1835, American settlers in Texas revolted against Mexican rule and in 1836, set up the republic of Texas.

Setting the Scene

News of fighting in Texas spread to the United States in late 1835. People heard how Americans in Texas were rebelling against Mexico. "I was at Chicago, Illinois, practicing medicine," recalled Joseph Barnard, a young doctor, "when the news of the Texan revolt from Mexico reached our ears." The news inspired him. The Texans, he wrote, "were in arms for a cause that I had always been taught to consider sacred, . . . Republican principles and popular institutions. They had entered into the contest with spirit and were carrying it on with vigor."

Along with hundreds of other Americans, Dr. Barnard made his way to Texas. There, he fought alongside other American settlers eager to win independence.

Fighting for independence

Americans in Mexican Texas

In the early 1800s, American farmers, especially from the South, looked eagerly at the vast region called Texas. At the time, Texas was part of the Spanish colony of Mexico.

At first, Spain refused to let Americans settle in Texas. Then in 1821, Spain gave Moses Austin a land grant there. Although Austin died before he could set up a colony, his son, Stephen, took over.

Before Stephen Austin could establish his colony, Mexico won independence from Spain. Austin went to Mexico City to make sure that the new government supported the land grant. The new leaders agreed to let Austin bring settlers to Texas. Mexico wanted settlers to develop the land and control Indian attacks. At the time, only about 4,000 Mexicans lived in Texas.

Austin gathered about 300 families to move to Texas. Starting in 1821, they began settling the colony. Many settlers came from the cotton country of the Southeast. Some built large cotton plantations and brought in slaves to work the land.

Independence for Texas

Key
← Texan forces
✸ Texan victories
← Mexican forces
✸ Mexican victories

Albers Equal-Area Projection
0   150   300 Miles
0 150 300 Kilometers

GEOGRAPHY *Skills*

After a brief but bloody war, Texas gained its independence from Mexico.

1. **Location** On the map, locate **(a)** Rio Grande, **(b)** Nueces River, **(c)** Gonzales, **(d)** San Antonio, **(e)** the Alamo, **(f)** Goliad, **(g)** San Jacinto.

2. **Movement** **(a)** Where did Santa Anna's army first fight the Texans? **(b)** Describe the movement of Mexican and Texan forces after the Alamo.

3. **Critical Thinking Comparing** Refer to the political map of the United States in the Reference Section. How do the boundaries of the Republic of Texas compare with the boundaries of Texas today?

As Austin's colony grew and succeeded, Mexico gave land grants to other people. Some were from Mexico, but the largest number came from the United States. By 1830, about 20,000 Americans had moved to Texas.

Conflict With Mexico

In return for land, Austin and the original American settlers agreed to become Mexican citizens and to worship in the Roman Catholic Church. Later American settlers, however, felt no loyalty to Mexico. They spoke little or no Spanish. Most were Protestant. These and other differences led to conflict between the settlers and the Mexican government.

Mexico Fears Losing Texas In 1830, Mexico barred any more Americans from settling in Texas. Mexico feared that the Americans would try to make Texas a part of the United States. It had good reason to fear this possibility. The United States had already tried twice to buy Texas.

To assert its authority, Mexico began to enforce laws that had long been ignored. One was the law requiring Texans to promise to worship in the Catholic Church. Another law banned slavery in Texas. American settlers resented these laws. Their anger grew when Mexico sent troops to enforce its will.

In 1833, General Antonio López de Santa Anna gained power in Mexico. Two years later, he threw out the Mexican constitution and became a dictator. A **dictator** is a ruler with absolute power and authority. Rumors spread that Santa Anna intended to drive the Americans out of Texas.

Texans Take Action With Santa Anna in power, Americans in Texas felt that the time had come for action. They had the support of many Tejanos (teh HAH nohs), people of Mexican descent born in in Texas. Tejanos did not necessarily want independence from Mexico. They did, however, want to be rid of the dictator, Santa Anna.

In October 1835, Texans in the town of Gonzales (gahn ZAH lehs) clashed with Mexican troops. They forced the troops to withdraw. Inspired by that victory, Stephen Austin vowed to "see Texas forever free from Mexican domination." Two months later, Texans occupied the city of San Antonio. Determined to stamp out the rebellion, Santa Anna marched north with a large army.

While Santa Anna was on the move, a group of Texans declared independence for the Republic of Texas on March 2, 1836. Sam Houston was given command of the army. Volunteers from the United States and from other nations, along with African Americans and Tejanos, joined the fight for Texan independence.

San Antonio, Texas

The Alamo

Each year, millions of tourists visit the Alamo in San Antonio, Texas. Few of them realize just how close the building came to collapsing into ruin. After 1836, the Alamo was used as a warehouse and a general store. Since 1905, however, the Alamo has been managed by the Daughters of the Republic of Texas. Three buildings house exhibits on Texas's struggle for independence.

Go Online
PHSchool.com

Virtual Field Trip For an interactive look at the Alamo, visit PHSchool.com, **Web Code mfd-1302.**

Siege at the Alamo

By the time Santa Anna reached San Antonio, the Texans had taken up positions in an old Spanish mission called the **Alamo.** There they waited for the Mexican attack.

Against Great Odds The Texans were poorly equipped. Their supplies of ammunition, food, water, and medicine were low. Only about 150 Texans faced a force of 6,000 Mexican troops!

Inside the mission, young William B. Travis was in command. Among the volunteers at the Alamo were the famous frontiersmen Jim Bowie and Davy Crockett. Several Tejano families, two Texan women, and two young male slaves were also there.

"Victory or Death!" On February 23, 1836, Mexican troops began the siege of the Alamo. In a **siege,** enemy forces try to capture a city or fort, often by surrounding and bombarding it. The Texan defenders bravely held out as cannon pounded the walls. Still, Travis knew that without help, the defenders were doomed. He sent a messenger through the Mexican lines with a letter addressed "to the People of Texas and all the Americans in the World":

> 66 *I shall never surrender or retreat.*
>
> I call on you in the name of Liberty, of patriotism, and of everything dear to the American character to come to our aid with all [speed]. . . . *Victory or Death!* 99
>
> —William B. Travis, Letter, February 24, 1836

Recognize Multiple Causes

Target Skill

A cause makes something happen. Sometimes an effect can have more than one cause. Read the subsections "Siege at the Alamo" and "Texan Independence" to discover the connection between the Alamo and the independence of Texas. Add this information to your chart.

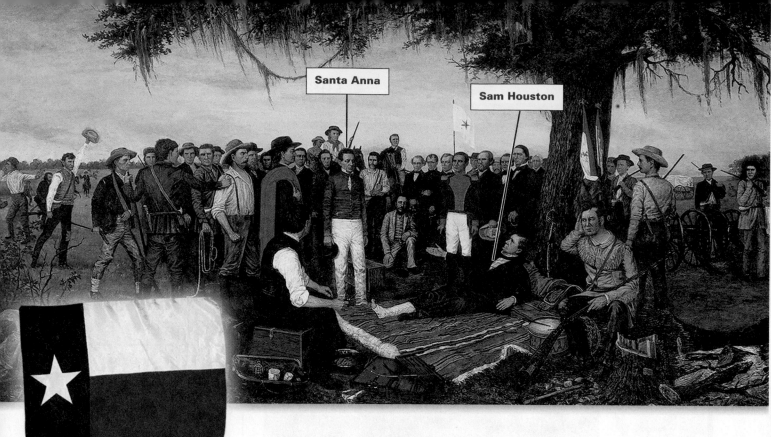

Santa Anna

Sam Houston

Viewing History

Winning Texas Independence

San Jacinto, Texas

Sam Houston was wounded in the leg during the Battle of San Jacinto. Despite tremendous pain and a boot full of blood, Houston fought on to victory. This painting shows Houston accepting the surrender of the Mexican commander Santa Anna. The flag is that of the Lone Star Republic. **Drawing Conclusions** *Why was San Jacinto a turning point in Texas history?*

Travis also sent scouts to find more volunteers and food. About 40 men managed to slip through enemy lines and join the fighters in the Alamo. Still, no large force arrived.

For 12 days, the Mexican bombardment continued. At dawn on March 6, Mexican cannons shattered the mission walls. Santa Anna now launched an all-out attack. Thousands of Mexican soldiers poured over the broken walls, shouting "Viva Santa Anna!" Attackers and defenders battled in hand-to-hand combat. In the end, about 180 Texans and almost 1,500 Mexicans lay dead. Most of the handful of Texan survivors were executed.

Texan Independence

The fall of the Alamo ignited cries for revenge. Texan fury grew a few weeks later, when Mexican troops killed several hundred soldiers fighting for the Texan cause after they had surrendered at Goliad. News of these events inspired new volunteers to join the Texan forces. Many came from the United States. Houston worked hard to turn the volunteers into an effective army. The Texans were eager to attack, but Houston held them back until the time was right.

Houston soon found the chance to attack Santa Anna. Scouts reported that the Mexican general and his army were camped near the San Jacinto (juh SIN toh) River. On the afternoon of April 21, 1836, the Texans caught their enemies by surprise. With cries of "Remember the Alamo!" and "Remember Goliad!" Texans charged into battle.

The **Battle of San Jacinto** lasted only 18 minutes. Although the Texans were outnumbered, they killed 630 Mexicans and captured 700 more. The next day, they captured Santa Anna, forcing him to sign a treaty granting Texas independence.

The Lone Star Republic

In battle, Texans had carried a flag with a single white star. After winning independence, they nicknamed their nation the **Lone Star Republic.** They wrote a constitution using the United States Constitution as a model. In September 1836, voters elected Sam Houston president of the Republic of Texas.

The new country faced several serious problems. First, the government of Mexico refused to accept the treaty that Santa Anna had signed. For Mexicans, Texas was still a part of their country. Second, Texas was nearly bankrupt. Third, Comanches and other Indian groups threatened to attack small Texan communities. Most Texans thought that the best way to solve their problems was to become part of the United States.

In the United States, people were divided about whether to **annex,** or add on, Texas. The arguments reflected sectional divisions in the country. White southerners generally favored the idea. Many northerners opposed it. At issue was slavery.

By the 1830s, antislavery feeling was growing in the North. Because many Texans owned slaves, northerners feared that Texas would join the Union as a slave-owning state. In addition, President Andrew Jackson worried that annexing Texas would lead to war with Mexico. As a result, Congress refused to annex Texas.

For the next nine years, leaders of the Lone Star Republic worked to attract new settlers. The new Texas government encouraged immigration by offering settlers free land. During the Panic of 1837, thousands of Americans moved to Texas. Settlers also arrived from Germany and Switzerland. They helped the new nation grow and prosper. By the 1840s, about 140,000 people lived in Texas, including many African Americans and some Mexicans.

★ ★ ★ Section 2 Assessment ★ ★ ★

Recall

1. **Identify** Explain the significance of **(a)** Stephen Austin, **(b)** Antonio López de Santa Anna, **(c)** Tejano, **(d)** Sam Houston, **(e)** Alamo, **(f)** William B. Travis, **(g)** Battle of San Jacinto, **(h)** Lone Star Republic.
2. **Define** **(a)** dictator, **(b)** siege, **(c)** annex.

Comprehension

3. Describe two causes of the conflict between American settlers and Mexico.
4. How did the fighting at the Alamo inspire Texans to win their independence?

5. Why did Texas not join the United States after San Jacinto?
6. Explain two problems that Texans tried to solve after winning independence.

Critical Thinking and Writing

7. **Exploring the Main Idea** Review the Main Idea statement at the beginning of this section. Then, write at least five headlines to mark events described in this section.
8. **Supporting a Point of View** As a Texan in 1838, you must vote to support or to oppose Texas's annexation by the United States. Write a position paper stating your opinion.

ACTIVITY

Go Online PHSchool.com

Connecting to Today
Use the Internet to find out what programs are underway today to preserve the Alamo. Then, write a paragraph that describes these efforts. For help in completing the activity, visit PHSchool.com, **Web Code mfd-1303.**

Determining Patterns and Distributions on Maps

Maps can help to make clear much of the information that historians collect. For example, a distribution map shows how people or things are spread over an area. A distribution map is a kind of thematic map—a map that presents certain themes. The theme of this map is settlement patterns in the newly formed Republic of Texas.

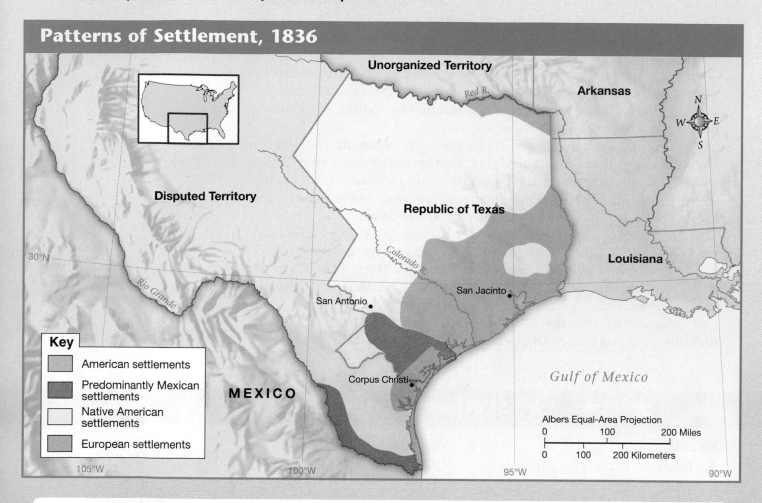

Patterns of Settlement, 1836

Key
- American settlements
- Predominantly Mexican settlements
- Native American settlements
- European settlements

Learn the Skill *To determine patterns and distribution on a map, use the following steps:*

1. **Read the title.** A map title provides a summary of the information shown on the map. In the case of a distribution map, the title should provide information about where people or things are located.

2. **Study the map key.** The key, or legend, tells what the different symbols on the map represent.

3. **Determine patterns.** Note which groups dominate in different areas.

4. **Analyze the information.** Put together what the map shows and what you already know about the subject to draw conclusions or make predictions.

Practice the Skill *Answer the following questions based on the map above:*

1. What is the title of the map?

2. (a) What color indicates Native American settlements on the map? (b) How are American settlements shown?

3. (a) Where were the Mexican settlements? (b) What was the smallest settlement in terms of area in 1836?

4. Analyze the reasons why people settled in Texas where they did by 1836.

Apply the Skill *See the Chapter Review and Assessment.*

3 California and the Southwest

Prepare to Read

Objectives

In this section, you will
- Explain why Americans took an interest in the New Mexico Territory.
- Describe life for Native Americans on California's missions and ranches.
- Summarize why many Americans supported the idea of westward expansion.

Key Terms

New Mexico Territory

Santa Fe Trail

self-sufficient

vaquero

Manifest Destiny

Target Reading Skill

Comparison and Contrast Copy this incomplete Venn diagram. As you read, write key facts about the Southwest and California in the 1840s in the appropriate sections.

SOUTHWEST
- Includes all or parts of Arizona, New Mexico, Nevada, Utah, Colorado
- Santa Fe is capital
- •
- •

• Settled by the Spanish
- •
- •

CALIFORNIA
- Region of contrasts in land, climate, and rainfall
- •
- •

Main Idea As Americans learned more about California and the Southwest in the 1840s, many came to think that the United States should expand its borders to the Pacific Ocean.

Setting the Scene Richard Henry Dana reached California after 150 days at sea. His ship had sailed from Boston around the tip of South America. One "fine Saturday afternoon," Dana and his crewmates sailed into Monterey Bay. "Everything was as green as nature could make it—the grass, the leaves, and all; the birds were singing in the woods and great numbers of wild fowl were flying over our heads. . . . The Mexican flag was flying from the little square Presidio, and the drums and trumpets of the soldiers . . . sounded over the water and gave life to the scene."

Dana wrote about his experiences in the book *Two Years Before the Mast*, which appeared in 1840. Dana's book contains a detailed description of life on the California coast. In it, Dana gives close attention to the daily lives of the peoples of California: Latino, Native American, and European.

At the time, California belonged to Mexico. With the help of books like *Two Years Before the Mast*, however, many Americans began to think that the United States should take control of all the lands between the Atlantic and Pacific oceans.

Life in Old California

New Mexico Territory

In the early 1840s, Mexico ruled not only California but all of the Southwest. The Southwest included most of present-day Arizona and New Mexico, all of Nevada and Utah, and parts of Colorado. This huge region was called New Mexico Territory.

Much of the Southwest is hot and dry with deserts and mountains. In some areas, thick grasses grow. Before the Spanish arrived, the Zuñi (ZOON yee) and other Indians farmed using irrigation. Other Native Americans, such as the Apaches, lived mainly by hunting.

The Spanish explorer Juan de Oñate (ohn YAH tay) claimed the region for Spain in 1598. In the early 1600s, the Spanish built Santa Fe and made it the capital of the territory. In time, Santa Fe grew into a busy trading town.

Spain, however, would not let Americans settle in Santa Fe or anywhere else in New Mexico. Only after Mexico became independent in 1821 were Americans welcome there. William Becknell, a merchant and adventurer, was the first American to head for Santa Fe. In 1821, he led some traders from Franklin, Missouri, across the plains to the New Mexico town. Other Americans soon followed Becknell's route. It became known as the Santa Fe Trail.

California's Missions and Ranches

California, too, was ruled first by Spain and then by Mexico. Spanish explorers had reached California in 1542, long before the English settled in Jamestown. Spanish and Native American cultures shaped life in California.

A String of Missions As you have read, Spanish soldiers and missionaries built the first European settlements in California. In 1769, Captain Gaspar de Portolá led an expedition up the Pacific coast. With him was Father Junípero Serra (hoo NEE peh roh SEHR rah). Father Serra built his first mission at San Diego. Later he and other missionaries set up a string of 21 missions along the California coast.

Each mission included a church and the surrounding land. Each became self-sufficient, producing enough for its own needs. Spanish soldiers built forts near the missions. The missions supplied meat, grain, and other foods to the forts.

California Missions and Ranches Before the Spanish arrived, California Indians lived in small, scattered groups. As a result, they had little success resisting the Spanish soldiers who forced them to work on mission lands.

Native Americans herded sheep and cattle and raised crops for the missions. In return, they lived at the missions and learned about the Roman Catholic faith. Many missionaries were dedicated to converting the Indians to Christianity. However, mission life was hard. Thousands of Native Americans died from overwork and diseases.

In the 1820s, newly independent Mexico decided that California's economy was growing too slowly. Hoping to speed up growth, the government took land from the missions and gave it to wealthy individuals. These people set up huge cattle ranches in California.

Native Americans did most of the work on the ranches, tending cattle and other animals. A new culture developed on the ranches— the culture of the vaqueros. Vaqueros were the Indian and Mexican cowhands who worked on the ranches. They were excellent riders and ropers, and their traditions strongly influenced later cowhands.

Support for Expansion

In the mid-1840s, only about 700 people from the United States lived in California. Every year, however, more Americans began moving west. On several occasions, the United States government offered to

Compare and Contrast

As you read the subsection "California's Missions and Ranches," note the similarities and differences between California and the Southwest. Add this information to your Venn diagram.

Primary Source

A Vaquero Roundup

Many of our traditions of cattle herding began with the vaqueros, Latino ranch hands in the Southwest and California. In this selection, a rancher describes some of the skills of the vaqueros:
"It was my good fortune to be taken on [a roundup]. . . . Even on the ground covered with grass, a huge cloud of dust envelopes everything, and nothing is heard but the thundering bank ahead. This is kept up for two or three hours, when the horsemen managed to get into the center of the flying herd. When the dust finally cleared, here and there over the plains could be seen colts and young mares, their forelegs tied to prevent them from escaping, which the vaqueros had lassoed . . ."

—Ygnacio Pedro Villegas,
Roundup, 1895

Analyzing Primary Sources
What is Villegas's (vee YAY gahs) attitude toward the vaqueros?

buy California from Mexico. Some officials were eager to gain control of the ports at San Francisco and San Diego.

The Idea of Manifest Destiny There was another reason for wanting to purchase California. Many Americans saw their nation and its democratic government as the best in the world. They believed that Americans had the right and the duty to spread their culture across the continent all the way to the Pacific Ocean.

In the 1840s, a newspaper in New York called this belief Manifest Destiny. Manifest means clear or obvious. Destiny means something that is sure to happen. Americans who believed in Manifest Destiny thought that expansion would also open new opportunities for the United States economy.

Manifest Destiny had a negative side. Many white Americans believed that they were superior to Native Americans and Mexicans. They used this belief to justify taking lands belonging to people whom they considered inferior.

Election of 1844 Manifest Destiny played a role in the election of 1844. The Whigs nominated Henry Clay for President. Clay was a well-known national leader. The Democrats chose a little-known candidate, James K. Polk.

Voters soon labeled Polk the candidate who favored expansion. Polk wanted to add Texas and Oregon to the United States. Clay, on the other hand, opposed the annexation of Texas.

The Democrats made Oregon a campaign issue. Britain and the United States held Oregon jointly. Polk demanded the whole region as far north as latitude 54°40'N. "Fifty-four forty or fight!" became the Democrats' campaign cry. On election day, Americans showed their support for expansion by choosing James Polk President.

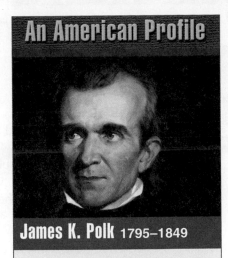

An American Profile

James K. Polk 1795–1849

It is easy to forget just how hard life could be 200 years ago. Consider this: As a teenager, James Polk suffered from severe stomach pains. A doctor discovered gallstones and recommended surgery. Anesthesia was unknown at the time. In 1812, when he was 17, Polk was strapped to a table and operated on while he was awake.

James Polk was a very determined person. Although he had little formal education, he mastered Latin and Greek, graduated with honors from the University of North Carolina, and became a lawyer.

What qualities did Polk show in early life that might serve him well as President?

★ ★ ★ **Section 3 Assessment** ★ ★ ★

Recall

1. **Identify** Explain the significance of **(a)** New Mexico Territory, **(b)** William Becknell, **(c)** Santa Fe Trail, **(d)** Junípero Serra, **(e)** Manifest Destiny, **(f)** James K. Polk.
2. **Define** **(a)** self-sufficient, **(b)** vaquero.

Comprehension

3. Why were Americans attracted to the New Mexico Territory?
4. How did mission and ranch life affect Native Americans in California?
5. Why did many Americans feel strongly about expansion to the Pacific Ocean?

Critical Thinking and Writing

6. **Exploring the Main Idea** Review the Main Idea statement at the beginning of this section. Then, write a newspaper editorial that might have appeared in the 1840s for or against expansion.
7. **Supporting a Point of View** You are a supporter of one of the major candidates for President in the election of 1844. Write a paragraph stating whether you support Polk or Clay. Give reasons to support your choice.

ACTIVITY

Drawing a Political Cartoon Draw a political cartoon about Manifest Destiny from the point of view of the people of the Southwest.

4 The Mexican War

Prepare to Read

Objectives

In this section, you will
- Explain how the United States gained Oregon and Texas.
- List the causes and results of the Mexican War.
- Name the new lands the United States acquired as a result of the Mexican War.
- Describe how a mix of cultures shaped California and the Southwest.

Key Terms

Bear Flag Republic

Chapultepec

Treaty of Guadalupe-Hidalgo

cede

Mexican Cession

Gadsden Purchase

Target Reading Skill

Cause and Effect As you read, complete the following chart to show some of the causes and effects of the Mexican War.

CAUSES
1. United States annexes Texas
2.
3.

MEXICAN WAR

EFFECTS
1. Treaty of Guadalupe-Hidalgo
2. United States acquires vast new lands
3.

Main Idea As a result of the Mexican War, the United States expanded its borders to the Pacific Ocean.

Wartime spirit

Setting the Scene American troops marched off to war with Mexico in 1846. Many of them proudly sang new words to the popular tune "Yankee Doodle": "They attacked our men upon our land, / And crossed our river too, sir. / Now show them all with sword in hand / What yankee boys can do, sir."

The bloody Mexican War would last 20 months. When it ended, the United States had expanded its borders to the Pacific Ocean. In the end, the war helped the United States achieve its dream of Manifest Destiny.

War Clouds Over Oregon and Texas

James K. Polk took office in March 1845 on a wave of support for expansion. Acting on his campaign promise, Polk took steps to gain control of Oregon. That move brought close the possibility of war with Britain.

Dividing Oregon Polk did not really want to fight Britain. Instead, in 1846, he agreed to a compromise. Oregon was divided at latitude 49°N. Britain got the lands north of the line, and the United States got the lands south of the line.

The United States named its lands the Oregon Territory. Later, the states of Oregon (1859), Washington (1889), and Idaho (1890) were carved out of the Oregon Territory.

Annexing Texas Texas proved a more difficult problem. As you have read, the United States at first had refused to annex Texas. Then, in 1844, Texan president Sam Houston signed a treaty of annexation with the United States. However, the Senate again refused to ratify the treaty. Senators feared that annexing Texas would cause a war with Mexico.

Sam Houston would not give up. To pressure the United States to annex Texas, he pretended that Texas might ally itself with Britain. The trick worked. Americans did not want Britain to gain a foothold in Texas. In 1845, Congress passed a joint resolution admitting Texas to the Union.

The United States and Mexico Clash

The annexation of Texas outraged Mexicans. They had never accepted Texan independence. They also worried that Americans might encourage rebellions in California and New Mexico as they had in Texas.

At the same time, Americans resented Mexico. They were annoyed when Mexico rejected President Polk's offer of $30 million to buy California and New Mexico. Many Americans felt that Mexico stood in the way of Manifest Destiny.

War Begins A border dispute finally sparked war. Both the United States and Mexico claimed control over the land between the Rio Grande and the Nueces (noo AY says) River. In January 1846, Polk ordered General Zachary Taylor to set up posts in the disputed area. (See the map above.) Polk knew that the move might lead to war. In April 1846, Mexican troops crossed the Rio Grande and clashed with the Americans. Soldiers on both sides were killed.

When Polk heard about the fighting, he asked Congress to declare war. "Mexico," he said, "has passed the boundary of the United States, has invaded our territory, and shed American blood upon American soil." At Polk's urging, Congress declared war on Mexico.

Americans Respond Americans were divided over the war. Many people in the South and West were eager to fight, hoping to win new lands. Some northerners, however, opposed the war. They saw it as a southern plot to add slave states to the Union. The writer Henry David Thoreau refused to pay taxes because he thought the war was unjust. For this, Thoreau was arrested and imprisoned. Still, the war was generally popular. When the army called for volunteers, thousands of young recruits flocked to the cause. A large number came from the South and West.

Fighting in Mexico

During the Mexican War, the United States attacked on several fronts at once. President Polk hoped this strategy would win a quick victory. General Taylor crossed the Rio Grande into northern Mexico.

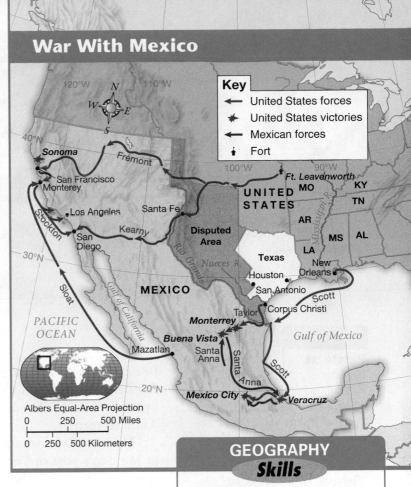

War With Mexico

Key
⟵ United States forces
✴ United States victories
⟵ Mexican forces
⚑ Fort

GEOGRAPHY Skills

Fighting along a disputed border between Texas and Mexico triggered the Mexican War.

1. **Location** On the map, locate **(a)** Rio Grande, **(b)** Nueces River, **(c)** Buena Vista, **(d)** Veracruz, **(e)** Mexico City.

2. **Movement** Describe the movements of each of the following American commanders: **(a)** Winfield Scott, **(b)** Stephen Kearny, **(c)** John C. Frémont.

3. **Critical Thinking Drawing Inferences** Based on the map, was sea power important to the United States in the Mexican War? Explain.

Viewing History

Battle at Buena Vista

Early in the Battle of Buena Vista, the Americans faced a determined Mexican attack. An American officer cried out to General Zachary Taylor: "General, we are whipped." "I know it," replied Taylor. "But the volunteers don't know it. Let them alone. We'll see what they do." The Americans drove the Mexicans back and won the battle. In this picture, Taylor, at center, gives instructions to his artillery.
Drawing Inferences *Do you think Taylor really believed that his forces were "whipped"?*

Understand Effects An effect is what happens as a result of a specific cause or factor. Read the subsection "Peace Brings New Lands" to learn about the effects of the Mexican War. Add the information to your chart.

In February 1847, he met Mexican General Santa Anna at the Battle of Buena Vista. The Americans were outnumbered more than two to one but were better armed and led. After fierce fighting, they forced Santa Anna to retreat.

Meanwhile, a second army under General Winfield Scott landed at Mexico's port of Veracruz. After a long battle, the Americans took the city. Scott then headed toward Mexico City, the capital.

Revolt in California A third army, led by General Stephen Kearny, captured Santa Fe without firing a shot. Kearny hurried on to San Diego. After several battles, he won control of southern California early in 1847.

Even before hearing of the war, Americans in northern California had begun a revolt against Mexican rule. The rebels declared California an independent republic on June 14, 1846. They nicknamed their new nation the Bear Flag Republic.

Led by a young American officer, John C. Frémont (FREE mont), rebel forces then drove the Mexican troops out of northern California. Frémont later joined forces with United States troops.

The Final Battle By 1847, the United States controlled all of New Mexico and California. General Scott, meanwhile, had reached Mexico City. There, his forces faced fierce resistance.

Young Mexican soldiers made a heroic stand at Chapultepec (chah POOL tuh pehk), a fort just outside the capital. Today, Mexicans honor those young soldiers as heroes.

Peace Brings New Lands

With Mexico City in American hands, the Mexican government moved to make peace. In 1848, it signed the Treaty of Guadalupe-Hidalgo (gwah duh LOOP ay ih DAHL goh). Mexico had to cede, or give up, all of California and New Mexico to the United States. These lands were called the Mexican Cession. In return, the United States paid Mexico $15 million and agreed to respect the rights of Spanish-speaking people in the Mexican Cession.

A few years later in 1853, the United States paid Mexico $10 million for a strip of land in present-day Arizona and New Mexico. The Americans needed the land to complete a railroad. The land was called the **Gadsden Purchase.** With the Gadsden Purchase, many Americans felt that their dream of Manifest Destiny had been fulfilled.

A Mix of Cultures

After 1848, English-speaking settlers flocked to the Southwest. They brought their own culture, including ideas about democracy. Still, the newcomers had much to learn from earlier residents. Mexican Americans taught them how to mine silver and irrigate crops. Many Spanish and Native American words—such as stampede, buffalo, tortilla, soda, and tornado—were added to the English language.

The newcomers often treated Mexican Americans and Native Americans poorly. Earlier residents tried hard to protect their traditions and rights. However, when Mexican Americans went to court to defend their property, they often lost their cases. Mariano Vallejo (vah YAY hoh), whose family had settled in California long before the Mexican War wrote that American settlers "took advantage of laws which they understood, but which were new to the Spaniards."

In the Southwest, however, Americans kept some Mexican laws. One law said that a husband and wife owned property jointly. In the rest of the United States, married women could not own property. Another Mexican law prevented landowners from cutting off water to their neighbors. This law was especially important in the desert Southwest, where water was scarce.

Viewing History

The Bear Flag

California

As a symbol of their freedom, the California rebels raised this "Bear Flag." It remains California's state flag today. **Analyzing Primary Sources** *(a) Why do you think the flag makers put a single star on the flag? (b) Why do you suppose they chose a grizzly bear as their main symbol?*

★ ★ ★ **Section 4 Assessment** ★ ★ ★

Recall

1. **Identify** Explain the significance of (a) Zachary Taylor, (b) Winfield Scott, (c) Stephen Kearny, (d) Bear Flag Republic, (e) John C. Frémont, (f) Chapultepec, (g) Treaty of Guadalupe-Hidalgo, (h) Mexican Cession, (i) Gadsden Purchase.
2. **Define** cede.

Comprehension

3. Describe how the United States gained (a) Oregon, (b) Texas.
4. Describe two causes of the Mexican War.
5. What new lands were added to the United States as a result of the Mexican War?

6. Name three groups whose cultures influenced California and the Southwest, and describe some of their influences.

Critical Thinking and Writing

7. **Exploring the Main Idea** Review the Main Idea statement at the beginning of this section. Then, write a paragraph or two summarizing how the Mexican War helped the United States expand.
8. **Identifying Alternatives** Do you think the United States could have avoided going to war with Mexico in 1846? Explain.

ACTIVITY

Mental Mapping Study the map showing war with Mexico on page 395. On a piece of paper, draw your own sketch map of the region. Label the major bodies of water and the routes of U.S. and Mexican forces. Show the location of U.S. victories and forts. Use colors to outline and shade each country and area.

5 Americans Rush West

Prepare to Read

Objectives

In this section, you will
- Explain why the Mormons moved to Utah.
- Describe how the gold rush affected life in California.
- Summarize why California developed such a diverse population.

Key Terms

Mormons
Nauvoo
refuge
Sutter's Mill
forty-niner
vigilante
lynch

Target Reading Skill

Cause and Effect As you read, complete the following chart to show the effects of the gold rush on California.

```
                    GOLD RUSH
        ┌──────────┬──────────┬──────────┬──────────┐
     Flood of    Law-and-    Changes in
     settlers   order issues  government
     •            •            •
     •            •            •
```

Main Idea In the late 1840s, thousands of Americans headed west, including the Mormons who went to Utah and the forty-niners who headed to California.

Entering the new land

Setting the Scene In 1848, exciting news reached the people of Toishan in southern China. Mountains of gold had been discovered across the Pacific Ocean, in a place called California. The gold was there just for the digging!

At the time, strict laws forbade Chinese citizens from leaving the country. Anyone caught leaving could be beheaded. Still, tens of thousands of Chinese risked their lives to sail across the Pacific to California. There, they joined the flood of people arriving from Europe, South America, and other parts of the United States. All were eager to find gold.

Gold was not the only attraction of the West. By 1848, California, New Mexico Territory, Oregon Country, and Texas had all been added to the United States. Pioneers set out hoping to make new lives. There, they put their hopes and dreams into building homes and working to make a living.

Mormons Settle in Utah

The largest group of settlers to move into the Mexican Cession were the Mormons. Mormons belonged to the Church of Jesus Christ of Latter-Day Saints. The church was founded by Joseph Smith in 1830. Smith, a farmer in upstate New York, attracted many followers to his faith.

Troubles With Neighbors Smith was an energetic, popular man. His teachings, however, angered many non-Mormons. For example, Mormons at first believed that property should be owned in common. Smith also said that a man could have more than one wife. Angry neighbors forced the Mormons to leave New York.

The Mormons moved west to Ohio. There, too, they faced opposition. From Ohio, they went to Missouri and then to Illinois. In the 1840s, the Mormons built a community called Nauvoo on the banks of the Mississippi River in Illinois. Once again, the Mormons and their neighbors clashed. In 1844, an angry mob killed Joseph Smith. The Mormons then chose Brigham Young as their new leader.

Young realized that the Mormons needed to find a **refuge,** a place where they would be safe from persecution. He had read about a valley between the Rocky Mountains and the Great Salt Lake in Utah. Young hoped that this isolated valley might make a good home for the Mormons.

A Difficult Journey To move 15,000 men, women, and children from Illinois to Utah was an awesome challenge. Relying on religious faith and careful planning, Brigham Young achieved his goal. In 1847, Young led an advance party into the valley of the Great Salt Lake. Later, waves of Mormon families followed. For several years, Mormon wagon trains struggled across the plains and over the Rockies to Utah. When they ran short of wagons or their oxen died, the families made the long trip pulling their gear in handcarts.

Life in the Desert In Utah, the Mormons had to learn how to survive in the desert climate. Harsh as the environment was, Young was convinced that Utah was Zion, or the promised land for the Mormons:

> 66 We will raise our wheat, build our houses, fence our farms, plant our vineyards and orchards, and produce everything that will make our bodies comfortable and happy and in this manner we intend to build up Zion on the earth. 99
>
> —Brigham Young, "Building Up and Adornment of Zion by the Saints," February 23, 1862

To meet these goals, Young planned an irrigation system to bring water to farms. He also drew up plans for a large city, called Salt Lake City, to be built in the desert.

The Mormon settlements in Utah grew quickly. Like other white settlers, however, Mormons took over Native American land, usually paying nothing for it.

Congress recognized Brigham Young as governor of the Utah Territory in 1850. Later, as non-Mormons began moving into the area, trouble broke out. In time, though, peace was restored, and Utah became a state in 1896.

California Gold Rush

While the Mormons were making the long trek to Utah, thousands of other Americans were racing even farther west to California. The great attraction there was gold.

Cause *and* Effect

Causes

- Oregon has fertile land
- Texas is ideal for raising cattle and growing cotton
- Many Americans believe in Manifest Destiny
- Mormons seek a safe home
- Gold is discovered in California

WESTWARD MOVEMENT

Effects

- Texas wins war for independence
- United States annexes Texas
- Britain and United States divide Oregon
- United States defeats Mexico in war
- Cotton Kingdom spreads

Effects Today

- United States stretches from sea to sea
- California and Texas are the most populous states
- Mexican American culture enriches the United States

GRAPHIC ORGANIZER
Skills

Westward movement increased at a tremendous rate in the mid-1800s.

1. **Comprehension** List two attractions that drew Americans to the West.

2. **Critical Thinking Drawing Conclusions** According to this chart, was Manifest Destiny successful? Explain.

Understand Effects Skim the subheadings in this section. Then, predict how the gold rush would affect the population in the West. Read to learn new information about population change in the West.

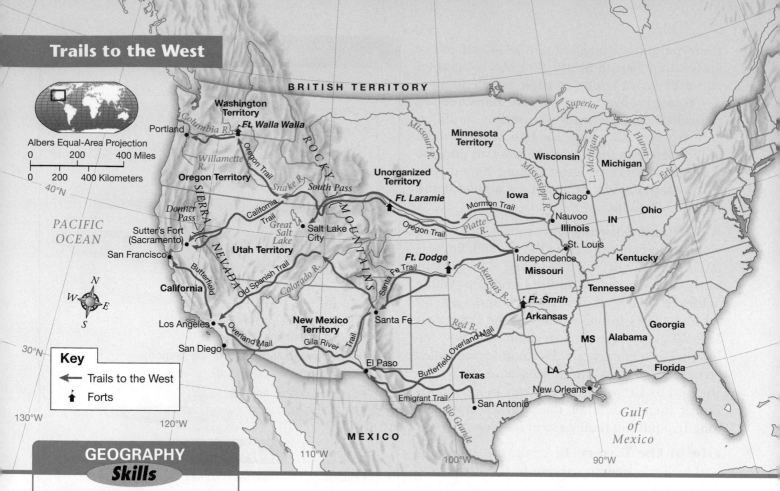

Trails to the West

BRITISH TERRITORY

Albers Equal-Area Projection
0   200   400 Miles
0   200   400 Kilometers

Key
← Trails to the West
⚑ Forts

PACIFIC OCEAN

Washington Territory
Portland
Ft. Walla Walla
Oregon Territory
Oregon Trail
Willamette R.
Columbia R.
Snake R.
South Pass
SIERRA NEVADA
Donner Pass
California Trail
Sutter's Fort (Sacramento)
San Francisco
Great Salt Lake
Salt Lake City
Utah Territory
California
Butterfield
Old Spanish Trail
Colorado R.
Los Angeles
San Diego
Overland Mail
New Mexico Territory
Gila River Trail
El Paso
Emigrant Trail
Rio Grande
MEXICO

ROCKY MOUNTAINS
Missouri R.
Unorganized Territory
Ft. Laramie
Oregon Trail
Platte R.
Ft. Dodge
Santa Fe Trail
Santa Fe
Arkansas R.
Red R.
Butterfield Overland Mail
Texas
San Antonio

Minnesota Territory
Wisconsin   Michigan
Iowa   Chicago
Mormon Trail
Nauvoo
Illinois
St. Louis
Independence
Missouri
Ft. Smith
Arkansas
MS   Alabama
LA
New Orleans

L. Superior
L. Michigan
L. Huron
L. Erie
Ohio
IN
Kentucky
Tennessee
Georgia
Florida
Gulf of Mexico

40°N
30°N
130°W   120°W   110°W   100°W   90°W

GEOGRAPHY Skills

In the 1800s, Americans followed a number of different trails to the West. Mountain passes allowed settlers to cross the Rockies and Sierra Nevada.

1. **Location** On the map, locate (a) Santa Fe, (b) Santa Fe Trail, (c) Sierra Nevada, (d) Rocky Mountains, (e) San Diego, (f) San Francisco, (g) Salt Lake City.

2. **Movement** Which trails ended in cities in California?

3. **Critical Thinking Applying Information** (a) What would be the best route for a pioneer family to take from Independence, Missouri, to Sutter's Fort, California? (b) What mountains would they have to cross? (c) In which community might they seek shelter along the way?

Sutter's Mill In 1848, John Sutter was having a sawmill built on the American River, north of Sacramento, California. Sutter had hired James Marshall to supervise the job. Early on January 24, Marshall set out to inspect a ditch his crew was digging. He later recalled the events of that day:

    66 It was a clear, cold morning; I shall never forget that morning. As I was taking my usual walk, . . . my eye was caught with the glimpse of something shining in the bottom of the ditch. There was about a foot of water running then. I reached my hand down and picked it up; it made my heart thump, for I was certain it was gold. 99

—James Marshall, quoted in *Hutchings' Illustrated California Magazine,* 1857–1858

At first, Sutter tried to keep the news a secret. His efforts failed. Within a few days, news reached San Francisco that gold had been found at **Sutter's Mill.** Carpenters threw down their saws. Bakers left bread in their ovens. Schools emptied as teachers and students joined the rush to the gold fields.

From San Francisco, the news spread across the United States and to the rest of the world. Thousands of Americans caught "gold fever." People from Europe, China, Australia, and South America joined in the great gold rush. More than 80,000 people made the long journey to California in 1849. They became known as **forty-niners.**

Working the Gold Fields At first, gold was easy to find near the surface of the Earth. Miners could dig it out with knives. Later on, miners found a better way to get the gold out of riverbeds. They loaded sand and gravel from the riverbed into a washing pan. Then, they held the pan under water, gently swirling it. The water washed away the gravel, leaving the heavier gold in the pan. This process was known as "panning for gold."

Very few miners actually struck it rich. Many went broke trying to make their fortunes in the gold fields. Still, although many miners left the gold fields, they stayed in California. In time, they found jobs or took up farming.

Women joined the gold rush, too. Some staked claims and mined for gold. Others took advantage of economic opportunities in the mining camps. Women ran boardinghouses, took in laundry, sewed for the miners, and opened bakeries.

A New State The gold rush brought big changes to California. Almost overnight, San Francisco grew from a sleepy town to a bustling city as newcomers poured in from all over the world. In the gold fields, towns sprang up just as quickly.

Greed led some forty-niners into crime. Murders and robberies plagued many mining camps. As the crime wave grew, miners and even some city-dwellers formed vigilance committees. **Vigilantes** (vihj uh LAN teez), or self-appointed law enforcers, dealt out punishment even though they had no legal right to do so. Sometimes, a person accused of a crime was **lynched**—hanged without a legal trial.

Californians soon realized that they needed a strong government to stop such lawlessness. In 1849, they drafted a state constitution. They then asked to be admitted to the Union. Their request caused an uproar in the United States. Many people wanted to know whether the new state would allow slavery. As you will read, after a heated debate, California was admitted to the Union in 1850 as a free state.

A Diverse Population

The gold rush changed California in many ways. It brought diverse groups of people to the West. Most of the newcomers were white Americans. However, California's mining camps included runaway slaves from the South, Native Americans, and New Englanders. There were also people from Hawaii, China, Peru, Chile, France, Germany, Italy, Ireland, and Australia.

Mexican Americans and Indians Before the gold rush, California's population included large numbers of Mexicans. Due to the efforts of people such as José Carrillo (cah REE yoh), much of their culture was preserved. Carillo came from an old California family. In part through his efforts, the state's first constitution was written in both Spanish and English. Despite such efforts, many Mexican Americans faced serious hardships. During the 1850s and 1860s, many lost land that their families had owned for generations.

Native Americans fared even worse. Many were driven off the lands where they lived. Without any means to earn a living, large

Connecting to Today

California's Water Wars

Pioneer settlers in California sometimes fought over water rights. Although tempers have cooled since then, control of water still creates conflict in California.

Today, farmers, city dwellers, and environmentalists compete for the state's limited water resources. Farmers use 80 percent of the state's water to grow crops and support the economy. Cities want more water to supply a growing population. Environmental groups want to cut water usage to preserve rivers and wetlands and the plants and animals that depend on them.

These three groups have to compete to achieve their goals. In the long run, however, they will have to work together if California is to make the best use of its limited water resources.

Describe one thing people in California can do to solve the state's water problems.

numbers died of starvation or diseases brought by the newcomers. Still others were murdered.

In 1850, about 100,000 Indians lived in California. By the 1870s, the state's Indian population had dropped to 17,000.

Chinese Americans Attracted by the tales of a "mountain of gold," thousands of Chinese sailed across the Pacific to California. At first, the Chinese were welcomed because California needed workers. When the Chinese staked claims in the gold fields, however, white miners often drove them off.

Chinese Americans and, later, other immigrants from Asia, faced prejudice in California. Despite the harsh treatment, many Chinese Americans stayed in California. They helped the state to grow. They drained swamplands and dug irrigation systems to turn dry land into fertile farmland. They also helped build the railroads that linked California with other parts of the country.

African Americans Free blacks, too, joined the gold rush in California, hoping to strike it rich. Some became well-off. In fact, by the 1850s, California had the richest African American population of any state. Yet, African Americans faced discrimination and were denied certain rights. For example, under California law, African Americans and other minorities were denied the right to testify against whites in court. After a long struggle, African Americans won this right in 1863.

In spite of these problems, California continued to grow and prosper. Settlers from other states and immigrants from all over the world kept arriving. With their diverse backgrounds, the newcomers added to California's unique culture. By 1860, the state's population was about 300,000.

★ ★ ★ **Section 5 Assessment** ★ ★ ★

Recall

1. **Identify** Explain the significance of (a) Mormons, (b) Joseph Smith, (c) Nauvoo, (d) Brigham Young, (e) Sutter's Mill.
2. **Define** (a) refuge, (b) forty-niner, (c) vigilante, (d) lynch.

Comprehension

3. Why did Brigham Young decide to lead the Mormons to Utah?
4. Describe two effects of the gold rush on California.
5. How did California's population become so diverse?

Critical Thinking and Writing

6. **Exploring the Main Idea** Review the Main Idea statement at the beginning of this section. Then, write at least two paragraphs describing how settlers in California and Utah modified their environment.
7. **Linking Past and Present** California is still a diverse land. In the 1990s, almost 30 percent of immigrants to the United States settled in California. Most came from Asia. (a) Why do you think California still attracts many immigrants? (b) Why might many Asian immigrants settle in California?

ACTIVITY

Go Online
PHSchool.com

Visualizing the Gold Rush
Use the Internet to learn more about the California gold rush. Look for photos and paintings. Then, describe life in: (a) the gold fields, (b) a gold-rush city. For help in completing the activity, visit PHSchool.com, **Web Code mfd-1304.**

Women and the California Gold Rush

Women as well as men had the vision and willpower to make a profit in the mining towns of the California gold rush. One enterprising woman was Luzena Stanley Wilson, who in 1849 arrived at the gold mines near Sacramento with her husband and two sons. At first, the Wilsons built and ran a hotel in Sacramento, but lost it in a flood. Then, the family moved to Nevada City, where Luzena started a new business.

Miners' tools

Working a claim

"I determined to set up [another] hotel. So I bought two boards from a precious pile belonging to a man who was building the second wooden house in town. With my own hands I chopped stakes, drove them into the ground, and set up my table. I bought provisions at a neighboring store, and when my husband came back at night he found, mid the weird light of the pine torches, twenty miners eating at my table. Each man as he rose put a dollar in my hand and said I might count him as a permanent customer. I called my hotel 'El Dorado.'

"From the first day it was well patronized, and I shortly after took my husband into partnership."

ACTIVITY

Luzena Wilson wanted to run her own business. What were the advantages of running her own business? Divide a piece of paper into two columns, "Advantages" and "Disadvantages." List four items in each column.

CHAPTER SUMMARY

Section 1
In the early 1800s, fur trappers hunted the rich forests of Oregon Country. By the 1840s, missionaries and pioneers arrived to settle the region.

Section 2
The presence of a growing number of Americans in Texas led to tension with Mexico. After revolting, the settlers won a short war against Mexico. The victors established the independent republic of Texas.

Section 3
Spain built missions along the West coast of North America. Later, Mexico controlled the New Mexico Territory and California. Many Americans moved into this area, driven there by the idea of Manifest Destiny.

Section 4
A compromise with Britain gave the United States the Oregon Territory. The United States annexed Texas, and it took control of California and most of the Southwest after its victory in the Mexican War.

Section 5
In the late 1840s, the Mormons moved to Utah to escape religious persecution. Thousands of other Americans were drawn to California by the gold rush, thus turning California into a land of diverse peoples.

Building Vocabulary

Review the chapter vocabulary words listed below. Then, use the words and their definitions to create a matching quiz. Exchange quizzes with another student.

1. **mountain man**
2. **rendezvous**
3. **dictator**
4. **siege**
5. **annex**
6. **cede**
7. **forty-niner**
8. **vigilante**

For additional review and enrichment activities, see the interactive version of *The American Nation,* available on the Web and on CD-ROM.

Chapter Self-Test For practice test questions for Chapter 13, visit PHSchool.com, **Web Code mfa-1305.**

Reviewing Key Facts

9. Describe the life of the mountain men in Oregon Country. (Section 1)
10. How did Texans force Santa Anna to grant Texas independence? (Section 2)
11. Why was the idea of Manifest Destiny important to many Americans? (Section 3)
12. How did the Treaty of Guadalupe-Hidalgo affect the United States? (Section 4)
13. Why did California try to become a state in 1849? (Section 5)

Critical Thinking and Writing

14. **Analyzing Information** Analyze the relationship between Manifest Destiny and the westward growth of the United States.
15. **Understanding Causes and Effects** Write a paragraph explaining one result of the battle of San Jacinto.
16. **Drawing Conclusions** Explain how the Alamo was both a defeat and a victory for Texas.
17. **Connecting to Geography: Regions** Use the map at the beginning of this chapter that shows the growth of the United States to 1853. **(a)** List three of today's states that were added to the United States between 1820 and 1860. **(b)** How did westward expansion change the borders of the United States?

Read this excerpt from President Polk's speech asking for a declaration of war, and then answer the questions that follow:

> ❝ [Mexico] has invaded our territory and shed American blood upon the American soil. She has proclaimed that hostilities have commenced, and that the two nations are now at war. As war exists, and, [despite] all our efforts to avoid it, exists by the act of Mexico herself, we are called upon by every consideration of duty and patriotism to [clear] . . . the honor, the rights, and the interests of our country. ❞
>
> —James K. Polk, Message to Congress, May 11, 1846

18. Whom does Polk blame for the fighting?
- **A.** France
- **B.** Spain
- **C.** Mexico
- **D.** the United States

19. According to Polk, the United States and Mexico are already at war because
- **A.** Congress had declared war right before his speech.
- **B.** of Mexico's actions.
- **C.** Manifest Destiny holds that peace between the two nations is impossible.
- **D.** negotiations to avoid war have failed.

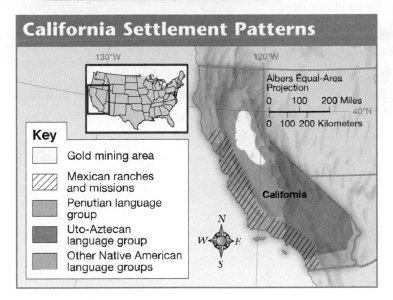

California Settlement Patterns

Key
- Gold mining area
- Mexican ranches and missions
- Penutian language group
- Uto-Aztecan language group
- Other Native American language groups

20. Which of the following regions covers the smallest land area?
- **A.** areas where the main language is Penutian
- **B.** areas where the main language is English
- **C.** areas where the main language is Uto-Aztecan
- **D.** areas where the main language is Spanish

21. **(a)** Which of the regions on the map is the most recently established? **(b)** Does this map show conditions in 1800? 1825? 1850? Explain your answer.

ACTIVITIES

Connecting With . . .
Geography

Describing Expansion Locate the following places on the map on the chapter-opening page: **1.** Louisiana Purchase, **2.** Gadsden Purchase, **3.** Oregon Country, **4.** Mexican Cession. After locating these places, describe at least four steps by which the United States expanded its borders from the Mississippi River to the Pacific Ocean.

Go Online
PHSchool.com

Connecting to Today

Transferring Information Use the Internet to find the Census Bureau's estimate of the Hispanic population of the United States today. Then, use the Bureau's historical statistics to create a chart showing how that population has grown since the 1850 census. For help in starting this activity, visit PHSchool.com, **Web Code mfd-1306.**

Writing a Journal Entry

Examining the Texan Struggle for Independence Use the Internet to find sites that offer eyewitness accounts of the Texas war for independence. Choose one eyewitness account and identify the author's point of view. Then, write a journal entry that tells of the person's experiences. For help in starting this activity, visit PHSchool.com, **Web Code mfd-1307.**

North and South

1820–1860

1 **Industry in the North**
2 **Life in the North**
3 **Cotton Kingdom in the South**
4 **Life in the South**

A railroad advertisement

Cotton press used to make cotton bales

1830

The growth of railroads changes the way goods are shipped. With railroads, goods can be shipped quickly and cheaply.

1840s

The invention of the cotton gin increases the production of cotton. The cotton boom increases the spread of slavery.

1820s

Skilled workers begin to organize unions.

AMERICAN EVENTS

John Quincy Adams

Martin Van Buren

Presidential Terms: James Monroe 1817–1825 | 1825–1829 | Andrew Jackson 1829–1837 | 1837–1841

1820 • **1830** • **1840**

WORLD EVENTS

1829 ▲
A steam-powered locomotive in England travels 30 miles per hour.

1840 ▲
The World Anti-Slavery Convention is held in Great Britain.

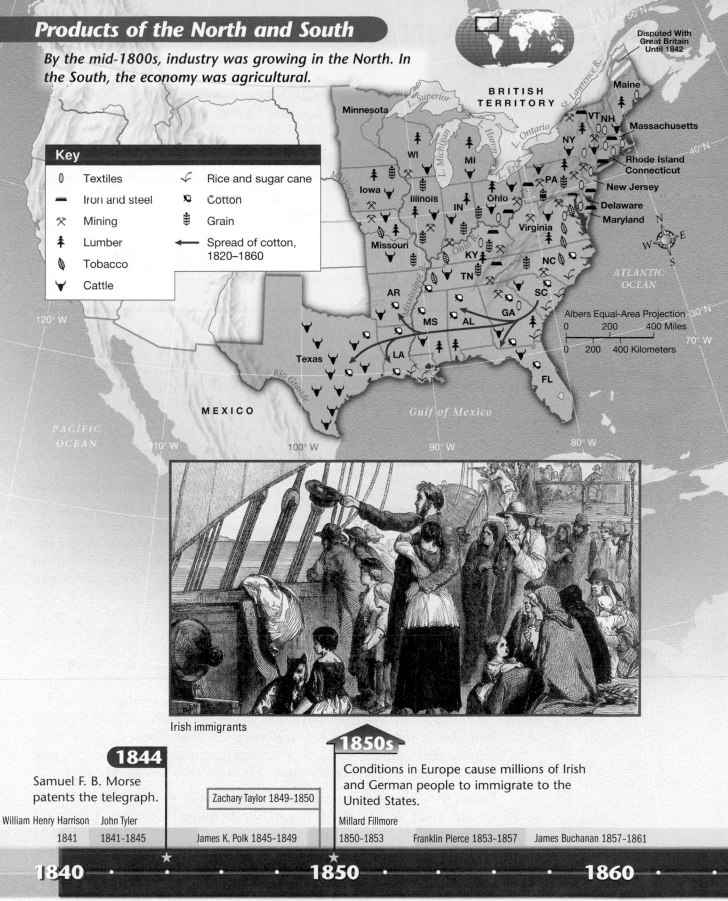

Products of the North and South

By the mid-1800s, industry was growing in the North. In the South, the economy was agricultural.

Disputed With Great Britain Until 1842

BRITISH TERRITORY

Key

Textiles		Rice and sugar cane	
Iron and steel		Cotton	
Mining		Grain	
Lumber		Spread of cotton, 1820–1860	
Tobacco			
Cattle			

Minnesota

Maine

VT NH

Massachusetts

WI

MI

NY

Rhode Island
Connecticut

Iowa

Illinois

IN

Ohio

PA

New Jersey

Delaware

Maryland

Missouri

Virginia

KY

TN

NC

AR

SC

MS

AL

GA

Texas

LA

FL

ATLANTIC OCEAN

Albers Equal-Area Projection

0   200   400 Miles

0   200   400 Kilometers

PACIFIC OCEAN

MEXICO

Rio Grande

Gulf of Mexico

Irish immigrants

1844

Samuel F. B. Morse patents the telegraph.

1850s

Conditions in Europe cause millions of Irish and German people to immigrate to the United States.

Zachary Taylor 1849–1850

William Henry Harrison 1841

John Tyler 1841–1845

James K. Polk 1845–1849

Millard Fillmore 1850–1853

Franklin Pierce 1853–1857

James Buchanan 1857–1861

1840

1850

1860

▲ 1848

In revolutions in Germany, rebels demand national unity and social and economic reforms.

1 Industry in the North

Prepare to Read

Objectives

In this section, you will
- Summarize how new inventions changed manufacturing and farming in the North.
- Identify the difficulties faced by the first railroads.
- Explain how railroads and clipper ships helped the northern economy.

Key Terms

telegraph

locomotive

clipper ship

Target Reading Skill

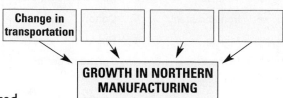

Cause and Effect Copy the chart below. As you read, complete the chart to show the causes that led to a change in manufacturing in the North. Add as many boxes as you need.

Change in transportation → GROWTH IN NORTHERN MANUFACTURING

Main Idea New inventions and faster transportation changed the way goods were manufactured and shipped.

A cast-iron stove from the 1800s

Setting the Scene Susan Blunt's New Hampshire neighbors were suspicious when she brought home a new stove in the autumn of 1838. Was she really going to cook meals on it, instead of over the kitchen fire?

Soon, however, the advantages of the cast-iron stove became clear. Instead of hanging kettles over a fire, Blunt tended them at waist height, on the stove top. The oven heated food more evenly, too. In the end, Susan Blunt recalled: "In a year or two all the neighbors had one, after they saw that we came out all right in the spring."

Susan Blunt's cast-iron stove was only one sign of the way northern factories were changing the lives of ordinary people. Northern industry grew steadily in the mid-1800s. Most northerners still lived on farms. However, more and more of the northern economy began to depend on manufacturing and trade.

New Inventions

The 1800s brought a flood of new inventions in the North. "In Massachusetts and Connecticut," a European visitor exclaimed, "there is not a laborer who has not invented a machine or a tool."

In 1846, Elias Howe patented a sewing machine. A few years later, Isaac Singer improved on Howe's machine. Soon, clothing makers bought hundreds of the new sewing machines. Workers could now make dozens of shirts in the time it took a tailor to sew one by hand.

Farm Machines Some new inventions made work easier for farmers. In 1825, Jethro Wood began the manufacture of an iron plow with replaceable parts. John Deere improved on the idea when he invented a lightweight steel plow. Earlier plows made of heavy iron or wood had to be pulled by slow-moving oxen. A horse could pull a steel plow through a field more quickly.

In 1847, Cyrus McCormick opened a factory in Chicago that produced mechanical reapers. The reaper was a horse-drawn machine that mowed wheat and other grains. McCormick's reaper could do the work of five people using hand tools.

Other farm machines followed. There was a mechanical drill to plant grain, a threshing machine to beat grain from its husk and a horse-drawn hay rake. These machines helped farmers raise more grain with fewer hands. As a result, thousands of farmworkers left the countryside. Some went west to start farms of their own. Others found jobs in new factories in northern cities.

The Telegraph Samuel F. B. Morse received a patent for a "talking wire," or **telegraph** in 1844. The telegraph was a device that sent electrical signals along a wire. The signals were based on a code of dots, dashes, and spaces. Later, this system of dots and dashes became known as the Morse code.

Congress gave Morse funds to run wire from Washington, D.C., to Baltimore. On May 24, 1844, Morse set up his telegraph in the Supreme Court chamber in Washington. As a crowd of onlookers watched, Morse tapped out a short message: "What hath God wrought!" A few seconds later, the operator in Baltimore tapped back the same message. The telegraph worked!

Morse's invention was an instant success. Telegraph companies sprang up everywhere. Thousands of miles of wire soon stretched across the country. As a result of the telegraph, news could now travel long distances in a matter of minutes.

The telegraph helped many businesses to thrive. Merchants and farmers could have quick access to information about supply, demand, and prices of goods in different areas of the country. For example, western farmers might learn of a wheat shortage in New York and ship their grain east to meet the demand.

The First Railroads

At first, railroads were used to provide transportation to canals. In time, however, the railroad became a more practical means of transportation. The first railroads were built in the early 1800s. Horses or mules pulled cars along wooden rails covered with strips of iron. Then, in 1829, an English family developed a steam-powered locomotive engine to pull rail cars. The engine, called the Rocket, barreled along at 30 miles per hour.

Early Difficulties Not all Americans welcomed the new railroads. Workers who moved freight on horse-drawn wagons feared that they would lose their jobs. People who invested in canals worried that competition from the railroads might cause them to lose their investments.

There were problems with the early railroads. They were not always safe or reliable. Soft roadbeds and weak bridges often led to accidents. Locomotives often broke down. Even when they worked, their smokestacks belched thick black smoke and hot embers. The embers sometimes burned holes in passengers' clothing or set nearby buildings on fire.

Viewing History

Elias Howe and the Sewing Machine

Bridgeport, Connecticut

Once clothing manufacturers started using Elias Howe's invention, the time it took to make a shirt was reduced from 14 hours to little more than one hour. **Drawing Conclusions** *Why would tailors be unhappy with Howe's invention?*

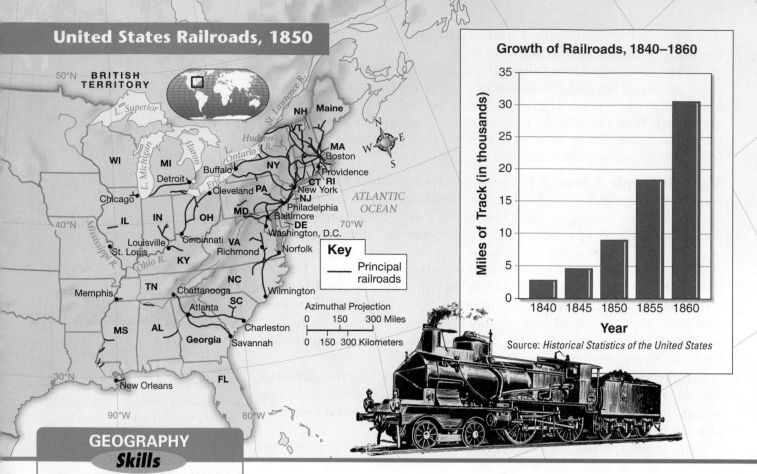

United States Railroads, 1850

BRITISH TERRITORY

Growth of Railroads, 1840–1860

Source: *Historical Statistics of the United States*

Key — Principal railroads

Azimuthal Projection
0   150   300 Miles
0 150 300 Kilometers

GEOGRAPHY Skills

There were about 23 miles of railroad tracks in 1830. From 1840 to 1860, railroad construction increased greatly. Goods could be transported more quickly by rail than by canals, and railroads were in service all year-round.

1. **Location** On the map, locate (a) New York, (b) Lake Erie, (c) Chicago, (d) Mississippi River, (e) Wisconsin.

2. **Movement** How many principal railroads ran through Atlanta?

3. **Critical Thinking Applying Information** What area of the country had the most railroad mileage? Explain.

Part of the problem was the way in which railroads were built. Often, instead of two tracks being laid—one for each direction—only one was set. This increased the likelihood of a collision.

A Railroad Boom Gradually, railroad builders overcame problems and removed obstacles. Engineers learned to build sturdier bridges and solid roadbeds. They replaced wooden rails with iron rails. Such improvements made railroad travel safer and faster.

By the 1850s, railroads crisscrossed the nation. The major lines were concentrated in the North and West. New York, Chicago, and Cincinnati became major rail centers. The South had much less track than the North.

Yankee Clippers

Railroads increased commerce within the United States. At the same time, trade also increased between the United States and other nations. At seaports in the Northeast, captains loaded their ships with cotton, fur, wheat, lumber, and tobacco. Then, they sailed to other parts of the world.

Speed was the key to successful trade at sea. In 1845, an American named John Griffiths launched the *Rainbow,* the first of the **clipper ships.** These sleek vessels had tall masts and huge sails that caught every gust of wind. Their narrow hulls clipped swiftly through the water.

In the 1840s, American clipper ships broke every speed record. One clipper sped from New York to Hong Kong in 81 days, flying past older ships that took five months to reach China. The speed of the clippers helped the United States win a large share of the world's sea trade in the 1840s and 1850s.

The golden age of the clipper ship was brief. In the 1850s, Britain launched the first oceangoing iron steamships. These sturdy vessels carried more cargo and traveled even faster than clippers.

The Northern Economy Expands

By the 1830s, factories began to use steam power instead of water power. Machines that were driven by steam were powerful and cheap to run. Also, factories that used steam power could be built almost anywhere, not just along the banks of swift-flowing rivers. As a result, American industry expanded rapidly.

At the same time, new machines made it possible to produce more goods at a lower cost. These more affordable goods attracted eager buyers. Families no longer had to make clothing and other goods in their homes. Instead, they could buy factory-made products.

Railroads allowed factory owners to transport large amounts of raw materials and finished goods cheaply and quickly. Also, as railroads stretched across the nation, they linked distant towns with cities and factories. These towns became new markets for factory goods.

The growth of railroads also affected northern farming. Railroads brought cheap grain and other foods from the West to New England. New England farmers could not compete with this new source of cheap foods. Many left their farms to find new jobs as factory workers, store clerks, and sailors.

Recognize Multiple Causes

Which factors causing the expansion of the northern economy are discussed in this subsection? Add this information to your chart.

★ ★ ★ Section 1 Assessment ★ ★ ★

Recall

1. **Identify** Explain the significance of (a) Elias Howe, (b) John Deere, (c) Cyrus McCormick, (d) Samuel F. B. Morse, (e) John Griffiths.
2. **Define** (a) telegraph, (b) locomotive, (c) clipper ship.

Comprehension

3. What new inventions made work easier for farmers?
4. Why was safety a major concern with the first railroads?
5. How did steam power and railroads change the northern economy?

Critical Thinking and Writing

6. **Exploring the Main Idea** Review the Main Idea statement at the beginning of this section. Then, write a paragraph about how the new inventions affected the rapid growth of factories in the North.
7. **Understanding Cause and Effect** How do you think life might have changed in a small Ohio town after a railroad linked it to New York City in 1840?

The Telegraph

Like the Internet today, the telegraph had a revolutionary effect on communication. Before the telegraph, messages were hand carried. With the telegraph, people could communicate across great distances almost instantly.

The telegraph used electricity that traveled along wires. Operators sent messages by using a device to transmit short and long bursts of electricity with spaces in between. These bursts translated letters into the dots and dashes of the Morse code. At the receiving end, a telegraph operator translated the dots and dashes of Morse code back into letters.

In 1861, transcontinental telegraph lines were erected along the route of the Pony Express. The Pony Express had operated between St. Joseph, Missouri, and Sacramento, California. Riding relays of fast horses, Pony Express riders could deliver a letter from point to point in ten days or less. Once the telegraph lines were completed, the Pony Express was no longer needed.

ACTIVITY

Working with a partner, create your own Morse code. Then, use it to write a brief message from one to the other.

2 Life in the North

Prepare to Read

Objectives

In this section, you will
- Describe factory conditions in the 1840s.
- Identify what factory workers hoped to accomplish by joining together.
- Describe the new immigrants.
- Explain how free African Americans were treated in the North.

Key Terms

artisan

trade union

strike

famine

nativist

Know-Nothing party

discrimination

Target Reading Skill

Main Idea As you read, prepare an outline of this section. Use roman numerals to indicate the major headings of this section, capital letters for the subheadings, and numbers for the supporting details.

> I. Factory Conditions Become Worse
>   A. A change in values
>   1. Factory workers feel differently about their jobs
>   2.
>   B. Families in factories
>   1.
>   2.
>   C. Hazards at work
>   1.
>   2.

Main Idea Industry in the North changed with the arrival of new immigrants and the efforts of factory workers to improve their working conditions.

Setting the Scene Alzina Parsons never forgot her thirteenth birthday. The day began as usual, with work in the local spinning mill. Suddenly, Alzina cried out. She had caught her hand in the spinning machine, badly mangling her fingers. The foreman summoned the factory doctor. He cut off one of the injured fingers and sent the girl back to work.

Twenty years earlier, such an incident probably would not have occurred. Factory work was hard, but mill owners treated workers like human beings. By the 1840s, however, there was an oversupply of workers. Many factory owners now treated workers like machines.

Factory workers

Factory Conditions Become Worse

Factories of the 1840s and 1850s were very different from the mills of the early 1800s. The factories were larger, and they used steam-powered machines. Laborers worked longer hours for lower wages. Usually, workers lived in dark, dingy houses in the shadow of the factory.

A Change in Values The emphasis on mass production changed the way workers felt about their jobs. Before the growth of factories, skilled workers, or **artisans,** were proud of the goods they made. The factory owner, however, was more interested in how much could be produced than in how well it was made. Workers could not be creative. Furthermore, unlike the artisan who could have his own business, the factory worker was not likely to rise to a management position.

Families in Factories As the need for workers increased, entire families labored in factories. In some cases, a family agreed to work for one year. If even one family member broke the contract, the entire family might be fired.

The factory day began when a whistle sounded at 4 A.M. The entire family—father, mother, and children—headed off to work. Many factories, at that time, employed young children. The workday did not end until 7:30 P.M., when a final whistle sent the workers home.

Hazards at Work Factory workers faced discomfort and danger. Few factories had windows or heating systems. In summer, the heat and humidity inside the factory were stifling. In winter, the extreme cold contributed to frequent sickness.

Factory machines had no safety devices, and accidents were common. There were no laws regulating factory conditions, and injured workers often lost their jobs.

Workers Join Together

Poor working conditions and low wages led workers to organize. The first workers to organize were artisans.

Trade Unions and Strikes In the 1820s and 1830s, artisans in each trade united to form **trade unions.** The unions called for a shorter workday, higher wages, and better working conditions. Sometimes, unions went on strike to gain their demands. In a **strike,** union workers refuse to do their jobs.

At the time, strikes were illegal in many parts of the United States. Strikers faced fines or jail sentences. Employers often fired strike leaders.

Progress for Artisans Slowly, however, workers made progress. In 1840, President Van Buren approved a ten-hour workday for government employees. Workers celebrated another victory in 1842 when a Massachusetts court declared that they had the right to strike.

Artisans won better pay because factory owners needed their skills. Unskilled workers, however, were unable to bargain for better wages since their jobs required little or no training. Because these workers were easy to replace, employers did not listen to their demands.

Women Workers Organize The success of trade unions encouraged other workers to organize. Workers in New England textile mills were especially eager to protest cuts in wages and unfair work rules. Many of these workers were women.

Women workers faced special problems. First, they had always earned less money than men did. Second, most union leaders did not want women in their ranks. Like many people at the time, they believed that women should not work outside the home. In fact, the goal of many unions was to raise men's wages so that their wives could leave their factory jobs.

Despite these problems, women workers organized. They staged several strikes at Lowell, Massachusetts, in the 1830s. In the 1840s, Sarah Bagley organized the Lowell Female Labor Reform Association. The group petitioned the state legislature for a ten-hour workday.

An American Profile

Sarah Bagley 1806–1870?

Sarah Bagley had left her New Hampshire home to work in the textile mills of Lowell, Massachusetts. Over the years, her health—like that of other workers—suffered. She decided to do something about it.

In 1844, Bagley began to organize women workers. About 500 formed a group called the Lowell Female Labor Reform Association—the first American organization of working women. As the group's president, she testified to the Massachusetts legislature about working in the mills. She spoke out against the long workdays and short meal breaks. Bagley also traveled to other factory towns and urged women workers there to organize. She wrote articles promoting workers' rights.

By 1846, the state legislature had still refused to act. Bagley left the mills and entered a new industry, becoming the first woman telegraph operator.

In what way was Bagley a pioneer?

A New Wave of Immigrants

By the late 1840s, many factory workers in the North were immigrants. An immigrant is a person who enters a new country in order to settle there. In the 1840s and 1850s, about 4 million immigrants arrived in the United States. Among them were immigrants from Great Britain who came to the United States to earn higher wages. There was a greater demand for skilled machinists, carpenters, and miners.

From Ireland and Germany In the 1840s, a disease destroyed the potato crop in Ireland, which was the main food of the poor people. Other crops, such as wheat and oats, were not affected. At the time, Ireland was under British rule and most Irish crops were exported to Great Britain. When a large part of the potato crop was lost to disease, British landowners continued to ship the wheat and oats to England. There was little left for the Irish to eat. This situation caused a **famine,** or severe food shortage. Thousands of people died of starvation. Nearly as many died from disease. Between 1845 and 1860, over 1.5 million Irish fled to the United States.

Meanwhile, many Germans were also arriving in the United States. Harsh weather conditions from 1829 to 1830 resulted in severe food shortages. By 1832, more than 10,000 Germans were coming to the United States in a single year. In 1848, revolutions had broken out in several parts of Germany. The rebels fought for democratic reforms. When the revolts failed, thousands had to flee. Many other German immigrants came simply to make a better life for themselves. Between 1848 and 1860, nearly one million Germans arrived in the United States.

Enriching the Nation Immigrants supplied much of the labor that helped the nation's economy grow. Although most of the Irish immigrants had been farmers, few had money to buy farmland. Many settled in the northern cities where low-paying factory jobs were available. Other Irish workers helped build many new canals and railroads. Irish women often worked as servants in private homes.

Immigrants from Germany often had enough money to move west and buy good farmland. Others were artisans and merchants. Towns of the Midwest such as St. Louis, Milwaukee, and Cincinnati had German grocers, butchers, and bakers.

A small minority of the immigrants from Germany were Jewish. German Jews began immigrating to the United States in the 1820s. By the early 1860s, there were about 150 communities in the United States with large Jewish populations.

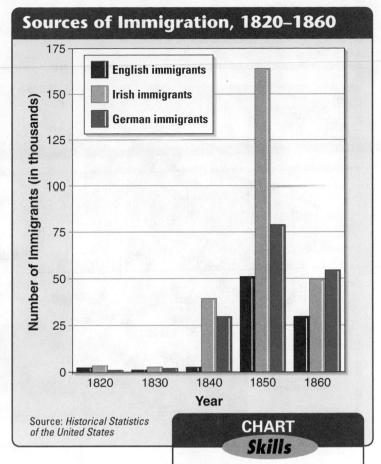

Sources of Immigration, 1820–1860

Number of Immigrants (in thousands) vs. Year

- English immigrants
- Irish immigrants
- German immigrants

Source: *Historical Statistics of the United States*

CHART Skills

Throughout the 1800s, immigrants from Great Britain, Ireland, and Germany came to the United States. From 1840 to 1850, the numbers increased as more immigrants wanted to escape the political and economic difficulties in Europe.

1. **Comprehension**
   (a) About how many more Irish immigrants arrived in 1850 than did in 1860?
   (b) In 1860, how many more German immigrants than Irish immigrants arrived?

2. **Critical Thinking**
   Synthesizing Information Why do you think fewer immigrants came from Great Britain than from Ireland and Germany during the 1800s?

Civics

Portsmouth, New Hampshire

Portsmouth Black Heritage Trail

The first known African to arrive in Portsmouth, New Hampshire, land-ed in 1645 at a wharf (shown here) near what is now Prescott Park. For the next 350 years, African Ameri-cans, both enslaved and free, would be part of this seacoast town. Visi-tors can tour the communities where Portsmouth's African Ameri-can population lived, worked, and served their town and state.

Go Online
PHSchool.com

Virtual Field Trip For an interac-tive look at the Black Heritage Trail, visit PHSchool.com, **Web Code mfd-1401.**

Identify Supporting Details

Which details in the paragraphs on this page reveal how some Americans felt about new immi-grants? Add these details to your outline.

A Reaction Against Immigrants Not everyone welcomed the flood of immigrants. One group of Americans, called **nativists,** want-ed to preserve the country for native-born, white citizens. Using the slogan "Americans must rule America," they called for laws to limit immigration. They also wanted to keep immigrants from voting until they had lived in the United States for 21 years. At the time, new-comers could vote after only 5 years in the country.

Some nativists protested that newcomers "stole" jobs from native-born Americans because they worked for lower pay. Furthermore, when workers went out on strike, factory owners often hired immigrant workers to replace them. Many distrusted the dif-ferent language, customs, and dress of the immigrants. Others blamed immigrants for the rise in crime in the growing cities. Still others mistrusted Irish newcomers because many of them were Catholics. Until the 1840s, the majority of immigrants from Europe had been Protestants.

By the 1850s, hostility to immigrants was so strong that nativists formed a new political party. Members of the party were anti-Catholic and anti-immigrant. Many meetings and rituals of the party were kept secret. It was called the **Know-Nothing party** because members answered, "I know nothing," when asked about the party. The message of the party did gain supporters. In 1856, the Know-Nothing candidate for President won 21 percent of the popular vote. Soon after, however, the party died out. Still, many Americans con-tinued to blame the nation's problems on immigrants.

African Americans in the North

During the nation's early years, slavery was legal in the North. By the early 1800s, however, all the northern states had outlawed slavery. As a result, thousands of free African Americans lived in the North.

Denied Equal Rights Free African Americans in the North faced discrimination. **Discrimination** is a policy or an attitude that denies equal rights to certain groups of people. As one writer pointed out, African Americans were denied "the ballot-box, the jury box, the halls of the legislature, the army, the public lands, the school, and the church."

Even skilled African Americans had trouble finding good jobs. One black carpenter was turned away by every furniture maker in Cincinnati. At last, a shop owner hired him. However, when he entered the shop, the other carpenters dropped their tools. Either he must leave or they would, they declared. Similar experiences occurred throughout the North. In addition, African Americans faced competition from immigrants who settled in northern cities.

Some Success Despite such obstacles, some African Americans achieved notable success in business. William Whipper grew wealthy as the owner of a lumberyard in Pennsylvania. He devoted much of his time and money to help bring an end to slavery. Henry Boyd operated a profitable furniture company in Cincinnati.

African Americans made strides in other areas as well. Henry Blair invented a corn planter and a cottonseed planter. In 1845, Macon Allen became the first African American licensed to practice law in the United States. After graduating from Bowdoin College in Maine, John Russwurm became one of the editors of *Freedom's Journal,* the first African American newspaper.

★ ★ ★ Section 2 Assessment ★ ★ ★

Recall
1. **Identify** Explain the significance of **(a)** Sarah Bagley, **(b)** Know-Nothing party, **(c)** William Whipper, **(d)** Henry Boyd, **(e)** Macon Allen, **(f)** John Russwurm.
2. **Define** **(a)** artisan, **(b)** trade union, **(c)** strike, **(d)** famine, **(e)** nativist, **(f)** discrimination.

Comprehension
3. Describe factory conditions in the 1840s.
4. How did factory workers improve working conditions?
5. Why did German and Irish immigrants come to the United States in the mid-1800s?

6. **(a)** How did discrimination affect free African Americans in the North? **(b)** What successes did they have?

Critical Thinking
7. **Exploring the Main Idea** Review the Main Idea statement at the beginning of this section. Then, prepare a cause-and-effect chart about the effects of immigration on the United States from 1820 to 1860. The first entry in the "Causes" box can be "Famine in Ireland."
8. **Making Inferences** How would a nativist define a "real" American?

ACTIVITY

Delivering a Speech
You are a worker in a northern factory. Prepare a speech urging other workers to strike. Deliver your finished speech to the class.

3 Cotton Kingdom in the South

Prepare to Read

Objectives

In this section, you will
- Identify how the cotton gin improved cotton production in the South.
- Explain how the South became an agricultural economy.
- Describe the ways in which the South was dependent on the North.

Key Terms

boom

cultivate

Target Reading Skill

Clarifying Meaning Copy the concept web below. As you read, fill in the blank ovals with important facts about the southern economy in the 1800s. Add as many ovals as you need.

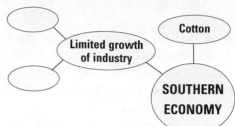

Main Idea Cotton was the leading crop in the agricultural economy of the South.

A cotton plant

Setting the Scene An Englishman, Basil Hall, traveled through much of the South aboard a riverboat in 1827. He complained that the southerners he met were interested in only one thing—cotton:

> 66 All day and almost all night long, the captain, pilot, crew and passengers were talking of nothing else; and sometimes our ears were so wearied with the sound of cotton! cotton! cotton! that we gladly hailed fresh . . . company in hopes of some change—but alas! . . . 'What's cotton at?' was the first eager inquiry. 99
>
> —Basil Hall, *Travels in North America in the Years 1827 and 1828*

Cotton became even more important to the South in the years after Hall's visit. It was so profitable, southerners did not even feel a need to invest in factories. Even though southerners grew other crops, cotton remained the region's leading export. Cotton plantations—and the slave system on which they depended—shaped the way of life in the South.

Cotton Gin, Cotton Boom

The Industrial Revolution greatly increased the demand for southern cotton. Textile mills in the North and in Britain needed more and more cotton to make cloth. At first, southern planters could not meet the demand. They could grow plenty of cotton because the South's soil and climate were ideal. However, removing the seeds from the cotton by hand was a slow process. Planters needed a better way to clean cotton.

Eli Whitney's Invention Eli Whitney, a young Connecticut schoolteacher, was traveling to Georgia in 1793. He was going to be a tutor on a plantation. At that time, there were few public schools in the South. When Whitney learned of the planters' problem, he decided to build a machine to clean cotton.

In only 10 days, Whitney came up with a model. His cotton engine, or gin, had two rollers with thin wire teeth. When cotton was swept between the rollers, the teeth separated the seeds from the fibers.

The simple cotton gin had an enormous effect on the southern economy. A single worker using a gin could do the work of 50 people cleaning cotton by hand. Because of the gin, planters could now grow cotton at a huge profit.

Cotton Kingdom and Slavery The cotton gin led to a **boom,** or swift growth, in cotton production. In 1792, planters grew only 6,000 bales of cotton a year. By 1850, the figure was over 2 million bales.

Planters soon learned that soil wore out if planted with cotton year after year. They needed new land to **cultivate,** or prepare for planting. After the War of 1812, cotton planters began to move west.

By the 1850s, there were cotton plantations extending in a wide band from South Carolina through Alabama and Mississippi to Texas. This area of the South became known as the Cotton Kingdom.

Tragically, as the Cotton Kingdom spread, so did slavery. Even though cotton could now be cleaned by machine, it still had to be planted and picked by hand. The result was a cruel cycle in which the work of slaves brought profits to planters, who then used the profits to buy more land and more slaves.

An Agricultural Economy

Cotton was the South's most profitable cash crop. However, the best conditions for growing cotton could be found mostly in the southernmost portion of the region. In other areas of the South, rice, sugar cane, and tobacco were major crops. In addition, southerners raised much of the nation's livestock.

Rice was an important crop along the coasts of South Carolina and Georgia. Sugar cane was important in Louisiana and Texas. Growing rice and sugar cane required expensive irrigation and drainage systems. Cane growers also needed costly machinery to grind their harvest. Small-scale farmers could not afford such expensive equipment, however. As a result, the plantation system dominated sugar and rice production just as it did cotton production.

Tobacco had been an export of the South since 1619, and it continued to be planted in Virginia, North Carolina, and Kentucky. However, in the early 1800s, the large tobacco plantations of colonial days had given way to small tobacco farms. On these farms, a few field hands tended five or six acres of tobacco.

In addition to the major cash crops of cotton, rice, sugar, and tobacco, the South also led the nation in livestock production. Southern livestock owners profited from hogs, oxen, horses, mules, and beef cattle. Much of this livestock was raised in areas that were unsuitable for growing crops, such as the pine woods of North Carolina. Kentucky developed a rural economy that included the breeding of horses.

Primary Source

The Cotton Gin

Thomas Jefferson was secretary of state and inspector of patents in 1793. He received a request for a patent from a schoolteacher named Eli Whitney. Interested in learning more about it, Jefferson asked Whitney the following questions:

"Has the machine been thoroughly tried in the ginning of cotton, or is it as yet but a machine in theory? What quantity of cotton has it cleaned on an average of several days, worked by hand, and by how many hands? . . . Favorable answers to these questions would induce me to engage one of them to be forwarded to Richmond for me."

—Thomas Jefferson, from "That With This Ginn," 1793

Analyzing Primary Sources
Why do you think Jefferson was interested in the cotton gin?

Cotton Production and Slavery

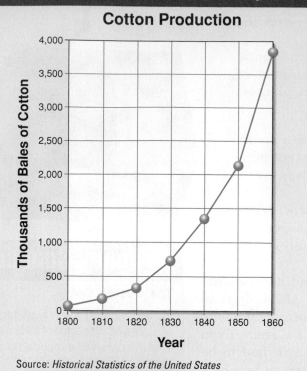

Cotton Production

Source: *Historical Statistics of the United States*

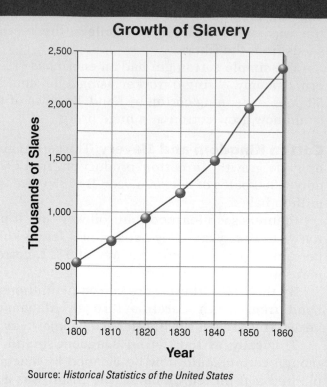

Growth of Slavery

Source: *Historical Statistics of the United States*

GRAPH *Skills*

As cotton production increased in the South, so did the number of enslaved African Americans.

1. **Comprehension**
   (a) How many more bales of cotton were produced in 1850 than in 1820? **(b)** In which decade did the number of slaves increase the most?

2. **Critical Thinking Making Predictions** In what way do you think ending slavery would affect the southern economy?

Economics $

Limited Industry Most of the industry in the South remained small and existed only to meet the needs of a farming society. Agricultural tools such as cotton gins, planters, and plows were manufactured. Factories also made goods such as ironware, hoes, and materials made of hemp, which were used to make bags for holding bales of cotton. Cheap cotton cloth was made for use in slaves' clothing. Some southerners wanted to encourage the growth of industry in the South. William Gregg, for example, modeled his cotton mill in South Carolina on the mills in Lowell, Massachusetts. Gregg built houses and gardens for his workers and schools for their children.

The South also developed a few other successful industries. In Richmond, Virginia, for example, the Tredegar Iron Works turned out railroad equipment, machinery, tools, and cannons. Flour milling was another important southern industry.

Even so, the South lagged behind the North in manufacturing. Rich planters preferred to invest their money in land and slaves rather than in factories.

Slavery also reduced the need for southern industry. In the North, most people had enough money to buy factory goods. In the South, however, millions of slaves could not buy anything. As a result, the demand for manufactured goods in the South was not as great as it was in the North.

Southern Cities Although the South was mainly rural, there were some cities. The major ones were New Orleans, Louisiana; Charleston, South Carolina; and Richmond, Virginia. These cities had the same problems as northern cities, including poor housing and poor sanitation.

Fewer than 8 percent of white southerners lived in towns of more than 4,000 people. However, many free African Americans lived in towns and cities.

Economically Dependent

With little industry of its own, the South came to depend more and more on the North and on Europe. Southern planters often borrowed money from northern banks in order to expand their plantations. They also purchased much of their furniture, farm tools, and machines from northern or European factories.

Many southerners resented this situation. One southerner described a burial to show how the South depended on the North for many goods in the 1850s:

> 66 The grave was dug through solid marble, but the marble headstone came from Vermont. It was in a pine wilderness but the pine coffin came from Cincinnati. An iron mountain overshadowed it but the coffin nails and the screws and the shovel came from Pittsburgh. . . . A hickory grove grew nearby, but the pick and shovel handles came from New York. . . . That country, so rich in underdeveloped resources, furnished nothing for the funeral except the corpse and the hole in the ground. 99
>
> —Henry Grady, Speech to the Bay Street Club, Boston, 1889

Still, most southerners were proud of the booming cotton industry in their region. As long as cotton remained king, southerners believed, they could look to the future with confidence.

Reread Reread this quote to make sure you understand how the writer's description shows the South's dependence on the North. Add this information to your concept web.

★ ★ ★ Section 3 Assessment ★ ★ ★

Recall

1. **Identify** Explain the significance of **(a)** Eli Whitney, **(b)** Cotton Kingdom, **(c)** William Gregg.
2. **Define (a)** boom, **(b)** cultivate.

Comprehension

3. How did the cotton gin lead to the spread of slavery?
4. Explain the importance of cotton as a cash crop in the southern economy.
5. Why was there limited growth of industry in the South?

Critical Thinking and Writing

6. **Exploring the Main Idea** Review the Main Idea statement at the beginning of this section. Then, list the positive and negative effects of cotton production on life in the South.
7. **Drawing Conclusions** Although most southerners owned no slaves, many defended slavery. Why do you think this was so?

ACTIVITY

Go Online
PHSchool.com

Connecting to Today
Today, cotton is still widely used in fabrics. Use the Internet to find out more about cotton. Write a brief report with interesting cotton facts. For help in completing the activity, visit PHSchool.com, **Web Code mfd-1402**.

4 Life in the South

Prepare to Read

Objectives

In this section, you will
- Name the groups of white southerners that made up southern society.
- Describe how free African Americans and enslaved African Americans were treated.
- Explain how African Americans resisted slavery.

Key Terms

"cottonocracy"

slave codes

extended family

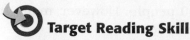

Target Reading Skill

Comparison and Contrast Copy this table. As you read, complete the table with information about the white southerners and the African American southerners. The first entry is done for you.

WHITE SOUTHERNERS	AFRICAN AMERICAN SOUTHERNERS
• Rich southern planter • Owned slaves •	• •

Main Idea Most white southerners were not plantation owners; however, the plantation system and slavery were at the center of southern life.

Katie Darling

Setting the Scene In 1937, at the age of 88, Katie Darling recalled her life growing up as an enslaved person in East Texas:

> 66 Miss Stella, my young mistress, got all our ages down in a Bible, that is how I knows I was born in 1849. . . . Mammy died in slavery, and Pappy run away. . . . By the time I was big enough to tote a cow pail they put me to milking. Master had over a hundred head of cows and most of the time me and Violet, another house girl, did all the milking. We was up before five. By five we better be in that cow pen. We better milk all of them cows too or they'd bull-whip us. 99
>
> —Katie Darling, Interview, August 2, 1937

With her brothers and sisters, Darling worked from dawn to dusk and often on Sundays. She was only one of millions of African Americans throughout the South who suffered the anguish of slavery.

White Southerners

The Old South is often pictured as a land of vast plantations worked by hundreds of slaves. Such grand estates did exist in the South. However, most white southerners were not rich planters. In fact, most whites owned no slaves at all.

The "Cottonocracy" A planter was someone who owned at least 20 slaves. In 1860, only one white southerner in 30 belonged to a planter family. An even smaller number—less than 1 percent—owned 50 or more slaves. These wealthy families were called the "cottonocracy" because they made huge amounts of money from cotton. Though few in number, their views and way of life dominated the South.

The richest planters built elegant homes and filled them with expensive furniture from Europe. They entertained lavishly. They tried to dress and behave like European nobility.

Because of their wealth and influence, many planters became political leaders. They devoted many hours to local, state, and national politics. Planters hired white overseers to run day-to-day affairs on their plantations and to manage the work of enslaved Africans.

Small Farmers About 75 percent of southern whites were small farmers. These "plain folk" owned the land they farmed. They might also own one or two enslaved Africans. Unlike planters, plain folk worked with their slaves in the fields.

Among small farmers, helping each other was an important duty. "People who lived miles apart counted themselves as neighbors," wrote a farmer in Mississippi. "And in case of sorrow or sickness, there was no limit to the service neighbors provided."

Poor Whites Lower on the social ladder was a small group of poor whites. They did not own the land they farmed. Instead, they rented it, often paying the owner with part of their crop. Many barely made a living.

Poor whites often lived in the hilly, wooded areas of the South. They planted crops such as corn, potatoes, and other vegetables. They also herded cattle and pigs. Poor whites had hard lives, but they enjoyed rights that were denied to all black people, enslaved or free.

African American Southerners

Both free and enslaved African Americans lived in the South. Although free under the law, free African Americans faced harsh discrimination. Enslaved African Americans had no rights at all.

Free African Americans Most free African Americans were descendants of slaves freed during and after the American Revolution. Others had bought their freedom. In 1860, over 200,000 free blacks lived in the South. Most lived in Maryland and Delaware, where slavery was in decline. Others lived in cities such as New Orleans, Richmond, and Charleston.

Slave owners did not like free African Americans living in the South. They feared that free African Americans set a bad example, encouraging slaves to rebel. Also, slave owners justified slavery by claiming that African Americans could not take care of themselves. Free African American workers proved this idea wrong.

To discourage free African Americans, southern states passed laws that made life even harder for them. Free African Americans were not allowed to vote or travel. In some southern states, they had to move out of the state or risk the chance of being kidnapped and enslaved.

Despite these limits, free African Americans were able to make a life for themselves. Some even made valuable contributions to southern life. For example, Norbert Rillieux (RIHL yoo) invented a machine that revolutionized the way sugar was refined. Another inventor, Henry Blair, patented a seed planter.

An American Profile

Norbert Rillieux
1804–1894

In the early 1800s, sugar was refined by boiling sugar cane in huge vats. Moving the hot liquid between vats was dangerous.

Norbert Rillieux invented a machine that cooked the sugar in closed vats under low air pressure. Since pipes moved the liquid from one vat to another, there was no danger to workers. Rillieux's machine made better sugar, too. The method quickly spread across Louisiana and to Mexico and Cuba. Factories today use essentially the same technique. Rillieux also invented a machine that improved the processing of sugar from sugar beets.

Was Rillieux's method less or more costly to operate than the old technique? Why?

Identify Contrasts How was life in the South different for free African Americans than it was for whites? How did white southerners make life difficult for free African Americans? Add this information to your table.

Enslaved African Americans By 1860, enslaved African Americans made up one third of the South's population. Most worked as field hands on cotton plantations. Both men and women cleared new land and planted and harvested crops. Children helped by pulling weeds, collecting wood, and carrying water to the field hands. By the time they were teenagers, they worked between 12 and 14 hours a day.

On large plantations, some African Americans became skilled workers, such as carpenters and blacksmiths. A few worked in cities and lived almost as if they were free. Their earnings, however, belonged to their owners.

Life Without Freedom

The life of enslaved African Americans was determined by strict laws and the practices of individual slave owners. Conditions varied from plantation to plantation. Some owners made sure their slaves had clean cabins, decent food, and warm clothes. Other planters spent as little as possible on their slaves.

Slave Codes Southern states passed laws known as slave codes to keep slaves from either running away or rebelling. Under the codes, enslaved African Americans were forbidden to gather in groups of more than three. They could not leave their owner's land without a written pass. They were not allowed to own guns.

Viewing History

Two Ways of Life
Wealthy southern planters lived in large, beautiful homes with many slaves and acres of fertile land. More typical of the South during the 1800s was the small farmer who lived in a modest home and worked hard to make a living. Most white farmers did not have slaves. **Synthesizing Information** *Why do you think rich planters thought of themselves as aristocrats?*

424

Slave codes also made it a crime for slaves to learn how to read and write. Owners hoped that this law would make it hard for African Americans to escape slavery. They reasoned that uneducated runaway slaves would not be able to use maps or read train schedules. They would not be able to find their way north.

Some laws were meant to protect slaves, but only from the worst forms of abuse. However, enslaved African Americans did not have the right to testify in court. As a result, they were not able to bring charges against owners who abused them.

Enslaved African Americans had only one real protection against mistreatment. Owners looked on their slaves as valuable property. Most slave owners wanted to keep this human property healthy and productive.

Hard Work Even the kindest owners insisted that their slaves work long, hard days. Slaves worked from "can see to can't see," or from dawn to dusk, up to 16 hours a day. Frederick Douglass, who escaped slavery, recalled his life under one harsh master:

> 66 We were worked in all weathers. It was never too hot or too cold; it could never rain, blow, hail, or snow too hard for us to work in the field. Work, work, work. . . . The longest days were too short for him and the shortest nights too long for him. 99
> —Frederick Douglass, *Narrative of the Life of Frederick Douglass, An American Slave*

Family Life It was hard for enslaved African Americans to keep their families together. Southern laws did not recognize slave marriages or slave families. As a result, owners could sell a husband and wife to different buyers. Children were often taken from their parents and sold.

On large plantations, many enslaved families did manage to stay together. For those African Americans, the family was a source of strength, pride, and love. Grandparents, parents, children, aunts, uncles, and cousins formed a close-knit group. This idea of an **extended family** had its roots in Africa.

Enslaved African Americans preserved other traditions as well. Parents taught their children traditional African stories and songs. They used folk tales to pass on African history and moral beliefs.

Religion Offers Hope By the 1800s, many enslaved African Americans were devout Christians. Planters often allowed white ministers to preach to their slaves. African Americans also had their own preachers and beliefs.

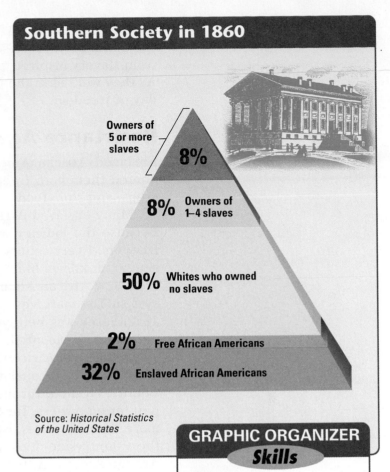

Southern Society in 1860

Owners of 5 or more slaves — 8%

8% Owners of 1–4 slaves

50% Whites who owned no slaves

2% Free African Americans

32% Enslaved African Americans

Source: *Historical Statistics of the United States*

GRAPHIC ORGANIZER
Skills

This social pyramid represents the structure of southern society in 1860. At the top are wealthy and powerful planters. At the bottom are millions of enslaved African Americans.

1. **Comprehension** Which group in southern society was most numerous?

2. **Critical Thinking Analyzing Information** How did the social structure of the South reflect the importance of slavery?

Economics $

Religion helped African Americans cope with the harshness of slave life. Bible stories about how the ancient Hebrews had escaped from slavery inspired a new type of religious song called a spiritual. As they worked in the fields, slaves would often sing about a coming day of freedom.

Resistance Against Slavery

Enslaved African Americans struck back against the system that denied them both freedom and wages. Some broke tools, destroyed crops, and stole food.

Many enslaved African Americans tried to escape to the North. Because the journey was long and dangerous, very few made it to freedom. Every county had slave patrols and sheriffs ready to question an unknown black person.

A few African Americans used violence to resist the brutal slave system. Denmark Vesey, a free African American, planned a revolt in 1822. Vesey was betrayed before the revolt began. He and 35 other people were executed.

In 1831, an African American preacher named Nat Turner led a major revolt. An enslaved worker on a plantation in Southampton County, Virginia, Turner believed his mission was to take revenge on plantation owners. Turner led his followers through Virginia, killing more than 57 whites. For nearly two months terrified whites hunted the countryside looking for Turner. They killed many innocent African Americans before catching and hanging him.

Nat Turner's revolt increased southern fears of an uprising of enslaved African Americans. Revolts were rare, however. Since whites were cautious and well armed, a revolt by African Americans had almost no chance of success.

★ ★ ★ **Section 4 Assessment** ★ ★ ★

Recall

1. **Identify** Explain the significance of **(a)** Norbert Rillieux, **(b)** Henry Blair, **(c)** Denmark Vesey, **(d)** Nat Turner.
2. **Define** **(a)** "cottonocracy," **(b)** slave codes, **(c)** extended family.

Comprehension

3. Describe the way of life of each of the following groups in the South: **(a)** rich planters, **(b)** small farmers, **(c)** poor whites.
4. How did laws restrict the freedom of both free and enslaved African Americans?

5. In what ways did enslaved African Americans struggle against slavery?

Critical Thinking and Writing

6. **Exploring the Main Idea** Review the Main Idea statement at the beginning of this section. Then, write a paragraph discussing the importance of plantations in the southern economy.
7. **Synthesizing Information** Few southerners were planters. Why do you think this small group was able to dominate the political and social life of the South?

Making Generalizations

You can extend your understanding of how new technology affected American life by making generalizations. Making generalizations means taking a number of examples and facts and arriving at a general statement.

This passage tells about the daguerreotype, an image printed on a chemically treated copper plate, and developed by a Frenchman named Louis Daguerre in 1839:

In 1847, two Americans began a collaboration that would advance science on several fronts. The men were John A. Whipple, a photographer, and William Cranch Bond, an astronomer who headed the Harvard College Observatory. Whipple had already developed a technique for making paper prints from the daguerreotype images. Bond had just acquired the world's largest telescope. The collaborators' goal was to photograph the sky through the telescope. Although their first attempts were unsuccessful, Whipple and Bond finally produced the first astronomical daguerreotype—an image of the star Vega. This was soon followed by pictures of the moon. Bond and Whipple then toured Europe to great acclaim, distributing copies of the exciting new images to observatories on the continent.

The chart shows how to organize facts to make a generalization based on the passage.

Making Generalizations

Facts

- Whipple developed a technique for making paper prints of daguerreotypes.
- Bond, an astronomer, acquired the world's largest telescope.
- Bond and Whipple worked together to create photographic images of the moon and the stars.

Generalization

Learn the Skill *To make generalizations, use the following steps:*

1. **Identify the main idea and details.** What information is being given?

2. **Compile a list of relevant facts.** You may find that not every fact given is necessary for a generalization.

3. **Find a common element.** Look for a single feature that is true of all the facts you have listed.

4. **Make a generalization.** Make a general statement based on the facts. Accurate generalizations often include words such as *many, most, often, usually, some, few,* and *sometimes.* Faulty generalizations may include words such as *all, none, always, never,* or *every.*

Practice the Skill *Answer the following questions about the passage and chart:*

1. What is the subject of the passage?

2. **(a)** Identify a fact that is not relevant to those listed on the chart. **(b)** Identify a relevant fact that fits with those given on the chart.

3. How are the facts on the chart related?

4. Write a generalization based on the facts. Use a clue word.

Apply the Skill *See the Chapter Review and Assessment.*

CHAPTER SUMMARY

Section 1
A flood of new inventions in the 1800s aided the growth of industry in the North. Railroads and clipper ships increased both domestic and international commerce.

Section 2
Workers formed unions to battle poor conditions in northern factories. Nativists tried to keep immigrants out of the United States. The end of slavery in the North freed African Americans there.

Section 3
The invention of the cotton gin in 1793 helped to make cotton the South's leading crop. The South's economy was dependent on agriculture, not industry.

Section 4
The "cottonocracy" that developed in the South strengthened the institution of slavery in that region. Some African Americans resisted slavery.

Interactive Textbook
For additional review and enrichment activities, see the interactive version of *The American Nation*, available on the Web and on CD-ROM.

Go Online
PHSchool.com

Chapter Self-Test For practice test questions for Chapter 14, visit PHSchool.com, **Web Code mfa-1404.**

Building Vocabulary

Write sentences using the chapter vocabulary words listed below, leaving blanks where the vocabulary words would go. Exchange your sentences with another student and fill in the blanks in each other's sentences.

1. **telegraph**
2. **locomotive**
3. **clipper ship**
4. **trade union**
5. **strike**
6. **nativist**
7. **discrimination**
8. **"cottonocracy"**
9. **slave codes**
10. **extended family**

Reviewing Key Facts

11. Describe three inventions that caused the North's economy to expand. (Section 1)
12. Give two reasons for Irish and German immigration to the United States in the 1840s and 1850s. (Section 2)
13. Explain how the cotton gin changed life in the South. (Section 3)
14. Discuss the difference between the planter and the small farmer. (Section 4)

Critical Thinking and Writing

15. **Comparing** Compare two inventions that you think had the greatest impact on American life during the mid-1800s. Explain your answer.
16. **Evaluating Information** Why is transportation important to economic progress?
17. **Analyzing Information** How did the political, social, and economic situation of free African Americans and enslaved African Americans differ?
18. **Connecting to Geography: Regions** Make a comparison chart that shows how economic differences affected life in the North and in the South.

Frederick Law Olmsted, who often wrote about social issues, gives his view on poor white women working in the South. Read the excerpt. Then, answer the questions that follow:

  ❝ Poor white girls never hired themselves out to do servants' work, but they would come and help another white woman with her sewing or quilting, and take wages for it. . . . That their condition is not as unfortunate by any means as that of Negroes, however, is most obvious, since among them, people may sometimes elevate themselves to positions and habits of usefulness and respectability. ❞

—Frederick Law Olmsted,
A Journey in the Seaboard Slave States, 1856

19. According to Olmsted, poor white girls
  A. never hired themselves out as servants.
  B. competed with African American women for the same jobs.
  C. were worse off than African American women.
  D. could do nothing to improve their lives.

20. Why do you think poor white girls would refuse to be hired as servants?
  A. They didn't like their bosses.
  B. The work was "beneath" them.
  C. It would take too long to travel to the job.
  D. They would have to leave their homes.

Read the following passage about steamboats. Then, answer the questions that follow:

  ❝ The western steamboat carried both freight and passengers; but it won its greatest fame as a way to travel. The most luxurious boats, called 'floating palaces,' offered accommodations far beyond the experience of the average American. Steamboats also provided the cheapest form of inland transportation before the Civil War.

  Despite the discomforts of swarming mosquitoes, heat from the boilers, and noisy engines at all hours of the night, observers agreed that journeying by steamboat was far more pleasant than taking a stagecoach, the principal alternative in the West before 1850. ❞

—Davidson, et al., *Nation of Nations*

21. What is the main idea of the passage?
  A. Steamboat travel was costly.
  B. Steamboats are the best way to travel.
  C. Steamboats carried freight and people.
  D. Steamboat travel was comfortable.

22. Make a generalization based on the passage.

ACTIVITIES

Connecting With . . . Culture

Understanding the Nation in the 1800s Read the following quotations. Determine which person or event is being referred to. Then, write a brief paragraph describing how each person or event affected American society.

"The roads, the canals, and the mails play [an important] part in the prosperity of the Union. . . ."

"I thank God I am not property now, but am regarded as a man like yourself. . . ."

Go Online
PHSchool.com

Becoming a Citizen

A Citizenship Pamphlet Immigrants in the mid-1800s had to live in the United States for five years before gaining voting privileges. Use the Internet to find out how immigrants can become citizens today. Present the information in a pamphlet. For help in starting this activity, visit PHSchool.com, **Web Code mfd-1406.**

Incidents in the Life of a Slave Girl

Harriet A. Jacobs

Harriet Jacobs

Introduction Born in Edenton, North Carolina, in the early 1800s, Harriet Jacobs did not realize she was a slave until she was six years old. When Jacobs was 11, her mistress died and she was sent to a new master, Dr. James Norcom. Jacobs found her new situation at the Norcom household unbearable. In 1835, she escaped from Norcom and went into hiding in her hometown. For seven years, she hid in the cramped space of an attic in her grandmother's house. The following selection describes her life in the attic.

Vocabulary Before you read the selection, find the meanings of these words in a dictionary: **benumb, delirious, stupefy, kindle.**

I suffered much more during the second winter than I did during the first. My limbs were benumbed by inaction, and the cold filled them with cramp. I had a very painful sensation of coldness in my head; even my face and tongue stiffened, and I lost the power of speech. Of course it was impossible, under the circumstances, to summon any physician. My brother William came and did all he could for me. Uncle Philip also watched tenderly over me; and poor grandmother crept up and down to inquire whether there were any signs of returning life. I was restored to full consciousness by the dashing of cold water on my face, and found myself leaning against my brother's arm, while he bent over me with streaming eyes. He afterwards told me he thought I was dying, for I had been in an unconscious state for sixteen hours. I next became delirious, and was in great danger of betraying myself and my friends. To prevent this, they stupefied me with drugs. I remained in bed for six weeks, weary in body and sick at heart. How to get medical advice was the question. William finally went to a Thompsonian doctor, and described himself as having all my pains and aches. He returned with herbs, roots, and ointment. He was especially charged to rub on the ointment by a fire, but how could a fire be made in my little den? Charcoal in a furnace was tried, but there was no outlet for the gas, and it nearly cost my life. Afterwards coals, already kindled, were brought up in an iron pan, and placed on bricks. I was so weak, and it was so long since I had enjoyed the warmth of a fire, that those few coals actually made me weep. I think the medicines did me some good; but my recovery was very slow. Dark thoughts passed through my mind as I lay there day after day. I tried to be thankful for my little cell, dismal as it was, and even to love it, as part of the price I had paid for the redemption of my children. Sometimes I thought God was a compassionate Father, who would forgive my sins for the sake of my sufferings. At other times, it seemed to me there was no justice or mercy in the divine government. I asked why the curse of slavery was permitted to exist, and why I had been so persecuted and wronged from youth upward. These things took the shape of mystery, which is to this day not so clear to my soul as I trust it will be hereafter.

In the midst of my illness, grandmother broke down under the weight of anxiety and

This house was a "station" where runaway slaves could hide.

toil. The idea of losing her, who had always been my best friend and a mother to my children, was the sorest trial I had yet had. O, how earnestly I prayed that she might recover! How hard it seemed, that I could not tend upon her, who had so long and so tenderly watched over me!

One day the screams of a child nerved me with strength to crawl to my peeping-hole, and I saw my son covered with blood. A fierce dog, usually chained, had seized and bitten him. A doctor was sent for, and I heard the groans and screams of my child while the wounds were being sewed up. O, what torture to a mother's heart, to listen to this and be unable to go to him!

But childhood is like a day in spring, alternately shower and sunshine. Before long Benny was bright and lively, threatening the destruction of the dog; and great was his delight when the doctor told him the next day that the dog had bitten another boy and been shot. Benny recovered from his wounds; but it was long before he could walk.

Analyzing Literature

1. What hardships did Harriet endure the second winter in the attic?
   - **A** She was always hungry and lonely.
   - **B** Her body was stiff from cold and she could not talk.
   - **C** The attic was too warm and she could not communicate with anyone.
   - **D** She was not able to let anyone know that she was ill.

2. How did Harriet's brother help her?
   - **A** He helped her send messages to the doctor.
   - **B** He sealed the cracks in the walls of the attic.
   - **C** He managed to bring her ointments.
   - **D** He brought her children to the attic.

3. **Critical Thinking Drawing Inferences** What inner conflicts does Harriet experience?

15 Reform and a New American Culture

1820–1860

1 **The Reforming Spirit**
2 **Opposing Slavery**
3 **A Call for Women's Rights**
4 **American Art and Literature**

Religious revival meeting

William Lloyd Garrison
and his antislavery vow

AMERICAN EVENTS

Early 1800s
The Second Great Awakening sweeps the nation. At outdoor revival meetings, converts promise to reform their lives.

1831
William Lloyd Garrison begins publishing his antislavery newspaper, *The Liberator.*

1837
Horace Mann pushes for education reform in Massachusetts.

Presidential Terms: James Monroe 1817–1825 | John Quincy Adams 1825–1829 | Andrew Jackson 1829–1837 | Martin Van Buren 1837–1841

1820 · · · · **1830** · · · · · **1840**

WORLD EVENTS

▲ 1820
American Colonization Society begins transporting free blacks to colonize Liberia in western Africa.

1837 ▲
First kindergarten opens in Germany.

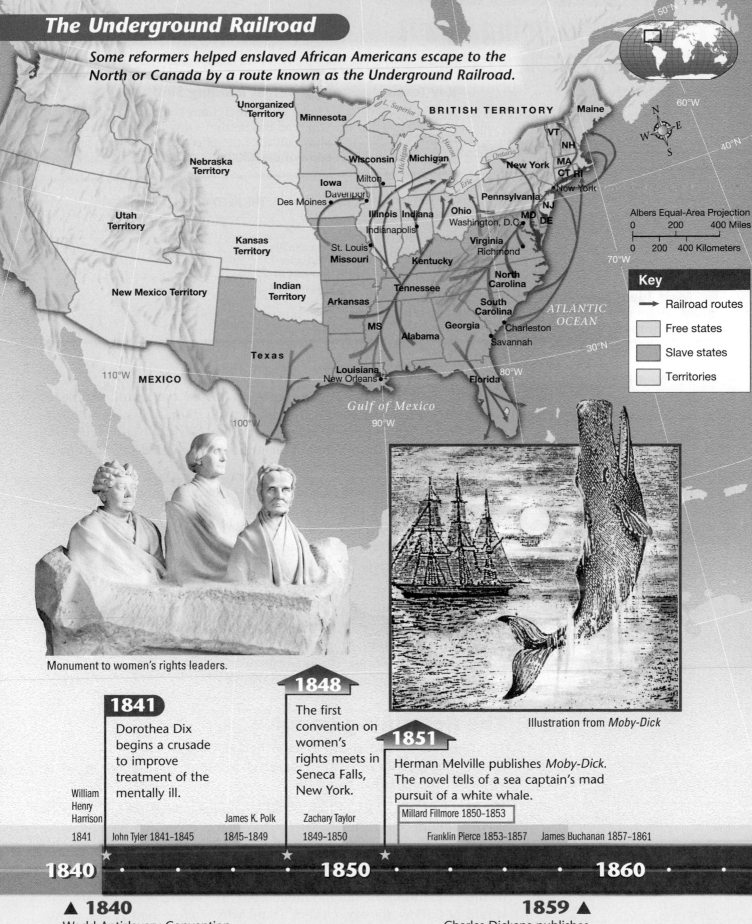

The Underground Railroad

Some reformers helped enslaved African Americans escape to the North or Canada by a route known as the Underground Railroad.

Key
→ Railroad routes
◻ Free states
◼ Slave states
◻ Territories

Albers Equal-Area Projection
0   200   400 Miles
0   200   400 Kilometers

Monument to women's rights leaders.

Illustration from *Moby-Dick*

1841
Dorothea Dix begins a crusade to improve treatment of the mentally ill.

1848
The first convention on women's rights meets in Seneca Falls, New York.

1851
Herman Melville publishes *Moby-Dick*. The novel tells of a sea captain's mad pursuit of a white whale.

William Henry Harrison
1841 John Tyler 1841–1845 James K. Polk 1845–1849 Zachary Taylor 1849–1850

Millard Fillmore 1850–1853
Franklin Pierce 1853–1857   James Buchanan 1857–1861

1840   **1850**   **1860**

▲ **1840**
World Antislavery Convention opens in London.

1859 ▲
Charles Dickens publishes *A Tale of Two Cities*.

1 The Reforming Spirit

Prepare to Read

Objectives

In this section, you will
- Explain how political and religious ideals provided inspiration for reform.
- Summarize reforms sought for criminals and the mentally ill.
- Identify the goals of the temperance movement.
- Describe how reformers improved education.

Key Terms

social reform

predestination

Second Great Awakening

revival

debtor

temperance movement

Target Reading Skill

Cause and Effect Copy the chart below. As you read this section, complete the chart to show some of the effects of the reforming spirit of the 1800s.

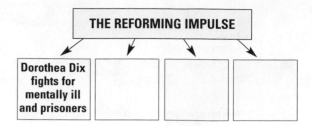

THE REFORMING IMPULSE

Dorothea Dix fights for mentally ill and prisoners

Main Idea Between 1820 and 1860, a wide variety of reform movements sprang up to improve conditions in the United States.

Caves at Newgate prison

Setting the Scene Two reporters entered the small, ordinary-looking brick hut. Opening a trapdoor in the floor, they peered down the dark shaft of an abandoned copper mine. Nervously, they climbed 50 feet down an old wooden ladder until they reached the bottom:

> 66 Lighting the candles . . . I led the way down a series of stone steps. . . . The roof was very low, and the candle gave so little light, that I was compelled to feel my way forward with my walking-stick. . . . [I] groped forward twenty or thirty feet into the caverns . . . where the prisoners used to sleep. 99
>
> —quoted in Phelps, *Newgate of Connecticut*

Years earlier, these cramped caves had served as Connecticut's state prison, Newgate. It was shut down in 1827.

In the mid-1800s, some Americans began to condemn the way prisoners were treated. Prison reform was just one of many movements that sprang up to cure the nation's ills.

The Reforming Impulse

The impulse toward social reform had both political and religious roots. **Social reform** is an organized attempt to improve what is unjust or imperfect in society.

Political Ideals As you have read, during the Jackson era, politics was becoming more democratic. More people could vote and take part in government than ever before.

Still, some critics said American society was not democratic enough. They pointed to the promise of liberty and equality expressed in the Declaration of Independence. A true democracy, they argued, would not allow slavery. Others asked why women had fewer rights than men. By changing such injustices, reformers hoped to move the nation closer to its political ideals.

The Second Great Awakening During the colonial era, many American Protestants believed in **predestination.** According to this idea, God decided in advance which people would attain salvation after death. This belief led many people to worry that they could do nothing to be saved.

In the early 1800s, a dynamic religious movement known as the **Second Great Awakening** swept the nation. Its leaders stressed free will rather than predestination. They taught that individuals could choose to save their souls by their own actions.

To stir religious feelings, preachers held **revivals,** huge outdoor meetings. Revivals might last for days and attract thousands of people. A witness recalled the excitement of a revival at Cane Ridge, Kentucky:

> **66** The vast sea of human beings seemed to be agitated as if by storm. I counted seven ministers all preaching at once. . . . Some of the people were singing, others praying, some crying for mercy. **99**
>
> —James B. Finley, *Autobiography*

One leader of the Second Great Awakening was a minister named Charles Grandison Finney. A powerful speaker, Finney taught that individual salvation was the first step toward "the complete reformation of the whole world." Such teachings inspired new efforts to improve society.

Hospital and Prison Reform

One of the most vigorous social reformers was Dorothea Dix, a Boston schoolteacher. She turned her attention to what one minister called the "outsiders" in society: criminals and the mentally ill.

Reforms for the Mentally Ill In 1841, Dix visited a jail for women near Boston. She was outraged to discover that some of the prisoners were not criminals, but mentally ill. Dix demanded to know why these women were locked in small, dark, unheated cells. The jailer replied that "lunatics" did not feel the cold.

During the next 18 months, Dix visited every jail, poorhouse, and hospital in Massachusetts. Her shocking reports helped persuade state legislators to fund a new mental hospital:

> **66** I proceed, gentlemen, briefly to call your attention to the present state of Insane Persons confined . . . in cages, closets, cellars, stalls, pens! Chained, naked, beaten with rods, and lashed into obedience. **99**
>
> —Dorothea Dix, "Memorial to the State Legislators of Massachusetts"

Dix went on to inspect jails as far away as Louisiana and Illinois. Her reports persuaded most legislatures to treat the mentally ill as patients, not criminals.

Roots of Reform

The Reform Movement

Political Origins
- The ideals of liberty and equality in the Declaration of Independence inspire people to try to improve society
- During Jackson era, more people can vote than ever before
- Critics say slavery and other injustices violate democratic ideals

Religious Influences
- Second Great Awakening stresses free will rather than predestination
- Revivals encourage people to reform their lives
- Finney teaches that individual salvation is the first step to the reform of a society

GRAPHIC ORGANIZER
Skills

Both political and religious ideas inspired Americans to work for reform.

1. **Comprehension** Identify one political change in the country that encouraged reform.

2. **Critical Thinking Identifying Causes and Effects** Why might a belief in free will inspire a spirit of reform?

Civics

POLITICAL CARTOON
Skills

A Call for Temperance Temperance leaders believed a ban on alcoholic beverages would benefit society. This cartoon appeared in 1855.

1. **Comprehension** What object in this cartoon symbolizes temperance?

2. **Understanding Main Ideas** According to the cartoon, what are some of the ways temperance would benefit society?

3. **Critical Thinking Drawing Inferences** Why do you think the cartoonist included a school and a church?

Prison Reform Dix also joined a growing movement to improve conditions in prisons. Men, women, and children were often crammed together in cold, damp rooms. When food supplies were low, prisoners went hungry—unless they had money to buy meals from jailers.

Five out of six people in northern jails were **debtors,** or people who could not pay money they owed. While behind bars, debtors had no way to earn money to pay back their debts. As a result, many debtors remained in prison for years.

Dix and others called for changes in the prison system. As a result, some states built prisons with only one or two inmates to a cell. Cruel punishments were banned, and people convicted of minor crimes received shorter sentences. Slowly, states stopped treating debtors as criminals.

The Temperance Movement

Alcohol abuse was widespread in the early 1800s. At political rallies, weddings, and funerals, men, women, and sometimes even children drank heavily. Men could buy whiskey in candy stores or barbershops.

The **temperance movement,** a campaign against alcohol abuse, took shape in the late 1820s. Women often took a leading role in the battle. They knew that "demon rum" could lead to wife beating, child abuse, and the breakup of families.

Some temperance groups urged people to drink less. Others sought to end drinking altogether. They won a major victory in 1851, when Maine banned the sale of alcohol. Eight other states passed "Maine laws." Most states later repealed the laws, but the temperance crusade would gain new strength in the late 1800s.

Improving Education

In 1800, few American children attended school. Massachusetts was the only state that required free public schools supported by the community. Teachers were poorly trained and ill paid. Students of all ages crowded together in a single room.

As more men won the right to vote, reformers acted to improve education. They argued that a republic required educated citizens.

Growth of Public Schools New York State took the lead in improving public education. In 1814, the state passed a law requiring local governments to set up tax-supported school districts.

Horace Mann became head of the Massachusetts board of education in 1837. He hounded legislators to provide more money for education. Under his leadership, Massachusetts built new schools, extended the school year, and raised teachers' pay. The state also opened three colleges to train teachers.

Other states followed the lead of Massachusetts and New York. By the 1850s, most northern states had set up free tax-supported elementary schools. Schools in the South improved more slowly. In both the North and the South, schooling usually ended in the eighth grade. There were few public high schools.

Education for African Americans In most areas, African Americans had little chance to attend school. A few cities, like Boston and New York, set up separate schools for black students. However, these schools received less money than schools for white students did. In the North, African American men and women often opened their own schools to educate their children.

Some attempts to educate African Americans met with hostility. In the 1830s, Prudence Crandall, a Connecticut Quaker, began a school for African American girls. Crandall continued to teach even as rocks smashed through the window. Finally, a mob broke in one night and destroyed the school.

Despite such obstacles, some African Americans went on to attend private colleges such as Harvard, Dartmouth, and Oberlin. In 1854, Pennsylvania chartered the first college for African American men.

Educating People With Disabilities Some reformers improved education for people with disabilities. In 1817, Thomas Gallaudet (gal uh DEHT) set up a school for the deaf in Hartford, Connecticut.

Samuel Gridley Howe founded the first American school for the blind in 1832. Howe used a system of raised letters to enable students to read with their fingers. One of Howe's pupils, Laura Bridgman, was the first deaf and blind student to receive a formal education.

 **Understand Effects** Read the paragraphs in the subsection "Improving Education." Explain the changes reformers made to education in the 1800s. Add this information to your chart.

★ ★ ★ **Section 1 Assessment** ★ ★ ★

Recall

1. **Identify** Explain the significance of **(a)** Second Great Awakening, **(b)** Charles Grandison Finney, **(c)** Dorothea Dix, **(d)** Horace Mann, **(e)** Thomas Gallaudet, **(f)** Samuel Gridley Howe, **(g)** Laura Bridgman.
2. **Define** **(a)** social reform, **(b)** predestination, **(c)** revival, **(d)** debtor, **(e)** temperance movement.

Comprehension

3. Why did the reforming spirit grow in the 1800s?
4. How did Dorothea Dix help improve treatment of the mentally ill?

5. Why did many women join the temperance movement?
6. Describe two educational reforms of the mid-1800s.

Critical Thinking and Writing

7. **Exploring the Main Idea** Review the Main Idea statement at the beginning of this section. Then, write a paragraph evaluating the possible impact of one reform movement on American society.
8. **Linking Past and Present** List two ways that religious groups promote social reform in the United States today.

ACTIVITY

Go Online
PHSchool.com

Connecting to Today
Many organizations today combat alcohol or drug abuse. Use the Internet to find out about one such organization. Report to the class on its goals and methods. For help in completing the activity, visit PHSchool.com, **Web Code mfd-1501.**

An American Classroom

In colonial times, many schoolhouses were one-room log cabins with paper covering a few small windows. They were often supported by churches or private charities. But by the mid-1800s, all northern states began supporting public education. What were these early classrooms like?

Public schools taught large numbers of students from different backgrounds. Students wrote their lessons on slate boards. Memorization and recitation were common. Here, students "toe the line"— standing behind a line on the floor as they recite their daily lessons.

Fast Facts

- Girls and boys were usually taught together in elementary school. In high school, however, they were often separated.
- New technologies, such as the invention of the steel pen and the blackboard, changed classrooms in the 1800s.
- Physical punishment was common in schoolrooms. A popular saying advised, "Spare the rod and spoil the child."

PICTORIAL PRIMER

| 9 and 9 make 18 | 10 and 10 make 20 |

STEAMBOAT.

Here is a Steamboat full of passengers, how swift it glides along, and makes the water foam. Steamboats were invented by Robert Fulton, and the first one was built in New-York.

PICTORIAL PRIMER

Boy Flying a Kite.

Here is a boy just coming from school, he has learned his lesson well, and his teacher has rewarded him with a kite. He will raise it very high in the air, it will not fall down while the wind blows. Kites are made of paper.

In elementary schools, students learned their lessons from picture books called primers. These pages from an 1845 primer combine lessons in arithmetic, reading, and history.

ACTIVITY

With a partner, design two pages for a modern primer for elementary-school students. Use the one shown at left as a model. Include illustrations and a variety of subjects.

2 Opposing Slavery

Prepare to Read

Objectives

In this section, you will
- Explain how the antislavery movement began and grew.
- Describe the Underground Railroad.
- Identify why so many white northerners and southerners opposed abolition.

Key Terms

American Colonization Society

abolitionist

The Liberator

Underground Railroad

Target Reading Skill

Reading Process As you read, prepare an outline of this section. Use roman numerals for the major headings, capital letters for the subheadings, and numbers for the supporting details.

> I. Roots of the Antislavery Movement
>   A. Early efforts
>   1. Quakers protest
>   2.
>   B. Colonization movement
>   1.
>   2.
> II. The Abolitionist Movement Grows
>   A.
>   B.

Main Idea In the 1830s and 1840s, reformers became more active in calling for an end to slavery in the United States.

Setting the Scene

As the spirit of reform spread, many young people joined antislavery efforts. In Providence, Rhode Island, white and black girls met together every week, starting in 1834. As they sewed, one member would read aloud from an antislavery newspaper. By selling their needlework, the girls raised $90 for the antislavery cause in a single year.

The idea quickly spread. In Albany, New York, black students pledged six cents a month. Members of the Pittsburgh Juvenile Society pledged a "cent a week."

Today, a penny a week doesn't seem like much. But it was a great deal for a boy or girl whose family was lucky to earn fifty or a hundred dollars for the entire year. The spread of such organizations showed that in the North, many black and white Americans had come to believe that slavery must end.

Antislavery medallion

Roots of the Antislavery Movement

In the Declaration of Independence, Thomas Jefferson had written that "all men are created equal." Yet many Americans, including Jefferson himself, did not believe that this statement applied to enslaved African Americans. In the 1800s, a growing number of reformers began to think differently.

Early Efforts Religious beliefs led some Americans to oppose slavery. Since colonial times, Quakers had taught that it was a sin for one human being to own another. All people, they said, were equal in the sight of God. Later, during the Second Great Awakening, ministers like Charles Grandison Finney called on Christians to join a crusade to stamp out slavery.

In the North, slavery gradually came to an end. By 1804, all the states from Pennsylvania through New England had promised to free their slaves over time. Still, there were only 50,000 slaves in the North in 1800, compared with nearly one million in the South.

Colonization Movement The American Colonization Society proposed to end slavery by setting up an independent colony in Africa for freed slaves. In 1822, President Monroe helped the society found the nation of Liberia in western Africa.

Some African Americans favored colonization, believing that they would never have equal rights in the United States. Most, however, opposed the movement. Nearly all, enslaved or free, had been born in the United States. They wanted to stay in their homeland. In the end, only a few thousand African Americans settled in Liberia.

The Abolitionist Movement Grows

A growing number of reformers, known as abolitionists, wanted to end slavery completely in the United States. Some abolitionists favored a gradual end to slavery. They expected slavery to die out if it was kept out of the western territories. Other abolitionists demanded that slavery end everywhere, at once.

African American Abolitionists
Free African Americans played a key role in the abolitionist movement. Some tried to end slavery through lawsuits and petitions. In the 1820s, Samuel Cornish and John Russwurm set up an abolitionist newspaper, *Freedom's Journal.* They hoped to turn public opinion against slavery by printing stories about the brutal treatment of enslaved African Americans.

Other African American abolitionists called for stronger measures. In *An Appeal to the Colored Citizens of the World,* David Walker encouraged enslaved African Americans to free themselves by any means necessary. Walker's friend Maria Stewart also spoke out against slavery. Stewart was the first American woman to make public political speeches.

Frederick Douglass
The best-known African American abolitionist was Frederick Douglass. Douglass was born into slavery in Maryland. As a child, he defied the slave codes by learning to read.

Douglass escaped in 1838 and made his way to New England. One day at an antislavery meeting, he felt a powerful urge to speak. Rising to his feet, he talked about the sorrows of slavery and the meaning of freedom. The audience was moved to tears. Soon, Douglass was lecturing across the United States and Britain. In 1847, he began publishing an antislavery newspaper, the *North Star.*

William Lloyd Garrison
The most outspoken white abolitionist was a fiery young man named William Lloyd Garrison. To Garrison, slavery was an evil to be ended immediately. In 1831, Garrison launched *The Liberator,* the most influential antislavery newspaper. On the first page of the first issue, Garrison revealed his commitment:

> 66 I will be as harsh as truth, and as uncompromising as justice. . . . I am in earnest. . . . I will not excuse—I will not retreat a single inch—and I WILL BE HEARD. 99
>
> —William Lloyd Garrison, *The Liberator,* January 1831

A year later, Garrison helped to found the New England Anti-Slavery Society. Members included Theodore Weld, a young minister

An American Profile

Frederick Douglass
1817–1895

Even while he was still enslaved, Frederick Douglass bravely fought slavery. He suffered beatings for resisting commands and was once jailed for trying to escape. Even after he finally did escape, Douglass was in constant danger of being recaptured and returned to the South. Despite the risk, he did not hesitate to speak out against slavery.

In 1845, Douglass wrote his autobiography. Fearing for Douglass's life, an abolitionist friend warned him not to publish it. Douglass did so anyway. Two years later, friends raised money to buy Douglass his freedom at last.

What risks did Frederick Douglass take by publishing his autobiography?

Bethel AME Church

Founded in 1816, the African Methodist Episcopal Church was a center of African American life. The Bethel AME Church in the African American community of Springtown, New Jersey, became a key station on the Underground Railroad. Harriet Tubman herself often led runaways from Maryland and Delaware there to spend a safe night on their way to freedom.

Go Online
PHSchool.com

Virtual Field Trip For an interactive look at the Underground Railroad, visit PHSchool.com, **Web Code mfd-1502.**

and follower of Charles Grandison Finney. Weld brought the energy of a religious revival to antislavery meetings.

The Grimké Sisters Angelina and Sarah Grimké were the daughters of a South Carolina slaveholder. Hating slavery, they moved to Philadelphia to work for abolition. Their lectures drew large crowds.

Some people, including other abolitionists, objected to women speaking out in public. "Whatsoever it is morally right for a man to do," replied Sarah Grimké, "it is morally right for a woman to do." As you will see, this belief helped spark a crusade for women's rights.

The Underground Railroad

Some abolitionists formed the Underground Railroad. It was not a real railroad, but a network of black and white abolitionists who secretly helped slaves escape to freedom in the North or Canada.

"Conductors" guided runaways to "stations" where they could spend the night. Some stations were homes of abolitionists. Others were churches or even caves. Conductors sometimes hid runaways under loads of hay in wagons with false bottoms.

One daring conductor, Harriet Tubman, had escaped slavery herself. Risking her freedom and her life, Tubman returned to the South 19 times. She led more than 300 slaves, including her parents, to freedom. Admirers called Tubman the "Black Moses" after the biblical leader who led the Israelites out of slavery in Egypt. Slave owners offered a $40,000 reward for her capture.

Predict

Before you read this section, predict the reactions of northerners and southerners to the abolitionist movement. Then, read to see whether your predictions were correct.

Opposition to Abolition

By the mid-1800s, slavery existed only in the South. Still, abolitionists like Douglass and Garrison made enemies in the North as well.

Reaction in the North Northern mill owners, bankers, and merchants depended on cotton from the South. They saw attacks on slavery as a threat to their livelihood. Some northern workers also opposed abolition. They feared that African Americans might come north and take their jobs by working for low pay.

In northern cities, mobs sometimes broke up antislavery meetings or attacked homes of abolitionists. At times, the attacks backfired and won support for the abolitionists. One night, a Boston mob dragged William Lloyd Garrison through the streets at the end of a rope. A witness wrote, "I am an abolitionist from this very moment."

Reaction in the South Most white southerners were disturbed by the growing abolitionist movement. They accused abolitionists of preaching violence. Many southerners blamed Nat Turner's rebellion on William Lloyd Garrison, who had founded *The Liberator* only a few months earlier. David Walker's call for a slave revolt seemed to confirm the worst fears of southerners.

Slave owners responded to the abolitionist crusade by defending slavery even more. If slaves were treated well, wrote one slave owner, they would "love their master and serve him . . . faithfully." Others argued that slaves were better off than northern workers who labored long hours in dusty, airless factories.

Even some southerners who owned no slaves defended slavery. To them, slavery was essential to the southern economy. Many southerners believed northern support for the antislavery movement was stronger than it really was. They began to fear that northerners wanted to destroy their way of life.

★ ★ ★ Section 2 Assessment ★ ★ ★

Recall

1. **Identify** Explain the significance of (a) American Colonization Society, (b) David Walker, (c) Frederick Douglass, (d) William Lloyd Garrison, (e) *The Liberator,* (f) Grimké sisters, (g) Underground Railroad, (h) Harriet Tubman.
2. **Define** abolitionist.

Comprehension

3. Describe two ways reformers fought against slavery.
4. How did the Underground Railroad work?
5. (a) Why did some northerners oppose abolition? (b) Describe two effects of the abolitionist movement in the South.

Critical Thinking and Writing

6. **Exploring the Main Idea** Review the Main Idea statement at the beginning of this section. Then, write a paragraph explaining what you think was the most powerful reason for ending slavery.
7. **Identifying Alternatives** Some abolitionists favored a gradual end to slavery rather than immediate abolition. List two possible arguments for and two possible arguments against this position.

ACTIVITY

Sending a Secret Message You are a conductor on the Underground Railroad. You have a cousin in New Jersey whose home you want to use as a station. Write a letter describing what your cousin will need to do. Include a map showing the route you will be taking. (See the map at the beginning of this chapter.)

Making Decisions

We make decisions all the time, but some are much more difficult than others. One way to learn decision-making skills is to look at the choices that others have made. What would you have decided if you had been living as a slave and had seen the chance to escape?

James Adams escaped from a plantation in Virginia as a teenager. Years later, he described the journey:

> **" After crossing the road, we came out from the mountains to a level cleared place of farms and houses. Then we were afraid, and put ourselves on guard, resolving to travel by night. . . . We would follow a road until it bent away from the north; then we would leave it and go by the compass. This caused us to meet many rivers and streams where there were no bridges; some we could wade over, and some we crossed by swimming. . . . Our feet were now sore with long travelling. "**
>
> —James Adams, quoted in
> *The Underground Railroad* (Hansen)

A table like this one can help you weigh the pros and cons of a decision.

PROS AND CONS OF ESCAPING SLAVERY	
Arguments For	**Arguments Against**
becoming free	being caught, punished, or killed
escaping hardship	undergoing a dangerous trip
escaping abuse	leaving family behind

Reward poster
for runaway slave

Learn the Skill *To learn decision-making skills, use the following steps:*

1. **Identify the problem.** What is the issue you want to resolve or the goal you want to achieve?

2. **Identify the facts.** Gather enough information to make an informed decision.

3. **List options.** What choices of action are there?

4. **Predict consequences.** What are the pros and cons of each alternative?

5. **Make a decision.** Choose a course of action based on the facts and evidence you have found.

Practice the Skill *Use the passage, poster, and table above to answer the following questions:*

1. What was James Adams's goal?

2. **(a)** What benefits did the Underground Railroad offer? **(b)** What were two dangers that people faced when escaping?

3. What alternatives did enslaved people have?

4. Identify two possible consequences of trying to escape.

5. What decision would you have made about escaping? Give reasons for your answer.

Apply the Skill *See the Chapter Review and Assessment.*

3 A Call for Women's Rights

Prepare to Read

Objectives

In this section, you will
- Explain why some women called for equal rights in the 1800s.
- List the goals that were set at the Seneca Falls Convention.
- Summarize how women won new educational opportunities.

Key Terms

Seneca Falls Convention

women's rights movement

Target Reading Skill

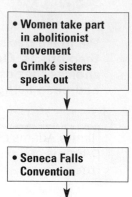

Sequence Copy this flow-chart. As you read, fill in the boxes with information about the development of the women's rights movement. Two boxes have been begun to help you get started.

- Women take part in abolitionist movement
- Grimké sisters speak out

↓

↓

- Seneca Falls Convention

↓

Main Idea The abolitionist movement helped spark a new reform movement that sought equality for women.

Sarah and Angelina Grimké

Setting the Scene

As you have read, Sarah and Angelina Grimké became powerful speakers against slavery. However, their bold activities shocked many people, including some male abolitionists. Many ministers refused to let the Grimkés speak in their churches. One minister did allow them to speak—but left as soon as he introduced them. He announced that he would rather rob a chicken coop than hear a woman speaking in public.

A friend of the Grimkés made fun of such attitudes in a poem:

> 66 They've taken a notion to speak for themselves,
> . . . And are wielding the tongue and the pen;
> They've mounted the rostrum; the [quarrelsome] elves!
> . . . And—oh horrid!—are talking to men! 99
> —Maria Chapman, "The Times That Try Men's Souls"

More determined than ever, the Grimkés continued their crusade. "Can you not see," Angelina asked one abolitionist, "that woman could do and would do a hundred times more for the slave, if she were not fettered?" Now, however, the Grimkés had a second topic to lecture about: women's rights.

Seeking Equal Rights

Women had few political or legal rights in the mid-1800s. They could not vote or hold office. When a woman married, her husband became owner of all her property. If a woman worked outside the home, her wages belonged to her husband. A husband also had the right to hit his wife as long as he did not seriously injure her.

Many women, like the Grimkés, had joined the abolitionist movement. As these women worked to end slavery, they became aware that they lacked full social and political rights themselves. Both black and white abolitionists, men and women, joined the struggle for women's rights.

Sojourner Truth One of the most effective women's rights leaders was born into slavery in New York. Her original name was Isabella. After gaining freedom, she came to believe that God wanted her to fight slavery. Vowing to sojourn, or travel, across the land speaking the truth, she took the name Sojourner Truth.

Truth was a spellbinding speaker. Her exact words were rarely written down. However, her message spread by word of mouth. According to one witness, Truth ridiculed the idea that women were inferior to men by nature:

> **66** I have as much muscle as any man, and can do as much work as any man. I have plowed and reaped and husked and chopped and mowed, and can any man do more than that? **99**
>
> —Sojourner Truth, speech at Akron women's rights convention, 1851

Mott and Stanton Other abolitionists also turned to the cause of women's rights. The two most influential were Lucretia Mott and Elizabeth Cady Stanton. Lucretia Mott was a Quaker and the mother of five children. A quiet speaker, she won the respect of many listeners with her persuasive logic. Mott also used her organizing skills to set up petition drives across the North.

Elizabeth Cady Stanton was the daughter of a New York judge. As a child, she was an excellent student and an athlete. However, her father gave her little encouragement. Stanton later remarked that her "father would have felt a proper pride had I been a man."

In 1840, Stanton and Mott joined a group of Americans at a World Antislavery Convention in London. However, convention officials refused to let women take an active part in the proceedings. Female delegates were even forced to sit behind a curtain, hidden from view. After returning home, Mott and Stanton took up the cause of women's rights with new energy.

Seneca Falls Convention

Even in London, Mott and Stanton had begun thinking about holding a convention to draw attention to the problems women faced. "The men . . . had [shown] a great need for some education on that question," Stanton later recalled. The meeting finally took place in 1848 in Seneca Falls, New York.

"Women Are Created Equal" About 200 women and 40 men attended the Seneca Falls Convention. The delegates approved a *Declaration of Sentiments,* modeled on the Declaration of Independence. It proclaimed, "We hold these truths to be self-evident: that all men and women are created equal."

The women and men at Seneca Falls voted for resolutions that demanded equality for women at work, at school, and at church. Only one resolution met with any opposition at the convention. It demanded that women be allowed to vote. Even the bold reformers at Seneca Falls hesitated to take this step. In the end, the resolution narrowly passed.

An American Profile

Elizabeth Cady Stanton
1815–1902

Elizabeth Cady's first memory was of adult visitors sympathizing with her parents on the birth of her younger sister. Another girl! Witty, energetic Elizabeth was viewed as a rebellious daughter who loved riding horses, detested sewing, and enjoyed spending time in her father's law office. There, the clerks teased her by reading aloud laws that denied basic rights to women.

In 1839, Cady met abolitionist Henry Stanton. At their wedding ceremony, the couple removed the word "obey" from their vows. Elizabeth Cady Stanton chose to obey only her sense of right and wrong.

How did her childhood experiences influence Stanton's career?

▲ Past

▲ Present

Viewing History

Reforming Fashions

In the 1800s, tightly laced dresses that crushed women's rib cages often caused them to faint. Journalist Amelia Bloomer promoted a new fashion: loose-fitting trousers. Many Americans objected to these "bloomers" (left). Today, Amelia Bloomer would be pleased to see that women wear comfortable clothes every day.

Linking Past and Present
Do changing fashions ever cause controversy today? Give examples.

A Long Struggle The Seneca Falls Convention marked the start of an organized campaign for equal rights, or the **women's rights movement.** Other leaders took up the struggle. Susan B. Anthony built a close working partnership with Elizabeth Cady Stanton. While Stanton usually had to stay at home with her seven children, Anthony was free to travel across the country. Anthony was a tireless speaker. Even when audiences heckled her and threw eggs, she always finished her speech.

In the years after 1848, women worked for change in many areas. They won additional legal rights in some states. For example, New York passed laws allowing married women to keep their own property and wages. Still, many men and women opposed the women's rights movement. The struggle for equal rights would last many years.

New Opportunities in Education

The women at Seneca Falls believed that education was a key to equality. Elizabeth Cady Stanton said:

66 The girl must be allowed to romp and play, climb, skate, and swim. Her clothing must be more like those of the boy—strong, loose-fitting garments, thick boots. . . . She must be taught to look forward to a life of self-dependence and, like the boy, prepare herself for some [profitable] trade profession. 99

—Elizabeth Cady Stanton, Letter, 1851

Such an idea was startling in the early 1800s. Women from poor families had little hope of learning even to read. Middle-class girls who went to school learned dancing and drawing rather than science or mathematics. After all, people argued, women were expected to care for their families. Why did they need an education?

Schools for Women Reformers worked to improve education for women. Emma Willard opened a high school for girls in Troy, New York. Here, young women studied "men's" subjects, such as mathematics and physics.

Mary Lyon opened Mount Holyoke Female Seminary in Massachusetts in 1837. She did not call the school a college because many people thought it was wrong for women to attend college. In fact, however, Mount Holyoke was the first women's college in the United States.

New Careers At about this time, a few men's colleges began to admit women. As their education improved, women found jobs teaching, especially in grade schools.

A few women entered fields such as medicine. Elizabeth Blackwell attended medical school at Geneva College in New York. To the surprise of school officials, she graduated first in her class. Women had provided medical care since colonial times, but Blackwell was the first woman in the United States to earn a medical degree. She later helped found the nation's first medical school for women.

Women made their mark in other fields as well. Maria Mitchell was a noted astronomer. Sarah Josepha Hale edited *Godey's Lady's Book*, an influential magazine for women. Antoinette Blackwell became the first American woman ordained a minister. She also campaigned for abolitionism, temperance, and women's right to vote.

Identify Sequence
What events led to more educational opportunities for girls and women? Put these events on your flowchart.

★ ★ ★ Section 3 Assessment ★ ★ ★

Recall

1. **Identify** Explain the significance of (a) Sojourner Truth, (b) Elizabeth Cady Stanton, (c) Seneca Falls Convention, (d) Emma Willard, (e) Elizabeth Blackwell.
2. **Define** women's rights movement.

Comprehension

3. What legal rights did women lack in the early 1800s?
4. (a) Why did Mott and Stanton organize a women's rights convention? (b) Describe two resolutions passed by the convention.

5. How did reformers change education for women?

Critical Thinking and Writing

6. **Exploring the Main Idea** Review the Main Idea statement at the beginning of this section. Then, write a sentence summarizing the link between the abolitionist and women's rights movements.
7. **Making Predictions** How do you think the growth of educational opportunities in the mid-1800s would affect the future of the women's rights movement later in the century? Write a paragraph explaining the reasons for your prediction.

ACTIVITY

Designing a Banner
With a partner, design a banner to be displayed at the Seneca Falls Convention. Make a clever and attractive design that expresses the feelings of early women's rights crusaders. Include a brief slogan.

4 American Art and Literature

Prepare to Read

Objectives

In this section, you will
- Describe the new style of American painting.
- Summarize themes that American writers explored.
- Identify why the "inner light" was important to Emerson and Thoreau.

Main Idea In the mid-1800s, American writers and artists began to create a new vision that reflected the continuity and change of American life.

Key Terms

Hudson River School

transcendentalist

individualism

civil disobedience

Target Reading Skill

Main Idea Copy the concept web below. As you read, fill in the blank ovals with information about American art and literature. Add as many ovals as you need.

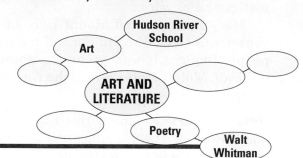

Setting the Scene In 1820, a Scottish minister named Sydney Smith deplored what he saw as a lack of culture in the United States:

> 66 In the four quarters of the globe, who reads an American book? Or goes to an American play? Or looks at an American picture or statue? What does the world yet owe to Americans? 99
>
> —Sydney Smith, *The Edinburgh Review*

Even as Smith wrote these words, American artists and writers were breaking free of European traditions to create a unique American vision. At the same time, their work expressed universal themes—such as the love of nature or the desire for liberty—that appealed to audiences far beyond the United States.

Painter's easel and equipment

American Painters

Before 1800, most American painters studied in Europe. Benjamin West of Philadelphia was appointed historical painter to King George III. Many American painters journeyed to London to study with West. Two of them, Charles Willson Peale and Gilbert Stuart, later painted famous portraits of George Washington.

By the mid-1800s, American artists began to develop their own style. The first group to do so became known as the **Hudson River School.** Artists such as Thomas Cole and Asher B. Durand painted vivid landscapes of New York's Hudson River region. African American artist Robert S. Duncanson reflected the style of the Hudson River School.

Other artists painted scenes of hard-working country people. George Caleb Bingham of Missouri created a timeless picture of frontier life along the rivers that feed the great Mississippi. George Catlin and Alfred Jacob Miller traveled to the Far West to record the daily life of Indians on the Great Plains and in the Rockies.

The Poetry of Democracy

Henry Wadsworth Longfellow was the favorite poet of Americans in the mid-1800s. Longfellow based many poems on events from the past. "Paul Revere's Ride" honored the Revolutionary War hero. "The Song of Hiawatha" idealized Native American life.

Other poets spoke out on social issues. John Greenleaf Whittier, a Quaker from Massachusetts, and Frances Watkins Harper, an African American woman from Maryland, used their pens to make readers aware of the evils of slavery.

Walt Whitman published only one book of poems, *Leaves of Grass*. However, he added to it over a period of 27 years. Whitman had great faith in the common people. His poetry celebrated democracy. He wrote proudly of being part of a "nation of many nations":

> 66 At home on the hills of Vermont or in the
> woods of Maine, or the Texan ranch,
> Comrade of Californians, comrade of free
> North-Westerners. . . .
> Of every hue and caste am I, of every rank
> and religion. 99
>
> —Walt Whitman, *Song of Myself*

Only seven of Emily Dickinson's more than 1,700 poems were published in her lifetime. A shy woman who rarely left her home, Dickinson called her poetry "my letter to the world / That never wrote to me." Today, she is recognized as one of the nation's greatest poets.

Novels and Stories

Like painters, early American writers also depended on Europe for their ideas and inspiration. In the 1820s, however, a new crop of writers began to write stories with American themes.

Two Early Writers One of the most popular American writers was Washington Irving, a New Yorker. Irving first became known for *The Sketch Book,* a collection of tales published in 1820. Two of his best-loved tales are "Rip Van Winkle" and "The Legend of Sleepy Hollow."

The exciting novels of James Fenimore Cooper were also set in the American past. In *The Deerslayer* and *The Last of the Mohicans,* Cooper created Natty Bumppo, a heroic model of a strong, solitary frontiersman. The novels gave an idealized view of relations between whites and Native Americans on the frontier.

Viewing History

Hudson River School
In his 1849 painting *Kindred Spirits,* Asher B. Durand depicts the grandeur of New York's Catskill Mountains. The two men shown are nature poet William Cullen Bryant and Durand's fellow painter Thomas Cole. **Analyzing Information** *What kinds of emotions might a painting like this stir?*

The stories of Cooper and Irving gave Americans a sense of the richness of their past. Their appeal went beyond the United States, however. Washington Irving was the first American writer to enjoy fame in Europe.

Later Writers In 1851, Herman Melville published *Moby-Dick*. The novel tells the story of Ahab, the crazed captain of a whaling ship. Ahab vows revenge on the white whale that years earlier bit off his leg. *Moby-Dick* had only limited success when it was first published. Today, however, critics rank it among the finest American novels.

Nathaniel Hawthorne often drew on the history of New England in his novels and short stories. In *The Scarlet Letter*, published in 1850, Hawthorne explored Puritan notions of sin and salvation. The novel shows how a young man is consumed by guilt when he tries to hide his wrongdoing from the world.

Edgar Allan Poe became famous for his many tales of horror. His short story "The Tell-Tale Heart" is about a murderer, driven mad by guilt, who imagines he can hear his victim's heartbeat. Poe is also known as the "father of the detective story" for his mystery stories, such as "The Murders in the Rue Morgue."

William Wells Brown was the first African American to earn his living as a writer. He published *Clotel*, a novel about slave life, in 1853. Brown also wrote a play inspired by his own experiences as a fugitive slave and a conductor on the Underground Railroad. His lectures and readings drew large audiences in Europe as well as throughout the North.

Identify Supporting Details

Which details in this paragraph give examples of the types of novels written during the mid-nineteenth century? Add these details to your concept web.

Viewing History

Sleepy Hollow

"The Legend of Sleepy Hollow," by Washington Irving, remains one of the most popular American stories. This modern statue depicts the Headless Horseman that terrified schoolteacher Ichabod Crane. **Linking Past and Present** *Why do you think this story is so popular?*

Women Writers Many best-selling novels of the period were written by women. Some novels told about young women who gained wealth and happiness through honesty and self-sacrifice. Others showed the hardships faced by widows and orphans.

Few of these novels are read today. However, writers like Catherine Sedgwick and Fanny Fern earned far more than Hawthorne or Melville. Hawthorne complained about the success of a "mob of scribbling women."

The "Inner Light"

In New England, a small but influential group of writers and thinkers emerged. They called themselves **transcendentalists** because they believed that the most important truths in life transcended, or went beyond, human reason. Transcendentalists valued the spark of deeply felt emotions more than reason. They believed that each individual should live up to the divine possibilities within. This belief influenced many transcendentalists to support social reform.

Emerson The leading transcendentalist was Ralph Waldo Emerson. Emerson was the most popular essayist and lecturer of his day. Audiences flocked to hear him talk on subjects such as self-reliance and character. Emerson believed that the human spirit was reflected in nature. Civilization might provide material wealth, he said, but nature exhibited higher values that came from God.

In his essays and lectures, Emerson stressed individualism, or the importance of each individual. Each person, Emerson said, has an "inner light." He urged people to use this inner light to guide their lives and improve society. "Trust thyself," he wrote. "Every heart vibrates to that iron string."

Thoreau Henry David Thoreau (thuh ROW), Emerson's friend and neighbor, believed that the growth of industry and the rise of cities were ruining the nation. He urged people to live as simply and as close to nature as possible. In *Walden*, his best-known work, Thoreau describes spending a year alone in a cabin on Walden Pond in Massachusetts.

Like Emerson, Thoreau believed that each individual must decide what is right or wrong. "If a man does not keep pace with his companions," he wrote, in *Walden*, "perhaps it is because he hears a different drummer. Let him step to the music he hears."

Thoreau's "different drummer" told him that slavery was wrong. He argued in favor of civil disobedience, the idea that people have a right to disobey unjust laws if their consciences demand it. He once went to jail for refusing to pay taxes to support the Mexican War, which he felt promoted slavery. Thoreau's writings on civil disobedience and nonviolence later influenced Mohandas Gandhi and Martin Luther King, Jr.

Primary Source

Civil Disobedience

In his famous essay "Civil Disobedience," Henry David Thoreau discussed his refusal to pay taxes to support the Mexican War:
"I have paid no poll tax for six years. I was put into a jail once on this account, for one night; and, as I stood considering the walls of solid stone, two or three feet thick, the door of wood and iron, a foot thick, and the iron grating which strained the light, I could not help being struck with the foolishness of that institution which treated me as if I were mere flesh and blood and bones, to be locked up. . . . I was not born to be forced. I will breathe after my own fashion. Let us see who is the strongest."

—Henry David Thoreau, "Civil Disobedience"

Analyzing Primary Sources
How does this passage show Thoreau's belief in the individual conscience?

★ ★ ★ **Section 4 Assessment** ★ ★ ★

Recall
1. **Identify** Explain the significance of (a) Hudson River School, (b) Emily Dickinson, (c) Washington Irving, (d) Herman Melville, (e) William Wells Brown, (f) Ralph Waldo Emerson, (g) Henry David Thoreau.
2. **Define** (a) transcendentalist, (b) individualism, (c) civil disobedience.

Comprehension
3. How did American painting change in the mid-1800s?
4. Describe the themes explored by two of the following: (a) Henry Wadsworth Longfellow, (b) Walt Whitman, (c) James Fenimore Cooper, (d) Nathaniel Hawthorne.
5. Identify the reasons for and the impact of Thoreau's idea of civil disobedience.

Critical Thinking and Writing
6. **Exploring the Main Idea** Review the Main Idea statement at the beginning of this section. Then, analyze how the work of one writer reflected continuity or change in American life.
7. **Drawing Conclusions** List two themes expressed by American writers. For each one, give reasons why it was also meaningful to audiences outside the United States.

ACTIVITY

Go Online
PHSchool.com

Writing a Museum Guide
Use the Internet to find other examples of American painting from 1800–1865. Choose one work, and write a description that might appear in a museum guide. Include the title, artist, and date, as well as a description of the subject matter. For help in completing the activity, visit PHSchool.com, **Web Code mfd-1503.**

CHAPTER SUMMARY

Section 1
A reforming impulse led to the Second Great Awakening. It also produced leaders who attacked problems in hospitals, prisons, politics, and education. The temperance movement battled alcohol abuse.

Section 2
The abolitionist movement arose in the North. The Underground Railroad helped slaves escape to freedom. Southerners opposed the abolitionists.

Section 3
The women's rights movement was born at the Seneca Falls Convention of 1848. New educational and career opportunities opened for women in the 1800s.

Section 4
A first wave of U.S. painters, poets, and writers with an American-inspired vision emerged in the 1800s. New England transcendentalists gave birth to two new ideas: individualism and civil disobedience.

Building Vocabulary

Use the chapter vocabulary words listed below to create a crossword puzzle. Exchange puzzles with a classmate. Complete the puzzles, and then check each other's answers.

1. social reform
2. predestination
3. revival
4. debtor
5. abolitionist
6. Underground Railroad
7. women's rights movement
8. individualism

Reviewing Key Facts

9. What were the effects of the Second Great Awakening? (Section 1)

10. How did public education improve in the early 1800s? (Section 1)

11. How did abolitionists achieve their goals? (Section 2)

For additional review and enrichment activities, see the interactive version of *The American Nation,* available on the Web and on CD-ROM.

Chapter Self-Test For practice test questions for Chapter 15, visit PHSchool.com, **Web Code mfa-1504.**

12. What ideas were contained in the Seneca Falls Declaration of Sentiments? (Section 3)

13. Identify two writers who explored the American past in their work. (Section 4)

Critical Thinking and Writing

14. **Drawing Inferences** In his *Appeal to the Colored Citizens of the World*, David Walker wrote that "all men are created equal; that they are endowed by their Creator with certain inalienable rights." **(a)** From which document did Walker borrow this idea? **(b)** Write a paragraph explaining why he included this phrase.

15. **Comparing** Compare the abolitionist movement and the women's rights movement in terms of causes and impact.

16. **Connecting to Geography: Place** Look at the painting from the Hudson River School in Section 4. Write down five adjectives that describe the geographic setting of the painting. Then, list five places or types of landform found in the United States that you think would attract landscape painters.

17. **Synthesizing Information** Write a paragraph explaining how the Second Great Awakening, the educational reform movement, and the work of Emerson and Thoreau all stressed the importance of the individual.

At an 1852 abolitionist meeting in Rochester, New York, Frederick Douglass denounced the continuing slave trade in the United States:

❝ Fellow citizens, this murderous traffic is, today, in active operation in this boasted republic. In the solitude of my spirit, I see clouds of dust raised on the highways of the South; I see the bleeding footsteps; I hear the doleful [sad] wail of fettered humanity on the way to the slave markets where victims are to be sold like horse, sheep, and swine. . . . My soul sickens at the sight. ❞

—Frederick Douglass,
"What, to the Slave, Is the Fourth of July?"

18. What emotion is Douglass trying to stir up?
   A. joy   **C.** outrage
   B. complacency   **D.** despair
19. What point is Douglass making by using the phrase *boasted republic?*
   A. The United States should be proud of its plentiful livestock.
   B. The United States leads the way in opposing murder.
   C. The United States is home to brave individuals who carry on despite their hardships.
   D. The existence of slavery undermines the U.S. boast that the nation is a land of the free.

ARGUMENTS FOR	ARGUMENTS AGAINST
A. Men, women, and children live in poor conditions	**C.** Cost of building new prisons is too high
B. Eighth Amendment prohibits "cruel and unusual" punishment	**D.** Tax money should be used to benefit law-abiding citizens

You are a state legislator trying to decide whether to use state money to build new prisons. Copy the table above. Add any arguments for or against. Then, answer the following questions:

20. Argument B is most closely linked to
   A. Second Great Awakening
   B. Declaration of Independence
   C. Bill of Rights
   D. Economics
21. Would you have voted in favor of funding new prisons? Explain your decision.

ACTIVITIES

Connecting With . . .
Culture

Writing a Song With a group of students, write a marching song that might have been used at one of the following events: a temperance rally, an abolitionist meeting, a march for women's rights. Use a familiar tune, or write your own. Write words. Include a refrain, or repeated phrase, that emphasizes the main goal of the song. Gather musical instruments, and perform the song in class.

Go Online
PHSchool.com

Researching

Preparing a Biographical Sketch Use the Internet to find information on one of the following women: Antoinette Blackwell, Sara Josepha Hale, Emily Blackwell, Elizabeth Blackwell, Amelia Bloomer, Myra Bradwell, Margaret Fuller, Mary Ann Cary, Maria Mitchell, or Lucy Stone. Write a brief sketch explaining her contribution to women's rights. Include a timeline of major events in her life. For help in starting this activity, visit PHSchool.com, **Web Code mfd-1506.**

TEST PREPARATION

1 "Individual reform is the first step toward social reform." This statement represents a key idea of what reform movement?

A The Second Great Awakening

B The temperance movement

C The abolitionist movement

D The women's rights movement

Use the quotation **and** your knowledge of social studies to answer the following question.

Daniel Webster, Reply to Robert Hayne, 1830 (adapted)

"While the people choose to maintain the Constitution as it is, while they are satisfied with it, and refuse to change it, who has given, or who can give, to the state legislatures a right to alter it?"

---

2 What idea or policy is the subject of Webster's speech?

A Nullification

B Manifest Destiny

C Federalism

D Civil disobedience

3 What was one result of the rise of the Cotton Kingdom?

A Slavery began to decline.

B The South developed an industrial economy.

C Eli Whitney invented the cotton gin.

D Large planters gained political influence.

Use the map **and** your knowledge of social studies to answer the following question.

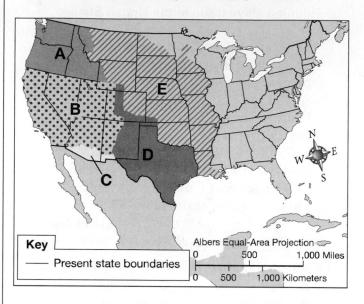

4 Which two areas shown on this map did the United States acquire by the same method?

A A and B

B C and E

C B and D

D C and D

5 How were the works of James Fenimore Cooper similar to those of Henry Wadsworth Longfellow?

A Both were best known for their poetry.

B Both used their pens to oppose slavery.

C Both explored historical subjects in their work.

D Both were transcendentalists.

6 Which statement is true of both Texas and California?

  A It was admitted to the Union as a slave state.

  B American settlers there rebelled against Mexican rule.

  C It became part of the United States as a result of the Mexican War.

  D Its annexation was an important issue in the election of 1844.

Use the graph <u>and</u> your knowledge of social studies to answer the following question.

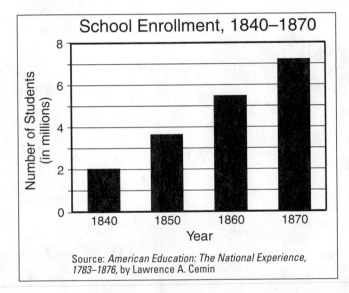

School Enrollment, 1840–1870

Source: *American Education: The National Experience, 1783–1876,* by Lawrence A. Cemin

7 The trend shown on this graph is most closely related to what development?

  A The expansion of voting rights

  B Increased immigration from Ireland

  C The abolitionist movement

  D The rise of the Hudson River School

8 Which slogan best reflects the main beliefs of the Know-Nothing party?

  A "Fifty-four forty or fight!"

  B "America for Americans!"

  C "To the victor go the spoils!"

  D "Stamp out demon rum!"

9 Which was one result of Andrew Jackson's Native American policy?

  A The Seminole nation was completely destroyed.

  B The United States annexed Florida and Texas.

  C Few Native Americans remained east of the Mississippi.

  D War broke out between the United States Army and the Cherokees.

Writing Practice

10 Describe and evaluate one political, one social, and one economic effect of westward expansion.

11 Analyze the impact of transportation systems on the nation. Choose at least two advances in transportation and explain how each one affected the growth, development, or urbanization of the United States.

Unit 5

Division and Reunion

The Soldiers of the Civil War
In *A Rainy Day in Camp* by Winslow Homer, Civil War soldiers find time to gather around a campfire.

“Union! I can more easily conceive of the Lion and Lambs lying down together, than of a union of the North and South.”

—Sarah Chase, Massachusetts teacher in the South (1866)

CHAPTER 16
Slavery Divides the Nation

1820–1861

1 Slavery in the Territories
2 The Compromise of 1850
3 The Crisis Deepens
4 The Republican Party Emerges
5 A Nation Divides

Family escaping slavery

RAN AWAY!

FROM THE SUBSCRIBER. My Mulatto Boy, GEORGE. Said George is 5 feet 8 inches in height, brown curly Hair, dark coat. I will give $400 for him alive, and the same sum for satisfactory proof that he has been killed.
Vide **ANTHONY & ELLIS' MAMMOTH** "UNCLE TOM'S CABIN." WM. HARRIS.

Fugitive slave poster

AMERICAN EVENTS

1820
The Missouri Compromise maintains the balance of free and slave states in the Union.

John Quincy Adams	1825–1829
Andrew Jackson	1829–1837
Martin Van Buren	1837–1841
William Henry Harrison	1841

1850
Congress passes the Compromise of 1850. One new law requires all Americans to help recapture fugitive slaves.

1848
The Free-Soil party is formed to oppose the extension of slavery in the West.

Presidential Terms: James Monroe 1817–1825 · John Tyler 1841–1845 · James K. Polk 1845–1849 · Zachary Taylor 1849–1850

1820 · · · 1845 · · · 1850

WORLD EVENTS

▲ **1833**
Slavery is abolished in the British Empire.

1850 ▲
Civil war breaks out in China.

Slave and Free States, 1850

As new states entered the Union, the balance between slave and free states became harder to maintain.

BRITISH TERRITORY

Oregon Territory

Minnesota Territory

Unorganized Territory

Utah Territory

California (1850)

New Mexico Territory

Indian Territory

ME (1820)
VT (1791)
NH (1788)
MA (1788)
RI (1790)
CT (1788)
NY (1788)
PA (1787)
NJ (1787)
DE (1787)
MD (1788)

WI (1848)
MI (1837)
Iowa (1846)
Illinois (1818)
IN (1816)
Ohio (1803)

Missouri (1821)
KY (1792)
Virginia (1788)
NC (1789)
TN (1796)
SC (1788)

Arkansas (1836)
MS (1817)
AL (1819)
Georgia (1788)
LA (1812)

Texas (1845)

FL (1845)

Washington, D.C. (slave trade banned)

L. Superior
L. Michigan
L. Huron
L. Ontario
L. Erie
Missouri R.
Mississippi R.

ATLANTIC OCEAN

PACIFIC OCEAN

MEXICO

Gulf of Mexico

Albers Equal-Area Projection

0   200   400 Miles
0   200   400 Kilometers

50°N
40°N
30°N
20°N
110°W
90°W
80°W
70°W

Key

	Free states
	Slave states
	Territories
1787	Date of entry into Union

Stephen Douglas

Flag from Fort Sumter

1854

Senator Stephen Douglas proposes the Kansas-Nebraska Act, allowing new territories to decide whether or not to permit slavery.

1857

In *Dred Scott* v. *Sandford*, the Supreme Court rules that Congress cannot ban slavery in any territory.

1861

The Confederate States of America is formed. Confederate troops later fire on Fort Sumter, South Carolina, where this flag flew. The bombardment marks the beginning of the Civil War.

Millard Fillmore 1850–1853

Franklin Pierce 1853–1857

James Buchanan 1857–1861

Abraham Lincoln 1861–1865

1850 · · **1855** · · **1860** · · ·

1854 ▲
Slavery is abolished in Venezuela.

1861 ▲
Czar Alexander II frees all Russian serfs.

1 Slavery in the Territories

Prepare to Read

Objectives

In this section, you will
- Describe the purpose of the Missouri Compromise.
- Explain why conflict arose over the issue of slavery in the western territories.
- Identify why the Free-Soil party was founded.

Key Terms

Missouri Compromise

Wilmot Proviso

popular sovereignty

Free-Soil party

Target Reading Skill

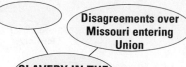

Reading Process Copy the concept web below. Include three or four blank ovals. As you read, fill in each blank oval with important facts about slavery in the territories.

Disagreements over Missouri entering Union

SLAVERY IN THE TERRITORIES

Free-Soil party opposes extension of slavery

Main Idea The Missouri Compromise attempted to settle the issue of whether slavery should be allowed in the western territories.

Jefferson at 78

Setting the Scene When he reached his seventies, Thomas Jefferson vowed "never to write, talk, or even think of politics." Still, in 1820 at the age of 77, he broke this vow. Jefferson voiced alarm at the fierce debate going on in Congress:

❀ This momentous question, like a fire bell in the night, awakened and filled me with terror. I considered it at once as the [funeral bells] of the Union. . . . We have the wolf by the ears, and we can neither hold him, nor safely let him go. ❀

—Thomas Jefferson, Letter to John Holmes, April 22, 1820

Jefferson knew the "wolf," or the issue of slavery, could tear the North and South apart. As settlers moved west, Congress faced an agonizing decision. Should it ban slavery in the territories and later admit them to the Union as free states? Or should it permit slavery in the territories and later admit them as slave states? This was the critical question that filled Jefferson with terror in the night.

The Missouri Compromise

There were 11 free states and 11 slave states in 1819. That year, Congress considered Missouri's application to join the Union as a slave state. Immediately, a crisis erupted. Missouri's admission would give the South a majority in the Senate. Determined not to lose power, northerners opposed letting Missouri enter as a slave state.

The argument lasted many months. Finally, Senator Henry Clay made a proposal. During the long debate, Maine had also applied for statehood. Clay suggested admitting Missouri as a slave state and Maine as a free state. His plan, called the Missouri Compromise, kept the number of slave and free states equal.

As part of the Missouri Compromise, Congress drew an imaginary line across the southern border of Missouri at latitude 36°30′ N.

Slavery was permitted in the part of the Louisiana Purchase south of that line. It was banned north of the Missouri Compromise line. The only exception to this was Missouri itself.

Slavery in the West

The Missouri Compromise applied only to the Louisiana Purchase. In 1848, the Mexican War added vast western lands to the United States. Once again, the question of slavery in the territories arose.

Wilmot Proviso Many northerners feared that the South would extend slavery into the West. David Wilmot, a member of Congress from Pennsylvania, called for a law to ban slavery in any territories won from Mexico. Southern leaders angrily opposed this Wilmot Proviso. They said that Congress had no right to ban slavery in the West.

The House passed the Wilmot Proviso in 1846, but the Senate defeated it. As a result, Americans continued to argue about slavery in the West even while their army fought in Mexico.

Opposing Views As the debate heated up, people found it hard not to take sides. Abolitionists wanted slavery banned throughout the country. They insisted that slavery was morally wrong.

Southern slaveholders thought that slavery should be allowed in any territory. They also demanded that slaves who escaped to the North be returned to them. Even white southerners who did not own slaves generally agreed with these ideas.

Between these two extreme views were more moderate positions. Some moderates argued that the Missouri Compromise line should be extended across the Mexican Cession to the Pacific. Any new state north of the line would be a free state. Any new state south of the line could

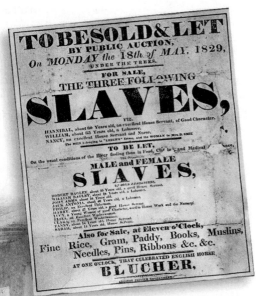

Viewing History

A Family for Sale

As Americans debated the issue of slavery, slave auctions continued in the South. The family members on the auction block here might never see each other again. **Drawing Inferences** *What do the poster (above) and the painting (left) suggest about the attitude of slaveholders toward slaves?*

allow slavery. Other moderates supported the idea of **popular sovereignty,** or the right of people to create their government. Under popular sovereignty, voters in a new territory would decide for themselves whether or not to allow slavery.

The Free-Soil Party

The debate over slavery led to the birth of a new political party. By 1848, many northern Democrats and Whigs opposed the spread of slavery. However, the leaders of both parties refused to take a stand. They did not want to lose any southern votes. Some also feared that the slavery issue would split the nation.

In 1848, antislavery members of both parties met in Buffalo, New York. There, they founded the **Free-Soil party.** The main goal of the Free-Soil party was to keep slavery out of the western territories. Only a few Free-Soilers were abolitionists who wanted to end slavery in the South.

In the 1848 presidential campaign, Free-Soilers named former President Martin Van Buren as their candidate. Democrats chose Lewis Cass of Michigan. The Whigs selected Zachary Taylor, a hero of the Mexican War.

For the first time, slavery was an important election issue. Van Buren called for a ban on slavery in the Mexican Cession. Cass supported popular sovereignty. Taylor did not speak on the issue. However, because he was a slave owner from Louisiana, many southern voters assumed that he supported slavery.

Zachary Taylor won the election. Still, Van Buren took 10 percent of the popular vote, and 13 other Free-Soil candidates won seats in Congress. The success of the new Free-Soil party showed that slavery had become a national issue.

Predict
What does the success of the Free-Soil party suggest about the future of the slavery issue?

★ ★ ★ **Section 1 Assessment** ★ ★ ★

Recall

1. **Identify** Explain the significance of (a) Missouri Compromise, (b) Wilmot Proviso, (c) Free-Soil party, (d) Zachary Taylor.
2. **Define** popular sovereignty.

Comprehension

3. What was the Missouri Compromise?
4. Describe three conflicting views on slavery in the West.
5. Why did voters leave the Whig and Democratic parties to join the Free-Soil party in 1848?

Critical Thinking and Writing

6. **Exploring the Main Idea** Review the Main Idea statement at the beginning of this section. Then, write a paragraph explaining whether the Missouri Compromise settled the issue of slavery in the western territories.
7. **Drawing Conclusions** The goals of the Free-Soil party pleased some northerners but not others. Write a paragraph explaining why some northerners were pleased and others displeased by the Free-Soil party.

ACTIVITY

Drawing a Political Cartoon With a partner, plan and sketch a political cartoon about the issue of slavery in the western territories. Assume one of the opposing viewpoints described in this section: southern slaveholder, abolitionist, supporter of extending the Missouri Compromise line across the country, or supporter of popular sovereignty. Then, create a cartoon that represents your point of view.

2 The Compromise of 1850

Prepare to Read

Objectives

In this section, you will
- Explain why the slavery debate erupted again in 1850.
- Describe the impact of the Compromise of 1850.
- Summarize how *Uncle Tom's Cabin* affected attitudes toward slavery.

Key Terms

secede

fugitive

civil war

Compromise of 1850

Fugitive Slave Act

Uncle Tom's Cabin

🎯 Target Reading Skill

Cause and Effect As you read, complete the chart at right to show some of the causes and effects of the Compromise of 1850.

```
┌───── CAUSES ─────┐
I. California seeks statehood
2.
3.

  COMPROMISE OF 1850

┌───── EFFECTS ─────┐
I. North reacts to Fugitive
   Slave Act
2.
3.
```

🇺🇸 **Main Idea** The Compromise of 1850, which was supposed to save the Union, only inflamed tensions.

Setting the Scene Tempers in Congress had reached the boiling point. California had applied to be admitted to the Union as a free state in 1850. Senator Thomas Hart Benton of Missouri supported California's request. He denounced Senator Henry Foote of Mississippi for opposing California's admission.

In response, Senator Foote rose angrily, picked up a pistol, and aimed it at Benton. As other senators watched in horror, Benton turned toward Foote and roared, "Let him fire. Stand out of the way and let the assassin fire!"

No blood was shed in the Senate that day. However, even as Congress tried to reach a new compromise, many Americans began to fear that a peaceful solution to the slavery issue was impossible.

Violence threatens in the Senate

The Slavery Debate Erupts Again

For a time after the Missouri Compromise, both slave and free states entered the Union peacefully. However, when California requested admission to the Union as a free state in 1850, the balance of power in the Senate was once again threatened.

California's Impact In 1849, there were 15 slave states and 15 free states in the nation. If California entered the union as a free state, the balance of power would be broken. Furthermore, it seemed quite possible that Oregon, Utah, and New Mexico might also join the Union as free states.

Many southerners feared that the South would be hopelessly outvoted in the Senate. Some even suggested that southern states might want to **secede**, or **remove** themselves, from the United States. Northern congressmen, meanwhile, argued that California should enter the Union as a free state because most of the territory lay north of the Missouri Compromise line.

It was clear that the nation faced a crisis. Many in Congress looked to Senator Henry Clay for a solution.

Balance of Free and Slave States

Free States	Slave States
California (1850)	
Wisconsin (1848)	Texas (1845)
Iowa (1846)	Florida (1845)
Michigan (1837)	Arkansas (1836)
Maine (1820)	Missouri (1821)
Illinois (1818)	Alabama (1819)
Indiana (1816)	Mississippi (1817)
Ohio (1803)	Louisiana (1812)
Vermont (1791)	Tennessee (1796)
Rhode Island	Kentucky (1792)
New York	Virginia
New Hampshire	North Carolina
Massachusetts	South Carolina
Connecticut	Maryland
New Jersey	Georgia
Pennsylvania	Delaware

■ Original 13 states

John C. Calhoun

Daniel Webster   Henry Clay

Viewing History

Crisis in the Senate

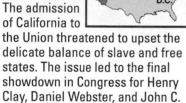

The admission of California to the Union threatened to upset the delicate balance of slave and free states. The issue led to the final showdown in Congress for Henry Clay, Daniel Webster, and John C. Calhoun. **Analyzing Primary Sources** *Why do you think the gallery was filled with spectators to hear this debate?*

Clay vs. Calhoun Clay had won the nickname "the Great Compromiser" for working out the Missouri Compromise. Now, nearly 30 years later, the 73-year-old Clay was frail and ill. Still, he pleaded for the North and South to reach an agreement. If they failed to do so, Clay warned, the nation could break apart.

Senator John C. Calhoun of South Carolina replied to Clay. Calhoun was dying of tuberculosis and could not speak loudly enough to address the Senate. He stared defiantly at his northern foes while Senator James Mason of Virginia read his speech.

Calhoun refused to compromise. He insisted that slavery be allowed in the western territories. In addition, Calhoun demanded that **fugitive,** or runaway, slaves be returned to their owners. He wanted northerners to admit that southern slaveholders had the right to reclaim their "property."

If the North rejected the South's demands, Calhoun told the Senate, "let the states . . . agree to part in peace. If you are unwilling that we should part in peace, tell us so, and we shall know what to do." Everyone knew what Calhoun meant. If an agreement could not be reached, the South would use force to leave the Union.

Webster Calls for Unity Daniel Webster of Massachusetts spoke next. He supported Clay's plea to save the Union. Webster stated his position clearly:

66 I speak today not as a Massachusetts man, nor as a northern man, but as an American. . . . I speak today for the preservation of the Union. . . . There can be no such thing as a peaceable secession. 99

—Daniel Webster, Speech in the U.S. Senate, July 17, 1850

Webster feared that the states could not separate without starting a bloody civil war. A **civil war** is a war between people of the same country.

Like many northerners, Webster viewed slavery as evil. The breakup of the United States, however, he believed was worse. To save the Union, Webster was willing to compromise. He would support southern demands that northerners be forced to return fugitive slaves.

Compromise of 1850

In 1850, as the debate raged, Calhoun died. His last words reportedly were "The South! The poor South! God knows what will become of her now!" President Taylor also died in 1850. The new President was Millard Fillmore. Unlike Taylor, he supported Clay's compromise plan.

The Compromise Passes Henry Clay gave more than 70 speeches in favor of a compromise. At last, however, he became too sick to continue. Stephen Douglas, of Illinois, took up the fight for him and guided Clay's plan, the **Compromise of 1850,** through Congress.

The Compromise of 1850 had five parts. First, it allowed California to enter the Union as a free state. Second, it divided the rest of the Mexican Cession into the territories of New Mexico and Utah. Voters in each would decide the slavery question according to popular sovereignty. Third, it ended the slave trade in Washington, D.C., the nation's capital. Congress, however, declared that it had no power to ban the slave trade between slave states. Fourth, it included a strict fugitive slave law. Fifth, it settled a border dispute between Texas and New Mexico.

Fugitive Slave Act The **Fugitive Slave Act** of 1850 required all citizens to help catch runaway slaves. People who let fugitives escape could be fined $1,000 and jailed. The new law also set up special courts to handle the cases of runaways. Suspects were not allowed a jury trial. Judges received $10 for sending an accused runaway to the South but only $5 for setting someone free. Lured by the extra money, some judges sent African Americans to the South whether or not they were runaways.

Reaction The Fugitive Slave Act enraged antislavery northerners. By forcing them to catch runaways, the law made northerners feel as if they were part of the slave system. In several northern cities, crowds tried to rescue fugitive slaves from their captors.

Despite the compromise, tensions remained high because neither side got everything that it wanted. The new Fugitive Slave Act was especially hard for northerners to accept. Each time the act was

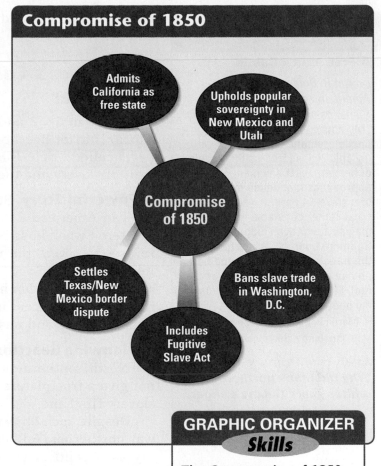

Compromise of 1850

- Admits California as free state
- Upholds popular sovereignty in New Mexico and Utah
- Compromise of 1850
- Settles Texas/New Mexico border dispute
- Includes Fugitive Slave Act
- Bans slave trade in Washington, D.C.

GRAPHIC ORGANIZER
Skills

The Compromise of 1850 was a desperate attempt to save the Union.

1. **Comprehension** Which parts of the Compromise would have been favored by the South?

2. **Critical Thinking Identifying Points of View** Would an abolitionist approve of the Compromise of 1850? Why or why not?

Civics

 **Identify Causes and Effects**

Which factors on this page were effects of the Compromise of 1850? Add these to your chart.

A Free Man's Castle

Martin R. Delany, an African American newspaper editor, responds to the Fugitive Slave Act: "My house is my castle; in that castle are none but my wife and my children, as free as the angels of heaven. . . . If any man approaches that house in search of a slave—I care not who he may be, whether constable or sheriff, magistrate or even judge of the Supreme Court . . . if he crosses the threshold of my door, and I do not lay him a lifeless corpse at my feet, I hope the grave may refuse my body a resting place."

—Martin R. Delany, speech given in Pittsburgh, September 30, 1850

Analyzing Primary Sources
Why did many northern whites share Delany's anger?

enforced, it convinced more northerners that slavery was immoral and evil.

Uncle Tom's Cabin: An Antislavery Bestseller

An event in 1852 added to the growing antislavery mood of the North. Harriet Beecher Stowe, a New England woman, published a novel called *Uncle Tom's Cabin.* Stowe wrote the novel to show the evils of slavery and the injustice of the Fugitive Slave Act.

A Powerful Story Stowe told the story of Uncle Tom, an enslaved African American noted for his kindness and piety. Tom's world is shattered when he is bought by the brutal Simon Legree. When Tom refuses to reveal the whereabouts of two runaways, Legree whips him to death.

Uncle Tom's Cabin had wide appeal among northern readers. The first printing sold out in just two days. Eventually, the book sold millions of copies and was translated into dozens of languages.

Nationwide Reaction Although *Uncle Tom's Cabin* was popular in the North, southerners objected to the book. They claimed that it did not give a true picture of slave life. Indeed, Stowe had seen little of slavery firsthand.

Despite such objections, *Uncle Tom's Cabin* helped to change the way northerners felt about slavery. No longer could they ignore slavery as a political problem for Congress to settle. More and more northerners now saw slavery as a moral problem facing every American. For this reason, *Uncle Tom's Cabin* was one of the most important books in American history.

★ ★ ★ Section 2 Assessment ★ ★ ★

Recall

1. **Identify** Explain the significance of (a) Stephen Douglas, (b) Compromise of 1850, (c) Fugitive Slave Act, (d) Harriet Beecher Stowe, (e) *Uncle Tom's Cabin.*
2. **Define** (a) secede, (b) fugitive, (c) civil war.

Comprehension

3. How did the issue of admitting California to the Union in 1850 again raise the debate over slavery?
4. How did Americans respond to the Compromise of 1850?
5. What was the impact of *Uncle Tom's Cabin?*

Critical Thinking and Writing

6. **Exploring the Main Idea** Review the Main Idea statement at the beginning of this section. Then, write a letter to a newspaper editor explaining whether you think the Compromise of 1850 was a success or a failure. Give reasons for your answer.
7. **Summarizing** For each of the following leaders, write one sentence summarizing his attitude toward the need for a compromise in 1850: (a) Calhoun, (b) Webster, (c) Clay.

ACTIVITY

Making a Decision You are a northerner during the 1850s. There is a knock at your door. It's a fugitive slave! Will you help the runaway, or will you turn the person in to the authorities? Write a brief statement explaining the reasons for your decision.

Uncle Tom's Cabin

Harriet Beecher Stowe saw the horrors of slavery while living in Cincinnati. Across the Ohio River was Kentucky, a slave state. Her hatred of slavery led her to write *Uncle Tom's Cabin*. The novel had an impact that lasted long after slavery ended.

Harriet Beecher Stowe

Uncle Tom Defies Simon Legree

"Well, Tom!" said Legree, walking up and seizing him grimly by the collar of his coat, and speaking through his teeth, in a paroxysm of determined rage, "do you know I've made up my mind to KILL you?"

"It's very likely, Mas'r," said Tom, calmly.

"I have," said Legree, with grim terrible calmness, "done—just—that—thing, Tom, unless you tell me what you know about these yer gals!"

Tom stood silent.

"D'ye hear?" said Legree, stamping with a roar like that of an incensed lion. "Speak!"

"I han't got nothing to tell, Mas'r," said Tom with a slow, firm deliberate utterance.

"Do you dare to tell me, ye old black Christian, ye don't know?"...

"I know, Mas'r; but I can't tell anything. I can die!"

— Harriet Beecher Stowe,
Uncle Tom's Cabin, Chapter 40

Fast Facts

- The character of Tom was inspired by Josiah Henson, a Methodist preacher who had escaped slavery.
- Some southerners wrote "anti-Tom" novels to defend slavery.
- The first movie of *Uncle Tom's Cabin* was made in 1903.

In this poster for a stage version of *Uncle Tom's Cabin*, the fugitive slave Eliza flees across an icy river.

Uncle Tom and Simon Legree

ACTIVITY

You are hosting a dinner honoring Harriet Beecher Stowe. Prepare a brief speech introducing Stowe. Explain how her book reflects divisions in the United States.

3 The Crisis Deepens

Prepare to Read

Objectives

In this section, you will
- Identify the goal of the Kansas-Nebraska Act.
- Explain why violence erupted in Kansas and in the Senate.
- Summarize the impact of the Dred Scott case on the nation.

Key Terms

Kansas-Nebraska Act

Border Ruffians

guerrilla warfare

lawsuit

Dred Scott v. *Sandford*

Target Reading Skill

Cause and Effect As you read, complete the following chart to show some of the causes that directly led the United States to become a more divided nation.

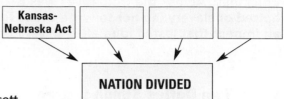

Main Idea In the 1850s, violence in Kansas and the Dred Scott decision inflamed tensions over slavery.

An election in Kansas

Setting the Scene

Americans had hoped that the Compromise of 1850 would end the debate over slavery in the West. Before long, though, proslavery and antislavery forces were battling for control of the territory of Kansas. An observer described election day in one Kansas district in 1855:

66 On the morning of the election, before the polls were opened, some 300 or 400 Missourians and others were collected in the yard . . . where the election was to be held, armed with bowie-knives, revolvers, and clubs. They said they came to vote, and whip the . . . Yankees, and would vote without being sworn. Some said they came to have a fight, and wanted one. 99

—Report of the Congressional Committee, July 1, 1856

Hearing of events in Kansas, Abraham Lincoln, then a young lawyer in Illinois, predicted that "the contest will come to blows, and bloodshed." Once again, the issue of slavery in the territories divided the nation.

Kansas-Nebraska Act

The Compromise of 1850 dealt mainly with lands that were part of the Mexican Cession. It did not resolve the issue of slavery in lands that had been part of the Louisiana Purchase. In January 1854, Senator Stephen Douglas introduced a bill to set up a government for the Nebraska Territory. This territory stretched from Texas north to Canada, and from Missouri west to the Rockies.

Douglas knew that white southerners did not want to add another free state to the Union. He proposed that the Nebraska Territory be divided into two territories, Kansas and Nebraska. The settlers living in each territory would then be able to decide the issue of slavery by popular sovereignty. Douglas's bill was known as the **Kansas-Nebraska Act.**

Support for the Act The Kansas-Nebraska Act seemed fair to many people. After all, the Compromise of 1850 had applied popular sovereignty in New Mexico and Utah. Southern leaders especially supported the Kansas-Nebraska Act. They were sure that slave owners from neighboring Missouri would move with their slaves across the border into Kansas. In time, they hoped, Kansas would become a slave state.

President Franklin Pierce, a Democrat elected in 1852, also supported the bill. With the President's help, Douglas pushed the Kansas-Nebraska Act through Congress. He did not realize it at the time, but he had lit a fire under a powder keg.

Northern Outrage Many northerners were unhappy with the new law. The Missouri Compromise had already banned slavery in Kansas and Nebraska, they insisted. In effect, the Kansas-Nebraska Act would repeal the Missouri Compromise.

The northern reaction to the Kansas-Nebraska Act was swift and angry. Opponents of slavery called the act a "criminal betrayal of precious rights." Slavery could now spread to areas that had been free for more than 30 years. Some northerners protested by openly challenging the Fugitive Slave Act.

The Crisis Turns Violent

Kansas now became a testing ground for popular sovereignty. Stephen Douglas hoped that settlers would decide the slavery issue peacefully on election day. Instead, proslavery and antislavery forces sent settlers to Kansas to fight for control of the territory.

GEOGRAPHY
Skills

The issue of whether to allow slavery in the territories created tension between the North and the South.

1. **Location** On the map, locate **(a)** Missouri Compromise Line, **(b)** Kansas Territory, **(c)** Nebraska Territory.

2. **Region** **(a)** Which territories were open to slavery after 1854? **(b)** Which territories were closed to slavery?

3. **Critical Thinking Making Predictions** How would the balance of power in the Senate change if western territories became slave states?

Slavery After the Kansas-Nebraska Act

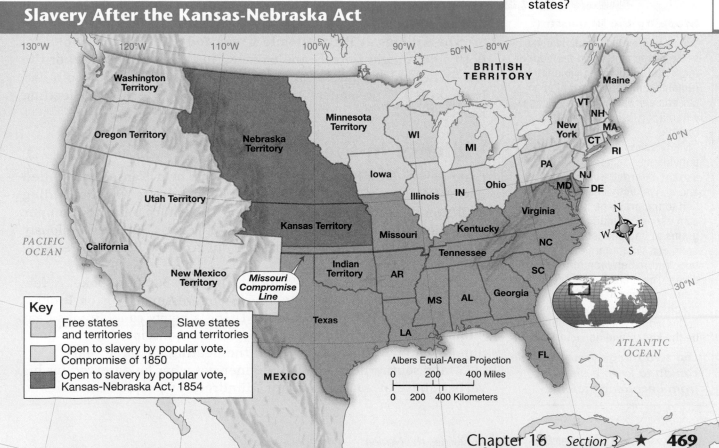

Key

- Free states and territories
- Slave states and territories
- Open to slavery by popular vote, Compromise of 1850
- Open to slavery by popular vote, Kansas-Nebraska Act, 1854

Albers Equal-Area Projection

0   200   400 Miles

0   200   400 Kilometers

Most of the new arrivals were farmers from neighboring states. Their main interest in moving to Kansas was to acquire cheap land. Few of these settlers owned slaves. At the same time, abolitionists brought in more than 1,000 settlers from New England.

Proslavery settlers moved into Kansas as well. They wanted to make sure that antislavery forces did not overrun the territory. Proslavery bands from Missouri often rode across the border. These **Border Ruffians,** as they were called, battled the antislavery forces in Kansas.

Two Governments In 1855, Kansas held elections to choose lawmakers. Hundreds of Border Ruffians crossed into Kansas and voted illegally. They helped to elect a proslavery legislature.

The new legislature quickly passed laws to support slavery. One law said that people could be put to death for helping slaves escape. Another made speaking out against slavery a crime punishable by two years of hard labor.

Antislavery settlers refused to accept these laws. They elected their own governor and legislature. With two rival governments, Kansas was in chaos. Armed gangs roamed the territory looking for trouble.

"Bleeding Kansas" A band of proslavery men raided the town of Lawrence, an antislavery stronghold, in 1856. The attackers destroyed homes and smashed the press of a Free-Soil newspaper.

John Brown, an abolitionist, decided to strike back. Brown had moved to Kansas to help make it a free state. He claimed that God had sent him to punish supporters of slavery.

Brown rode with his four sons and two other men to the town of Pottawatomie (paht uh WAHT uh mee) Creek. In the middle of the night, they dragged five proslavery settlers from their beds and murdered them.

The killings at Pottawatomie Creek led to even more violence. Both sides fought fiercely and engaged in **guerrilla warfare,** or the use of hit-and-run tactics. By late 1856, more than 200 people had been killed. Newspapers started calling the territory "Bleeding Kansas."

Violence in the Senate

Even before John Brown's attack, the battle over Kansas had spilled into the Senate. Charles Sumner of Massachusetts was the leading abolitionist senator. In one speech, the sharp-tongued Sumner denounced the proslavery legislature of Kansas. He then viciously criticized his southern foes, singling out Andrew Butler, an elderly senator from South Carolina.

Butler was not in the Senate on the day Sumner spoke. A few days later, however, Butler's nephew, Congressman Preston Brooks, marched into the Senate chamber. Using a heavy cane, Brooks beat Sumner until he fell down, bloody and unconscious, to the floor. Sumner did not fully recover from the beating for three years.

Many southerners felt that Sumner got what he deserved for his verbal abuse of another senator. Hundreds of people sent canes to

Brooks to show their support. To northerners, however, the brutal act was more evidence that slavery led to violence.

The Dred Scott Case

With Congress in an uproar, many Americans looked to the Supreme Court to settle the slavery issue and restore peace. In 1857, the Court ruled on a case that involved an enslaved person named Dred Scott. Instead of bringing harmony, however, the Court's decision further divided the North and the South.

Dred Scott had been enslaved for many years in Missouri. Later, he moved with his owner to Illinois and then to the Wisconsin Territory, where slavery was not allowed. After they returned to Missouri, Scott's owner died. Antislavery lawyers helped Scott to file a **lawsuit**, a legal case brought to settle a dispute between people or groups. Scott's lawyers argued that, because Scott had lived in a free territory, he had become a free man.

The Supreme Court's Decision In time, the case reached the Supreme Court as *Dred Scott* v. *Sandford.* The Court's decision shocked and dismayed Americans who opposed slavery. First, the Court ruled that Scott could not file a lawsuit because, as an enslaved person, he was not a citizen. Also, the Court's written decision clearly stated that slaves were considered to be property.

The Court's ruling did not stop there. Instead, the Justices went on to make a sweeping decision about the larger issue of slavery in

Viewing History

Bleeding Kansas

In 1856, the slavery issue sparked bloodshed in Kansas. Here, Border Ruffians attack antislavery settlers. Abolitionists like John Brown also committed acts of violence. **Identifying Bias** *What details in the picture suggest that the artist favored the antislavery settlers?*

the territories. According to the Court, Congress did not have the power to outlaw slavery in any territory. The Court's ruling meant that the Missouri Compromise was unconstitutional.

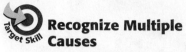

Recognize Multiple Causes

Why did the Dred Scott decision drive the North and South apart? Add this information to your chart.

The Nation Reacts White southerners rejoiced at *Dred Scott* v. *Sandford*. It meant that slavery was legal in all the territories. This was just what white southerners had been demanding for years.

African Americans responded angrily to the Dred Scott decision. In the North, many held public meetings to condemn the ruling. At one meeting in Philadelphia, a speaker hoped that the ruling would lead more whites to "join with us in our efforts to recover the long lost boon of freedom."

White northerners were also shocked by the ruling. Many had hoped that slavery would eventually die out if it were restricted to the South. Now, however, slavery could spread throughout the West. Even northerners who disliked abolitionists felt that the ruling in *Dred Scott* v. *Sandford* was wrong. A newspaper in Cincinnati declared, "We are now one great . . . slaveholding community."

Abolitionist Frederick Douglass also spoke out against *Dred Scott* v. *Sandford*: "This infamous decision," he declared, "maintains that slaves . . . are property in the same sense that horses, sheep, and swine are property . . . that [people] of African descent are not and cannot be citizens of the United States." He told his listeners:

❝ All I ask of the American people is that they live up to the Constitution, adopt its principles, [take in] its spirit, and enforce its provisions. When this is done . . . liberty . . . will become the inheritance of all the inhabitants of this highly favored country. ❞

—Frederick Douglass, *Collected Speeches*, 1857

★ ★ ★ **Section 3 Assessment** ★ ★ ★

Recall

1. **Identify** Explain the significance of (a) Kansas-Nebraska Act, (b) Franklin Pierce, (c) Border Ruffians, (d) Charles Sumner, (e) *Dred Scott* v. *Sandford*.
2. **Define** (a) guerrilla warfare, (b) lawsuit.

Comprehension

3. Why did Stephen Douglas propose the Kansas-Nebraska Act?
4. How did the Kansas-Nebraska Act lead to violence?
5. How did white southerners, African Americans, and white northerners react to the Dred Scott decision?

Critical Thinking and Writing

6. **Exploring the Main Idea** Review the Main Idea statement at the beginning of this section. Then, make a list of five statements from this section that support the main idea.
7. **Analyzing Primary Sources** After the Kansas-Nebraska Act was passed, Stephen Douglas stated: "The struggle for freedom was forever banished from the halls of Congress to the western plains." Rewrite Douglas's statement in your own words. Then, explain why you agree or disagree with it.

ACTIVITY

Go Online
PHSchool.com

Connecting to Today
Use the Internet to find out more about a recent Supreme Court decision involving the rights of workers, minorities, or students. Write a brief summary describing both sides of the issue and what the court decided. For help in completing the activity, visit PHSchool.com, **Web Code mfd-1601.**

4 The Republican Party Emerges

Prepare to Read

Objectives

In this section, you will
- Explain why the Republican party was founded.
- Explain the rapid emergence of Abraham Lincoln as a Republican leader.
- Describe the reaction to John Brown's raid on Harpers Ferry.

Key Terms

Republican party

arsenal

treason

martyr

Target Reading Skill

Comparison and Contrast As you read, complete this table listing the conflicting views of Abraham Lincoln and Stephen Douglas.

LINCOLN'S VIEWS	DOUGLAS'S VIEWS
• Slavery was morally wrong	•
•	• Western territories should decide slavery issue by popular sovereignty
•	•

 Main Idea Abraham Lincoln emerged as a leader of the new Republican party, which was dedicated to halting the spread of slavery.

Setting the Scene The tall lawyer stood before a political convention in Springfield, Illinois. People in the packed hall listened carefully as he addressed the number one issue of the day—slavery:

> ❝ A house divided against itself cannot stand. I believe this government cannot endure permanently half slave and half free. I do not expect the Union to be dissolved—I do not expect the house to fall—but I do expect it will cease to be divided. It will become all one thing, or all the other. ❞
>
> —Abraham Lincoln, Speech, June 16, 1858

Few people outside of Illinois had heard of Abraham Lincoln. Yet, his speech became famous. Many northerners were soon repeating his prediction about the "house divided." Lincoln and the new party he represented—the Republican party—moved to the forefront of the debate over slavery.

Figure of Abraham Lincoln

The Republican Party

By the mid-1850s, people who opposed slavery in the territories sought a new political voice. Neither Whigs nor Democrats, they argued, would take a strong stand against slavery. "We have submitted to slavery long enough," an Ohio Democrat declared.

A group of Free-Soilers, northern Democrats, and antislavery Whigs gathered in Michigan in 1854. There they formed the Republican party. Its main goal was to keep slavery out of the western territories. A few Republicans were abolitionists. They hoped to end slavery in the South as well. Most Republicans, however, wanted only to stop the spread of slavery.

The new party grew quickly. By 1856, it was ready to challenge the older parties for power. Republicans selected John C. Frémont to run for President. Frémont was a frontiersman who had fought for

The Election of 1856 In this 1856 cartoon, Millard Fillmore steps in between John C. Frémont (left) and James Buchanan (right).

1. **Comprehension** What accusations do Frémont and Buchanan make against one another?

2. **Finding the Main Idea** How does the cartoonist show that the slavery issue stirred strong feelings?

3. **Critical Thinking Identifying Points of View** Which candidate do you think the cartoonist favored? Explain.

California's independence. He had little political experience, but he opposed the spread of slavery.

Frémont's main opponent was Democrat James Buchanan of Pennsylvania. Many Democrats saw Buchanan as a "northern man with southern principles." They hoped that he would attract voters in both the North and the South. Former President Millard Fillmore also ran as the candidate of the American, or "Know-Nothing," party. A strong supporter of the Union, Fillmore feared that a Republican victory would split the nation apart.

Buchanan won the election with support from a large majority of southerners and many northerners. Still, the Republicans made a strong showing in the election. Without the support of a single southern state, Frémont won one third of the popular vote. Southerners worried that their influence in the national government was fading.

Abe Lincoln of Illinois

The next test for the Republican party came in 1858 in Illinois. Abraham Lincoln, a Republican, challenged Democrat Stephen Douglas for his seat in the Senate. Because most Americans expected Douglas to run for President in 1860, the race captured the attention of the whole nation.

From the Backwoods of Kentucky Abraham Lincoln was born on the Kentucky frontier. Like many frontier people, his parents moved often to find better land. The family lived in Indiana and later in Illinois. As a child, Lincoln spent only a year in school. Still, he taught himself to read, poring over his books by firelight.

After Lincoln left home, he opened a store in Illinois. There, he studied law on his own and launched a career in politics. He served eight years in the state legislature and one term in Congress. Bitterly opposed to the Kansas-Nebraska Act, he decided to run for the Senate in 1858.

When the race began, Lincoln was not a national figure. Still, people in Illinois knew him well and liked him. To them, he was "just folks"—someone who enjoyed picnics, wrestling contests, and all their favorite pastimes. His honesty, wit, and plain-spoken manner made him a good speaker.

Lincoln-Douglas Debates During the Senate campaign, Lincoln challenged Douglas to a series of debates. Douglas was not eager to accept, but he did. During the campaign, the two debated seven times. Slavery was the important issue.

Douglas wanted to settle the slavery question by popular sovereignty. He personally disliked slavery, but stated that he did not care whether people in the territories voted "down or up" for it.

Lincoln, like nearly all whites of his day, did not believe in "perfect equality" between blacks and whites. He did, however, believe that slavery was wrong:

> 66 There is no reason in the world why the negro is not entitled to all the natural rights [listed] in the Declaration of Independence, the right to life, liberty, and the pursuit of happiness. . . . In the right to eat the bread, without the leave of anybody else, which his own hand earns, he is my equal and the equal of Judge Douglas, and the equal of every living man. 99
>
> —Abraham Lincoln, Speech at Ottawa, Illinois, August 21, 1858

Since slavery was a "moral, social, and political wrong," said Lincoln, Douglas and other Americans should not treat it as an unimportant question to be voted "down or up." Lincoln was totally opposed to slavery in the territories. Still, he was not an abolitionist. He had no wish to interfere with slavery in the states where it already existed.

A Leader Emerges Week after week, both men spoke nearly every day to large crowds. Newspapers reprinted their campaign speeches. The more northerners read Lincoln's words, the more they thought about the injustice of slavery.

In the end, Douglas won the election by a slim margin. Still, Lincoln was a winner, too. He was now known throughout the country. Two years later, the two rivals would again meet face to face—both seeking the office of President.

John Brown's Raid

In the meantime, more bloodshed inflamed divisions between the North and the South. In 1859, the radical abolitionist John Brown carried his antislavery campaign from Kansas to the East. He led a group of followers, including five African Americans, to the town of Harpers Ferry, Virginia.

Compare and Contrast

Read the paragraphs following "Lincoln-Douglas Debates." How did Douglas and Lincoln differ on the issue of slavery? Add this information to your chart.

Primary Source

Douglas Debates Lincoln

In his first debate with Lincoln, Stephen Douglas defended the principle of popular sovereignty: "We have settled the slavery question as far as we are concerned; we have prohibited it in Illinois forever, . . . but when we settled it for ourselves, we exhausted all our power over that subject. We must leave each and every other state to decide for itself the same question. . . . Now, my friends, if we will only act conscientiously and rigidly upon this great principle of popular sovereignty, we will continue at peace, one with another."

—Stephen Douglas, Speech at Ottawa, Illinois, August 21, 1858

Analyzing Primary Sources
How might an abolitionist respond to Douglas?

There, Brown planned to raid a federal **arsenal,** or gun warehouse. He thought that enslaved African Americans would flock to him at the arsenal. He would then give them weapons and lead them in a revolt.

Sentenced to Death Brown quickly gained control of the arsenal. No slave uprising took place, however. Instead, troops under the command of Robert E. Lee killed ten raiders and captured Brown.

Most people, in both the North and the South, thought that Brown's plan to lead a slave revolt was insane. After all, there were few enslaved African Americans in Harpers Ferry. Furthermore, after seizing the arsenal, Brown did nothing further to encourage a slave revolt. At his trial, however, Brown seemed perfectly sane. He sat quietly as the court found him guilty of murder and **treason,** or actions against one's country. Before hearing his sentence, he gave a moving defense of his actions. He showed no emotion as he was sentenced to death.

Hero or Villain? Because he conducted himself with such dignity during his trial, John Brown became a hero to many northerners. Some considered him a **martyr** because he was willing to give up his life for his beliefs. On the morning he was hanged, church bells rang solemnly throughout the North. In years to come, New Englanders would sing a popular song with the chorus: "John Brown's body lies a mold'ring in the grave, but his soul is marching on."

To white southerners, the northern response to John Brown's death was outrageous. People were singing the praises of a man who had tried to lead a slave revolt! Many southerners became convinced that the North wanted to destroy slavery—and the South along with it. The nation was poised for a violent clash.

★ ★ ★ Section 4 Assessment ★ ★ ★

Recall

1. **Identify** Explain the significance of **(a)** Republican party, **(b)** John C. Frémont, **(c)** James Buchanan, **(d)** Abraham Lincoln, **(e)** Harpers Ferry.
2. **Define** **(a)** arsenal, **(b)** treason, **(c)** martyr.

Comprehension

3. What issue led to the founding of the Republican party?
4. How did Abraham Lincoln emerge as a Republican leader?
5. How did northerners and southerners respond to John Brown's raid?

Critical Thinking and Writing

6. **Exploring the Main Idea** Review the Main Idea statement at the beginning of this section. Then, write a paragraph explaining how the views of the Republican party differed from the views of earlier parties.
7. **Supporting a Point of View** Lincoln said the nation could not "endure permanently half slave and half free." Do you agree that slavery was too important an issue to allow differences among the states? Write a paragraph explaining the reasons for your opinion.

Identifying Bias

Was John Brown a hero or a villain? That depends on your point of view. To evaluate historical evidence correctly, you must be able to identify *bias*, strong beliefs that prejudice someone's point of view.

A North Carolina newspaper ran this editorial after the execution of John Brown:

The Execution of Brown

❝ We give to-day full accounts of the scenes attending the execution of the traitor, murderer, and thief, John Brown. He died, as he lived, a hardened criminal. [When] his wretched confederates shall have paid the penalty of their crimes, we hope that their allies and sympathizers at the North will realize the fact that the South has the power to protect her soil and property, and will exercise it in spite of all the measures which can be leveled at her by the abolitionists and their [supporters]. ❞

—Raleigh, North Carolina, *Register,* December 9, 1859

In this abolitionist painting, John Brown pauses on his way to his execution to kiss an enslaved woman's baby.

Learn the Skill *To identify bias, use the following steps:*

1. **Identify the sources.** Knowing a person's background helps you evaluate that person's attitudes.

2. **Identify main ideas.** What is the main point that is being made?

3. **Distinguish facts from opinions.** Remember, facts are statements that can be proven, while opinions are someone's beliefs.

4. **Look for emotion-packed words or images.** How information is presented is an important clue to the point of view.

5. **Identify bias.** How do the writer's or artist's feelings and beliefs affect his or her presentation?

Practice the Skill *Answer the following questions about the editorial and picture above:*

1. Where was the newspaper published?

2. What are the points of view of the editorial and the painting?

3. **(a)** Which statements made by the writer can be proven as facts? **(b)** Which are opinions?

4. **(a)** Evaluate the language the writer uses to describe John Brown. **(b)** What emotions do the images in the painting create?

5. **(a)** What bias does the editorial show? **(b)** What bias does the painting show?

Apply the Skill *See the Chapter Review and Assessment.*

5 A Nation Divides

Prepare to Read

Objectives

In this section, you will
- Explain how the 1860 election reflected sectional divisions.
- Describe how the South reacted to the election results.
- Identify how the Civil War began in 1861.

Key Term

unamendable

Target Reading Skill

Main Idea As you read, prepare an outline of this section. Use roman numerals to indicate the major headings, capital letters for the subheadings, and numbers for the supporting details.

> I. The Election of 1860
>   A. Candidates and political parties
>   1.
>   2.
>   3.
>   4.
>   B. Results of the election
>   1.
>   2.
> II. The South Reacts
>   A. Secession
>   1.
>   2.

Main Idea The election of Abraham Lincoln as President in 1860 led a number of southern states to secede from the Union.

Lincoln campaign badge

Setting the Scene Thousands of people swarmed into Chicago, Illinois, for the 1860 Republican national convention. They filled all of the city's 42 hotels. When beds ran out, people slept on billiard tables. All were there to find out one thing: Who would win the Republican nomination for President—William Seward of New York or Abraham Lincoln of Illinois?

On the third day of the convention, a delegate rushed to the roof of the hall. There, a man stood waiting next to a cannon. "Fire the salute," ordered the delegate. "Old Abe is nominated!" Amid the celebration, though, a delegate from Kentucky struck a somber note. "Gentlemen, we are on the brink of a great civil war."

The Election of 1860

The Democrats held their convention in Charleston, South Carolina. Southerners wanted the party to support slavery in the territories. However, northern Democrats refused to do so. In the end, the party split in two. Northern Democrats chose Stephen Douglas to run for President. Southern Democrats picked John Breckinridge of Kentucky.

Some Americans tried to heal the split between the North and the South by forming a new party. The Constitutional Union party chose John Bell of Tennessee to run for President. Bell was a moderate who wanted to keep the Union together. He got support only in a few southern states that were still seeking a compromise.

Douglas was sure that Lincoln would win. However, he believed that Democrats "must try to save the Union." He urged southerners to stay with the Union, no matter who was elected.

When the votes were counted, Lincoln had carried the North and won the election. Southern votes did not affect the outcome at all. Lincoln's name was not even on the ballot in 10 southern states. Northerners outnumbered southerners and outvoted them.

The South Reacts

Lincoln's election brought a strong reaction in the South. A South Carolina woman described how the news was received:

> 66 The excitement was very great. Everybody was talking at the same time. One . . . more moved than the others, stood up saying . . . 'No more vain regrets—sad forebodings are useless. The stake is life or death—.' 99
>
> —Mary Boykin Chesnut, *A Diary From Dixie,* 1860

To many southerners, Lincoln's election meant that the South no longer had a voice in national government. They believed that the President and Congress were now set against their interests—especially slavery. Even before the election, South Carolina's governor had written to other southern governors. If Lincoln won, he wrote, it would be their duty to leave the Union.

Secession Senator John Crittenden of Kentucky made a last effort to save the Union. In December 1860, he introduced a bill to extend the Missouri Compromise line to the Pacific. Crittenden also proposed an amendment to the Constitution that was **unamendable,** one that could not be changed. Such an amendment would guarantee forever the right to hold slaves in states south of the compromise line.

The compromise bill received little support. Slavery in the West was no longer the issue. Many southerners believed that the North had put an abolitionist in the White House. They felt that secession was their only choice. Most Republicans also were unwilling to surrender what they had won in the national election.

GEOGRAPHY *Skills*

Abraham Lincoln won the election of 1860 with less than 40 percent of the popular vote.

1. **Location** On the map, locate **(a)** Kentucky, **(b)** Illinois, **(c)** South Carolina.

2. **Region** **(a)** Which political party did the northern states support? **(b)** Which party did most southern states support?

3. **Critical Thinking Drawing Conclusions** Did the results of the popular vote weaken or strengthen Lincoln's chances of effectively leading the nation? Explain.

Election of 1860

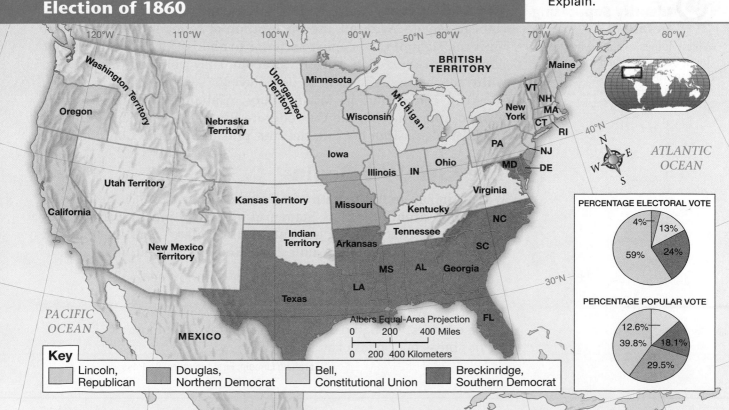

PERCENTAGE ELECTORAL VOTE

4% 13% 59% 24%

PERCENTAGE POPULAR VOTE

12.6% 39.8% 18.1% 29.5%

Albers Equal-Area Projection
0   200   400 Miles
0   200 400 Kilometers

Key
- Lincoln, Republican
- Douglas, Northern Democrat
- Bell, Constitutional Union
- Breckinridge, Southern Democrat

Charleston, South Carolina

Fort Sumter

The Civil War began in 1861 when Confederate forces bombarded and captured Fort Sumter in Charleston Harbor, South Carolina. Later in the war, Union gunships reduced Sumter to rubble. The fort was rebuilt, and it remained part of the seacoast defenses until 1947. Today, Fort Sumter is a national monument. Tour boats to the fort leave regularly from downtown Charleston.

Go Online
PHSchool.com

Virtual Field Trip For an interactive look at Fort Sumter, visit PHSchool.com, **Web Code mfd-1603.**

On December 20, 1860, South Carolina became the first state to secede. By late February, 1861, Alabama, Florida, Georgia, Louisiana, Mississippi, and Texas had also seceded.

The Confederacy Most southerners believed that they had every right to secede. After all, the Declaration of Independence said that "it is the right of the people to alter or to abolish" a government that denies the rights of its citizens. Lincoln, they believed, would deny white southerners the right to own slaves.

At a convention in Montgomery, Alabama, the seven states formed a new nation, the Confederate States of America. Jefferson Davis of Mississippi became the first president of the Confederacy.

The Civil War Begins

When Lincoln took the oath of office on March 4, 1861, he faced a dangerous situation. In his inaugural address, Lincoln warned that "no state . . . can lawfully get out of the Union." Still, he pledged that there would be no war unless the South started it:

> 66 In YOUR hands, my dissatisfied fellow-countrymen, and not in MINE, is the momentous issue of civil war. . . . We are not enemies, but friends. We must not be enemies. Though passion may have strained, it must not break our bonds of affection. 99
>
> — Abraham Lincoln, First Inaugural Address

Identify Supporting Details

Target Skill

Which details explain why the South believed it had the right to secede from the Union? Add these details to your outline.

Lincoln's Difficult Decision Jefferson Davis, however, had already ordered Confederate forces to begin seizing federal forts in the South. President Lincoln faced a difficult decision. Should he let the Confederates take over federal property? If he did, he would seem to be admitting that states had the right to leave the Union. On the other hand, if he sent troops to hold the forts, he might start a civil war. He might also lose the support of the eight slave states that had not seceded from the Union.

In April, the Confederacy forced Lincoln to make up his mind. By then, Confederate troops controlled nearly all forts, post offices, and other federal buildings in the South. The Union held only three forts off the Florida coast and Fort Sumter in South Carolina. Fort Sumter was important to the Confederacy because it guarded Charleston Harbor.

Bombardment of Fort Sumter President Lincoln learned that food supplies at Fort Sumter were running low. He notified the governor of South Carolina that he was going to ship food to the fort. Lincoln promised not to send troops or weapons.

The Confederates, however, felt that they could not leave the fort in Union hands. On April 11, 1861, they demanded that Fort Sumter surrender. Major Robert Anderson, the Union commander, refused to give in until he had run out of food or was ordered to surrender by the United States government. Confederate guns then opened fire. The Union troops quickly ran out of ammunition. On April 13, Anderson surrendered the fort.

When Confederate troops shelled Fort Sumter, people in Charleston gathered on their rooftops to watch. To many, it was like a fireworks show. No one knew that the fireworks marked the start of a civil war that would last four terrible years.

An American Profile

Jefferson Davis
1808–1889

After service in the Mexican War, Jefferson Davis became a United States Senator from Mississippi. Here, he championed states' rights. Then, as secretary of war, he influenced President Pierce to sign the Kansas-Nebraska Act. But Davis opposed splitting the Union. As tensions grew between the South and the North, he urged southern states not to secede.

They disregarded his advice. When Mississippi left the Union in 1861, Davis left the Senate and became president of the Confederacy.

Why do you think Jefferson Davis opposed secession?

★ ★ ★ Section 5 Assessment ★ ★ ★

Recall
1. **Identify** Explain the significance of **(a)** John Breckinridge, **(b)** John Bell, **(c)** John Crittenden, **(d)** Jefferson Davis.
2. **Define** unamendable.

Comprehension
3. How did the four candidates for President in 1860 reflect the nation's sectional differences?
4. Why did many southerners support secession after Lincoln won the presidency in 1860?
5. What happened at Fort Sumter in 1861 to begin the Civil War?

Critical Thinking and Writing
6. **Exploring the Main Idea** Review the Main idea statement at the beginning of this section. Then, write a newspaper editorial about Lincoln's election that might have appeared in a southern newspaper in November 1860.
7. **Solving Problems** Write an outline for a compromise plan that tries to save the Union in 1861. Your plan should offer advantages to both the North and the South.

ACTIVITY

Planning a Political Campaign You are a political campaign manager in 1860. Write a campaign slogan for each of the four candidates in the presidential election of 1860. Or, choose one of the candidates and design a campaign poster for that candidate.

CHAPTER SUMMARY

Section 1
The Missouri Compromise addressed slavery in the Louisiana Purchase. The issue was unresolved in lands that were part of the Mexican Cession. Abolitionists founded the Free-Soil party.

Section 2
The balance of power between North and South came to the forefront again when western territories applied for statehood. The Compromise of 1850 failed to completely satisfy either side. Tensions continued to build.

Section 3
Popular sovereignty did not solve the slavery issue in the new territories. Proslavery and antislavery forces clashed violently in Kansas. The Dred Scott case further divided North and South.

Section 4
During the 1858 Illinois Senate race, veteran politician Stephan Douglas and newcomer Abraham Lincoln debated the slavery issue. John Brown's raid drove the North and South farther apart.

Section 5
Seven southern states seceded from the Union after Abraham Lincoln was elected President. The Confederacy's attack on Fort Sumter marked the beginning of the Civil War.

For additional review and enrichment activities, see the interactive version of *The American Nation,* available on the Web and on CD-ROM.

Chapter Self-Test For practice test questions for Chapter 16, visit PHSchool.com, **Web Code mfa-1604.**

Reviewing Key Facts

11. Describe three positions on slavery held by Americans in the 1840s. (Section 1)
12. What were the five parts of the Compromise of 1850? (Section 2)
13. How did Kansas gain the nickname "Bleeding Kansas"? (Section 3)
14. What groups combined to form the Republican party? (Section 4)
15. Why did South Carolina secede from the Union? (Section 5)

Building Vocabulary

Review the chapter vocabulary words listed below. Then, use the words and their definitions to create a matching quiz. Exchange quizzes with another student. Check each other's answers when you are finished.

1. popular sovereignty
2. fugitive
3. civil war
4. guerrilla warfare
5. lawsuit
6. arsenal
7. treason
8. martyr
9. Missouri Compromise
10. Kansas-Nebraska Act

Critical Thinking and Writing

16. **Connecting to Geography: Regions** Study the map of the election of 1860 in Section 5. **(a)** From which regions did Lincoln draw his support? **(b)** Does the map show from what regions Douglas drew most of his support? Why or why not?
17. **Supporting a Point of View** Write two brief statements summarizing one argument for and one argument against Daniel Webster's support of the Fugitive Slave Act.
18. **Identifying Causes and Effects** **(a)** List two causes for the split in the Democratic party in the 1860 election. **(b)** List two effects of the election.

Look at this drawing that appeared in northern newspapers in 1856.

19. The beating of Charles Sumner by Preston Brooks resulted in
   A. northern support of slavery.
   B. southern support of abolition.
   C. dismissal of both men from the Senate.
   D. a wider rift between North and South.
20. What was the national mood in 1856?
   A. Most Americans supported slavery.
   B. Many Americans felt strongly about slavery.
   C. Americans did not care about slavery.
   D. Most Americans were abolitionists.

The election of 1860 outraged white southerners. They were especially upset that a President had been elected without any southern electoral votes. According to an Augusta, Georgia, newspaper editor, the Republican party:

“ stands forth today, hideous, revolting, loathsome, a menace not only to the Union of these states, but to Society, to Liberty, and to Law. It has drawn to it the corrupt, the vile, and [immoral], the [wasteful], the lawless. . . . It is a fiend, the type of lawless Democracy, a law unto itself, its only Lord King Numbers, its decrees but the will of a wild mob. ”

—Augusta, Georgia, *Chronicle*, November 1860, quoted in "Michael Holt, the Political Crisis of the 1850s"

21. Which of the following titles best reflects the viewpoint of the editorial writer?
   A. A Tribute to the Republicans
   B. A Loathsome Menace
   C. Separation of Powers
   D. Dangers of the Party System
22. What does this editorial tell you about the state of relations between the North and the South in November 1860?

ACTIVITIES

Connecting With . . . Economics

Transferring Information to Charts By 1861, the North had 65 percent of the farmland, 71 percent of the railroad track, 85 percent of the factories, 92 percent of the industrial workers, and 63 percent of the population of the United States. Create a series of pie charts comparing the resources of the North and the South.

35%
65%
■ Farmland in North
▨ Farmland in South

Researching a Biography

Ranking Lincoln Web Sites Use the Internet to find sites relating to Abraham Lincoln. Write a report listing the resources you found on these sites that make them valuable for a Lincoln biography. List five sites, and rank them in order of usefulness. For help in starting this activity, visit PHSchool.com, **Web Code mfd-1606.**

CHAPTER 17

The Civil War

1861–1865

1 **The Conflict Takes Shape**
2 **No Easy Victory**
3 **A Promise of Freedom**
4 **Hardships of War**
5 **The War Ends**

The Battle of Bull Run

1861
The first major battle of the war takes place at Bull Run on July 21.

1862
Union gunboats capture New Orleans and Memphis.

1863
The Battle of Gettysburg ends the Confederate drive into the North.

AMERICAN EVENTS

Presidential Terms: Abraham Lincoln 1861–1865

1861

1862

1863

WORLD EVENTS

▲ **1861**
The Russian czar frees the serfs.

▲ **1862**
Great Britain refuses to recognize the Confederacy.

Choosing Sides

In April 1861, eight slave states were still in the Union. These states would have to decide whether to remain in the Union or join the Confederacy.

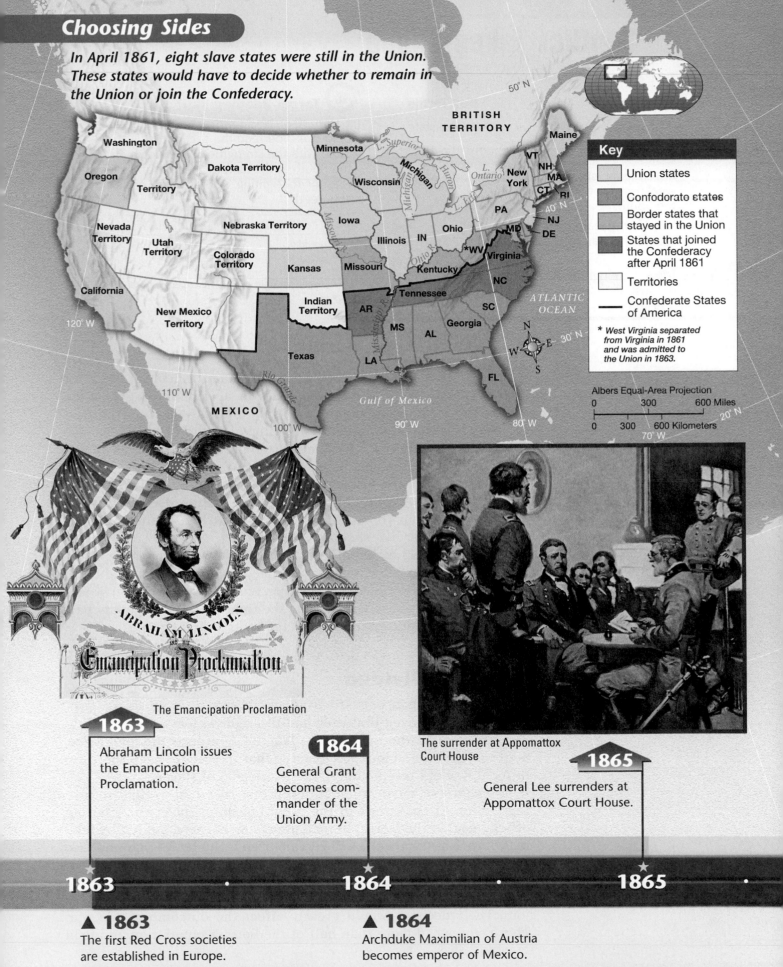

Key

- Union states
- Confederate states
- Border states that stayed in the Union
- States that joined the Confederacy after April 1861
- Territories
- Confederate States of America

* West Virginia separated from Virginia in 1861 and was admitted to the Union in 1863.

Albers Equal-Area Projection

0   300   600 Miles

0   300   600 Kilometers

The Emancipation Proclamation

1863
Abraham Lincoln issues the Emancipation Proclamation.

1864
General Grant becomes commander of the Union Army.

The surrender at Appomattox Court House

1865
General Lee surrenders at Appomattox Court House.

1863 ★ 1864 ★ 1865

▲ **1863**
The first Red Cross societies are established in Europe.

▲ **1864**
Archduke Maximilian of Austria becomes emperor of Mexico.

1 The Conflict Takes Shape

Prepare to Read

Objectives

In this section, you will
- Explain the issues that divided the nation.
- Describe the strengths and weaknesses of the North and the South.
- Identify the leaders of each side in the war.

Key Terms

border state

martial law

 Target Reading Skill

Comparison and Contrast Copy the table below. As you read the section, fill in the table with the strengths of the North and the South at the start of the war and their reasons for fighting. Add as many entries as you need.

NORTH	SOUTH
Strengths • • Reasons for fighting • •	Strengths • • Reasons for fighting • •

Main Idea Although both sides believed that their cause was just, the North had important advantages at the start of the war.

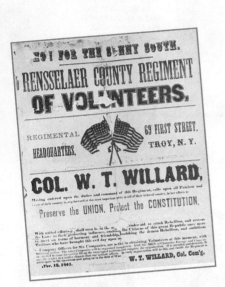

A poster calling for volunteers

Setting the Scene President Abraham Lincoln called for 75,000 volunteers to serve as soldiers in a campaign against the South. The term of enlistment was only 90 days—most northerners believed that the war would be over quickly. In the words of one confident Union supporter, "We shall crush out this rebellion as an elephant would trample on a mouse."

Southerners were just as convinced that a Confederate victory would be quick. A Confederate in North Carolina predicted, "Just throw three or four [bomb]shells among those blue-bellied Yankees and they'll scatter like sheep."

With flags held high, both northerners and southerners marched off to war. Most felt certain that a single, gallant battle would bring a quick end to the conflict. Few suspected that the Civil War would last four terrible years. By the time the fighting was over, every part of American society would be affected by the Civil War.

A Nation Divided

When the war began, each side was convinced that its cause was just. Southerners believed that they had the right to leave the Union. In fact, they called the conflict the War for Southern Independence. Southerners wanted independence so that they could keep their traditional way of life—including the institution of slavery.

Northerners, meanwhile, believed that they had to fight to save the Union. At the outset of the war, abolishing slavery was not an official goal of the North. In fact, many northerners, guided by feelings of racism, approved of slavery. Racism is the belief that one race is by nature superior to another.

In April 1861, eight slave states were still in the Union. As the war began, they had to make the difficult decision of which side to join. Their decision would greatly affect the outcome of the war. These states had more than half of the South's population and food crops. In addition, many of the South's factories were in these states.

Four of these states—Virginia,* North Carolina, Tennessee, and Arkansas—quickly joined the Confederacy. However, after some wavering between the North and South, the four **border states**—Kentucky, Missouri, Maryland, and Delaware—decided to remain in the Union. Maryland was especially critical to the Union cause since it bordered the nation's capital at Washington, D.C.

Still, there were some citizens of the border states who supported the South. In April 1861, pro-Confederate mobs attacked Union troops in Baltimore, Maryland. In response, President Lincoln declared **martial law,** or rule by the army instead of the elected government. Many people who sided with the South were arrested.

Strengths and Weaknesses

Both sides in the conflict had strengths and weaknesses as the war began. The South had the strong advantage of fighting a defensive war. "We seek no conquest," said Confederate President Jefferson Davis. "All we ask is to be let alone." If the North did not move its forces into the South, the Confederacy would remain a separate country.

The South White southerners believed that they were fighting a war for independence, similar to the American Revolution. Defending their homeland and their way of life gave them a strong reason to fight. "Our men must prevail in combat," one Confederate said, "or they will lose their property, country, freedom—in short, everything."

Confederate soldiers also enjoyed an advantage because they knew the southern countryside better. Friendly civilians often guided soldiers along obscure roads that did not appear on maps. Much of the South was wooded, too. Confederate forces used the woods for cover as they defended themselves against invading Union troops.

The South, however, had serious economic weaknesses. It had few factories to produce weapons and other vital supplies. It also had few railroads to move troops and supplies. The railroads that it did have often did not connect to one another. Tracks simply ran between two points and then stopped.

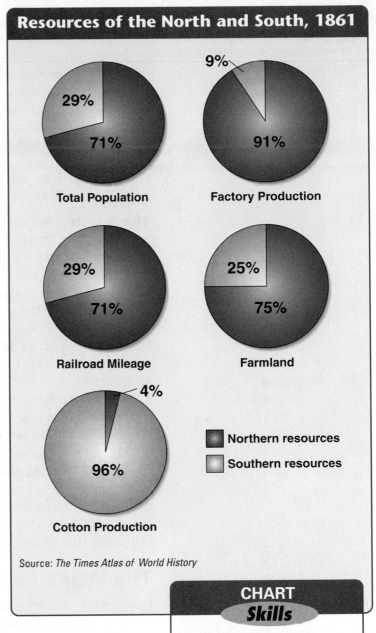

Resources of the North and South, 1861

29% / 71% — **Total Population**

9% / 91% — **Factory Production**

29% / 71% — **Railroad Mileage**

25% / 75% — **Farmland**

4% / 96% — **Cotton Production**

■ Northern resources
□ Southern resources

Source: *The Times Atlas of World History*

CHART
Skills

As the Civil War began, the North had a number of economic advantages over the South.

1. **Comprehension (a)** How much farmland did each side have? **(b)** What percentage of the nation's factories did the South have?

2. **Critical Thinking Making Predictions (a)** Which side had more railroad track? **(b)** How would this affect the war?

Economics

---

*In western Virginia, where there were few slave owners, many people supported the Union. When Virginia seceded, westerners formed their own government. West Virginia became a state of the Union in 1863.

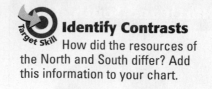

Identify Contrasts
How did the resources of the North and South differ? Add this information to your chart.

The South also had political problems. The Confederate constitution favored states' rights and limited the authority of the central government. As a result, the Confederate government often found it difficult to get things done. On one occasion, for example, the governor of Georgia insisted that only Georgian officers should command Georgian troops.

Finally, the South had a small population. Only about 9 million people lived in the Confederacy, compared with 22 million in the Union. More than one third of the southern population were enslaved African Americans. As a result, the South did not have enough people to serve as soldiers and to support the war effort.

The North The North had almost four times as many free citizens as the South. Thus, it had a large source of volunteers. It also had many people to grow food and to work in factories making supplies.

Industry was the North's greatest resource. Before the war, northern factories produced more than 90 percent of the nation's manufactured goods. Once the war began, these factories quickly began making guns, bullets, cannons, boots, uniforms, and other supplies for the Union army. In addition, the North had more than 70 percent of the nation's rail lines, which it used to transport both troops and supplies.

The North benefited from a strong navy and a large fleet of trading ships. With few warships and only a small merchant fleet, the South was unable to compete with the North at sea.

Despite these advantages, the North faced a difficult military challenge. To bring the South back into the Union, northern soldiers had to conquer a huge area. Instead of defending their homes, they were invading unfamiliar land. As Union armies marched into the South, their lines of supply would be much longer than those of the Confederates and thus more open to attack.

The War's Leaders

Leadership was a crucial factor in the Civil War. President Jefferson Davis of the Confederacy, President Abraham Lincoln of the Union, and military leaders on both sides played key roles in determining the war's outcome.

President Jefferson Davis Many people thought that Davis was a stronger leader than Lincoln. Davis's experience prepared him for the position. However, he did not want it. As one observer stated:

> 66 Mr. Davis's military instincts still predominate, and his eager wish was to have joined the army instead of being elected President. 99
>
> —Arthur James Freemantle, from *The Freemantle Diary*

Davis had attended the United States Military Academy at West Point. He had served as an officer in the Mexican War. Later, he served as Secretary of War under President Franklin Pierce. Furthermore, Davis was widely respected for his honesty and courage.

Davis, however, did not like to turn over to others the details of military planning. As a result, he spent much time worrying about small matters and arguing with his advisers.

President Abraham Lincoln At first, some northerners had doubts about Abraham Lincoln's ability to lead. He did not have much experience in national politics or military matters. However, Lincoln proved to be a patient but strong leader and a fine war planner.

Day by day, Lincoln gained the respect of those around him. Many liked his sense of humor. They noted that Lincoln even accepted criticism with a smile. When Secretary of War Edwin Stanton called Lincoln a fool, Lincoln commented, "Did Stanton say I was a fool? Then I must be one, for Stanton is generally right and he always says what he means."

Military Leaders As the war began, army officers in the South had to decide whether to stay in the Union army and fight against their home states, or join the Confederate forces.

Robert E. Lee of Virginia faced this dilemma when Lincoln asked him to command the Union army. He explains in a letter to a friend:

> 66 If Virginia stands by the old Union, so will I. But if she secedes . . . , then I will still follow my native State with my sword and, if need be, with my life. 99
> —Robert E. Lee, quoted in Carl Sandburg, *Abraham Lincoln*

Virginia did secede and Lee refused Lincoln's offer. Later, Lee became commander of the Confederate army.

Many of the army's best officers served the Confederacy. As a result, President Lincoln had trouble finding generals to match those of the South.

An American Profile

Robert E. Lee 1807–1870

Robert E. Lee came from a distinguished Virginia family. After graduating with honors from West Point, he served in the Army Corps of Engineers. During the Mexican War, his superior officer described him as "the very best soldier I ever saw in the field." Despite that, Lee hated the horror of war.

When the Civil War broke out, Lee was torn between the Union and his home state of Virginia. In the end, he chose Virginia. "I have not been able to make up my mind to raise my hand against my relatives, my children, my home," he said.

Why did Lee choose to side with the Confederacy?

★ ★ ★ Section 1 Assessment ★ ★ ★

Recall
1. **Identify** Explain the significance of **(a)** Abraham Lincoln, **(b)** Jefferson Davis, **(c)** Robert E. Lee.
2. **Define** **(a)** border state, **(b)** martial law.

Comprehension
3. What were the goals of each side as the war began?
4. Describe two advantages that the North had over the South at the start of the Civil War.
5. Describe one strength and one weakness of **(a)** President Abraham Lincoln, **(b)** President Jefferson Davis.

Critical Thinking and Writing
6. **Exploring the Main Idea** Review the Main Idea statement at the beginning of this section. Then, list five statements from the section that support the main idea.
7. **Making Decisions** Imagine that you are an army officer from the South at the beginning of the war. Would you side with the Union or with the Confederacy? Give at least two reasons for your decision.

ACTIVITY

Analyzing a Chart
Study the chart on page 487. Then, use the information on the chart to write a report analyzing the strengths and weaknesses of each side at the start of the Civil War. Based on your analysis, which side do you think will win the war? Explain.

2 No Easy Victory

Prepare to Read

Objectives

In this section, you will
- Describe the strategies each side adopted to win the war.
- Explain how early encounters dispelled hopes for a quick end to the war.
- Identify the victories of the Confederates.
- List the victories of the Union.

Key Terms

Battle of Bull Run

Virginia

Monitor

Battle of Antietam

Battle of Fredericksburg

Battle of Chancellorsville

Battle of Shiloh

Target Reading Skill

Main Idea As you read, prepare an outline of the section. Use roman numerals to indicate major headings, capital letters for subheadings, and numbers for supporting details.

> I. **Strategies for Victory**
>   A. **Union plans**
>   1.
>   2.
>   3.
>   B. **Confederate plans**
>   1.
>   2.
> II. **Early Encounters**

Main Idea Despite hopes for a quick victory, both northerners and southerners soon learned that they were in for a long, difficult struggle.

Bullet caught in a shoulder plate

Setting the Scene At first, the armies of the North and the South marched proudly off to war. Each side expected a quick and painless victory. The reality of war soon shattered this expectation. Over and over, soldiers wrote home describing the awful face of battle:

> 66 I never saw so many broken down and exhausted men in all my life. I was sick as a horse, and as wet with blood and sweat as I could be. . . . Our tongues were parched and cracked for water, and our faces blackened with powder and smoke. 99
> —quoted by Shelby Foote in *The Civil War: A Narrative*

It soon became clear that there would be no quick end to the struggle. Both sides began to dig in for a long, difficult war.

Strategies for Victory

The North and South had different strategies for victory. The Union planned an aggressive campaign against the South. The South, meanwhile, planned to hold tight until the North lost the will to fight.

Union Plans First, the Union planned to use its navy to blockade southern ports. This would cut off the South's supply of manufactured goods from Europe.

In the East, Union generals aimed to seize Richmond, Virginia, the Confederate capital. They thought that they might end the war quickly by capturing the Confederate government.

In the West, the Union planned to seize control of the Mississippi River. This would prevent the South from using the river to supply its troops. It would also separate Arkansas, Texas, and Louisiana from the rest of the Confederacy.

Confederate Plans The South's strategy was simpler: The Confederate army would fight a defensive war until northerners tired of fighting. If the war became unpopular in the North, President Lincoln would have to stop the war and recognize the South's independence.

The Confederacy counted on European money and supplies to help fight the war. Southern cotton was important to the textile mills of England and other countries. Southerners were confident that Europeans would recognize the Confederacy as an independent nation and continue to buy southern cotton for their factories.

Early Encounters

"Forward to Richmond! Forward to Richmond!" Every day for more than a month, the influential *New York Tribune* blazed this war cry across its front page. At last, responding to popular pressure, President Lincoln ordered an attack.

Battle of Bull Run On July 21, 1861, Union troops set out from Washington, D.C., for Richmond, about 100 miles away. Hundreds of Washingtonians, in a festive mood, rode out along with them to watch the battle.

The Union troops had not gone far when they met up with Confederate soldiers. A battle quickly followed. It took place near a small Virginia stream known as Bull Run.

At first, Union forces succeeded in breaking up Confederate battle lines. "The war is over!" yelled some soldiers from Massachusetts. But General Thomas Jackson rallied the Virginia troops on a nearby hill. "Look!" cried a Confederate officer to his men, "There is Jackson standing like a stone wall! Rally behind the Virginians!" From that day on, the general was known as "Stonewall" Jackson.

In the end, it was the Union troops who panicked and ran. "Off they went," reported one observer, "across fields, toward the woods, anywhere, everywhere, to escape." For most of the soldiers, the retreat did not stop until they reached Washington, D.C.

The Battle of Bull Run showed both the Union and the Confederacy that their soldiers needed training. It also showed that the war would be long and bloody.

Caution, Delay, and Retreat After the shocking disaster at Bull Run, President Lincoln appointed General George McClellan as commander of the Union army of the East, known as the Army of the Potomac. McClellan, a superb organizer, transformed inexperienced recruits into an army of trained soldiers prepared for battle.

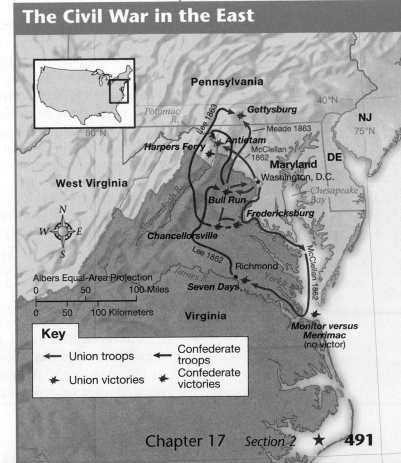

GEOGRAPHY Skills

Early in the war, Union armies were unsuccessful in their attempts to capture Richmond, the Confederate capital.

1. **Location** On the map, locate (a) Washington, D.C., (b) Richmond, (c) Bull Run, (d) Chancellorsville.

2. **Movement** Describe the route that General McClellan took when he tried to capture Richmond in 1862.

3. **Critical Thinking Making Decisions** Do you think that the Confederacy made a wise decision in locating its capital at Richmond? Explain.

The Civil War in the East

Pennsylvania

Potomac R.

Lee 1863

Gettysburg

Meade 1863

NJ

Harpers Ferry

Antietam

McClellan 1862

40°N

75°N

West Virginia

Maryland

Washington, D.C.

DE

Chesapeake Bay

Shenandoah R.

Bull Run

Fredericksburg

Chancellorsville

Lee 1862

James R.

Richmond

York R.

McClellan 1862

Albers Equal-Area Projection

0   50   100 Miles

0   50   100 Kilometers

Seven Days

Virginia

Monitor versus Merrimac (no victor)

Key

← Union troops

← Confederate troops

★ Union victories

★ Confederate victories

N W E S

80°N

McClellan, however, was very cautious. He delayed leading his troops into battle. Newspapers reported "all quiet along the Potomac" so often that the phrase became a national joke. Finally, President Lincoln lost patience. "If General McClellan does not want to use the army," the President snapped, "I would like to borrow it."

At last, in March 1862, McClellan and most of his troops left Washington and sailed down the Potomac River. After landing south of Richmond, McClellan began inching slowly toward the Confederate capital.

Learning of the Union approach, General Robert E. Lee launched a series of counterattacks. At the same time, Lee sent General Stonewall Jackson north to threaten Washington. As a result, Lincoln was prevented from sending the rest of the Union army to help McClellan. Cautious as usual, McClellan abandoned the attack and retreated.

Naval Action Early in the war, Union ships blockaded southern ports. At first, some small, fast ships slipped through the blockade. These "blockade runners" brought everything from matches to guns to the Confederacy.

In time, however, the blockade became more effective. Trade through southern ports dropped by more than 90 percent. The South desperately needed a way to break the Union blockade. One method it tried was the ironclad ship.

Confederates took over an abandoned Union warship, the USS *Merrimack.* They covered it with iron plates and renamed it the *Virginia.* On its first day out in March 1862, the *Virginia* destroyed two Union ships and drove three more aground. Union cannonballs bounced harmlessly off the *Virginia's* metal skin.

The Union countered with its own ironclad, the *Monitor.* The two ships clashed in the waters off Hampton Roads, Virginia. Despite an exhausting battle, neither vessel seriously damaged the other, and both withdrew. Two months later Confederates had to sink the *Virginia* when the Union captured Norfolk. The Union eventually built more than 50 ironclads.

Ironclad ships changed naval warfare. However, the South was never again able to mount a serious attack against the Union navy. The Union blockade held throughout the war.

Antietam In September 1862, General Lee took the offensive and marched his troops north into Maryland. He believed that a southern victory on northern soil would be a great blow to northern morale.

Luck was against Lee, however. At an abandoned Confederate campsite, a Union officer found a copy of Lee's battle plan. It was wrapped around three cigars, left behind by a careless general. General McClellan was overjoyed to have the information. "If I cannot whip 'Bobbie Lee,' I will be willing to go home," he boasted.

However, McClellan was slow to act. Finally, after a few days, he attacked Lee's main force at Antietam (an TEE tuhm) on September 17. In the day-long battle that followed, more than 23,000 Union and Confederate soldiers were killed or wounded.

Antietam National Battlefield

On September 17, 1862, Union and Confederate troops faced one another at Antietam Creek near Sharpsburg, Maryland.

Today, 103 monuments at Antietam honor those who fought there. Most of the monuments were built by Civil War veterans. The barrels of 500 cannons, which were used in the Civil War, are on the battlefield. These mark the location of artillery during the battle.

Go Online
PHSchool.com

Virtual Field Trip For an interactive look at the Antietam battle site, visit PHSchool.com, **Web Code mfd-1701.**

On the night of September 18, Lee ordered his troops to slip back into Virginia. The Confederates breathed a sigh of relief when they saw that McClellan was not pursuing them.

Neither side was a clear winner at the Battle of Antietam. The North was able to claim victory, though, because Lee had ordered his forces to withdraw. As a result, northern morale increased. Still, President Lincoln was keenly disappointed. General McClellan had failed to follow up his victory by pursuing the Confederates. In November, Lincoln appointed General Ambrose Burnside to replace McClellan as commander of the Army of the Potomac.

Confederate Victories in the East

Two stunning victories for the Confederacy came in late 1862 and 1863. In December 1862, Union forces set out once again toward Richmond.

Meeting Burnside's army outside Fredericksburg, Virginia, Lee's forces dug into the crest of a hill. There, in a strong defensive position, Confederate guns mowed down wave after wave of charging Union troops. The Battle of Fredericksburg was one of the Union's worst defeats. (See page 495.)

Half a year later, in May 1863, Lee, aided by Stonewall Jackson, again outmaneuvered Union forces. The Battle of Chancellorsville took place on thickly wooded ground near Chancellorsville, Virginia. Lee and Jackson defeated the Union troops in three days. Victory came at a high price for the South, however. During the battle, nervous

An American Profile

Ulysses S. Grant 1822–1885

General Ulysses S. Grant's troops had the Confederates surrounded at Fort Donelson. Confederate General Simon Bolivar Buckner wanted to discuss terms of surrender.

Grant's response was to the point: "No terms except an unconditional and immediate surrender can be accepted." Buckner immediately surrendered the fort. Grant's victory caused great celebration in the North. It also earned him the nickname "Unconditional Surrender" Grant.

What characteristics did Grant reveal by his actions at Fort Donelson?

Confederate sentries fired at what they thought was an approaching Union soldier. The "Union soldier" was General Stonewall Jackson. Several days later, Jackson died as a result of his injuries.

Union Victories in the West

In the West, Union forces met with better success. As you have read, the Union strategy was to seize control of the Mississippi River. General Ulysses S. Grant began moving toward that goal. In February 1862, Grant attacked and captured Fort Henry and Fort Donelson in Tennessee. These Confederate forts guarded two important tributaries of the Mississippi.

Grant now pushed south to Shiloh, a village on the Tennessee River. There, on April 6, he was surprised by Confederate forces. By the end of the day, the Confederates had driven the Union troops back toward the river.

Grant now showed the toughness and determination that would enable him to win many battles in the future. That night, one of Grant's soldiers approached him. The officer thought Union forces should retreat. But, seeing Grant's stubborn face, the officer only said, "Well, Grant, we've had the devil's own day, haven't we?"

"Yes," Grant replied. "Lick 'em tomorrow, though."

And they did. With the aid of reinforcements, Grant beat back the Confederates and won the **Battle of Shiloh.** It was, however, one of the bloodiest encounters of the Civil War.

While Grant was fighting at Shiloh, the Union navy moved to gain control of the Mississippi River. In April 1862, Union gunboats captured New Orleans. Other ships seized Memphis, Tennessee. By capturing these two cities, the Union controlled both ends of the Mississippi. The South could no longer use the river as a supply line.

★ ★ ★ Section 2 Assessment ★ ★ ★

Recall

1. **Identify** Explain the significance of **(a)** Stonewall Jackson, **(b)** Battle of Bull Run, **(c)** George McClellan, **(d)** *Virginia,* **(e)** *Monitor,* **(f)** Battle of Antietam, **(g)** Battle of Fredericksburg, **(h)** Battle of Chancellorsville, **(i)** Ulysses S. Grant, **(j)** Battle of Shiloh.

Comprehension

2. **Describe (a)** the North's three-part plan for defeating the South, **(b)** the South's plan to defeat the North.
3. What did both sides learn from the Battle of Bull Run?

4. Why was the Confederate victory at Fredericksburg critical?
5. How did Union victories at New Orleans and Memphis affect the South?

Critical Thinking and Writing

6. **Exploring the Main Idea** Review the Main Idea statement at the beginning of this section. Make a list of five events and their results during the first two years of the war.
7. **Analyzing Ideas** Analyze the meaning of this statement: "The South could win the war by not losing, but the North could win only by winning."

ACTIVITY

Connecting to Today
Both the Union and Confederate navies developed ironclad ships during the Civil War. Use the Internet to research technological advances in modern naval vessels. Prepare an oral class presentation including pictures. For help in completing the activity, visit PHSchool.com, **Web Code mfd-1702.**

The Battle of Fredericksburg

Fredericksburg, Virginia, was located between Washington, D.C., and Richmond, the Confederate capital. Taking Fredericksburg was a step toward capturing Richmond.

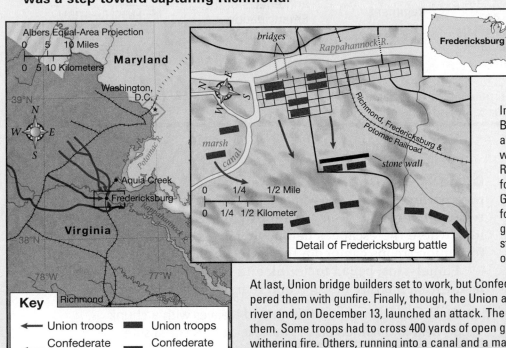

Detail of Fredericksburg battle

Key

← Union troops
← Confederate troops
┼┼┼┼ Key railroads
▬ Union troops
▬ Confederate troops

In the fall of 1862, General Ambrose Burnside began moving his Union army toward Fredericksburg. They were stopped by the Rappahannock River. While the Union troops waited for engineers to bridge the river, General Robert E. Lee's Confederate forces occupied the city and the high ground behind it. They took up a strong position, overlooking a large, open field.

At last, Union bridge builders set to work, but Confederate snipers peppered them with gunfire. Finally, though, the Union army got across the river and, on December 13, launched an attack. The terrain was against them. Some troops had to cross 400 yards of open ground in the face of withering fire. Others, running into a canal and a marsh, were forced to attack the Confederate line at its strongest point—the top of a hill.

The battle was a disaster for the Union army. For hours, soldiers marched up the hill only to be mowed down by gunfire. Finally, Burnside halted the attack. His army had lost 13,000 men, compared with only 5,000 for Lee's.

ACTIVITY

You are a correspondent for a northern or southern newspaper, and you saw the Battle of Fredericksburg. Write a description of the battle that explains how geography affected the outcome.

3 A Promise of Freedom

Prepare to Read

Objectives

In this section, you will
- Identify Lincoln's primary goal in the war.
- Describe the effects of the Emancipation Proclamation.
- Explain African Americans' contribution to the war effort both in the Union army and behind Confederate lines.

Key Terms

emancipate

Emancipation Proclamation

54th Massachusetts Regiment

Fort Wagner

Target Reading Skill

Cause and Effect Copy the chart. As you read, complete the chart to show the causes and effects of the Emancipation Proclamation.

```
              ┌─ CAUSES ─┐
              1.
              2. Lincoln wanted to weaken
                 the Confederacy's ability to
                 fight

              ┌ EMANCIPATION ┐
              │ PROCLAMATION │

              ┌─ EFFECTS ─┐
              1. Union fighting to end slavery
              2.
```

Main Idea By issuing the Emancipation Proclamation, Lincoln expanded the goals of the war to include the ending of slavery.

African American soldier

Setting the Scene John Finnely heard the news first thing in the morning: Ten slaves had run off the night before. Finnely, a twelve-year-old slave on a plantation in Alabama, had a pretty good idea where the escapees had gone. Most certainly, they had headed for Union troops camped a few miles to the north—and freedom.

Finnely, too, began to "think and think 'bout gittin' freedom." At last, with a mixture of hope and fear, he decided to make the break:

> ❝ I makes up my mind to go and I leaves with a chunk of meat and cornbread . . . half skeert to death. I sure have my eyes open and my ears forward, watchin' for the [Confederate slave patrols]. I step off the road in the night, at the sight of anything, and in the day I take to the woods. ❞
>
> —John Finnely, quoted in *Remembering Slavery*

At first, the Civil War was not a war against slavery. But as thousands of slaves like John Finnely rushed into the arms of Union troops with the hope of freedom, some northerners began to rethink the aims of the war.

Lincoln's Goal

The Civil War began as a war to restore the Union, not to end slavery. President Lincoln made this point clear in a letter that was widely distributed:

> ❝ If I could save the Union without freeing any slave, I would do it; and if I could save it by freeing all the slaves, I would do it; and if I could do it by freeing some and leaving others alone, I would also do that. ❞
>
> —Abraham Lincoln, August 22, 1862, quoted in Carl Sandburg, *Abraham Lincoln*

Lincoln had a reason for handling the slavery issue cautiously. As you have read, four slave states remained in the Union. The President did not want to do anything that might cause these states to shift their loyalty to the Confederacy. The resources of the border states might allow the South to turn the tide of the war.

The Emancipation Proclamation

By mid-1862, Lincoln came to believe that he could save the Union only by broadening the goals of the war. He decided to emancipate, or free, enslaved African Americans living in the Confederacy. In the four loyal slave states, however, slaves would not be freed. Nor would slaves be freed in Confederate lands that had already been captured by the Union, such as the city of New Orleans.

Motives and Timing Lincoln had practical reasons for his emancipation plan. At the start of the Civil War, more than 3 million slaves labored for the Confederacy. They helped grow the food that fed Confederate soldiers. They also worked in iron and lead mines that were vital to the South's war effort. Some served as nurses and cooks for the army. Lincoln knew that emancipation would weaken the Confederacy's ability to carry on the war.

However, Lincoln did not want to anger slave owners in the Union. Also, he knew that many northerners opposed freedom for enslaved African Americans. Lincoln hoped to introduce the idea of emancipation slowly, by limiting it to territory controlled by the Confederacy.

The President had another motive. As you read in Chapter 16, Lincoln believed that slavery was wrong. When he felt that he could act to free slaves without threatening the Union, he did so.

Lincoln was concerned about the timing of his announcement. The war was not going well for the Union. He did not want Americans to think he was freeing slaves as a desperate effort to save a losing cause. He waited for a victory to announce his plan.

On September 22, 1862, following the Union victory at Antietam, Lincoln issued a preliminary proclamation. He issued the formal Emancipation Proclamation on January 1, 1863.

Impact of the Proclamation Because the rebelling states were not under Union control, no slaves actually gained their freedom on January 1, 1863. Still, the Emancipation Proclamation changed the purpose of the war. Now, Union troops were fighting to end slavery as well as to save the Union.

The opponents of slavery greeted the proclamation with joy. In Boston, African American abolitionist Frederick Douglass witnessed one of the many emotional celebrations that took place:

> ❝ The effect of this announcement was startling . . .
> and the scene was wild and grand. . . . My old friend
> Rue, a Negro preacher, . . . expressed the heartfelt emo-
> tion of the hour, when he led all voices in the anthem,
> 'Sound the loud timbrel o'er Egypt's dark sea, Jehovah
> hath triumphed, his people are free!' ❞
> —Frederick Douglass, *Life and Times of Frederick Douglass*

Primary Source

The Emancipation Proclamation

On January 1, 1863, President Lincoln issued the Emancipation Proclamation. The document declared the following:
"On the 1st day of January, in the year of our Lord 1863, all persons held as slaves within any state or . . . part of a state [whose] people . . . shall then be in rebellion against the United States, shall be then, thenceforward, and forever free."

Analyzing Primary Sources
Were all enslaved African Americans freed? Explain.

Understand Effects
Which effects of the Emancipation Proclamation are discussed in this paragraph? Add these to your chart.

Viewing History

Assault on Fort Wagner

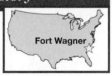

Fort Wagner

In this painting by Tom Lovell, African American soldiers of the 54th Massachusetts Regiment charge Confederate troops at Fort Wagner. Nearly half the regiment died in the failed attack, including the regiment's commander, Colonel Robert Gould Shaw. **Applying Information** *Why did African Americans have their own regiments?*

In the South, Lincoln's proclamation was seen as a "fiend's act" that destroyed expensive property. The proclamation won the sympathy of Europeans, especially workers. As a result, it became less likely that Britain or any other European country would come to the aid of the South.

African American Contributions

When the war began, thousands of free blacks volunteered to fight for the Union. At first, federal law forbade African Americans to serve as soldiers. When Congress repealed that law in 1862, however, both free African Americans and escaped slaves enlisted in the Union army.

In the Union Army The army assigned African American volunteers to all-black units, commanded by white officers. At first, the black troops served only as laborers. They performed noncombat duties such as building roads and guarding supplies. Black troops received only half the pay of white soldiers.

African American soldiers protested against this policy of discrimination that denied them the same treatment as other soldiers. Gradually, conditions changed. By 1863, African American troops were fighting in major battles against the Confederates. In 1864, the United States War Department announced that all soldiers would receive equal pay. By the end of the war, about 200,000 African Americans had fought for the Union. Nearly 40,000 lost their lives.

Acts of Bravery One of the most famous African American units in the Union army was the **54th Massachusetts Regiment.** The 54th accepted African Americans from all across the North. Frederick Douglass helped recruit troops for the regiment, and two of his sons served in it.

On July 18, 1863, the 54th Massachusetts Regiment led an attack on **Fort Wagner** near Charleston, South Carolina. Under heavy fire, troops fought their way into the fort before being forced to withdraw. In the desperate fighting, almost half the regiment was killed.

The courage of the 54th Massachusetts and other regiments helped to win respect for African American soldiers. Sergeant William Carney of the 54th Massachusetts was the first of 16 African American soldiers to win the Medal of Honor in the Civil War. Such soldiers had "proved themselves among the bravest of the brave," Secretary of War Edwin Stanton told Lincoln.

Behind Confederate Lines Despite the Emancipation Proclamation, African Americans still worked in the South as slaves on plantations. However, many slaves slowed down their work or refused to work at all. In this way, they hoped to weaken the South's war effort. They knew that when victorious Union troops arrived in their area, they would be free.

Thousands of enslaved African Americans took direct action to free themselves. Whenever a Union army appeared, slaves from all over the area would flee their former masters. They crossed the Union lines to freedom. By the end of the war, about one fourth of the South's enslaved population had escaped to freedom.

★ ★ ★ Section 3 Assessment ★ ★ ★

Recall

1. **Identify** Explain the significance of **(a)** Emancipation Proclamation, **(b)** 54th Massachusetts Regiment, **(c)** Fort Wagner.
2. **Define** emancipate.

Comprehension

3. Why was President Lincoln cautious about making the abolition of slavery a goal of the war?
4. How did the Emancipation Proclamation affect the status of enslaved African Americans?
5. How did enslaved African Americans help to hurt the Confederate war effort?

Critical Thinking and Writing

6. **Exploring the Main Idea** Review the Main Idea statement at the beginning of this section. Write a newspaper article explaining why Lincoln issued the Emancipation Proclamation.
7. **Analyzing Primary Sources** In 1861, Frederick Douglass said, "This is no time to fight with one hand when both hands are needed. This is no time to fight with only your white hand, and allow your black hand to remain tied!" **(a)** What did Douglass mean by this statement? **(b)** Did the United States Congress agree with Douglass? Explain.

ACTIVITY

Writing a Poem A monument is being built to honor the courageous African American soldiers of the Civil War. Write a poem to be inscribed on the monument, mentioning some of the facts you learned in this section.

4 Hardships of War

Prepare to Read

Objectives

In this section, you will
- Describe conditions for Confederate and Union soldiers.
- Explain what problems each side faced at home.
- Summarize how the war affected the economies of the North and the South.
- Identify the role women played in the war.

Key Terms

Copperhead

draft

habeas corpus

income tax

inflation

profiteer

Target Reading Skill

Comparison and Contrast Copy this incomplete Venn diagram. As you read, fill in key facts about conditions in the North and South during the Civil War. Write common characteristics in the overlapping section.

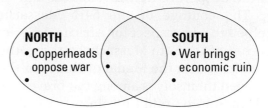

NORTH
- Copperheads oppose war
-

SOUTH
- War brings economic ruin
-

Main Idea The demands of the war hurt civilians as well as soldiers on both sides, but the problems were worse in the Confederate States.

Homecoming

Setting the Scene John Jones knew that he was not alone in the hardships he experienced. All he had to do was look around in the Confederate capital of Richmond. Some of the city's residents, he noted, looked "like vagabonds . . . gaunt and pale with hunger." As for his own family:

> 66 My daughter's cat is staggering today, for want of animal food. Sometimes I fancy I stagger myself. We do not average two ounces of meat daily; and some do not get any for several days together. 99
> —John B. Jones, *A Rebel War Clerk's Diary*

The Civil War caused hardships not only for soldiers but for people at home as well. Southerners were especially hard hit, because most of the fighting took place in the South. But for both North and South, the war affected every area of life.

The Hard Life of Soldiers

On both sides, most soldiers were under the age of 21. War, however, quickly turned gentle boys into tough men. Soldiers drilled and marched for long hours. They slept on the ground even in rain and snow. In combat, boys of 18 learned to stand firm as cannon blasts shook the earth and bullets whizzed past their ears.

As the death toll rose, the age restrictions for soldiers were relaxed. The South drafted boys as young as 17 and men as old as 50.

New technology added to the horror of war. Cone-shaped bullets made rifles twice as accurate. Improved cannons hurled exploding shells several miles. The new weapons had deadly results. In most battles, one fourth or more of the soldiers were killed or wounded.

Sick and wounded soldiers faced other horrors. Medical care on the battlefield was crude. Surgeons routinely amputated injured arms and legs. At the time, doctors did not know how germs cause infection and disease. As a result, minor wounds often became infected. In addition, poor sanitary conditions in the army camps allowed disease to spread rapidly. Diseases such as pneumonia and malaria killed more men than guns or cannons did.

On both sides, prisoners of war faced horrifying conditions. At Andersonville, a prison camp in Georgia, many Union prisoners died of disease or starvation.

The difficult life of soldiers led many to desert. One out of every seven Union soldiers and one out of every nine Confederate soldiers deserted.

Opposition to War in the North

Some northerners opposed using force to keep the South in the Union. Supporters of the war called these people Copperheads, after the poisonous snake. Other northerners supported the war but opposed the way Lincoln was conducting it.

The Draft Law As the war dragged on, public support dwindled. When the war began, the North offered men money to enlist. However, some men abused the system. They would sign up, collect the money, and then desert. Soon, however, there was a shortage of volunteers to serve in the Union army.

Viewing History

Battlefield Medicine

United States

Improved weapons during the Civil War made the injuries suffered by soldiers worse. Soldiers hit with the Minié ball suffered severe bone damage. Shown at left are the tools used by surgeons to amputate the limb. Unlike today, surgeons at that time worked without gloves, antiseptic, or masks. Now, there are better ways to care for wounds and, as shown at right, improved surgical procedures. **Drawing Conclusions** *How has technology been an advantage and a disadvantage in war?*

LINKING PAST AND PRESENT

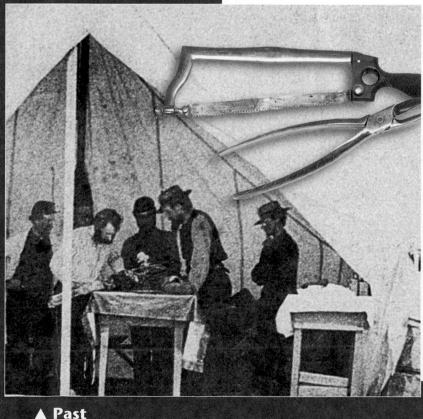

▲ Past

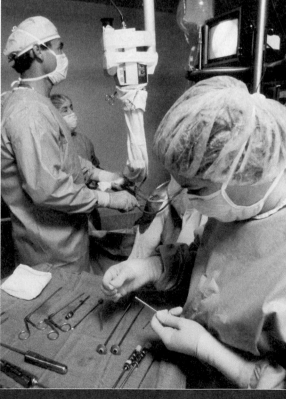

▲ Present

Congress passed a **draft** law in 1863. It required all able-bodied males between the ages of 20 and 45 to serve in the military if they were called. Under the law, a man could avoid the draft by paying the government $300 or by hiring someone to serve in his place. This angered many people, who began to see the Civil War as "a rich man's war and a poor man's fight."

Riots in the Cities Opposition to the draft law led to riots in several northern cities. The law had gone into effect soon after Lincoln issued the Emancipation Proclamation. Some white northerners, especially recent immigrants in the cities, believed that they were being forced to fight to end slavery. They also worried that they would have to compete with free African Americans for jobs.

The worst riot took place in New York City during July 1863. For four days, white workers attacked free blacks. Rioters also attacked rich New Yorkers who had paid to avoid serving in the army. At least 74 people were killed during the riot.

President Lincoln moved to stop the riots and other "disloyal practices." Several times, he suspended **habeas corpus** (HAY bee uhs KOR puhs), the right to be charged or have a hearing before being jailed. Lincoln argued that the Constitution allowed him to deny people their rights "when in the cases of rebellion or invasion, the public safety may require it." The President also said that those arrested could be tried under the stricter rules of a military court. Eventually, nearly 14,000 people were arrested. However, most were never charged with a specific crime or brought to trial.

Problems in the South

President Davis, meanwhile, struggled to create a strong federal government for the Confederacy. Many southerners firmly believed in states' rights. They resisted paying taxes to a central government. At one point, Georgia even threatened to secede from the Confederacy!

Like the North, the South was forced to pass a draft law to fill its army. However, men who owned or supervised more than 20 slaves did not have to serve. Southern farmers who had few or no slaves resented this law.

Near the end of the war, the South no longer had enough white men to fill the ranks. Robert E. Lee urged that enslaved African Americans be allowed to serve as soldiers. Desperate, the Confederate congress finally agreed. The war ended, however, before any enslaved people put on Confederate uniforms.

The Northern Economy

The Civil War cost far more than any previous war. The Union had to use several strategies to raise money. In some ways, however, war helped the North's economy.

Taxation and Inflation To pay for the war, Congress established the nation's first **income tax,** or tax on people's earnings, in 1861. A new agency, the Internal Revenue Bureau, oversaw the collection process. The Union also issued bonds worth millions of dollars. Still,

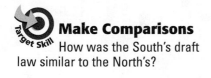
Make Comparisons
How was the South's draft law similar to the North's?

taxes and bonds did not raise enough money. To get the funds it needed, the North printed more than $400 million in paper money.

As the money supply increased, each dollar was worth less. In response, businesses charged more for their goods. The North was experiencing **inflation,** a rise in prices and a decrease in the value of money. During the war, prices for goods nearly doubled in the North.

Economic Benefits The war helped the North's economy in several ways. Since many farmers went off to fight, there was a greater need for machines to plant and harvest crops. The purchase of reapers rose to nearly 165,000 during the war. As a result, farm production actually went up during the war.

The wartime demand for clothing, shoes, guns, and other goods helped many northern industries. Some manufacturers made fortunes by profiteering. **Profiteers** charged excessive prices for goods that the government desperately needed for the war.

The Southern Economy

For the South, war brought economic ruin. The South had to struggle with the cost of the war, the loss of the cotton trade, and severe shortages brought on by the Union blockade.

The Economy Suffers To raise money, the Confederacy imposed an income tax and a tax-in-kind. The tax-in-kind required farmers to turn over one tenth of their crops to the government. The government took crops because it knew that southern farmers had little money.

Like the North, the South printed paper money. It printed so much that wild inflation set in. By 1865, one Confederate dollar was worth only two cents in gold. Prices were especially high in Richmond, where a barrel of flour was $275 in early 1864, potatoes were $25 a bushel, and butter was $15 a pound.

The war did serious damage to the cotton trade, the South's main source of income. Early in the war, President Davis halted cotton shipments to Britain. He hoped to force Britain to side with the South in return for renewed shipments of cotton. The tactic backfired. Britain simply bought more cotton from Egypt and India. Davis succeeded only in cutting the South's income.

Effects of the Blockade The Union blockade created severe shortages in the South. Confederate armies sometimes had to wait weeks for supplies of food and clothing. With few factories of its own, the South bought many of its weapons in Europe. However, the

---

Cause *and* Effect

Causes

- Issue of slavery in the territories divides the North and South
- Abolitionists want slavery to end
- South fears it will lose power in the national government
- Southern states secede after Lincoln's election
- Confederates bombard Fort Sumter

THE CIVIL WAR

Effects

- Lincoln issues the Emancipation Proclamation
- Northern economy booms
- South loses its cotton trade with Britain
- Total war destroys the South's economy
- Hundreds of thousands of Americans killed

Effects Today

- Disagreements over states' rights persist
- African Americans have equal protection under the Constitution
- Millions of Americans visit Civil War battlefields each year

GRAPHIC ORGANIZER
Skills

The Civil War was a major turning point in the history of the United States.

1. **Comprehension** How did the war affect the northern and southern economies?

2. **Critical Thinking Identifying Causes and Effects** Describe another cause or effect that could be added to this chart.

blockade cut off most deliveries from across the Atlantic. To acquire goods, the government began building and running factories. Private manufacturers were offered contracts and draft exemptions for their workers if they started making war goods.

For civilians, the blockade brought food shortages. The production of food became critical to the economy. Many plantations switched from growing cotton to raising grain and livestock, or animals raised for food. In some states, cotton production was limited.

Women in the War

Women of both the North and the South played vital roles during the war. As men left for the battlefields, women took jobs in industry and on farms.

Women's aid societies helped supply the troops with food, bedding, clothing, and medicine. Throughout the North, women held fairs and other fundraising events to pay for supplies.

Nursing the Wounded Women on both sides worked as nurses. At first, doctors were unwilling to permit even trained nurses to work in military hospitals. When wounded men began to swamp army hospitals, however, this attitude soon changed. In fact, women performed so well that nursing became an accepted occupation for women after the war.

Dorothea Dix, famous for her work reforming prisons and mental hospitals, and Clara Barton, who later founded the American Red Cross, both became nurses for the Union army. Sojourner Truth, the African American antislavery leader, worked in Union hospitals and in camps for freed slaves. In the South, Sally Tompkins set up a hospital in Richmond, Virginia.

★ ★ ★ **Section 4 Assessment** ★ ★ ★

Recall

1. **Identify** Explain the significance of **(a)** Copperhead, **(b)** Dorothea Dix, **(c)** Clara Barton, **(d)** Sojourner Truth, **(e)** Sally Tompkins.
2. **Define** **(a)** draft, **(b)** habeas corpus, **(c)** income tax, **(d)** inflation, **(e)** profiteer.

Comprehension

3. Describe three hardships faced by soldiers during the Civil War.
4. **(a)** Why did some northerners oppose the war? **(b)** How did the blockade affect the southern economy?

5. Describe three ways in which women contributed to the war effort.

Critical Thinking and Writing

6. **Exploring the Main Idea** Review the Main Idea statement at the beginning of this section. Then, write a diary entry describing conditions in the South during the later days of the Civil War.
7. **Linking Past and Present** **(a)** What advances in technology made Civil War battles deadly? **(b)** In what ways would war today be even more deadly?

ACTIVITY

Go **O**nline
PHSchool.com

Writing a Report
Use the Internet to find out more about Civil War medicine. Among the topics you might research are nurses, surgeons, field hospitals, battle wounds, and disease. Then, write a report about battlefield medicine during the Civil War. For help in completing the activity, visit PHSchool.com, **Web Code mfd-1703.**

5 The War Ends

Prepare to Read

Objectives

In this section, you will
- Explain why the Union victories at Vicksburg and Gettysburg were important.
- Describe Grant's plan for ending the war.
- Identify Lincoln's hopes for the Union after his reelection.
- Summarize why the Civil War was a major turning point in U.S. history.

Key Terms

siege

Battle of Gettysburg

Pickett's Charge

Gettysburg Address

total war

Appomattox Court House

Target Reading Skill

Sequence Copy the flowchart. As you read the section, fill in the boxes with information about the conclusion of the war.

Vicksburg
• Grant makes many attempts to capture
• Grant has brilliant plan
•

↓

Gettysburg
•
•

↓

↓

Main Idea Under the leadership of General Ulysses S. Grant, Union armies used their resources and manpower to defeat the Confederacy.

Setting the Scene

To General Ulysses S. Grant, every problem had a solution. For example, he needed telegraph lines to coordinate the march of his Union troops into the South. So, he had them strung as his troops advanced. Some of Grant's operators even learned to receive messages without a telegraph station. Touching the ends of the bare wires to their tongues, these resourceful men picked up the faint spark of the Morse Code signals.

In 1864, President Lincoln had appointed Ulysses S. Grant commander in chief of the Union army. "The art of war is simple," Grant said. "Find out where your enemy is, get at him as soon as you can and strike him as hard as you can, and keep moving on." It seemed the President had finally found the general who could lead the Union to victory.

The Fall of Vicksburg

As you have read, Confederate armies won major battles at Fredericksburg in December 1862 and at Chancellorsville in May 1863. These were gloomy days for the North. Then, in July 1863, the tide of war turned against the South as Union forces won major victories in both the East and the West.

In the West, Union triumph came along the Mississippi River. The Union, which had captured New Orleans and Memphis, already controlled both ends of the Mississippi River. Still, the Confederates held Vicksburg, Mississippi. Vicksburg sat on a cliff high above the river.

Early in 1863, Grant's forces tried again and again to seize Vicksburg. The Confederates held out bravely. At last, Grant devised a brilliant plan. Marching his troops inland, he launched a surprise attack on Jackson, Mississippi. Then, he turned west and attacked Vicksburg from the rear. (See the map on page 507.)

Civil War soldier on a telegraph pole

For more than six weeks, Grant's forces lay siege to Vicksburg. A **siege** is a military encirclement of an enemy position and blockading or bombarding it in order to force it to surrender. Finally, on July 4, 1863, the Confederates surrendered Vicksburg.

On July 9, Union forces also captured Port Hudson, Louisiana. The entire Mississippi was now under Union control. The Confederacy was split into two parts. Texas, Arkansas, and Louisiana were cut off from the rest of the Confederate states.

Union Victory at Gettysburg

Meanwhile, in the East, after his victory at Chancellorsville, General Lee moved his army north into Pennsylvania. He hoped to take the Yankees by surprise. If he succeeded in Pennsylvania, Lee planned to swing south and capture Washington, D.C.

On June 30, 1863, a Union force under General George C. Meade met part of Lee's army at the small town of Gettysburg, Pennsylvania. Both sides quickly sent in reinforcements. The three-day Battle of Gettysburg that followed was one of the most important battles of the Civil War.

On the first day of battle, July 1, the Confederates drove the Union forces out of Gettysburg. The Yankees, however, took up strong positions on Cemetery Ridge, overlooking the town.

The next day, Lee ordered an attack on both ends of the Union line. Southern troops fought hard, but the Union army was well prepared for Lee's offensive. At the end of a day of savage fighting, Lee's forces had suffered heavy casualties but failed to dislodge the Union army from its strong position.

Pickett's Charge Despite his losses, Lee decided to attack again. He wanted to "create a panic and virtually destroy the [Union] army." On July 3, he ordered General George Pickett to lead 15,000 men in a daring charge against the center of the Union line. To reach their target, Pickett's men would have to march 1,000 yards across open ground and climb up a steep slope within clear view of the enemy.

This last attack led by Pickett is known as Pickett's Charge. Pickett gave the order to charge. As the men rushed forward, Union guns opened fire. Row after row of soldiers fell to the ground, dead. The battle noise, one soldier recalled, was "strange and terrible, a sound that came from thousands of human throats . . . like a vast mournful roar."

Pickett's Charge failed. The steady barrage of bullets and shells kept all but a few Confederate soldiers from reaching the Union lines. The next day, a Union officer trying to ride over the battlefield could not because "the dead and wounded lay too thick to guide a horse through them."

As the survivors limped back, Lee rode among them. "It's all my fault," he admitted humbly. Lee had no choice but to retreat. After they were defeated at Gettysburg, the Confederates would never invade the North again.

Geography and History

The Vicksburg Campaign

Set on high bluffs overlooking the Mississippi River, Vicksburg was a major strategic target during the Civil War. If Union forces captured Vicksburg, they would control the river and split the Confederacy into two parts. "Vicksburg is the key!" said President Lincoln.

The swamps, rivers, and bluffs around Vicksburg made a direct attack almost impossible. At the same time, Confederate artillery, perched high above the Mississippi, could easily blast Union ships attempting to sail past the city.

In the end, General Grant determined that the only way to subdue Vicksburg was to lay siege to the city. After 48 days of being cut off from all supplies and of constant hammering by cannon fire, the Confederates finally surrendered.

Analyze the effect of geography on the Battle of Vicksburg.

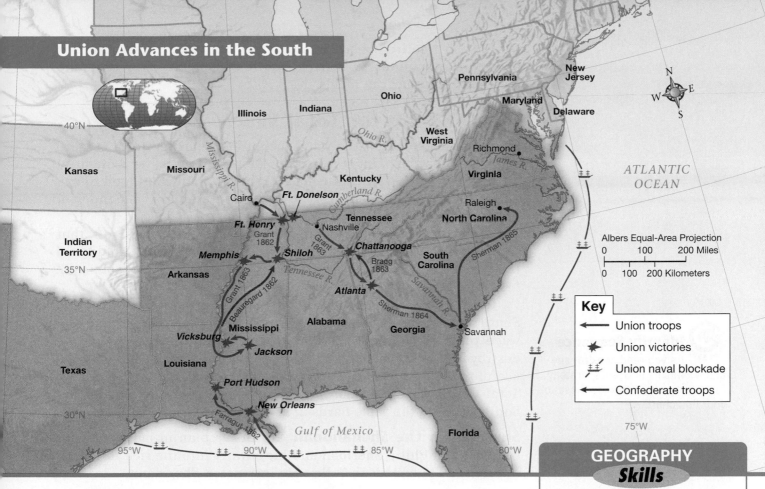

Union Advances in the South

Key
← Union troops
✷ Union victories
⚓ Union naval blockade
← Confederate troops

General Meade was proud of the victory. Lincoln, however, was disappointed. He felt that the Union army had once again allowed the Confederate troops to get away.

The Union victories at Vicksburg and Gettysburg marked the turning point of the Civil War. It seemed just a matter of time before the Confederacy would fall. However, the South was still determined to fight. The war would last another two years.

The Gettysburg Address

The Battle of Gettysburg left more than 50,000 dead or wounded. On November 19, 1863, there was a ceremony to dedicate a cemetery to the memory of those soldiers who died in the battle. President Lincoln attended the ceremony. He delivered a speech now known as the Gettysburg Address. Lincoln said that the Civil War was a test of whether or not a democratic nation could survive. He reminded Americans that their nation was founded on the belief that "all men are created equal." Lincoln told the audience:

❝ We here highly resolve that these dead shall not have died in vain—that this nation, under God, shall have a new birth of freedom—and that government of the people, by the people, for the people, shall not perish from the earth. ❞

—Abraham Lincoln, Gettysburg Address, November 19, 1863

GEOGRAPHY Skills

As the Civil War dragged on, Union armies advanced deeper and deeper into the South. General Sherman marched his troops through Georgia and the Carolinas.

1. **Location** On the map, locate **(a)** Vicksburg, **(b)** Atlanta, **(c)** Savannah.

2. **Place** What three Confederate states were cut off from the rest of the Confederacy after Union forces gained control of the Mississippi River?

3. **Critical Thinking Applying Information** Based on the map, why would the South suffer more damage than the North—no matter who won the war?

Lincoln's entire speech was only ten sentences long and took about three minutes to deliver, but it is honored as a profound statement of American ideals.

Grant's Plan for Total War

Since the beginning of the war, Lincoln had searched for a general who could lead the Union to victory. More and more, he thought of Ulysses S. Grant. After capturing Vicksburg, Grant continued to win battles in the West. In 1864, Lincoln appointed him commander of the Union forces.

Some questioned the choice, but President Lincoln felt that "Unconditional Surrender" Grant was the general who would end the war in the Union's favor. "I can't spare this man," Lincoln said. "He fights."

Grant had a plan for ending the war. He wanted to destroy the South's ability to fight. To achieve this, Grant ordered his generals to wage **total war** against the South. He wanted the Union army to destroy food, equipment, and anything else they found that might be useful to the enemy. In the past, war had been restricted to soldiers. Total war, however, did not make any distinctions. Civilians in the South suffered the same hardships as the army.

Sheridan in the Shenandoah To set his plan in motion, Grant sent General Philip Sheridan and his cavalry into the rich farmland of Virginia's Shenandoah Valley. He instructed Sheridan:

> **66** Leave nothing to invite the enemy to return. Destroy whatever cannot be consumed. Let the valley be left so that crows flying over it will have to carry their rations along with them. **99**
> —Ulysses S. Grant, quoted in Bruce Catton, *Grant Takes Command*

Sheridan obeyed. In the summer and fall of 1864, he marched through the valley, destroying farms and livestock. During the campaign, Sheridan's troops burned 2,000 barns filled with grain. There was nothing left for Lee's troops or for southern civilians.

Sherman's March to the Sea Grant also ordered General William Tecumseh Sherman to capture Atlanta, Georgia, and then march to the Atlantic coast. Like Sheridan, Sherman had orders to destroy everything useful to the South.

Sherman's troops captured Atlanta in September 1864. They began their campaign by turning the people of Atlanta out of their homes and burning a large part of the city. Then, Sherman began his "march to the sea."

As they marched through Georgia, Sherman's troops ripped up railroad tracks, built bonfires from the ties, then heated and twisted the rails. They killed livestock and tore up fields. They burned barns, homes, bridges, and factories.

Lincoln Is Reelected

Lincoln ran for reelection in 1864. At first, his defeat seemed, in his own words, "exceedingly probable." Before the capture of Atlanta,

Identify Sequence As you read, look for specific examples of Grant's strategy for waging total war. Add these to your flowchart.

Union chances for victory looked bleak. Lincoln knew that many northerners were unhappy with his handling of the war. He thought that this might cost him the election.

The Democrats nominated General George McClellan to oppose Lincoln. They adopted a resolution demanding the immediate "cessation of hostilities" against the South. Although he had commanded the Union army, McClellan was willing to compromise with the Confederacy. If peace could be achieved, he was ready to restore slavery.

Then, in September, Sherman took Atlanta, and the North rallied around Lincoln. Sheridan's smashing victories in the Shenandoah Valley in October further increased Lincoln's popular support. In the election in November, the vote was close, but Lincoln remained President.

In his second Inaugural Address, Lincoln looked forward to the coming of peace:

66 With malice toward none, with charity for all . . . let us strive . . . to bind up the nation's wounds . . . to do all which may achieve a just and a lasting peace among ourselves and with all nations. 99

—Abraham Lincoln, Second Inaugural Address

The Civil War Ends

Grant had begun a drive to capture Richmond in May 1864. Throughout the spring and summer, he and Lee fought a series of costly battles.

Northerners read with horror that 60,000 men were killed or wounded in a single month at the battles of the Wilderness, Spotsylvania, and Cold Harbor. Still, Grant pressed on. He knew that the Union could replace men and supplies. The South could not.

Lee dug in at Petersburg, near Richmond. Here, Grant kept Lee under siege for nine months. At last, with a fresh supply of troops, Grant took Petersburg on April 2, 1865. The same day, Richmond fell.

Lee and his army withdrew to a small Virginia town called **Appomattox Court House.** There, a week later, they were trapped by Union troops. Lee knew that his men would be slaughtered if he kept fighting. On April 9, 1865, Lee surrendered.

At Appomattox Court House, Grant offered generous terms of surrender to the defeated Confederate army. Soldiers were required to turn over their rifles, but officers were allowed to keep their pistols. Soldiers who had horses could keep them. Grant knew that southerners would need the animals for spring plowing. Finally, ordered Grant, "each officer and man will be allowed to return to his home, not to be disturbed by the United States authorities."

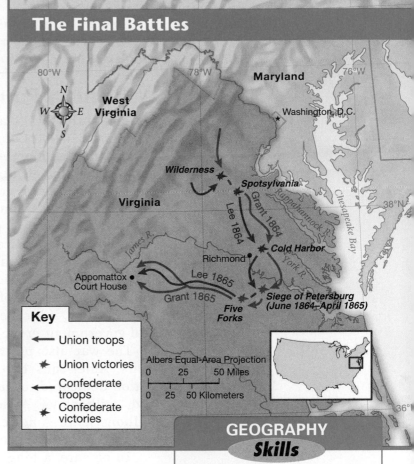

The Final Battles

Key

← Union troops

✴ Union victories

← Confederate troops

✴ Confederate victories

Albers Equal-Area Projection
0 25 50 Miles
0 25 50 Kilometers

GEOGRAPHY *Skills*

The final battles of the Civil War pitted Grant against Lee in Virginia. Finally, on April 9, 1865, Lee surrendered at Appomattox Court House.

1. **Location** On the map, locate (a) Richmond, (b) Petersburg, (c) Appomattox Court House.

2. **Place** Where did Grant lay siege to Lee's forces for nine months?

3. **Critical Thinking Applying Information** Which battle took place first: Cold Harbor or Spotsylvania? Explain.

As the Confederates surrendered, Union soldiers began to cheer. Grant ordered them to be silent. "The war is over," he said. "The rebels are our countrymen again."

A Turning Point in American History

The toll of the Civil War was immense. More than 360,000 Union soldiers and 250,000 Confederate soldiers lost their lives. No war has ever resulted in more American deaths. In dollars, the war's cost was about 20 billion. That was more than 11 times the entire amount spent by the federal government between 1789 and 1861!

The Civil War was a major turning point in American history. The balance of power was changed. The Democratic party lost its influence and the Republicans were in a commanding position. No longer would Americans speak of the nation as a confederation of states. Before the war, Americans referred to "*these* United States." After, they began speaking of "*the* United States." The idea that each state might secede, if it chose, was dead. As a result, the power of the federal government grew.

The war also put an end to slavery in the United States. For years, Americans had debated whether slavery could exist in a nation dedicated to the ideals of liberty and equality. By the war's end, millions of African Americans had gained their freedom. Millions more Americans, both North and South, began to think about what it meant to be free and equal.

To be sure, a long and difficult struggle for equality lay ahead. Yet, Lincoln's words at Gettysburg were prophetic: "We here highly resolve . . . that this nation, under God, shall have a new birth of freedom." From out of a cruel, bitter, often heart-rending war, the United States did indeed emerge a stronger, freer nation.

★ ★ ★ Section 5 Assessment ★ ★ ★

Recall

1. **Identify** Explain the significance of **(a)** Battle of Gettysburg, **(b)** Pickett's Charge, **(c)** Gettysburg Address, **(d)** Ulysses S. Grant, **(e)** William Tecumseh Sherman, **(f)** Appomattox Court House.
2. **Define** **(a)** siege, **(b)** total war.

Comprehension

3. Which Union victories were a turning point?
4. What was Grant's plan for ending the war?
5. What ideals did Lincoln express in the Gettysburg Address and his Second Inaugural Address?
6. How did the Civil War change the United States?

Critical Thinking and Writing

7. **Exploring the Main Idea** Review the Main Idea statement at the beginning of this section. Then, make a list of the major events of the years 1863–1865 of the Civil War. Indicate the importance of each.
8. **Supporting a Point of View** Some people believe that Grant's decision to wage total war on the South was wrong because it caused great suffering among civilians. Do you agree or disagree? Explain.

ACTIVITY

Writing a Speech
Suppose that you are President of the United States at the end of the Civil War. Write a speech summarizing the important events of the war and explaining what you believe the Union victory accomplished.

When the Civil War began, photography was just beginning. Pioneer photographers shouldered their bulky cameras and followed armies into battle. The result was the first detailed photographic record of a war.

These Civil War photographs, like all photographs, are valuable primary source documents. Just as with other primary sources, however, we must learn to evaluate them for accuracy and bias.

In this photograph, a family gathers at a Union Army camp in 1862.

Learn the Skill *To analyze a photograph, use the following steps:*

1. **Identify the subject.** What does the photograph show?

2. **Look for details.** What evidence does the photograph include about people, daily life, the weather, events, or the environment?

3. **Analyze the photographer's intent.** Why did the photographer take this picture? How did the photographer feel about the subject?

4. **Draw conclusions.** What can you learn from this photograph? How does it add to your understanding of history?

Practice the Skill *Answer the following questions about the photograph above:*

1. **(a)** Who are the people in the photograph? **(b)** Where are they?

2. **(a)** What tools, utensils, and furniture do you see? **(b)** Where are the people living? **(c)** What other details do you see?

3. **(a)** Why do you think the photographer took this picture? **(b)** How do you think the photographer felt about families and war?

4. What did you learn from this photograph?

Apply the Skill *See the Chapter Review and Assessment.*

CHAPTER SUMMARY

Section 1
At the start of the Civil War, both the North and the South had strengths and weaknesses. The North, however, had a larger population and industries that could make war supplies.

Section 2
The Union and Confederacy had different plans for winning the war. Early on, the Confederacy won some important eastern battles, but the Union had victories in the west.

Section 3
Lincoln issued the Emancipation Proclamation, which freed slaves in Confederate states under Union control. African American soldiers and civilians played an important role in the war.

Section 4
New technologies added to the horror of war. On both sides civilians and soldiers suffered. The southern economy fell into ruin. Many women contributed to the war effort.

Section 5
Grant's plan for total war produced a string of important Union victories. Lincoln was reelected in 1864. The war's end in 1865 represented a turning point in American history.

Building Vocabulary

Review the meaning of the vocabulary words listed below. Then, write a sentence for each word in which you define the word and describe its relationship to the Civil War.

1. border state
2. martial law
3. emancipate
4. draft
5. habeas corpus
6. inflation
7. profiteer
8. total war

Reviewing Key Facts

9. Why did each side go to war? (Section 1)
10. Why was President Lincoln unhappy with General McClellan? (Section 2)

For additional review and enrichment activities, see the interactive version of *The American Nation,* available on the Web and on CD-ROM.

Chapter Self-Test For practice test questions for Chapter 17, visit PHSchool.com, **Web Code mfa-1704.**

11. **(a)** What did the Emancipation Proclamation provide? **(b)** How did it change the nature of the war? (Section 3)
12. **(a)** Why did some northerners object to the draft law? **(b)** What was the response to the draft law in the South? (Section 4)
13. How did the Union wage total war on the South in 1864 and 1865? (Section 5)

Critical Thinking and Writing

14. **Making Generalizations** Make a generalization about the strengths and weaknesses of the North and South at the start of the war. List three facts to support your generalization.
15. **Summarizing** Write one or two sentences summarizing Lincoln's attitudes toward slavery and the war.
16. **Making Comparisons** How did the North's General Grant and the South's General Lee compare as military leaders?
17. **Connecting to Geography: Movement** Describe the effects of the Union blockade of southern ports.
18. **Synthesizing Information** Review the excerpt from Lincoln's Second Inaugural Address on page 509. How did Grant's treatment of the defeated Confederate army at Appomattox Court House reflect the ideas in the Inaugural Address?

The Union blockade caused great difficulty for southern families. Dr. Paul Barringer recalls how his family managed.

> **66** Almost at once we began to feel the pinch of war. White sugar disappeared immediately; . . . there was no sugar for the table. There was, however, an unlimited quantity of sorghum syrup, and around the barrels of sorghum, a thick crust of brown sugar often formed. This was carefully scraped off to be served with coffee and berries, the fluid product going to the slaves. **99**
>
> —Dr. Paul B. Barringer, *The Natural Bent: The Memories of Dr. Paul Barringer*

19. According to Barringer, how soon were southerners affected by the blockade?
    A. about one year later
    B. almost at once
    C. right after South Carolina seceded
    D. before Lincoln's inauguration in March 1861
20. What substitute was used for white sugar?
    A. berries
    B. a pinch of table salt
    C. liquid sorghum syrup
    D. brown sugar

Mathew Brady took this picture of Abraham Lincoln and his son, Tad, in 1864. Look at the picture. Then, answer the questions that follow.

21. What details are emphasized in the photograph?
    A. Lincoln's position in the chair.
    B. His son's lack of interest in the book.
    C. The concentration of Lincoln and his son.
    D. Tad's hand resting on his father's chair.
22. What can you learn about Lincoln from this photograph?

ACTIVITIES

Connecting With . . .
Economics

Making a Chart You are the graphic illustrator for an economics magazine. Create a flowchart to illustrate how the high cost of the Civil War led to inflation.

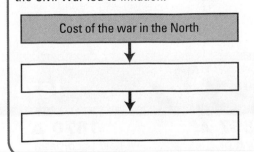

Cost of the war in the North

Connecting to Today
Planning a TV Documentary The Civil War ended slavery for African Americans. Use the Internet to find out how African Americans fight for equality today. Use what you learn to write an outline for a TV documentary on the person of your choice. For help in starting this activity, visit PHSchool.com, **Web Code mfd-1705.**

Researching Civil War Photos
Creating a Photo Essay Photographers like Mathew Brady took thousands of pictures documenting the Civil War. Use the Internet to find photographs taken of the war. Then, download selected pictures to create a photo essay of the war. For help in starting this activity, visit PHSchool.com, **Web Code mfd-1706.**

Reconstruction and the Changing South

1863–1896

1 **Early Steps to Reunion**

2 **Radical Reconstruction**

3 **The South Under Reconstruction**

4 **The End of Reconstruction**

Reward poster (left) and chair in which Lincoln was shot (right)

Thaddeus Stevens

1865

Lincoln is assassinated five days after the war ends. As the nation mourns, the issue of readmitting southern states remains unresolved.

1867

Radical Reconstruction begins. Republican leaders in Congress like Thaddeus Stevens call for harsh measures against the South.

1863

President Abraham Lincoln proposes a mild Reconstruction plan for readmitting southern states after the Civil War.

AMERICAN EVENTS

Presidential Terms:			
Abraham Lincoln	1861–1865	Andrew Johnson 1865–1869	Ulysses S. Grant 1869–1877

1860 · · **1865** · · **1870**

WORLD EVENTS

1867 ▲
The Dominion of Canada is formed.

1870 ▲
Italy becomes a unified nation.

The South After the Civil War

One by one, southern states rejoined the Union after the Civil War.

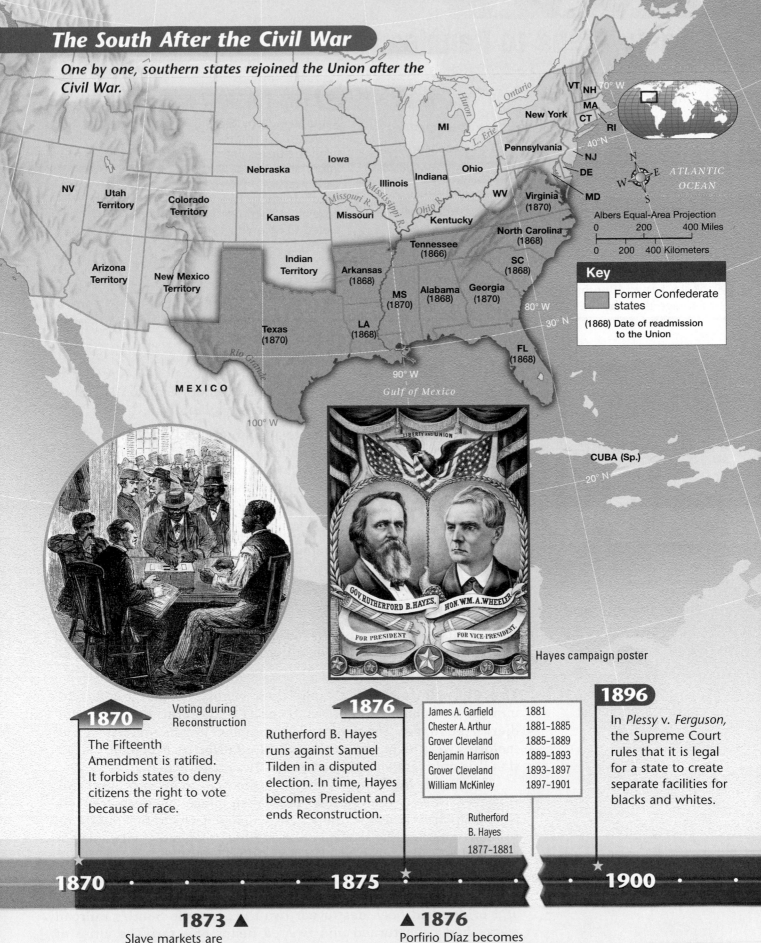

MI

New York

Pennsylvania

Ohio

Indiana

Illinois

Iowa

Nebraska

MN

NV

Utah Territory

Colorado Territory

Kansas

Missouri

Kentucky

WV

Virginia (1870)

North Carolina (1868)

Tennessee (1866)

Arizona Territory

New Mexico Territory

Indian Territory

Arkansas (1868)

MS (1870)

Alabama (1868)

Georgia (1870)

SC (1868)

Texas (1870)

LA (1868)

FL (1868)

MEXICO

Gulf of Mexico

CUBA (Sp.)

ATLANTIC OCEAN

Albers Equal-Area Projection

0 200 400 Miles

0 200 400 Kilometers

Key

Former Confederate states

(1868) Date of readmission to the Union

Hayes campaign poster

GOV. RUTHERFORD B. HAYES. FOR PRESIDENT

HON. WM. A. WHEELER. FOR VICE-PRESIDENT.

LIBERTY AND UNION

1870

Voting during Reconstruction

The Fifteenth Amendment is ratified. It forbids states to deny citizens the right to vote because of race.

1876

Rutherford B. Hayes runs against Samuel Tilden in a disputed election. In time, Hayes becomes President and ends Reconstruction.

James A. Garfield	1881
Chester A. Arthur	1881–1885
Grover Cleveland	1885–1889
Benjamin Harrison	1889–1893
Grover Cleveland	1893–1897
William McKinley	1897–1901

Rutherford B. Hayes 1877–1881

1896

In *Plessy* v. *Ferguson*, the Supreme Court rules that it is legal for a state to create separate facilities for blacks and whites.

1870 • **1875** • **1900** •

1873 ▲
Slave markets are abolished in Zanzibar.

▲ **1876**
Porfirio Díaz becomes the leader of Mexico.

1 Early Steps to Reunion

Prepare to Read

Objectives

In this section, you will
- Describe the nation's postwar problems.
- List the early steps that were taken toward Reconstruction.
- Explain how the assassination of Lincoln and the inauguration of a new President led to conflict.

Key Terms

freedmen

Reconstruction

Ten Percent Plan

amnesty

Wade-Davis Bill

Freedmen's Bureau

Thirteenth Amendment

Target Reading Skill

Sequence Copy this flowchart. As you read, fill in the boxes with information about the early years of Reconstruction. Two boxes have been completed to help you get started.

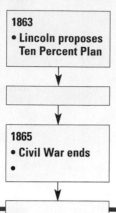

```
1863
• Lincoln proposes
  Ten Percent Plan
      ↓
┌──────────────┐
└──────────────┘
      ↓
1865
• Civil War ends
•
      ↓
┌──────────────┐
└──────────────┘
```

Main Idea After the Civil War, the country had to repair the damage done by the fighting and find a way to rebuild.

Ruined plantation house

Setting the Scene

At the end of the Civil War, the future looked bleak to many southerners. Susan Dabney Smedes described the scene facing her father, once a wealthy planter:

> 66 My father had come home to a house stripped of nearly every article of furniture and to a plantation stripped of the means of cultivating . . . it. A few mules and one cow were all that were left of the stock. 99
>
> —Susan Dabney Smedes, *Memorials of a Southern Planter*

Across the South, cities and farms lay in ruins. All southerners, black or white, faced an unfamiliar new world. At the same time, a shattered nation had to find a way to become whole again.

Postwar Problems

After four years of war, both northerners and southerners had to adjust to a changed world. The adjustment was far more difficult in the South.

The Victorious North Despite their victory, northerners faced a number of economic problems. Some 800,000 returning Union soldiers needed jobs. The government was canceling its war orders, and factories were laying off workers. Still, the North's economic disruption was only temporary. Boom times quickly returned.

The North lost more soldiers in the war than the South did. However, only a few battles had taken place on northern soil. Northern farms and cities were hardly touched. One returning Union soldier remarked, "It seemed . . . as if I had been away only a day or two, and had just taken up . . . where I had left off."

The Defeated South Confederate soldiers had little chance of taking up where they had left off. In some areas, every house, barn, and bridge had been destroyed. Two thirds of the South's railroad tracks had been turned into twisted heaps of scrap. The cities of

Columbia, Richmond, and Atlanta had been leveled.

The war wrecked the South's financial system. After the war, Confederate money was worthless. People who had loaned money to the Confederacy were never repaid. Many southern banks closed, and depositors lost their savings.

The war changed southern society forever. Almost overnight, there was a new class of nearly four million people known as **freedmen**—men and women who had been slaves. Under slavery, they had been forbidden to own property and to learn to read and write. What would become of them? How could the South cope with this sudden, drastic change?

Early Steps Toward Reconstruction

President Lincoln was worried about **Reconstruction,** or the rebuilding of the South. He wanted to make it fairly easy for southerners to rejoin the Union. The sooner the nation was reunited, Lincoln believed, the faster the South would be able to rebuild.

Lincoln's Reconstruction Plan As early as 1863, Lincoln outlined his **Ten Percent Plan** for Reconstruction. Under this plan, a southern state could form a new government after 10 percent of its voters swore an oath of loyalty to the United States. The new government had to abolish slavery. Voters could then elect members of Congress and take part in the national government once again.

Lincoln's plan also offered **amnesty,** or a government pardon, to Confederates who swore loyalty to the Union. Amnesty would not apply to the former leaders of the Confederacy, however.

A Rival Proposal Many Republicans in Congress felt that the Ten Percent Plan was too generous toward the South. In 1864, they passed the **Wade-Davis Bill,** a rival plan for Reconstruction. It required a majority of white men in each southern state to swear loyalty to the Union. It also denied the right to vote or hold office to anyone who had volunteered to fight for the Confederacy. Lincoln refused to sign the Wade-Davis Bill because he felt it was too harsh.

The Freedmen's Bureau Congress and the President did agree on one proposal. One month before Lee surrendered, Congress passed a bill creating the **Freedmen's Bureau,** a government agency to help former slaves. Lincoln signed the bill.

The Freedmen's Bureau gave food and clothing to former slaves. It also tried to find jobs for freedmen. The bureau helped poor whites as well. It provided medical care for more than one million people.

Viewing History

Richmond in Ruins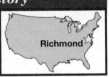

After the Civil War, some of the South's most important cities lay in ruins. This picture shows the devastation in Richmond, Virginia. **Drawing Conclusions** *What effect do you think this kind of devastation had on southerners?*

Washington, D.C.

Ford's Theatre

On April 14, 1865, John Wilkes Booth crept into Abraham Lincoln's box at Ford's Theatre. As the President watched the comedy Our American Cousin, *Booth shot him. Today, park rangers at the restored theatre recount the story of the tragic assassination. You can visit a museum devoted to Lincoln's death—and even attend a play.*

Virtual Field Trip For an interactive look at Ford's Theatre, visit PHSchool.com, **Web Code mfd-1801.**

Identify Sequence
As you read, identify the major goals and accomplishments of the Freedmen's Bureau. Add these items to your flowchart.

One of the bureau's most important tasks was to set up schools for freedmen. Most of the teachers were volunteers, often women, from the North. Grandparents and grandchildren sat side by side in the classroom. Charlotte Forten, an African American volunteer from Philadelphia, wrote:

❝ It is wonderful how a people who have been so long crushed to the earth . . . can have so great a desire for knowledge, and such a capacity for attaining it. ❞
—Charlotte Forten, article in the *Atlantic Monthly*

The Freedmen's Bureau laid the foundation for the South's public school system. It also created colleges for African Americans, including Howard, Morehouse, and Fisk. Many of the graduates of these schools became teachers themselves. By the 1870s, African Americans were teaching in grade schools throughout the South.

Lincoln Is Assassinated

President Lincoln hoped to persuade Congress to accept his Reconstruction plan. However, he never got the chance.

On April 14, 1865, just five days after Lee's surrender, the President attended a play at Ford's Theatre in Washington, D.C. A popular actor from the South, John Wilkes Booth, crept into the President's box and shot Lincoln in the head. Lincoln died the next morning. Booth was later caught and killed in a barn outside the city.

The nation was plunged into grief. Millions who had been celebrating the war's end now mourned Lincoln's death. "Now he belongs to the ages," commented Secretary of War Edwin Stanton.

The New President

Vice President Andrew Johnson was now President. Johnson had represented Tennessee in Congress. When his state seceded, Johnson had remained loyal to the Union.

Johnson's Plan Republicans in Congress believed Johnson would support a strict Reconstruction plan. But his plan was much milder than expected. It called for a majority of voters in each southern state to pledge loyalty to the United States. Each state also had to ratify the Thirteenth Amendment, which Congress had approved in January 1865. It banned slavery throughout the nation. (As you read, the Emancipation Proclamation did not free slaves in states loyal to the Union.)

Congress Rebels The southern states quickly met Johnson's conditions. As a result, the President approved their new state governments in late 1865. Voters in the South then elected representatives to Congress. Many of those elected had held office in the Confederacy. For example, Alexander Stephens, the former vice president of the Confederacy, was elected senator from Georgia.

Republicans in Congress were outraged. The men who had led the South out of the Union were being elected to the House and Senate. Also, no southern state allowed African Americans to vote.

When the new Congress met, Republicans refused to let southern representatives take their seats. Instead, they set up a Joint Committee on Reconstruction to form a new plan for the South. The stage was set for a showdown between Congress and the President.

★ ★ ★ Section 1 Assessment ★ ★ ★

Recall

1. **Identify** Explain the significance of **(a)** Reconstruction, **(b)** Ten Percent Plan, **(c)** Wade-Davis Bill, **(d)** Freedmen's Bureau, **(e)** John Wilkes Booth, **(f)** Andrew Johnson, **(g)** Thirteenth Amendment.
2. **Define** **(a)** freedmen, **(b)** amnesty.

Comprehension

3. Describe two problems faced by the South after the Civil War.
4. What early Reconstruction measure did Lincoln and Congress agree upon?

5. Why did Republicans in Congress oppose Johnson's Reconstruction plan?

Critical Thinking and Writing

6. **Exploring the Main Idea** Review the Main Idea statement at the beginning of this section. Then, write a letter to President Lincoln supporting or opposing his Reconstruction plan.
7. **Drawing Inferences** One teacher said that freedmen "will starve themselves in order to send their children to school." Write a paragraph explaining why you think education meant so much to the freedmen.

Solving Problems

Learning how to solve problems is an important skill for both citizens and government leaders. Just as the solutions to problems of the past affect the present, the solutions you choose today will have consequences in the future.

African American writer W.E.B. DuBois described some of the problems faced by the Freedmen's Bureau:

> ❝Here, at a stroke of the pen, was erected a government of millions of men,—and not ordinary men, either, but black men [weakened] by a peculiarly complete system of slavery, centuries old; and now, suddenly, violently, they come into a new birthright, at a time of war and passion, in the midst of the stricken, embittered population of their former masters. Any man might well have hesitated to assume charge of such a work, with vast responsibilities, indefinite powers, and limited resources . . . for Congress had appropriated no money for salaries and expenses.❞
>
> —W.E.B. DuBois, "The Freedmen's Bureau"

As it set up new schools throughout the South, the Freedmen's Bureau faced the problem of finding enough teachers for so many eager new students.

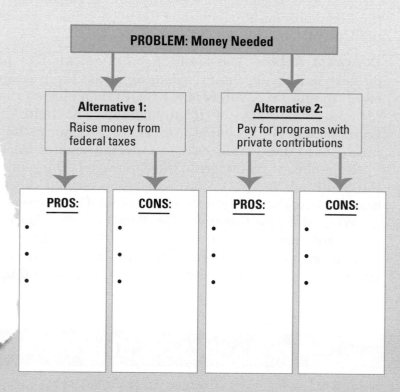

Learn the Skill *To learn problem-solving skills, use the following steps:*

1. **Identify the problem.** State the problem you want to solve as simply and completely as possible.

2. **List possible solutions.** There is usually more than one way to solve a problem. Identify your alternatives.

3. **Review the alternatives.** What resources would be needed to implement the solution? What would the consequences be?

4. **Choose a course of action.** Decide how you will resolve the problem.

Practice the Skill *Use the information above to answer the following questions:*

1. According to DuBois what was one problem that the Freedmen's Bureau faced?

2. **(a)** What two alternatives are shown on the chart? **(b)** Can you think of a third alternative? Explain.

3. **(a)** What might be some of the pros and cons of Alternative 1? **(b)** What might be some of the pros and cons of Alternative 2?

4. What solution to the problem would you have favored? Why?

Apply the Skill *See the Chapter Review and Assessment.*

2 Radical Reconstruction

Prepare to Read

Objectives

In this section, you will
- Describe how Congress reacted to the passage of black codes in the South.
- Explain how Radical Republicans gained power in Congress.
- Identify why President Johnson was impeached.

Key Terms

black codes

Radical Republican

Fourteenth Amendment

Radical Reconstruction

Reconstruction Act

impeach

Fifteenth Amendment

Target Reading Skill

Cause and Effect Copy the chart below. As you read, complete the chart to show some of the effects of the rise of Radical Republicans in Congress. Add as many boxes as you need.

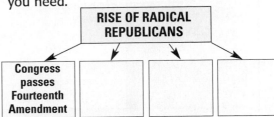

Main Idea Angered by the South's response to President Johnson's Reconstruction program, Republicans in Congress put in place a harsher plan.

Setting the Scene In New Orleans, Confederate flags were being sold in the streets. In Mississippi, the governor refused to fly the American flag over the state capitol. Many southerners were singing, "I'm a good old rebel, that's what I am / And I don't want no pardon for anything I done." Hearing such reports in 1866, Republicans decided to take harsh measures against the South.

Black Codes Anger Congress

After the war, most southern states promptly ratified the Thirteenth Amendment. However, southern legislatures also passed **black codes,** laws that severely limited the rights of freedmen.

Rights and Restrictions The black codes did grant some rights. For example, African Americans could marry legally and own some kinds of property. Still, the codes were clearly meant to keep freedmen from gaining political or economic power.

Black codes forbade freedmen to vote, own guns, or serve on juries. In some states, African Americans were permitted to work only as servants or farm laborers. In others, they had to sign contracts for a year's work. Those without contracts could be arrested and sentenced to work on a plantation.

Congress Reacts Republicans charged that Johnson's lenient Reconstruction plan had encouraged southern legislatures to pass the black codes. Republicans were also outraged by reports of violence against freedmen. In 1866, angry whites burned homes, churches, and schoolhouses in a black section of Memphis, Tennessee. More than 40 African Americans were killed. Similar riots broke out in New Orleans when freedmen met to support the right to vote.

A report by the Joint Committee on Reconstruction accused the South of trying to "preserve slavery . . . as long as possible." When

Confederate flag

Rival Plans for Reconstruction

Plan	Ten Percent Plan	Wade-Davis Bill	Johnson Plan	Reconstruction Act
Proposed by	President Abraham Lincoln (1863)	Republicans in Congress (1864)	President Andrew Johnson (1865)	Radical Republicans (1867)
Conditions for Former Confederate States to Rejoin Union	• 10 percent of voters must swear loyalty to Union • Must abolish slavery	• Majority of white men must swear loyalty • Former Confederate volunteers cannot vote or hold office	• Majority of white men must swear loyalty • Must ratify Thirteenth Amendment • Former Confederate officials may vote and hold office	• Must disband state governments • Must write new constitutions • Must ratify Fourteenth Amendment • African American men must be allowed to vote

GRAPHIC ORGANIZER
Skills

In the early years of Reconstruction, federal leaders debated several plans for readmitting southern states to the Union.

1. **Comprehension**
   (a) Identify one similarity between the Wade-Davis Bill and President Johnson's plan. **(b)** Identify one difference.

2. **Critical Thinking**
   Evaluating Information Which of the plans shown here seems to be the harshest toward the South? Explain.

Civics 🏛

President Johnson ignored the report, members of Congress called Radical Republicans vowed to take control of Reconstruction.

Rise of the Radicals

The Radicals were led by Thaddeus Stevens of Pennsylvania in the House and Charles Sumner of Massachusetts in the Senate. Radical Republicans had two main goals. First, they wanted to break the power of wealthy planters who had long ruled the South. Second, they wanted to ensure that freedmen received the right to vote.

Republican Control Radicals needed the support of moderate Republicans, the largest group in Congress. Moderates and Radicals disagreed on many issues, but they shared a strong political motive. Most southerners were Democrats. With southerners barred from Congress, Republicans could control both houses.

To combat the black codes, Congress passed the Civil Rights Act in April 1866. It gave citizenship to African Americans. When Johnson vetoed the bill, Congress overrode the veto.

Fourteenth Amendment Republicans feared that the Supreme Court might use its power of judicial review to declare the Civil Rights Act unconstitutional. In the Dred Scott decision of 1857, the Court had ruled that African Americans were not citizens. To avoid a similar ruling, Republicans proposed the Fourteenth Amendment. It defined citizens as "all persons born or naturalized in the United States." (The amendment did not apply to most Native Americans.) It guaranteed citizens "equal protection of the laws" and forbade states to "deprive any person of life, liberty, or property without due process of law." Thus, states could not legally discriminate against a citizen on unreasonable grounds, such as race.

Under the Fourteenth Amendment, any state that denied any male citizen age 21 or older the right to vote would have its representation in Congress reduced. Republicans believed that freedmen would be able to defend their rights if they could vote.

Republicans hoped the amendment would secure basic political rights for African Americans in the South. That goal would take a century to achieve. In the 1950s, the Fourteenth Amendment became a powerful tool in the struggle for citizenship rights.

Radicals in Power

President Johnson encouraged former Confederate states to reject the Fourteenth Amendment. He also decided to make the amendment an issue in the 1866 congressional elections.

Election of 1866 Across the North, Johnson urged voters to reject the Radicals. When a heckler yelled for Johnson to hang Jefferson Davis, Johnson shouted, "Why not hang Thad Stevens?" Many northerners criticized the President for losing his temper.

In July, white mobs in New Orleans killed 34 African Americans. The violence convinced many northerners that stronger measures were needed. In the end, the elections were a disaster for Johnson. Republicans won majorities in both houses of Congress.

The Radical Program In 1867, Republicans in Congress prepared to take charge of Reconstruction. With huge majorities in both houses, Congress could easily override a veto. The period that followed is often called **Radical Reconstruction.**

Congress passed the first **Reconstruction Act** in March 1867. It threw out the state governments that had refused to ratify the Fourteenth Amendment—all the former Confederate states except Tennessee. The act also divided the South into five military districts. Army commanders were given broad powers to enforce Reconstruction. Many southerners bitterly resented the imposition of military rule.

To rejoin the Union, former Confederate states had to write new constitutions and ratify the Fourteenth Amendment. The Reconstruction Act also required that southern states allow African Americans to vote.

With the new constitutions in place, reconstructed states held elections to set up new state governments. Former Confederate officials were barred from voting. Many other white southerners stayed away from the polls in protest. Protected by the army, freedmen proudly exercised their new right to vote. As a result, Republicans gained control of all of the new southern state governments.

Impeachment and a New President

Congress passed other Reconstruction acts over Johnson's veto. As President, Johnson had a duty to execute the new laws. However, Johnson did what he could to limit their effect. He fired several military commanders who supported Radical Reconstruction. Republicans in Congress decided to remove Johnson from office.

Trial On February 24, 1868, the House of Representatives voted to **impeach,** or bring formal charges against, Johnson. According to the Constitution, the House may impeach a President for "treason,

Primary Source

The Impeachment of Andrew Johnson

At the impeachment trial of President Johnson, Senator James Grimes of Iowa voted against conviction. Here, he explains why:
"Nor can I suffer my judgment of the law governing this case to be influenced by political considerations. I cannot agree to destroy the harmonious working of the Constitution for the sake of getting rid of an unacceptable President. Whatever may be my opinion of [Johnson], I cannot consent to trifle with the high office he holds. I can do nothing which, by implication, may be [seen as] an approval of impeachment as a part of future political machinery."

—James Grimes, quoted in *Trial of Andrew Johnson* (Poore)

Analyzing Primary Sources

Write a sentence summarizing the main reason that Grimes voted against the removal of President Johnson.

bribery, or other high crimes and misdemeanors." The President is removed from office if found guilty by two thirds of the Senate.

During Johnson's trial, it became clear that he was not guilty of high crimes and misdemeanors. Even Charles Sumner, Johnson's bitter foe, admitted that the charges were "political in character."

Despite intense pressure, seven Republican senators refused to vote for conviction. The Constitution, they said, did not allow Congress to remove a President just because they disagreed with him. In the end, the vote was 35 to 19—one vote shy of the two thirds needed to convict.

A New President Johnson served out the few remaining months of his term. In 1868, Republicans nominated the Union's greatest war hero, Ulysses S. Grant, for President.

By election day, most southern states had rejoined the Union. As Congress demanded, the southern governments allowed African American men to vote. About 500,000 blacks voted—nearly all of them for Grant. He easily won the election.

Fifteenth Amendment In 1869, Congress proposed the Fifteenth Amendment. It forbade any state to deny any citizen the right to vote because of "race, color, or previous condition of servitude."

Republicans had moral and political reasons for supporting the Fifteenth Amendment. They remembered the great sacrifices made by African American soldiers in the Civil War. They also felt it was wrong to let African Americans vote in the South but not in the North. In addition, Republicans knew that if African Americans could vote in the North, they would help Republicans win elections there.

The Fifteenth Amendment was ratified in 1870. At last, all African American men over age 21 had the right to vote.

★ ★ ★ Section 2 Assessment ★ ★ ★

Recall

1. **Identify** Explain the significance of **(a)** Radical Republicans, **(b)** Thaddeus Stevens, **(c)** Charles Sumner, **(d)** Fourteenth Amendment, **(e)** Radical Reconstruction, **(f)** Reconstruction Act, **(g)** Fifteenth Amendment.
2. **Define** **(a)** black codes, **(b)** impeach.

Comprehension

3. Why did the black codes anger Republicans in Congress?
4. How did Radical Republicans win control of Congress?

5. Why did Congress impeach President Johnson?

Critical Thinking and Writing

6. **Exploring the Main Idea** Review the Main Idea statement at the beginning of this section. Then, write two sentences evaluating the Reconstruction Act—one from Andrew Johnson's viewpoint, the other from a Radical Republican's viewpoint.
7. **Supporting a Point of View** Write a note from one member of Congress to another explaining why you think the Fourteenth or Fifteenth Amendment is necessary.

ACTIVITY

Drawing a Political Cartoon Draw a political cartoon that might have appeared during the congressional elections of 1866. Your cartoon should express a point of view about the conflict between Radical Republicans and the President over control of Reconstruction.

The Power of the Fourteenth Amendment

The Fourteenth Amendment was originally intended to grant citizenship to former slaves and to ensure their rights. As society changed, the Court's interpretation of the Fourteenth Amendment changed as well.

> **66** ...No State shall make or enforce any law which shall abridge the privileges or immunities of citizens of the United States; nor shall any State deprive any person of life, liberty, or property, without due process of law; nor deny to any person within its jurisdiction the equal protection of the laws. **99**
>
> —Fourteenth Amendment

1905

Lochner v. New York

The Supreme Court strikes down a law regulating working hours. The Court rules that **equal protection** means that employers have the right to make contracts with workers freely. This ruling is later reversed.

1954

Brown v. Board of Education of Topeka

The Supreme Court rules that having separate schools for white and black students discriminates against African Americans and is a violation of **equal protection.** The ruling ends school segregation and becomes a landmark in the fight for equal rights.

1963

Gideon v. Wainwright

The Supreme Court rules that **due process** means that all people accused of a crime have the right to an attorney. If a person cannot afford an attorney, the state must provide one for her or him.

1971

Reed v. Reed

The Supreme Court strikes down an Idaho law giving men automatic preference over women in certain situations. The Court rules that **equal protection** means that men and women must be treated equally before the law.

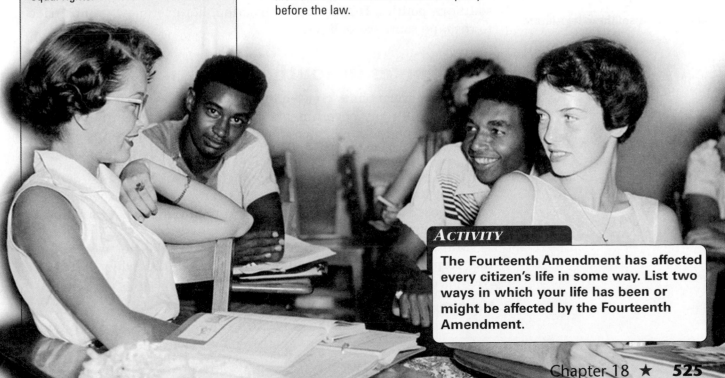

ACTIVITY

The Fourteenth Amendment has affected every citizen's life in some way. List two ways in which your life has been or might be affected by the Fourteenth Amendment.

3 The South Under Reconstruction

Prepare to Read

Objectives

In this section, you will
- Identify new forces in southern politics.
- Describe how southern Conservatives resisted Reconstruction.
- List the challenges facing Reconstruction governments.
- Explain why sharecropping led to a cycle of poverty.

Key Terms

scalawag

carpetbagger

Conservatives

Ku Klux Klan

sharecropper

Target Reading Skill

Clarifying Meaning As you read, prepare an outline of this section. Use roman numerals to indicate the major headings, capital letters for the subheadings, and numbers for the supporting details.

I. New Forces in Southern Politics
  A. White southern Republicans
    1. Opposed secession
    2.
  B. Northerners
    1.
    2.
  C.
II. Conservatives Resist
  A.
  B.

Main Idea Reconstruction governments tried to rebuild the South despite sometimes fierce opposition.

Meeting of a southern legislature

Setting the Scene White superintendents in Virginia's tobacco factories were puzzled. Suddenly, many of their black workers were absent from their jobs. White households experienced the same problem. With their servants missing, they were forced "to cook their own dinners or content themselves with a cold lunch."

What was going on? In 1867, as southern states began writing new constitutions, African American delegates took an active part. On days when important issues were debated, freedmen from all around flocked to watch. In Alabama, a political convention of freedmen declared, "We claim exactly the same rights, privileges and immunities as are enjoyed by white men."

Before the Civil War, a small group of rich planters had dominated southern politics. During Reconstruction, however, new groups tried to reshape southern politics.

New Forces in Southern Politics

The state governments created during Radical Reconstruction were different from any governments the South had known before. The old leaders had lost much of their influence. Three groups stepped in to replace them.

White Southern Republicans Some white southerners supported the new Republican governments. Many were businesspeople who had opposed secession in 1860. They wanted to forget the war and get on with rebuilding the South.

Many whites in the South felt that any southerner who helped the Republicans was a traitor. They called the white southern Republicans **scalawags,** a word used for small, scruffy horses.

Northerners Northerners who came to the South after the war were another important force. White southerners accused the new arrivals of hoping to get rich from the South's misery. Southerners claimed that these northerners were in such a hurry they had time only to fling a few clothes into cheap suitcases, or carpetbags. As a result, they became known as **carpetbaggers.**

In fact, northerners went south for various reasons. A few did hope to profit as the South was being rebuilt. Many more, however, were Union soldiers who had grown to love the South's rich land. Others, both white and black, were teachers, ministers, and reformers who sincerely wanted to help the freedmen.

African Americans African Americans were the third major new group in southern politics. Before the war, they had no voice in southern government. During Reconstruction, they not only voted in large numbers, but they also ran for and were elected to public office in the South. African Americans became sheriffs, mayors, and legislators in the new state and local governments. Sixteen African Americans were elected to Congress between 1869 and 1880.

Two African Americans, both representing Mississippi, served in the Senate. Hiram Revels, a clergyman and teacher, became the nation's first black senator in 1870. He completed the unfinished term of former Confederate president Jefferson Davis. In 1874, Blanche K. Bruce became the first African American to serve a full term in the Senate.

Freedmen had less political influence than many whites claimed, however. Only in South Carolina did African Americans win a majority in one house of the state legislature. No state elected a black governor.

Conservatives Resist

Most white southerners who had held power before the Civil War resisted Reconstruction. These **Conservatives** resented the changes imposed by Congress and enforced by the military. They wanted the South to change as little as possible. Conservatives were willing to let African Americans vote and hold a few offices. Still, they were determined that real power would remain in the hands of whites.

A few wealthy planters tried to force African Americans back onto plantations. Many small farmers and laborers wanted the government to take action against freedmen, who now competed with them for land and power.

Most of these white southerners were Democrats. They declared war on anyone who cooperated with the Republicans. "This is a white man's country," declared one southern senator, "and white men must govern it."

Spreading Terror Some white southerners formed secret societies to help them regain power. The most dangerous was the **Ku Klux Klan,** or KKK. The Klan worked to keep African Americans and white Republicans out of office.

Dressed in white robes and hoods to hide their identities, Klansmen rode at night to the homes of African American voters, shouting threats and burning wooden crosses. When threats did not work, the Klan turned to violence. Klan members murdered hundreds of African Americans and their white allies.

An American Profile

Hiram Revels 1822–1901

Hiram Revels was born to free parents in North Carolina. Yet, he had to learn to read in secret because the law banned education for free blacks as well as slaves. Moving north, he became a minister and educator with the African Methodist Episcopal Church. He recalled, "I was imprisoned in Missouri in 1854, for preaching the gospel to Negroes, though I was never subjected to violence." During the Civil War, he helped recruit the first two black regiments in Maryland. This life of service paved the way for Revels to become the first African American in the Senate.

How might his previous experience have prepared Hiram Revels for service in the Senate?

POLITICAL CARTOON
Skills

The Ku Klux Klan
The KKK used terror and violence to keep African Americans from voting. Northern cartoonist Thomas Nast attacked the Klan and other secret societies in this cartoon.

1. **Comprehension** Identify two Klan activities shown in this cartoon.

2. **Understanding Main Ideas** How does Nast show the impact of the Ku Klux Klan and similar groups on African Americans?

3. **Critical Thinking Identifying a Point of View** What details in this cartoon show Nast's view of the Ku Klux Klan?

Congress Responds Many moderate southerners condemned the violence of the Klan. Yet, they could do little to stop the Klan's reign of terror. Freedmen turned to the federal government for help. In Kentucky, African American voters wrote to Congress:

66 We believe you are not familiar with the Ku Klux Klan's riding nightly over the country spreading terror wherever they go by robbing, whipping, and killing our people without provocation. 99

— Records of the U.S. Senate, April 11, 1871

In 1870, Congress made it a crime to use force to keep people from voting. Although Klan activities decreased, the threat of violence remained. Some African Americans continued to vote and hold office, but others were frightened away from the ballot box.

The Challenge of Rebuilding

Despite political problems, Reconstruction governments tried to rebuild the South. They built public schools for both black and white children. Many states gave women the right to own property. In addition, Reconstruction governments rebuilt railroads, telegraph lines, bridges, and roads. Between 1865 and 1879, the South put down 7,000 miles of railroad track.

Rebuilding cost money. Before the war, southerners paid low taxes. Reconstruction governments raised taxes sharply. This created discontent among many southern whites.

Southerners were further angered by widespread corruption in the Reconstruction governments. One state legislature, for example, voted $1,000 to cover a member's bet on a horse race. Other items billed to the state included hams, perfume, and a coffin.

Corruption was not limited to the South. After the Civil War, dishonesty plagued northern governments, as well. Most southern officeholders, however, served their states honestly.

A Cycle of Poverty

In the first months after the war, freedmen left the plantations on which they had lived and worked. They found few opportunities, however.

"Nothing but Freedom" Some Radical Republicans talked about giving each freedman "40 acres and a mule." Thaddeus Stevens suggested breaking up big plantations and distributing the land. Most Americans opposed the plan, however. In the end, former slaves received—in the words of a freedman—"nothing but freedom."

Through hard work or good luck, some freedmen were able to become landowners. Most, however, had little choice but to return to where they had lived in slavery. At the same time, some large planters found themselves with land but nobody to work it.

Sharecropping During Reconstruction, many freedmen and poor whites went to work on the large plantations. These **sharecroppers** rented and farmed a plot of land. Planters provided seed, fertilizer, and tools in return for a share of the crop at harvest time. To many freedmen, sharecropping offered a measure of independence. Many hoped to own their own land one day.

In fact, most sharecroppers and small landowners became locked in a cycle of poverty. Each spring, they received supplies on credit. In the fall, they had to repay what they had borrowed. If the harvest did not cover what they owed, they sank deeper into debt. Many farmers lost their land and became sharecroppers themselves.

Paraphrasing Paraphrasing can help you understand what you read. When you paraphrase, you restate what you have read in your own words. Paraphrase the paragraphs under "A Cycle of Poverty." Add the information to your outline.

★ ★ ★ Section 3 Assessment ★ ★ ★

Recall
1. **Identify** Explain the significance of (a) Hiram Revels, (b) Blanche K. Bruce, (c) Conservatives, (d) Ku Klux Klan.
2. **Define** (a) scalawag, (b) carpetbagger, (c) sharecropper.

Comprehension
3. What role did freedmen play in Reconstruction governments?
4. What was the goal of groups like the Ku Klux Klan?
5. Describe two economic problems faced by Reconstruction governments in the South.

6. Why did many farmers become sharecroppers?

Critical Thinking and Writing
7. **Exploring the Main Idea** Review the Main Idea statement at the beginning of this section. Then, list two accomplishments of Reconstruction governments. Evaluate the impact of each on the South.
8. **Making Decisions** If you had been an African American during Reconstruction, would you have tried to vote despite threats? Write a paragraph explaining your reasons.

ACTIVITY

Writing a Welcoming Speech You are a Republican member of Congress in 1870. You have been asked to write a brief speech welcoming one of the first African Americans elected to the House of Representatives. Your speech should highlight the importance of this occasion.

4 The End of Reconstruction

Prepare to Read

Objectives

In this section, you will
- List the events that led to the end of Reconstruction.
- Explain how the rights of African Americans were restricted in the South after Reconstruction.
- Identify industries that flourished in the "New South."

Key Terms

poll tax
literacy test
grandfather clause
segregation
Jim Crow laws
Plessy v. *Ferguson*
"New South"

 Target Reading Skill

Main Idea Copy the concept web below. As you read, fill in the blank ovals with information about the aftermath of Reconstruction. Add as many ovals as you need.

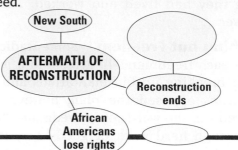

Main Idea When the North lost interest in protecting the goals of Reconstruction, the era came to an end.

Frederick Douglass

Setting the Scene Americans flocked to the great Centennial Exposition held in Philadelphia in 1876. Fairgoers gazed at the latest wonders of modern industry—the elevator, a giant steam engine, and the telephone ("Of what use is such an invention?" asked the New York *Tribune*).

At the opening ceremony, Frederick Douglass was invited to sit on the platform. But when the famed abolitionist tried to take his place, a policeman barred the way. The officer could not believe that a black man belonged on stage. Finally, a United States Senator persuaded the policeman to let Douglass pass.

By 1876, Americans were looking ahead to a bright future. Eager to put the past behind them, many northerners lost interest in Reconstruction. For African Americans in the South, the end of Reconstruction meant a slow erosion of their hard-won rights.

The End of Reconstruction

By the 1870s, Radical Republicans were losing power. Many northerners grew weary of trying to reform the South. It was time to let southerners run their own governments, they said—even if it meant that African Americans in the South might lose their rights.

Radicals in Decline Disclosure of widespread corruption also hurt Republicans. President Grant had appointed many friends to government offices. Some used their position to steal large sums of money from the government. Grant won reelection in 1872, but many northerners lost faith in Republicans and their policies.

Congress passed the Amnesty Act in 1872. It restored the right to vote to nearly all white southerners. They voted solidly Democratic. At the same time, threats of violence kept many African Americans from voting. By 1876, only three southern states—South Carolina, Florida, and Tennessee—remained under Republican control.

Election of 1876 The end of Reconstruction came with the election of 1876. The Democrats nominated Samuel Tilden, governor of New York, for President. The Republicans chose Ohio governor Rutherford B. Hayes. Both candidates vowed to fight corruption.

Tilden won the popular vote. However, he had only 184 electoral votes, one short of the number needed to win. The outcome of the election hung on 20 disputed votes. All but one came from the three southern states still controlled by Republicans.

As inauguration day drew near, the nation still had no one to swear in as President. Congress set up a special commission to settle the crisis. The commission, made up mostly of Republicans, decided to give all the disputed electoral votes to Hayes.

Southern Democrats could have fought the decision. Hayes, however, had privately agreed to end Reconstruction. Once in office, he removed all remaining federal troops from Louisiana, South Carolina, and Florida. Reconstruction was over.

Impact of Reconstruction Reconstruction had a deep and lasting impact on southern politics. White southerners had bitter memories of Radical Republican policies and military rule. For the next hundred years, the South remained a stronghold of the Democratic party. At the same time, black southerners steadily lost most of their political rights.

Restricted Rights

As Conservatives tightened their grip on southern governments, states found new ways to keep African Americans from exercising their rights. Many of these laws restricted the right to vote.

GEOGRAPHY Skills

The 1876 presidential election hinged on the disputed votes of three southern states. Although Samuel Tilden won the popular vote, Rutherford B. Hayes was declared the winner of the election.

1. **Location** On the map, locate **(a)** Florida, **(b)** Louisiana, **(c)** South Carolina.

2. **Regions** Which candidate carried the southern states where the vote was not disputed?

3. **Critical Thinking Drawing Inferences** Based on this map, do you think the Civil War ended sectionalism in the United States? Explain.

Election of 1876

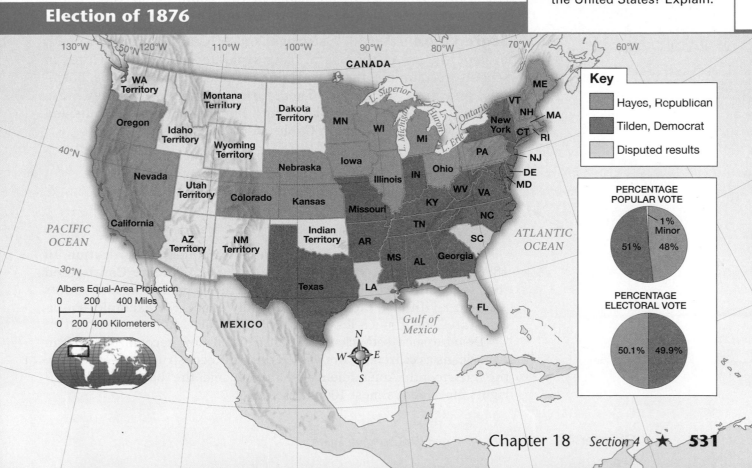

Key
- Hayes, Republican
- Tilden, Democrat
- Disputed results

PERCENTAGE POPULAR VOTE
51% 48% 1% Minor

PERCENTAGE ELECTORAL VOTE
50.1% 49.9%

Viewing History

A Port in the New South

Shreveport

After Reconstruction, the economy of the South slowly began to recover. This print, made in the 1870s, shows the port of Shreveport, Louisiana. **Analyzing Information** *How does this picture suggest that the South was recovering from the effects of the war?*

Voting Restrictions Over time, many southern states passed **poll taxes,** requiring voters to pay a fee each time they voted. As a result, poor freedmen could rarely afford to vote. States also imposed **literacy tests** that required voters to read and explain a section of the Constitution. Since most freedmen had little education, such tests kept them away from the polls.

Many poor whites could not pass the literacy test. To increase the number of white voters, states passed **grandfather clauses.** These laws stated that if a voter's father or grandfather had been eligible to vote on January 1, 1867, the voter did not have to take a literacy test. Since no African Americans in the South could vote before 1868, grandfather clauses ensured that only white men could vote.

Segregation After 1877, **segregation,** or legal separation of races, became the law of the South. Laws separated blacks and whites in schools, restaurants, theaters, trains, streetcars, playgrounds, hospitals, and even cemeteries. These **Jim Crow laws,** as they were known, trapped southern blacks in a hopeless situation. Louisiana novelist George Washington Cable described segregation as:

> **66** A system of oppression so rank that nothing could make it seem small except the fact that [African Americans] had already been ground under it for a century and a half. **99**
>
> — George Washington Cable, "The Freedman's Case in Equity"

African Americans brought lawsuits to challenge segregation. In 1896, in the case of *Plessy* v. *Ferguson,* the Supreme Court ruled that segregation was legal so long as facilities for blacks and whites were equal. In fact, facilities were rarely equal. For example, southern states spent much less on schools for blacks than for whites.

Despite such setbacks, the Constitution now recognized African Americans as citizens. Laws passed during Reconstruction—especially the Fourteenth Amendment—would become the basis of the civil rights movement almost 100 years later.

Industry in the "New South"

During Reconstruction, the South made some progress toward rebuilding its economy. Cotton production, long the basis of the South's economy, slowly recovered. By 1880, planters were growing as much cotton as they had in 1860.

A new generation of southern leaders worked to expand the economy. In stirring speeches, Atlanta journalist Henry Grady described a "New South" that used its vast natural resources to build up its own industry instead of depending on the North.

Agricultural Resources In 1880, the entire South still produced fewer finished textiles than Massachusetts. In the next decade, more and more communities started building textile mills to turn cotton into cloth.

The tobacco industry also grew. In North Carolina, James Duke used new machinery to revolutionize the manufacture of tobacco products. Duke's American Tobacco Company eventually controlled 90 percent of the nation's tobacco industry.

New Industries The South also tapped its mineral resources. With its large deposits of iron ore and coal, Alabama became a center of the steel industry. Oil refineries sprang up in Louisiana and Texas. Other states produced copper, granite, and marble.

By the 1890s, many northern forests had been cut down. The southern yellow pine competed with the northwestern white pine as a lumber source. Southern factories turned out cypress shingles and hardwood furniture.

The South had developed a more balanced economy by 1900. "We find a South wide awake with business," wrote a visitor, "eagerly laying lines of communication, rapidly opening mines, building furnaces, foundries, and all sorts of shops." Still, the South could not keep up with even more rapid growth in the North and the West.

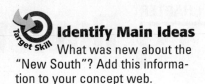

Identify Main Ideas What was new about the "New South"? Add this information to your concept web.

★ ★ ★ Section 4 Assessment ★ ★ ★

Recall

1. **Identify** Explain the significance of **(a)** Rutherford B. Hayes, **(b)** Jim Crow laws, **(c)** *Plessy* v. *Ferguson,* **(d)** Henry Grady, **(e)** "New South," **(f)** James Duke.
2. **Define** **(a)** poll tax, **(b)** literacy test, **(c)** grandfather clause, **(d)** segregation.

Comprehension

3. Why did the Radical Republicans lose their power?
4. Describe two ways in which African Americans in the South lost political rights.

5. How did the southern economy change after Reconstruction?

Critical Thinking and Writing

6. **Exploring the Main Idea** Review the Main Idea statement at the beginning of this section. Then, evaluate the ways in which Reconstruction was both a success and a failure.
7. **Making Predictions** Write a paragraph predicting how the Supreme Court decision in *Plessy* v. *Ferguson* might affect later efforts by African Americans to achieve equality.

ACTIVITY

Go Online
PHSchool.com

Connecting to Today
Choose one of the former Confederate states. Then, use the Internet to find out what the major industries and resources of that state are. Use this information to create a chart. For help in completing the activity, visit PHSchool.com, **Web Code mfd-1803.**

CHAPTER SUMMARY

Section 1
The South had a more difficult time recovering from the Civil War than the North. Lincoln's Reconstruction plan met with some resistance. Andrew Johnson became President after Lincoln's assassination.

Section 2
The South's black codes restricted the rights of freed African Americans. Congress responded by passing harsh Reconstruction measures. President Johnson survived an impeachment attempt.

Section 3
Southern and northern groups competed to control the South in the postwar period. The effort to rebuild the South created a cycle of poverty that affected freed African Americans and poor whites.

Section 4
Reconstruction did little to improve the condition of freed African Americans. However, new industries helped to improve the economy of the South.

For additional review and enrichment activities, see the interactive version of *The American Nation,* available on the Web and on CD-ROM.

Chapter Self-Test For practice test questions for Chapter 18, visit PHSchool.com, **Web Code mfa-1804.**

Building Vocabulary

Review the meaning of the chapter vocabulary words listed below. Then, write a sentence for each word in which you define the word and describe its relation to the postwar South.

1. freedmen
2. amnesty
3. black codes
4. scalawag
5. carpetbagger
6. sharecropper
7. poll tax
8. literacy test
9. grandfather clause
10. segregation

Reviewing Key Facts

11. Describe Lincoln's plan for Reconstruction. (Section 1)
12. Describe two accomplishments of the Freedmen's Bureau. (Section 1)
13. What did the Fifteenth Amendment state? (Section 2)
14. Why did many northerners go to the South during Reconstruction? (Section 3)
15. What were the results of the presidential election of 1876? (Section 4)

Critical Thinking and Writing

16. **Drawing Conclusions** If Abraham Lincoln had lived, do you think he would have supported Radical Reconstruction? Write a paragraph explaining your answer and giving reasons.
17. **Supporting a Point of View** Do you think former Confederate officeholders should have been barred from serving in Congress? Write a position statement giving reasons for your point of view.
18. **Identifying Causes and Effects** Analyze the causes and effects of the passage of the Fourteenth Amendment.
19. **Linking Past and Present** **(a)** What action did the federal government take to stop violence by groups like the Ku Klux Klan? **(b)** List two ways governments and individuals work to end hate crimes today.
20. **Connecting to Geography: Place** Analyze the effect of geographic factors on the rise of the "New South." List at least three specific examples.

In an 1876 speech, Senator Blanche K. Bruce of Mississippi discussed the hopes that African Americans had for the future:

66 Although many of us are uneducated in the schools, we are informed and advised as to our duties to the government, our state, and ourselves. . . . With scrupulous respect for the rights of others, and with the hopefulness of political youth, we are determined that the great government that gave us liberty and rendered its gift valuable by giving us the ballot shall not find us wanting in a sufficient response to any demand that humanity or patriotism may make upon us. 99

—Blanche K. Bruce, Record of the 44th Congress, 1876

21. According to Bruce, what is African Americans' most important duty?
    A. to go to school in order to get an education
    B. to remain politically youthful
    C. to do what patriotism demands
    D. to cherish the gift of the vote
22. What government actions does Bruce praise?
    A. keeping African Americans informed
    B. giving African Americans their freedom and the right to vote
    C. trying to keep African Americans hopeful that their condition will improve in the future
    D. opening new schools in African American neighborhoods

Examine the chart below, and answer the questions that follow.

The Cycle of Poverty

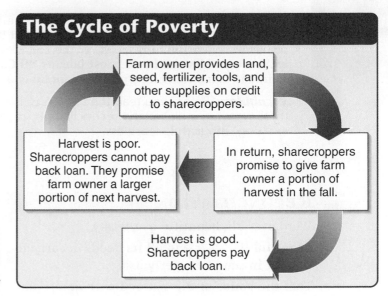

Farm owner provides land, seed, fertilizer, tools, and other supplies on credit to sharecroppers.

In return, sharecroppers promise to give farm owner a portion of harvest in the fall.

Harvest is good. Sharecroppers pay back loan.

Harvest is poor. Sharecroppers cannot pay back loan. They promise farm owner a larger portion of next harvest.

23. What problem is the main topic of this chart?
    A. Poor harvest
    B. Scarcity of supplies
    C. Sharecroppers' rising debt
    D. Inability to get credit
24. Suggest and evaluate one possible solution to the problem shown on the chart.

ACTIVITIES

Connecting With . . .
Government and Citizenship

Creating a Poster Choose one of the three Civil War amendments to the Constitution discussed in this chapter. With a partner, create a poster that expresses the key ideas of that amendment and its importance to Americans. Include both images and words. You may include modern images that reflect the importance of the amendment today.

Go Online
PHSchool.com

Connecting to Today
Giving a Report Use the Internet to find out about the nation's Historically Black Colleges and Universities (HBCUs). Report to the class on the location, history, and current goals of one of these schools. For help in starting this activity, visit PHSchool.com, **Web Code mfd-1805.**

History Through Literature

Leaves of Grass
Walt Whitman

Introduction One of the best-loved of all American poets, Walt Whitman served as a Union nurse in the Civil War. The following poems were written in response to the end of the war and the death of Abraham Lincoln. In the most famous, "O Captain! My Captain!" Whitman compares Lincoln to the captain of a ship.

Vocabulary Before you read the selections, find the meanings of these words in a dictionary: **reconciliation, carnage, incessantly, exulting, mournful, ceaseless.**

Walt Whitman

RECONCILIATION

Word over all, beautiful as the sky,

Beautiful that war and all its deeds of carnage
   must in time be utterly lost,

That the hands of the sisters Death and Night
   incessantly softly wash again, and ever, this
   soil'd world;

For my enemy is dead, a man divine as myself
   is dead,

I look where he lies white-faced and still in
   the coffin—I draw near,

Bend down and touch lightly with my lips the
   white face in the coffin.

O CAPTAIN! MY CAPTAIN!

O Captain! My Captain! our fearful trip is
done,

Our ship has weather'd every rack,* the
   prize we sought is won,

The port is near, the bells I hear, the people all
   exulting,

While follow eyes the steady keel, the vessel
   grim and daring;

   But O heart! heart! heart!

      O the bleeding drops of red,

         Where on the deck my Captain lies,

            Fallen cold and dead.

O Captain! My Captain! rise up and hear the
   bells;

Rise up—for you the flag is flung—for you
   the bugle trills,

For you bouquets and ribbon'd wreaths—for
   you the shores a-crowding,

For you they call, the swaying mass, their
   eager faces turning;

   Here Captain! dear father!

      This arm beneath your head!

         It is some dream that on the deck

            You've fallen cold and dead.

My Captain does not answer, his lips are pale
   and still,

My father does not feel my arm, he has no
   pulse nor will,

The ship is anchor'd safe and sound, its voyage
   closed and done,

From fearful trip the victor ship comes in with
   object won;

   Exult O shores, and ring O bells!

      But I with mournful tread,

         Walk the deck my Captain lies,

            Fallen cold and dead.

*rack: storm

HUSH'D BE THE CAMPS TO-DAY (MAY 4, 1865)

Hush'd be the camps to-day,

And soldiers let us drape our war-worn
    weapons,

And each with musing soul retire to celebrate

Our dear commander's death.

No more for him life's stormy conflicts,

Nor victory, nor defeat—no more time's dark
    events,

Charging like ceaseless clouds across the sky.

But sing poet in our name,

Sing of the love we bore him—because you,
    dweller in camps, know it truly.

As they invault the coffin there,

Sing—as they close the doors of earth upon
    him—one verse,

For the heavy hearts of soldiers.

Statue at the Lincoln Memorial

Analyzing Literature

1. In "Reconciliation," how would you describe the speaker's attitude toward the enemy?
   - **A** Triumphant
   - **B** Forgiving
   - **C** Vengeful
   - **D** Fearful

2. In "Oh Captain! My Captain!" the people are rejoicing because
   - **A** Lincoln is dead
   - **B** Lincoln has issued the Emancipation Proclamation
   - **C** the Union has been preserved
   - **D** the South has been destroyed

3. **Critical Thinking and Writing Applying Information** How does Whitman's depiction of Abraham Lincoln reflect what you have learned about his role as a leader during the Civil War? Refer to at least two lines from Whitman's poems.

Use the map <u>and</u> your knowledge of social studies to answer the following question.

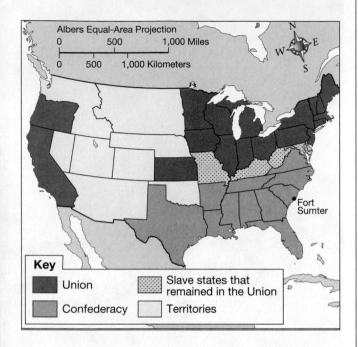

Albers Equal-Area Projection

0   500   1,000 Miles

0   500   1,000 Kilometers

Fort Sumter

Key

- Union
- Confederacy
- Slave states that remained in the Union
- Territories

1 Which conclusion can you draw from this map?

A More people lived in the Union than in the Confederacy.

B The Confederacy occupied most of the Atlantic Coast.

C Most of the fighting in the Civil War took place in the South.

D All slave states seceded from the Union.

2 Which of the following was not a goal of Radical Reconstruction?

A Break the power of southern planters

B Guarantee the vote to freedmen

C End slavery

D Strengthen Republican control of Congress

3 In which of the following pairs was the first event a cause of the second?

A Fort Sumter is fired upon; South Carolina secedes

B California applies for statehood; Compromise of 1850 passed

C Fighting erupts in Kansas; Kansas-Nebraska Act passed

D John Brown leads raid on Harpers Ferry; Republican party is formed

4 What was one major effect of the Emancipation Proclamation?

A It immediately freed slaves in the North.

B It immediately freed slaves in the South.

C It allowed African Americans to enlist in the Union army.

D It increased support for the Union cause in Europe.

5 With which of these statements would both Abraham Lincoln and Stephen Douglas have agreed?

A "The Kansas-Nebraska Act will help save the Union."

B "The Union must be preserved."

C "The people of each state have the right to decide whether to allow slavery."

D "The nation cannot survive half-slave, half-free."

Use the statements below **and** your knowledge of social studies to answer the following question.

- "All persons formerly held as slaves shall have the right to own, sell, purchase, and inherit property."

- "No one other than white men shall be permitted to serve on juries, hold office, or vote in any election."

---

6 Where would you be most likely to find *both* of the above statements?

   A The Wade-Davis Bill

   B The Reconstruction Act

   C One of the black codes

   D The Supreme Court decision in *Plessy* v. *Ferguson*

7 Which of the following individuals would have been most likely to agree with the Dred Scott decision?

   A Harriet Beecher Stowe

   B Frederick Douglass

   C John C. Calhoun

   D John Brown

8 Which of the following explained which people were considered to be American citizens?

   A Thirteenth Amendment

   B Fourteenth Amendment

   C Fifteenth Amendment

   D Gettysburg Address

Use the table **and** your knowledge of social studies to answer the following question.

Casualties of Selected Civil War Battles

Battle Site	Union Casualties	Confederate Casualties
Gettysburg	23,053	28,063
Antietam	12,410	10,316
Shiloh	13,047	10,694
Fredericksburg	12,653	5,309

Source: *The Civil War,* Time-Life Books

9 Which battle had the largest percentage of Union casualties?

   A Antietam

   B Gettysburg

   C Shiloh

   D Fredericksburg

Writing Practice

10 "Slavery was the chief cause of the Civil War." Agree or disagree with this statement. Give reasons for your answer.

11 Describe one social, one political, and one economic effect of the Civil War on the South. Explain which effect you think had the greatest impact.

Epilogue: The United States Since 1865

1865–PRESENT

1 **Entering Modern Times**
2 **A New Role for the Nation**
3 **The Great Depression and World War II**
4 **The Cold War and the Civil Rights Era**
5 **Into the Future**

Completion of the transcontinental railroad

World War I recruiting poster

1869

The nation's first railroad stretching from coast to coast is completed. The transcontinental railroad contributes to the growth of the West.

1917

Three years after World War I begins in Europe, the United States enters the war.

1901

Progressive reformer Theodore Roosevelt becomes President.

1929

The Great Depression begins.

AMERICAN EVENTS

1865 • • • • • • 1900 • • • • 1935

WORLD EVENTS

▲ **1870s**
The Age of Imperialism begins.

1917 ▲
The Russian Revolution brings Communists to power in Russia.

The United States Since 1865

Between 1867 and 1959, a total of 14 new states entered the Union.

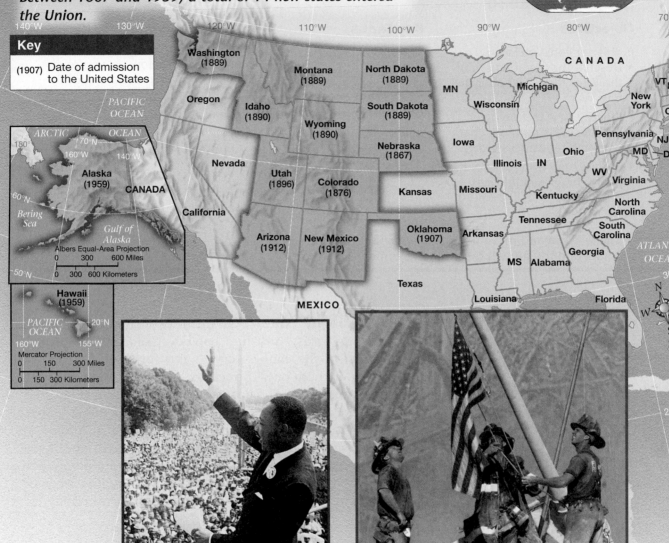

Key
(1907) Date of admission to the United States

Washington (1889)
Montana (1889)
North Dakota (1889)
MN
Michigan
CANADA
ME
VT
NH
Oregon
Idaho (1890)
South Dakota (1889)
Wisconsin
New York
MA
CT
RI
Wyoming (1890)
Pennsylvania
NJ
Nevada
Utah (1896)
Nebraska (1867)
Iowa
Illinois
IN
Ohio
MD
DE
WV
Virginia
California
Colorado (1876)
Kansas
Missouri
Kentucky
North Carolina
Arizona (1912)
New Mexico (1912)
Oklahoma (1907)
Arkansas
Tennessee
South Carolina
MS
Alabama
Georgia
ATLANTIC OCEAN
Texas
Louisiana
Florida
MEXICO

PACIFIC OCEAN

ARCTIC OCEAN
Alaska (1959)
CANADA
Bering Sea
Gulf of Alaska
Albers Equal-Area Projection
0   300   600 Miles
0   300   600 Kilometers

Hawaii (1959)
PACIFIC OCEAN
Mercator Projection
0   150   300 Miles
0   150   300 Kilometers

Martin Luther King, Jr.

Firefighters in the rubble of the World Trade Center

1941
After the Japanese bombing of Pearl Harbor, the United States enters World War II.

1963
Martin Luther King, Jr., leads the March on Washington in support of civil rights for African Americans.

2001
After attacks on New York's World Trade Center and the Pentagon, President George W. Bush vows to defeat terrorism.

1935 · · · · · **1970** · · · · · **Present** · · ·

▲ **1939**
World War II begins in Europe.

▲ **1954**
Vietnam throws off French rule.

1991 ▲
The collapse of the Soviet Union ends the Cold War.

1 Entering Modern Times

Prepare to Read

Objectives

In this section, you will
- Describe how settlement of the West increased after the Civil War.
- Identify new technologies and business methods that helped big business grow.
- Explain how rising immigration led to the growth of cities.

Key Terms

Homestead Act
transcontinental railroad
corporation
capital
monopoly
American Federation of Labor
urbanization

Target Reading Skill

Clarifying Meaning Complete the concept web below. As you read the section, fill in the blank ovals with information about changes after the Civil War. Add as many ovals as you need.

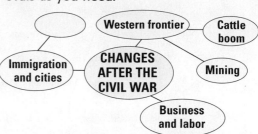

Main Idea Westward movement, expanding industry, increased immigration, and the growth of cities transformed the nation.

Texas longhorn

Setting the Scene "Here was all these cheap long-horned steers over-running Texas," recalled cowboy "Teddy Blue" Abbott. "Here was the rest of the country crying out for beef—and no railroads in Texas to get them out." Ranchers saw only one way to meet the nation's demands: Bring the cattle to the rail centers.

The long cattle drives gave birth to one of the most popular American heroes—the cowboy. In spite of his romantic image, the cowboy's life was rough and dangerous. He spent months on the trail, facing roaring rivers, grass fires, and the threat of stampede. When a cowboy got to town after a long drive, his first thoughts were of a good meal, a haircut, and showy new clothes. Abbott recalled:

> 66 I had a new white Stetson hat that I paid ten dollars for and new pants that cost twelve dollars, and a good shirt and fancy boots. They had colored tops, red and blue, with a half-moon and star on them. . . . I thought I was dressed right for the first time in my life. 99
>
> —"Teddy Blue" Abbott, quoted in *The West* (Burns)

The cattle boom lasted only about 20 years, but it helped change the West forever. At the same time, the nation's cities and factories were also undergoing great changes.

Settlement of the West

Since the Louisiana Purchase of 1803, the nation had expanded steadily westward. After the Civil War, westward movement sped up. Many Americans hoped to find new lives in the wide prairies. The West, however, was already home to many Native Americans.

Moving West The mining boom that began with the California gold rush continued. Valuable strikes of silver or gold brought prospectors to Nevada, the Dakotas, even as far as Alaska. Some mining "boomtowns" grew into permanent settlements. Parts of the West organized as territories, which later became new states.

Cattle ranching became a "boom" industry in the 1870s. For years, herds of longhorns had roamed the open range in Texas and the Southwest. Now, a growing population needed more meat. Ranchers hired cowhands to herd the cattle from grazing lands to railroad lines in the north. Ranching soon spread throughout the Great Plains.

The federal government encouraged settlers. The **Homestead Act** of 1862 gave land to anyone who would farm it for five years. Eager for land, families from the East endured hardships and harsh weather. African Americans also moved West, looking for freedom they did not have in the South. Farmers plowed grassland with efficient new steel plows. They also built fences, leading to clashes with ranchers.

Railroads carried supplies and settlers to the West. To encourage railroad building, the government granted land and money. In 1869, two railroad companies completed the nation's first **transcontinental railroad.** Now it was possible for settlers to travel by train all the way from the Atlantic coast to the Pacific.

Indians Lose Their Land Westward movement spelled disaster for Native Americans in the West. The many Indian nations there had rich, varied cultures. While some Indians farmed, many more depended on the huge herds of bison, or buffalo, that roamed the Great Plains. The buffalo supplied meat for food and skins for clothing, warm rugs, and tepees.

As miners and settlers moved onto Native American lands, they broke treaties that the government had made with the Indians. Soldiers and hunters wiped out the huge buffalo herds. Native

GEOGRAPHY
Skills

Mining, railroad building, and cattle ranching all played a major role in changing the West.

1. **Location** On the map, locate **(a)** Comstock Lode, **(b)** Central Pacific Railroad, **(c)** Chisholm Trail.

2. **Movement** Describe the route of the Goodnight-Loving Trail.

3. **Critical Thinking Drawing Conclusions** Why do you think most railroad lines in the West were built to run east–west rather than north–south?

The Changing West

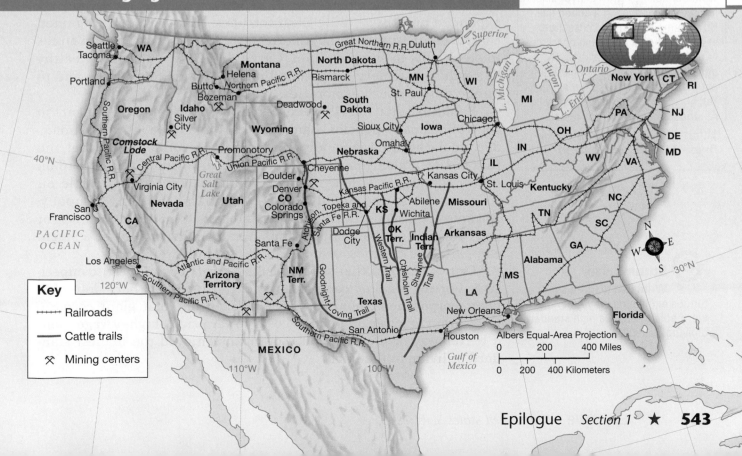

Americans tried to resist the loss of their land and their way of life. Leaders such as Sitting Bull and Crazy Horse of the Lakota Sioux and Geronimo of the Apaches led their people in wars against government troops. In the end, however, the federal government gradually forced western Indians onto reservations.

Business and Labor

American business and industry boomed after the Civil War. New technology fueled this rapid growth. Inventions such as refrigeration and the telephone changed both business and daily life. Thomas Edison and his workers invented products that shaped today's world—not only the first practical light bulb but also the electric power plant, the phonograph, and motion pictures. Late in the 1800s, inventors in the United States and Europe built the first automobiles.

Growth of Big Business The railroad industry dominated the American economy. A network of rail lines crossed the country. Powerful "railroad barons" such as Cornelius Vanderbilt bought up smaller lines and built great railroad empires. Some railroad owners abused their power by fixing prices and bribing public officials. Nonetheless, the railroads created jobs and spurred the growth of industry.

To expand, businesses organized as corporations. A **corporation** is a business owned by investors. The company sells shares of stock in exchange for **capital**, or money to invest in future growth. If the business prospers, the value of the stock grows. Investors in corporations faced fewer risks than owners of private businesses. If a private business goes bankrupt, the owners must pay all the debts. By law, stockholders cannot be held responsible for the debts of a corporation.

In the 1850s, scientists developed the Bessemer process, a method of making stronger steel at lower cost. The steel industry expanded quickly, creating great fortunes. Andrew Carnegie gained control of all aspects of the American steel industry, from iron mines to steel mills to shipping lines. Carnegie believed that the wealthy had a duty to society. He gave millions of dollars to charities and to public projects such as libraries.

Banks invested heavily in corporations, which allowed bankers to control company policies. Banker J. P. Morgan bought up railroads and steel companies, including Carnegie's. He formed U.S. Steel, the first billion-dollar American business. Other fortunes were based on a new resource, oil. John D. Rockefeller, starting with a single oil refinery, built the highly successful Standard Oil Company. Rockefeller organized his business interests to control the stock of rival companies. Standard Oil thus became a **monopoly**, or a single company that controls or dominates an entire industry.

Critics charged that these business practices reduced competition, hurting smaller companies and consumers. Others defended giant corporations, however. They pointed out that giant corporations brought lower production costs, lower prices, higher wages, and a better way of life. By 1900, Americans enjoyed the highest standard of living in the world.

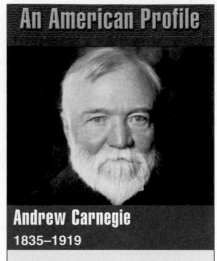

An American Profile

Andrew Carnegie
1835–1919

In Scotland, Andrew Carnegie's father wove linen on a hand loom. His mother cobbled shoes. But, new technology was driving such artisans into poverty. Even after immigrating to the United States, the family continued to plunge deeper into debt.

Young Andrew decided to work *with* technology rather than against it. First, he got a job in a cotton mill. He became a telegram messenger at age 14, then a telegraph operator for the Pennsylvania Railroad. By age 23, Carnegie was superintendent of the railroad's western division. Yet, his greatest success—as the American Steel King—lay ahead.

What qualities do you think helped Carnegie succeed?

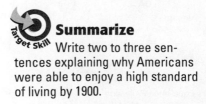

Summarize
Write two to three sentences explaining why Americans were able to enjoy a high standard of living by 1900.

Rise of Organized Labor Factory conditions could be harsh and dangerous. Workers, including young children, labored long hours in crowded sweatshops for low pay. Unsafe conditions were common. In 1911, a deadly fire broke out in the Triangle Shirtwaist Factory in New York City. Nearly 150 workers, mostly young immigrant women, died because the owners had locked the doors.

Workers began to organize for better conditions, shorter hours, and an end to child labor. In 1886, the American Federation of Labor (AFL) brought together trade unions, which represented skilled workers. Some unions used strikes to gain better pay. In the beginning, public officials and the courts generally sided with factory owners. Still, union membership grew steadily.

Immigration and the Growth of Cities

In the late 1800s, millions of immigrants streamed into the United States. Many were fleeing poverty at home. They hoped for factory jobs or farmland. A large number of Jews and Armenian Christians arrived, driven from their homelands by religious persecution.

The New Immigrants Before the Civil War, most immigrants came from northern and western Europe. In the late 1800s, this pattern changed. More people came from southern or eastern Europe—Italy, Poland, Russia, and other countries. A growing number of Asians, mainly Chinese, landed on the West Coast. By the 1890s, most Europeans came through the immigration station at Ellis Island in New York Harbor. Their first sight of the American "promised land" was the Statue of Liberty, with these words inscribed on its base:

> 66 Give me your tired, your poor,
> Your huddled masses yearning to breathe free,
> The wretched refuse of your teeming shore.
> Send these, the homeless, tempest-tossed to me:
> I lift my lamp beside the golden door. 99
>
> —Emma Lazarus, "The New Colossus"

Viewing History

Immigrants in a New Land Above are just some of the millions of European immigrants who first entered the United States at Ellis Island. Inspectors wrote down each immigrant's name and country of origin. **Drawing Conclusions** *Based on your reading and this picture, how do you think these immigrants felt as they arrived in the United States?*

Primary Sources

See Jacob Riis, "How the Other Half Lives," on page 608 of the Reference Section.

Language, religion, and culture set newcomers apart from their neighbors. People of one ethnic group clustered together in city neighborhoods. While older immigrants kept traditional ways, their children hurried to learn English and become citizens.

Many Americans opposed the flood of immigrants. These nativists said that the newcomers competed with Americans for jobs and would never fit into American culture. On the West Coast, anti-Chinese feelings were especially strong. An 1882 federal law barred most Chinese immigrants. Other laws set limits on immigration.

Growing Cities Immigration fueled the rapid growth of cities. The United States was once mainly a rural nation. That changed as people flocked to the cities for jobs in factories, stores, and offices. This process of population shifting from farms to cities is called **urbanization.** African American migrants from the South formed thriving communities in northern cities such as Chicago and Detroit.

Cities themselves changed with the building of skyscrapers and great public parks. Streetcar lines linked cities and suburbs. In 1897, the nation's first subway line opened in Boston. Cities offered a wide variety of attractions, from music halls and museums to sports.

City life was very different for rich and poor. The poor often lived in small, dark, crowded tenement apartments. In these unhealthy conditions, diseases like tuberculosis spread easily. Middle-class families, on the other hand, lived in comfortable houses. The very wealthy built mansions far from the crowds.

Reformers worked to improve the terrible conditions in the slums. They fought for better city services, such as safe water and clean streets. In Chicago, Jane Addams led the settlement house movement, which offered education and other services. Religious groups such as the Salvation Army also aided the poor.

★ ★ ★ Section 1 Assessment ★ ★ ★

Recall

1. **Identify** Explain the significance of (a) Homestead Act, (b) Thomas Edison, (c) Andrew Carnegie, (d) American Federation of Labor, (e) Jane Addams.
2. **Define** (a) transcontinental railroad, (b) corporation, (c) capital, (d) monopoly, (e) urbanization.

Comprehension

3. What groups of people contributed to the settlement of the West?
4. (a) How did the growth of big business benefit the nation? (b) Why did some people argue against monopolies?

5. Why did immigrants come to the United States?

Critical Thinking and Writing

6. **Exploring the Main Idea** Review the Main Idea statement at the beginning of this section. Then, list three ways in which modern American life might be different if one of the changes described in this section had not taken place.
7. **Making a Decision** If you were an investor in the late 1800s, would you buy stock or put your money into a privately owned business? Write a letter to another investor explaining your decision.

ACTIVITY

Connecting to Today
Choose five American cities, including one in your home state. Then, use the Internet to find out about population growth in those cities. Create a database of tables or graphs showing the population of each city in 1850, 1900, 1950, and 2000. For help in completing the activity, visit PHSchool.com, **Web Code mfd-3101.**

2 A New Role for the Nation

Prepare to Read

Objectives

In this section, you will
- Identify the changes that Progressive reformers supported.
- Explain how the United States assumed a greater role in world affairs.
- List the causes and results of World War I.

Key Terms

Progressives

muckraker

civil service

Nineteenth Amendment

isolationism

imperialism

Spanish-American War

Roosevelt Corollary

World War I

Target Reading Skill

Main Idea As you read, prepare an outline of this section. Use roman numerals to indicate the major headings, capital letters for the sub-headings, and numbers for the supporting details. The sample below will help you get started.

> I. The Progressive Era
>   A. Progressive reformers
>   1. Muckrakers
>   2. Political reforms
>   3.
>   B. Presidents back reform
>   1.
>   2.
> II. Becoming a World Power
>   A.
>   B.

Main Idea As the government began to take on a larger role in people's lives, the nation also became more involved in world affairs.

Setting the Scene

Theodore Roosevelt was no ordinary politician. He had been a cattle rancher in North Dakota and head of the New York City police department. He had led the Rough Riders, a volunteer cavalry unit in a war with Spain.

With his dynamic personality, "Teddy" became a popular hero—and he used his popularity to push for an ambitious program of reforms. In an election speech, he promised:

> 66 The principles for which we stand are the principles of fair play and a square deal for every man and every woman in the United States. 99
>
> —Theodore Roosevelt, Address to the Boys' Progressive League, July 3, 1913

Under the leadership of Roosevelt and his successors, the federal government began to take on a new, larger role in people's lives. At the same time, the United States itself took on a new role as a growing world power.

Theodore Roosevelt

The Progressive Era

In the decades following the Civil War, industrial growth helped create a period of prosperity known as the "Gilded Age." Still, American society had many problems. In the Progressive Era, from 1898 to 1917, reformers worked to reduce the power of big business, improve social conditions, and clean up political corruption.

Progressive Reformers The Progressives were men and women who wanted to improve society, though they had different targets. Crusading journalists known as muckrakers reported on slum conditions and unsafe meatpacking plants. Other Progressives backed political reforms such as primary elections. In 1913, Progressives won passage of two constitutional amendments. The Sixteenth

POLITICAL CARTOON
Skills

Women Win the Vote
The Nineteenth Amendment, giving women the right to vote, was ratified in 1920. This cartoon by Rollin Kirby appeared that year.

1. **Comprehension**
   (a) What does the ladder represent? **(b)** What is the woman standing on?

2. **Understanding Main Ideas** **(a)** Based on this cartoon, was the woman's climb easy or difficult? **(b)** What is her mood?

3. **Critical Thinking Identifying Points of View** Based on this cartoon, do you think Rollin Kirby favored the Nineteenth Amendment? Support your answer.

Civics 🏛

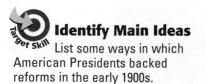
Identify Main Ideas
List some ways in which American Presidents backed reforms in the early 1900s.

Amendment gave Congress the power to impose an income tax. The Seventeenth Amendment called for senators to be elected directly by the people, rather than by state legislatures.

Reformers also attacked corruption in government. As you have read, under the spoils system, most government jobs went to loyal party workers. One early reform set up a **civil service** system that awarded federal jobs on the basis of examination scores, not political influence. Reformers also tried to limit the power of big business. In 1890, Congress passed the Sherman Antitrust Act. Its goal was to limit business monopolies that hurt competition. However, the act proved ineffective at first.

During the Progressive Era, the long campaign for women's suffrage gained strength. In the late 1800s, women gained the right to vote in four western states: Wyoming, Utah, Colorado, and Idaho. As more women entered the work force after 1900, leaders like Carrie Chapman Catt stepped up the campaign. At last, in 1920, the Nineteenth Amendment to the Constitution guaranteed women's right to vote.

Presidents Back Reform In 1901, Theodore Roosevelt became President after the assassination of William McKinley. As President, Roosevelt pushed through a series of Progressive reforms. He enforced the Sherman Antitrust Act against what he saw as unfair monopolies, and he supported organized labor. He also backed laws to conserve natural resources and to make food products and medicines safer.

Roosevelt's successors, William Howard Taft and Woodrow Wilson, also supported reforms. Wilson supported laws to encourage business competition. At Wilson's urging, Congress also passed laws to regulate the banking system.

Seeking Equality Minority groups gained little from Progressive reforms. Since the end of Reconstruction, African Americans had lost many political rights. They faced prejudice and segregation in schools, housing, and jobs. Two leaders offered different answers. Booker T. Washington advised African Americans to accept segregation, at least for the time being. He urged them to concentrate on education, economic self-improvement, and gradual progress.

Educator and writer W.E.B. DuBois disagreed. DuBois believed instead that African Americans should work actively against discrimination. DuBois joined with white reformers to found the National Association for the Advancement of Colored People (NAACP) to work for equal rights for African Americans.

Becoming a World Power

In his Farewell Address, George Washington had advised Americans to "steer clear of permanent alliances." Later Presidents continued this policy of **isolationism,** or limited involvement in the world's affairs. But, as American trade expanded in the late 1800s, so did American interest in the rest of the world.

By the 1870s, many European nations had launched the Age of Imperialism. **Imperialism** is the policy of powerful countries seeking to control the political and economic affairs of weaker countries or regions. European powers took over most of Africa and parts of Asia.

Some American politicians believed that the United States should expand overseas, too. Albert Beveridge of Indiana argued:

66Today we are raising more than we can consume. Today we are making more than we can use. Today our industrial society is congested; there are more workers than there is work. . . . Therefore we must find new markets for our produce, new occupations for our capital, new work for our labor.99

—Albert Beveridge, quoted in *Modern Eloquence* (Reed)

Expansion in the Pacific Once Americans reached the Pacific coast, they looked toward trade and territory around the Pacific Ocean. In the 1850s, the United States Navy forced Japan to open its ports to trade with the West. In 1867, the United States purchased the resource-rich Alaska territory from Russia.

Cause *and* Effect

Causes

- Western frontier closes
- Businesses seek raw materials and new markets
- European nations compete for resources and markets

OVERSEAS EXPANSION

Effects

- United States develops strong navy
- Open Door Policy protects trade with China
- United States governs lands in Caribbean and Pacific
- United States builds Panama Canal
- United States sends troops to Latin American nations to protect its interests

Effects Today

- United States is global superpower
- Alaska and Hawaii are 49th and 50th states
- Puerto Rico, American Samoa, Guam, and U.S. Virgin Islands remain United States territories
- United States has close economic ties with Latin America and Pacific Rim

GRAPHIC ORGANIZER
Skills

In the late 1800s, the United States gradually became more involved in foreign affairs.

1. **Comprehension** Which of the effects listed here involved Latin America?

2. **Critical Thinking Ranking** Which of the Effects Today listed here do you think is the most important? Explain.

Expansion in the Pacific rested on naval power. The United States acquired the islands of Midway and Samoa, where ships bound for Asia could refuel. The next large acquisition was the island chain of Hawaii. Starting in the mid-1800s, Americans had set up large sugar plantations in Hawaii. In 1893, with the help of United States Marines, the planters overthrew the last Hawaiian queen, Liliuokalani (lih lee oo oh kah LAH nee). The United States soon annexed the islands.

In mainland Asia, the United States competed with European nations for influence in China. The United States supported an "Open Door Policy" that guaranteed access to Chinese ports and trade.

Relations With Latin America Backers of expansion now looked closer to home. In nearby Cuba, people were rebelling against rule by Spain. Sensational newspaper stories made many Americans want to help the rebels. In 1898, after the American battleship *Maine* blew up in Havana harbor, the United States declared war on Spain. American forces won a quick victory in the Spanish-American War. The peace settlement gave Americans their first taste of overseas empire. The United States gained Cuba, Puerto Rico, Guam, and the Philippines. Cubans were given self-rule, though under American control.

Teddy Roosevelt favored American expansion. One of his goals was to build a canal across the narrow Isthmus of Panama. It would let ships sail between the Atlantic and Pacific oceans without going around South America. Taking advantage of a local rebellion, Roosevelt got land for the canal. Despite tropical diseases and engineering challenges, the Panama Canal was completed by 1914.

Roosevelt took another step in establishing an American role in Latin America. As you have read, the Monroe Doctrine of 1823 established the idea that the United States would oppose European interference in Latin America. Roosevelt expanded the Monroe Doctrine. He stated that the United States had the right to intervene in Latin American affairs. This policy became known as the Roosevelt Corollary. In the following decade, Presidents sent troops to protect United States interests in Haiti, the Dominican Republic, and other Caribbean countries.

World War I

In 1914, long-standing tensions in Europe erupted into the largest war the world had yet seen. Imperialism was one cause—major nations were competing for territory. Within those empires, various nationalist groups wanted independence. To maintain power, nations built up their armed forces. They also made alliances with one another, promising support if their allies were attacked.

In June 1914, a Serbian nationalist killed the heir to the Austro-Hungarian throne. Austria-Hungary blamed the Serbian government and declared war. Russia stepped in to protect Serbia. The alliance system drew one country after another into war. The war pitted the Central Powers—Germany; Austria-Hungary; and the Ottoman, or Turkish, Empire—against the Allied Powers of France, Britain, and Russia. In time, more than 20 countries were involved. Across Europe, millions of soldiers fought in long, deadly offensives. People called it the Great War, although we now call it World War I.

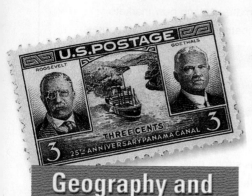

Geography and History

Building the Panama Canal

For American engineers and workers, building a canal across Panama was a gigantic undertaking.

- The canal extends 50.72 miles from the Atlantic Ocean to the Pacific Ocean.
- Workers removed 262 million cubic yards of earth and rock in constructing the canal.
- Some 56,600 workers used hand shovels, pickaxes, dynamite, and giant steam shovels to cut through jungles, hills, and swamps.
- The greatest obstacle to construction was disease: Work could begin only after scientists wiped out the mosquitoes that spread yellow fever.
- The canal saved 7,873 miles of travel for a ship bound from New York to California.

What other kinds of building projects present geographic challenges?

The United States Enters the War President Woodrow Wilson tried to keep the United States neutral. Most Americans viewed the war as a European problem. Soon, though, American opinion shifted. President Wilson angrily denounced German submarine attacks on ships crossing the Atlantic Ocean.

Finally, in April 1917, Wilson asked Congress to declare war on Germany. "The world must be made safe for democracy," he declared.

Americans quickly prepared for war. The government built and trained an army. Industries mobilized to produce weapons and supplies. Other programs boosted food production. On the home front, people bought Liberty Bonds to help pay for the war effort. Many women went to work to fill important jobs. To encourage unity, the government made it a crime to criticize United States involvement in the war.

Results of World War I When the United States joined the war, things looked bad for the Allies—Britain, France and Russia. Then, Russia withdrew from the war after a revolution overthrew the tsar's government. American troops landed in France to reinforce British and French armies. By June 1918, the Germans were in retreat. The war ended in November.

The costs of the war were staggering. More than 8 million people had died of wounds or disease, and millions more were wounded. Much of Europe was in ruins.

President Wilson tried to shape the peace settlement. His "Fourteen Points" plan proposed an end to alliances. It outlined a League of Nations that would settle international disputes. However, the final peace treaty left out many of Wilson's ideas. Instead, the Treaty of Versailles imposed harsh terms on Germany.

In the United States, Congress rejected membership in the League of Nations. Many politicians wanted a return to isolationism.

★ ★ ★ Section 2 Assessment ★ ★ ★

Recall

1. **Identify** Explain the significance of (a) Theodore Roosevelt, (b) Progressives, (c) Nineteenth Amendment, (d) Woodrow Wilson, (e) Booker T. Washington, (f) W.E.B. DuBois, (g) Spanish-American War, (h) Roosevelt Corollary, (i) World War I.
2. **Define** (a) muckraker, (b) civil service, (c) isolationism, (d) imperialism.

Comprehension

3. Describe three Progressive reforms.
4. What new territories did the United States gain?

5. Why did the United States enter World War I?

Critical Thinking and Writing

6. **Exploring the Main Idea** Review the Main Idea statement at the beginning of this section. Then, write two pairs of sentences about events described in this section. Label the first sentence in each pair "BEFORE" and the second sentence in each pair "AFTER."
7. **Drawing Conclusions** Write a paragraph explaining why reformers thought a competitive civil service examination might help solve the problem of government corruption.

ACTIVITY

Drawing a Political Cartoon Reread the statement by Albert Beveridge in this section. Then, draw a political cartoon that might have appeared in an American newspaper at the time. Your cartoon should either support or disagree with Beveridge's point of view.

Honoring Our Veterans

World War I ended on November 11, 1918. Today, we celebrate that date as Veterans Day, a holiday to honor all of those who served in the armed forces in war or peace.

> ❝ *Veterans deserve to know that we as a people honor their service. Please honor their sacrifice. Pay tribute each day to their irreplaceable gift to our nation. And take a moment to thank tomorrow's veterans. It's never too early to let them know how deeply we recognize their passionate commitment to keep America safe.* ❞
> —2000 Veterans Day Speech, Army Public Affairs Division

The first "unknown soldier" was one of four American dead taken from the French battlefields of World War I. He was honored at Arlington National Cemetery in 1921. Since then, unknowns from World War II and the Korean War have been buried in the "Tomb of the Unknowns." Here, a Marine solemnly stands guard at the tomb.

The Veterans of Foreign Wars (VFW) was begun in 1899 by veterans of the Spanish-American War. Its membership now numbers more than 2 million. This nonprofit organization offers support to veterans. It also sponsors community projects, such as an annual essay contest for seventh, eighth, and ninth graders. Here, VFW members salute a passing parade.

ACTIVITY

With a group of classmates, plan a Veterans Day ceremony. Prepare the opening paragraph of a speech. (If you like, you may choose to focus on a specific veteran you know.) Design a banner or poster, and suggest a list of special activities for your community.

3 The Great Depression and World War II

Prepare to Read

Objectives

In this section, you will
- Explain how the Great Depression began.
- Describe how the New Deal affected American life.
- List the causes of World War II.

Key Terms

jazz
margin buying
Great Depression
New Deal
Social Security
deficit spending
totalitarian state
Holocaust
World War II
D-Day

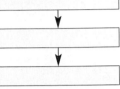 Target Reading Skill

Reading Process Copy this flow-chart. As you read, fill in the boxes with information about the events discussed in this section. One box has been partly filled in to help you get started.

1920s
• Postwar decade
• Business expansion
• Jazz Age
•

↓

↓

Main Idea In the 1930s and 1940s, Americans endured the nation's greatest economic crisis as well as World War II.

Setting the Scene Long before World War I, Americans had begun to fall in love with the automobile. A popular song from 1905 showed that the car was already part of American culture:

“Come away with me, Lucille,
In my merry Oldsmobile.
Down the road of life we'll fly,
Automo-bubbling you and I.”
—Vincent Bryan, "In My Merry Oldsmobile"

1925 automobile

By the 1920s, the automobile was an indispensable part of American life. Mass production made cars more affordable. Car ownership ended the isolation of rural families. Gas stations, motels, and roadside restaurants sprang up.

The car boom was just one sign of the prosperous economy and optimistic spirit of the 1920s. However, Americans would soon be plunged into two crises that threatened their entire way of life.

From Prosperity to Depression

The 1920s began as a hopeful, prosperous time. President Calvin Coolidge declared, "The chief business of the American people is business." The postwar economy grew quickly.

The Prosperous Twenties The auto industry was important in the booming economy. Factories turned out new consumer goods such as radios, vacuum cleaners, and refrigerators. Many people also invested in the stock market for the first time. Stock prices rose steadily.

Women could now vote. More women also joined the work force. Young women known as flappers shocked older Americans with their short skirts and reckless behavior.

Jazz was an original American musical style that blended West African rhythms, European harmonies, and African American work songs and spirituals. It became so popular that the 1920s are often called the "Jazz Age."

The Crash Some of the prosperity was built on shaky ground. Farmers, miners, and factory workers faced hard times. The soaring stock market encouraged a practice called **margin buying.** Investors would buy stock for a small down payment, borrowing the rest from their brokers, and then sell for a profit when the price of the stock rose. Margin buying worked as long as prices kept rising.

Then, the economy began to slow. Because fewer people could afford to buy goods, factories laid off workers or closed. Worried investors began to sell their stocks. As prices fell, brokers demanded full payment for stocks bought on margin. Many investors had to sell at a loss. On October 29, 1929, the stock market crashed.

The economy plunged into the worst economic slump in American history, the **Great Depression,** which deepened through the early 1930s. Banks closed, wiping out people's savings. Unemployment soared. Hungry people lined up at soup kitchens.

President Herbert Hoover tried to restore confidence in the economy by predicting better times ahead. However, like most Presidents since the time of Jefferson, he did not believe that the government should become directly involved in the economy. In the end, Hoover did take steps to fight the Great Depression with public works programs. Still, people blamed him for the hard times.

The New Deal

In 1932, Americans elected a new President, Franklin Delano Roosevelt. FDR promised to take action against hard times. "I pledge myself to a new deal for the American people," he said.

FDR's Program Roosevelt instituted a series of bold new programs called the **New Deal.** The New Deal had three main goals: relief for the unemployed, plans for recovery, and reforms to prevent another severe depression. The WPA (Works Progress Administration), for example, built schools and public buildings and gave work to artists and writers. The Tennessee Valley Authority (TVA) built dams to supply electric power and control floods in parts of the South. The Federal Deposit Insurance Corporation (FDIC) protected the funds people deposited in their bank accounts.

Unlike most other industrial nations, the United States had no insurance for retired workers. In 1935, the **Social Security** system began. It provided benefits for retired or disabled people.

Impact of the New Deal The New Deal did not end the Great Depression. Still, some New Deal programs did place the nation's banks on a firmer footing, protect farmers, and provide work for millions of people.

The New Deal changed people's relationship with the federal government. Government grew bigger, with more influence on everyday life. Many people came to believe that government had a

---

Primary Source

FDR's First Inaugural Address

In his first speech as President, Franklin Roosevelt tried to reassure the American people:
"This is preeminently a time to speak the truth, the whole truth, frankly and boldly. Nor need we shrink from honestly facing conditions in our country today. This great Nation will endure as it has endured, will revive and will prosper. So, first of all, let me assert my firm belief that the only thing we have to fear is fear itself—nameless, unreasoning, unjustified terror which paralyzes needed efforts to convert retreat into advance."
—Franklin Delano Roosevelt, First Inaugural Address

Analyzing Primary Sources

Why do you think FDR told Americans that the only thing they had to fear was fear?

Unemployment, 1929–1941

Percentage of Workers (y-axis): 0, 2, 4, 6, 8, 10, 12, 14, 16, 18, 20, 22, 24, 26

Year (x-axis): 1929, 1931, 1933, 1935, 1937, 1939, 1941

Source: *Historical Statistics of the United States*

The Great Depression threw millions of Americans out of work. Bread lines (right) were common in every major American city.

1. **Comprehension** In which year was unemployment at its worst?

2. **Critical Thinking Making Generalizations** Based on this graph (left), make two generalizations about the changing rate of unemployment.

Economics $

responsibility to help all its citizens. Supporters of the New Deal argued that social programs had helped people keep their faith in democracy during the crisis.

Some critics argued that the New Deal went too far. They were alarmed that, in order to support massive programs, the government was spending more money than it was taking in. This practice is known as **deficit spending.** Critics also argued that the growing size and power of the federal government threatened traditional American freedoms. Former President Herbert Hoover warned:

66 Either we shall have a society based upon ordered liberty and the initiative of the individual, or we shall have a planned society that means dictation no matter what you call it or who does it. There is no half-way ground. 99

—Herbert Hoover, speech to the Republican National Convention, 1936

The debate about the size of the federal government that began during the New Deal continues to this day.

World War II

Americans and Europeans hoped to avoid another war as destructive as World War I. During the depression, Americans returned to isolationism, focusing on troubles at home. World events soon made neutrality impossible, however.

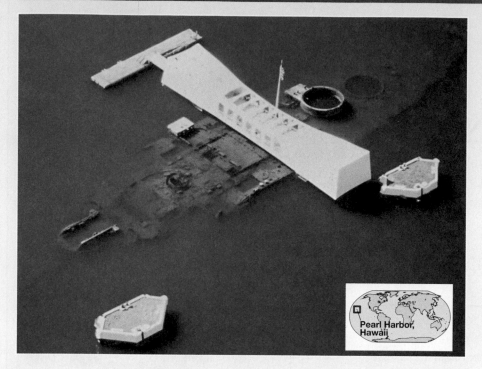

USS *Arizona* Memorial

On December 7, 1941, Japanese planes bombed the United States fleet anchored at Pearl Harbor, Hawaii. The battleship *Arizona* sank with more than 1,100 sailors aboard. Today, you can view the sunken hull of the *Arizona*. At the "remembrance exhibit," you can pay tribute to the first Americans to die in World War II.

Pearl Harbor, Hawaii

The Rise of Dictators In the 1920s and 1930s, totalitarian governments gained power in many nations. A **totalitarian state** is one in which a single party controls the government and every aspect of people's lives. In the Soviet Union, Joseph Stalin built a powerful communist dictatorship. Military leaders in Japan began to build an empire in East Asia.

In Italy, Benito Mussolini and his Fascist party played on extreme nationalist feelings. In Germany, Adolf Hitler blamed Germany's losses in the war on Jews and others. His National Socialist, or Nazi, party was brutal and militaristic. During the war years, Hitler and his officers carried out his systematic plan to destroy European Jews. In what is now called the **Holocaust,** more than 6 million Jews, as well as millions of others, died or were killed in concentration camps.

Use Prior Knowledge

How was the response of Americans to the start of World War II similar to the response of Americans to the start of World War I?

The War Begins Hitler's armies began to invade neighboring countries one by one. At first, Britain and France gave in to Hitler's demands in order to avoid war. However, when Hitler invaded Poland in 1939, they declared war. **World War II** pitted the Axis powers—Germany, Italy, and Japan—against the Allies. The Allies included Britain, France, China, the Soviet Union, and many others.

Hitler's armies quickly overran most of Europe. Soon Britain stood alone. In Asia, the Japanese carried out a program of aggression despite American protests.

At first, the United States tried to remain neutral. As the war continued, President Roosevelt pushed programs to send economic aid to the Allies. Then, on December 7, 1941, Japan launched a surprise attack on the American Pacific fleet at Pearl Harbor, in Hawaii. The next day, the United States entered the war on the Allied side.

The Home Front The nation mobilized for war quickly. Factories converted to war production. To conserve supplies for the military, the government rationed meat, gasoline, sugar, clothing, and other goods. Millions of women went to work in defense jobs. People from every part of the country and every ethnic group worked for victory.

War fears led to tragedy for many Japanese Americans. Saying that they might be disloyal, the government moved about 110,000 Japanese Americans on the West Coast into relocation camps. They lost homes and businesses. Years later, Congress agreed to pay Japanese American citizens who had lost their homes and farms.

The Allied Victory In 1942, the Allies faced losses everywhere. German forces held most of Europe and were besieging the Soviet Union. Japan occupied islands in the Pacific.

Several Allied victories marked turning points in the war. The United States Navy turned back the Japanese at Midway Island. The Russians withstood the German siege of Stalingrad, and the British drove back the Germans in North Africa. In 1943, the Allies invaded Italy, as Mussolini's government collapsed. The major invasion of Western Europe came on **D-Day**, June 6, 1944. Allied troops landed on the coast of Normandy, France, and pressed eastward toward Germany.

Roosevelt died in April 1945, but Allied advances went on. In May, Hitler committed suicide and Germany surrendered. FDR's successor, Harry Truman, decided to use a powerful new weapon, the atomic bomb, against Japan. The bombing of Hiroshima and Nagasaki in August 1945 brought about Japan's surrender.

★ ★ ★ Section 3 Assessment ★ ★ ★

Recall
1. **Identify** Explain the significance of **(a)** Great Depression, **(b)** Herbert Hoover, **(c)** Franklin D. Roosevelt, **(d)** New Deal, **(e)** Social Security, **(f)** Adolf Hitler, **(g)** Holocaust, **(h)** World War II, **(i)** D-Day.
2. **Define** **(a)** jazz, **(b)** margin buying, **(c)** deficit spending, **(d)** totalitarian state.

Comprehension
3. What were the causes of the Great Depression?
4. Describe the three goals of the New Deal.

5. **(a)** How did World War II begin in Europe? **(b)** Why did the United States enter the war?

Critical Thinking and Writing
6. **Exploring the Main Idea** Review the Main Idea statement at the beginning of this section. Then, write a paragraph explaining whether you think a depression or a war is a greater threat to a nation.
7. **Supporting a Point of View** **(a)** Summarize one argument for and one argument against the New Deal. **(b)** Write a letter to FDR telling him why you do or do not support his goals.

ACTIVITY

Go Online
PHSchool.com

Making a Map
Use the Internet to find out about the D-Day landing. Then, make a map showing the movement of Allied forces. For help in completing the activity, visit PHSchool.com, **Web Code mfd-3103**.

4 The Cold War and the Civil Rights Era

Prepare to Read

Objectives

In this section, you will
- List the causes of the Cold War.
- Identify the successes that the civil rights movement achieved.
- Explain how the Vietnam War affected the United States.

Key Terms

Cold War

Marshall Plan

Korean War

Cuban missile crisis

civil rights movement

Brown v. Board of Education

Vietnam War

Target Reading Skill

Reading Process Copy the concept web below. As you read, fill in the blank ovals with information about the aftermath of World War II. Add as many ovals as you need.

Korean War — Brown v. Board of Education — Cold War — Civil rights movement — Berlin divided — POSTWAR CHALLENGES — Vietnam War

Main Idea After World War II, Americans faced the challenges of the Cold War abroad and the civil rights movement at home.

American and Soviet flags

Setting the Scene

British statesman Winston Churchill had warned early on of the Nazi menace. Now, in March 1946, Churchill came to Fulton, Missouri, to speak of a new threat to peace. The Soviet Union, he said, had seized control of most of Eastern Europe:

> ❝ From Stettin in the Baltic to Trieste in the Adriatic, an iron curtain has descended across the Continent. . . . All these famous cities and the populations around them lie in what I must call the Soviet sphere. ❞
>
> —Winston Churchill, "The Sinews of Peace"

In the audience, President Harry Truman nodded in agreement. Under Truman's leadership, the United States began a long commitment to stop Soviet aggression and the spread of communism.

The Cold War Begins

The United States, Britain, and the Soviet Union were allies in World War II. Still, the two democracies distrusted the Soviet communist dictatorship. Stalin and other Soviet leaders had boasted that they would spread their revolutionary ideas throughout the world.

At the end of the war, the Allies divided Germany into occupation zones. They also divided the city of Berlin, deep inside the Soviet zone. In addition, Soviet troops stayed in Eastern Europe. Stalin set up communist governments in nations such as Poland and Czechoslovakia. In response, President Truman resolved to contain Soviet expansion. He sent aid to anticommunist groups in other countries.

For the next 46 years, the United States and the Soviet Union clashed in a conflict known as the Cold War. The two superpowers did not face each other directly in battle. Instead, they competed for influence around the world. As both nations spent billions on defense and weapons, an arms race sped up. People on both sides worried about the outbreak of a nuclear war.

Postwar Crises In 1947, Secretary of State George C. Marshall proposed a plan to rebuild Europe. With some $12 billion of **Marshall Plan** help, Western Europe began to recover. Stalin, however, kept Eastern Europe from taking American aid.

In 1948, the Western powers united their zones of Germany. In response, the Soviets blockaded supplies coming into West Berlin. Truman's answer was the Berlin Airlift. For nearly a year, American planes dropped tons of food and supplies in West Berlin. Stalin lifted the blockade, but Berlin remained a trouble spot. In 1961, East Germany built a wall dividing East and West Berlin.

The Korean War After World War II, communism gained a foothold in Asia. Communists led by Mao Zedong took control of China in 1949. On the Korean peninsula, a Soviet-backed government ruled the North, above the 38th parallel. The United States backed a noncommunist government in South Korea.

In June 1950, North Korean troops invaded the South. Truman asked for a United Nations force to stop them. Most of the UN forces were American. The **Korean War** dragged on until a truce was negotiated in 1953; however, Korea remained divided.

Cold War Fears Many Americans worried that Communists were working inside the United States. Truman ordered loyalty checks for government workers, and Congress carried on investigations.

In 1950, Wisconsin Senator Joseph McCarthy made dramatic charges about Communists in government, in schools, and even in the army. Although he was able to supply little real evidence, many people lost their jobs.

GEOGRAPHY Skills

During the Cold War, the United States and the Soviet Union competed for influence around the world. In many hot spots, the rivalry sparked armed conflict.

1. **Location** On the map, locate **(a)** Soviet Union, **(b)** Germany, **(c)** Korea, **(d)** Cuba, **(e)** Vietnam.

2. **Regions** What continent was most evenly divided into American and Soviet spheres of influence?

3. **Critical Thinking Drawing Conclusions** Why would Americans be concerned about Soviet influence in Cuba?

The Cold War

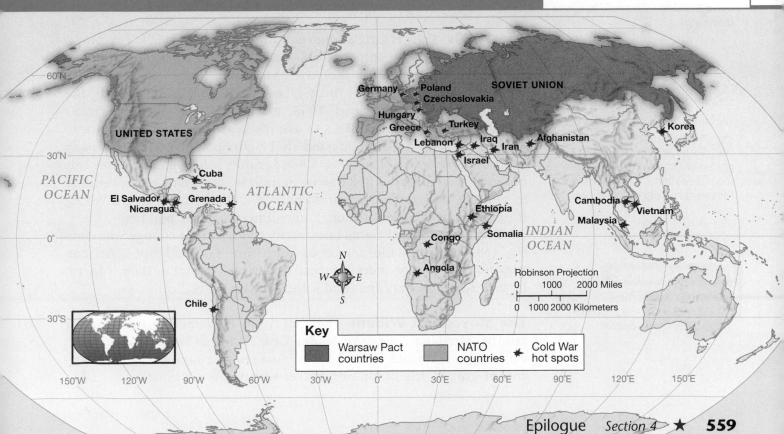

Key
- Warsaw Pact countries
- NATO countries
- ★ Cold War hot spots

Robinson Projection

Viewing History

Working for Civil Rights

The South

In the early 1960s, black and white protesters rode together on buses throughout the South. Many of these "freedom riders" were from the North. They risked assault and arrest in their struggle for civil rights. **Drawing Inferences** *Why do you think these freedom riders held hands as they sang?*

Set a Purpose for Reading

When you set a purpose for reading, you give yourself a focus. If your purpose is to learn about post-war challenges, how does the subsection "The Civil Rights Movement" help you meet your goal?

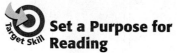

Primary Sources

See Martin Luther King, Jr., "I Have a Dream," on page 609 of the Reference Section.

Cuba In 1959, the communist threat came closer to home. Fidel Castro led a revolution in Cuba, taking over businesses and private property. Thousands of Cubans fled to the United States as exiles. The Soviet Union sent Castro economic aid.

In October 1962, the Soviets attempted to ship weapons to Castro. President John F. Kennedy then announced that American ships would stop any Soviet ships taking missiles to Cuba. After a tense few days, the Soviet ships turned back. The **Cuban missile crisis** was one of the hottest moments of the Cold War.

The Civil Rights Movement

After World War II, African Americans increased their fight for equal rights. This effort became known as the **civil rights movement.**

The Movement Begins As you read, in 1896 the Supreme Court ruled in *Plessy* v. *Ferguson* that states could legally segregete blacks and whites. Segregation became the law in southern states.

The NAACP sued to end segregation. In *Brown* v. *Board of Education* (1954), the Supreme Court overturned *Plessy* v. *Ferguson,* declaring that "separate educational facilities are inherently unequal." The court ordered schools everywhere to integrate. Despite some protests, the federal government enforced the order.

In 1955, African American Rosa Parks was arrested in Montgomery, Alabama, when she refused to give up her seat on a bus to a white man. In response, African Americans organized a boycott of the city's segregated bus system. During the boycott, Martin Luther King, Jr., emerged as a compelling national leader. A Baptist minister, King urged the use of nonviolent protests against unjust laws. His ideas about civil disobedience were strongly influenced by the writings of Henry David Thoreau. (See Chapter 15.)

The 1960s The civil rights movement grew in the 1960s. The movement drew young people, both black and white. Most protests were peaceful but were often met with violence. Homes and churches were bombed. Civil rights workers were killed or injured. Still, the movement grew. In August 1963, more than 200,000 Americans marched on Washington, D.C., to ask for laws to end discrimination.

President Kennedy supported civil rights policies. After Kennedy was assassinated in November 1963, Lyndon Johnson carried on this program. A Texan who had been a Senate leader, Johnson was skilled at getting laws passed. Congress passed a Civil Rights Act, a Voting Rights Act, and a constitutional amendment against poll taxes.

Despite new civil rights laws, many thought that change was coming too slowly. Leaders such as Malcolm X called upon African Americans to take more aggressive action. In April 1968, Martin Luther King, Jr., was shot and killed in Memphis, Tennessee.

The Movement Widens The civil rights movement inspired other groups. Mexican American leader César Chávez organized migrant workers to form the United Farm Workers. Through a national boycott of grapes, the union won better working conditions.

The women's rights movement also grew. Women often earned less money than men for doing the same jobs. Many professional schools gave preference to male applicants. Congress passed several laws to protect women's rights. The Civil Rights Act of 1964 outlawed discrimination in hiring based on gender as well as race.

The Vietnam War

Early in the 1960s, the American fight against communism led the nation into a painful era. Involvement in Vietnam, a former French colony in Southeast Asia, began slowly.

American Involvement In 1954, Vietnam was divided into a communist North and a noncommunist South. The United States backed the South. Many peasants in South Vietnam, however, joined the pro-communist Vietcong guerrillas.

Gradually, Presidents Kennedy and Johnson sent more and more military aid to South Vietnam. The Vietnam War turned into the longest war in American history. Between 1961 and 1973, more than 58,000 American troops lost their lives. There were few clear-cut victories as Americans fought unseen guerrillas in the jungle.

Impact at Home Americans were bitterly divided over the Vietnam War. Some "hawks" wanted an all-out victory over the communist North. "Doves," however, believed that the United States should not be in Vietnam at all. Antiwar protests were widespread, especially among college students.

Many blamed President Johnson for the worsening war, and he did not run again in 1968. Antiwar protests and violence disrupted the political conventions. The next President, Richard Nixon, promised to end the war. However, as the fighting continued, protests at home increased. Finally, in 1974, the last American troops left Vietnam. The following year, North Vietnam defeated South Vietnam.

★ ★ ★ Section 4 Assessment ★ ★ ★

Recall

1. **Identify** Explain the significance of (a) Cold War, (b) Marshall Plan, (c) Korean War, (d) Joseph McCarthy, (e) Cuban missile crisis, (f) *Brown* v. *Board of Education*, (g) Martin Luther King, Jr., (h) Lyndon Johnson, (i) César Chávez, (j) Vietnam War.
2. **Define** civil rights movement.

Comprehension

3. How did the Cold War begin?
4. Describe two gains made by the civil rights movement.

5. How did the Vietnam War divide Americans?

Critical Thinking and Writing

6. **Exploring the Main Idea** Review the Main Idea statement at the beginning of this section. Then, list two facts that support the following statement: Both the Cold War and the civil rights movement were related to a belief in American democracy.
7. **Contrasting** List two ways that American attitudes toward World War II differed from attitudes toward the Vietnam War.

ACTIVITY

Interviewing Write a list of 5–7 questions about the civil rights movement or the Vietnam War. Then, interview three older relatives or acquaintances who lived through those times. Keep a written or electronic record of their responses, and share them with the class.

5 Into the Future

Prepare to Read

Objectives

In this section, you will
- Summarize the events and ideas that sparked the conservative movement.
- Explain how the Cold War ended.
- Describe how terrorist attacks in 2001 affected Americans.
- Identify the changes and challenges that Americans have faced in recent times.

Key Terms

Watergate affair

Reaganomics

détente

free market economy

Persian Gulf War

terrorism

North American Free Trade Agreement

environmentalist

Target Reading Skill

Clarifying Meaning As you read, prepare an outline of this section. Use roman numerals to indicate the major headings, capital letters for the subheadings, and numbers for the supporting details. The sample at right will help you get started.

> I. The Conservative Movement
>   A. Politics of the 1970s
>   1. Watergate
>   2.
>   B. The Reagan Revolution
>   1. Conservative goals
>   2.
>   C.
> II. New Directions in Foreign Policy
>   A.
>   B.

Main Idea In the late 1900s, the United States took new directions politically, economically, and in world affairs.

Reagan campaign button

Setting the Scene Beset by economic woes and overseas crises, voters in 1980 turned to Ronald Reagan. A former movie actor and California governor, Reagan won people over with his genial smile, relaxed style, and open patriotism. One of his main targets was the growth of the federal government. He said:

> 66 Government is not the solution to our problem, government is the problem. . . . It is not my intention to do away with government. It is, rather, to make it work— work with us, not over us; to stand by our side, not ride on our back. 99
>
> —Ronald Reagan, First Inaugural Address, 1981

As President, Reagan united a new generation of conservatives. The "Reagan Revolution" brought enormous changes in how government worked.

The Conservative Movement

Federal government programs expanded in the 1960s and 1970s. Some laws created equal opportunities for women and minorities. Others helped the poor or protected consumers, workers, and the environment. Such programs did not always succeed. To pay for them, the government increased taxes. Businesses complained that regulation cost too much. A reaction against "big government" began.

Politics of the 1970s The unpopular Vietnam War helped bring Richard Nixon, a Republican, to office in 1969. In response to economic problems—rising prices, slow growth, and high unemployment—Nixon cut back spending. Then, political scandal rocked his administration. In 1972, burglars connected with Nixon's reelection campaign broke into Democratic headquarters in the Watergate office building. A congressional investigation showed that Nixon and his advisers had taken steps to cover up the Watergate affair. Faced with the threat of impeachment, Nixon stepped down in August 1974—the first President to resign from office.

Economic problems continued to plague Nixon's successors, Gerald Ford and Jimmy Carter. Under Carter, inflation reached 10 percent a year or more. With prices rising, many families had trouble paying for food, clothing, and shelter. In 1979, a foreign policy crisis further eroded Carter's popularity. Revolutionaries in Iran took over the American embassy and held Americans hostage for over a year. In 1980, discouraged voters turned to Ronald Reagan's upbeat message and promise of change.

The Reagan Revolution The conservatives who elected Reagan had various goals. All wanted a smaller federal government and less government regulation. Some conservatives focused on morality and a return to traditional family values. Many belonged to evangelical Christian churches.

As President, Reagan cut taxes, slowed down spending on social programs, and eliminated many regulations on business. This economic policy became known as Reaganomics. At the same time, he increased military spending to put pressure on the Soviet Union. After Reagan served two terms, his Vice President, George H.W. Bush, was elected in 1988. He continued many of Reagan's policies.

New Directions In 1992, former Arkansas governor Bill Clinton defeated Bush. A Democrat, Clinton was often at odds with the Republican Congress. He vetoed attempts to cut social programs and environmental laws. Clinton and Congress did work together to balance the federal budget.

A strong and growing economy helped keep Clinton's popularity high. Still, conservatives distrusted him. An investigation of Clinton's financial dealings turned up evidence of his improper relationship with a White House intern, which he at first denied. For only the second time in history, the House of Representatives voted to impeach a President, charging him with lying under oath. In February 1999, the Senate acquitted Clinton.

In 2000, Clinton's Vice President, Albert Gore, ran against Texas Governor George W. Bush, a son of the former President. Bush ran on a platform of "compassionate conservatism" and promised a large tax cut. Gore pointed to his political experience and the strong economy. Gore won the popular vote by a narrow margin. The electoral vote, however, remained in doubt as Gore contested Bush's victory in Florida. After the Supreme Court stopped further recounts, Gore conceded. George W. Bush became President in 2001.

Election of 2000

Percentage National Popular Vote

48.39% | 47.88% | 3.73% Other

Percentage Florida Popular Vote

48.85% | 48.84% | 2.31% Other

■ Gore, Democrat
■ Bush, Republican

CANDIDATE	TOTAL NATIONAL VOTE	TOTAL FLORIDA VOTE
Gore	50,996,039	2,912,253
Bush	50,456,141	2,912,790
Other	3,928,486	138,037

Source: Federal Election Commission

GRAPH Skills

The presidential election of 2000 was the most disputed race since 1876.

1. **Comprehension** What was the difference in the popular vote between Bush and Gore?

2. **Critical Thinking Drawing Conclusions** What role did candidates of other parties play in the election?

 Civics

New Directions in Foreign Policy

From the late 1940s on, the Cold War dominated foreign policy. Then, communist rule began to crumble all over Europe. By the mid-1990s, communism was no longer a major threat. New kinds of conflicts erupted in trouble spots all over the world.

The Cold War Ends The Cold War began to thaw in the Nixon administration. A strong anticommunist, Nixon established ties with Communist China and visited the Soviet Union. The policy of **détente,** or relaxation of tensions, continued under Ford and Carter. A Soviet invasion of Afghanistan in 1980 ended détente. President Reagan took a hard line, calling the Soviet Union an "evil empire." Tensions once again increased.

In 1985, a new Soviet leader set great changes in motion. Mikhail Gorbachev relaxed controls on free speech and political opposition. Starting in 1989, communist governments in Eastern Europe began to collapse. The Berlin Wall was torn down, and Germany was reunited under a democratic government.

Finally, in 1991, the Soviet Union itself broke apart. The United States tried to help Russia and the other republics build democracy. It also helped the former communist states develop a **free market economy,** in which individuals rather than the government made decisions about what to produce and sell.

New World Conflicts When the communist government of Yugoslavia fell, old ethnic and religious hatreds flared up in the Balkans. In 1991, the republics of Croatia and Bosnia split off from Yugoslavia. Millions of people were displaced as Serbs, Croats, and Bosnians fought one another. War again erupted in 1998, between Serbs and Albanians in Kosovo. NATO forces intervened, and American soldiers joined European troops as peacekeepers.

The Middle East was another hot spot. One source of trouble was hostility between the Jewish state of Israel and its Arab neighbors. Another was ongoing violence between Israelis and Palestinians within Israel. Presidents Carter, Clinton, and George W. Bush worked to bring peace. Still, violence between Israelis and Palestinians continued to rise.

American support for Israel angered many Arabs. In 1973, oil-producing Arab countries cut off oil shipments, causing shortages and high prices. Concern about the supply of oil also led to the brief **Persian Gulf War** in 1991. Saddam Hussein, the dictator of Iraq, invaded neighboring oil-rich Kuwait. President Bush organized a UN coalition led by the United States. After six weeks, Iraqi troops withdrew from Kuwait. Still, Hussein remained in power.

The Fight Against Terrorism

After the 1960s, terrorist bombings, kidnappings, and hijackings became more common in Europe, the Middle East, and elsewhere. **Terrorism** is the deliberate use of random acts of violence, often against civilians, in order to achieve a political goal.

Americans and Terrorism In the Middle East, a number of radical Muslim groups sponsored terrorism. These extremists opposed

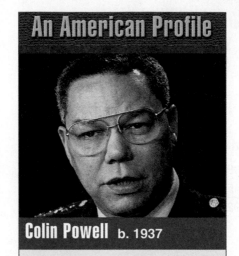

An American Profile

Colin Powell b. 1937

As Chairman of the Joint Chiefs of Staff, General Colin Powell helped direct American strategy in the Persian Gulf War. It was just one of many victories in his life.

Powell was the son of garment workers in New York City's Harlem. Every child in his family was expected to work for a college education. After college, Powell joined the army, earning a Purple Heart in Vietnam. Later in life, he helped found an organization that encouraged Americans to volunteer for pubic service. In 2001, he was named Secretary of State.

What qualities do you think made Colin Powell a strong leader?

American policies in the Middle East and western influence on their culture. As a result, Americans overseas sometimes became targets of terrorism. In 1988, a bomb exploded on an American airliner over Scotland, killing 270 people. Later, bombings hit two United States embassies in Africa and a navy ship off the coast of Yemen.

Terrorism also became a threat within the United States itself. In 1993, a bomb rocked the World Trade Center in New York City. Six Arab men were later convicted of the crime. Not all acts of terror were linked to the Middle East, however. In 1995, two Americans who resented the government exploded a bomb that destroyed a federal office building in Oklahoma City, killing 168 people.

Attacks on the United States On September 11, 2001, terrorists seized control of four American passenger airplanes. The hijackers crashed two of the planes into the Twin Towers of the World Trade Center, the tallest buildings in New York City. As onlookers watched in horror, the two skyscrapers burned, then collapsed. A third hijacked airliner crashed into American military headquarters at the Pentagon near Washington, D.C. The fourth airplane crashed in Pennsylvania after courageous passengers attacked the hijackers.

More than 3,000 people were killed in the terrorist attacks. In New York, the victims included many heroic police and firefighters trying to save people from the burning towers.

Americans Respond American citizens were quick to respond to the tragedy. Millions lined up to give blood and aided in rescue efforts.

President George W. Bush voiced the nation's outrage. The attacks, he said, were "acts of war." He committed the nation to an all-out campaign against terrorism.

Early on, the government blamed the attacks on a network of terrorists led by Osama bin Laden, a wealthy Saudi hiding in Afghanistan. American forces attacked military targets and terrorist training camps in Afghanistan. As the search for bin Laden continued, President Bush vowed to wipe out terrorism everywhere.

As part of his fight against terrorism, President Bush continued to pressure Saddam Hussein, dictator of Iraq, to stop developing weapons of mass destruction such as chemical, biological, and nuclear arms. In March 2003, the United States invaded Iraq. Lightning air and ground strikes by a coalition of forces led by the United States toppled the Iraqi regime in just six weeks. Iraqi leaders, including Saddam, went into hiding. One by one, many of the top leaders were tracked down. In December 2003, Saddam was captured. However, guerrilla activities persisted in Iraq. It seemed that the tough task of rebuilding the country would take many years.

Changes and Challenges

The nation faced other challenges and changes. Trade and technology made the world smaller and more interdependent.

A Global Economy Foreign trade became important in the economies of most countries. The United States now competes for trade with European and Asian nations that have strong economies. Some people want to use tariffs to protect American companies and

---

Primary Source

The Nation Is Attacked

President Bush addressed Congress and the nation on September 20, 2001:
"We have seen the state of our union in the endurance of rescuers working past exhaustion. We've seen the unfurling of flags, the lighting of candles, the giving of blood, the saying of prayers in English, Hebrew, and Arabic.... The entire world has seen for itself the state of our union, and it is strong.

Tonight we are a country awakened to danger and called to defend freedom. Our grief has turned to anger and our anger to resolution. Whether we bring our enemies to justice or bring justice to our enemies, justice will be done."

— George W. Bush, Address to Congress, September 20, 2001

Analyzing a Primary Source
Restate the main point of the last sentence above in your own words.

Go to **United We Stand** for updated articles and lessons to guide your classroom discussions of September 11 and beyond. Go to PHSchool.com, **Web Code mfd-3104.**

Summarize

Summarize two of the challenges that the world faces today.

jobs. Others, however, favor free trade. In 1993, Congress approved the North American Free Trade Agreement (NAFTA). It reduced trade barriers among the United States, Canada, and Mexico.

New Technology The first computers were built after World War II. By the 1980s, smaller and faster computers had become a fixture in homes and offices around the world. The Internet brought people and nations closer together. The possibilities of these technologies seem endless.

Space exploration sparked other new technologies. The United States began its space program in the 1950s as part of its rivalry with the Soviet Union. In 1969, two American astronauts became the first people to walk on the moon. The launching of the first reusable space shuttle in 1981 opened up possibilities for further discovery.

The Environment Environmental issues affect the entire world. Since the 1970s, environmentalists have worked to reduce pollution, protect resources, and improve the quality of air and water. Energy use and climate change remain serious issues. Burning fossil fuels—coal, oil, and natural gas—sends carbon dioxide into the atmosphere. Other human-made chemicals were blamed for damaging the ozone layer of the atmosphere. The ozone layer blocks out harmful radiation from the sun.

New Immigration Patterns The face of the United States has also changed. After the fall of the Soviet Union, many Russians and other former Soviet citizens moved to the United States. Conflicts like those in Asia and the Balkans created many refugees, who sought safety here. Today, most new immigrants come from Latin America, the Caribbean, and Asia. By 2000, Latinos had become the largest ethnic minority in the United States.

★ ★ ★ Section 5 Assessment ★ ★ ★

Recall

1. **Identify** Explain the significance of **(a)** Ronald Reagan, **(b)** Watergate affair, **(c)** Reaganomics, **(d)** Bill Clinton, **(e)** George W. Bush, **(f)** Persian Gulf War, **(g)** North American Free Trade Agreement.
2. **Define** **(a)** détente, **(b)** free market economy, **(c)** terrorism, **(d)** environmentalist.

Comprehension

3. Why did conservatives object to "big government"?
4. What event marked the end of the Cold War?

5. How did Americans respond to terrorist attacks in September 2001?
6. How did the American economy change?

Critical Thinking and Writing

7. **Exploring the Main Idea** Review the Main Idea statement at the beginning of this section. Then, list what you see as the three biggest changes described in this section.
8. **Drawing Conclusions** List four ways in which your life would be different today if computers had not been invented.

ACTIVITY

Writing a Speech You have been asked to write a speech welcoming new immigrants from Russia after the breakup of the Soviet Union. Describe the benefits that they will find in the United States and what will be expected of them as citizens.

Transferring Information

Historical information comes in many forms. Sometimes, it is helpful to organize information so that you can compare it with other data.

The data below relate to sources of immigration in 1900. These data have been used to create the pie chart below.

Asia	4 percent
Americas	1.2 percent
Europe	94.7 percent
Africa	less than 1 percent
Other	less than 1 percent

The paragraph below describes modern immigration trends.

Immigration patterns have changed. In 1998, the largest percentage (45.2) came from the Americas. Another sizable percentage (33.2) were people from Asia. Africans now made up 6.2 percent, while Europeans accounted for 13.7 percent. About 1.7 percent of immigrants came from other places.

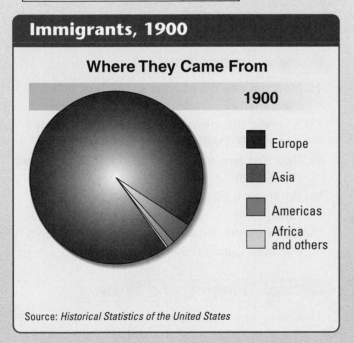

Immigrants, 1900

Where They Came From

1900

- Europe
- Asia
- Americas
- Africa and others

Source: *Historical Statistics of the United States*

Where They Came From, 1998

Learn the Skill *To learn how to transfer information, use the following steps:*

1. **Identify the raw data.** As you read a selection, note the facts given. If many statistics are included, think about how you might organize them so that they are easier to see and use.

2. **List the data.** Compile a list of the facts that you might use. Organize the percentages from greatest to least.

3. **Transfer the data.** To make a pie chart, divide a circle into parts that add up to 100 percent. Color each part to represent the percentage you want to include. Label the chart.

4. **Draw conclusions based on the data.** What can you learn by looking at the data in this form?

Practice the Skill *Use the information above to answer the following questions:*

1. **(a)** What kind of data does the paragraph provide? **(b)** What percentage of immigrants to the United States in 1998 were from Europe? From Asia?

2. **(a)** Order the data in the paragraph in order of percentage. **(b)** Where did the largest group of immigrants come from in 1998?

3. Copy the blank pie chart, and fit the data from the paragraph into it. Use the same color code as in the completed pie chart.

4. Describe how immigration patterns changed between 1900 and 1998.

Apply the Skill *See the Chapter Review and Assessment.*

Review and Assessment

CHAPTER SUMMARY

Section 1
Many western territories were settled and admitted as states in the post-Civil War decades. The United States was transformed by the emergence of big business and labor as well as by the flow of immigrants.

Section 2
The Progressive Era transformed the role of government. Because the nation had become a world power by the turn of the century, the U.S. entry into World War I turned the tide of the European conflict.

Section 3
Roosevelt's New Deal programs failed to bring an end to the Great Depression. The United States and its allies defeated the Axis powers in World War II.

Section 4
The Cold War pitted the U.S. against the Soviet Union in the decades after World War II. The civil rights movement fought for equal rights for African Americans. The Vietnam War divided the country.

Section 5
The conservative movement sought to reduce the role of the federal government in people's lives. With the end of the Cold War, new challenges, including the threat of terrorism, confronted the nation.

For additional review and enrichment activities, see the interactive version of *The American Nation,* available on the Web and on CD-ROM.

Chapter Self-Test For practice test questions for the Epilogue, visit PHSchool.com, **Web Code mfa-3105.**

Reviewing Key Facts

11. How did city life change in the late 1800s? (Section 1)
12. How did the views of Booker T. Washington and W.E.B. DuBois differ? (Section 2)
13. Describe two effects of the Great Depression. (Section 3)
14. What were the causes of the Korean War? (Section 4)
15. Describe the outcome of the 2000 presidential election. (Section 5)

Critical Thinking and Writing

16. **Connecting to Geography: Movement** Look at the physical map of the United States in the Reference Section. Identify one major obstacle that builders would have faced in completing the first transcontinental railroad.
17. **Contrasting** List three ways in which totalitarian states, such as those of the Soviet Union or Nazi Germany, differ from a democratic government like that of the United States.
18. **Drawing Conclusions** Events such as the bombing of Pearl Harbor in 1941 or the terrorist attacks in 2001 often stir Americans to a sense of unity and patriotism. Write a paragraph saying why you think this is so.

Building Vocabulary

Write sentences using the chapter vocabulary words listed below, leaving blanks where the vocabulary words would go. Exchange your sentences with another student, and fill in the blanks in each other's sentences.

1. corporation
2. monopoly
3. muckraker
4. isolationism
5. imperialism
6. deficit spending
7. civil rights movement
8. détente
9. free market economy
10. terrorism

Analyzing Primary Sources

Mary Antin, a Russian Jewish immigrant, came to the United States in 1890. Here, she speaks of the opportunities in her new home:

> 66Education was free. That subject my father had written about repeatedly, as comprising his chief hope for us children, the essence of American opportunity, the treasure that no thief could touch, not even misfortune or poverty. It was the one thing that he was able to promise us when he sent for us; surer, safer than bread or shelter. . . . No application made, no questions asked, no examinations, rulings, exclusions; no machinations, no fees. The doors stood open for every one of us.99
>
> —Mary Antin, *The Promised Land*

19. What is the main idea of this passage?
    A. Poverty prevails in America.
    B. The United States is a land of thieves, who are constantly stealing people's valuables.
    C. Education is a free gift available to everybody who wants to take advantage of it.
    D. The doors of school buildings are never closed in the United States.

20. Why did immigrants value education so highly?
    A. It allowed individuals to better themselves.
    B. Schools paid all of their relocation costs.
    C. Schools provided teaching jobs.
    D. Schools never asked questions.

Transferring Information

The chart below gives raw data about United States exports in 1999. Examine the data, and answer the questions that follow.

United States Exports by Region

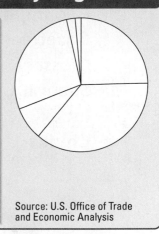

REGION	PERCENTAGE OF U.S. EXPORTS
Europe	24.7
NAFTA (Canada and Mexico)	36.4
Other Latin American Countries	8.0
Asia	27.4
Australia and Oceania	2.1
Africa	1.4

Source: U.S. Office of Trade and Economic Analysis

21. What percentage of United States exports went to Canada and Latin America in 1999?
    A. 36.4 percent
    B. 8 percent
    C. 44.4 percent
    D. Cannot tell from the data given

22. Copy the blank pie chart shown here. Use the data given in the table to create a pie chart.

ACTIVITIES

Connecting With . . .
Culture

Designing a Poster The motto of the United States is *E pluribus unum,* a Latin phrase that means "Out of many, one." Design a poster about how people of various ethnic, racial, religious, and national groups have contributed to our national identity. Include three different examples chosen from this chapter or from earlier chapters in the textbook.

Evaluating the Validity of Internet Sites

Reviewing Sites About World War II Use the Internet to find sites relating to World War II. Write a review evaluating one site in terms of source, type of information, visuals, overall usefulness, and reliability. Then, explain whether you consider that site a valid source of information. For help in starting this activity, visit PHSchool.com, **Web Code mfd-3107.**

Reference Section

Washington Crossing the Delaware

Primary Sources and Literature

The River

Pare Lorentz

In 1937, filmmaker Pare Lorentz told the history of the Mississippi River in his film *The River*. As the film begins, the audience hears the prologue, or introductory words.

Vocabulary Before you read the selection, find the meanings of these words in a dictionary: **glacier, rill, rivulet.**

Main Idea The prologue describes the journey of the Mississippi as it progresses from small tributaries to a wide river emptying into the Gulf of Mexico.

A winding river

From as far West as Idaho,
   Down from the glacier peaks of the Rockies—
From as far East as New York,
   Down from the turkey ridges of the Alleghenies
Down from Minnesota, twenty-five hundred miles,
   The Mississippi River runs to the Gulf.
Carrying every drop of water, that flows down two-thirds of the continent,
Carrying every brook and rill, rivulet and creek,
Carrying all the rivers that run down two-thirds of the continent
The Mississippi runs to the Gulf of Mexico.
Down the Yellowstone, the Milk, the White and Cheyenne;
The Cannonball, the Musselshell, the James and the Sioux;
Down the Judith, the Grand, the Osage, and the Platte,
The Skunk, the Salt, the Black, and Minnesota;
Down the Rock, the Illinois, and the Kankakee . . .
Down the Arkansas fifteen hundred miles from the Great Divide;
Down the Red, a thousand miles from Texas;
Down the great Valley, twenty-five hundred miles from Minnesota,
   Carrying every rivulet and brook, creek and rill,
Carrying all the rivers that run down two-thirds of the continent—
The Mississippi runs to the Gulf.

Analyzing Literature

1. Into what body of water does the Mississippi River empty?

   A The Wabash

   B The Ohio

   C The Gulf of Mexico

   D The Missouri

2. Three states mentioned in the prologue include:

   A Idaho, New York, and Texas

   B Missouri, Ohio, and New York

   C Arkansas, Colorado, and Idaho

   D New Mexico, New York, and Texas

3. Critical Thinking and Writing Analyzing Ideas Based on the prologue, what kind of story do you think the movie will tell about the Mississippi River?

Primary Sources and Literature

Democracy in America

Alexis de Tocqueville

Alexis de Tocqueville came to the United States in 1831 to study the prison system. However, during the nine months he spent there, he observed and studied much more. In a series of notebooks, he recorded his impressions of the people he met and what he saw. Eventually, this collection became *Democracy in America*. The following is an excerpt from one of the entries.

Vocabulary Before you read the selection, find the meanings of these words in a dictionary: **compatriots, sedentary, zeal.**

Main Idea Tocqueville praises Americans' commitment to education and working hard.

Of all the countries in the world, America is that in which the spread of ideas and of human industry is most continual and most rapid. There is not an American but knows the resources of all the parts of the vast land that he inhabits; all the able men in the Union know each other by reputation, many of them personally. I have often been struck by astonishment to find how far that is the case. I can say that it has never happened to me to speak to an American about one of his compatriots without finding that he was up-to-date in knowing both how he was now placed and the story of his life.

I know that this intense industrial and intellectual movement is particularly encouraged by education, by the sort of government America enjoys, and by the altogether special situation in which the Americans find themselves. In America populations are not at all sedentary, . . . almost all of them are real industrial entrepreneurs who feel the need for means of communication with a liveliness and use them with a zeal which one could never expect from the routine and lazy spirit of our peasants. The effect of a road or a canal is therefore more noticeable and above all more immediate in America than it would be in France.

Alexis de Tocqueville

Analyzing Primary Sources

1. According to Tocqueville, how has the rapid spread of ideas affected Americans?

   A It shows that Americans communicate too often.

   B Most Americans are well informed.

   C People living in the countryside are not up-to-date.

   D Most Americans are not well educated.

2. How would Tocqueville define an American entrepreneur?

   A A person who works very hard

   B An educated person who welcomes new opportunities

   C A person who is sedentary

   D An educated government worker

3. **Critical Thinking and Writing** **Drawing Inferences** Why does Tocqueville feel that the effect of canals and roads is "more noticeable" and "immediate" in the United States than in France?

The Constitution of the Iroquois

The Iroquois constitution helped put an end to destructive fighting among the five Iroquois nations. It gave each of the Five Nations full control over its own affairs, but it set up two Grand Councils to deal with all matters that affected the Iroquois in general—for example, peace or war. Here are excerpts from the Iroquois constitution.

Vocabulary Before you read the selection, find the meanings of these words in a dictionary: **confederate, defection, manifest, upbraid, heeded, divest, titleship, vested, mentors.**

Main Idea The constitution of the Iroquois confederation provides a blueprint for the people to live together in peace.

. . . All the business of the Five Nations Confederate Council shall be conducted by the two combined bodies of Confederate Lords. . . . If any Confederate Lord neglects or refuses to attend the Confederate Council, the other Lords of the Nation of which he is a member shall require their War Chief to request the female sponsors of the Lord so guilty of defection to demand his attendance of the Council. If he refuses, the women holding the title shall immediately select another candidate for the title. If at any time it shall be manifest that a Confederate Lord has not in mind the welfare of the people, . . . the men or women of the Confederacy . . . shall come to the council and upbraid the erring Lord through his War Chief. If the complaint of the people through the War Chief is not heeded the first time it shall be uttered again and then if no attention is given a third complaint and warning shall be given. If the Lord is [defiant], the matter shall go to the council of the War Chiefs. The War Chiefs shall then divest the erring Lord of his title by order of the women in whom the titleship is vested. . . . The Lords of the Confederacy of the Five Nations shall be mentors of the people for all time. . . . Their hearts shall be full of peace and good will and their minds filled with a yearning for the welfare of the people of the Confederacy.

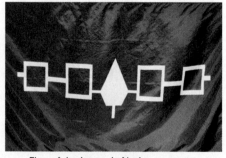

Flag of the Iroquois Nation

Analyzing Primary Sources

1. Matters of concern to all Iroquois will be considered by

  A the lords of the Mohawk and Cayuga nations

  B a Grand Council made up of all Iroquois

  C two Grand Councils made up of important lords

  D any Iroquois elected in free elections

2. If a member of the grand council does not obey the rules, he

  A cannot attend any more meetings

  B will be exiled to a neighboring group

  C can be criticized by the men and women of the League

  D will be allowed to finish his term on the council

3. Critical Thinking Analyzing Information How did the constitution ensure that the concerns of the people were addressed?

The Printing Press: "New Makers of Books"

William Fichet

Printing was probably the most important new technology developed during the Renaissance. The invention of the printing press helped spread learning throughout Europe. No one had a more important role in this new technology than a German printer named Johannes Gutenberg (GOO tun berg). Gutenberg's press used type in which each letter of the alphabet was on a separate piece of metal. The following selection comes from a letter written by William Fichet (fee SHAY), the man who brought Gutenberg's invention to Paris.

Vocabulary Before you read the selection, find the meanings of these words in a dictionary: **devised, Muses, mortals, transcribed, posterity.**

Main Idea Fichet praises Gutenberg's contribution to humankind.

Great light has been thrown by the breed of new makers of books, whom, within our memory, Germany has broadcast into every quarter. For they say that there, not far from the city of Mainz, there appeared a certain John whose surname was Gutenberg, who first of all men, devised the art of printing, whereby books are made, not by a reed, as did the ancients, nor with a quill pen, as do we, but with metal letters, and that swiftly, neatly, beautifully. Surely this man is worthy to be loaded with divine honors by all the Muses, all the arts, all the tongues of those who delight in books, and is all the more to be preferred to gods and goddesses in that he has put the means of choice within reach of letters themselves and of mortals devoted to culture. . . .

But that great Gutenberg has discovered things far more pleasing and more divine, in carving out letters in such fashion that whatever can be said or thought can by them be written down at once and transcribed and committed to the memory of posterity.

An early printing press

Analyzing Primary Sources

1. According to Fichet, how were books made by "the ancients"?

   A Using styluses

   B Using reeds

   C Using quills

   D Using pens

2. Which of these statements describes Fichet's opinion of Gutenberg?

   A Gutenberg lived near Mainz, Germany.

   B Until now, Europeans wrote books by using quill pens.

   C Gutenberg is worthy of divine honors.

   D Thanks to Gutenberg, ideas can be preserved for the future.

3. **Critical Thinking and Writing Making Predictions** List three ways in which the invention of the printing press will change life in Europe.

Historical Document

A Brief Account of the Devastation of the Indies
Bartolomé de Las Casas

In 1542, Bartolomé de Las Casas returned to Spain to report on Spanish treatment of Native Americans. Although some historians think Las Casas exaggerated some of the facts, no one disputes that his account had a powerful impact.

Vocabulary Before you read the selection, find the meanings of these words in a dictionary: **guileless, duplicity, embroilments, rancors, complaisant, malady, ravening.**

Main Idea Las Casas argues that the greed and cruelty of the Spanish conquerors had a deadly effect on Caribbean Indians.

And of all the infinite universe of humanity, [the Indians] are the most guileless, the most devoid of wickedness and duplicity, the most obedient and faithful to their native masters and to the Spanish Christians whom they serve. They are by nature the most humble, patient, and peaceable, holding no grudges, free from embroilments, neither excitable nor quarrelsome. These people are the most devoid of rancors, hatreds, or desire for vengeance of any people in the world. And because they are so weak and complaisant, they are less able to endure heavy labor and soon die of no matter what malady. . . .

Yet into this sheepfold, into this land of meek outcasts there came some Spaniards who immediately behaved like ravening wild beasts, wolves, tigers, or lions that had been starved for many days. And Spaniards behaved no other way during the past forty years, down to the present time, for they are still acting like ravening beasts, killing, terrorizing, afflicting, torturing, and destroying the native peoples, doing all this with the strangest and most varied methods of cruelty, never seen or heard of before, and to such a degree that this Island of Hispaniola once so populous (having a population that I estimated to be more than three million), has now a population of barely two hundred persons.

A Spanish coin

Analyzing Primary Sources

1. Las Casas is mainly interested in presenting the Indians as

 A faithful workers

 B innocent victims

 C proud warriors

 D good Christians

2. Which word best describes the attitude of Las Casas toward the Spanish?

 A Admiring

 B Forgiving

 C Angry

 D Afraid

3. Critical Thinking and Writing Evaluating Information (a) What effect did Las Casas hope his report would have? **(b)** List three ways in which he uses words to stir strong emotions.

Eyewitness Account

The General History of Virginia

John Smith

In 1624, John Smith published *The General History of Virginia*, one of our main sources of information about the founding of Jamestown. Here, Smith describes what happened after the ship that brought the colonists in 1607 returned to England.

Vocabulary Before you read the selection, find the meanings of these words in a dictionary: **pilfer, sassafras, palisades, provision.**

Main Idea The Jamestown colony suffered from exhaustion, a lack of food, and poor leadership.

While the ships stayed, our allowance was somewhat bettered by a daily proportion of biscuits, which the sailors would pilfer to sell, give, or exchange with us for money, sassafras, furs. . . . But when they departed, there remained neither tavern, [nor] beer, [nor] house, nor place of relief, but the [community cooking pot]. . . . and that was half a pint of wheat, and as much barley boiled with water for a man a day, and this having fried some twenty-six weeks in the ship's hold, contained as many worms as grains . . .

With this lodging and diet, our extreme toil in bearing and planning palisades so strained and bruised us, and our continual labor in the extremity of the heat had so weakened us, as were cause sufficient to have made us as miserable in our native country, or any other place in the world.

From May to September, those that escaped lived upon sturgeon, and sea crabs. Fifty in this time we buried. . . .

But now was all our provision spent, the sturgeon gone, all helps abandoned, each hour expecting the fury of the savages; when God, the Patron of all good endeavors in that desperate extremity so changed the hearts of the savages that they brought such plenty of their fruits and provision as no man wanted.

John Smith

Analyzing an Eyewitness Account

1. How did the colonists survive before the ships left?

  A They hunted and fished.

  B They ate crab and sturgeon.

  C The sailors shared or sold food.

  D They had extra provisions.

2. Who supplied the food that finally saved the colonists from starvation?

  A Sailors

  B Native Americans

  C The Spanish

  D John Smith

3. Critical Thinking and Writing Evaluating Information Smith wrote this history more than 15 years after the events described here. Would you consider it a reliable account of the early years of Jamestown? Why or why not?

Historical Document

Fundamental Orders of Connecticut

As the first written plan of government in 1639, the Fundamental Orders of Connecticut provided for a representative form of government with a governor, a legislative assembly, and courts. Three of the orders are given below.

Vocabulary Before you read the selection, find the meanings of these words in a dictionary: **Freemen, deputies, Jurisdiction, levied.**

Main Idea The Fundamental Orders of Connecticut provide for each town to be represented in the General Court.

It is Ordered . . . that Windsor, Hartford, and Wethersfield shall have power . . . to send four of their Freemen as their deputies to every General Court; and Whatsoever other Town shall be . . . added to this Jurisdiction, they shall send so many deputies as the Court shall judge meet, a reasonable proportion to the number of Freemen that are in the said Towns being to be attended therein; which deputies shall have the power of the whole Town to give their votes and allowance to all such laws and orders as may be for the public good . . .

It is Ordered, sentenced, and decreed, that the deputies thus chosen shall have power and liberty to appoint a time and a place of meeting together before any General Court, to advise and consult of . . . things as may concern the good of the public . . .

It is Ordered . . . that when any General Court upon the occasions of the Commonwealth have agreed upon any sum, or sums of money to be levied upon the several Towns within this Jurisdiction, that a committee be chosen to set out and appoint what shall be the proportion of every town to pay of the said levy . . .

Colonists settle in Connecticut

Analyzing Primary Sources

1. In what way was the system of government in Connecticut similar to our system today?

   A Each town has a say in decisions through its representatives.

   B Each town government makes its own laws.

   C Only Freemen may be in the government.

   D Every town pays the same amount of taxes to the colonial government.

2. How will the amount of taxes to be collected from each town be decided?

   A The town representative will decide the sum.

   B The General Court will choose an amount that all towns will pay.

   C A chosen committee will decide the sum.

   D The towns will vote.

3. **Critical Thinking and Writing Evaluating Information** Do you think the Freemen from each town represented all the people? Explain.

Eyewitness Account

Autobiography
Benjamin Franklin

At 17, Benjamin Franklin left his home in Boston to seek his fortune in Philadelphia. After several years, he owned his own printing shop and had gained a reputation as a hard worker and a successful businessman. Always eager to improve his city, Franklin introduced several new ideas in Philadelphia, including that of a lending library.

Vocabulary Before you read the selection, find the meanings of these words in a dictionary: **render, commencing, manifested, utility.**

Main Idea Benjamin Franklin decides to start a public lending library in Philadelphia.

At the time I establish'd myself in Pennsylvania, there was not a good bookseller's shop in any of the colonies to the southward of Boston. In New York and [Philadelphia] the printers were indeed stationers; they sold only paper, etc., almanacs, ballads, and a few common school-books. Those who lov'd reading [had to] send for their books from England; the members of the [club] had each a few. We . . . hired a room to hold our club in. I propos'd that we should all of us bring our books to that room, where they would not only be ready to consult in our conferences, but become a common benefit, each of us being at liberty to borrow such as he wish'd to read at home. This was . . . done, and for some time contented us.

Finding the advantage of this little collection, I propos'd to render the benefit from books more common by commencing a public subscription library. I drew a sketch of the plan and rules that would be necessary . . . each subscriber engag'd to pay a certain sum down for the first purchase of books, and an annual contribution for increasing them. . . . The library was opened one day in the week for lending to the subscribers. . . . The institution soon manifested its utility, [and] was imitated by other towns, and in other provinces. . . . Reading became fashionable. . . .

Benjamin Franklin

Analyzing an Eyewitness Account

1. Why did Franklin feel a place to buy books was necessary?
   A Printers sold books only in Boston.
   B Books arrived in the colonies monthly.
   C Most colonial cities were without bookshops.
   D Colonists had to buy books from France.

2. How was the first library run?
   A Subscribers paid for each book.
   B Subscribers contributed money and then borrowed books free of charge.
   C Subscribers could borrow five books.
   D Anyone could borrow books.

3. **Critical Thinking and Writing Synthesizing Information** Benjamin Franklin believed in the ideas of the Enlightenment. How did his founding of the public library advance those ideas?

Historical Document

The English Bill of Rights

When Americans wrote their Bill of Rights, they were inspired by the English Bill of Rights of 1689. This was a list of rights that the English government guaranteed to citizens. It ensured that Parliament, not the monarchy, was the most important branch of government.

Vocabulary Before you read the selections, find the meanings of these words in a dictionary: **regal, consent, levying, petition, proceedings, excessive, inflicted, redress, amending.**

Main Idea The English Bill of Rights of 1689 limited the power of the monarchy.

And thereupon the said lords . . . asserting their ancient rights and liberties, declare:

That the . . . power of suspending of laws, or the execution of laws, by regal authority, without consent of parliament, is illegal.

That levying money for or to the use of the crown, . . . without grant of parliament, . . . is illegal.

That it is the right of the subjects to petition the King, and all commitments and prosecutions for such petitioning are illegal.

That the raising or keeping a standing army within the kingdom in a time of peace, unless it be with consent of parliament, is against the law.

That election of members of parliament ought to be free.

That the freedom of speech, and debates or proceedings in parliament, ought not to be . . . questioned in any court or place out of parliament.

That excessive bail ought not to be required, nor excessive fines imposed; nor cruel and unusual punishments inflicted.

And that for redress of all grievances, and for the amending, strengthening and preserving of the laws, parliaments ought to be held frequently.

Colonial protest

Analyzing Primary Sources

1. According to the English Bill of Rights, the power to levy money

  A belongs entirely to the monarchy

  B requires the approval of Parliament

  C belongs entirely to Parliament

  D belongs entirely to English towns and villages

2. What does the English Bill of Rights say about the rights of the people?

  A They can refuse to pay taxes.

  B They can petition the king without fear of persecution.

  C They can join the army.

  D They can be elected to Parliament.

Critical Thinking Analyzing Information List four ways in which the English Bill of Rights makes Parliament stronger than the monarch.

"Revolutionary Tea"

The Tea Act of 1773 placed a new tax on tea sold in the colonies. The song "Revolutionary Tea," written by an anonymous colonist, reveals how many colonists felt about the Tea Act and about their relationship with far-off Britain.

Vocabulary Before you read the selection, find the meanings of these words in a dictionary: **pence, conveyed, quoth, steeped.**

Main Idea A colonial song pokes fun at Britain, comparing it to a rich, old woman who forces her daughter to pay a tax.

There was an old lady lived over the sea.
And she was an Island Queen;
Her daughter lived off in a new country,
With an ocean of water between.
The old lady's pockets were full of gold,
But never contented was she,
So she called on her daughter to pay her a tax
Of three pence a pound on her tea,
Of three pence a pound on her tea. . . .

The tea was conveyed to the daughter's door,
All down by the ocean's side;
And the bouncing girl poured out every pound
In the dark and boiling tide.
And then she called out to the Island Queen,
"Oh, mother, dear mother," quoth she,
"Your tea you may have when 'tis steeped enough,
But never a tax from me.
But never a tax from me."

A colonial teapot

Analyzing Literature

1. What is the main point of "Revolutionary Tea"?
   A   The colonists will remain loyal to Britain.
   B   The British and the American colonists both love tea.
   C   Colonists resent the tax on tea.
   D   The American colonists are like disobedient children.

2. The "old lady" represents
   A   Massachusetts
   B   colonial tea merchants
   C   Britain
   D   redcoats in Boston

3. **Critical Thinking Identifying Points of View** Which point of view does the song represent, the British or the American? Give two examples from the song to support your answer.

Common Sense

Thomas Paine

At the request of Benjamin Franklin, Englishman Thomas Paine came to America in 1776 to help support the cause of independence. Soon after his arrival, Paine published a 47-page pamphlet, *Common Sense*. It played a key role in persuading the colonists to revolt against Great Britain.

Vocabulary Before you read the selection, find the meanings of these words in a dictionary: **advocate, reconciliation, derived, ineffectual, disdain, vanity, obstinancy.**

Main Idea Thomas Paine urges the colonists to break away from Great Britain.

I challenge the warmest advocate for reconciliation, to show, a single advantage that this continent can reap, by being connected with Great Britain. I repeat the challenge, not a single advantage is derived. Our corn will fetch its price in any market in Europe, and our imported goods must be paid for, buy them where we will. . . .

Every quiet method for peace hath been ineffectual. Our prayers have been rejected with disdain; and only tended to convince us, that nothing flatters vanity, or confirms obstinancy in Kings more than repeated petitioning and nothing hath contributed more than that very measure to make the Kings of Europe absolute. . . . Wherefore since nothing but blows will do . . . let us come to a final separation. . . .

As to government matters, it is not in the powers of Britain to do this continent justice: The business of it will soon be too weighty, and intricate, to be managed with any tolerable degree of convenience, by a power, so distant from us, and so very ignorant of us; for if they cannot conquer us, they cannot govern us. To be always running three or four thousand miles with a tale or a petition, waiting four or five months for an answer, which when obtained requires five or six more to explain it in, will in a few years be looked upon as folly and childishness. There was a time when it was proper, and there is a proper time for it to cease.

Thomas Paine

Analyzing Primary Sources

1. According to Paine, how has Great Britain responded to the colonies' attempts at peace?

  A Their petitions are carefully considered.

  B Their petitions are useless.

  C The King is ready to listen to colonial complaints.

  D Great Britain wants war.

2. What is one argument Paine gives for becoming independent of Great Britain?

  A There are too many laws to follow.

  B The distance between the two places makes it difficult to govern effectively.

  C The colonies have economic difficulties.

  D The colonists have to fight Britain's wars.

3. Critical Thinking and Writing Analyzing Information How might Paine's appeal persuade colonists to separate from Great Britain?

Historical Document

On the Care of the Wounded
Benjamin Rush

Dr. Benjamin Rush became Surgeon General of the Continental Army in April 1777. After inspecting the hospitals where the wounded soldiers were treated, Rush complained about the horrible conditions in a letter to General Washington.

Vocabulary Before you read the selection, find the meanings of these words in a dictionary: **redress, calamity, prolonged, contracted, perish, mortality.**

Main Idea Dr. Rush describes how the conditions at the hospitals are often an obstacle to recovery.

I have delayed troubling Your Excellency with the state of our hospitals in hopes you would hear it from the director general, whose business it is to correspond with Your Excellency upon this subject. . . . I beg leave therefore at last to look up to you, and through you to the Congress, as the only powers that can redress our grievances or do us justice.

I need not inform Your Excellency that we have now upward of 5,000 sick in our hospitals. This number would cease to be alarming if our hospitals could afford such accommodations to the poor fellows as would ensure them a speedy recovery. But this is far from being the case. There cannot be a greater calamity for a sick man than to come into our hospital at this season of the year. Old disorders are prolonged, and new ones contracted among us. This last is so much the case that I am safe when I assert that a great majority of those who die under our hands perish with diseases caught in our hospitals. When I consider the present army under Your Excellency's command as the last hope of America, I am more alarmed and distressed at these facts than I have words to express. I can see nothing to prevent the same mortality this winter among our troops that prevailed last year. Every day deprives us 4 or 5 patients out of 500 in a hospital under my care in this place. The same complaints are heard from every quarter. The surgeons have been blamed for these things, but without reason.

Benjamin Rush

Analyzing Primary Sources

1. According to Dr. Rush, why are the soldiers not recovering sooner?

   A Their injuries are too difficult to care for.

   B There are too many soldiers to treat.

   C They catch diseases during their stay in the hospital.

   D The food is poor.

2. What does Rush predict will happen if conditions in the hospitals do not improve?

   A More soldiers will die in the coming winter.

   B Soldiers will desert the army.

   C There will not be enough surgeons.

   D Rush will be forced to leave his position.

3. Critical Thinking and Writing Drawing Inferences Why does Rush call the army the "last hope of America"?

Eyewitness Account

Debates in the Federal Convention of 1787

James Madison

James Madison took detailed notes of all the debates at the Constitutional Convention of 1787. Here, he describes the final day of the convention.

Vocabulary Before you read the selection, find the meanings of these words in a dictionary: **notwithstanding, venerable, vicissitudes.**

Main Idea Although some delegates refuse to sign the Constitution, the majority agree to put aside their objections and approve the document.

The Liberty Bell

Mr. Randolph [of Virginia] then rose and . . . apologized for his refusing to sign the constitution, notwithstanding the vast majority and venerable names that would give sanction to its wisdom and its worth. He said, however, that he did not mean by this refusal to decide that he should oppose the Constitution [in public]. He meant only to keep himself free to be governed by his duty as it should be prescribed by his future judgment. . . .

Mr. Gouverneur Morris [PA] said that he too had objections, but, considering the present plan as the best that was to be attained, he should take it with all its faults. The majority had determined in its favor, and by that determination he should abide. . . .

The members then proceeded to sign the [document].

While the last members were signing it, Dr. Franklin, looking toward the President's chair, at the back of which a rising sun happened to be painted, observed to a few members near him that painters had found it difficult to distinguish in their art a rising from a setting sun. "I have," said he, "often, and often in the course of the session, and the vicissitudes of my hopes and fears as to its [result], looked at that behind the President without being able to tell whether it was rising or setting. But now at length I have the happiness to know that it is a rising and not a setting sun."

Analyzing an Eyewitness Account

1. How would you describe Randolph's attitude toward the Constitution?

A He approved of it.

B He had objections but agreed to sign it.

C He refused to sign it.

D He swore to oppose it.

2. How would you describe Morris's attitude toward the Constitution?

A He approved of it.

B He had objections but agreed to sign it.

C He refused to sign it.

D He swore to oppose it.

3. Critical Thinking and Writing Drawing Inferences **(a)** Restate the main idea of Franklin's story about the sun. **(b)** Why do you think he felt this way?

The Federalist Papers

Alexander Hamilton

The Federalist Papers is a name given to a series of essays written in 1787 by Alexander Hamilton, James Madison, and John Jay. The purpose of the essays was to win support for the new Constitution. This is an excerpt from the first essay, written by Hamilton.

Vocabulary Before you read the selection, find the meanings of these words in a dictionary: **unequivocal, inefficiency, subsisting, propriety.**

Main Idea Hamilton argues that the future of democratic government in the world depends on the success of the Constitution.

After an unequivocal experience of the inefficiency of the subsisting federal government, you are called upon to deliberate on a new Constitution for the United States of America. The subject speaks its own importance; comprehending in its consequences nothing less than the existence of the UNION, the safety and welfare of the parts of which it is composed, the fate of an empire in many respects the most interesting in the world. It has been frequently remarked that it seems to have been reserved to the people of this country, by their conduct and example, to decide the important question whether societies of men are really capable or not of establishing good government from reflection and choice, or whether they are forever destined to depend for their political constitutions on accident and force. If there be any truth in the remark, the crisis at which we are arrived may with propriety be regarded as the era in which that decision is to be made; and a wrong election of the part we shall act may, in this view, deserve to be considered as the general misfortune of mankind. . . .

It may perhaps be thought superfluous to offer arguments to prove the utility of the UNION . . . But the fact is that we already hear it whispered in the private circles of those who oppose the new Constitution, that the thirteen States are of too great extent for any general system, and that we must of necessity resort to separate confederacies . . .

Alexander Hamilton

Analyzing Primary Sources

1. According to Hamilton, Americans must prove to the world that
   A a colony can leave its parent country
   B the United States is superior to other nations
   C people can create their own government
   D the Articles of Confederation can work

2. What does Hamilton fear will happen if the Constitution fails?
   A The states will separate.
   B Britain will regain control.
   C The government will become inefficient.
   D A new Constitution will have to be written.

3. **Critical Thinking and Writing** **Supporting a Point of View** Do you agree that the American experiment with democratic government was important to the entire world? Explain.

Historical Document

Three State Constitutions

Each of the 50 states has its own constitution. The following are brief excerpts from the constitutions of New York, Texas, and California.

Vocabulary Before you read the selection, find the meanings of these words in a dictionary: **discrimination, rendered, incompetent, diffusion, conservation.**

Main Idea Some topics are common to all state constitutions, while others reflect the concerns of that particular state.

New York Bill of Rights
Sec. 3. The free exercise and enjoyment of religious profession and worship, without discrimination or preference, shall forever be allowed in this state to all mankind; and no person shall be rendered incompetent to be a witness on account of his opinions on matters of religious belief . . .
Sec. 5. Excessive bail shall not be required nor excessive fines imposed, nor shall cruel and unusual punishments be inflicted, nor shall witnesses be unreasonably detained.

Texas Article 7 (Education)
Sec. 1. A general diffusion of knowledge being essential to the preservation of the liberties and rights of the people, it shall be the duty of the Legislature of the State to establish and make suitable provision for the support and maintenance of an efficient system of public free schools.
Sec. 7. (a) One-fourth of the revenue derived from the State occupation taxes shall be set apart annually for the benefit of the public free schools. . . .

California Article 10 (Water)
Sec. 2. It is hereby declared that because of the conditions prevailing in this State the general welfare requires that the water resources of the State be put to beneficial use to the fullest extent of which they are capable, and that the waste or unreasonable use or unreasonable method of use of water be prevented, and that the conservation of such waters is to be exercised with a view to the reasonable and beneficial use thereof in the interest of the people and for the public welfare. . . .

State flags of New York, Texas, and California

Analyzing Primary Sources

1. Section 3 of the New York Bill of Rights is related to which amendment to the United States Constitution?

A The First Amendment

B The Second Amendment

C The Fifth Amendment

D The Thirteenth Amendment

2. The "conditions" referred to in the California constitution are most likely related to the state's

A geography

B history

C population

D government

3. Critical Thinking and Writing Solving Problems **(a)** What general goal is described in the above excerpt from the Texas constitution? **(b)** Describe one specific way in which the Texas constitution tries to meet that goal.

Twelve Angry Men

Reginald Rose

Twelve Angry Men takes place inside a jury room at a murder trial. A unanimous vote is needed to convict. Here, Juror #8—the only person to vote "not guilty"—has promised to go along with the others if they still want to vote "guilty." One juror then changes his vote.

Main Idea This play examines the attitudes of different jurors toward serving on a jury.

#11: Please. I would like to say something here. I have always thought that a man was entitled to have unpopular opinions in this country. This is the reason I came here. In my own country, I am ashamed to say . . .

#10: What do we have to listen to now, the whole history of your country?

#7: Yeah, let's stick to the subject. [*He turns to #5.*] Now I'm talking facts. What made you change your vote?

#9: There's nothing for him to tell you. He didn't change his vote. I did.

#7: No, I wouldn't like you to tell me why.

#9: Well, I'd like to make it clear anyway . . .

#10: Do we have to listen to this?

Foreman: The man wants to talk.

#9: . . . [Juror #8] has been standing alone against us. He doesn't say the boy is not guilty. He just isn't sure. Well it's not easy to stand alone against the ridicule of others, even when there's a worthy cause. So he gambled for support, and I gave it to him. I respect his motives. The boy on trial is probably guilty. But I want to hear more. Right now the vote is ten to two.

#11: Pardon. This fighting. This is not why we are here, to fight. We have a responsibility. This, I have always thought, is a remarkable thing about democracy. That we are, uh, what is the word? Notified. That we are notified by mail to come down to this place and decide on the guilt or innocence of a man we have never heard of before. We have nothing to gain or lose by our verdict. This is one of the reasons why we are strong. We should not make it a personal thing. . . . Thank you.

A lawyer and judge meet

Analyzing Literature

1. Which juror is a naturalized citizen?

   A Juror #7

   B Juror #9

   C Juror #10

   D Juror #11

2. Juror #9 changes his vote because he

   A believes the defendant is guilty

   B believes the defendant is not guilty

   C is not sure whether the defendant is guilty

   D is afraid to stand alone against the others

3. Critical Thinking and Writing Analyzing Information (a) What features of the American jury system does Juror #11 praise? **(b)** Why do you think he feels this way?

Historical Document

Farewell Address
George Washington

After serving two terms as President, George Washington wrote his famous Farewell Address in 1796. In it, he announced that he would not seek a third term. As he retired from public service, the outgoing President gave his views on the best policies for the young republic to follow.

Vocabulary Before you read the selection, find the meanings of these words in a dictionary: **discriminations, distract, ill-founded, primary, detached.**

Main Idea On leaving office, Washington urges the nation to reject political parties and keep out of Europe's affairs.

[On Political Parties]

I have already [told] you the danger of Parties in the State, with particular reference to the founding of them on Geographical discriminations. Let me now take a more [general] view, & warn you in the most solemn manner against the [harmful] effects of the Spirit of Party, generally.

. . . the common & continual mischiefs of the spirit of the Party are sufficient to make it the interest and the duty of a wise People to discourage and restrain it.

It serves always to distract the Public Councils and [weaken] the Public Administration. It [stirs up] the Community with ill-founded Jealousies and false alarms, kindles the [hatred] of one part against another . . .

[On Europe]

Europe has a set of primary interests, which to us have none, or a very remote relation. Hence she must be engaged in frequent controversies, the causes of which are essentially foreign to our concerns. . . .

Our detached & distant situation invites and enables us to pursue a different course. If we remain one People, under an efficient government, the period is not far off, when we may defy material injury. . . .

George Washington

Analyzing Primary Sources

1. What is Washington's view of political parties?

  A They cost too much money.

  B They cause dangerous divisions.

  C They result in the rise of monarchs.

  D They weaken the system of checks and balances.

2. What is Washington's advice on foreign policy?

  A Cancel treaties with European countries.

  B Avoid all links except trade with European countries.

  C Make alliances only with European democracies.

  D Join all foreign alliances.

3. Critical Thinking and Writing Evaluating Information Washington himself belonged to no political party. Did that increase or decrease the effectiveness of what he had to say? Explain.

A Letter to John Adams, 1796
Thomas Jefferson

Although they were political opponents, Thomas Jefferson and John Adams maintained a deep respect for one another. After their retirements, Jefferson lived in Virginia and Adams in Massachusetts. They corresponded for the rest of their lives—almost until the day when they both died, July 4, 1826.

Vocabulary Before you read the selection, find the meanings of these words in a dictionary: **magistracy, disinterestedness, esteem, contrived.**

Main Idea Jefferson congratulates Adams on winning the presidential election of 1796, even though Jefferson himself became Vice President.

DEAR SIR—The public and the public papers have been much occupied lately in placing us in a point of opposition to each other. I trust with confidence that less of it has been felt by ourselves personally. . . . I knew it impossible you should lose a vote North of the Delaware [River], and even if that of Pennsylvania should be against you in the mass, yet that you would get enough South of that to place your succession out of danger.

. . . No one then will congratulate you with purer disinterestedness than myself. The share indeed which I may have had in the late vote, I shall still value highly, as an evidence of the share I have in the esteem of my fellow citizens. . . . I have no ambition to govern men. It is a painful and thankless office. . . . I devoutly wish you may be able to shun for us this war by which our agriculture, commerce and credit will be destroyed. If you are, the glory will be all your own; and that your administration may be filled with glory and happiness to yourself . . . is the sincere wish of one who tho', in the course of our voyage thro' life, various little incidents have happened or been contrived to separate us, retains still for you the solid esteem of the moments when we were working for our independence, and sentiments of respect and affectionate attachment.

Thomas Jefferson

Analyzing Primary Sources

1. What was Jefferson's attitude toward Adams's election as President?

   A Congratulations from a supporter

   B Congratulations from an opponent, but admirer

   C Anger that the people of the United States had rejected him for President

   D Anger because the election was dishonest

2. Jefferson expected Adams to win the election because

   A he knew Adams to be strong in the North

   B he expected Adams to sweep the region south of the Delaware River

   C Jefferson had campaigned for him

   D Adams was a very good campaigner

3. **Critical Thinking and Writing Summarizing** In three sentences, summarize the ideas expressed by Jefferson in the final paragraph of the letter.

Historical Document

Marbury v. Madison

John Marshall

When William Marbury was denied an appointment as a federal judge in Thomas Jefferson's administration, he decided to sue James Madison. As Secretary of State, Madison had the power to allow the appointment to proceed.

Vocabulary Before you read the selection, find the meanings of these words in a dictionary: **province, opposition, conformably, paramount, void, obligatory, omnipotence.**

Main Idea Chief Justice Marshall's ruling in *Marbury* v. *Madison* expands the power of the Supreme Court and establishes judicial review.

It is, emphatically, the province and duty of the Judicial Department to say what the law is. . . . if a law be in opposition to the Constitution, if both the law and the Constitution apply to a particular case, so that the court must either decide that case conformably to the law, disregarding the Constitution, or conformably to the Constitution, disregarding the law, the court must determine which of these conflicting rules governs the case. This is of the very essence of judicial duty. If, then, the courts are to regard the Constitution, and the Constitution is superior to any ordinary act of the legislature, the Constitution, and not such ordinary act, must govern the case to which they both apply.

Those, then, who [argue] the principle that the Constitution is to be considered in court as a paramount law are reduced to the necessity of maintaining that courts must close their eyes on the Constitution and only see the law.

This doctrine would subvert the very foundation of all written constitutions. It would declare that an act which, according to the principles and theory of our government, is entirely void, is yet, in practice, completely obligatory. . . . It would be giving to the legislature a practical and real omnipotence, with the same breath which professes to restrict their powers within narrow limits. . . .

Bronze doors leading into the Supreme Court in Washington, D.C.

Analyzing Primary Sources

1. Which branch(es) of government are referred to in this decision?

   A Executive and judicial

   B Legislative and judicial

   C Executive and legislative

   D Judicial only

2. According to this decision, what can the Supreme Court do?

   A Decide what laws the states can propose

   B Write new laws

   C Decide if a law is constitutional

   D Propose new amendments

3. Critical Thinking and Writing Applying Information The idea of judicial review enables the Supreme Court to declare a law unconstitutional. How did this ruling change the balance of power among the branches of government?

Literature

"The Star-Spangled Banner"

Francis Scott Key

Francis Scott Key, a young lawyer, watched from the deck of the ship *Tonnant* as the Americans and the British fought at Fort McHenry in 1814. In the morning, Key could see that the American flag was still waving over Fort McHenry. Hastily, Key began to write a poem on the back of a letter he had in his pocket. The poem was later set to music and became the verses of "The Star-Spangled Banner."

Vocabulary Before you read the selection, find the meanings of these words in a dictionary: **perilous, ramparts, haughty, reposes.**

Main Idea Francis Scott Key describes his feelings when he sees the American flag at Fort McHenry.

Oh, say, can you see, by the dawn's early light,
What so proudly we hailed at the twilight's last gleaming,
Whose broad stripes and bright stars through the perilous fight,
O'er the ramparts we watched were so gallantly streaming?
And the rocket's red glare, the bombs bursting in air,
Gave proof through the night that our flag was still there.
Oh, say, does that star-spangled banner yet wave
O'er the land of the free, and the home of the brave?

On the shore, dimly seen through the mists of the deep,
Where the foe's haughty host in dread silence reposes,
What is that which the breeze, o'er the towering steep,
As it fitfully blows, half conceals, half discloses?
Now it catches the gleam of the morning's first beam,
In full glory reflected, now shines on the stream.
'Tis the star-spangled banner; oh, long may it wave
O'er the land of the free, and the home of the brave!

The United States Flag

Analyzing Literature

1. Francis Scott Key uses the word "flag" only once in the anthem. What phrase does he use to describe the flag?
   A Through the mists of the deep
   B Star-spangled banner
   C The gleam of the morning's first beam
   D The breeze o'er the towering steep

2. What seems to be most important to Key about the Americans winning this battle?
   A That the American flag remain at other forts
   B That the Americans gain British land
   C That Americans be able to conquer other nations
   D That Americans protect their freedom

3. **Critical Thinking and Writing Evaluating Information** What description in "The Star-Spangled Banner" most impresses you? Explain.

Literature

Life on the Mississippi
Mark Twain

Mark Twain's *Life on the Mississippi* combines a true account of his experiences as a river pilot with an account of his visit to the Mississippi made nearly 20 years after he left the Midwest to live in the East. In this selection, Twain describes a steamboat trip down the Mississippi as a young man. At the time, Twain wanted to be a steamboat pilot. His admiration for the skill and confidence of the pilot, Mr. Bixby, is clear.

Vocabulary Before you read the selection, find the meanings of these words in a dictionary: **imminent, intent, apex.**

Main Idea	With coolness under pressure and years of experience, Mr. Bixby manages to guide his steamboat over some very treacherous shallows on the Mississippi.

Mark Twain

. . . Now the engines were stopped altogether, and we drifted with the current. Not that I could see the boat drift, for I could not, the stars being all gone by this time. This drifting was the dismalest work; it held one's heart still. Presently I discovered a blacker gloom than that which surrounded us. It was the head of the island. We were closing right down upon it. We entered its deeper shadow, and so imminent seemed the peril that I was likely to suffocate; and I had the strongest impulse to do SOMETHING, anything, to save the vessel. But still Mr. Bixby stood by his wheel, silent, intent as a cat, and all the pilots stood shoulder to shoulder at his back. . . .

The water grew shallower and shallower, by the leadsman's cries, till it was down to- "Eight-and-a-half! . . . E-i-g-h-t feet! . . . E-i-g-h-t feet! . . . Seven-and— . . ."

We touched bottom! Instantly Mr. Bixby set a lot of bells ringing, shouted through the tube, "NOW, let her have it—every ounce you've got!" . . . The boat rasped and ground her way through the sand, hung upon the apex of disaster a single tremendous instant, and then over she went! And such a shout went up at Mr. Bixby's back never loosened the roof of a pilot-house before!

Analyzing Literature

1. In the dark night, Twain "discovered a blacker gloom than that which surrounded us." What had he discovered?

  A Another steamboat drifting in the night

  B A large log floating down river

  C A large island right in their path

  D A person who had fallen overboard

2. What was the job of the leadsman?

  A Call out the depth of the water

  B Watch out for floating objects

  C Maintain discipline on board the boat

  D Provide leadership for the deckhands

3. Critical Thinking and Writing Comparing Compare Mr. Bixby's skill and calm with an impressive deed you have personally witnessed or read about.

Historical Document

The Monroe Doctrine

James Monroe

As the nations of Latin America gained their independence in the 1820s, the United States became concerned that Spain or other European nations would attempt to establish colonies in the region. In 1823, President James Monroe issued a warning to European powers not to colonize in the Western Hemisphere. The doctrine has helped shape American foreign policy to this day.

Vocabulary Before you read the selection, find the meanings of these words in a dictionary: **henceforth, colonization, candor, amicable, dependencies, interposition, manifestation, disposition.**

Main Idea President James Monroe warns European nations not to attempt to set up any new colonies in the Western Hemisphere.

[T]he occasion has been judged proper for asserting, as a principle in which the rights and interests of the United States are involved, that the American continents, by the free and independent condition which they have assumed and maintain, are henceforth not to be considered as subjects for future colonization by any European powers. . . .

We owe it, therefore, to candor and to the amicable relations existing between the United States and those [European] powers to declare that we should consider any attempt on their part to extend their system to any portion of this hemisphere as dangerous to our peace and safety. With the existing colonies or dependencies of any European power we have not interfered and shall not interfere. But with the Governments who have declared their independence and maintain it, and whose independence we have, on great consideration and on just principles, acknowledged, we could not view any interposition for the purpose of oppressing them, or controlling in any other manner their destiny, by any European power in any other light than as the manifestation of an unfriendly disposition toward the United States. . . .

James Monroe

Analyzing Primary Sources

1. What is the main point of the Monroe Doctrine?

   A It recognizes nations in Latin America.

   B It warns Europe against further colonization in the Americas.

   C It permits Russia to settle in the Northwest.

   D It warns Spain against invading Portugal.

2. How does this doctrine continue the policy suggested by George Washington?

   A Both advise European alliances.

   B Both suggest trade with Spain.

   C Both advise no alliances.

   D Both suggest alliances with Great Britain.

3. **Critical Thinking and Writing** **Linking Past and Present** Does the Monroe Doctrine have any value today? Give two reasons to support your point of view.

Primary Sources and Literature

The Inauguration of Andrew Jackson

Mrs. Samuel Harrison Smith

With the inauguration of Andrew Jackson in 1829, a democratic spirit swept through the nation. Thousands of his supporters traveled to Washington, D.C., to celebrate his arrival at the White House. Mrs. Samuel Harrison Smith, an important member of Washington society, attended the celebration.

Vocabulary Before you read the selection, find the meanings of these words in a dictionary: **immense, lodgings, hogshead.**

Main Idea Mrs. Samuel Harrison Smith gives her account of the Jackson inauguration in a letter to a friend.

Andrew Jackson

. . . [I] will give you an account of the inauguration in mere detail. The whole of the preceding day, immense crowds were coming into the city from all parts, lodgings could not be obtained, and the newcomers had to go to Georgetown which soon overflowed . . .

The President, after having been *literally* nearly pressed to death and almost suffocated and torn to pieces by the people in their eagerness to shake hands with Old Hickory, had retreated through the back way, or south front, and had escaped to his lodgings at Gadsby's. Cut glass and china to the amount of several thousand dollars had been broken in the struggle to get the refreshments. Punch and other articles had been carried out in tubs and buckets, but had it been in hogsheads it would have been insufficient; ice creams and cake and lemonade made for 20,000 people, for it is said that number were there, though I think the estimate exaggerated. Ladies fainted, men were seen with bloody noses, and such a scene of confusion took place as is impossible to describe: . . .

. . . Ladies and gentlemen only had been expected at this levee, not the people *en masse*. But it was the people's day, and the people's President, and the people would rule. God grant that one day or other the people do not put down all rule and rulers.

Analyzing an Eyewitness Account

1. Which statement describes the situation the day before the inauguration?

  A People slept at the White House.

  B Many people had no place to stay.

  C Only wealthy people had lodgings in the city.

  D People brought food to the celebration.

2. How do you know that the attendance at the inauguration was more than expected?

  A The reception was very long; people were tired.

  B There was a long line of people to shake hands with the President.

  C There was not enough food.

  D Some people brought extra dishes.

3. Critical Thinking and Writing Identifying Points of View How do you think Mrs. Harrison felt about what happened at the inauguration? Explain.

Historical Document

The Second Reply to Hayne
Daniel Webster

States' rights was a critical issue during the mid-1800s. The crisis of the Tariff of 1828 led to a major debate in the Senate, between **Robert Hayne** of South Carolina and **Daniel Webster** of Massachusetts, about the right of a state to declare a federal law unconstitutional.

Vocabulary Before you read the selection, find the meanings of these words in a dictionary: **sovereign, behold, dissevered, discordant, belligerent, rent, fraternal, ensign, lustre, delusion, folly, sentiment.**

Main Idea Daniel Webster argues that the states cannot act independently of the federal government.

The people of the United States have declared that the Constitution shall be the supreme law. We must either admit the proposition, or dispute their authority. The States are . . . not affected by this supreme law. But the State legislatures . . . are . . . not sovereign over the people. So far as the people have given the power to the general government . . . and the government holds of the people, and not of the State governments. . . .

While the Union lasts, we have high, exciting, gratifying prospects spread out before us and our children. Beyond that I seek not to penetrate the veil. God grant that in my day, at least, that curtain may not rise! . . . When my eyes shall be turned to behold for the last time the sun in heaven, may I not see him shining on the broken and dishonored fragments of a once glorious Union; on States dissevered . . . on a land rent with civil feuds, or drenched . . . in fraternal blood! Let their last feeble and lingering glance rather behold the gorgeous ensign of the republic . . . not a stripe erased or polluted, not a single star obscured, bearing for its motto, no such miserable interrogatory as "What is all this worth?" nor those other words of delusion and folly, "Liberty first and Union afterwards"; but everywhere, spread all over in characters of living light . . . as they float over the sea and over the land, and in every wind under the whole heavens, that other sentiment, dear to every true American heart, Liberty *and* Union, now and for ever, one and inseparable!

Daniel Webster

Analyzing Primary Sources

1. According to the first paragraph, what does Webster see as the limit of state governments?

 A The state can act without the consent of the people.

 B The state can ignore federal laws.

 C The states must follow the people's will.

 D The state governments can declare laws unconstitutional.

2. What does Webster hope never to see?

 A Liberties taken from some states

 B The Union dissolved

 C The states denying people liberties

 D The states with more power than the federal government

3. Critical Thinking and Writing Drawing Inferences Webster rejects the idea of "Liberty first and Union afterwards." What does he believe instead? Explain.

Historical Document

Women and the Oregon Trail

Hundreds of Americans found their way to the West over the Oregon Trail. How many died along the trail we will never know. The number varied from year to year. Cholera, caused by contaminated water, killed more travelers than anything else. As you will read in these excerpts from women who journeyed the trail, there were many dangers facing the traveler.

Vocabulary Before you read the selection, find the meanings of these words in a dictionary: **drove, dropsy, heart rendering, submission, seclusion.**

Main Idea The Oregon Trail was filled with danger. Many pioneers experienced tragic losses while traveling along the trail.

Snake River Crossing

"... our worst trouble at these large rivers, is swimming the stock over, often after swimming nearly halfway over, the poor things, will turn and come out again, at this place, however, there are Indians who swim the river from morning till night it is fun for them, there is many a drove of cattle that could not be got over without their help, by paying them a small sum, they will take a horse by the bridle or halter, and swim over with him, the rest of the horses all follow, and by driving ... the cattle they will most always follow the horses, sometimes they fail and turn back."

—Amelia Stewart Knight, August 5, 1853

Dear Little Willie

"... Our dear little Willie is not expected to live 12 hours as he evidently has the Cholera Infantum or dropsy in the brain the Doctor tells us it is in vain to administer any medicine as he must surely die. This to us is heart rendering, but God's ways are not our ways neither is his thoughts our thoughts! O! may we bow with submission to his will.

"... Last night our darling Willie was called from earth, to vie with angels around the throne of God. He was buried to-day upon an elevated point, one hundred and fifty feet above the plain in a spot of sweet seclusion. ... He was four years of age ..."

—Abigail Scott, August 25–28, 1852

A woman pioneer

Analyzing Primary Sources

1. According to Amelia Stewart Knight, the worst trouble at large rivers was

A getting horses and cattle across the river

B guarding against Indian attack

C finding the trail on the other side

D keeping the wagons from being swept away

2. "Little Willie" was Abigail Scott's

A cousin who was left back in Independence, Missouri

B ox who broke his leg during the first two weeks of the trip

C father, who refused to leave his home

D four-year-old son who died of cholera

3. Critical Thinking and Writing Making Generalizations Make two generalizations based on the experiences of Abigail Scott and Amelia Stewart Knight. Support the generalizations with facts from the two selections.

The Luck of Roaring Camp

Bret Harte's 1866 short story "The Luck of Roaring Camp" provides a vivid picture of a mining camp in the days of the California gold rush. In the story, miners in the town of Roaring Camp adopt a baby whose mother has died. Soon after, the town begins to benefit from a burst of good luck.

Vocabulary Before you read the selection, find the meanings of these words in a dictionary: **prefix, regeneration, imperceptibly, quarantine, mortification, sloughed, debarred, prudential, innovation, ablutions.**

Main Idea Miners in Roaring Camp develop a greater sense of community with the arrival of an infant boy.

. . . Oakhurst one day declared that the baby had brought "the luck" to Roaring Camp. It was certain that of late they had been successful. "Luck" was the name agreed upon, with the prefix of Tommy for greater convenience. . . .

And so the work of regeneration began in Roaring Camp. Almost imperceptibly a change came over the settlement. The cabin assigned to "Tommy Luck"—or "The Luck," as he was more frequently called—first showed signs of improvement. It was kept scrupulously clean and white-washed. . . .

Stumpy imposed a kind of quarantine upon those who aspired to the honor and privilege of holding "The Luck." It was a cruel mortification to Kentuck—who, in the carelessness of a large nature and the habits of frontier life, had begun to regard all garments as a second [skin], which, like a snake's, only sloughed off through decay—to be debarred this privilege from certain prudential reasons. Yet such was the subtle influence of innovation that he thereafter appeared regularly every afternoon in a clean shirt, and face still shining from his ablutions. . . .

"Tommy," . . . must not be disturbed by noise. The shouting and yelling which had gained the camp its [crude] title were not permitted within hearing distance of Stumpy's.

Miners in California

Analyzing Literature

1. How did the baby get his name?
   - **A** He was named after Thomas Jefferson.
   - **B** He was named for the roaring brook near the town.
   - **C** He was named after the miner "Kentuck."
   - **D** He brought good luck to the town.

2. Why did Kentuck change his ways?
   - **A** He wanted to hold the baby.
   - **B** He wanted to change his luck.
   - **C** He was expecting to run for mayor.
   - **D** He was planning to move to a larger camp.

3. **Critical Thinking and Writing Drawing Inferences** What do you think will happen to the town if "Tommy" ever leaves it? Explain.

Historical Document

Factory Rules From the Handbook to Lowell, 1848

Established in 1813, the textile factory in Lowell, Massachusetts, became the most famous center of textile manufacturing in the country. Employing mostly young women from New England farm families, Lowell represented a model work community. The female workers, or "mill girls," were closely supervised. They were also required to follow the factory rules.

Main Idea All employees at the Lowell factory must follow company rules.

All persons in the employ of the Hamilton Manufacturing Company, are to observe the regulations of the room where they are employed. They are not to be absent from their work without the consent of the overseer, except in cases of sickness, and then they are to send him word of the cause of their absence. They are to board in one of the houses of the company and give information at the counting room, where they board, when they begin, or, whenever they change their boarding place; and are to observe the regulations of their boarding-house.

Those intending to leave the employment of the company, are to give at least two weeks' notice thereof to their overseer.

All persons entering into the employment of the company, are considered as engaged for twelve months, and those who leave sooner, or do not comply with all these regulations, will not be entitled to a regular discharge.

The company will not employ any one who is habitually absent from public worship on the Sabbath, or known to be guilty of immorality.

A physician will attend once in every month at the counting-room, to vaccinate all who may need it, free of expense.

Any one who shall take from the mills or the yard, any yarn, cloth or other article belonging to the company, will be considered guilty of stealing and be liable for prosecution. . . .

Workers at a textile mill

Analyzing Primary Sources

1. Where must the employees live?
   A In apartments near the factory
   B With friends in the area
   C In housing provided by the company
   D In housing chosen by the employee

2. Which statement best describes the rules listed here?
   A Only women are hired.
   B Most of the rules protect the company from loss of property on workers' time.
   C Injured workers are paid.
   D The worker must complete 18 months of service.

3. Critical Thinking and Writing Applying Information How would you describe the relationship between the employer and the employee at the Lowell factory in 1848? Explain.

Eyewitness Account

Life and Times of Frederick Douglass

Frederick Douglass

Born into slavery, Frederick Douglass was in his twenties before he escaped to freedom in Bedford, Massachusetts. A self-educated man, he became a well-known abolitionist and orator. He gave lectures about the evils of slavery in the United States, London, and the West Indies. *Life and Times of Frederick Douglass* is one of his three autobiographies.

Vocabulary Before you read the selection, find the meanings of these words in a dictionary: **lodged, ample.**

Main Idea Frederick Douglass describes his childhood experience as a slave.

As before intimated, I received no severe treatment from the hands of my master, but the insufficiency of both food and clothing was a serious trial to me. . . . In hottest summer and coldest winter, I was kept almost in a state of nudity. My only clothing—a little coarse sackcloth or tow-linen sort of shirt, scarcely reaching to my knees, was worn night and day and changed once a week. In the daytime I could protect myself by keeping on the sunny side of the house, or in stormy weather, in the corner of the kitchen chimney. But the great difficulty was to keep warm during the night. The pigs in the pen had leaves, and the horses in the stable had straw, but the children had no beds. They lodged anywhere in the ample kitchen. I slept generally in a little closet, without even a blanket to cover me. In very cold weather I sometimes got down the bag in which corn was carried to the mill, and crawled into that. . . . Our cornmeal mush, which was our only regular if not all-sufficing diet, . . . was placed in a large tray or trough. This was set down on the floor of the kitchen, or out of doors on the ground, and the children were called like so many pigs, and . . . would come, some with oyster-shells, some with pieces of shingle, but none with spoons. . . . He who could eat the fastest got most, and he that was strongest got the best place, but few left the trough really satisfied.

Frederick Douglass

Analyzing an Eyewitness Account

1. According to Douglass, what was his main discomfort as a slave?
   A His sleeping area was too warm.
   B His sackcloth was not changed often enough.
   C He was repeatedly beaten.
   D He was usually cold and hungry.

2. Aside from insufficient food, why were mealtimes difficult for the slave children?
   A The children had to compete with the farm animals for food.
   B The weakest children suffered most.
   C The mush was served to the oldest children first.
   D The strongest children received less.

3. Critical Thinking and Writing Analyzing Information What qualities did Douglass need in order to survive his life in slavery?

Historical Document

Declaration of Sentiments
Elizabeth Cady Stanton and Lucretia Mott

When Elizabeth Cady Stanton and Lucretia Mott attended the World Anti-Slavery Convention in 1840, they had to sit and listen from a curtained gallery because women were not allowed on the main convention floor. Outraged, both women vowed to hold a convention for women's rights. Eight years later, Stanton and Mott organized a convention at Seneca Falls, New York.

Vocabulary Before you read the selection, find the meanings of these words in a dictionary: **endowed, inalienable, usurpations, candid, franchise.**

Main Idea Stanton and Mott presented their case for women's rights in the Declaration of Sentiments.

We hold these truths to be self-evident: that all men and women are created equal; that they are endowed by their Creator with certain inalienable rights; that among these are life, liberty, and the pursuit of happiness; that to secure these rights governments are instituted, deriving their just powers from the consent of the governed. . . .

The history of mankind is a history of repeated injuries and usurpations on the part of man toward woman, having in direct object the establishment of an absolute tyranny over her. To prove this, let facts be submitted to a candid world.

He has never permitted her to exercise her inalienable right to the elective franchise.

He has compelled her to submit to laws, in the formation of which she had no voice.

He has withheld from her rights which are given to the most ignorant and degraded men—both natives and foreigners.

Having deprived her of this first right of a citizen, the elective franchise, thereby leaving her without representation in the halls of legislation, he has oppressed her on all sides.

He has made her, if married, in the eye of the law, civilly dead.

He has taken from her all right in property, even to the wages she earns. . . .

Lucretia Mott and Elizabeth Cady Stanton

Analyzing Primary Sources

1. What truth is obvious according to the Declaration of Sentiments?
   A Women have natural rights.
   B Men and women have natural rights.
   C Women have a right to protest.
   D None of the above

2. According to the Declaration, of which of the following rights do women feel they have been deprived?
   A The right to property
   B The right to submit to laws in which they had a voice
   C The right to money they have earned
   D All of the above

3. Critical Thinking and Writing Analyzing Information Why do you think the Declaration of Sentiments is based on the Declaration of Independence?

Moby-Dick
Herman Melville

In 1820, a whale hunting ship, the *Essex*, sank after being attacked by a giant whale. Only eight crew members survived. Herman Melville knew of the story, and ten years later it would become part of his best-known seafaring novel, *Moby-Dick*.

Vocabulary Before you read the selection, find the meanings of these words in a dictionary: **dismasted, razeed, imprecations, perdition, splice.**

Main Idea Ahab is the captain of the whale ship *Pequod*. In this scene, Ahab has offered gold to the first sailor who sees the white whale, Moby-Dick.

"It's a white whale, I say," resumed Ahab, as he threw down the [hammer]: "a white whale. Skin your eyes for him, men; look sharp for white water; if ye see but a bubble, sing out." . . .

"Captain Ahab," said Starbuck . . . "Captain Ahab, I have heard of Moby-Dick—but it was not Moby-Dick that took off thy leg?"

"Who told thee that?" cried Ahab; then pausing, "Aye, Starbuck; aye, my hearties all round; it was Moby-Dick that dismasted me; Moby-Dick that brought me to this dead stump I stand on now. Aye, aye," he shouted with a terrific, loud, animal sob, like that of a heart-stricken moose; "Aye, aye! It was that accursed white whale that razeed me; made a poor pegging lubber of me for ever and a day!" Then tossing both arms, with measureless imprecations he shouted out: "Aye, aye! and I'll chase him round Good Hope, and round the Horn, and round the Norway Maelstrom, and round perdition's flames before I give him up. And this is what ye have shipped for, men! to chase that white whale on both sides of land, and over all sides of earth, till he spouts black blood and rolls fin out. What say ye, men, will ye splice hands on it, now? I think ye do look brave."

"Aye, aye!" shouted the harpooneers and seamen, running closer to the excited old man: "A sharp eye for the white whale; a sharp lance for Moby-Dick!"

A painting of the whale, Moby-Dick

Analyzing Literature

1. What does the excerpt explain about Ahab and Moby-Dick?
   A   Ahab believes Moby-Dick is a gentle whale.
   B   Ahab believes the white whale is harmless.
   C   Ahab has never seen the white whale.
   D   Moby-Dick previously attacked Ahab.

2. How do the sailors react to Ahab's offer?
   A   They decide Ahab is not serious.
   B   They join in Ahab's enthusiasm.
   C   They do not believe there is a white whale.
   D   They try to persuade Ahab to give up the idea.

3. **Critical Thinking and Writing Drawing Inferences** Why do you think Ahab is determined to find Moby-Dick? What does this tell you about the kind of man Ahab is?

A Slave Escapes
Levi Coffin

Levi Coffin was an abolitionist who spent a lifetime helping slaves escape on the Underground Railroad. In his *Reminiscences of Levi Coffin* (1876), he describes how he helped an escaped African American man named Louis avoid being returned to slavery. Louis had been recaptured and faced a hearing under the Fugitive Slave Law.

Vocabulary Before you read the selection, find the meanings of these words in a dictionary: **intently, sexton, secreted.**

Main Idea — Aided by abolitionists, a slave named Louis makes his escape to freedom.

When the time set for the decision arrived, the court-room was crowded with interested listeners, white and black. . . . Louis . . . to gain more room, slipped his chair back a little way. Neither his master nor the marshal noticed the movement, as they were intently listening to the judge, and he slipped his chair again, until he was back of them. . . . Next he rose quietly to his feet and took a step backward. Some abolitionist friendly to his cause gave him an encouraging touch on the foot, and he stepped farther back. Then . . . he quietly and cautiously made his way around the south end of the room . . .

He was well acquainted with the different streets, and made his way quickly, . . . to Avondale, where he knew the sexton of the colored burying ground. . . .

[*Coffin and other abolitionists now attempt to smuggle Louis, disguised in woman's dress, into a church.*]

I passed on to Vine Street and joined the throng of people going to evening service. Louis followed, at a short distance, and was conducted to the church previously mentioned. I passed in at a side gate and went into the basement of the church. Louis followed me and was soon safely secreted in one of the committee rooms, where he remained for several weeks. The officers of the law made vigorous efforts to find him, but gained no clue to his hiding place. . . .

Fugitive slaves

Analyzing an Eyewitness Account

1. Louis escaped from the courtroom by

  A getting up from his chair and quietly walking out

  B jumping out of a window

  C disguising himself as a policeman

  D taking a hostage

2. Abolitionists helped Louis by doing which of the following?

  A Providing a wagon to take him to Avondale

  B Hiding him in a church

  C Disguising him as a minister

  D Assisting him to the train station

3. Critical Thinking and Writing Drawing Conclusions Based on these excerpts, what qualities of character did Louis possess?

Primary Sources and Literature

Dred Scott v. Sandford (1857)

Dred Scott v. *Sandford* was a landmark Supreme Court case which did much to pave the way for the Civil War. In its decision, the Court ruled that African Americans were not United States citizens. The Court also determined that an important part of the Missouri Compromise of 1820 was unconstitutional. The ruling raised anger between the North and the South to the point where it exploded into fighting in 1861.

Vocabulary Before you read the selection, find the meanings of these words in a dictionary: **express, prohibition, dominion.**

Main Idea According to the Dred Scott decision, any act that deprived a citizen of the United States of his slaves was unconstitutional because it violated the Fifth Amendment to the Constitution.

. . . The rights of property are united with the rights of person, and placed on the same ground by the 5th amendment to the Constitution, which provides that no person shall be deprived of life, liberty, and property, without due process of law. And an act of Congress which deprives a citizen of the United States of his liberty or property, merely because he came himself or brought his property into a particular Territory of the United States, and who had committed no offence against the laws, could hardly be dignified with the name of due process of law. . . .

The powers over person and property of which we speak are not only not granted to Congress, but are in express terms denied, and they are forbidden to exercise them. And this prohibition is not confined to the States, but the words are general, and extend to the whole territory over which the Constitution gives it power to legislate, including those portions of it remaining under Territorial Government, as well as that covered by States. It is a total absence of power everywhere within the dominion of the United States, and places the citizens of a Territory, so far as these rights are concerned, on the same footing with citizens of the States. . . . And if Congress itself cannot do this—if it is beyond the powers conferred on the Federal Government—it will be admitted, we presume, that it could not authorize a Territorial Government to exercise them.

Dred Scott

Analyzing Primary Sources

1. What portion of the Constitution provides that no person shall be deprived of life, liberty, and property without due process of law?

  A The First Amendment

  B The Third Amendment

  C The Fifth Amendment

  D The Seventh Amendment

2. According to the ruling, the power to take away a person's property just because he moves to a Territory of the United States

  A belongs to the President

  B is granted to Congress

  C is denied to Congress

  D belongs to the Court

3. Critical Thinking and Writing Summarizing Using your own words, write three sentences to summarize the ideas expressed in the Dred Scott decision.

Literature

The Red Badge of Courage
Stephen Crane

Born six years after the Civil War ended, Stephen Crane never fought in a war. Yet, his portrayal of Henry Fleming as a young Union soldier who manages to overcome his fear during the war is realistic and convincing.

Vocabulary Before you read the selection, find the meanings of these words in a dictionary: **urchin, menacing, regiment, welded.**

Main Idea After spending time in camp, participating in military drills, Henry Fleming is finally thrust into the heat of a real battle.

The captain of the company had been pacing excitedly to and fro in the rear. He coaxed in schoolmistress fashion, as to a congregation of boys with primers. His talk was an endless repetition. "Reserve your ire, boys—don't shoot till I tell you—save your fire—wait till they get close up—don't be damned fools—"

Perspiration streamed down the youth's face, which was soiled like that of a weeping urchin. He frequently, with a nervous movement, wiped his eyes with his coat sleeve. His mouth was still a little ways open.

He got the one glance at the foe-swarming field in front of him, and instantly ceased to debate the question of his piece being loaded. Before he was ready to begin—before he had announced to himself that he was about to fight—he threw the obedient, well-balanced rifle into position and fired a first wild shot. Directly he was working at his weapon like an automatic affair.

He suddenly lost concern for himself, and forgot to look at a menacing fate. He became not a man but a member. He felt that something of which he was a part—a regiment, an army, a cause, or a country—was in a crisis. He was welded into a common personality which was dominated by a single desire. For some moments he could not flee no more than a little finger can commit a revolution from a hand.

Stephen Crane

Analyzing Literature

1. How does Henry feel as he begins to take part in the battle?
   A He is excited and ready.
   B He is sweating, but confident.
   C He is nervous and fearful.
   D He is unable to act.

2. What happens as Henry prepares to shoot his rifle?
   A He loses control and continues to fire wildly.
   B He chooses a target and takes aim.
   C He fires aimlessly once, and then begins to control his shots.
   D He cannot load the rifle.

3. **Critical Thinking and Writing Analyzing Information** What does Henry learn about himself during the battle?

Historical Document

The Gettysburg Address
Abraham Lincoln

On November 19, 1863, President Abraham Lincoln gave a brief speech at the dedication of a battlefield at Gettysburg. Lincoln's "Gettysburg Address" is today considered one of the most important and moving statements of American ideals.

Vocabulary Before you read the selection, find the meanings of these words in a dictionary: **score, proposition, consecrate, hallow, detract.**

Main Idea Lincoln argues that the best way to honor the Union dead is to keep alive the principles of democracy.

Four score and seven years ago our fathers brought forth on this continent, a new nation, conceived in liberty, and dedicated to the proposition that all men are created equal. Now we are engaged in a great civil war, testing whether that nation, or any nation so conceived and so dedicated, can long endure. We met on a great battlefield of that war. We have come to dedicate a portion of that field, as a final resting place for those who here gave their lives that that nation might live. It is altogether fitting and proper that we should do this. But, in a larger sense, we can not dedicate, we can not consecrate, we can not hallow, this ground. The brave men, living and dead. who struggled here, have consecrated it, far above our poor power to add or detract. The world will little note, nor long remember what we say here, but it can never forget what they did here. It is for us the living, rather, to be dedicated here to the unfinished work which they who fought here have thus far so nobly advanced. It is rather for us to be here dedicated to the great task remaining before us, that from these honored dead we take increased devotion to that cause for which they gave the last full measure of devotion, that we here highly resolve that these dead shall not have died in vain, that this nation, under God, shall have a new birth of freedom, and that government of the people, by the people, for the people, shall not perish from the earth.

Statue of Abraham Lincoln

Analyzing Primary Sources

1. From what document does Lincoln quote in his opening sentence?

   A   The Declaration of Independence

   B   The Bill of Rights

   C   The "Star-Spangled Banner"

   D   The Emancipation Proclamation

2. Lincoln argues that "we cannot consecrate . . . this ground" because

   A   it is not fitting and proper to do so

   B   the world will little note nor long remember Gettysburg

   C   those who fought at Gettysburg have already consecrated it

   D   the soldiers at Gettysburg died in vain

3. **Critical Thinking and Writing Analyzing Ideas** Give three examples of how Lincoln uses this speech to try to remind people of the ideals upon which the United States was founded.

Eyewitness Account

Ten Years on a Georgia Plantation Since the War
Frances Butler Leigh

Frances Butler Leigh was the daughter of a Georgia planter. In this account, she recalls journeying from the North back to her home in 1866.

Main Idea Leigh's account describes both the physical and emotional impact that the Civil War had on the South.

The Southern railroads were many of them destroyed for miles, not having been rebuilt since the war, and it was very questionable how we were to get as far as Savannah, a matter we did accomplish however, in a week's time, after the following adventures, of which I find an account in my letters written at the time. We stopped one day in Washington, and went all over the new Capitol, which had been finished since I was there five years ago.

On Saturday we left, reaching Richmond at four o'clock on Sunday morning. I notice that it is a peculiarity of Southern railroads that they always either arrive, or start, at four o'clock in the morning. That day we spent quietly there, and sad enough it was, for besides all the associations with the place which crowded thick and fast upon one's memory, half the town was a heap of burnt ruins, showing how heavily the desolation of war had fallen upon it. And in the afternoon I went out to the cemetery, and after some search found the grave I was looking for. There he lay, with hundreds of others who had sacrificed their lives in vain, their resting place marked merely by small wooden headboards, bearing their names, regiments, and the battles in which they fell. The grief and excitement made me quite ill, so that I was glad to leave the town before daylight the next morning, and I hope I may never be there again.

Richmond, Virginia, after the Civil War

Analyzing an Eyewitness Account

1. Upon what evidence does Leigh base her account?

   A Her memory only

   B Letters she wrote at the time

   C Official records

   D Newspaper accounts

2. This passage describes all of the following effects of the Civil War on the South EXCEPT the

   A destruction of railroads

   B destruction of cities

   C destruction of plantations

   D heavy casualties

3. Critical Thinking and Writing Drawing Conclusions (a) What emotions does Leigh feel as she visits Richmond? **(b)** Do you think her reaction was typical of many southerners at the time? Explain.

Plessy v. Ferguson

Henry B. Brown and John M. Harlan

In 1892, Homer Plessy boarded a streetcar in Louisiana. He had a first-class ticket. When asked to leave the car because he was African American, Plessy refused. He was arrested. Eventually, the case went to the Supreme Court. Plessy argued that his rights under the Fourteenth Amendment were violated.

Main Idea Justice Brown and Justice Harlan were two of seven judges on the Supreme Court who heard the case. Justice Brown delivers the opinion that establishes segregation in the South for over 50 years. Justice Harlan is the only judge to disagree.

Judge Henry B. Brown

The object of the [Fourteenth Amendment] was undoubtedly to enforce the absolute equality of the two races before the law, but in the nature of things it could not have been intended to abolish distinctions based upon color, or to enforce social . . . equality. . . . Laws permitting, and even requiring, separation [of races] in places . . . do not necessarily imply the inferiority of either race to the other, and have been generally, if not universally, recognized as within the competency of the state legislatures in the exercise of their police powers.

Judge John M. Harlan

The Thirteenth Amendment . . . decreed universal civil freedom in this country. But that amendment having been found inadequate . . . was followed by the Fourteenth Amendment . . .

These notable additions to the fundamental law were welcomed by the friends of liberty throughout the world. This Court has further said, "that the law in the states shall be the same for the black as for the white . . . and, in regard to the colored race, for whose protection the amendment was primarily designed, that no discrimination shall be made against them by law because of their color."

Justice John M. Harlan

Analyzing Primary Sources

1. According to Justice Brown, what is not guaranteed under the Fourteenth Amendment?

  A Voting rights

  B Social equality of all races

  C The power of state legislatures

  D The civil rights of African Americans

2. According to Justice Harlan, why was the Fourteenth Amendment passed?

  A It further protected the rights of formerly enslaved African Americans.

  B It ended slavery.

  C The Thirteenth Amendment was unconstitutional.

  D It gave the states additional rights.

3. Critical Thinking and Writing Summarizing Using your own words, summarize the arguments of Justice Brown and Justice Harlan in four or five sentences. How were African Americans affected?

Eyewitness Account

How the Other Half Lives
Jacob Riis

After years of drifting from one low-paying job to another, Jacob Riis became a police reporter for *The New York Times*. Most of his stories were about events in poor neighborhoods. Dissatisfied with writing about the events, Riis decided to tell his stories through photography.

Vocabulary Before you read the selection, find the meanings of these words in a dictionary: **notorious, cosmopolitan, successor, scavenger, monopolizes, bootblacking, hod, alderman.**

Main Idea	In "How the Other Half Lives," published in 1890, Riis shows the lives of immigrants through pictures and words. In the following passage, he describes the diversity of immigrants in the city.

Immigrants arriving in the United States

When once I asked the agent of a notorious Fourth Ward alley how many people might be living in it I was told: One hundred and forty families, one hundred Irish, thirty-eight Italian, and two that spoke the German tongue. Barring the agent herself, there was not a native-born individual in the court. The answer was characteristic of the cosmopolitan character of lower New York. . . . One may find for the asking an Italian, a German, a French, African, Spanish, Bohemian, Russian, Scandinavian, Jewish, and Chinese colony. . . .

The German ragpicker of thirty years ago, quite as low in the scale as his Italian successor, is the thrifty tradesman or prosperous farmer of today.

The Italian scavenger of our time is fast graduating into exclusive control of the corner fruit stands, while his black-eyed boy monopolizes the bootblacking industry, in which a few years ago he was an intruder. The Irish hod carrier in the second generation has become a brick layer, if not the alderman of his ward; while the Chinese [peasant] is in almost exclusive possession of the laundry business. The poorest immigrant comes here with the ambition to better himself, and, given half a chance, might be reasonably expected to make the most of it.

Analyzing an Eyewitness Account

1. How had lower New York changed by 1890?

  A Only native-born people were there.

  B There were nearly all immigrants living there.

  C Most of the people living there were Russian and Chinese.

  D Half of the population was native-born.

2. What happened as generations of immigrants remained in the city?

  A All family members worked in factories.

  B Most wanted to return home.

  C No important change took place; each generation lived the same way.

  D Each group made economic improvements.

3. Critical Thinking and Writing Comparing (a) How were the immigrants who came to America different? (b) How were they the same?

I Have a Dream
Martin Luther King, Jr.

To celebrate the one hundredth anniversary of the Emancipation Proclamation, civil rights leaders planned a march to Washington, D.C. On August 28, 1963, nearly 200,000 marchers arrived in Washington. The keynote speaker was the well-known civil rights leader, Dr. Martin Luther King, Jr.

Vocabulary Before you read the selection, find the meanings of these words in a dictionary: **creed, prodigious, hamlet.**

Main Idea In his speech, Dr. King describes his dream for racial harmony.

I have a dream that one day this nation will rise up and live out the true meaning of its creed: "We hold these truths to be self-evident: that all men are created equal."

I have a dream that one day on the red hills of Georgia the sons of former slaves and the sons of former slaveowners will be able to sit down together at the table of brotherhood. . . .

I have a dream that my four children will one day live in a nation where they will not be judged by the color of their skin but by the content of their character.

I have a dream today. . . .

So let freedom ring from the prodigious hilltops of New Hampshire. . . .

But not only that; let freedom ring from Stone Mountain of Georgia!

Let freedom ring from Lookout Mountain of Tennessee!

Let freedom ring from every hill and every molehill of Mississippi. From every mountainside, let freedom ring.

When we let freedom ring, when we let it ring from every village and every hamlet, from every state and every city, we will be able to speed up that day when all of God's children, black men and white men, Jews and Gentiles, Protestants and Catholics, will be able to join hands and sing in the words of the old Negro spiritual, "Free at last! free at last! thank God Almighty, we are free at last!"

Dr. Martin Luther King, Jr.

Analyzing Primary Sources

1. Why does Dr. King believe the United States is not living out the meaning of its creed?
   A African American men are denied freedom.
   B White women are denied civil liberties.
   C Only men are treated fairly.
   D Not all Americans are treated equally.

2. What is King's hope for his children?
   A They should be judged as individuals, not by their race.
   B They should be judged racially and by character.
   C They should be judged as King's children.
   D All of the above

3. **Critical Thinking and Writing Evaluating Information** Describe the way in which Dr. King uses words and rhythms to make his point.

Presidents of the United States

1 George Washington (1732–1799)

Years in office:
1789–1797
Party:
none
Elected from:
Virginia
Vice President:
John Adams

2 John Adams (1735–1826)

Years in office:
1797–1801
Party:
Federalist
Elected from:
Massachusetts
Vice President:
Thomas
    Jefferson

3 Thomas Jefferson (1743–1826)

Years in office:
1801–1809
Party:
Democratic
    Republican
Elected from:
Virginia
Vice President:
1) Aaron Burr,
2) George Clinton

4 James Madison (1751–1836)

Years in office:
1809–1817
Party:
Democratic
    Republican
Elected from:
Virginia
Vice President:
1) George Clinton,
2) Elbridge Gerry

5 James Monroe (1758–1831)

Years in office:
1817–1825
Party:
Democratic
    Republican
Elected from:
Virginia
Vice President:
Daniel Tompkins

6 John Quincy Adams (1767–1848)

Years in office:
1825–1829
Party:
National
    Republican
Elected from:
Massachusetts
Vice President:
John Calhoun

7 Andrew Jackson (1767–1845)

Years in office:
1829–1837
Party:
Democratic
Elected from:
Tennessee
Vice President:
1) John Calhoun,
2) Martin Van
    Buren

8 Martin Van Buren (1782–1862)

Years in office:
1837–1841
Party:
Democratic
Elected from:
New York
Vice President:
Richard Johnson

9 William Henry Harrison* (1773–1841)

Years in office:
1841
Party:
Whig
Elected from:
Ohio
Vice President:
John Tyler

10 John Tyler (1790–1862)

Years in office:
1841–1845
Party:
Whig
Elected from:
Virginia
Vice President:
none

11 James K. Polk (1795–1849)

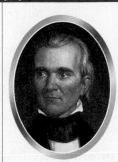

Years in office:
1845–1849
Party:
Democratic
Elected from:
Tennessee
Vice President:
George Dallas

12 Zachary Taylor* (1784–1850)

Years in office:
1849–1850
Party:
Whig
Elected from:
Louisiana
Vice President:
Millard Fillmore

*Died in office

13 Millard Fillmore (1800–1874)

Years in office:
1850–1853
Party:
Whig
Elected from:
New York
Vice President:
none

14 Franklin Pierce (1804–1869)

Years in office:
1853–1857
Party:
Democratic
Elected from:
New Hampshire
Vice President:
William King

15 James Buchanan (1791–1868)

Years in office:
1857–1861
Party:
Democratic
Elected from:
Pennsylvania
Vice President:
John Breckinridge

16 Abraham Lincoln** (1809–1865)

Years in office:
1861–1865
Party:
Republican
Elected from:
Illinois
Vice President:
1) Hannibal
   Hamlin,
2) Andrew
   Johnson

17 Andrew Johnson (1808–1875)

Years in office:
1865–1869
Party:
Republican
Elected from:
Tennessee
Vice President:
none

18 Ulysses S. Grant (1822–1885)

Years in office:
1869–1877
Party:
Republican
Elected from:
Illinois
Vice President:
1) Schuyler
   Colfax,
2) Henry Wilson

19 Rutherford B. Hayes (1822–1893)

Years in office:
1877–1881
Party:
Republican
Elected from:
Ohio
Vice President:
William Wheeler

20 James A. Garfield** (1831–1881)

Years in office:
1881
Party:
Republican
Elected from:
Ohio
Vice President:
Chester A. Arthur

21 Chester A. Arthur (1829–1886)

Years in office:
1881–1885
Party:
Republican
Elected from:
New York
Vice President:
none

22 Grover Cleveland (1837–1908)

Years in office:
1885–1889
Party:
Democratic
Elected from:
New York
Vice President:
Thomas
   Hendricks

23 Benjamin Harrison (1833–1901)

Years in office:
1889–1893
Party:
Republican
Elected from:
Indiana
Vice President:
Levi Morton

24 Grover Cleveland (1837–1908)

Years in office:
1893–1897
Party:
Democratic
Elected from:
New York
Vice President:
Adlai Stevenson

**Assassinated

25 William McKinley** (1843–1901)

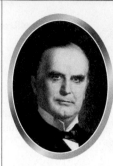

Years in office:
1897–1901
Party:
Republican
Elected from:
Ohio
Vice President:
1) Garret Hobart,
2) Theodore Roosevelt

26 Theodore Roosevelt (1858–1919)

Years in office:
1901–1909
Party:
Republican
Elected from:
New York
Vice President:
Charles Fairbanks

27 William Howard Taft (1857–1930)

Years in office:
1909–1913
Party:
Republican
Elected from:
Ohio
Vice President:
James Sherman

28 Woodrow Wilson (1856–1924)

Years in office:
1913–1921
Party:
Democratic
Elected from:
New Jersey
Vice President:
Thomas Marshall

29 Warren G. Harding* (1865–1923)

Years in office:
1921–1923
Party:
Republican
Elected from:
Ohio
Vice President:
Calvin Coolidge

30 Calvin Coolidge (1872–1933)

Years in office:
1923–1929
Party:
Republican
Elected from:
Massachusetts
Vice President:
Charles Dawes

31 Herbert C. Hoover (1874–1964)

Years in office:
1929–1933
Party:
Republican
Elected from:
California
Vice President:
Charles Curtis

32 Franklin D. Roosevelt* (1882–1945)

Years in office:
1933–1945
Party:
Democratic
Elected from:
New York
Vice President:
1) John Garner,
2) Henry Wallace,
3) Harry S Truman

33 Harry S Truman (1884–1972)

Years in office:
1945–1953
Party:
Democratic
Elected from:
Missouri
Vice President:
Alben Barkley

34 Dwight D. Eisenhower (1890–1969)

Years in office:
1953–1961
Party:
Republican
Elected from:
New York
Vice President:
Richard M. Nixon

35 John F. Kennedy** (1917–1963)

Years in office:
1961–1963
Party:
Democratic
Elected from:
Massachusetts
Vice President:
Lyndon B. Johnson

36 Lyndon B. Johnson (1908–1973)

Years in office:
1963–1969
Party:
Democratic
Elected from:
Texas
Vice President:
Hubert Humphrey

*Died in office
**Assassinated

37 Richard M. Nixon*** (1913–1994)

Years in office:
1969–1974
Party:
Republican
Elected from:
New York
Vice President:
1) Spiro Agnew,
2) Gerald R. Ford

38 Gerald R. Ford (b. 1913)

Years in office:
1974–1977
Party:
Republican
Appointed from:
Michigan
Vice President:
Nelson
    Rockefeller

39 Jimmy Carter (b. 1924)

Years in office:
1977–1981
Party:
Democratic
Elected from:
Georgia
Vice President:
Walter Mondale

40 Ronald W. Reagan (b. 1911)

Years in office:
1981–1989
Party:
Republican
Elected from:
California
Vice President:
George H.W.
    Bush

41 George H.W. Bush (b. 1924)

Years in office:
1989–1993
Party:
Republican
Elected from:
Texas
Vice President:
J. Danforth
    Quayle

42 William J. Clinton (b. 1946)

Years in office:
1993–2001
Party:
Democratic
Elected from:
Arkansas
Vice President:
Albert Gore, Jr.

43 George W. Bush (b. 1946)

Years in office:
2001–
Party:
Republican
Elected from:
Texas
Vice President:
Richard Cheney

***Resigned

Presidents of the United States ★ **613**

The American Flag

The Flag That Inspired Our National Anthem

During the War of 1812, Mary Young Pickersgill was hired to make a new flag for Fort McHenry in Baltimore harbor. She was told to make a huge flag. Pickersgill and her 13-year-old daughter, Caroline, spent several weeks in the hot summer of 1813 sewing and stitching. When it came time to assemble the flag, Pickersgill realized that she did not have enough space in her workshop. She arranged to finish the sewing in a nearby brewery. Every evening after the brewery had closed for the day, Pickersgill and her daughter worked by candlelight on the flag.

When Pickersgill's flag was hung at Fort McHenry, it could be seen far and wide. In fact, Francis Scott Key could see the flag from eight miles away during the bombardment of the fort by British warships. Its "broad stripes and bright stars" inspired him to write the poem, "The Star-Spangled Banner." Key later suggested that the poem be sung to a popular British tune. A Baltimore music store owner published the poem together with the music, and by 1861, "The Star-Spangled Banner" could be heard at most patriotic events. It was not until 1931, however, that Congress passed a law making "The Star-Spangled Banner" the national anthem of the United States.

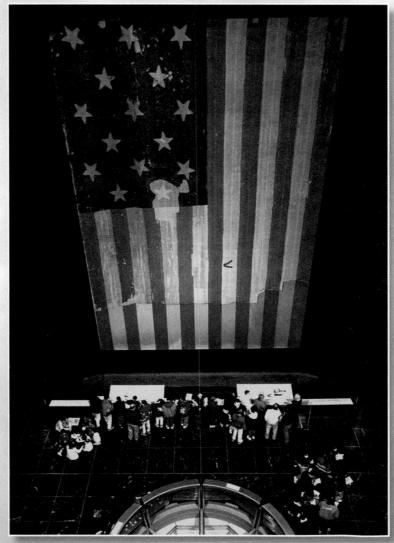

"By the dawn's early light," it flew over Fort McHenry. Today, the Star-Spangled Banner hangs at the Smithsonian Institution in Washington, D.C.

Ten Rules for Respecting the American Flag

The American flag should be treated with respect and great care at all times. Following the rules in the Flag Code honors our citizens and our traditions.

1. The flag should be treated courteously, as if it were a person.

2. The flag of the United States of America should be at the center and at the highest point of the group when a number of flags of states or localities are displayed.

3. The flag is usually displayed in the open from sunrise to sunset.

4. The flag should never be displayed upside down except as a signal of distress when there is extreme danger to life or property.

5. When a flag is displayed at half-staff, the flag should first be hoisted briskly to the peak of the staff and then lowered slowly.

6. The flag should never be used as wearing apparel, bedding, or drapery.

7. The flag should never be displayed, used, or stored in such a way that would permit it to be easily torn, soiled, or damaged.

8. The flag should never be used as a covering for a ceiling.

9. The flag should never be used for advertising purposes. It should not be embroidered on such articles as cushions or handkerchiefs.

10. When a flag is no longer in good enough condition to be displayed, it should be destroyed in a dignified way, preferably by burning.

—Adapted from the Federal Flag Code

The Pledge of Allegiance

The Pledge of Allegiance should be said standing at attention, facing the flag, with the right hand over the heart. I pledge allegiance to the Flag of the United States of America, and to the Republic for which it stands, one nation under God, indivisible, with liberty and justice for all.

The High School Student Who Changed Our Flag

Our present 50-star flag was designed by a 17-year-old high school student. In 1958, Robert Heft was a shy high school junior in Lancaster, Ohio. At the time, the United States had 48 states. However, talk of Alaska and Hawaii becoming states led him to design a 50-star flag as a school project. He arranged the 50 stars in alternating rows of six stars and five stars. His teacher was not impressed. He gave Robert a B-minus grade for the project but said he would improve the grade if Heft could get Congress to accept the design. Heft took on the challenge. He sent the flag to his representative in Congress. In 1960, President Dwight D. Eisenhower phoned Heft to tell him that his design had been selected to be the nation's new flag. And Heft's grade? True to his promise, the teacher changed the grade to an A!

The Fifty States

State	Date of Entry to Union (Order of Entry)	Land Area in Square Miles	Population (In Thousands)	Number of Representatives in House*	Capital	Largest City
Alabama	1819 (22)	50,750	4,447	7	Montgomery	Birmingham
Alaska	1959 (49)	570,374	627	1	Juneau	Anchorage
Arizona	1912 (48)	113,642	5,131	8	Phoenix	Phoenix
Arkansas	1836 (25)	52,075	2,673	4	Little Rock	Little Rock
California	1850 (31)	155,973	33,872	53	Sacramento	Los Angeles
Colorado	1876 (38)	103,730	4,301	7	Denver	Denver
Connecticut	1788 (5)	4,845	3,406	5	Hartford	Bridgeport
Delaware	1787 (1)	1,955	784	1	Dover	Wilmington
Florida	1845 (27)	53,997	15,982	25	Tallahassee	Jacksonville
Georgia	1788 (4)	57,919	8,186	13	Atlanta	Atlanta
Hawaii	1959 (50)	6,423	1,212	2	Honolulu	Honolulu
Idaho	1890 (43)	82,751	1,294	2	Boise	Boise
Illinois	1818 (21)	55,593	12,419	19	Springfield	Chicago
Indiana	1816 (19)	35,870	6,080	9	Indianapolis	Indianapolis
Iowa	1846 (29)	55,875	2,926	5	Des Moines	Des Moines
Kansas	1861 (34)	81,823	2,688	4	Topeka	Wichita
Kentucky	1792 (15)	39,732	4,042	6	Frankfort	Louisville
Louisiana	1812 (18)	43,566	4,469	7	Baton Rouge	New Orleans
Maine	1820 (23)	30,865	1,275	2	Augusta	Portland
Maryland	1788 (7)	9,775	5,296	8	Annapolis	Baltimore
Massachusetts	1788 (6)	7,838	6,349	10	Boston	Boston
Michigan	1837 (26)	56,809	9,938	15	Lansing	Detroit
Minnesota	1858 (32)	79,617	4,919	8	St. Paul	Minneapolis
Mississippi	1817 (20)	46,914	2,845	4	Jackson	Jackson
Missouri	1821 (24)	68,898	5,595	9	Jefferson City	Kansas City
Montana	1889 (41)	145,556	902	1	Helena	Billings
Nebraska	1867 (37)	76,878	1,711	3	Lincoln	Omaha
Nevada	1864 (36)	109,806	1,998	3	Carson City	Las Vegas
New Hampshire	1788 (9)	8,969	1,236	2	Concord	Manchester
New Jersey	1787 (3)	7,419	8,414	13	Trenton	Newark
New Mexico	1912 (47)	121,365	1,819	3	Santa Fe	Albuquerque
New York	1788 (11)	47,224	18,976	29	Albany	New York
North Carolina	1789 (12)	48,718	8,049	13	Raleigh	Charlotte
North Dakota	1889 (39)	68,994	642	1	Bismarck	Fargo
Ohio	1803 (17)	40,953	11,353	18	Columbus	Columbus
Oklahoma	1907 (46)	68,679	3,451	5	Oklahoma City	Oklahoma City
Oregon	1859 (33)	96,003	3,421	5	Salem	Portland
Pennsylvania	1787 (2)	44,820	12,281	19	Harrisburg	Philadelphia
Rhode Island	1790 (13)	1,045	1,048	2	Providence	Providence
South Carolina	1788 (8)	30,111	4,012	6	Columbia	Columbia
South Dakota	1889 (40)	75,898	755	1	Pierre	Sioux Falls
Tennessee	1796 (16)	41,220	5,689	9	Nashville	Memphis
Texas	1845 (28)	261,914	20,852	32	Austin	Houston
Utah	1896 (45)	82,168	2,233	3	Salt Lake City	Salt Lake City
Vermont	1791 (14)	9,249	609	1	Montpelier	Burlington
Virginia	1788 (10)	39,598	7,079	11	Richmond	Virginia Beach
Washington	1889 (42)	66,582	5,894	9	Olympia	Seattle
West Virginia	1863 (35)	24,087	1,808	3	Charleston	Charleston
Wisconsin	1848 (30)	54,314	5,364	8	Madison	Milwaukee
Wyoming	1890 (44)	97,105	494	1	Cheyenne	Cheyenne
District of Columbia		61	572	1 (nonvoting)		

Self-Governing Areas, Possessions, and Dependencies	Land Area in Square Miles	Population (In Thousands)	Capital
Puerto Rico	3,515	809	San Juan
Guam	209	155	Agana
U.S. Virgin Islands	132	121	Charlotte Amalie
American Samoa	77	65	Pago Pago

Sources: Department of Commerce, Bureau of the Census   *As of 108th Congress.

State Flags

 Alabama
 Alaska
 Arizona
 Arkansas

 Colorado
 Connecticut
 Delaware
 Florida
 Georgia

 Hawaii
 Idaho
 Illinois
 Indiana
 Iowa

 Kansas
 Kentucky
 Louisiana
 Maine
 Maryland

 Massachusetts
 Michigan
 Minnesota
 Mississippi
 Missouri

 Montana
 Nebraska
 Nevada
 New Hampshire
 New Jersey

 New Mexico
 New York
 North Carolina
 North Dakota
 Ohio

 Oklahoma
 Oregon
 Pennsylvania
 Rhode Island

 South Dakota
 Tennessee
 Texas
 Utah

 Virginia
 Washington
 West Virginia
 Wisconsin
 Wyoming

The Fifty States

Geographic Atlas

80°N   160°W   140°W   120°W   100°W   80°W   60°W

ARCTIC OCEAN

Greenland
(Den.)

Yukon R.

Alaska (U.S.)

60°N

Mackenzie R.

CANADA

**NORTH
AMERICA**

Ottawa   Montréal

40°N

Chicago   New York

San Francisco   Washington, DC

UNITED STATES

Los Angeles   Bermuda (U.K.)

Midway Is. (U.S.)   Houston

New
Orleans

ATLANTIC OCEAN

20°N

**Hawaii
(U.S.)**

MEXICO

Mexico City

See inset map

Caracas   **GUYANA**

VENEZUELA

Equator   0°

Bogotá   Georgetown   Paramaribo

COLOMBIA   French
Guiana
(Fr.)

Galápagos Is.
(Ecuador)

Quito

SURINAME

PACIFIC OCEAN

ECUADOR

Negro R.

**SOUTH
AMERICA**

SAMOA   **PERU**

American
Samoa (U.S.)   French Polynesia
(Fr.)   Lima   **BRAZIL**

Amazon R.

TONGA   **BOLIVIA**

Cook Is.
(N.Z.)   La Paz   Brasilia

20°S   Pitcairn I. (U.K.)   Sucre

Rio Francisco R.

PARAGUAY

Asunción   Rio de Janeiro
São Paulo

CHILE

Easter I.
(Chile)

Santiago   Buenos   **URUGUAY**
Aires   Montevideo

40°S

ARGENTINA

Falkland Is.
(U.K.)

S. Georgia
(U.K.)

60°S

ANTARCTICA

Caribbean

**UNITED
STATES**

Azimuthal Projection

0   150   300 Miles

0   150   300 Kilometers

Gulf of Mexico

Miami

Nassau

B
A
H
A
M
A
S

Havana

CUBA

Turks and
Caicos Is. (U.K.)

Br. Virgin Is.
(U.K.)

Cayman
Islands
(U.K.)   **DOMINICAN
REPUBLIC**

MEXICO   Kingston   Port-au-Prince   Puerto
Rico
(U.S.)   **ANTIGUA
AND BARBUDA**

Belmopan   **JAMAICA**   **HAITI**   Santo
Domingo   Guadeloupe (Fr.)

BELIZE   Virgin Islands (U.S.)

ST. KITTS AND NEVIS

GUATEMALA   **DOMINICA**

HONDURAS   *Caribbean Sea*   Martinique (Fr.)

Guatemala   Tegucigalpa   Neth. Antilles (Neth.)   **ST. LUCIA**

San Salvador   **NICARAGUA**   Aruba
(Neth.)   **ST. VINCENT AND
THE GRENADINES**   **BARBADOS**

EL SALVADOR   Managua   **GRENADA**

*ATLANTIC
OCEAN*

**COSTA
RICA**   San José   Caracas   Port of Spain   **TRINIDAD
AND
TOBAGO**

Panamá

PANAMA   **VENEZUELA**

COLOMBIA   **GUYANA**

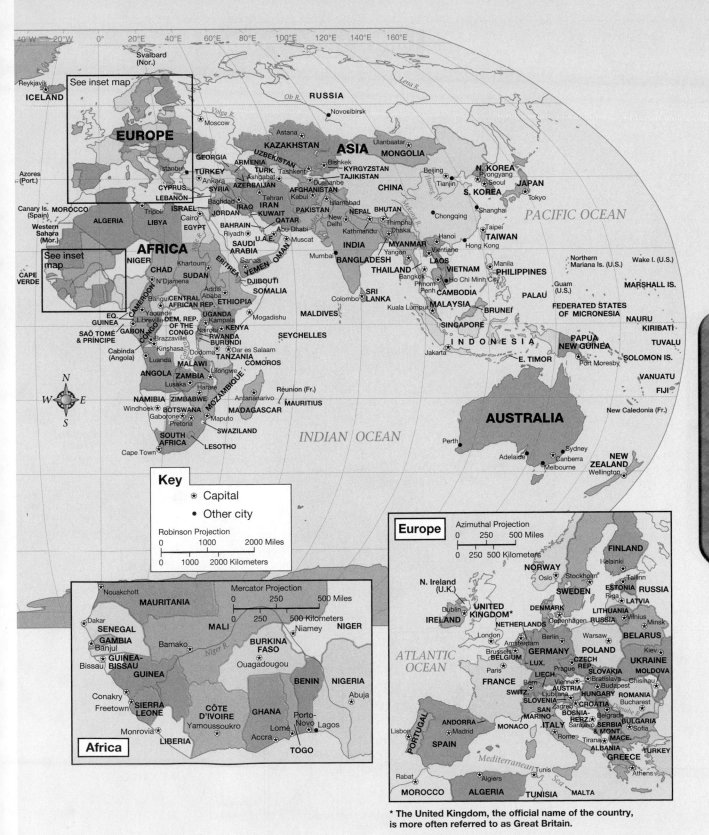

Key

⊛ Capital
• Other city

Robinson Projection

0   1000   2000 Miles

0   1000   2000 Kilometers

Europe

Azimuthal Projection

0   250   500 Miles

0   250 500 Kilometers

Mercator Projection

0   250   500 Miles

0   250   500 Kilometers

Africa

* The United Kingdom, the official name of the country,
is more often referred to as Great Britain.

Geographic Atlas

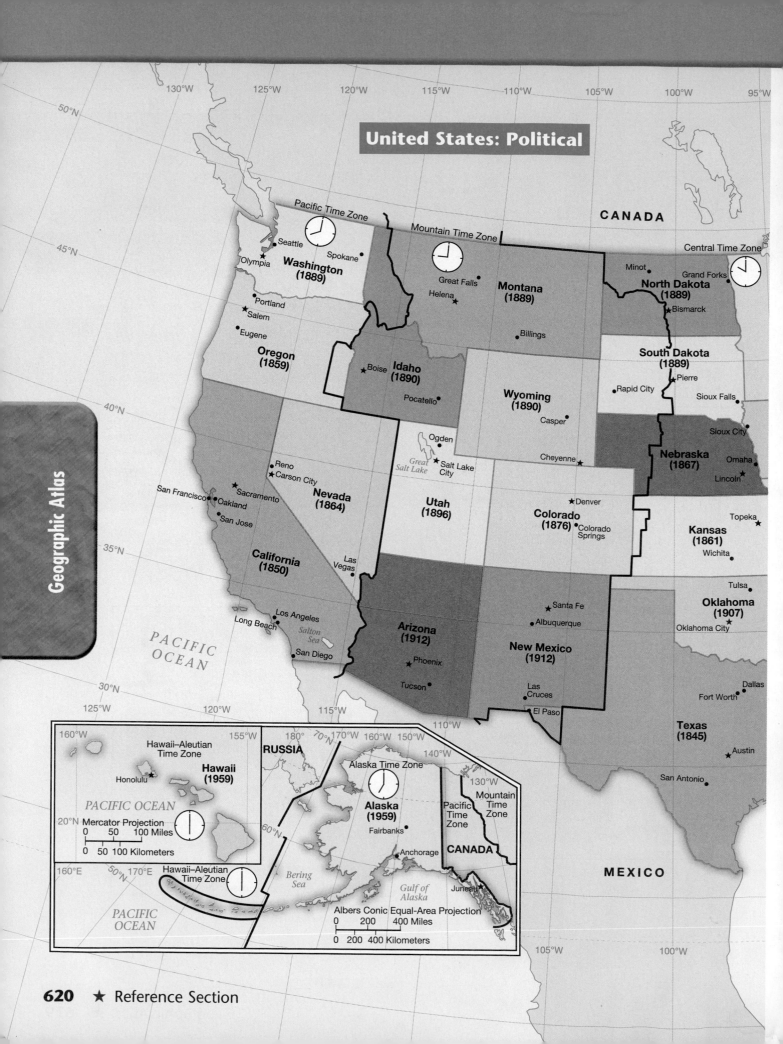

United States: Political

CANADA

Pacific Time Zone

Mountain Time Zone

Central Time Zone

Washington (1889)
- Seattle
- Spokane
- Olympia

Oregon (1859)
- Portland
- Salem
- Eugene

Montana (1889)
- Great Falls
- Helena
- Billings

Idaho (1890)
- Boise
- Pocatello

Wyoming (1890)
- Casper
- Cheyenne

North Dakota (1889)
- Minot
- Grand Forks
- Bismarck

South Dakota (1889)
- Pierre
- Rapid City
- Sioux Falls

Nebraska (1867)
- Sioux City
- Omaha
- Lincoln

Nevada (1864)
- Reno
- Carson City

Utah (1896)
- Ogden
- Salt Lake City
- Great Salt Lake

California (1850)
- San Francisco
- Oakland
- Sacramento
- San Jose
- Las Vegas
- Los Angeles
- Long Beach
- Salton Sea
- San Diego

Colorado (1876)
- Denver
- Colorado Springs

Kansas (1861)
- Topeka
- Wichita

Oklahoma (1907)
- Tulsa
- Oklahoma City

Arizona (1912)
- Phoenix
- Tucson

New Mexico (1912)
- Santa Fe
- Albuquerque
- Las Cruces
- El Paso

Texas (1845)
- Dallas
- Fort Worth
- Austin
- San Antonio

PACIFIC OCEAN

MEXICO

Hawaii–Aleutian Time Zone

Hawaii (1959)
- Honolulu

PACIFIC OCEAN

Mercator Projection
0   50   100 Miles
0   50 100 Kilometers

Hawaii–Aleutian Time Zone

PACIFIC OCEAN

RUSSIA

Alaska Time Zone

Alaska (1959)
- Fairbanks
- Anchorage
- Juneau

Pacific Time Zone

Mountain Time Zone

CANADA

Bering Sea

Gulf of Alaska

Albers Conic Equal-Area Projection
0   200   400 Miles
0   200 400 Kilometers

Geographic Atlas

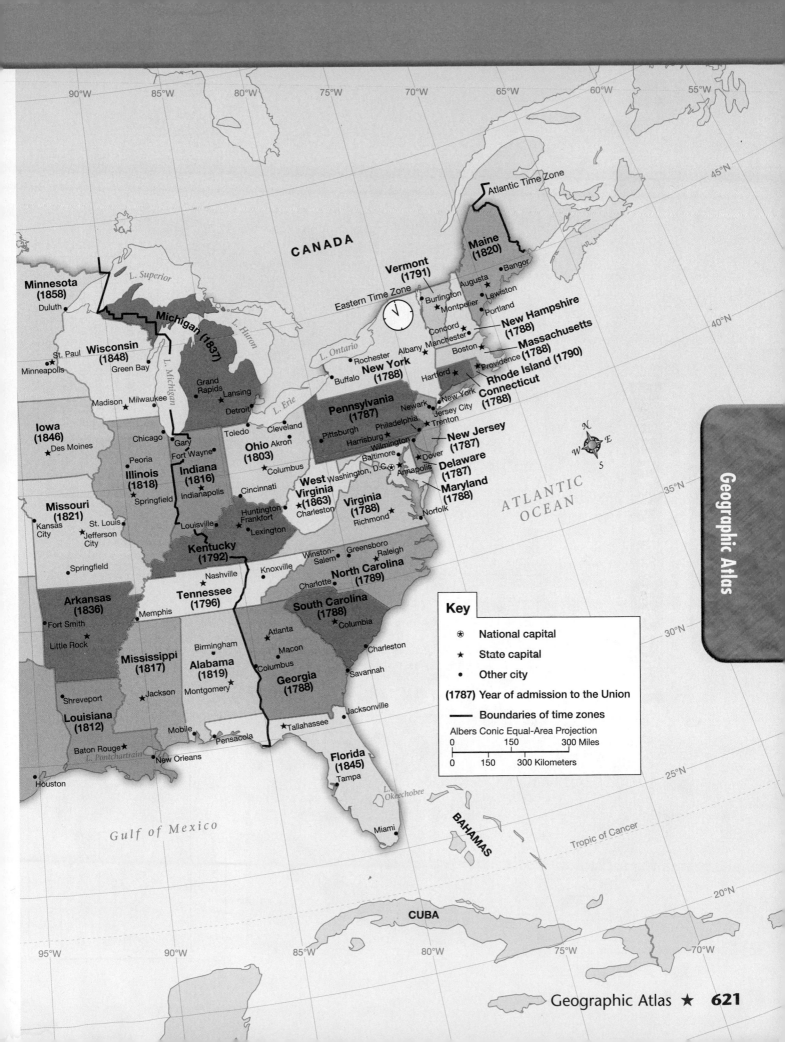

Atlantic Time Zone

**Maine
(1820)**
• Bangor

**Vermont
(1791)**
Augusta
Burlington • Lewiston
Montpelier • Portland

Eastern Time Zone

CANADA

L. Superior

**Minnesota
(1858)**
Duluth

Michigan (1837)

**Wisconsin
(1848)**
St. Paul
Minneapolis
Green Bay

L. Huron
L. Michigan

Grand
Rapids • Lansing
Madison • Milwaukee
Detroit

Concord
Manchester
Albany • Boston

**New Hampshire
(1788)**
**Massachusetts
(1788)**
Providence
Hartford • **Rhode Island (1790)**
**Connecticut
(1788)**

**New York
(1788)**
Rochester
Buffalo

L. Ontario

L. Erie

**Iowa
(1846)**
Chicago
Des Moines

Gary
Fort Wayne

Peoria

**Illinois
(1818)**
Springfield

**Indiana
(1816)**
Indianapolis

Toledo
Cleveland

Ohio Akron
(1803)
Columbus

Cincinnati

**Pennsylvania
(1787)**
Pittsburgh
Harrisburg
Philadelphia

Newark
Jersey City
Trenton

New York

**New Jersey
(1787)**

**Missouri
(1821)**
Kansas
City
St. Louis
Jefferson
City

Springfield

Louisville

Wilmington
Baltimore
Washington, D.C.
Annapolis

Dover
**Delaware
(1787)**
**Maryland
(1788)**

**West
Virginia
(1863)**
Charleston

Huntington
Frankfort
Lexington

**Virginia
(1788)**
Richmond

Norfolk

**Kentucky
(1792)**

Nashville

Knoxville

Winston-
Salem
Charlotte

Greensboro
Raleigh

**North Carolina
(1789)**

**Arkansas
(1836)**
Fort Smith

Little Rock

Memphis

**Tennessee
(1796)**

**ATLANTIC
OCEAN**

**Missouri
(1821)**

**Mississippi
(1817)**

Birmingham

**Alabama
(1819)**
Montgomery

Jackson

Atlanta
Macon

Columbus

**South Carolina
(1788)**
Columbia

Charleston

Savannah

**Georgia
(1788)**

Shreveport

**Louisiana
(1812)**

Mobile
Pensacola

Jacksonville

Baton Rouge
L. Pontchartrain
New Orleans

Houston

Tallahassee

**Florida
(1845)**
Tampa

L.
Okeechobee

Gulf of Mexico

BAHAMAS

Miami

Tropic of Cancer

CUBA

Key

⊛ National capital

★ State capital

• Other city

(1787) Year of admission to the Union

——— Boundaries of time zones

Albers Conic Equal-Area Projection

0	150	300 Miles
0	150	300 Kilometers

Geographic Atlas

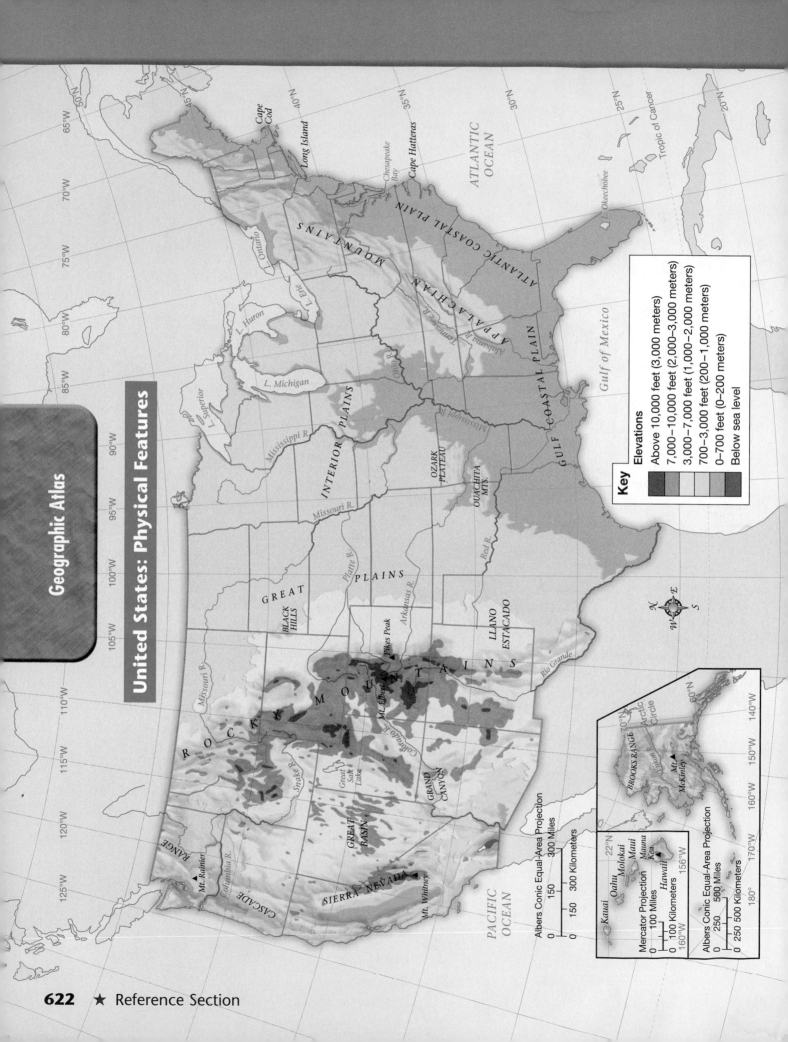

Geographic Atlas

United States: Physical Features

Cape Cod
Long Island
Chesapeake Bay
Cape Hatteras
ATLANTIC OCEAN
Tropic of Cancer
L. Okeechobee

APPALACHIAN MOUNTAINS
ATLANTIC COASTAL PLAIN
Gulf of Mexico
GULF COASTAL PLAIN

L. Ontario
L. Erie
L. Huron
L. Michigan
L. Superior
Tennessee R.
Ohio R.
Alabama R.
Mississippi R.

INTERIOR PLAINS
Mississippi R.
Missouri R.
OZARK PLATEAU
OUACHITA MTS.
Red R.

GREAT PLAINS
BLACK HILLS
Platte R.
Arkansas R.
LLANO ESTACADO
Pikes Peak
Mt. Elbert
Colorado R.
Rio Grande

Missouri R.
ROCKY MOUNTAINS
Snake R.
Columbia R.
Great Salt Lake
GREAT BASIN
GRAND CANYON

CASCADE RANGE
Mt. Rainier
SIERRA NEVADA
Mt. Whitney
PACIFIC OCEAN

Key

Elevations

- Above 10,000 feet (3,000 meters)
- 7,000–10,000 feet (2,000–3,000 meters)
- 3,000–7,000 feet (1,000–2,000 meters)
- 700–3,000 feet (200–1,000 meters)
- 0–700 feet (0–200 meters)
- Below sea level

N
W   E
S

Albers Conic Equal-Area Projection
0   150   300 Miles
0   150   300 Kilometers

BROOKS RANGE
Arctic Circle
Yukon R.
Mt. McKinley
Albers Conic Equal-Area Projection
0   250   500 Miles
0   250   500 Kilometers

Kauai
Oahu
Molokai
Maui
Mauna Kea
Hawaii
Mercator Projection
0   100 Miles
0   100 Kilometers

United States: Natural Resources

Key

Bauxite	Coal	Cobalt	Copper

Gold	Iron ore	Lead	Manganese

Mercury	Molybdenum	Natural Gas	Oil

Silver	Sulfur	Uranium	Zinc

Geographic Atlas

Albers Equal-Area Projection

0   150   300 Miles

0   150   300 Kilometers

Hawaii
Mercator Projection

0   100 Miles

0   100 Kilometers

Albers Conic Equal-Area Projection

0   250   500 Miles

0   250   500 Kilometers

ATLANTIC OCEAN

Gulf of Mexico

PACIFIC OCEAN

Tropic of Cancer

Geographic Atlas

United States: Land Use

Key

- Manufacturing and trade
- Ranching or grazing
- Crops and livestock
- Forest products
- Little or no commercial activity

Albers Conic Equal-Area Projection

0 150 300 Miles

0 150 300 Kilometers

ATLANTIC OCEAN

Tropic of Cancer

Gulf of Mexico

PACIFIC OCEAN

Alaska

Albers Conic Equal-Area Projection

0 250 500 Miles

0 250 500 Kilometers

Arctic Circle

Anchorage

Yukon R.

Hawaii

Mercator Projection

0 100 Miles

0 100 Kilometers

Honolulu

Maine
VT
NH
MA
CT
RI
Boston
New York
Philadelphia
NJ
DE
MD
Richmond
New York
Pennsylvania
Pittsburgh
Baltimore
Washington, D.C.
Virginia
WV
North Carolina
South Carolina
Georgia
Atlanta
Florida
Miami
Ohio
Indianapolis
Indiana
Kentucky
Tennessee
Memphis
Alabama
MS
Detroit
Michigan
Lake Michigan
Chicago
Illinois
St. Louis
Ohio R.
Mississippi R.
Arkansas
Arkansas R.
Louisiana
New Orleans
Lake Erie
Lake Huron
Lake Superior
Lake Ontario
Wisconsin
Minnesota
Minneapolis
Iowa
Missouri
Kansas City
Kansas
Oklahoma
Red R.
Dallas
Texas
Houston
North Dakota
South Dakota
Missouri R.
Platte R.
Nebraska
Denver
Colorado
New Mexico
Rio Grande
Montana
Wyoming
Idaho
Snake R.
Utah
Salt Lake City
Colorado R.
Arizona
Phoenix
Nevada
Las Vegas
Los Angeles
San Francisco
California
Columbia R.
Oregon
Washington
Seattle
Alabama R.
Tennessee R.

N
E
S
W

United States: Population Density

Key

Per sq. km	Per sq. mile
0–1	0–2
1–10	2–25
10–25	25–65
25–50	65–130
50–100	130–250
Over 100	Over 250

Albers Conic Equal-Area Projection

300 Miles
0   150   300 Kilometers
0   150

Geographic Atlas

ATLANTIC OCEAN

Gulf of Mexico

PACIFIC OCEAN

Alaska

Anchorage

Arctic Circle

Albers Conic Equal-Area Projection
0   250   500 Miles
0   250 500 Kilometers

Hawaii
Honolulu

Mercator Projection
0   100 Miles
0   100 Kilometers

Gazetteer of American History

This gazetteer, or geographic dictionary, lists places that are important in American history. The approximate latitude and longitude are given for cities, towns, and other specific locations. See text page 4 for information about latitude and longitude. In the Gazetteer, after the description of each place, there are usually two numbers in parentheses. The first number refers to the text page where you can find out more about the place. The second appears in slanted, or *italic*, type and refers to a map (*m*) where the place is shown.

See text page 4 for information about latitude and longitude.

A

Africa Second largest continent in the world. (p. 52, *m51*)

Alabama 22nd state. Nicknamed the Heart of Dixie or the Cotton State. (p. 616, *m620–621*)

Alamo (29°N/99°W) Former mission in San Antonio, Texas, where 255 rebels died during the Texas war for independence. (p. 387, *m386*)

Alaska 49th state. Unofficially nicknamed the Last Frontier. Purchased from Russia in 1867. (p. 616, *m620–621*)

Albany (43°N/74°W) Capital of New York. (p. 143, *m142*)

Andes Rugged mountain chain in South America. (p. 39)

Appalachian Mountains Mountain chain that stretches from Georgia to Canada. (p. 13, *m12*)

Appomattox Court House (37°N/79°W) Town in Virginia where Lee surrendered to Grant. (p. 509, *m507*)

Arctic Ocean World's fourth-largest ocean. (p. 11, *m12*)

Argentina Country in South America. (p. 349, *m349*)

Arizona 48th state. Nicknamed the Grand Canyon State. (p. 616, *m620–621*)

Arkansas 25th state. Nicknamed the Land of Opportunity. (p. 616, *m620–621*)

Asia Largest of the world's continents. (p. 50, *m618–619*)

Atlanta (34°N/84°W) Capital and largest city of Georgia. Burned by Sherman during the Civil War. (p. 508, *m470*)

Atlantic Ocean World's second largest ocean. (p. 11, *m618–619*)

Atlantic Plain Low-lying area that stretches along the eastern coast of the United States. (p. 13, *m12*)

B

Baltimore (39°N/77°W) Port city in Maryland. (p. 323, *m323*)

Bering Sea Narrow sea between Asia and North America. Scientists think a land bridge was here during the last ice age. (p. 69, *m37*)

Boston (42°N/71°W) Seaport and industrial city in Massachusetts. (p. 102, *m103*)

Brazil Largest country in South America. (p. 350, *m349*)

Breed's Hill (42°N/71°W) Overlooks Boston harbor. Site of fighting during the Battle of Bunker Hill. (p. 170)

Buena Vista (26°N/101°W) City in Mexico. Site of an American victory in the Mexican War. (p. 396, *m395*)

Buffalo (43°N/79°W) City in New York State on Lake Erie. (p. 341, *m340*)

Bunker Hill (42°N/71°W) Overlooks Boston harbor. Site of first major battle of the Revolution. (p. 170)

C

Cahokia (39°N/90°W) British fort captured by George Rogers Clark during the American Revolution. (p. 189, *m187*)

California 31st state. Nicknamed the Golden State. Ceded to the United States by Mexico in 1848. (p. 616, *m620–621*)

Canada Northern neighbor of the United States. Second largest nation in the world. (p. 145, *m618–619*)

Canadian Shield Lowland region that lies mostly in eastern Canada. (p. 13, *m12*)

Caribbean Sea Tropical sea in the Western Hemisphere. (p. 69, *m76*)

Central America The part of Latin America made up of Guatemala, Honduras, El Salvador, Nicaragua, Costa Rica, Panama, and Belize. (p. 40, *m349*)

Central Plains Large region of the United States located between the Rocky Mountains in the west and the Appalachian Mountains in the east. (p. 13, *m12*)

Chancellorsville (38°N/78°W) Site in Virginia of a Confederate victory in 1863. (p. 493, *m491*)

Charleston (33°N/80°W) City in South Carolina. Site of battles in both the American Revolution and the Civil War. (p. 115, *m115*)

Chesapeake Bay Large inlet of the Atlantic Ocean in Virginia and Maryland. (p. 114, *m115*)

Chicago (42°N/88°W) City in Illinois on Lake Michigan. (p. 410, *m620–621*)

China Country in East Asia. (p. 53, *m618–619*)

Cincinnati (39°N/84°W) City in southern Ohio on the Ohio River. (p. 410, *m620–621*)

Coastal Plains Region consisting of the Atlantic Plain and the Gulf Plain along the Gulf of Mexico. (p. 13, *m12*)

Colorado 38th state. Nicknamed the Centennial State. (p. 616, *m620–621*)

Colorado River River that begins in the Rocky Mountains and flows into Gulf of California. (p. 15, *m12*)

Columbia River Chief river of the Pacific Northwest. (p. 309, *m308*)

Concord (43°N/71°W) Village in Massachusetts where battle occurred between the British and Americans at the start of the American Revolution. (p. 159, *m170*)

Connecticut One of the original 13 states. Nicknamed the Constitution State or the Nutmeg State. (p. 616, *m620–621*)

Cowpens (35°N/82°W) In South Carolina, site of an American victory in the Revolutionary War. (p. 192, *m192*)

Cumberland Gap (37°N/84°W) Pass in the Appalachian Mountains near the borders of Virginia, Kentucky, and Tennessee. (p. 148, *m329*)

Cuzco (14°S/72°W) Capital of the Incan empire. (p. 39, *m35*)

D

Dallas (33°N/97°W) Major city in north central Texas. (p. 7, *m620–621*)

Delaware One of the original 13 states. Nicknamed the First State or the Diamond State. (p. 616, *m620–621*)

Gazetteer

Delaware River Flows into the Atlantic Ocean through Delaware Bay. (p. 85, *m90*)

Detroit (42°N/83°W) Largest city in Michigan. (p. 321, *m323*)

District of Columbia Located on the Potomac River. Seat of the federal government of the United States. (p. 281, *m620–621*)

E

England Part of Great Britain. (p. 81, *m82*)

Equator Line of latitude labeled 0° on maps. Separates the Northern and Southern hemispheres. (p. 4, *m618–619*)

Erie Canal Linked the Hudson and Mohawk rivers with Buffalo and Lake Erie in New York State. Built between 1817 and 1825. (p. 340, *m340*)

Europe World's second smallest continent. (p. 68, *m618–619*)

F

Florida 27th state. Nicknamed the Sunshine State. (p. 616, *m620–621*)

Fort Donelson (37°N/88°W) Located in Tennessee. Captured by Grant in 1862. (p. 494, *m503*)

Fort Henry (37°N/88°W) Located in Tennessee. Captured by Grant in 1862. (p. 494, *m503*)

Fort McHenry (39°N/77°W) Located in Baltimore harbor. British bombardment there in 1814 inspired Francis Scott Key to write "The Star-Spangled Banner." (p. 323)

Fort Necessity (40°N/79°W) British fort during the French and Indian War. (p. 143, *m142*)

Fort Pitt (40°N/80°W) British fort in the 1700s on the site of present-day Pittsburgh. (p. 144, *m187*)

Fort Sumter (33°N/80°W) Guarded Charleston harbor in South Carolina. First shots of the Civil War fired there in 1861. (p. 481, *m503*)

Fort Ticonderoga (44°N/74°W) Fort at the south end of Lake Champlain. Captured from the British by Ethan Allen in 1775. (p. 144, *m142*)

France Country in Western Europe. (p. 83, *m618–619*)

Fredericksburg (38°N/78°W) Located in eastern Virginia. Site of a Confederate victory in 1862. (p. 493, *m491*)

G

Gadsden Purchase Land purchased from Mexico in 1853. Now part of Arizona and New Mexico. (p. 397, *m379*)

Georgia One of the original 13 states. Nicknamed the Peach State or the Empire State of the South. (p. 616, *m620–621*)

Germany Country in central Europe (p. 415, *m618–619*)

Gettysburg (40°N/77°W) Town in southern Pennsylvania. Site of a Union victory in 1863 and Lincoln's Gettysburg Address. (p. 506, *m491*)

Goliad (29°N/97°W) Texas town where Mexicans killed several hundred Texans during the Texas war for independence. (p. 388, *m386*)

Gonzales (29°N/97°W) City in Texas near San Antonio. Site of the first Texan victory over Mexico in 1835. (p. 386, *m386*)

Great Britain Island nation of Western Europe. Includes England, Scotland, Wales, and Northern Ireland. (p. 142, *m618–619*)

Great Colombia Country that existed from 1822 to 1830, made up of present-day Ecuador, Venezuela, Panama, and Colombia. (p. 349, *m349*)

Great Lakes Chain of five lakes in central North America. Lakes Superior, Michigan, Huron, Ontario, and Erie. (p. 15, *m12*)

Great Plains Western part of the Interior Plains. (p. 13, *m12*)

Great Salt Lake (41°N/113°W) Lake in northern Utah with highly saline water. (p. 399, *m400*)

Great Wagon Road Early pioneer route across the Appalachians. (p. 112, *m115*)

Gulf of Mexico Body of water along the southern coast of the United States. (p. 14, *m12*)

Gulf Plain Low-lying area stretching along the coast of the Gulf of Mexico. (p. 13, *m12*)

H

Haiti Country in the West Indies. The nation won independence from France in the early 1800s. (p. 307, *m618–619*)

Harpers Ferry (39°N/78°W) Town in West Virginia. John Brown raided the arsenal there in 1859. (p. 475, *m491*)

Hawaii Newest of the 50 states. Nicknamed the Aloha State. (p. 616, *m620–621*)

Hawaiian Islands Region in the Pacific Ocean composed of a group of eight large islands and many small islands. (p. 14, *m12*)

Houston (29°N/95°W) Inland port and largest city in Texas. (p. 7, *m395*)

Hudson River Largest river in New York State. (p. 82, *m90*)

I

Idaho 43rd state. Nicknamed the Gem State. Acquired as part of the Oregon Territory. (p. 616, *m620–621*)

Illinois 21st state. Nicknamed the Inland Empire. Settled as part of the Northwest Territory. (p. 616, *m620–621*)

Indiana 19th state. Nicknamed the Hoosier State. Settled as part of the Northwest Territory. (p. 616, *m620–621*)

Interior Plains Region of the central United States that stretches from the Rockies to the Appalachians. (p. 13, *m12*)

Intermountain Region Rugged region from the Rocky Mountains to the Sierra Nevada and coastal mountains of the western United States. (p. 12, *m12*)

Iowa 29th state. Nicknamed the Hawkeye State. Acquired as part of the Louisiana Purchase. (p. 616, *m620–621*)

Ireland Country in northern Europe occupying part of an island west of Great Britain. (p. 415, *m618–619*)

Italy Country in southern Europe. (p. 545, *m618–619*)

J

Jamestown (37°N/77°W) First successful English colony in North America. (p. 87, *m90*)

K

Kansas 34th state. Nicknamed the Sunflower State. Acquired as part of the Louisiana Purchase. (p. 616, *m620–621*)

Kaskaskia (38°N/90°W) British fort on the Mississippi River captured by George Rogers Clark during the American Revolution. (p. 189, *m187*)

Kentucky 15th state. Nicknamed the Bluegrass State. (p. 616, *m620–621*)

Kilwa (8°S/39°E) East African trading state in the 1400s. (p. 52, *m51*)

Kings Mountain (35°N/81°W) In South Carolina, site of an American victory in the Revolutionary War. (p. 191, *m192*)

L

Lancaster Turnpike Road built in the 1790s linking Philadelphia and Lancaster, Pennsylvania. (p. 339, *m329*)

Latin America Name for those parts of the Western Hemisphere where Latin languages such as Spanish, French, and Portuguese are spoken. Includes Mexico, Central America, South America, and the islands of the Caribbean. (p. 348, *m349*)

Lexington (42°N/71°W) Village in Massachusetts. Site of the first clash between minutemen and British troops in 1775. (p. 160, *m170*)

Gazetteer

Liberia Country in West Africa. Set up in 1822 as a colony for free African Americans. (p. 440, *m618–619*)

London (51°N/0°) Capital of United Kingdom. (*m618–619*)

Long Island Located in New York. Site of a British victory in the Revolution. (p. 181, *m182*)

Los Angeles (34°N/118°W) City in southern California. First settled by Spanish missionaries. (p. 7, *m76*)

Louisbourg (46°N/60°W) Fort in eastern Canada that played a major role in the French and Indian War. (p. 144, *m142*)

Louisiana 18th state. Nicknamed the Pelican State. First state created out of the Louisiana Purchase. (p. 616, *m620–621*)

Lowell (43°N/83°W) City in Massachusetts. Important site of Industrial Revolution. (p. 333)

M

Maine 23rd state. Nicknamed the Pine Tree State. Originally part of Massachusetts. (p. 616, *m620–621*)

Mali Kingdom in West Africa. Reached its peak between 1200 and 1400. (p. 52)

Maryland One of the original 13 states. Nicknamed the Old Line State or the Free State. (p. 616, *m620–621*)

Mason-Dixon Line Boundary between Pennsylvania and Maryland surveyed and marked in the 1760s. (p. 113)

Massachusetts One of the original 13 states. Nicknamed the Bay State or the Old Colony. (p. 616, *m620–621*)

Memphis (35°N/90°W) City in Tennessee on the Mississippi River. Captured by Union forces in 1862. (p. 494, *m503*)

Mexican Cession Lands acquired by the United States from Mexico under the Treaty of Guadalupe Hidalgo in 1848. (p. 396, *m379*)

Mexico Southern neighbor of the United States. Gained independence from Spain in 1821. (p. 348, *m618–619*)

Mexico City (19°N/99°W) Capital of Mexico. (p. 396, *m77*)

Michigan 26th state. Nicknamed the Great Lake State or the Wolverine State. Settled as part of the Northwest Territory. (p. 616, *m620–621*)

Minnesota 32nd state. Nicknamed the Gopher State. Most of it was acquired as part of the Louisiana Purchase from France. (p. 616, *m620–621*)

Mississippi 20th state. Nicknamed the Magnolia State. (p. 616, *m620–621*)

Mississippi River Longest river in the United States. Links the Great Lakes with the Gulf of Mexico. (p. 14, *m12*)

Missouri 24th state. Nicknamed the Show Me State. Acquired as part of the Louisiana Purchase. (p. 616, *m620–621*)

Missouri River Second longest river in the United States. Rises in the northern Rocky Mountains and joins the Mississippi River near St. Louis, Missouri (p. 14, *m12*)

Montana 41st state. Nicknamed the Treasure State. Acquired in part through the Louisiana Purchase. (p. 616, *m620–621*)

Montreal (46°N/74°W) Major city in Canada. Located in the province of Quebec. (p. 319, *m323*)

N

National Road Early road to the West that began in Cumberland, Maryland, and eventually reached Illinois. (p. 339, *m329*)

Nauvoo (41°N/91°W) Town founded by the Mormons in Illinois in the 1840s. (p. 398, *m400*)

Nebraska 37th state. Nicknamed the Cornhusker State. Acquired as part of the Louisiana Purchase. (p. 616, *m620–621*)

Nevada 36th state. Nicknamed the Sagebrush State or the Battle Born State. Acquired at the end of the Mexican War. (p. 616, *m620–621*)

New Amsterdam (41°N/74°W) Town established by Dutch settlers on Manhattan Island in the early 1600s. Renamed New York by the British. (p. 85)

New England Region of northeastern United States, including the states of Maine, New Hampshire, Vermont, Massachusetts, Rhode Island, and Connecticut. (p. 93, *m101*)

New France Colony established by France in North America. (p. 83, *m82*)

New Hampshire One of the original 13 states. Nicknamed the Granite State. (p. 616, *m620–621*)

New Jersey One of the original 13 states. Nicknamed the Garden State. (p. 616, *m620–621*)

New Mexico 47th state. Nicknamed the Land of Enchantment. Acquired at the end of the Mexican War. (p. 616, *m620–621*)

New Netherland Dutch colony on the Hudson River. Seized by the English and renamed New York in 1664. (p. 85)

New Orleans (30°N/90°W) Port city in Louisiana near the mouth of the Mississippi River. Settled by the French in the 1600s. (p. 84, *m76*)

New Spain Area in the Americas ruled by Spain for some 300 years. Included much of present-day western United States. (p. 77, *m77*)

New York One of the original 13 states. Nicknamed the Empire State.

(p. 616, *m620–621*)

New York City (41°N/74°W) Port city at the mouth of the Hudson River. (p. 109, *m111*)

Norfolk (37°N/76°W) City and port in southeastern Virginia. (p. 492, *m620–621*)

North America World's third largest continent. (p. 11, *m618–619*)

North Carolina One of the original 13 states. Nicknamed the Tar Heel State or the Old North State. (p. 616, *m620–621*)

North Dakota 39th state. Nicknamed the Sioux State or the Flickertail State. Acquired as part of the Louisiana Purchase. (p. 616, *m620–621*)

Northwest Territory Name for lands north of the Ohio River. Acquired by the Treaty of Paris in 1783. (p. 203, *m203*)

Nueces River Claimed by Mexico in the Mexican War as the southern border of Texas. (p. 395, *m395*)

O

Ohio 17th state. Nicknamed the Buckeye State. Settled as part of the Northwest Territory. (p. 616, *m620–621*)

Ohio River Important transportation route. Begins at Pittsburgh and flows to the Mississippi River. (p. 141, *m142*)

Oklahoma 46th State. Nicknamed the Sooner State. Acquired as part of the Louisiana Purchase. (p. 616, *m620–621*)

Oregon 33rd state. Nicknamed the Beaver State. Acquired as part of the Oregon Territory. (p. 616, *m620–621*)

Oregon Trail Overland route from Independence, Missouri, to the Columbia River valley. (p. 383, *m400*)

P

Pacific Coast Highest and most rugged region of the United States. Includes the Cascades and the Sierra Nevada. (p. 12, *m12*)

Pacific Ocean World's largest ocean. (p. 11, *m618–619*)

Panama Country on the isthmus separating North and South America. Gained independence from Colombia in 1903. (p. 550, *m618–619*)

Panama Canal Canal dug through the Isthmus of Panama to link the Atlantic and Pacific oceans. (p. 550)

Paris (49°N/2°E) Capital of France. (p. 183, *m618–619*)

Pennsylvania One of the original 13 states. Nicknamed the Keystone State. (p. 616, *m620–621*)

Petersburg (37°N/78°W) City in Virginia. Union forces kept the city under siege for nine months during the Civil War. (p. 509, *m507*)

Philadelphia (40°N/75°W) Major port and chief city in Pennsylvania. (p. 110, *m111*)

Philippine Islands Group of islands in the Pacific Ocean. Acquired by the United States in 1898. Gained independence in 1946. (p. 550, *m618–619*)

Pikes Peak (39°N/105°W) Mountain located in the Rocky Mountains of central Colorado. (p. 310, *m308*)

Plymouth (42°N/71°W) New England colony founded in 1620 by Pilgrims. (p. 94, *m90*)

Portugal Country in Western Europe. (p. 60, *m59*)

Potomac River Forms part of the Maryland-Virginia border. Flows through Washington, D.C., and into Chesapeake Bay. (p. 492, *m491*)

Prime Meridian Line of longitude labeled 0° on maps. (p. 5)

Princeton (40°N/75°W) City in New Jersey. Site of an American victory during the Revolution. (p. 182, *m182*)

Puerto Rico (18°N/67°W) Island in the Caribbean Sea. A self-governing commonwealth of the United States. (p. 550, *m618–619*)

Q

Quebec (47°N/71°W) City in eastern Canada. (p. 83, *m82*)

R

Rhode Island One of the original 13 states. Nicknamed Little Rhody or the Ocean State. (p. 616, *m620–621*)

Richmond (38°N/78°W) Capital of Virginia. Capital of the Confederate States of America during the Civil War. (p. 490, *m491*)

Rio Grande River that forms the border between the United States and Mexico. (p. 15, *m12*)

Roanoke Island (36°N/76°W) Island off North Carolina. Site of English "lost colony" founded in 1587. (p. 87, *m90*)

Rocky Mountains Mountains extending through the western United States and Canada. (p. 13, *m12*)

Russia Largest country in the world, spanning Europe and Asia. (p. 545, *m618–619*)

S

Sacramento (39°N/122°W) Capital of California. Developed as a gold rush boomtown. (p. 400, *m400*)

St. Augustine (30°N/81°W) City in Florida. Founded by Spain in 1565. Oldest European settlement in the United States. (p. 77, *m77*)

St. Lawrence River Waterway from the Great Lakes to the Atlantic Ocean. Forms part of the border between the United States and Canada. (p. 15, *m82*)

St. Louis (38°N/90°W) City in Missouri on the Mississippi River. Lewis and Clark began their expedition there. (p. 309, *m308*)

Salt Lake City (41°N/112°W) Largest city in Utah. Founded in 1847 by Mormons. (p. 399, *m400*)

San Antonio (29°N/99°W) City in southern Texas. Site of the Alamo. (p. 386, *m386*)

San Diego (33°N/117°W) City in southern California. Founded as the first Spanish mission in California. (p. 392, *m400*)

San Francisco (38°N/122°W) City in northern California. Boomtown of the California gold rush. (p. 393, *m400*)

Santa Fe (35°N/106°W) Capital of New Mexico. First settled by the Spanish. (p. 77, *m76*)

Santa Fe Trail Overland trail from Independence to Santa Fe. Opened in 1821. (p. 392, *m400*)

Saratoga (43°N/75°W) City in eastern New York. The American victory there in 1777 was a turning point in the Revolution. (p. 183, *m182*)

Savannah (32°N/81°W) Oldest city in Georgia, founded in 1733. (p. 116, *m115*)

Sierra Nevada Mountain range mostly in California. (p. 12, *m12*)

Songhai West African kingdom in the 1400s. (p. 53, *m35*)

South America World's fourth largest continent. (p. 11, *m67*)

South Carolina One of the original 13 states. Nicknamed the Palmetto State. (p. 616, *m620–621*)

South Dakota 40th state. Nicknamed the Coyote State or the Sunshine State. Acquired as part of the Louisiana Purchase. (p. 616, *m620–621*)

Spain Country in southwestern Europe. (p. 60, *m82*)

Spanish Florida Part of New Spain. Purchased by the United States in 1821. (p. 350, *m363*)

T

Tennessee 16th state. Nicknamed the Volunteer State. Gained statehood after North Carolina ceded its western lands to the United States. (p. 616, *m620–621*)

Tenochtitlán (19°N/99°W) Capital of the Aztec empire. Now part of Mexico City. (p. 38, *m35*)

Texas 28th state. Nicknamed the Lone Star State. Proclaimed independence from Mexico in 1836. Was a separate republic until 1845. (p. 616, *m620–621*)

Timbuktu (17°N/3°W) City on the Niger River in Africa. (p. 53, *m51*)

Trenton (41°N/74°W) Capital of New Jersey. Site of an American victory in the Revolution. (p. 182, *m182*)

U

United Kingdom See Great Britain. (*m618–619*)

Utah 45th state. Nicknamed the Beehive State. Settled by Mormons. (p. 616, *m620–621*)

V

Valley Forge (40°N/76°W) Winter headquarters for the Continental Army in 1777–1778. Located near Philadelphia. (p. 185, *m182*)

Veracruz (19°N/96°W) Port city in Mexico on the Gulf of Mexico. (p. 396, *m395*)

Vermont 14th state. Nicknamed the Green Mountain State. (p. 616, *m620–621*)

Vicksburg (42°N/86°W) City in Mississippi. Site of a Union victory in 1863. (p. 505, *m503*)

Vietnam Country in Southeast Asia. Site of a war involving the United States during the Cold War. (p. 562, *m618–619*)

Vincennes (39°N/88°W) City in Indiana. British fort there was captured by George Rogers Clark in 1779. (p. 189, *m187*)

Virginia One of the original 13 states. Nicknamed the Old Dominion. (p. 616, *m620–621*)

W

Washington 42nd state. Nicknamed the Evergreen State. Acquired as part of Oregon Territory. (p. 616, *m620–621*)

Washington, D.C. (39°N/77°W) Capital of the United States since 1800. (p. 281, *m323*)

West Indies Islands in the Caribbean Sea. Explored by Columbus. (p. 69, *m77*)

West Virginia 35th state. Nicknamed the Mountain State. Separated from Virginia early in the Civil War. (p. 616, *m620–621*)

Wisconsin 30th state. Nicknamed the Badger State. Settled as part of the Northwest Territory. (p. 616, *m620–621*)

Wyoming 44th state. Nicknamed the Equality State. (p. 616, *m620–621*)

Y

Yorktown (37°N/76°W) Town in Virginia. Site of the British surrender in 1781. (p. 193, *m192*)

Gazetteer

Glossary

This glossary defines all vocabulary words and many important historical terms and phrases. These words and terms appear in blue type the first time that they are used in the text. The page number(s) after each definition refers to the page(s) on which the word or phrase is defined in the text. For other references, see the index.

Pronunciation Key

When difficult names or terms first appear in the text, they are respelled to help you with pronunciation. A syllable printed in small capital letters receives the greatest stress. The pronunciation key below lists the letters and symbols that will help you pronounce the word. It also includes examples of words using each of the sounds and shows how each word would be pronounced.

Symbol	Example	Respelling
a	hat	(hat)
ay	pay, late	(pay), (layt)
ah	star, hot	(stahr), (haht)
ai	air, dare	(air), (dair)
aw	law, all	(law), (awl)
eh	met	(meht)
ee	bee, eat	(bee), (eet)
er	learn, sir, fur	(lern), (ser), (fer)
ih	fit	(fiht)
i	mile	(mīl)
ir	ear	(ir)
oh	no	(noh)
oi	soil, boy	(soil), (boi)
oo	root, rule	(root), (rool)
or	born, door	(born), (dor)
ow	plow, out	(plow), (owt)

Symbol	Example	Respelling
u	put, book	(put), (buk)
uh	fun	(fuhn)
yoo	few, use	(fyoo), (yooz)
ch	chill, reach	(chihl), (reech)
g	go, dig	(goh), (dihg)
j	jet, gently bridge	(jeht), (JEHNT lee), (brihj)
k	kite, cup	(kīt), (kuhp)
ks	mix	(mihks)
kw	quick	(kwihk)
ng	bring	(brihng)
s	say, cent	(say), (sehnt)
sh	she, crash	(shee), (krash)
th	three	(three)
y	yet, onion	(yeht), (UHN yuhn)
z	zip, always	(zihp), (AWL wayz)
zh	treasure	(TREH zher)

A

abolitionist person who wanted to end slavery completely in the United States (p. 440)

Act of Toleration a 1649 law passed by the Maryland assembly that provided religious freedom for all Christians (p. 114)

Adams-Onís Treaty an 1821 treaty between Spain and the United States in which Spain agreed to give Florida to the United States in exchange for $5 million (p. 350)

adobe sun-dried brick (p. 41)

Alamo old Spanish mission in Texas where Mexican forces under Santa Anna besieged American rebels, who were fighting to make Texas independent of Mexico in 1836 (p. 387)

Albany Plan of Union proposal by Benjamin Franklin to create one government for the 13 colonies (p. 143)

Alien and Sedition acts in 1798, Federalist-supported laws that permitted the President to expel foreigners, made it harder for immigrants to become citizens, and allowed for citizens to be fined or jailed if they criticized the government or its officials (p. 293)

alliance agreement between nations to aid and protect one another (p. 85)

ally nation that works with another nation for a common purpose (p. 183)

altitude height above sea level (p. 15)

amend change (p. 218)

American Colonization Society organization in the early 1800s that proposed to end slavery by helping African Americans move to Africa (p. 440)

American Federation of Labor organization of trade unions (p. 545)

American System program for economic growth promoted by Henry Clay in the early 1800s; called for high tariffs on imports and federal funds to improve transportation (p. 345)

amnesty government pardon (p. 517)

annex to add on (p. 389)

anthropology the study of how people and cultures develop (p. 30)

Antifederalists people who opposed

the Constitution and a strong national government (p. 215)

appeal to ask that a decision be reviewed by a higher court (p. 256)

Appomattox Court House Virginia town that was the site of the Confederate surrender in 1865 (p. 509)

apprentice person who learns a trade or craft from a master (p. 128)

archaeology the study of evidence left by early peoples in order to find out about their way of life (p. 22)

arsenal place where guns are stored (p. 476)

Articles the main body of the Constitution, divided into seven sections, which establishes the framework for the United States government (p. 249)

Articles of Confederation first American constitution, passed in 1777, which created a loose alliance of 13 independent states (p. 201)

artifact object made by humans (p. 22)

artisan skilled worker (p. 413)

astrolabe navigational instrument used to determine latitude while at sea (p. 59)

authenticity the quality or condition of being genuine (p. 21)

B

Bacon's Rebellion a 1676 raid led by Nathaniel Bacon against the governor and Native Americans in Virginia (p. 114)

Bank of the United States bank set up in 1791 to hold government deposits, to issue paper money to pay government bills, and to make loans to farmers and businesses (p. 281)

Battle of Antietam an 1862 Civil War battle in Maryland; in the day-long battle, more than 23,000 soldiers were killed or wounded (p. 493)

Battle of Bull Run first major battle of the Civil War; fought in Virginia in 1861 (p. 491)

Battle of Bunker Hill in 1775, first major battle of the Revolution (p. 170)

Battle of Chancellorsville an 1863 Civil War battle in Virginia; important victory for the Confederacy (p. 493)

Battle of Cowpens a 1781 battle in South Carolina, where Americans won an important victory over the British (p. 192)

Battle of Fredericksburg an 1862 Civil War battle in Virginia; one of the Union's worst defeats (p. 493)

Battle of Gettysburg an 1863 Civil War battle in Pennsylvania that left more

than 50,000 soldiers dead or wounded; the Confederates never invaded the North again (p. 506)

Battle of Lake Erie In the War of 1812, an American victory led by Oliver Perry against the British (p. 322)

Battle of Long Island a 1776 battle in New York in which more than 1,400 Americans were killed, wounded, or captured (p. 181)

Battle of New Orleans At the end of the War of 1812, a battle between British and American forces that ended in an American victory (p. 324)

Battle of San Jacinto an 1836 battle between Texans and Mexicans during the Texas war for independence from Mexico (p. 388)

Battle of Saratoga in 1777, the first major American victory in the Revolution, which ended the British threat to New England (p. 183)

Battle of Shiloh an 1862 Civil War battle in Tennessee that ended in a Union victory; one of the bloodiest encounters of the Civil War (p. 494)

Battle of Tippecanoe In 1811, battle over white settlement in the Indiana Territory (p. 318)

Battle of Trenton a 1776 battle in New Jersey in which George Washington's troops captured a Hessian encampment in a surprise attack (p. 182)

Battle of Yorktown final battle in the Revolution; this 1781 American victory in Virginia forced the British to surrender (p. 193)

battles of Lexington and Concord in 1775, conflicts between Massachusetts colonists and British soldiers that started the Revolutionary War (p. 160)

Bear Flag Republic nickname for California after it declared independence from Mexico in 1846 (p. 396)

Bessemer process method developed in the 1850s for making stronger steel at a lower cost (p. 544)

bias a leaning toward or against a certain person, group, or idea (p. 22)

bill proposed law (p. 253)

bill of rights written list of freedoms that a government promises to protect (pp. 123, 200)

Bill of Rights first 10 amendments to the United States Constitution (p. 218)

black codes laws passed by southern states that severely limited the rights of African Americans after the Civil War (p. 521)

blockade the shutting of a port to keep people or supplies from moving in or out (p. 171)

bond certificate that promises to repay money loaned, plus interest, on a certain date (p. 280)

boom period of swift economic growth (p. 419)

Border Ruffians proslavery bands from Missouri who often rode across the border into Kansas to battle the antislavery forces there (p. 470)

border state slave state that remained in the Union during the Civil War (p. 487)

Boston Massacre a 1770 conflict between colonists and British troops in which five colonists were killed (p. 152)

Boston Tea Party a 1773 protest in which colonists dressed as Indians dumped British tea into Boston harbor (p. 157)

boycott refusal to buy certain goods and services (p. 150)

Brown v. Board of Education 1954 Supreme Court case that brought about the end of legal segregation in public schools (p. 560)

burgess representative to the colonial Virginia government (p. 90)

C

Cabinet group of officials who head government departments and advise the President (p. 279)

capital money raised for a business venture (pp. 331, 544)

capitalist person who invests in a business in order to make a profit (p. 331)

caravan group of people who travel together for safety (p. 52)

carpetbagger uncomplimentary nickname for a northerner who went to the South after the Civil War (p. 527)

cartographer mapmaker (p. 8)

cash crop crop sold for money at market (p. 111)

cash economy economy in which people exchange money for goods and services (p. 27)

caucus private meeting; often a political meeting (p. 364)

causeway raised road made of packed earth (p. 38)

cavalry troops on horseback (p. 184)

cede to give up (pp. 202, 396)

Chapultepec fort outside of Mexico City that was the site of an 1847 battle between the United States and Mexico during the Mexican War (p. 396)

charter legal document giving certain rights to a person or company (p. 88)

checks and balances principle of the U.S. Constitution that safeguards against abuse of power by giving each branch of government the power to check the other branches (p. 251)

chronology sequence of events over time (p. 25)

circumnavigate travel all the way around the Earth (p. 71)

citizen person who owes loyalty to a particular nation and is entitled to all its rights and protections (p. 265)

city-state large town that has its own government and controls the surrounding countryside (p. 52)

civic virtue the willingness to work for the good of the nation or community even at great sacrifice (p. 266)

civics the study of the rights and responsibilities of citizens (p. 29)

civil relating to lawsuits involving the private rights of individuals, as opposed to criminal lawsuits (p. 261)

civil disobedience idea that people have a right to disobey laws they consider to be unjust if their consciences demand it (p. 451)

civil rights movement the efforts of African Americans to win equal rights (p. 560)

civil service system of government employment that awards federal jobs on the basis of examination scores, not political influence (p. 548)

civil war war between people of the same country (p. 465)

Civil War amendments the Thirteenth, Fourteenth, and Fifteenth amendments to the United States Constitution, which abolished slavery, guaranteed citizenship to former slaves, and gave African American men the right to vote (p. 261)

civilian nonmilitary (p. 249)

clan group of two or more related families (p. 48)

Clermont steamboat built in 1807; first steamboat to be commercially successful in American waters (p. 339)

climate average weather of a place over a period of 20 to 30 years (p. 15)

clipper ship fast-sailing ship of the mid-1800s (p. 410)

Cold War long period of intense rivalry after World War II between the Soviet Union and the United States (p. 558)

colony group of people who settle in a distant land but are still ruled by the government of their native land (p. 70)

Columbian Exchange the global exchange of goods and ideas resulting from the encounter between the peoples of the Eastern and the Western hemispheres (p. 71)

committee of correspondence letter-writing campaign that became

a major tool of protest in the colonies (p. 153)

Common Sense published in 1776, an essay by Thomas Paine that urged the colonies to declare independence (p. 173)

compromise settlement in which each side gives up some of its demands in order to reach an agreement (p. 208)

Compromise of 1850 agreement over slavery by which California joined the Union as a free state and a strict fugitive slave law was passed (p. 465)

confederation league of independent states or nations (p. 317)

conquistador name for the Spanish explorers who claimed lands in the Americas for Spain (p. 74)

Conservatives during Reconstruction, white southerners who resisted change (p. 527)

constitution document that sets out the laws, principles, organization, and processes of a government (p. 200)

Constitutional Convention gathering of state representatives on May 25, 1787, to revise the Articles of Confederation (p. 206)

constitutional initiative process by which citizens can petition for amendments to their state constitution (p. 263)

consumer user of goods and services (p. 27)

Continental Army army established by the Second Continental Congress to fight the British (p. 169)

continental divide mountain ridge that separates river systems flowing toward opposite sides of a continent (p. 309)

Copperhead northerner who opposed using force to keep the southern states in the Union (p. 501)

corduroy road road made of logs (p. 339)

corporation business owned by investors (p. 544)

"cottonocracy" name for the wealthy planters who made their money from cotton in the mid-1800s (p. 422)

coureur de bois French colonists who lived and worked in the woods as fur trappers (p. 83)

creole person born in Spain's American colonies to Spanish parents (pp. 78, 348)

Crusades between 1095 and 1300, series of wars fought by Christians to control the Holy Land (p. 58)

Cuban missile crisis major Cold War confrontation between the United States and the Soviet Union in 1962 when the United States blocked a Soviet attempt to install missiles in Cuba (p. 560)

culture entire way of life developed by a people (pp. 22, 40)

cultivate to prepare and use land for planting crops (p. 419)

culture area region in which people share a similar way of life (p. 42)

currency money (p. 202)

D

D-Day the invasion of western Europe on June 6, 1944, when American, British, and other allied troops landed on the coast of Normandy, France, and pressed eastward toward Germany (p. 557)

dame school private school run by a woman, usually in her home (p. 128)

debtor person who cannot pay money he or she owes (pp. 116, 436)

Declaration of Independence a 1776 document stating that the 13 English colonies were a free and independent nation (p. 175)

deficit spending government practice of spending more money than it takes in from taxes (p. 555)

democratic ensuring that all people have the same rights (p. 302)

Democratic Republican supporter of Thomas Jefferson, who favored a decentralized government (p. 289)

Democrats supporters of Andrew Jackson; included frontier farmers and factory workers (p. 364)

depression period when business activity slows, prices and wages fall, and unemployment rises (pp. 204, 373)

détente President Nixon's policy, continued under Presidents Ford and Carter, to reduce tensions between the superpowers (p. 564)

dictator ruler with absolute power and authority (p. 386)

dictatorship government in which one person or a small group holds complete authority (p. 212)

diffusion process of spreading ideas from one culture to another (p. 43)

direct democracy form of government in which ordinary citizens have the power to govern (p. 57)

discrimination policy or attitude that denies equal rights to certain groups of people (p. 417)

domestic tranquillity peace and order at home; one of the six goals defined in the Preamble to the United States Constitution (p. 249)

draft law requiring certain people to serve in the military (p. 502)

Dred Scott v. ***Sandford*** an 1857 Supreme Court case in which a slave,

E

Dred Scott, sued for his freedom and lost; case brought into question the federal power over slavery in the territories (p. 471)

economics the study of how people manage limited resources to satisfy their wants and needs (p. 26)

electoral college group of electors from every state who meet every four years to vote for the President and Vice President of the United States (p. 255)

elevation height above sea level (p. 13)

emancipate to set free (p. 497)

Emancipation Proclamation President Lincoln's 1863 declaration freeing slaves in the Confederacy (p. 497)

embargo ban on trade (p. 314)

Embargo Act an 1807 law that imposed a total ban on foreign trade (p. 314)

encomienda land grant given by the Spanish government to Spanish settlers that included the right to demand labor or taxes from Native Americans (p. 78)

English Bill of Rights a 1689 document that guaranteed the rights of English citizens (pp. 123, 213)

Enlightenment movement in Europe in the 1600s and 1700s that emphasized the use of reason (p. 129)

environmentalist person who works to reduce pollution and protect the environment (p. 566)

Era of Good Feelings the eight years of James Monroe's presidency, from 1817 to 1825, when the Democratic Republicans dominated the nation's politics (p. 343)

Erie Canal artificial waterway opened in 1825 linking Lake Erie to the Hudson River (p. 340)

erosion gradual wearing away (p. 13)

established church chosen religion of a state (p. 94)

executive branch branch of government that carries out laws (p. 208)

expedition long voyage of exploration (p. 308)

export trade product sent to markets outside a country (p. 120)

extended family family group that includes grandparents, parents, children, aunts, uncles, and cousins (pp. 53, 425)

F

faction opposing group within a party (p. 287)

factory system method of producing goods that brought workers and machinery together in one place (p. 331)

famine severe food shortage (p. 415)

Farewell Address final official speech of Presidents as they leave office (p. 286)

federalism a principle of the United States Constitution that establishes the division of power between the federal government and the states (p. 251)

Federalist supporter of the Constitution, who favored a strong federal, or national, government (pp. 215, 289)

The Federalist Papers series of essays by Federalists James Madison, Alexander Hamilton, and John Jay in support of ratifying the Constitution (p. 216)

feudalism system of rule by lords who ruled their own lands but owed loyalty and military service to a monarch (p. 58)

Fifteenth Amendment an 1869 amendment to the United States Constitution that forbids any state to deny African Americans the right to vote because of race (p. 524)

54th Massachusetts Regiment African American unit in the Union Army (p. 499)

First Amendment amendment to the United States Constitution that safeguards basic individual liberties including freedom of religion, speech, and the press (p. 260)

First Continental Congress in 1774, meeting in Philadelphia of delegates from 12 colonies (p. 158)

first global age era at the beginning of the 1400s, when long-distance trade and travel increased dramatically, linking far-off parts of the world (p. 50)

flatboat boat with a flat bottom used for transporting heavy loads on inland waterways (p. 337)

foreign policy actions that a nation takes in relation to other nations (p. 285)

Fort Wagner fort in South Carolina that was the site of an attack by the African American 54th Massachusetts Regiment in 1863 (p. 499)

forty-niner one of the more than 80,000 people who joined the gold rush to California in 1849 (p. 400)

Founding Fathers James Madison, Thomas Jefferson, and other leaders who laid the groundwork for the United States (p. 211)

Fourteenth Amendment an 1868 amendment to the United States Constitution that gives citizenship to all persons born in the United States and guarantees equal protection of the laws (p. 522)

free enterprise system in which the government plays a limited role in the economy (p. 28)

free market economy economic system in which individuals, rather than the government, decide what and how much to produce and sell (pp. 303, 564)

Free-Soil party bipartisan, antislavery party founded in the United States in 1848 to keep slavery out of the western territories (p. 462)

freedmen men and women who had been slaves (p. 517)

Freedmen's Bureau United States government agency founded during Reconstruction to help former slaves (p. 517)

French and Indian War a war that took place from 1754 to 1763 between England and France, both aided by Native American allies, that led to the end of French power in North America (p. 142)

French Revolution a 1789 rebellion in France that ended the French monarchy for a time (p. 284)

frigate fast-sailing ship with many guns (p. 292)

fugitive runaway (p. 464)

Fugitive Slave Act law passed in 1850 that required all citizens to aid in the capture of runaway slaves (p. 465)

Fundamental Orders of Connecticut a 1639 plan of government in the Puritan colony in Connecticut; expanded the idea of representative government in the English colonies (p. 104)

G

Gadsden Purchase strip of land in present-day Arizona and New Mexico for which the United States paid Mexico $10 million in 1853 (p. 397)

General Court elected representative assembly in the Massachusetts Bay Colony (p. 103)

general welfare well-being of all the citizens of a nation; one of the six goals defined in the Preamble to the United States Constitution (p. 249)

gentry highest social class in the 13 English colonies (p. 126)

geography the study of people, their environments, and their resources (p. 4)

Gettysburg Address speech made by President Lincoln in 1863 after the Battle of Gettysburg (p. 507)

Glossary

Gibbons v. Ogden an 1824 case in which the Supreme Court upheld the power of the federal government to regulate interstate commerce (p. 346)

glacier thick sheet of ice (p. 36)

Glorious Revolution in 1688, movement that brought William and Mary to the throne of England and strengthened the rights of English citizens (p. 123)

grandfather clause law that excused a voter from a literacy test if his father or grandfather had been eligible to vote on January 1, 1867; protected the voting rights of southern whites, but not those of southern blacks (p. 532)

Great Awakening religious movement in the English colonies in the early 1700s (p. 127)

Great Compromise plan at the Constitutional Convention that settled the differences between large and small states (p. 208)

Great Depression worst period of economic decline in United States history, beginning in 1929 and lasting until the start of World War II (p. 554)

Green Mountain Boys Vermont colonial militia led by Ethan Allen, which made a surprise attack on Fort Ticonderoga, giving Americans control of the key route into Canada (p. 169)

guerrilla soldier who uses hit-and-run tactics (p. 192)

guerrilla warfare the use of hit-and-run military tactics (p. 470)

Gullah combination of English and West African languages spoken by African Americans in the South Carolina colony (p. 126)

H

habeas corpus the right that no person can be held in prison without first being charged with a specific crime (pp. 213, 502)

Hartford Convention gathering of New England delegates during the War of 1812 to protest the war by threatening to secede from the Union (p. 325)

Holocaust murder of millions of Jews and others by the government of Nazi Germany and its allies during World War II (p. 556)

Homestead Act an 1862 law that gave land to settlers to be developed as farms (p. 543)

House of Burgesses representative assembly in colonial Virginia (p. 90)

House of Representatives the larger of the two bodies that make up the legislative branch of the United States government; representation is based on population (p. 252)

Hudson River School group of American artists who painted landscapes of New York's Hudson River Valley in the mid-1800s (p. 448)

I

immigrant person who enters another country in order to settle there (p. 266)

impeach to bring charges of serious wrongdoing against a public official (pp. 257, 523)

imperialism policy of powerful countries seeking to control the political and economic affairs of weaker countries or regions (p. 549)

import trade product brought into a country (p. 120)

impressment practice of forcing people into military service (p. 313)

inauguration ceremony in which the President officially takes the oath of office (p. 278)

income tax a tax on people's earnings (p. 502)

incriminate to give evidence against (p. 260)

indentured servant person who agreed to work without wages for a period of time in exchange for passage to the colonies (p. 126)

Indian Removal Act law passed in 1830 that forced many Native Americans to move west of the Mississippi River (p. 372)

indigo plant used to make a valuable blue dye (p. 115)

individualism concept that stresses the importance of each individual (p. 451)

Industrial Revolution gradual process by which machines replaced hand tools, and steam and other new sources of power replaced human and animal power (p. 330)

inflation a rise in prices and a decrease in the value of money (p. 503)

infrastructure system of roads, bridges, and tunnels (p. 263)

interchangeable parts identical, machine-made parts for a tool or instrument (p. 332)

internal improvements improvements to roads, bridges, and canals (p. 346)

interstate commerce trade between different states (p. 346)

intervention direct involvement (p. 351)

Intolerable Acts series of laws passed in 1774 to punish Boston for the Tea Party (p. 157)

irrigation bringing water to dry lands (p. 6)

Islam monotheistic religion founded by the prophet Muhammad in the early A.D. 600s (p. 50)

isolationism policy of limiting involvement in the political affairs of foreign nations (p. 549)

isthmus narrow strip of land (p. 11)

J

Jay's Treaty a 1795 agreement between Britain and the United States that called for Britain to pay damages for seized American ships and to give up forts it still held in the West. In exchange, the United States would repay debts owed to British merchants (p. 286)

jazz original American music style that blends West African rhythms, European harmonies, and African American work songs and spirituals (p. 554)

Jim Crow laws laws that separated people of different races in public places in the South (p. 532)

judicial branch branch of government that decides if laws are carried out fairly (p. 208)

judicial review power of the Supreme Court to decide whether acts of a President or laws passed by Congress are constitutional (p. 305)

Judiciary Act a 1789 law that created the structure of the Supreme Court and set up a system of district courts and circuit courts for the nation (p. 279)

jury duty the responsibility of every citizen to serve on a jury when called (p. 268)

K

kachina masked dancer at religious ceremonies of the Southwest Indians (p. 47)

Kansas-Nebraska Act an 1854 law that established the territories of Nebraska and Kansas, giving the settlers the right of popular sovereignty to decide on the issue of slavery (p. 468)

Kentucky and Virginia resolutions declarations passed in 1798 and 1799 that claimed that each state has the right to decide whether a federal law is constitutional and to nullify laws deemed unconstitutional within a state's borders (p. 293)

kinship sharing a common ancestor (p. 53)

"kitchen cabinet" group of unofficial advisers to Andrew Jackson who met with him in the White House kitchen (p. 367)

Know-Nothing party political party of the 1850s that was anti-Catholic and anti-immigrant (p. 416)

Korean War conflict that lasted from 1950 to 1953 between North Korea, aided by China, and South Korea, aided by United Nations forces consisting primarily of United States troops (p. 559)

Ku Klux Klan secret society organized in the South after the Civil War to reassert white supremacy by means of violence (p. 527)

L

laissez faire idea that government should play as small a role as possible in economic affairs (p. 303)

Lancaster Turnpike road built in the 1790s by a private company, linking Philadelphia and Lancaster, Pennsylvania (p. 339)

Land Ordinance of 1785 law setting up a system for settling the Northwest Territory (p. 203)

latitude distance north or south from the equator (p. 4)

lawsuit legal case brought to settle a dispute between a person or group (p. 471)

League of the Iroquois alliance of the five Iroquois nations (p. 48)

legislative branch branch of government that passes laws (p. 208)

legislature group of people who have the power to make laws (p. 122)

libel act of publishing a statement that may unjustly damage a person's reputation (p. 130)

The Liberator most influential antislavery newspaper; begun by William Lloyd Garrison in 1831 (p. 440)

liberty freedom (p. 249)

limited government a principle of the United States Constitution that states that government has only the powers that the Constitution gives it (p. 250)

literacy test examination to see if a person can read and write; used in the past to restrict voting rights (p. 532)

local government government on the county, parish, city, town, village, or district level (p. 263)

locomotive engine that pulls a railroad train (p. 409)

Lone Star Republic nickname for Texas after it won independence from Mexico in 1836 (p. 389)

longitude distance east or west from the Prime Meridian (p. 4)

Louisiana Purchase vast territory between the Mississippi River and Rocky Mountains, purchased from France in 1803 (p. 308)

Lowell girl young woman who worked in the Lowell Mills in Massachusetts during the Industrial Revolution (p. 333)

Loyalist colonist who remained loyal to Britain (p. 170)

lynch to hang without a legal trial (p. 401)

M

Magna Carta signed in 1215, a British document that contains two basic ideas: Monarchs themselves have to obey the laws, and citizens have basic rights (pp. 90, 213)

majority more than half (p. 362)

Manifest Destiny belief held in the 1800s that Americans had the right and the duty to spread across the continent all the way to the Pacific Ocean (p. 393)

manor district ruled by a lord, including the lord's castle and the lands around it (p. 58)

map projection way of drawing Earth on a flat surface (p. 8)

Marbury v. Madison an 1803 court case in which the Supreme Court ruled that it had the power to decide whether laws passed by Congress were constitutional and to reject laws that it considered unconstitutional (p. 305)

margin buying practice by which investors buy stock for a small downpayment and borrow the rest from their brokers, hoping to sell for a profit when the price of the stock rises (p. 554)

Marshall Plan American plan to help European nations rebuild their economies after World War II (p. 559)

martial law rule by the army instead of the elected government (p. 487)

martyr person who dies for his or her beliefs (p. 476)

Mason-Dixon Line boundary between Pennsylvania and Maryland that divided the Middle Colonies from the Southern Colonies (p. 113)

Mayflower Compact a 1620 agreement for ruling the Plymouth Colony, signed by Pilgrims before they landed at Plymouth (p. 95)

McCulloch v. Maryland an 1819 case in which the Supreme Court ruled that states had no right to interfere with federal institutions within their borders (p. 346)

mercantilism theory that a nation's economic strength came from protecting and increasing its home economy by

keeping strict control over its colonial trade (p. 120)

mercenary soldier who fights merely for pay, often for a foreign country (p. 171)

mestizo in Spain's American colonies, person of mixed Spanish and Indian background (p. 78)

Mexican Cession Mexican territory of California and New Mexico given to the United States in 1848 (p. 396)

middle class in the 13 English colonies, a class that included skilled craftsworkers, farmers, and some tradespeople (p. 126)

militia army of citizens who serve as soldiers during an emergency (p. 158)

minuteman colonial militia volunteer who was prepared to fight at a minute's notice (p. 159)

mission religious settlement run by Catholic priests and friars (p. 78)

missionary person who tries to spread certain religious beliefs among a group of people (pp. 56, 84)

Missouri Compromise agreement, proposed in 1819 by Henry Clay, to keep the number of slave and free states equal (p. 460)

Monitor ironclad Union warship (p. 492)

monopoly a single company that controls or dominates an entire industry (p. 544)

Monroe Doctrine President Monroe's foreign policy statement warning European nations not to interfere in Latin America (p. 351)

Mormons members of the Church of Jesus Christ of Latter-Day Saints founded by Joseph Smith in 1830 (p. 398)

Mound Builders the name for various North American cultures that built large earth mounds beginning about 3,000 years ago (p. 41)

mountain man trapper who explored and hunted in Oregon in the early 1800s (p. 381)

muckraker journalist who exposed corruption and other problems of the late 1800s and early 1900s in the United States (p. 547)

mudslinging the use of insults to attack an opponent's reputation (p. 374)

N

national debt total amount of money that a government owes to others (p. 280)

National Road first federally funded national road project, begun in 1811 (p. 339)

Glossary (sidebar)

nationalism devotion to one's country (p. 318)

nativist person who wanted to limit immigration and preserve the United States for native-born, white citizens (p. 416)

natural resources materials that humans can take from the environment to survive and satisfy their needs (p. 5)

natural rights rights that belong to all people from birth (p. 175)

naturalize to complete the official process for becoming a citizen (p. 265)

Nauvoo Mormon community built on the banks of the Mississippi River in Illinois in the 1840s (p. 398)

Navigation Acts series of laws passed by the English Parliament in the 1650s that regulated trade between England and its colonies (p. 121)

Negro Fort settlement of escaped African American slaves in the Spanish colony of Florida (p. 350)

neutral not taking sides in a conflict (p. 285)

Neutrality Proclamation a 1793 statement by President Washington that the United States would not support or aid either France or Britain in their European conflict (p. 285)

New Deal program of President Franklin D. Roosevelt to end the Great Depression (p. 554)

New Jersey Plan plan at the Constitutional Convention, favored by smaller states, that called for three branches of government with a single-chamber legislature (p. 208)

New Mexico Territory huge region in the Southwest owned by Mexico in the 1800s (p. 391)

"New South" term to describe the South in the late 1800s when efforts were made to expand the economy by building up industry (p. 533)

Nineteenth Amendment a 1920 amendment to the United States Constitution that guarantees women's right to vote (pp. 261, 548)

nominating convention meeting at which a political party chooses a candidate (p. 364)

Nonintercourse Act an 1809 law that allowed Americans to carry on trade with all nations except Britain and France (p. 314)

North American Free Trade Agreement (NAFTA) treaty among the United States, Canada, and Mexico to gradually remove tariffs and other trade barriers (p. 566)

Northwest Ordinance a 1787 article that set up a government for the Northwest Territory, guaranteed basic

rights to settlers, and outlawed slavery there (p. 203)

northwest passage a natural waterway through or around North America (p. 81)

nullification idea that a state has the right to nullify, or cancel, a federal law that the state leaders consider to be unconstitutional (p. 371)

Nullification Act act passed by South Carolina that declared the 1832 tariff illegal (p. 371)

nullify to cancel (p. 293)

O

Olive Branch Petition peace petition sent to King George by colonial delegates after the battles of Lexington and Concord, declaring their loyalty to the king and asking him to repeal the Intolerable Acts (p. 168)

Oregon Country term used in the early 1800s for the region west of the Rocky Mountains, including present-day Oregon, Washington, Idaho, and parts of Wyoming, Montana, and Canada (p. 380)

Oregon Trail route to Oregon used by wagon trains in the 1800s (p. 383)

override to overrule, as when Congress overrules a presidential veto (p. 257)

P

Parliament representative assembly in England (p. 90)

Patriot colonist who favored war against Britain (p. 169)

patriotism feeling of love and devotion toward one's country (p. 266)

patroon owner of a huge estate in a Dutch colony (p. 109)

peninsulare person from Spain who held a position of power in a Spanish colony (p. 78)

Pennsylvania Dutch German-speaking Protestants who settled in Pennsylvania (p. 110)

persecution mistreatment or punishment of a group of people because of their beliefs (p. 94)

Persian Gulf War war fought in 1991 between Iraq and a coalition of countries led by the United States to free oil-rich Kuwait from occupying Iraqi forces (p. 564)

petition formal written request to someone in authority, signed by a group of people (p. 149)

Pickett's Charge failed Confederate charge at the Battle of Gettysburg (p. 506)

Pilgrims in the 1600s, English settlers who sought religious freedom in the Americas (p. 93)

Pinckney Treaty a 1795 agreement with Spain that let Americans ship their goods down the Mississippi River and store them in New Orleans (p. 306)

pit house house in the Arctic region dug into the ground and covered with wood and skins (p. 43)

Plains of Abraham a field near Quebec; site of a major British victory over the French in the French and Indian War (p. 144)

plantation large estate farmed by many workers (p. 80)

Plessy v. Ferguson an 1896 court case in which the Supreme Court ruled that segregation in public facilities was legal as long as the facilities were equal (p. 532)

political science the study of government (p. 29)

poll tax tax required before a person can vote (p. 532)

Pontiac's War a 1763 conflict between Native Americans and the British over settlement of Indian lands in the Great Lakes area (p. 147)

popular sovereignty a principle of the United States Constitution that states that the people have the right to create, alter, and abolish their government; in the mid-1800s, a term referring to the idea that each territory could decide for itself whether or not to allow slavery (pp. 250, 462)

potlatch ceremonial dinner held by some Native Americans of the Northwest Coast to show off their wealth (p. 44)

preamble introduction to a declaration, constitution, or other official document (pp. 175, 248)

precedent an act or decision that sets the example for others to follow (pp. 96, 278)

precipitation water that falls in the form of rain, sleet, hail, or snow (p. 15)

predestination Protestant idea that God decided in advance which people would attain salvation after death (p. 435)

presidio fort where soldiers lived in the Spanish colonies (p. 77)

primary source firsthand information about people or events (p. 20)

Proclamation of 1763 law forbidding English colonists to settle west of the Appalachian Mountains (p. 147)

profiteer person who takes advantage of a crisis to make money (p. 503)

Progressives reformers who wanted to improve American life in the late

Glossary

1800s and early 1900s (p. 547)

proprietary colony English colony in which the king gave land to proprietors in exchange for a yearly payment (p. 109)

Protestant Reformation movement to reform the Roman Catholic Church in the 1500s; led to the creation of many different Christian churches (p. 83)

psychology the study of how people think and behave (p. 30)

public school school supported by taxes (p. 128)

pueblo a town in the Spanish colonies; Anasazi village (pp. 41, 77)

Puritans group of English Protestants who settled the Massachusetts Bay Colony (p. 102)

Q

Quakers Protestant reformers who believe in the equality of all people (p. 110)

Quebec Act law that set up a government for Canada and protected the rights of French Catholics (p. 158)

quipu device made of cord or string with knots that stood for quantities; used by the Incas to keep accounts and records (p. 40)

Quran sacred book of Islam (p. 51)

R

racism belief that one race is superior to another (p. 119)

radical person who wants to make drastic changes in society (p. 173)

Radical Reconstruction period beginning in 1867 when the Republicans, who had control in both houses of Congress, took charge of Reconstruction (p. 523)

Radical Republican member of Congress during Reconstruction who wanted to break the power of wealthy planters in the South and ensure that freedmen received the right to vote (p. 522)

ratify to approve (p. 194)

Reaganomics President Reagan's economic policy that cut taxes, slowed down spending on social programs, and eliminated many regulations on business (p. 563)

Reconstruction rebuilding of the South after the Civil War (p. 517)

Reconstruction Act an 1867 law that threw out the southern state governments that had refused to ratify the Fourteenth Amendment and required that former Confederate states allow African Americans to vote (p. 523)

refuge a place where one is safe from persecution (p. 399)

religious tolerance willingness to let others practice their own beliefs (p. 104)

Renaissance French word meaning rebirth; burst of learning in Europe from the late 1300s to about 1600 (p. 59)

rendezvous French word meaning "get-together"; yearly meeting where mountain men traded furs (p. 382)

repeal cancel (p. 150)

representative government political system in which voters elect representatives to make laws for them (p. 90)

republic system of government in which citizens choose representatives to govern them (pp. 57, 211)

Republic of Great Colombia independent state composed of the present-day nations of Venezuela, Colombia, Ecuador, and Panama; established in 1819 after the territory declared independence from Spain (p. 349)

Republican party political party established in the United States in 1854 with the goal of keeping slavery out of the western territories (p. 473)

resident alien noncitizen living in the country (p. 266)

revival huge outdoor religious meeting (p. 435)

Roosevelt Corollary policy established by President Theodore Roosevelt that extended the Monroe Doctrine by stating that the United States had the right to intervene in Latin American affairs (p. 550)

royal colony colony under the direct control of the English crown (p. 109)

rugged individualist person who follows his or her own independent course in life (p. 381)

S

Sabbath holy day of rest (p. 106)

sachem member of the tribal chief council in the League of the Iroquois (p. 48)

salvation everlasting life (p. 56)

Santa Fe Trail route to Santa Fe, New Mexico, that was used by traders in the 1800s (p. 392)

savanna region of grasslands (p. 52)

scalawag white southerner who supported the Republicans during Reconstruction (p. 526)

secede to withdraw from membership in a group (p. 463)

Second Amendment amendment to the United States Constitution related to the right to bear arms (p. 260)

Second Great Awakening widespread religious movement in the United States in the early 1800s (p. 435)

secondary source account provided after the fact by people who did not directly witness or participate in the event (p. 21)

sectionalism loyalty to a state or section rather than to the whole country (p. 345)

sedition stirring up rebellion against a government (p. 293)

segregation legal separation of races (p. 532)

self-sufficient able to produce enough for one's own needs (p. 392)

Seminole War conflict that began in Florida in 1817 between the Seminole Indians and the United States Army when the Seminoles resisted removal (p. 373)

Senate the smaller of the two bodies that make up the legislative branch of the United States government; based on equal representation, with two senators for each state (p. 253)

Seneca Falls Convention an 1848 meeting at which leaders of the women's rights movement called for equal rights for women (p. 445)

separation of powers principle by which the powers of government are divided among separate branches (p. 214)

sharecropper person who rents a plot of land from another person and farms it in exchange for a share of the crop (p. 529)

Shays' Rebellion a 1786 revolt in Massachusetts led by farmers in reaction to high taxes (p. 204)

siege military blockade or bombardment of an enemy town or position in order to force it to surrender (pp. 193, 387, 506)

Silk Road overland trade routes linking China to the Middle East (p. 52)

slave code laws that controlled the lives of enslaved African Americans and denied them basic rights (pp. 119, 424)

smuggling importing or exporting goods in violation of trade laws (p. 314)

social reform an organized attempt to improve what is unjust or imperfect in society (p. 434)

social sciences studies that relate to human society and social behavior (p. 29)

Social Security federal program begun in the 1930s to provide aid for the elderly and unemployed; the program was later expanded (p. 554)

sociology the study of how people behave in groups (p. 30)

Glossary

Spanish-American War an 1898 war between the United States and Spain over American expansion; enabled the United States to gain control of Cuba, Puerto Rico, Guam, and the Philippines (p. 550)

speculator someone who invests in a risky venture in the hope of making a large profit (p. 280)

spinning jenny machine developed in 1764 that could spin several threads at once (p. 331)

spoils system practice of rewarding supporters with government jobs (p. 366)

Stamp Act a 1765 law that placed new duties on legal documents and taxed newspapers, almanacs, playing cards, and dice (p. 149)

states' rights the right of states to limit the power of the federal government (pp. 293, 370)

strike refusal by workers to do their jobs until their demands are met (p. 414)

suffrage the right to vote (p. 361)

Supreme Court highest court in the United States established by the Constitution (p. 256)

surplus extra (p. 37)

Sutter's Mill location where gold was discovered in California in 1848, setting off the gold rush (p. 400)

Swahili language that blends Arab words and local African languages spoken widely in East Africa (p. 52)

T

tariff tax on foreign goods brought into a country (p. 281)

Tariff of Abominations tariff passed by Congress in 1828 that favored manufacturing in the North but hurt the farmers in the South (p. 370)

Tea Act a 1773 law that let the British East India Company bypass tea merchants and sell directly to colonists (p. 156)

Tejano person of Mexican descent born in Texas (p. 386)

telegraph communications device that sends electrical signals along a wire (p. 409)

temperance movement campaign against alcohol consumption (p. 436)

Ten Percent Plan President Lincoln's plan for Reconstruction that allowed a southern state to form a new government after 10 percent of its voters swore an oath of loyalty to the United States (p. 517)

terrace wide shelf of land cut into a hillside (p. 40)

terrorism deliberate use of random violence, especially against civilians, to achieve political goals (p. 564)

Thanksgiving day at the end of the harvest season set aside by the Pilgrims to give thanks to God (p. 97)

thematic map map that deals with a specific topic, such as population, natural resources, or elections (p. 9)

Thirteenth Amendment an 1865 amendment to the United States Constitution that bans slavery throughout the nation (p. 519)

Three-Fifths Compromise agreement at the Constitutional Convention that three fifths of the slaves in any state be counted in its population (p. 209)

total war all-out war that affects civilians at home as well as soldiers in combat (p. 508)

totalitarian state country where a single party controls the government and every aspect of people's lives (p. 556)

town meeting meeting in colonial New England where colonists discussed and voted on issues (p. 107)

Townshend Acts laws passed in 1767 that taxed goods such as glass, paper, paint, lead, and tea (p. 150)

trade union association of trade workers formed to gain higher wages and better working conditions (p. 414)

Trail of Tears forced journey of the Cherokee Indians from Georgia to a region west of the Mississippi during which thousands of Cherokees died (p. 372)

traitor person who betrays his or her country (p. 175)

transcendentalist member of the small, influential group of New England writers and thinkers who believed that the most important truths in life transcended, or went beyond, human reason (p. 450)

transcontinental railroad railroad that stretches across a continent (p. 543)

treason actions against one's country (p. 476)

Treaty of Ghent peace treaty signed by Britain and the United States at the end of the War of 1812 (p. 325)

Treaty of Greenville treaty signed by some Native Americans in 1795, giving up land that would later become part of Ohio in exchange for $20,000 and a promise of more money if they kept the peace (p. 317)

Treaty of Guadalupe-Hidalgo an 1848 treaty in which Mexico gave up California and New Mexico to the United States for $15 million (p. 396)

Treaty of Paris a 1763 agreement between Britain and France that ended the French and Indian War, and marked the end of French power in North America (p. 145); peace treaty between the United States and Britain, ratified in 1783, that recognized the United States as an independent nation (p. 194)

triangular trade colonial trade route between New England, the West Indies, and Africa (p. 121)

tribe community of people that share common customs, language, and rituals (p. 42)

tributary stream or smaller river that flows into a larger one (p. 15)

tribute bribe (p. 313)

turning point moment in history that marks a decisive change (p. 70)

turnpike road built by a private company that charges a toll to use it (p. 339)

tutor private teacher (p. 128)

Twenty-sixth Amendment amendment to the United States Constitution that lowered the minimum voting age from 21 to 18 (p. 261)

U

unamendable unable to change (p. 479)

Uncle Tom's Cabin an 1852 novel by Harriet Beecher Stowe written to show the evils of slavery and the injustice of the Fugitive Slave Act (p. 466)

unconstitutional not allowed under the Constitution (pp. 257, 288)

Underground Railroad network of black and white abolitionists who secretly helped slaves escape to freedom in the North or Canada (p. 441)

United Provinces of Central America federation of the present-day nations of Guatemala, El Salvador, Honduras, Nicaragua, and Costa Rica; established in 1823 after these states declared independence from Spain (p. 349)

urbanization process of a population's shifting from farms to cities (pp. 335, 546)

V

Valley Forge Pennsylvania site of Washington's Continental Army encampment during the winter of 1777–1778 (p. 185)

vaquero Indian or Mexican cowhand (p. 392)

veto reject, as when the President rejects a law passed by Congress (p. 257)

Glossary

Vietnam War military conflict between the communist forces of North Vietnam, supported by China and the Soviet Union, and the noncommunist forces of South Vietnam, supported by the United States; American involvement lasted from 1961 to 1973 (p. 561)

vigilante self-appointed enforcer of the law (p. 401)

Virginia ironclad warship used by the Confederates to break the Union blockade (p. 492)

Virginia Plan plan at the Constitutional Convention, favored by larger states, that called for a strong national government with three branches and a two-chamber legislature (p. 208)

W

Wade-Davis Bill an 1864 plan for Reconstruction that required a majority of white men in each southern state to swear loyalty to the Union and denied the right to vote or hold office to anyone who had volunteered to fight for the Confederacy (p. 517)

War Hawks members of Congress from the South and the West who called for war with Britain prior to the War of 1812 (p. 318)

Watergate affair series of scandals involving the administration of President Richard Nixon, including the burglarizing of the Democratic headquarters in the Watergate office building in Washington, D.C., in 1972; led to Nixon's resignation in 1974 (p. 563)

weather condition of Earth's atmosphere at a given time and place (p. 15)

Whigs members of John Quincy Adams's former National Republican party; included many business people, southern planters, and former Federalists (p. 363)

Whiskey Rebellion a 1794 protest over a tax on all liquor made and sold in the United States (p. 282)

Wilmot Proviso law passed in 1846 that banned slavery in any territories won by the United States from Mexico (p. 461)

women's rights movement organized campaign to win property, education, and other rights for women (p. 446)

World War I war fought from 1914 to 1918, in which Great Britain, France, Russia, Belgium, Italy, Japan, the United States, and other allies defeated Germany, Austria-Hungary, the Ottoman Empire, and Bulgaria (p. 550)

World War II war fought from 1939 to 1945, in which Great Britain, France, the Soviet Union, the United States, China, and other allies defeated Germany, Italy, Japan, and their allies (p. 556)

writ of assistance legal document that allowed British customs officials to inspect a ship's cargo without giving a reason (p. 150)

X

XYZ Affair a 1797 French attempt to bribe the United States by demanding payment before talks could begin on the issue of French seizure of neutral American ships (p. 292)

Y

Yankee nickname for New England merchants who dominated colonial trade (p. 121)

Glossary

Spanish Glossary

A

abolitionist/abolicionista persona que quería acabar completamente la esclavitud en los Estados Unidos (pág. 440)

Act of Toleration/Acta de Tolerancia ley aprobada por la asamblea de Maryland en 1649 que aseguraba la libertad religiosa para todos los cristianos (pág. 114)

Adams-Onís Treaty/Tratado de Adams-Onís tratado de 1821 entre España y los Estados Unidos según el cual España se comprometía a entregar Florida a los Estados Unidos a cambio de 5 millones de dólares (pág. 350)

adobe/adobe ladrillo secado al sol (pág. 41)

Alamo/Álamo vieja misión española situada en Texas donde las fuerzas mexicanas bajo las órdenes de Santa Anna asediaron a los rebeldes estadounidenses que luchaban en 1836 para que Texas se independizara de México (pág. 387)

Albany Plan of Union/Plan de Unión de Albany propuesta de Benjamin Franklin que consistía en crear un solo gobierno para las 13 colonias (pág. 143)

Alien and Sedition acts/Actas de Extranjería y de Sedición leyes apoyadas por los federalistas que permitían que el presidente expulsara a extranjeros, dificultara la obtención de la ciudadanía a los extranjeros, y multara o encarcelara a ciudadanos por criticar al gobierno o a sus funcionarios (pág. 293)

alliance/alianza acuerdo entre naciones para ayudarse y protegerse mutuamente (pág. 85)

ally/aliado (a) nación que trabaja con otra nación hacia una meta común (pág. 183)

altitude/altura elevación sobre el nivel del mar (pág. 15)

amend/reformar cambiar (pág. 218)

American Colonization Society/Sociedad de Colonización Americana organización de principios del 1800 que proponía acabar con la esclavitud ayudando a los afroamericanos a que se mudaran al Africa (pág. 440)

American Federation of Labor/Federación Americana del Trabajo organización de gremios (pág. 545)

American System/sistema estadounidense programa para fomentar el crecimiento económico, promovido por Henry Clay a principios del siglo XIX; proponía imponer altas tasas a las importaciones y usar fondos federales para mejorar el sistema de transportes (pág. 345)

amnesty/amnistía perdón del gobierno (pág. 517)

annex/anexar agregar (pág. 389)

anthropology/antropología estudio de cómo se desarrollan las personas y las culturas (pág. 30)

Antifederalists/antifederalistas personas que se oponían a la constitución y a un gobierno nacional fuerte (pág. 215)

appeal/apelar pedir a una corte de mayor autoridad que reconsidere una decisión (pág. 256)

Appomattox Court House/Appomattox Court House Ciudad de Virginia en donde la Confederación se rindió (pág. 509)

apprentice/aprendiz persona que aprende un oficio o artesanía de un maestro (pág.128)

archaeology/arqueología estudio de las evidencias dejadas por culturas antiguas con el objeto de conocer su forma de vida (pág. 22)

arsenal/arsenal depósito de armas (pág. 476)

Articles/artículos parte principal de la Constitución, que está dividida en siete secciones y establece la estructura del gobierno de los Estados Unidos (pág. 249)

Articles of Confederation/Artículos de la Confederación primera constitución americana, aprobada en 1777, que creó una alianza vaga entre los 13 estados independientes (pág. 201)

artifact/artefacto objeto hecho por seres humanos (pág. 22)

artisan/artesano trabajador manual calificado (pág. 413)

astrolabe/astrolabio instrumento de navegación que se usa para determinar la latitud en alta mar (pág. 59)

authenticity/autenticidad cualidad o condición de ser genuino (pág. 21)

B

Bacon's Rebellion/rebelión de Bacon revuelta liderada en 1676 por Nathaniel Bacon en contra del gobernador y de los americanos nativos de Virginia (pág. 114)

Bank of the United States/Banco de los Estados Unidos banco establecido en 1791 para retener los depósitos del gobierno, emitir papel moneda para el pago de las cuentas del gobierno y otorgar préstamos a granjeros y gentes de negocios (pág. 281)

Battle of Antietam/batalla de Antietam batalla librada en Maryland en 1862 durante la Guerra Civil; duró un día y murieron o resultaron heridos más de 23,000 soldados (pág. 493)

Battle of Bull Run/batalla de Bull Run primera gran batalla de la Guerra Civil, librada en Virginia en 1861 (pág. 491)

Battle of Bunker Hill/batalla de Bunker Hill batalla de 1775 que fue la primera gran batalla de la Revolución (pág. 170)

Battle of Chancellorsville/batalla de Chancellorsville batalla librada en Virginia en 1863 durante la Guerra Civil; fue una victoria importante para la Confederación (pág. 493)

Battle of Cowpens/batalla de Cowpens batalla de 1781 que tuvo lugar en Carolina del Norte y por la cual los colonos obtuvieron una victoria importante sobre los británicos (pág. 192)

Battle of Fredericksburg/batalla de Fredericksburg batalla librada en Virginia en 1862 durante la Guerra Civil; fue una de las peores derrotas de la Unión (pág. 493)

Battle of Gettysburg/batalla de Gettysburg batalla librada en Pennsylvania en 1863 durante la Guerra Civil que dejó más de 50,000 soldados muertos o heridos. Los Confederados nunca volvieron a invadir el Norte (pág. 506)

Battle of Lake Erie/batalla del lago Erie batalla de la guerra de 1812 contra los británicos, que terminó con la victoria de las fuerzas de los Estados Unidos lideradas por Oliver Perry (pág. 322)

Battle of Long Island/batalla de Long Island batalla de 1776 en Nueva York, en la que más de 1,400 colonos murieron, resultaron heridos o fueron capturados (pág. 181)

Battle of New Orleans/batalla de Nueva Orleáns batalla entre los británicos y los estadounidenses que terminó con la victoria de las fuerzas de los Estados Unidos, al final de la guerra de 1812 (pág. 324)

Battle of San Jacinto/batalla de San Jacinto una batalla de 1836 entre texanos y mexicanos que se produjo durante la guerra que llevó a cabo Texas para independizarse de México (pág. 388)

Battle of Saratoga/batalla de Saratoga primera victoria importante de la Revolución en la batalla de 1777, que acabó con la amenaza de los ingleses en Nueva Inglaterra (pág. 183)

Battle of Shiloh/batalla de Shiloh batalla librada en 1862 en Tennessee, que terminó con la victoria de la Unión; fue uno de los encuentros más sangrientos de la Guerra Civil (pág. 494)

Battle of Tippecanoe/batalla de Tippecanoe batalla de 1811 a propósito de las colonizaciones blancas en el territorio de Indiana (pág. 318)

Battle of Trenton/batalla de Trenton batalla de 1776 que tuvo lugar en Nueva Jersey, en la que las tropas de George Washington en un ataque sorpresa capturaron un campamento de Hessian (pág. 182)

Battle of Yorktown/batalla de Yorktown última batalla de la Revolución en 1781; esta victoria de los colonos en Virginia obligó a los ingleses a rendirse (pág. 193)

battles of Lexington and Concord/batallas de Lexington y Concord conflictos de 1775 entre colonos de Massachusetts y soldados británicos que dieron origen a la Revolución Americana (pág. 160)

Bear Flag Republic/República de la Bandera del Oso sobrenombre de California después de declararse independiente de México en 1846 (pág. 396)

Bessemer process/proceso de Bessemer método desarrollado en la década de 1850 para fabricar acero más resistente a un precio más bajo (pág. 544)

bias/prejuicio inclinación a favor o en contra de cierta persona, grupo o idea (pág. 22)

bill/proyecto de ley ley que se propone para su aprobación (pág. 253)

bill of rights/declaración de derechos lista escrita de las libertades que el gobierno promete proteger (págs. 123, 200)

Bill of Rights/Declaración de Derechos las primeras 10 enmiendas de la Constitución de Estados Unidos (pág. 218)

black codes/códigos de negros leyes aprobadas por los estados del Sur después de la Guerra Civil que limitaban con severidad los derechos de los afroamericanos (pág. 521)

blockade/bloqueo cierre de un puerto para que ni las personas ni las provisiones puedan entrar o salir (pág. 171)

bond/bono certificado que promete el pago de dinero que se ha prestado, más el interés, en una determinada fecha (pág. 280)

Border Ruffians/rufianes de frontera bandas proesclavistas de Missouri

que a menudo cruzaban la frontera con Kansas para combatir contra las fuerzas antiesclavistas de ese estado (pág. 470)

border state/estado de frontera estado esclavista que permaneció en la Unión durante la Guerra Civil (pág. 487)

Boston Massacre/masacre de Boston conflicto de 1770 entre colonos y tropas británicas en el que se dio muerte a cinco colonos (pág. 152)

Boston Tea Party/Fiesta del Té de Boston protesta de 1773 en la que los colonos se vistieron de indios y lanzaron el té de los británicos a la bahía de Boston (pág. 157)

boycott/boicot negarse a comprar ciertos bienes y servicios (pág. 150)

Brown v. Board of Education/Brown versus el Consejo de Educación caso de 1954 que llegó a la Corte Suprema, acabando con la segregación legal en las escuelas públicas (pág. 560)

burgess/burgués representante del gobierno colonial de Virginia (pág. 90)

C

Cabinet/gabinete grupo de funcionarios que dirigen departamentos gubernamentales y aconsejan al presidente (pág. 279)

capital/capital dinero con el que se inicia un negocio (págs. 331, 544)

capitalist/capitalista persona que invierte en un negocio con el fin de obtener beneficios (pág. 331)

caravan/caravana grupo de personas que viajaban juntas por razones de seguridad (pág. 52)

carpetbagger/*carpetbagger* sobrenombre despreciativo dado a los norteños que se mudaron al Sur después de la Guerra Civil (pág. 527)

cartographer/cartógrafo persona que hace mapas (pág. 8)

cash crop/cosecha de contado cosecha vendida por dinero en el mercado (pág. 111)

cash economy/cultivo comercial economía en la cual las personas intercambian dinero por mercancías y servicios (pág. 27)

caucus/reunión encuentro privado, a menudo de carácter político (pág. 364)

causeway/paso elevado camino elevado hecho con tierra comprimida (pág. 38)

cavalry/caballería tropas a caballo (pág. 184)

cede/ceder entregar (págs. 202, 396)

Chapultepec/Chapultepec fuerte en las afueras de Ciudad de México donde ocurrió una batalla entre los Estados Unidos y México durante la Guerra Mexicana en 1847 (pág. 396)

charter/carta legal documento que da ciertos derechos a una persona o compañía (pág. 88)

checks and balances/controlar y equilibrar principio de la Constitución de los Estados Unidos que ofrece protección contra los abusos de poder al dar a cada rama del gobierno la atribución de vigilar las otras (pág. 251)

chronology/cronología secuencia de sucesos o eventos a través del tiempo (pág. 25)

circumnavigate/circunnavegar viajar alrededor de la Tierra (pág. 71)

citizen/ciudadano persona que debe lealtad a una nación particular y se beneficia de la protección y de todos los derechos de dicha nación (pág. 265)

city-state/ciudad estado ciudad grande que tiene su propio gobierno y controla la zona de campo que la rodea (pág. 52)

civic virtue/virtud cívica deseo de trabajar por el bien de una nación o comunidad incluso a costa de grandes sacrificios (pág. 266)

civics/educación cívica estudio de los derechos y responsabilidades de los ciudadanos (pág. 29)

civil/civil se refiere a los juicios sobre derechos privados de los individuos, y no a los juicios criminales (pág. 261)

civil disobedience/desobediencia civil idea de que las personas tienen derecho a desobedecer las leyes que consideren injustas, si su conciencia lo exige (pág. 451)

civil rights movement/movimiento por los derechos civiles esfuerzo organizado de los afroamericanos para obtener derechos igualitarios (pág. 560)

civil service/servicio civil sistema de empleo gubernamental que otorga empleos federales con base en exámenes, en vez de influencia política (pág. 548)

civil war/guerra civil guerra entre personas del mismo país (pág. 465)

Civil War amendments/enmiendas de la Guerra Civil enmiendas número Trece, Catorce y Quince de la Constitución de los Estados Unidos que abolían la esclavitud, garantizaban la ciudadanía a los ex esclavos y daban el derecho al voto a los afroamericanos de sexo masculino (pág. 261)

civilian/civil no militar (pág. 249)

clan/clan grupo de dos o más familias emparentadas (pág. 48)

Clermont/Clermont barco a vapor construido en 1807 por Robert Fulton; fue el primer barco a vapor que obtuvo éxito comercial en aguas de los Estados Unidos (pág. 339)

Spanish Glossary

climate/clima promedio del tiempo de un lugar durante un período de entre 20 y 30 años (pág. 15)

clipper ship/clíper barco de mediados de los años 1800 que navegaba velozmente (pág. 410)

Cold War/Guerra Fría largo período caracterizado por intensa rivalidad entre los Estados Unidos y la Unión Soviética posterior a la Segunda Guerra Mundial (pág. 558)

colony/colonia grupo de personas que se establece en una tierra distante pero sigue bajo la dirección del gobierno de su tierra natal (pág. 70)

Columbian Exchange/intercambio colombino intercambio global de bienes e ideas que resulta del encuentro entre los pueblos de los hemisferios occidental y oriental (pág. 71)

committee of correspondence/ comité de correspondencia campaña que consistió en escribir cartas y se convirtió en un importante instrumento de protesta en la colonia (pág. 153)

Common Sense/Sentido común ensayo de Thomas Paine publicado en 1776 que instaba a las colonias a declarar la independencia (pág. 173)

compromise/compromiso documento en el que cada lado cede en algunas de sus posiciones para poder llegar a un acuerdo (pág. 208)

Compromise of 1850/Compromiso de 1850 acuerdo con respecto a la esclavitud según el cual California se sumó a la Unión como estado libre, y se aprobó una estricta ley sobre esclavos fugitivos (pág. 465)

confederation/confederación liga de estados o naciones independientes (pág. 317)

conquistador/conquistador término que se refiere a los exploradores españoles que ocuparon tierras en América y las declararon propiedad de España (pág. 74)

Conservatives/conservadores durante la Reconstrucción, los blancos del Sur que se resistían al cambio (pág. 527)

constitution/constitución documento que establece las leyes, principios, organización y sistema de un gobierno (pág. 200)

Constitutional Convention/ Convención Constitucional reunión de los representantes de los estados realizada el 25 de mayo de 1787 para revisar los Artículos de la Confederación (pág. 206)

constitutional initiative/iniciativa constitucional proceso para que los ciudadanos puedan pedir enmiendas a la constitución de su estado (pág. 263)

consumer/consumidor el que usa bienes y servicios (pág. 27)

Continental Army/Ejército Continental ejército establecido por el Segundo Congreso Continental para luchar contra los británicos (pág. 169)

continental divide/divisoria continental cadena de montañas que separa sistemas fluviales que corren en direcciones opuestas en un continente (pág. 309)

Copperhead/Copperhead norteño que se oponía el uso de la fuerza para mantener los estados del Sur dentro de la Unión (pág. 501)

corduroy road/camino de troncos camino hecho con troncos de árbol (pág. 339)

corporation/corporación negocio cuyos dueños son los inversionistas (pág. 544)

"cottonocracy"/"algodocracia" sobrenombre de los planteros ricos que hicieron su dinero con el algodón a mediados de los años 1800 (pág. 422)

coureur de bois/coureur de bois colonos franceses que vivían en los bosques y cazaban animales por sus pieles (pág. 83)

creole/criollo persona de padres españoles nacida en las colonias españolas de América (págs. 78, 348)

Crusades/Cruzadas series de guerras en las que los cristianos lucharon por el control de la Tierra Santa entre 1100 y 1300 (pág. 58)

Cuban missile crisis/crisis cubana de los misiles importante confrontación de 1962 entre los Estados Unidos y la Unión Soviética durante la Guerra Fría; los Estados Unidos bloquearon un intento soviético de instalar misiles en Cuba (pág. 560)

culture/cultura forma de vida desarrollada por un pueblo (págs. 22, 40)

culture area/área cultural región en la que las personas comparten una forma de vida similar (pág. 42)

currency/moneda dinero circulante (pág. 202)

D

D-Day/Día D invasión de Europa Occidental el 6 de junio de 1944 en la cual tropas de los Estados Unidos, Inglaterra y otros aliados desembarcaron en la costa de Normandía, Francia, y avanzaron en dirección este hacia Alemania (pág. 557)

dame school/escuela de damas escuela privada dirigida por una mujer, generalmente en su propia casa (pág. 128)

debtor/deudor persona que no puede pagar el dinero que debe (págs. 116, 436)

Declaration of Independence/ Declaración de Independencia documento de 1776 que declaraba que las 13 colonias formaban una nación libre e independiente (pág. 175)

deficit spending/gasto deficitario práctica gubernamental de gastar más dinero del que se recauda por impuestos (pág. 555)

democratic/democrático que asegura que todas las personas tengan los mismos derechos (pág. 302)

Democratic Republican/republicano demócrata partidario de Thomas Jefferson, quien apoyaba un gobierno descrentralizado (pág. 289)

Democrats/demócratas quienes apoyaban a Andrew Jackson, incluyendo granjeros de frontera y trabajadores de fábrica (pág. 364)

depression/depresión período en que la actividad comercial decrece, los precios y los salarios disminuyen, y aumenta el desempleo (págs. 204, 373)

détente/détente política del presidente Nixon continuada por los presidentes Ford y Carter, que procuraba reducir las tensiones entre los superpoderes (pág. 564)

dictator/dictador gobernante que tiene poder y autoridad absolutos (pág. 386)

dictatorship/dictadura gobierno en el cual una persona o pequeño grupo retiene toda la autoridad (pág. 212)

direct democracy/democracia directa forma de gobierno según la cual los ciudadanos comunes tienen el poder de gobernar (pág. 57)

discrimination/discriminación política o actitud que niega derechos igualitarios a ciertos grupos de personas (pág. 417)

domestic tranquility/tranquilidad interna orden y paz interna de una nación, uno de los seis objetivos definidos en el preámbulo de la Constitución de los Estados Unidos (pág. 249)

draft/leva ley que requiere que ciertas personas hagan el servicio militar (pág. 502)

Dred Scott* v. *Sandford*/*Dred Scott* versus *Sandford un caso que llegó a la Corte Suprema en 1857 en el cual un esclavo, Dred Scott, hizo un juicio para obtener su libertad y perdió; este caso puso en duda el poder federal con respecto a la esclavitud en los territorios (pág. 471)

E

economics/economía el estudio de cómo las personas manejan recursos limitados para satisfacer sus deseos y necesidades (pág. 26)

electoral college/colegio electoral grupo de electores de cada estado que cada cuatro años vota para elegir al presidente y vicepresidente de los Estados Unidos (pág. 255)

elevation/elevación altura por encima del nivel del mar (pág. 13)

emancipate/emancipar liberar (pág. 497)

Emancipation Proclamation/ Proclama de Emancipación declaración de 1863 del Presidente Lincoln que liberaba a los esclavos de la Confederación (pág. 497)

embargo/embargo prohibición de comerciar (pág. 314)

Embargo Act/Acta de Embargo ley de 1807 que impuso la prohibición total al comercio exterior (pág. 314)

encomienda/encomienda cesión de tierra otorgada por el gobierno español a los colonos españoles, que incluía el derecho a exigir trabajo o impuestos a los indígenas americanos (pág. 78)

English Bill of Rights/Declaración de Derechos Inglesa documento de 1689 que garantizaba los derechos de los ciudadanos ingleses (págs. 123, 213)

Enlightenment/Ilustración movimiento europeo de los siglos XVII y XVIII que enfatizaba el uso de la razón (pág. 129)

environmentalist/ambientalista persona que trabaja para reducir la polución y proteger el medio ambiente (pág. 566)

Era of Good Feelings/era de los buenos sentimientos los ocho años de la presidencia de James Monroe, desde 1817 a 1825, cuando los Demócratas Republicanos dominaban la política nacional (pág. 343)

Erie Canal/canal de Erie canal artificial construido en 1825 que conectaba el lago Erie con el río Hudson (pág. 340)

erosion/erosión desgaste gradual (pág. 13)

established church/iglesia oficial religión elegida por un estado (pág. 94)

execute/ejecutar llevar a cabo (pág. 201)

executive branch/rama ejecutiva rama del gobierno que hace cumplir las leyes (pág. 208)

expedition/expedición largo viaje de exploración (pág. 308)

export/producto de exportación artículo comercial que se envía a merca- dos extranjeros (pág. 120)

extended family/familia extendida grupo familiar que incluye abuelos, padres, hijos, tías, tíos y primos (págs. 53, 425)

F

faction/facción grupo de oposición dentro de un partido (pág. 287)

factory system/sistema de fábricas método de producción que reunió en un mismo lugar trabajadores y maquinaria (pág. 331)

famine/hambruna severa escasez de alimentos (pág. 415)

Farewell Address/discurso de despedida el último discurso de los presidentes al expirar sus mandatos (pág. 286)

federalism/federalismo principio de la Constitución de los Estados Unidos que establece la división de poderes entre el gobierno federal y los estados (pág. 251)

Federalist/federalista partidario de la Constitución quien estaba a favor de un gobierno federal o nacional fuerte (págs. 215, 289)

The Federalist Papers/Los Ensayos Federalistas series de ensayos escritos por los Federalistas James Madison, Alexander Hamilton y John Jay que apoyaban la ratificación de la Constitución (pág. 216)

feudalism/feudalismo sistema de gobierno en el que los señores o nobles regían sus propias tierras pero debían lealtad y servicio militar a un monarca (pág. 58)

54th Massachusetts Regiment/ regimiento 54° de Massachusetts unidad afroamericana del ejército de la Unión (pág. 499)

Fifteenth Amendment/Enmienda Decimoquinta enmienda a la Constitución de los Estados Unidos aprobada en 1869 que prohíbe a los estados negar a los afroamericanos el derecho al voto por causa de su raza (pág. 524)

First Amendment/Primera Enmienda enmienda a la Constitución de los Estados Unidos que protege las libertades individuales básicas, incluyendo la libertad religiosa, la libertad de expresión y la libertad de prensa (pág. 260)

First Continental Congress/Primer Congreso Continental reunión de delegados de 12 colonias en Filadelfia en 1774 (pág. 158)

first global age/primera era global época a comienzos del siglo XV en la que el comercio y los viajes aumentaron notablemente, conectando partes remotas del mundo (pág. 50)

flatboat/carguero de poco fondo embarcación que se usa para transportar carga pesada en rutas acuáticas de tierra adentro (pág. 337)

foreign policy/política exterior acciones de una nación en relación con otras naciones (pág. 285)

Fort Wagner/fuerte Wagner fuerte de Carolina del Sur objeto de un ataque en 1863 por parte del Regimiento 54° de Massachusetts (pág. 499)

forty-niner/persona del cuarenta y nueve una de los más de 80,000 personas que en 1849 se unieron a la fiebre del oro (pág. 400)

Founding Fathers/padres de la patria James Madison, Thomas Jefferson, y otros líderes que dieron los primeros pasos para la formación de los Estados Unidos (pág. 211)

Fourteenth Amendment/Enmienda Decimocuarta enmienda a la Constitución de los Estados Unidos aprobada en 1968 que otorga la ciudadanía a todas las personas nacidas en los Estados Unidos y les garantiza la protección igualitaria de las leyes (pág. 522)

free enterprise/libre empresa sistema en el cual el gobierno juega un rol limitado en la economía (pág. 28)

free market economy/economía de mercado libre sistema económico en el cual los individuos, en vez del gobierno, deciden qué y cuánto producir y vender (págs. 303, 564)

Free-Soil party/partido del territorio libre partido antiesclavista fundado en 1848 en los Estados Unidos, para mantener la esclavitud fuera de los territorios del oeste que incluía miembros de ambos partidos (pág. 462)

freedmen/libertos hombres y mujeres que habían sido esclavos (pág. 517)

Freedmen's Bureau/Oficina de Libertos agencia del gobierno de los Estados Unidos fundada durante la Reconstrucción para ayudar a los ex esclavos (pág. 517)

French and Indian War/Guerra Franco-Indígena guerra entre Inglaterra y Francia de 1754 a 1763 en la que ambos países tuvieron indios americanos como aliados y que acabó con el poder francés en América del Norte (pág.142)

French Revolution/Revolución Francesa rebelión que tuvo lugar en Francia en 1789 y que acabó con la monarquía (pág. 284)

frigate/fragata barco armado con muchos cañones que navega rápidamente (pág. 292)

fugitive/fugitivo persona que huye (pág. 464)

Fugitive Slave Act/Acta de los Esclavos Fugitivos ley de 1850 que exigía a todos los ciudadanos colaborar en la captura de esclavos fugitivos (pág. 465)

Fundamental Orders of Connecticut/Órdenes Fundamentales de Connecticut plan de gobierno de la Colonia puritana de Connecticut en 1639 que expandía la idea del gobierno representativo en las colonias inglesas (pág. 104)

G

Gadsden Purchase/Compra de Gadsden banda de tierra entre lo que es hoy Arizona y Nuevo México, por la cual los Estados Unidos pagó a México $10 millones en 1853 (pág. 397)

General Court/Corte General asamblea representativa electa de la Colonia de la bahía de Massachusetts (pág. 103)

general welfare/bienestar general bienestar de todos los ciudadanos de una nación, uno de los seis objetivos definidos en el preámbulo de la Constitución de Estados Unidos (pág. 249)

gentry/alta burguesía la clase social más alta en las 13 colonias inglesas (pág. 126)

geography/geografía el estudio de las personas, su medio ambiente y sus recursos (pág. 4)

Gettysburg Address/discurso de Gettysburg discurso pronunciado en 1863 por el Presidente Lincoln después de la Batalla de Gettysburg (pág. 507)

Gibbons v. Ogden/Gibbons versus Ogden caso judicial de 1814 en el que la Corte Suprema confirmó el poder del gobierno federal para regular el comercio (pág. 346)

glacier/glaciar capa gruesa de hielo (pág. 36)

Glorious Revolution/Revolución Gloriosa movimiento de 1688 que llevó a William y a Mary al trono de Inglaterra y reforzó los derechos de los ciudadanos ingleses (pág. 123)

grandfather clause/cláusula del abuelo ley que eximía a un votante de la prueba de alfabetización si su padre o su abuelo había sido elegible para votar el 1º de enero de 1867; la ley protegía el derecho a votar de los blancos pero no el de los negros del Sur (pág. 532)

Great Awakening/Gran Despertar movimiento religioso que tuvo lugar a principios del siglo XVIII en las colonias inglesas (pág. 127)

Great Compromise/Gran Compromiso plan de la Convención Constitucional que resolvió los conflictos entre los estados grandes y los pequeños (pág. 208)

Great Depression/gran depresión el peor período de decadencia económica en la historia de los Estados Unidos; comenzó en 1929 y duró hasta el comienzo de la Segunda Guerra Mundial (pág. 554)

Green Mountain Boys/los muchachos de *Green Mountains* milicia colonial de Vermont liderada por Ethan Allen que llevó a cabo un ataque sorpresa al Fuerte Ticonderoga, obteniendo para los colonos el control de la ruta clave hacia Canadá (pág. 169)

guerilla/guerrillero soldado que usa la táctica de atacar y retirarse (pág. 192)

guerrilla warfare/guerra de guerrillas el uso de tácticas militares basadas en atacar y retirarse rápidamente (pág. 470)

Gullah/*Gullah* combinación del idioma inglés y de lenguas de África Occidental que hablaban los afroamericanos en la colonia de Carolina de Sur (pág. 126)

H

habeas corpus/*habeas corpus* derecho por el cual no puede encarcelarse a ninguna persona por un crimen específico sin haber sido antes condenada (págs. 213, 502)

Hartford Convention/Convención de Hartford reunión de delegados de Nueva Inglaterra durante la guerra de 1812 que amenazó con separarse de la Unión como protesta contra la guerra (pág. 325)

Holocaust/holocausto asesinato de millones de judíos y otras personas por parte del gobierno de la Alemania nazi y sus aliados durante la Segunda Guerra Mundial (pág. 556)

Homestead Act/Acta de Posesión de Tierras ley de 1862 que dio tierras a los colonos para que las convirtieran en granjas (pág. 543)

House of Burgesses/Casa de los Burgueses asamblea de representantes de la Virginia colonial (pág. 90)

House of Representatives/Cámara de Representantes el mayor de los dos cuerpos que forman la rama legislativa del gobierno de los Estados Unidos; la representación se basa en el número de habitantes (pág. 252)

Hudson River School/escuela del río Hudson grupo de artistas de los Estados Unidos que pintaban paisajes del valle del río Hudson en Nueva York, a mediados de los años 1800 (pág. 448)

I

immigrant/inmigrante persona que se establece en otro país (pág. 266)

impeach/juicio político acusar formalmente de faltas serias a un funcionario del gobierno (págs. 257, 523)

imperialism/imperialismo política de los países poderosos para tratar de controlar los asuntos políticos y económicos de países o regiones más débiles (pág. 549)

import/producto de importación artículo comercial que se ha introducido a un país (pág. 120)

impressment/leva práctica de forzar a las personas a que hagan el servicio militar (pág. 313)

inauguration/toma de mando ceremonia en la cual el presidente jura su cargo (pág. 278)

income tax/impuesto a los ingresos un impuesto al dinero que las personas ganan (pág. 502)

incriminate/incriminar presentar evidencias en contra de alguien (pág. 260)

indentured servant/sirviente por contrato persona que aceptaba trabajar sin pago por un período de tiempo a cambio de un pasaje a las colonias (pág. 126)

Indian Removal Act/Acta de Reubicación de los Indios ley aprobada en 1830 que forzaba a muchos americanos nativos a mudarse hacia el oeste del río Mississippi (pág. 372)

indigo/índigo planta usada para hacer una valiosa tintura azul (pág. 115)

individualism/individualismo concepto que destaca la importancia de cada individuo (pág. 451)

Industrial Revolution/Revolución Industrial proceso gradual en el que las máquinas reemplazaron a las herramientas manuales, y el vapor y otras fuentes de energía reemplazaron a las personas y a los animales de carga (pág. 330)

inflation/inflación incremento de los precios y desvalorización del dinero (pág. 503)

infrastructure/infraestructura sistema de caminos, puentes y túneles (pág. 263)

interchangeable parts/partes intercambiables partes o repuestos idénticos para herramientas o instrumentos hechos a máquina (pág. 332)

internal improvements/mejoras internas mejoras hechas a caminos, puentes y canales (pág. 346)

interstate commerce/comercio interestatal comercio entre diferentes estados (pág. 346)

intervention/intervención participación directa (pág. 351)

Intolerable Acts/Actas Intolerables series de leyes aprobadas en 1774 para castigar a Boston por la Fiesta del té (pág. 157)

irrigation/irrigación riego de tierras áridas (pág. 6)

Islam/islam religión monoteísta fundada por el profeta Mahoma a principios del siglo VII (pág. 50)

isolationism/aislamiento política de limitar la ingerencia en los asuntos políticos de naciones extranjeras (pág. 549)

isthmus/istmo estrecha lengua de tierra (pág. 11)

J

Jay's Treaty/Tratado de Jay acuerdo de 1795 entre Gran Bretaña y los Estados Unidos que requería que Gran Bretaña pagara por los daños ocasionados por la captura de barcos estadounidenses, y devolviera los fuertes que aún ocupaba en el Oeste. Por su parte, los Estados Unidos pagaría las deudas contraídas con los comerciantes británicos (pág. 286)

jazz/jazz estilo musical original de los Estados Unidos que une ritmos del África Occidental, harmonías europeas, y canciones laborales y religiosas de los afroamericanos (pág. 554)

Jim Crow laws/leyes de Jim Crow leyes que separaban en los lugares públicos del Sur a las personas de diferentes razas (pág. 532)

judicial branch/rama judicial rama del gobierno que decide si las leyes se practican de manera justa (pág. 208)

judicial review/revisión judicial poder de la Corte Suprema para decidir si los actos de un presidente o las leyes aprobadas por el Congreso son constitucionales (pág. 305)

Judiciary Act/Acta judicial ley de 1789 que creó la estructura de la Corte Suprema y estableció un sistema de cortes de distrito y cortes de circuito a nivel nacional (pág. 279)

jury duty/el deber de ser jurado obligación de todo ciudadano de servir como jurado cuando se le llama (pág. 268)

K

kachina/kachina bailarín enmascarado que participaba en ceremonias religiosas de los indios americanos del Sudoeste (pág. 47)

Kansas-Nebraska Act/Acta de Kansas-Nebraska ley de 1854 que estableció los territorios de Kansas y Nebraska, dando a los colonos el derecho de soberanía popular para decidir con respecto a la esclavitud (pág. 468)

Kentucky and Virginia resolutions/Acuerdos de Kentucky y Virginia declaraciones aprobadas en 1798 y 1799 que reivindicaban para los estados el derecho de decidir si una ley federal era constitucional y de declararla nula dentro de los límites del estado si se decidía que era inconstitucional (pág. 293)

kinship/parentesco compartir antepasados (pág. 53)

"kitchen cabinet"/"gabinete de cocina" grupo de consejeros extra oficiales de Andrew Jackson que se reunía con él en la cocina de la Casa Blanca (pág. 367)

Know-Nothing Party/*Know-Nothing Party* partido político de la década de 1850 que estaba en contra del catolicismo y de la inmigración (pág. 416)

Korean War/Guerra de Corea conflicto que duró entre 1950 y 1953 entre Corea del Norte, apoyada por China, y Corea del Sur, apoyada por fuerzas de las Naciones Unidas que consistían principalmente en tropas de los Estados Unidos (pág. 559)

Ku Klux Klan/Ku Klux Klan sociedad secreta organizada en el Sur después de la Guerra Civil para afirmar la supremacía blanca por medio de la violencia (pág. 527)

L

laissez faire/*laissez faire* idea de que el gobierno debería jugar un rol tan mínimo como fuera posible en los asuntos económicos (pág. 303)

Lancaster Turnpike/carretera de peaje a Lancaster camino de peaje construido en la década de 1790 por una compañía privada, que conectaba Filadelfia con Lancaster, Pennsylvania (pág. 339)

Land Ordinance of 1785/Ordenanza de Tierras de 1785 ley que establecía un sistema para colonizar el Territorio del Noroeste (pág. 203)

latitude/latitud distancia hacia el norte o el sur del ecuador (pág. 4)

lawsuit/demanda caso legal iniciado para dirimir una disputa entre personas o grupos (pág. 471)

League of the Iroquois/Liga de los Iroquois alianza de las cinco naciones de los Iroquois (pág. 48)

legislative branch/rama legislativa rama del gobierno que aprueba las leyes (pág. 208)

legislature/legislatura grupo de personas que tiene el poder de hacer leyes (pág. 122)

libel/libelo acto de publicar afirmaciones que pueden dañar injustamente la reputación de una persona (pág. 130)

The Liberator/The Liberator el periódico antiesclavista más influyente, fundado por William Lloyd Garrison en 1831 (pág. 440)

liberty/libertad derecho de actuar de una manera u otra (pág. 249)

limited government/gobierno limitado principio de la Constitución de los Estados Unidos que establece que el gobierno sólo tiene los poderes que la constitución le otorga (pág. 250)

literacy test/prueba de alfabetización examen para ver si una persona puede leer y escribir; se usaba en el pasado para restringir el derecho al voto (pág. 532)

local government/gobierno local gobierno del condado, distrito de condado, ciudad, pueblo, villa o distrito (pág. 263)

locomotive/locomotora máquina que arrastra un tren (pág. 409)

Lone Star Republic/República de la Estrella Solitaria sobrenombre de Texas después que obtuvo su independencia de México en 1836 (pág. 389)

longitude/longitud distancia hacia el este o el oeste del primer meridiano (pág. 4)

Louisiana Purchase/Compra de Louisiana vasto territorio entre el río Mississippi y las Montañas Rocosas que se le compró a Francia en 1803 (pág. 308)

Lowell girl/chica Lowell mujer joven que trabajaba para Lowell Mills en Massachusetts durante la revolución industrial (pág. 333)

Loyalist/*loyalist* colono que permaneció leal a Gran Bretaña (pág. 170)

lynch/linchar colgar a alguien sin un juicio legal (pág. 401)

M

Magna Carta/Carta Magna documento británico de 1215 cuyas dos ideas básicas sostienen que incluso los monarcas tienen que obedecer la ley y que los ciudadanos tienen derechos básicos (págs. 90, 213)

majority/mayoría más de la mitad (pág. 362)

Manifest Destiny/destino manifiesto creencia que se diseminó en los años 1800 de que los estadounidenses tenían el derecho y la obligación de extenderse a través del continente hasta el Océano Pacífico (pág. 393)

manor/señorío distrito regido por un Señor que incluía su castillo y las tierras que lo rodeaban (pág. 58)

map projection/proyección cartográfica manera de dibujar la Tierra sobre una superficie plana (pág. 8)

Marbury v. Madison/Marbury versus Madison caso judicial de 1803 en el cual la Corte Suprema dictaminó que tenía el poder de decidir si las leyes aprobadas por el Congreso eran constitucionales y de rechazar las leyes que considerara inconstitucionales (pág. 305)

margin buying/comprar a crédito práctica según la cual los inversionistas compran acciones con un pequeño adelanto, y obtienen el resto en préstamo de un corredor de bolsa, con la esperanza de vender con una ganancia cuando suban los precios (pág. 554)

Marshall Plan/Plan Marshall plan de los Estados Unidos para ayudar a las naciones europeas a reconstruir sus economías después de la Segunda Guerra Mundial (pág. 559)

martial law/ley marcial gobierno por parte de los militares en vez de un gobierno electo (pág. 487)

martyr/mártir persona que muere por sus creencias (pág. 476)

Mason-Dixon Line/línea de Mason-Dixon límite entre Pennsylvania y Maryland que dividía las Colonias Centrales de las Colonias del Sur (pág. 113)

Mayflower Compact/acuerdo Mayflower acuerdo de 1620 para gobernar la colonia de Plymouth, firmado por los peregrinos antes de desembarcar en Plymouth (pág. 95)

McCulloch v. Maryland/McCulloch versus Maryland caso judicial de 1819 en el que la Corte Suprema dictaminó que los estados no tenían derecho a interferir en las instituciones federales aunque estuvieran dentro de sus límites (pág. 346)

mercantilism/mercantilismo teoría de que el poder económico de una nación provenía de proteger y aumentar la economía local manteniendo un estricto control sobre el comercio de sus colonias (pág. 120)

mercenary/mercenario soldado que lucha exclusivamente por dinero, a menudo para un país extranjero (pág. 171)

mestizo/mestizo en las colonias españolas de América, la persona que tiene mezcla de antepasados indios y españoles (pág. 78)

Mexican Cession/cesión mexicana territorio mexicano de California y Nuevo México que se entregó a los Estados Unidos en 1848 (pág. 396)

middle class/clase media en las 13 colonias inglesas, la clase social que incluía artesanos cualificados, granjeros y algunos comerciantes (pág. 126)

militia/milicia ejército de ciudadanos que sirven como soldados en una emergencia (pág. 158)

minuteman/miliciano de la Guerra de Independencia voluntario de una milicia colonial que estaba en todo momento preparado para luchar (pág. 159)

mission/misión colonia religiosa administrada por frailes y monjas católicas (pág. 78)

missionary/misionero persona que intenta transmitir ciertas creencias religiosas a un grupo de gente (págs. 56, 84)

Missouri Compromise/compromiso de Missouri acuerdo, propuesto en 1819 por Henry Clay, para mantener igual el número de estados que aceptaban o rechazaban la esclavitud (pág. 460)

Monitor/Monitor buque de guerra blindado de la Unión (pág. 492)

monopoly/monopolio una compañía que controla o domina toda una industria (pág. 544)

Monroe Doctrine/Doctrina Monroe declaración de política exterior del Presidente Monroe que prevenía a las naciones europeas para que no intervinieran en América Latina (pág. 351)

Mormons/mormones miembros de la Iglesia de Jesús Cristo de los Santos de los Últimos Días fundada en 1830 por Joseph Smith (pág. 398)

Mound Builders/constructores de montículos nombre de varias culturas de América del Norte que construyeron grandes montículos de tierra, comenzando hace unos 3,000 años (pág. 41)

mountain man/hombre de montaña cazador que exploraba Oregón a principios de los años 1800 (pág. 381)

muckraker/*muckraker* periodista que escribía sobre la corrupción y otros problemas de los Estados Unidos a fines de los años 1800 y principios de los años 1900 (pág. 547)

mudslinging/detractar uso de insultos para atacar la reputación de un oponente (pág. 374)

N

national debt/deuda nacional cantidad total de dinero que un gobierno debe a otros (pág. 280)

National Road/Caminos Nacionales primer proyecto nacional de caminos financiado federalmente, que se inició en 1811 (pág. 339)

nationalism/nacionalismo devoción hacia el propio país (pág. 318)

nativist/nativista persona que quería limitar la inmigración y reservar los Estados Unidos para los ciudadanos nativos blancos (pág. 416)

natural resources/recursos naturales materiales que los seres humanos pueden tomar del medio ambiente para sobrevivir y satisfacer sus necesidades (pág. 5)

natural rights/derechos naturales derechos que corresponden a todas las personas desde su nacimiento (pág. 175)

naturalize/naturalizarse completar el proceso oficial de convertirse en ciudadano (pág. 265)

Nauvoo/Nauvoo comunidad mormona formada en la década de 1840 en los bancos del río Mississippi en Illinois (pág. 398)

Navigation Acts/Actas de Navegación series de leyes aprobadas por el parlamento inglés a finales del siglo XVII que regulaban el comercio entre Inglaterra y sus colonias (pág. 121)

Negro Fort/Fuerte de los Negros asentamiento de esclavos afroamericanos fugitivos en la colonia española de Florida (pág. 350)

neutral/neutral que no toma partido en un conflicto (pág. 285)

Neutrality Proclamation/Declaración de neutralidad declaración de 1793 hecha por el presidente Washington que estipulaba que los Estados Unidos no apoyarían ni ayudarían a Francia ni a Gran Bretaña en su conflicto europeo (pág. 285)

New Deal/Nuevo Acuerdo programa del Presidente Franklin D. Roosevelt para acabar con la Gran Depresión (pág. 554)

New Jersey Plan/Plan de Nueva Jersey plan de la Convención Constitucional apoyado por los estados pequeños que requería tres ramas del gobierno con una legislatura de cámara única (pág. 208)

New Mexico Territory/territorio de Nuevo México extensa región del suroeste que pertenecía a México en los años 1800 (pág. 391)

"New South"/"Nuevo Sur" término de fines de los años 1800 que describía el Sur en un momento en que se esforzaba por expandir la economía a través de la industria (pág. 533)

Nineteenth Amendment/Enmienda Decimonovena enmienda de 1920 a la Constitución de los Estados Unidos que garantiza el derecho de votar a la mujer (págs. 261, 548)

nominating convention/convención de postulaciones reunión en la cual un partido político elige sus candidatos (pág. 364)

Nonintercourse Act/Acta de No Intercambio ley de 1809 que permitía a los estadounidenses comerciar con todas las naciones excepto Francia y Gran Bretaña (pág. 314)

North American Free Trade Agreement (NAFTA)/Tratado de Libre Comercio de América del Norte (TLC) tratado entre los Estados Unidos, Canadá y México para reducir gradualmente las tasas y otras barreras al comercio (pág. 566)

Northwest Ordinance/Ordenanza del Noroeste artículo de 1787 que establecía un gobierno para el Territorio del Noroeste, garantizaba derechos básicos a los colonos y declaraba que la esclavitud era allí ilegal (pág. 203)

northwest passage/pasaje noroeste pasaje de agua a través o alrededor de América del Norte (pág. 81)

nullification/anulación idea de que un estado tiene el derecho de anular o cancelar una ley federal que los líderes del estado consideran inconstitucional (pág. 371)

Nullification Act/Acta de Anulación acta aprobada por Carolina del Sur que declaraba ilegal la tasa de 1832 (pág. 371)

nullify/anular declarar nulo (pág. 293)

O

Olive Branch Petition/Petición de la Rama de Olivo petición de paz enviada al rey George por los delegados coloniales después de las batallas de Lexington y Concord, declarando su lealtad a la corona y pidiéndole que cancelara las Actas Intolerables (pág. 168)

Oregon Country/condado de Oregón término usado a principios de 1800 para designar a la extensa región situada al oeste de las Montañas Rocosas, incluyendo lo que es hoy Oregón, Washington, Idaho y partes de Wyoming, Montana y Canadá (pág. 380)

Oregon Trail/camino de Oregón ruta que llevaba a Oregón, usada por los trenes de carga en los años 1800 (pág. 383)

override/invalidar no admitir, como cuando el Congreso decide no admitir el veto presidencial (pág. 257)

P

Parliament/Parlamento en Inglaterra, asamblea representativa (pág. 90)

Patriot/patriota colono que estaba a favor de la guerra contra Gran Bretaña (pág. 169)

patriotism/patriotismo sentimiento de amor y devoción hacia el propio país (pág. 266)

patroon/patrón dueño de una gran propiedad en una colonia holandesa (pág. 109)

peninsulare/peninsular término que se refiere a un español que tenía una posición de poder en una colonia española (pág. 78)

Pennsylvania Dutch/holandeses de Pennsylvania protestantes de habla germana que se establecieron en Pennsylvania (pág. 110)

persecution/persecución maltrato o castigo a un grupo de personas a causa de sus creencias (pág. 94)

Persian Gulf War/Guerra del Golfo Persa guerra librada en 1991 entre Iraq y una alianza de países dirigida por los Estados Unidos para liberar Kuwait, un territorio rico en petróleo, de las fuerzas de ocupación iraquíes (pág. 564)

petition/petición solicitud formal firmada por un grupo de personas dirigida a alguien de mayor autoridad (pág. 149)

Pickett's Charge/Carga de Pickett ataque de la Confederación como parte de la Batalla de Gettysburg que fracasó (pág. 506)

Pilgrims/peregrinos colonos ingleses que, en el siglo XVII, procuraron libertad religiosa en las Américas (pág. 93)

Pinckney Treaty/Tratado de Pinckney acuerdo de 1795 con España que permitió a los Estados Unidos transportar sus mercancías por el río Mississippi y almacenarlas en Nueva Orleáns (pág. 306)

pit house/casa subterránea casa de la región Ártica cavada en la tierra y cubierta con madera y pieles (pág. 43)

Plains of Abraham/Planicies de Abraham campo cerca de Quebec donde en la Guerra Franco-Indígena tuvo lugar una importante victoria de los británicos frente a los franceses (pág. 144)

plantation/plantación gran propiedad cultivada por muchos trabajadores (pág. 80)

Plessy v. Ferguson/Plessy versus Ferguson un caso legal de 1896 en el cual la Corte Suprema dictaminó que la segregación en las instalaciones públicas era legal si las instalaciones eran iguales (pág. 532)

political science/ciencias políticas el estudio del gobierno (pág. 29)

poll tax/impuesto al voto impuesto que se requería antes de que las personas pudieran votar (pág. 532)

Pontiac's War/guerra de Pontiac conflicto de 1763 entre los indígenas americanos y los británicos sobre la colonización de tierras indias en el área de los Grandes Lagos (pág. 147)

popular sovereignty/soberanía popular principio de la Constitución de los Estados Unidos que establece que el pueblo tiene el derecho de crear, alterar o abolir su gobierno; a mediados de los años 1800, el término se refería a la idea de que cada territorio podía decidir por sí mismo si permitir o no la esclavitud (págs. 250, 462)

potlatch/*potlatch* cena ceremonial realizada por algunos americanos nativos de la costa noroeste para mostrar su riqueza (pág. 44)

preamble/preámbulo introducción a una declaración, constitución u otro documento oficial (págs. 175, 248)

precedent/precedente acta o decisión que sirve de ejemplo a las que siguen (págs. 96, 278)

precipitation/precipitación agua que cae en forma de lluvia, cellisca, granizo o nieve (pág. 15)

predestination/predestinación idea protestante según la cual Dios decidía de antemano quiénes, después de muertos, se salvarían (pág. 435)

presidio/presidio fuerte de las colonias españolas donde vivían los soldados (pág. 77)

primary source/fuente original información directa acerca de personas o eventos (pág. 20)

Proclamation of 1763/Proclama de 1763 ley que prohibía a los colonos ingleses establecerse al oeste de las montañas Apalaches (pág. 147)

profiteer/aprovechador persona que aprovecha una crisis para hacer dinero (pág. 503)

Progressives/progresistas reformadores que querían mejorar la vida en los Estados Unidos a fines de los años 1800 y principios de los años 1900 (pág. 547)

proprietary colony/colonia de propietarios colonia inglesa en la cual el rey daba tierras a propietarios a cambio de un pago anual (pág. 109)

Protestant Reformation/reforma protestante movimiento ocurrido en el siglo XVI para reformar la iglesia católica romana y que llevó a la creación de muchas iglesias cristianas diferentes (pág. 83)

psychology/sicología el estudio del modo de pensar y comportarse de los seres humanos (pág. 30)

public school/escuela pública escuela financiada por los impuestos (pág. 128)

pueblo/pueblo ciudad de las colonias españolas; aldea de los anasazi (págs. 41, 77)

Puritans/puritanos grupo de protestantes ingleses que se establecieron en la Colonia de la bahía de Massachusetts (pág. 102)

Q

Quakers/cuáqueros reformistas protestantes que creen en la igualdad de todas las personas (pág. 110)

Quebec Act/Acta de Quebec ley que establecía un gobierno para Canadá y protegía los derechos de los católicos franceses (pág. 158)

quipu/quipu artefacto hecho de cuerda o tiras con nudos que representaban cantidades, usado por los incas para sus registros y contabilidad (pág. 40)

Quran/Corán libro sagrado del islam (pág. 51)

R

racism/racismo creencia en la superioridad de una raza con respecto a otra (pág. 119)

radical/radical persona que quiere realizar cambios drásticos en la sociedad (pág. 173)

Radical Reconstruction/reconstrucción radical período que comenzó en 1867 cuando los Republicanos, que tenían el control de ambas cámaras, se hicieron cargo de la Reconstrucción (pág. 523)

Radical Republican/republicano radical en la época de la Reconstrucción, miembro del Congreso que quería quebrar el poder de los plantadores ricos del Sur y asegurarse de que los libertos recibieran el derecho a votar (pág. 522)

ratify/ratificar aprobar (pág. 194)

Reaganomics/reaganomics política económica del presidente Reagan que redujo los impuestos, limitó los gastos en programas sociales, y eliminó muchas reglas que se aplicaban a los negocios (pág. 563)

Reconstruction/reconstrucción reconstrucción del Sur después de la Guerra Civil (pág. 517)

Reconstruction Act/Acta de la Reconstrucción ley de 1867 que anuló los gobiernos de los estados del Sur que se habían negado a ratificar la Enmienda Decimocuarta y requirió que los ex-estados Confederados permitieran votar a los afroamericanos (pág. 523)

refuge/refugio lugar donde se está libre de persecuciones (pág. 399)

religious tolerance/tolerancia religiosa deseo de permitir que otros practiquen sus propias creencias (pág. 104)

Renaissance/Renacimiento explosión europea de aprendizaje que tuvo lugar desde finales del siglo XIV hasta el siglo XVI (pág. 59)

rendezvous/rendezvous palabra francesa que significa reunión; encuentro anual en el cual los hombres de montaña intercambiaban pieles (pág. 382)

repeal/revocar cancelar (pág. 150)

representative government/gobierno representativo sistema político según el cual los votantes eligen a los representantes que dictarán las leyes (pág. 90)

republic/república sistema de gobierno en el cual los ciudadanos eligen representantes para que los gobiernen (págs. 57, 211)

Republic of Great Colombia/República de la Gran Colombia estado independiente compuesto por lo que hoy son Venezuela, Colombia, Ecuador y Panamá; se fundó después de obtener la independencia de España en 1819 (pág. 349)

Republican party/partido republicano partido político establecido en 1854 en los Estados Unidos, con el fin de mantener la esclavitud fuera de los territorios del oeste (pág. 473)

resident alien/extranjero residente persona que vive en el país sin ser ciudadano (pág. 266)

revival/reunión evangelista gran encuentro religioso al aire libre (pág. 435)

Roosevelt Corollary/corolario de Roosevelt política establecida por el presidente Theodore Roosevelt que extendía la Doctrina Monroe afirmando que los Estados Unidos tenían el derecho a intervenir en los asuntos Latinoamericanos (pág. 550)

royal colony/colonia real colonia bajo el control directo de la corona inglesa (pág. 109)

rugged individualist/individualista recalcitrante persona que sigue en la vida su propio camino independiente (pág. 381)

S

Sabbath/sabbat día de descanso religioso (pág. 106)

sachem/sachem miembro del consejo tribal de jefes de la liga de los iroquois (pág. 48)

salvation/salvación vida eterna (pág. 56)

Santa Fe Trail/camino de Santa Fe ruta a Santa Fe, Nuevo México, que usaban los comerciantes en los años 1800 (pág. 392)

savanna/sabana región de pastos (pág. 52)

scalawag/scalawag blanco sureño que apoyaba a los Republicanos durante la Reconstrucción (pág. 526)

secede/separarse retirarse como miembro de un grupo (pág. 463)

Second Amendment/Segunda Enmienda enmienda a la Constitución de los Estados Unidos que se refiere al derecho a tener armas (pág. 260)

Second Great Awakening/Segundo Gran Despertar extenso movimiento religioso en los Estados Unidos a principios de los años 1800 (pág. 435)

secondary source/fuente secundaria relato de los hechos proporcionado por personas que no participaron directamente o presenciaron los hechos ocurridos (pág. 21)

sectionalism/seccionalismo lealtad a un estado o sección antes que a todo el país (pág. 345)

sedition/sedición rebelión en contra de un gobierno (pág. 293)

segregation/segregación separación legal de las razas (pág. 532)

self-sufficient/autosuficiente capaz de producir lo suficiente para satisfacer las necesidades propias (pág. 392)

Seminole War/guerra de los Seminoles conflicto que se inició en Florida entre los indios seminoles y el ejército de los Estados Unidos cuando los indios se resistieron a mudarse (pág. 373)

Senate/Senado el menor de los dos cuerpos que constituyen la rama legislativa del gobierno de los Estados Unidos; basada en la representación igualitaria de dos senadores por cada estado (pág. 253)

Seneca Falls Convention/convención de Seneca Falls un encuentro de 1848 en el cual líderes del movimiento por los derechos femeninos reclamaron derechos igualitarios para la mujer (pág. 445)

separation of powers/separación de poderes principio según el cual los poderes del gobierno se dividen en ramas separadas (pág. 214)

sharecropper/aparcero persona que alquila un terreno de otra persona y lo trabaja a cambio de parte de la cosecha (pág. 529)

Shays' Rebellion/rebelión de Shays revuelta de Massachussetts liderada por granjeros en 1786 en reacción a los altos impuestos (pág. 204)

siege/sitio cerco por parte del ejército de una ciudad o posición enemiga, seguido de bloqueo o bombardeo para obligarla a que se rinda (págs. 193, 387, 506)

Silk Road/Ruta de la Seda rutas terrestres que conectaban China con el Medio Oriente (pág. 52)

slave codes/códigos de la esclavitud leyes que controlaban la vida de los esclavos afroamericanos y les negaban los derechos básicos (págs. 119, 424)

smuggling/contrabando importar o exportar mercancías violando las leyes de comercio (pág. 314)

social reform/reforma social intento organizado de mejorar lo que es injusto o imperfecto en la sociedad (pág. 434)

social sciences/ciencias sociales estudios que se refieren a la sociedad y a la conducta social (pág. 29)

Social Security/seguridad social programa federal iniciado en la década de 1930 para proveeer ayuda a las personas mayores o sin empleo; el programa se expandió más adelante (pág. 554)

sociology/sociología estudio del comportamiento de las personas en grupos (pág. 30)

Spanish-American War/Guerra entre España y los Estados Unidos guerra de 1898 entre ambas naciones a causa del expansionismo de los Estados Unidos; permitió que los Estados Unidos obtuviera el control de Cuba, Puerto Rico, Guam y las Filipinas (pág. 550)

speculator/especulador alguien que invierte dinero en un negocio arriesgado con la esperanza de obtener grandes ganancias (pág. 280)

spinning jenny/hiladora de varios husos máquina inventada en 1764 que podía hilar varios hilos al mismo tiempo (pág. 331)

spoils system/sistema de sinecuras práctica que recompensaba a los partidarios de un gobierno otorgándoles empleos en dicho gobierno (pág. 366)

Stamp Act/Acta de los Sellos ley de 1765 que imponía nuevas obligaciones a los documentos legales y gravaba con impuestos los periódicos, almanaques, las cartas de jugar y los dados (pág. 149)

states' rights/derechos de los estados el derecho de los estados a limitar el poder del gobierno federal (págs. 293, 370)

strike/huelga acción, por parte de los trabajadores, de negarse a hacer su trabajo hasta que se acepten sus condiciones (pág. 414)

suffrage/sufragio derecho a votar (pág. 361)

Supreme Court/Corte Suprema corte de máxima autoridad de los Estados Unidos, establecida por la Constitución (pág. 256)

surplus/superávit excedente (pág. 37)

Sutter's Mill/*Sutter's Mill* lugar donde se descubrió oro en 1848, lo cual inició la fiebre del oro (pág. 400)

Swahili/swahili idioma que mezcla palabras árabes con las lenguas africanas locales, hablado en gran parte de África Oriental (pág. 52)

T

tariff/tasa de importación impuesto que afecta a bienes extranjeros que se importan a un país (pág. 281)

Tariff of Abomination/Tasa de Abominaciones tasa aprobada por el Congreso en 1828 que favorecía a la industria del Norte pero perjudicaba a los granjeros del Sur (pág. 370)

Tea Act/Acta del Té ley de 1773 que permitía a la Compañía Británica de las Indias Orientales prescindir de los comerciantes de té y vender sus productos directamente a los colonos (pág. 156)

Tejano/tejano persona nacida en Texas de origen mexicano (pág. 386)

telegraph/telégrafo mecanismo para comunicarse que envía señales eléctricas por un cable (pág. 409)

temperance movement/movimiento por la temperancia campaña en contra del consumo de alcohol (pág. 436)

Ten Percent Plan/Plan del Diez Por Ciento plan del presidente Lincoln para la Reconstrucción que permitía que un estado del Sur formara un nuevo gobierno después de que el 10 por ciento de sus votantes juraran lealtad a los Estados Unidos (pág. 517)

terrace/terraza amplio escalón de tierra que se cava en la ladera de una colina (pág. 40)

terrorism/terrorismo uso deliberado de violencia indiscriminada, especialmente contra civiles, para conseguir objetivos políticos

Thanksgiving/Día de Acción de Gracias día al final de la temporada de cosecha que los peregrinos reservaban para dar gracias a Dios (pág. 97)

thematic map/mapa temático mapa que trata de un tema específico, como población, recursos naturales o elecciones (pág. 9)

Thirteenth Amendment/Enmienda Decimotercera enmienda de 1865 a la Constitución de los Estados Unidos que prohíbe la esclavitud en toda la nación (pág. 519)

Three-Fifths Compromise/Compromiso de los Tres Quintos acuerdo al cual se llegó en la Convención Constitutional, según el cual las tres quintas partes de los esclavos de cada estado se contarían como parte de la población (pág. 209)

total war/guerra total guerra absoluta que afecta tanto a los civiles en sus casas como a los soldados en combate (pág. 508)

totalitarian state/estado totalitario país en el cual un solo partido controla el gobierno y todos los aspectos de la vida del pueblo (pág. 556)

town meeting/cabildo abierto reunión en Nueva Inglaterra durante la colonia donde los colonos discutían y votaban (pág. 107)

Townshend Acts/Actas de Townshend leyes aprobadas en 1767 que gravaban con impuestos bienes como vidrio, papel, pintura, plomo y té (pág. 150)

trade union/gremio asociación de trabajadores de un mismo oficio que se formaba para acceder a una paga mayor y a mejores condiciones de trabajo (pág. 414)

Trail of Tears/Ruta de Lágrimas viaje forzado de los indios cheroquíes desde Georgia hasta la región al oeste del Mississippi en el cual muchos indios murieron (pág. 372)

traitor/traidor persona que traiciona a su país (pág. 175)

transcendentalist/trascendentalista miembro del pequeño e influyente grupo de escritores de Nueva Inglaterra que creían que las verdades más importantes de la vida trascendían, o estaban más allá, de la razón humana (pág. 450)

transcontinental railroad/ferrocarril transcontinental ferrocarril que cruza un continente (pág. 543)

treason/traición acciones contra el propio país (pág. 476)

Treaty of Ghent/Tratado de Gante tratado de paz firmado por Gran Bretaña y los Estados Unidos a fines de la guerra de 1812 (pág. 325)

Treaty of Greenville/Tratado de Greenville tratado firmado por algunos indígenas americanos en 1795, por el cual entregaron tierra que más tarde formaría parte de Ohio a cambio de $20,000 y la promesa de más dinero si mantenían la paz (pág. 317)

Treaty of Guadalupe-Hidalgo/ Tratado de Guadalupe-Hidalgo tratado de 1848 por el cual México entregó California y Nuevo México a los Estados Unidos a cambio de $15 millones (pág. 396)

Treaty of Paris/Tratado de París acuerdo de 1763 entre Francia y Gran Bretaña que puso fin a la Guerra Franco-Indígena, y marcó el fin del poder de Francia en América del Norte (pág. 145); tratado de paz entre los Estados Unidos y Gran Bretaña ratificado en 1783, que reconoció a los Estados Unidos como una nación independiente (pág. 194)

triangular trade/comercio triangular ruta de comercio colonial entre Nueva Inglaterra, las Indias Occidentales y África (pág. 121)

tribe/tribu comunidad de personas que comparten costumbres, lenguaje y rituales (pág. 42)

tributary/tributario arroyo o río pequeño que desemboca en un río mayor (pág. 15)

tribute/tributo contribución de dinero (pág. 313)

turning point/momento decisivo momento histórico que indica un cambio fundamental (pág. 70)

turnpike/camino de peaje camino construido por una compañía privada que cobra un peaje por su uso (pág. 339)

tutor/tutor maestro privado (pág. 128)

Twenty-sixth Amendment/ Enmienda Vigesimosexta enmienda a la Constitución de los Estados Unidos que redujo de 21 a 18 años la edad mínima requerida para votar (pág. 261)

U

Uncle Tom's Cabin/La Cabaña del Tío Tom novela de Harriet Beecher Stowe escrita en 1852 que mostraba los horrores de la esclavitud y la injusticia del Acta de Esclavos Fugitivos (pág. 466)

unconstitutional/inconstitucional que no está permitido por la Constitución (págs. 257, 288)

Underground Railroad/Ruta Clandestina grupo de abolicionistas negros y blancos que trabajaban en secreto para ayudar a los esclavos a huir hacia la libertad en el norte de los Estados Unidos o Canadá (pág. 441)

United Provinces of Central America/Provincias Unidas de América Central federación que comprendía las actuales Guatemala, El Salvador, Honduras, Nicaragua y Costa Rica; fundada después de obtener la independencia de España en 1823 (pág. 349)

urbanization/urbanización proceso por el cual la población pasa de las granjas a las ciudades (págs. 335, 546)

V

Valley Forge/Valley Forge lugar de Pennsylvania donde estaba el campamento del Ejército Continental comandado por Washington durante el invierno de 1777 y 1778 (pág. 185)

vaquero/vaquero peón indio o mexicano que se ocupaba del ganado (pág. 392)

veto/veto rechazar, como cuando el presidente rechaza una ley que ha sido aprobada por el Congreso (pág. 257)

Vietnam War/Guerra de Vietnam conflicto militar entre las fuerzas comunistas de Vietnam del Norte, apoyadas por China y la Unión Soviética, y las fuerzas no comunistas de Vietnam del Sur, apoyadas por los Estados Unidos; los Estados Unidos participó en el conflicto entre 1961 y 1973 (pág. 561)

vigilante/vigilante alguien que se designa a sí mismo para hacer cumplir la ley (pág. 401)

Virginia/Virginia buque de guerra blindado que usaron los Confederados para quebrar el bloqueo de la Unión (pág. 492)

Virginia Plan/Plan de Virginia plan de la Convención Constitucional apoyado por los estados más grandes que recomendaba un gobierno nacional fuerte con tres ramas y una legislatura de dos cámaras (pág. 208)

W

Wade-Davis Bill/Proyecto de Wade-Davis plan de 1864 para la Reconstrucción, que requería que una mayoría de los hombres blancos de cada estado del Sur jurara lealtad a la Unión, y negaba el derecho al voto o el acceso a la función pública a quienes se habían ofrecido a luchar por la Confederación (pág. 517)

War Hawks/halcones de guerra miembros del Congreso que representaban al Oeste y al Sur y que instaban a la guerra contra Gran Bretaña antes de la guerra de 1812 (pág. 318)

Watergate affair/escándalo de Watergate serie de escándalos en los cuales estaba involucrada la administración del presidente Richard Nixon, incluyendo el robo a las oficinas centrales demócratas, situadas en el edificio Watergate en Washington, D.C., en 1972; llevó a la renuncia de Nixon en 1974 (pág. 563)

weather/tiempo condición de la atmósfera terrestre en un lugar y momento determinado (pág. 15)

Whigs/Whigs miembros del viejo Partido Republicano Nacional, liderado por John Quincy Adams, que incluía muchas personas de negocios, plantadores sureños y ex-federalistas (pág. 363)

Whiskey Rebellion/rebelión del whisky protesta de 1794 con respecto a un impuesto aplicado a todas las bebidas alcohólicas producidas y vendidas en los Estados Unidos (pág. 282)

Wilmot Proviso/cláusula de Wilmot ley aprobada en 1846 que proscribía la esclavitud en todos los territorios ganados a México por los Estados Unidos (pág. 461)

women's rights movement/ movimiento de los derechos de la mujer campaña organizada para obtener el derecho a la propiedad, la educación, y otros derechos para la mujer (pág. 446)

World War I/Primera Guerra Mundial guerra librada entre 1914 y 1918 en la cual Gran Bretaña, Francia, Rusia, Bélgica, Italia, Japón, los Estados Unidos y otros aliados vencieron a Alemania, el imperio Austrio-Húngaro, el imperio Otomano y Bulgaria (pág. 550)

World War II/Segunda Guerra Mundial guerra librada entre 1939 y 1945 en la cual Inglaterra, Francia, la Unión Soviética, los Estados Unidos y otros aliados derrotaron a Alemania, Italia, Japón y otros aliados (pág. 556)

writ of assistance/mandato de asistencia documento legal que permitía a los funcionarios de la aduana inglesa realizar la inspección de la carga de un barco sin tener que alegar razón alguna (pág. 150)

X

XYZ Affair/Affair XYZ intento francés de 1797 de sobornar a los Estados Unidos exigiendo pagos antes de que comenzaran las conversaciones sobre la captura por parte de los franceses de barcos estadounidenses neutrales (pág. 292)

Y

Yankee/yanki sobrenombre de los comerciantes de Nueva Inglaterra que dominaban el comercio colonial (pág. 121)

Index

Page numbers that are italicized refer to illustrations or quotations. An *m, p, c, g,* or *go* after a page number refers to a map *(m)*, picture *(p)*, chart *(c)*, graph *(g)*, or graphic organizer *(go)* on that page. A *q* refers to a quote within the text. A *ps* refers to a primary source feature.

Index

Index

Index

Index

Index

Index

Index

Index

Credits

Staff Credits

The people who made up *The American Nation* team—representing design services, editorial, editorial services, electronic publishing technology, manufacturing and inventory planning, market research, marketing services, online services and multimedia development, planning and budgeting, product planning, production services, project office, publishing processes, and rights and permissions—are listed below. Bold type denotes the core team members.

Ernest Albanese, Robert Aleman, Diane Alimena, **Margaret Antonini**, Rachel Avenia-Prol, Penelope Baker, Renée Beach, Rhett Conklin, **Lisa DelGatto**, Marlies Dwyer, Libby Forsyth, Doreen Galbraith, Catalina Gavilanes, **Nancy Gilbert**, Evan Holstrom, **John Kingston**, Vicki Lamb, Mary Sue Langan, Carol Lavis, **Marian Manners**, Vickie Menanteaux, Carrie O'Connor, James O'Neill, **Robert Prol, Maureen Raymond**, Bruce Rolff, Gerry Schrenk, Mildred Schulte, Melissa Shustyk, Annette Simmons, Robin Sullivan, Frank Tangredi.

Additional Credits

Greg Abrom, Susan Andariese, Rui Camarinha, John A. Carle, Orquidea Cepin, Lisa Ferrari, Jacki Hasko, Beth Hyslip, Raegan Keida, Elizabeth Kiszonas, Steve Lewin, Kathleen Mercandetti, Art Mkrtchyan, Kenneth Myett, Xavier W. Niz, Andrew Roney, Robert Siek, Jeff Zoda.

Text Credits

Grateful acknowledgment is made to the following for copyrighted material

The Mother of Nations Excerpt from *The Mother of Nations* by Joseph Bruchac. Copyright © 1989 by Joseph Bruchac. Published by The Crossing Press, 1989. Reprinted by permission.

I Have A Dream "I Have A Dream" by Dr. Martin Luther King, Jr. Copyright © 1963 by Martin Luther King, Jr. Copyright renewed 1991 by Coretta Scott King. Reprinted by arrangement with The Heirs to the Estate of Martin Luther King, Jr., c/o Writer's House, Inc. as agent for the proprietor.

Note: Every effort has been made to locate the copyright owner of material used in this textbook. Omissions brought to our attention will be corrected in subsequent editions.

Map and Art Credits

Maps: Mapping Specialists Limited; **Art: 18–19** John Edwards & Associates; **Charts and Graphs:** Kathleen Mercandetti.

Photo Credits

Photo Research: Omni-Photo Communications, Inc.

Cover and Title Page: Richard Walker/Pearson Education/PH School. Drum: Collections of the Fort Ticonderoga Museum; **ii** *m.* Collections of the Fort Ticonderoga Museum; *t.* Richard Walker/Pearson Education/PH School; **iv** Richard Walker/Pearson Education/PH School; **vi** *t.* North American kachina doll, Hopi tribe. Horniman Museum. ©Michael Holford; *b.* The Granger Collection, New York; **vii** *t.* Christy, Howard Chandler, *Scene at the Signing of the Constitution,* April 1940. Architect of the Capitol; *b.* Courtesy of The Bostonian Society, Old State House; **viii** *t.* ©Copyright 2003 PhotoDisc, Inc.; *b.* George Washington Banner: watercolor, graphite and pen ink on paper. .733 x .534 m. (28¾ in. x 21¹⁄₁₆ in.). Index of American Design, ©1993 National Gallery of Art. Photograph ©Board of Trustees, National Gallery of Art, Washington DC; **ix** *t.* National Museum of American History, Department of Social History, Political History Collection, Smithsonian Institution; *b.* ©1993 North Wind Picture Archives; **x** *t. Attack at Battery Wagner* © 1993 Tom Lovell © 1993 The Greenwich Workshop, Inc. Courtesy of The Greenwich Workshop, Inc., Shelton CT; **xi** *b.* The Granger Collection, New York; **xx** ©Copyright 2003 PhotoDisc, Inc. **xxiv** Michael Newman/PhotoEdit; **xxvii** Walter Hodges/Getty Images, Inc. **xl–1** Leigh, William Robinson. *Grand Canyon,* 1911. Oil on canvas, 66" x 99". Collection of The Newark Museum, Gift of Henry Washington Wack, 1930. Inv.: 30.203. The Newark Museum, Newark, New Jersey, USA. Art Resource, NY; **2** *l.* Jacques Le Moyne, *Chief Athore and Rene de Laudonniere.* Gouache and metallic pigments on vellum, with traces of black chalk outlines, 27 June 1564. Print Collection, Miriam and Ira D. Wallach Division of Art, Prints and Photographs, The New York Public Library, Astor, Lenox and Tilden Foundations; *r.* ©Hulton Getty/Archive Photos; **3** *l.* The Granger Collection, New York; *r.* Stone; **4** ©Bettmann/CORBIS; **6** ©H. De Lespinasse/The Image Bank; **11** ©1988 Addison Geary/Stock Boston; **13** ©UPI-Bettmann/CORBIS; **14** *t.* ©Adam Jones/Photo Researchers, Inc.; *m.* ©Ansel Adams Publishing Rights Trust/CORBIS; **20** Courtesy of Simon & Schuster; **21** ©Punch-Bill Tidy/Rothco; **23** *m.l.* Courtesy of the Massachusetts Historical Commission, Office of the Secretary of the Commonwealth, City Square Archaeological District, Boston; *m.r.* Courtesy of the Massachusetts Historical Commission, Office of the Secretary of the Commonwealth, American Glass Company site, South Boston; *b.* ©Cary Wolinsky/Stock Boston; **26** Stone; **27** *t.r.* ©2000 The Stock Market/Roger Ball; *t.* ©1997 The Stock Market/Bill Stormont; **28** Denise DeLuise/First Image West, Inc.; **31** *t.l.* ©Roman Soumar/CORBIS; Junior Achievement; *t.l.* Hulton Getty/Liaison Agency, Inc.; *t.r.* From the Walker Collection of A'Lelia Bundles; *t.r.* From the Walker Collection of A'Lelia Bundles; **34** The Granger Collection, New York; **35** *l.* © Dorling Kindersley. Courtesy of St. Bride Printing; *r.* Diego Rivera, *The Great City of Tenochtitlan,* 1945. Detail of mural, 4.92 x 9.71 m. Patio Corridor, National Palace, Mexico City, D.F., Mexico. Schalkwijk/Art Resource, NY; **36** ©Lowell Georgia/CORBIS; **40** ©North Wind Picture Archives; **41** ©Craig Aurness/CORBIS; **42** ©Denver Art Museum. Accession #1968.330A; **43** *t.r.* ©British Museum; *t.r.* ©British Museum; **45** *t.l.* Inuit polar bears, 14th–15th century. University of British Columbia/The Bridgeman Art Library, London/New York; *t.l.* Two Basket Hats .7464: Twined: hazel shoots, willow root, conifer root, bear grass, maidenhair, fern stems/ .7515: Twined: conifer root and bear grass wefts. The Brooklyn Museum 05.588.7464 + 05.588.7515 Museum Expedition 1905, Museum Collection Fund. ©Justin Kerr/The Brooklyn Museum; *t.l.* North American kachina doll, Hopi tribe. Horniman Museum. ©Michael Holford; *t.l.* The University Museum, University of Pennsylvania (Neg. T4-303); *t.r.* ©2003 British Museum; *t.r.* Werner Forman Archive, Smithsonian Institution, Washington, DC/Art Resource, NY; *t.r.* ©Canadian Museum of Civilization, Photo S93-9725; **46** Knife River Indian Villages National Historic Site, National Park Service Photo by Fred Armstrong; **47** Neg./Trans. no. K 10302. Courtesy Department of Library Services, American Museum of Natural History; **50** The Granger Collection, New York; **52** ©Aldona Sabalis/Photo Researchers, Inc.; **53** *b.r.* The Granger Collection, New York; *b.* ©ChinaStock Photo Library. All rights reserved; **55** The Granger Collection, New York; **57** Art Resource, NY; **58** Limbourg Brothers. The Month of October. Sowing. Detail. Chateau du Louvre. Tres Riches Heures du Duc de Berry. Musee Conde, Chantilly, France. Giraudon/Art Resource, NY; **60** Ivory salt cellar, Benin, 16th century. Nationalmuseet, Copenhagen, Denmark/Bridgeman Art Library, London/New York; **61** ©Copyright 2003 PhotoDisc, Inc.; **63** Florentine Codex, (16th century). Ms Palat. 218–220 Book IX Montezuma II (1466–1520) receiving tributes, from an account of the Aztecs written and illustrated by Bernardino de Sahagun, Spanish, mid 16th century. Biblioteca Medicea-Laurenziana, Florence, Italy/Bridgeman Art Library, London/New York; **64** Prentice Hall; **65** Courtesy Haudenosaunee Onondaga Nation and the New York State Museum; **66** *l.* Sebastiano del Piombo (ca. 1485–1547), *Christopher Columbus.* All rights reserved. Copyright © by the Metropolitan Museum of Art, NY; *r.* ©Wolfgang Kaehler/CORBIS; **67** Equity Management Inc.; **68** Werner Forman Archive/Statens Historiska Museum, Stockholm/ Art Resource, NY; **69** *b.r.* Rare Books Division, New York Public Library; *b.l.* Museum fur Kunst und Gewerbe, Hamburg;

74 Photograph courtesy Florida Division of Historical Resources, Bureau of Archaeological Research; **75** *Hernando Cortes (1485–1547, Spanish conquistador) meeting Indians of Tlaxcala region, Mexico, folio 207R of 1579 manuscript* Historia de las Indias by Diego Duran. ©The Art Archive/Biblioteca Nacional Madrid/Dagli Orti; **81** Image Select/Art Resource, NY; **83** *m.* ©Fotopic/Omni-Photo Communications, Inc.; *b.r.* ©North Wind Picture Archives; **85** The Granger Collection, New York; **86** ©Esbin/Anderson/Omni-Photo Communications, Inc.; **87** Courtesy of The Association for the Preservation of Virginia Antiquities; **88** *t.* ©Richard T. Nowitz/CORBIS; *t.l. Captain John Smith, 1st Governor of Virginia,* c. 1616 (oil on canvas) by English School (17th century). The Berger Collection at the Denver Art Museum, USA/The Bridgeman Art Library, London/New York; **89** *Pocahontas 1616* (detail), National Portrait Gallery, Smithsonian Institution/Art Resource, NY; **92** *b.* Jack Clifton, *First Legislature in the New World.* Oil on canvas. State Capitol, Commonwealth of Virginia. Courtesy The Library of Virginia; Courtesy Cassell & Co.; From "The Chronicle of Western Fashion" by John Peacock, published by Harry N. Abrams, Inc., New York. Used by permission of Thames & Hudson; **93** Courtesy of the Pilgrim Society, Plymouth, Massachusetts; **95** ©Bettmann/CORBIS; **96** ©Ted Curtin/Stock Boston; **100** *l.* The Granger Collection, New York; *r.* The Historical Society of Pennsylvania (HSP), *Silver Gorget* by Joseph Richardson [S-8-120]; **101** *l.* Peale, Charles Wilson (1741–1827), *Jonathan Edwards.* Engraved by J. D. Gross. Peale Museum; *r.* Courtesy of the Library of Congress; **102** John Lewis Stage; **104** ©Bettmann/CORBIS **105** The Granger Collection, New York; **106** ©Stone; **108** Chippendale mahogany side chair, Philadelphia, 1765–1770. From the collection of May and Howard Joynt/Christie's Images; **109** The Granger Collection, New York; **113** The Granger Collection, New York; **117** Photographer: Ron Blunt. Courtesy of Drayton Hall, Charleston, South Carolina. A property of the National Trust for Historic Preservation. All Rights Reserved; **118** Courtesy, American Antiquarian Society; **120** Culver Pictures, Inc.; **121** *Moses Marcy,* unknown artist. Oil on wood overmantel panel from the Moses Marcy House, Southbridge, MA, mid-18th century (no longer standing). Old Sturbridge Village, Southbridge, MA. [20.19.1] Photo by Henry E. Peach; **124** The Granger Collection, New York; **125** Brady/Prentice Hall, Inc.; **127** The Granger Collection, New York; **129** *t.l.* The Granger Collection, New York; *t.r.* ©Aaron Haupt/Photo Researchers, Inc.; **131** *t.* Chamberlin Mason (English, died 1787), *Portrait of Benjamin Franklin,* 1762 (detail). Oil on canvas, 50⅜" x 40¾". [56-88-1] Philadelphia Museum of Art: Gift of Mr. and Mrs. Wharton Sinkler; *b.l.* Courtesy of the Historical and Interpretive Collections of The Franklin Institute, Philadelphia, PA. Photo by Charles F. Penniman, Jr.; *b.r.* Courtesy of the Historical and Interpretive Collections of The Franklin

Institute, Philadelphia, PA. Photo by Charles F. Penniman, Jr.; *m.t.* Musee de l'Amitie Franco-Americaine, Bierancourt, France. ©Photograph by Erich Lessing/Art Resource, NY; *m.b.* Musee de l'Amitie Franco-Americaine, Bierancourt, France. ©Photograph by Erich Lessing/Art Resource, NY; **136–137** Art Resource, NY; **138** The Granger Collection, New York; **139** *l.* The Granger Collection, New York; *r.* The Granger Collection, New York; **140** The Granger Collection, New York; **141** The Granger Collection, New York; **146** Courtesy of the Library of Congress; **147** *b.l.* The Granger Collection, New York; *b.r.* The Granger Collection, New York; **149** Colonial Williamsburg Foundation; **151** *t.l.* Dawe, Phillip (c. 1750–c.1785). *The Bostonians Paying the Excise-Man or Tarring & Feathering.* London, 1774. Colored Engraving. The Gilder Lehman Collection on deposit at the Pierpont Morgan Library. GL 4961.01. Photography: Joseph Zehavi. The Pierpont Morgan Library. Art Resource, NY; *t.r.* AP Photo/Tony Dejak; **152** The Granger Collection, New York; **154** The Granger Collection, New York; **155** Courtesy, American Antiquarian Society; **156** Samuel Adams (1722–1803) American Revolutionary politician, chief agitator of the Boston Tea Party by Anonymous. Museum of Fine Arts, Boston, MA, USA/The Bridgeman Art Library, London/New York; **157** *t.* The Granger Collection, New York; *m.r.* Courtesy of The Bostonian Society, Old State House; **159** Lisa Poole/AP/Wide World Photos; **164** AP/Wide World Photos; **165** The Granger Collection, New York; **166** *l.* The Granger Collection, New York; *r.* Courtesy of The Bostonian Society, Old State House; **167** *l. Marquis de Lafayette* by Francesco-Guiseppe Casanova, ca. 1781–85, oil on canvas, 18.5 x 16.5 in., accession 1939.9. Collection of The New-York Historical Society; *r.* Gallery of the Republic; **168** West Point Museum Collections, United States Military Academy, West Point, New York. Presented by F. Donald Campbell, No 18,947. Photograph by Paul Warchol, New York; **169** The Granger Collection, New York; **172** The Granger Collection, New York; **173** *m.r.* Independence National Historical Park Collection; *m.r.* The Granger Collection, New York; **177** Letraset Phototone; **176–177** The Granger Collection, New York; **181** The Granger Collection, New York; **186** Unknown artist, *Black Privateer,* panel 4, panel reverse F, oil, ca. 1780. Courtesy of Alexander A. McBurney, M.D.; **187** Valentine Museum, Richmond, Virginia; **189** © Bettmann/CORBIS; **190** *t.l.* The Granger Collection, New York; *t.r.* ©1996 North Wind Picture Archives; *b.* The Granger Collection, New York; **191** Courtesy of Ted Speigel; **194** ©Christine Pemberton/Omni-Photo Communications, Inc.; **197** Courtesy of the Library of Congress; **198** *l.* The Granger Collection, New York; *r.* The Granger Collection, New York; *m.* National Museum of American History, Department of Social History, Political History Collection, Smithsonian Institution; **199** Bas-relief sculpture depicting the signing of the United States Constitution at the South

entrance of the Nebraska State Capitol, Lincoln, Nebraska. Image provided by Nebraska Capitol Collections; **200** *Thomas Jefferson.* Unknown artist. Oil on fragment of white marble. Photography by Jeff Goldman, 1986. Maryland Historical Society, Baltimore, Maryland; **202** ©Bettmann/CORBIS; **205** *m.r.* ©North Wind Picture Archives; *b.* ©North Wind Picture Archives; **206** ©Leif Skoogfors/Woodfin Camp & Associates; **207** ©Grace Davies/Omni-Photo Communications, Inc.; **208** Peale, Charles Wilson, *James Madison,* 1783. Courtesy of the Library of Congress; **209** Christy, Howard Chandler, *Scene at the Signing of the Constitution,* April 1940. Architect of the Capitol; **211** The Granger Collection, New York; **212** *t.* ©Nathan Beck/Omni-Photo Communications, Inc.; *t.l.* Jean-Antoine Houdon (1741–1828), *Benjamin Franklin* (ca. 1778). Plaster bust, 84.2 x 66.6 x 41.1 cm. Gift of the estate of George Francis Parkman, 1908. Boston Athenaeum; **215** National Museum of American History, Smithsonian Institution; **221** Courtesy of the American Antiquarian Society; **246** *l.* ©Joseph Sohm, Chromosohm Inc./CORBIS; *r.* The Granger Collection, New York; **247** *l.* National Museum of American History, Smithsonian Institution; *r.* ©Paul Conklin/PhotoEdit; **248** Cover, *Time Magazine,* Nov. 20, 2000, Vol. 156, No. 21.TimePix, Inc.; **249** *l.* ©Copyright 2001 PhotoDisc, Inc.; *r.* ©1997 Corbis Stock Market/Ed Wheeler; **252** The Granger Collection, New York; **255** ©Spencer Grant/Stock Boston; **257** ©Arthur Grace/Stock Boston; **259** ©Stock Boston; **262** ©Stephen Varone/Omni-Photo Communications, Inc.; **263** ©Michael Mancuso/Omni-Photo Communications, Inc.; **265** *People Weekly* ©1997 Andrew Kaufman; **266** Art Resource, NY; **267** ©The New Yorker Collection 2003, Barney Tobey, from cartoonbank.com. All Rights Reserved; **269** George Jones III/Photo Researchers, Inc. **274–275** John Hill, *Junction of the Erie and Northern (Champlain) Canals.* Aquatint, Number 34684. Courtesy of The New-York Historical Society; **276** *l. George Washington Banner:* watercolor, graphite and pen ink on paper. .733 x .534 m. (28¾ in. x 21¹/₁₆ in.). Index of American Design, ©1993 National Gallery of Art. Photograph ©Board of Trustees, National Gallery of Art, Washington DC; *r.* Courtesy of the Library of Congress; *c.* Courtesy of the Library of Congress; **277** Copyright © By the Metropolitan Museum of Art, NY **278** ©2000 North Wind Picture Archives; **279** ©Chromosohm/Sohm MCMXCII/Photo Researchers, Inc.; **280** The Granger Collection, New York; **283** *l.* Isaac Fowle (1818–1853), *Lady with a Scarf Figurehead.* Courtesy of The Bostonian Society/Old State House; *t.r. Swordsman Whirligig,* c. 1870. Carved, polychromed wood, 44.5 x 12.7 x 9.5 (excluding base) (17½ x 5 x 3¾). ©Shelburne Museum, Shelburne, Vermont (27.FW-43). Photograph by Ken Burris; *m.* The Granger Collection, New York; *b.r. Gabriel,* c. 1800. Sawn, polychromed wood with iron reinforcements. 33 x 85.1 x 1.3 (13 x 33½ x ½). Found in Ridgefield, Connecticut. ©Shelburne Museum, Shelburne, Vermont (27.FW-2). Photograph by Ken Burris; **284**

Credits

Society; **481** The Granger Collection, New York; **483** The Granger Collection, New York; **484** ©1997 North Wind Picture Archives; **485** *l.* Courtesy of the Library of Congress; *r.* Culver Pictures, Inc.; **486** West Point Museum Collections, United States Military Academy, West Point, New York; **489** ©Omni-Photo Communications, Inc.; **490** Smithsonian Institute; **494** Photograph by Matthew Brady. ©CORBIS; **495** ©2001 North Wind Picture Archives; **496** *Unidentified African-American Civil War soldier.* Tintype, unknown photographer, no date. Chicago Historical Society, ICHi-08068; **498** *Attack at Battery Wagner* © 1993 Tom Lovell © 1993 The Greenwich Workshop, Inc. Courtesy of The Greenwich Workshop, Inc., Shelton CT; **500** *Home Coming, 1865,* watercolor by William L. Sheppard. The Museum of the Confederacy, Richmond, Virginia. Copy Photography by Katherine Wetzel; *l.* Massachusetts Commandery, Military Order of the Loyal Legion and the U.S. Army Military History Institute; *t.l.* U.S. Army Military History Institute; *m.l.* U.S. Army Military History Institute; **501** *r.* ©Eric Kroll/ Omni-Photo Communications, Inc.; **505** ©CORBIS; **506** The Granger Collection, New York; **511** Courtesy of the Library of Congress; **513** Photograph by Matthew Brady. Culver Pictures, Inc.; **514** *l.* Culver Pictures, Inc.; *r.* Culver Pictures, Inc.; *m. Upholstered walnut parlor rocking chair.* Used by President Abraham Lincoln at Ford's Theatre, Washington, DC, April 14, 1865. H: 10.00 x 106.68 cm., W: 36.625 in., L: 34.5 in. (29.1451.1). From the Collections of Henry Ford Museum and Greenfield Village, No. 11-A-35(A); **515** *l.* The Granger Collection, New York; *r.* The Granger Collection, New York; **516** ©Bern Keating; **517** The Granger Collection, New York; **518** Courtesy of Ford's Theatre, Washington, DC. Photo by Andrew Lautman; **521** AP Photo/Lou Krasky; **523** The Granger Collection, New York; **525** *t.* ©Copyright 2001 PhotoDisc, Inc.; *b.* ©Bettmann/COR-BIS; **526** ©1994 North Wind Picture Archives; **527** The Granger Collection, New York; **528** The Granger Collection, New York; **530** SuperStock; **532** ©1998 North Wind Picture Archives; **536** The National Portrait Gallery, Smithsonian Institution; **537** ©Copyright 2003 PhotoDisc, Inc.; **540** *l.* Culver Pictures, Inc.; *r.* Courtesy of the Library of Congress; **541** *l.* ©Robert Mills/Bettmann/CORBIS; *r.,* ©2001 *The Record* (Bergen County, NJ) Thomas E. Franklin, staff photographer/CORBIS/SABA; **542** *m.l.* ©1996 North Wind Picture Archives; **544** *m.l.* The Granger Collection, New York; **545** *t.* ©Bettmann/CORBIS; *m.r.* East-Asiatic Company, Limited, Baltic America Line inspection card for immigration and steerage passengers. SS *Estonia.* Port of departure, Danzig, Poland. Date of departure, 20 November 1925. Stamped "Sent to Hospital, Dec. 4, 1925." National Park Service, Statue of Liberty National Monument; **547** *m.r.* Photo by R. Y. Young. Courtesy of the Library of Congress; **548** The Granger Collection, New York; **550** *t.l.* Equity Management Inc.; **552** *t.r.* ©Jack Kurtz/Impact Visuals; *inset* Courtesy of the Veterans of Foreign Wars of the United States; *b.* ©CORBIS; **553** *Vauxhall 30/98 Wensum, 1925* by Griffin, 1966. Private Collection./The Bridgeman Art Library, London/New York; **555** ©CORBIS; **556** *t.l.* ©H. K. Owen/Black Star; **558** *t.l.* Flag Research Center; *b.l.* The Granger Collection, New York; **560** Steve Schapiro/ Black Star; **562** National Museum of American History, Department of Social History, Political History Collection, Smithsonian Institution; **564** ©Ron Edmonds/AP/Wide World Photos; **570** Art Resource, NY; **571** ©Copyright 2003 PhotoDisc, Inc.; **572** ©Ansel Adams Publishing Rights Trust/CORBIS; ©Copyright 2003 PhotoDisc, Inc.; **573** The Granger Collection, New York; ©Copyright 2003 PhotoDisc, Inc.; **574** Courtesy Haudenosaunee Onondaga Nation and the New York State Museum; ©Copyright 2003 PhotoDisc, Inc.; **575** © Dorling Kindersley. Courtesy of St. Bride Printing; ©Copyright 2003 PhotoDisc, Inc; **576** Photograph courtesy Florida Division of Historical Resources, Bureau of Archaeological Research; ©Copyright 2003 PhotoDisc, Inc.; **577** *Captain John Smith, 1st Governor of Virginia,* c. 1616 (oil on canvas) by English School (17th century). The Berger Collection at the Denver Art Museum, USA/The Bridgeman Art Library, London/New York; ©Copyright 2003 PhotoDisc, Inc.; **578** The Granger Collection, New York; ©Copyright 2003 PhotoDisc, Inc.; **579** Chamberlin Mason (English, died 1787), *Portrait of Benjamin Franklin,* 1762 (detail). Oil on canvas, 50⅜" x 40¾". [56-88-1] Philadelphia Museum of Art: Gift of Mr. and Mrs. Wharton Sinkler; ©Copyright 2003 PhotoDisc, Inc.; **580** The Granger Collection, New York; ©Copyright 2003 PhotoDisc, Inc.; **581** Colonial Williamsburg Foundation; ©Copyright 2003 PhotoDisc, Inc.; **582** Independence National Historical Park Collection; ©Copyright 2003 PhotoDisc, Inc.; **583** Culver Pictures, Inc.; ©Copyright 2003 PhotoDisc, Inc.; **584** ©Leif Skoogfors/ Woodfin Camp & Associates; ©Copyright 2003 PhotoDisc, Inc.; **585** Culver Pictures, Inc.; ©Copyright 2003 PhotoDisc, Inc.; **586** *b.l.* Corel Professional Photos CD-ROM™; ©Copyright 2003 PhotoDisc, Inc.; **587** ©1997 Corbis Stock Market/Ed Wheeler; ©Copyright 2003 PhotoDisc, Inc.; **588** Art Resource, NY; ©Copyright 2003 PhotoDisc, Inc.; **589** *Thomas Jefferson.* Unknown artist. Oil on fragment of white marble. Maryland Historical Society, Baltimore, Maryland; ©Copyright 2003 PhotoDisc, Inc.; **590** Photograph ©1995 Fred J. Maroon; ©Copyright 2003 PhotoDisc, Inc.; **591** *t.* Donovan Reese/Stone; *b.* ©Copyright 2003 PhotoDisc, Inc.; **592** The Granger Collection, New York; ©Copyright 2003 PhotoDisc, Inc.; **593** The Granger Collection, New York; ©Copyright 2003 PhotoDisc, Inc.; **594** Index Stock Imagery, Inc.; ©Copyright 2003 PhotoDisc, Inc.; **595** Courtesy of the Library of Congress; ©Copyright 2003 PhotoDisc, Inc.; **596** ©2000 North Wind Picture Archives; ©Copyright 2003 PhotoDisc, Inc.; **597** Seaver Center for Western History Research, Natural History Museum of Los Angeles County. Museum Collection Number 277; ©Copyright 2003 PhotoDisc, Inc.; **598** The Granger Collection, New York; ©Copyright 2003 PhotoDisc, Inc.; **599** ©1998 North Wind Picture Archives; ©Copyright 2003 PhotoDisc, Inc.; **600** *r.* Culver Pictures, Inc.; ©Copyright 2003 PhotoDisc, Inc.; **601** The Granger Collection, New York; ©Copyright 2003 PhotoDisc, Inc.; **602** Eastman Johnson, *A Ride for Liberty—the Fugitive Slaves.* (detail) The Brooklyn Museum; ©Copyright 2003 PhotoDisc, Inc.; **603** The Granger Collection, New York; **604** The Granger Collection, New York; **605** National Portrait Gallery, Smithsonian Institution; **606** The Granger Collection, New York; **607** Culver Pictures, Inc.; *l.* ©CORBIS; **608** ©Bettmann/CORBIS; **609** ©Robert Mills/ Bettmann/ CORBIS; **610** *l.* National Portrait Gallery, Smithsonian Institution/Art Resource, NY; *m.l.* National Portrait Gallery, Smithsonian Institution/Art Resource, NY; *m.l.* White House Collection, copyright White House Historical Association; *m.t.* National Portrait Gallery, Smithsonian Institution/Art Resource, NY; *b.l.* National Portrait Gallery, Smithsonian Institution/Art Resource, NY; *t.r.* White House Collection, copyright White House Historical Association; *m.m.* National Portrait Gallery, Smithsonian Institution/ Art Resource, NY; *m.r.* National Portrait Gallery, Smithsonian Institution/Art Resource, NY; *m.m.* White House Collection, copyright White House Historical Association; *m.r.* National Portrait Gallery, Smithsonian Institution/Art Resource, NY; *m.b.* White House Collection, copyright White House Historical Association; *b.r.* National Portrait Gallery, Smithsonian Institution/ Art Resource, NY; **611** *t.l.* White House Collection, copyright White House Historical Association; *m.l.* White House Collection, copyright White House Historical Association; *m.l.* White House Collection, copyright White House Historical Association; *m.t.* National Portrait Gallery, Smithsonian Institution/Art Resource, NY; *t.r.* National Portrait Gallery, Smithsonian Institution/Art Resource, NY; *m.m.* White House Collection, copyright White House Historical Association; *m.r.* National Portrait Gallery, Smithsonian Institution/Art Resource, NY; *m.m.* National Portrait Gallery, Smithsonian Institution/Art Resource, NY; *m.r.* National Portrait Gallery, Smithsonian Institution/Art Resource, NY; *b.r.* White House Collection, copyright White House Historical Association; *m.b.* White House Collection, copyright White House Historical Association; *b.r.* White House Collection, copyright White House Historical Association; **612** *t.l.* National Portrait Gallery, Smithsonian Institution/Art Resource, NY; *m.l.* White House Collection, copyright White House Historical Association; *m.l.* White House Collection, copyright White House Historical Association; *b.l.* White House Collection, copyright White House Historical Association; *m.t.* National Portrait Gallery, Smithsonian Institution/Art Resource, NY; *t.r.* National Portrait Gallery, Smithsonian Institution/Art Resource, NY; *m.m.* White House Collection, copyright White House Historical Association; *m.r.* White House Collection, copyright White House Historical Association; *m.r.* White House Collection, copyright White House Historical

Credits